T0093372

Tobias on Locks and Insecurity Engineering

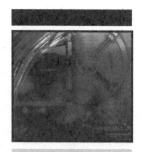

Tobias on Locks and Insecurity Engineering

Understanding and Preventing Design Vulnerabilities in Locks, Safes, and Security Hardware

Marc Weber Tobias, J.D.

Member of ASIS, ALOA, SAVTA, IAIL,
FBI InfraGard, AAPP, and APA;
technical advisor to AFTE; and
member of the Underwriters Laboratory Standards
Technical Panel on Locks and Safes

WILEY

Published by John Wiley & Sons, Inc., Hoboken, New Jersey.
Published simultaneously in Canada and the United Kingdom.

ISBNs: 9781119828259 (Hardback), 9781119828631 (ePDF), 9781119828266 (ePub)

For general information on our other products and services or for technical support, please contact our Customer Care Department within the United States at (800) 762-2974, outside the United States at (317) 572-3993 or fax (317) 572-4002.

Wiley also publishes its books in a variety of electronic formats. Some content that appears in print may not be available in electronic formats. For more information about Wiley products, visit our web site at www.wiley.com.

Library of Congress Control Number: 2023946543

Cover images: Vault: © mennovandijk/Getty Images
          Lights: © Tatiana Serebryakova/Getty Images
          Circuit Board: © DKosig/Getty Images
Cover design: Wiley

SKY10064813_011324

For Addi Wendt, one of the modern pioneers in the lock and security industry and a dear friend. He dedicated his life to developing and providing tools and advanced opening techniques for locksmiths and government services worldwide. And to the memory of Betty Mae Tobias, my beloved mother, who continually encouraged me to write this book before her passing.

About the Author

**Marc Weber Tobias J.D.,** is an investigative attorney and a physical security expert. His undergraduate major and degrees were in law enforcement and journalism, and he received his Juris Doctor degree from Creighton Law School in 1973.

He has authored seven law enforcement textbooks, including *Locks, Safes, and Security: An International Police Reference*, first and second editions, and *LSS+* (the Multimedia Edition). This is a primary reference for law enforcement, intelligence, locksmiths, and professional security officers.

He has contributed to Forbes for 12 years on matters of travel and security and has disclosed serious vulnerabilities in lock designs.

Marc has been granted 28 U.S. patents and has lectured worldwide on criminal investigations, liability, locks design, and bypass tools and techniques.

During his career, he has worked for government agencies as an investigator and prosecutor of major crimes. He and his colleagues also consult for many of the major lock manufacturers in the United States, Europe, and the Middle East. He directs a team that discovers vulnerabilities that can compromise the locks produced by his clients and then works with their design engineers to fix them.

Marc established the Security Engineering Laboratory at the University of Pittsburgh, School of Engineering, where senior engineering students work on security-related product designs.

He is a member of many professional organizations, including the Associated Locksmiths of America (ALOA), Safe and Vault Technicians Association (SAVTA), American Society for Industrial Security (ASIS), International Association of

Investigative Locksmiths (IAIL), American Association of Police Polygraphers (AAPP), American Polygraph Association (APA), Underwriters Laboratory Standards Technical Panel, and FBI InfraGard. He is a technical advisor to the Association of Firearms and Tool Marks Examiners (AFTE), the professional crime lab and forensic organization for law enforcement agencies worldwide.

Marc and his partners lectured at DefCon and other major cyber conferences for nine years on physical security, lock designs, and vulnerabilities. He has consulted with many law enforcement organizations and testified as an expert witness involving crimes related to the bypass of locks, including the major diamond theft in Antwerp, Belgium, and several homicide cases.

Books by the Author

A Field Manual of Criminal Law and Police Procedure, by Marc Weber Tobias and R. David Petersen, 1975

Locks, Safes, and Security, First Edition, 1970

Locks, Safes, and Security, Second Edition, 2000

Locks, Safes, and Security: The Multimedia Edition LSS+, 2002

Open in Thirty Seconds: Cracking One of the Most Secure Locks in America, by Marc Weber Tobias and Tobias Bluzmanis, 2008

Police Communications, 1974

Pre-Trial Criminal Procedure, by Marc Weber Tobias and R. David Petersen, 1972

Techno Security's Guide to Securing SCADA: A Comprehensive Handbook on Protecting the Critical Infrastructure, 2008

Acknowledgments

I would like to acknowledge the following people for helping to influence me in the writing of this book. The journey took me to many different countries to meet with specialists in locks, safes, and cybersecurity while making many friends along the way.

First, I'd like to thank the experts who have provided the most influence. Thank you to John Falle (Falle Safe Security); Enrico and Sascha Wendt (Lockmasters Germany); Alexandre Triffault (AT Security); Andreas Haberli (dormakaba); Clyde Roberson and Peter Field (Medeco); Eliot Springer (Israel Intel-Research and the New York Police Department [NYPD]); Lt. Mike Bach (NYPD TARU Unit); Graham Pulford; Harry Sher; Jacques Pyronnet; Jose Luis (Vicuna Tools); Juergen Kruehn (Ikon); Kloppers Burgert (South Africa Police Commander); Rami Almosnino, Nava Efrati, and Sam Shterenshus (MUL-T-LOCk); Eric Winter (University of Pittsburgh); David Moser, Torsten Quast, and Han Fey (ASSA ABLOY); Javier Roquero; Marc Handels and Juan Imedio (SaltoSystems Team); S. Ehlich-Adam (EVVA Locks); Urs Spani (KESO Locks); Bo Widen (inventor extraordinaire, Sweden); and Klaus Drumm (Geminy Locks).

Special recognition to Dr. Roger G. Johnston, Ph.D., retired Vulnerability Assessment team leader at Los Alamos and Argonne National Laboratories, for his insight into security and keeping America safe.

Second, my appreciation is given to Ross Anderson and the University of Cambridge for his expertise in cybersecurity and friendship, and Clayton Miller of Lockmasters (United States). Thanks also goes to Manfred Goth (Goth Forensic Laboratory), Nasser Al-Shamshi (Dubai Police Crime Lab), Tzachi Wiesenfeld, Tammy and Paul Davis (Videx), Vito Ruscigno (Italian Police inspector), and Jay Dean Smith (Denver Police Department).

Third, I thank all the lock innovators and creators for their covert-entry tool designs. Thanks also goes to Frederick Madelin (Madelin S.A.), Martin Newton (Safe Ventures in the UK), and Roy Saunders, the world's best safecracker (England).

Finally, my sincere thanks goes to those in the industry who helped make this book possible. Thank you sincerely to Dr. Alejandro Ojeda (Urban Alps), Aaron Fish, Barry Wels, Brock Self, Cedric Messequer, The Czech Locksmith Association, The European Locksmith Federation and Ona Gardemeister, Eric Michaud, Graham Pulford, Hans Milejeda, Harry Sferopoulos, Dr. Ilya Zeldes, Isabel Chernoff, Jacques Pyronnet, Jeff Proehl, Jean Marie Machefert, Jimmie Oxley and the University of Rhode Island, John Jackson, Mark Bloom (Spectrum Brands), Mary Besterfield-Sacre (Associate Dean, School of Engineering, University of Pittsburgh), Michael and Jane Tobias, Ralph Vasami (Builders Hardware Manufacturing Association), Reuven Borokovsky (Mul-T-Lock), and Governor William J. Janklow (South Dakota).

Finally, my colleague and co-conspirator, Tobias Alberto Bluzmanis, was invaluable because of the lock investigations we conducted, his brilliance as a locksmith, and the many patents we have received over the years. My work would have been impossible without Toby's ideas, input, and creativity.

Contents at a Glance

Foreword		xxxiii
Introduction		xxxv
Part I	Locks, Safes, and Insecurity Engineering	1
Chapter 1	Insecurity Engineering and the Design of Locks	3
Chapter 2	Insecurity Engineering: A Lack of Expertise and Imagination	25
Chapter 3	Vulnerability Assessment in Lock Designs	49
Chapter 4	The 3T2R Rule for Assessing the Security of a Lock	67
Part II	Legal and Regulatory Issues in Locks, Safes, and Security Systems	87
Chapter 5	Security Is All About Liability	89
Chapter 6	Legal Liability and Insecurity Engineering	103
Chapter 7	Standards for Locks and Safes	131
Chapter 8	Patents, Security, and the Protection of Intellectual Property	163
Chapter 9	Notification of Defects in Product Design	187
Chapter 10	Legal and Security Issues in Keying Systems	209
Part III	Basic Designs and Technologies for Mechanical and Electronic Locks	231
Chapter 11	A Brief History of Lock Design and Development	233
Chapter 12	Industry Definitions	257

Chapter 13   Modern Locking Mechanisms: A Merging of Old and New
              Technology   279

Chapter 14   A Comparison of High-Security Lock Designs   317

Part IV   Design and Insecure Engineering of Locks   339

Chapter 15   Attacks Against Locks: Then and Now   341

Chapter 16   An Overview: Vulnerability Analysis in Designs and Testing 379

Chapter 17   Destructive Attacks Against Locks and Related Hardware   395

Chapter 18   Covert Methods of Entry   417

Chapter 19   Attacks Against Electronic Locks   445

Chapter 20   Advanced Attacks Against High-Security Locks   459

Part V   Attacks on Key Control and Special Keying Systems   475

Chapter 21   Attacking Keys and Keying Systems   477

Chapter 22   Advanced Attacks on Key Control: 3D Printers and Special
              Software   507

Chapter 23   Digital Fingerprints of Locks: Electronic Decoding Systems 523

Chapter 24   Code-Setting Keys: A Case Study of an Attack on
              High-Security Key Control   537

Part VI   Specific Case Examples   545

Chapter 25   Case Examples from Part VII Rules   547

Chapter 26   Case Examples By Category   571

Part VII   Design Rules, Axioms, and Principles   597

Chapter 27   Design Rules, Axioms, and Guidelines   599

Epilogue   625

Appendix A   Patents Issued   627

Appendix B   Trademark Listing   629

Index   633

Contents

Foreword   **xxxiii**

Introduction   **xxxv**

Part I   **Locks, Safes, and Insecurity Engineering**   **1**

Chapter 1   **Insecurity Engineering and the Design of Locks**   **3**

               What Is Insecurity Engineering?   4

               Primary Responsibilities of Lock Manufacturers   4

                   Invent or Improve On State-of-the-Art Technology   5

                   Develop and Continue to Analyze and Improve On Earlier
                       Designs   5

                   Understand All Known Vulnerabilities and Imagine New Ones   6

                   Apply Expertise to Currently Manufactured and New Products   6

                   Protect Intellectual Property (IP) from Infringement   6

                   Ensure That IP Produced and Sold Is Secure and Will Not Cause
                       Injury or Harm   6

                   Do Not Produce Defective Products   6

                   Fully Understand Product Liability and Its Critical Importance   7

                   Initiate a Disclosure Program about Serious Vulnerabilities   7

               Examples of Insecurity Engineering Failures   7

               Important Design Rules   18

               Summary   24

Chapter 2   **Insecurity Engineering: A Lack of Expertise and Imagination**   **25**

               Basic Lock Types and Components   29

               Theory of Operation for Each Primary Lock Design Category   29

               Primary Security Classifications of Locks   31

               Lock Materials and Their Characteristics   33

               Standards and Their Criteria   34

               Security Features and Enhancements   34

Magnetics: Theory, Implementation, and Defeat   35
Bypass: Fundamental Expertise Requirements   35
  Mechanical Bypass of Locks and Systems   36
  Brute-Force Attacks   37
  Traditional Covert Entry   38
    Picking   38
    Impressioning   39
    Decoding   40
    Hybrid Attacks   42
  Keys and Keying Systems and Their Design and Compromise   42
  Attacks Against Shear Lines   44
Forensics and Evidence of Entry   45
  Evidence of Entry   46
  Audit Trails   46

Chapter 3   **Vulnerability Assessment in Lock Designs**   **49**
Vulnerability and Risks   51
  Defining a Vulnerability Assessment Plan   52
  VA Team Selection   53
The Vulnerability Assessment Process   57
  Insider Threats and Attacks   59
  Vulnerability Assessment Report   59
  Suggested Rules, Axioms, Guidelines, and Principles   61

Chapter 4   **The 3T2R Rule for Assessing the Security of a Lock**   **67**
The 3T2R Rule: Metrics, Security, and Liability   68
  Time   68
    Various Time Computations and Attack Vector Examples   69
    Time Delay, Security, and Liability   72
  Tools   72
    Forced Entry   73
    Covert and Surreptitious Entry   73
    Hybrid Attacks and the 3T2R Rule   75
    Tool Assessment and the 3T2R Rule: Simple,
      Complex, or Special Designs   77
  Training   79
  Reliability of the Exploit   81
  Repeatability of the Exploit   81
Overall Security Assessment and the 3T2R Rule and
  Numerical Scoring   82
    Security Ratings for Simple or Complex Attacks:
      Case Examples   83

Part II   **Legal and Regulatory Issues in Locks, Safes, and
Security Systems**   **87**

Chapter 5   **Security Is All About Liability**   **89**
Avoiding Legal Issues   89
Design Defects and Other Actions as the Basis of Product
  Liability   90

Design Defect Liability   90
How to Define Defectiveness   91
  Fraud and Misrepresentation   91
  False Representations   92
  Failure to Warn of a Dangerous Condition   92
  Failure to Foresee Product Use and Subsequent Liability   93
  Post-Sale Failure to Warn   93
  Post-Sale Duty to Remedy a Defect or Recall   94
  Failure to Disclose or Warn of a Known Defect   95
  Failure to Design Away Known Defects or Dangers   95
  Misconduct in Marketing   96
  Tortious Misrepresentation about a Product   96
  Failure to Adhere to Industry Standards, Cutting Corners,
    or Falsifying Test Results   96
  Negligence in Design or Manufacture, or Failure to Provide
    Adequate Warnings or Instructions   97
  Failure to Implement a Risk-Utility Test in Product Design   97
  Failure to Consider Alternative Designs   97
  Malfunctions and Liability   98
  Flagrant Disregard of Consumer Safety   98
  Failure to Exercise Due Care in Manufacturing   98
  Failure of a Manufacturer to Exercise Reasonable Care
    in Product Concept and Formulation   99
  Defective Product or Improper Consumer Use   99
  Summary of Specific Actions That Can Trigger Liability
    and Legal Issues   99
  Failure to Discourage a Culture of Arrogance in
    Engineering and Design   100

Chapter 6   Legal Liability and Insecurity Engineering   103
Development of Product Liability Law   104
Criminal, Civil, and Criminal Law   105
  Overview: Origins of Legal Liability for Product Designs   105
    Ancient Roman Law and the Twelve Tables   106
    The Emergence of a Standard of Care and an Extra-High
      Standard   106
    Privity of Contract: The Case of *Winterbottom v. Wright*   108
  Privity of Contract and Avoidance of Liability by
    Manufacturers: Implied Warranty Claims   109
Defective Products: What Are They, and Why Are They
  Important?   110
  Manufacturing Defects   111
  Design Defects   112
  Warning and Marketing Defects   113
  Post-Sale Issues and Duty to Warn   114
Exemption from Warnings: Sophisticated Users   114
Warranty of Merchantability, Defective Products, and
  Negligence   115

The Repair Doctrine: Liability for Subsequent Product
   Upgrades   116
Negligence vs. Privity of Contract   117
  MacPherson v. Buick Motor Car Company   117
Strict Liability vs. Negligence   118
  Strict Liability   118
  Who Can Sue for a Defective Product? Horizontal and
    Vertical Privity   119
The Malfunction Doctrine and a Defective Product   119
Failure to Implement an Alternative Design and Proof
  of Possibility   120
Risk-Utility Analysis of an Alternative Product Design   120
Knowingly Selling a Defective Product   121
User Misconduct Defenses   122
  Liability for Misuse of a Product   123
  State-of-the-Art or Defective?   124
Manufacturers Are Experts   126
  Reasonable Foreseeability   127
  Constructive Knowledge of Risk   127
  Due Care in Manufacturing   127
  Due Care in Design   127
    Industry Standards and Proof of Negligence   128
    Elements of Proof by a Manufacturer   128
    Elements of Proof by a Plaintiff   128
  Liability for Nonmanufacturers and Retailers   129
  Fraudulent or False Misrepresentation   129

Chapter 7   **Standards for Locks and Safes**   **131**
Basic Rules and Axioms Relating to Standards   133
U.S. Standards Organizations   137
  Underwriters Laboratory   137
  Builders Hardware Manufacturers Association   138
  American Society for Testing and Materials   138
Description and Analysis of U.S. Lock Standards: UL and
  BHMA   139
  UL 437: The Commercial Security Standard   139
    UL 437 Definitions and Test Requirements   139
    Attack-Resistance Times for Door Locks (Section 11.5)   141
  BHMA/ANSI 156.30 High-Security Standard   142
    Section 5: Key Control   143
    Section 6: Destructive Testing   144
    Section 7: Surreptitious-Entry Resistance   144
  BHMA 156.5 Cylinders and Input Devices for Locks   146
    Operational Tests Before and After Cycle Tests   146
    Cycle Test   147
    Strength Tests   147
    Electrified Input Devices   148

Deficiencies in the UL 437, BHMA 156.30, and 156.5
  Standards   148
  UL 437 Failures to Identify Vulnerabilities and Issues in
    Testing Protocols   148
    Key Control   149
    Pick, Bumping, and Impressioning Resistance   149
    Complex Forms of Picking   150
    Expertise Level of Those Performing Tests   151
    Forced-Entry Resistance   151
    Reliance on UL Standards: No Liability   151
    Bump Keys   152
    Decoding Attacks   152
    Key Control and 3D-Printed Keys   153
  Testing Deficiencies in the BHMA 156.30 Standard   153
    Forced Entry   153
    Mechanical Bypass of Locking Mechanisms   154
    Audit Trail for Electronic Locks   155
    Keys and Key Control   155
    Decoding   156
    Data From Within the Lock   157
    Data From Sources Outside the Cylinder   157
    Pick Resistance   158
    Exploit of Internal Tolerances   158
    Electronic Attacks and Testing   159
    Tools Commercially Available to Locksmiths   159
    Bumping and Rapping Resistance   160
  Recommendations for a High-Security Standard   160

Chapter 8 **Patents, Security, and the Protection of Intellectual Property**   **163**
  Patents and Their Relationship to the Security of an
    Invention   165
  Modifications to Existing Patented Products and Security   166
  History, Origins, Chronology, and Rationale for
    Patent Laws   166
    Relevant International Patent Treaties   167
      Paris Convention for the Protection of Industrial Property   168
      Patent Cooperation Treaty   168
      TRIPS Agreement: Trade-Related Aspects of Intellectual
        Property   168
  Overview: Current U.S. Patent Law   169
    The Definition of an Invention   170
    Types of Patents   170
      Utility Patents   170
      Design Patents   170
      Plant Patents   171
    Patent Rights and Their Value   171

Filing and Obtaining a Patent in the United States   172
    Provisional Applications   172
    Nonprovisional Applications   172
    Critical Steps to Take Before Filing a Nonprovisional
      Application   173
    Specific Legal Filing Requirements   173
    Proper Naming and Identification of the Inventor   174
Primary Parts of a Patent Application   175
    Specification   175
    Claims   175
Primary Statutory Criteria for the Issuance of a Patent   176
    Utility   176
    Novelty   177
    Nonobviousness   177
Patent Life and Validity   178
What Patent Rights Do Not Cover or Allow   178
Invalidation of a Patent Application: The Concept of Prior
    Art and Nondisclosure of Inventions   179
Filing for a Patent to Protect IP: Pros and Cons   181
    Advantages of Filing an Application   181
    Reasons Not to File an Application   182
    Patent Searches and Tools   182
Patent Classification System   183
Patent Infringement   183
    Summary of Criteria That Constitute Infringement   184
      Direct Infringement   184
      Indirect or Dependent Infringement   184
    Defenses to Infringement Actions   185
    Civil and Criminal Remedies for Infringement   186

Chapter 9   Notification of Defects in Product Design   187
Primary Rules and Questions   188
Internal Notifications   193
Assessing the Scope of the Issue or Problem   194
Action Items and Priority   195
Design Defects and Liability Considerations   195
Compensatory and Punitive Damages   197
Failure to Take Any Substantive Steps   197
Post-Sale Duty to Warn or Recall   197
The Protocol for the Notification of Defects in Locks   198
Threat-Level Criteria   198
Communications and Actions on Notification of a Defect   200
Special Cases: Consulting Agreements, Nondisclosure
    Agreements, and Extortion Attempts   201
Possible Extortion Attempts   202
Civil Remedies   204
Insider Threats as Part of a Scheme   207

| **Chapter 10** | **Legal and Security Issues in Keying Systems** | **209** |

How Manufacturers and Locksmiths Can Be Liable for
Damages   210

False or Misleading Advertising About Security and Key
Control   211

Key Control Procedures by Manufacturers   212

How Locksmiths and Key-Duplicating Shops Can Defeat
Key Control Schemes   213

    Cutting Keys on Counterfeit, Knockoff, or Legally Restricted
    Blanks   214

    Legal Restrictions   215

    Patent Infringement   215

    Contract Violation by Dealers   215

    Voiding of Warranty   215

    Potential Violation of City Ordinances   216

Identification of Counterfeit Blanks by Customers   216

Patent-Expired Blanks   216

Keyway Restrictions Are Often Easily Circumvented   216

Compromise of Physical Key Control: Duplication,
Simulation, and Replication of Credentials   217

    Duplication   218

        Sophisticated Computerized Key Machines   218

        Milling Machines   219

        3D Printers and Key Machines   219

    Simulation   220

    Visual Decoding of Keys   220

        Variable Key-Generation Systems   221

        Dimple Key Simulation and Overlay Bitting Insert   221

    Replication   222

    Decoding   222

    Impressioning   222

    Rights Amplification   223

    Inadequate Number of Differs   224

    Pinning Restrictions and Maximum Adjacent Cut
    Specifications   224

    Extrapolation of Top-Level Master Keys   225

        Defeat of Virtual Keyways   225

    Creation of Bump Keys and Lock Bumping   225

Legal Issues in Master Key Systems   226

    Extrapolation of Top-Level Master Keys   228

        Systems Protected by Side Bit Milling and Sidebar Codes   228

    Analysis of Multiple Keys in a System to Derive a Pattern or
    Sequence of Bitting   229

    Analysis of Many Keys in a Positional Master Keying System
    to Derive the Composite Master Key Code   229

Security Policies for Organizational Key Control   229

Part III	Basic Designs and Technologies for Mechanical and Electronic Locks	231
Chapter 11	**A Brief History of Lock Design and Development**	**233**
	From Blacksmiths to Locksmiths: The Development of the Technology of Locks	234
	The First Locking Systems	235
	The Original Egyptian Pin Tumbler Design	237
	Early Roman Locks and the Introduction of Wards	239
	Lock Designs in the Middle Ages: The Introduction of the Lever Tumbler	242
	Advancements in Lever Lock Designs	244
	Robert Barron: Double-Acting Lever Tumbler	244
	The Bramah Lock: No Direct Contact Between the Key and Bolt Mechanism	245
	The House of Chubb and the Detector Lock	246
	Parsons Balanced Lever Lock	247
	Newell Parautoptic Lock	247
	Hobbs Protector Lock	248
	Tucker and Reeves Safeguard Lock	249
	Yale Pin Tumbler Lock	250
	Disc Tumbler Lock	252
	Wafer Tumbler Lock	253
	Sidebar Locks: Briggs & Stratton	255
	Advancements in the Past 50 Years	255
Chapter 12	**Industry Definitions**	**257**
	Terminology	258
Chapter 13	**Modern Locking Mechanisms: A Merging of Old and New Technology**	**279**
	Conventional Mechanical Locks	283
	Wafer Tumbler Locks	284
	Hybrid Wafer Lock Designs with Sidebars	286
	Rotating Disc Designs	288
	Pin Tumbler Locks	288
	Components and Fundamental Operating Principles of a Conventional Pin Tumbler Lock	289
	Security Vulnerabilities of Conventional (and Some High-Security) Pin Tumbler Locks	291
	Hybrid Mechanical Designs	294
	Sidebars	294
	Dimple Locks and Telescoping Pins	294
	Axial Pin Tumblers	296
	Laser-Track Combinations	296
	Rotating Pin Tumblers and Sidebars	296
	Magnetic Fields and Rotating Discs	299

Security Enhancements to Conventional Locks   300
    Anti-Drill Pins and Barriers   300
    Blocking Access through the Keyway   300
    Anti-Bumping Pins   301
    Security Pins and False Gates or Notches   301
    Bitting Design   301
High-Security Mechanical Locks   302
    Attributes of High-Security Locks   304
Software- and Hardware-Based Keys, Locks, and
  Access Control   305
    Key-Based Digital Cylinders   305
        Assa Abloy CLIQ   306
        Assa Abloy eCLIQ   306
    Energy-Harvesting Locks   307
        iLOQ   308
        Abloy Pulse, eCLIQ, and Spark   310
Electronic Locks   310
Hybrid Electronic Locks with Biometric or Wireless
  Authentication   311
    Kwikset KEVO   311
    Wireless Door Locks, Access Control, and Authentication   312
Selecting Conventional or High-Security Locks   315

Chapter 14   **A Comparison of High-Security Lock Designs**   **317**
Criteria for Judging a Lock's Security   318
    Sidebars and Secondary Locking Systems   319
    Side Bit Milling and Sidebars   320
Assa Twin, V10, and Similar Sidebar Designs   321
    Unique Finger Pin Design   322
    Side Pins: Two Contact Points   322
    Sidebar Interaction with Side Pins   323
Schlage Primus   324
    Primus Sidebar and Finger Pin Design   325
Medeco Rotating Tumbler Sidebar Design   326
    Original Medeco Designs   328
    Medeco BIAXIAL   328
    Medeco m3   328
    Medeco M4: The Latest Adaptation of Side Bit Milling   332
EVVA Magnetic Code System (MCS)   334

Part IV   **Design and Insecure Engineering of Locks**   **339**

Chapter 15   **Attacks Against Locks: Then and Now**   **341**
The Origins of the Pin Tumbler Lock and Attacks on
  Its Security   344
Warded Lock Design and Insecurity   346
    Multiple Bolts for Warded Locks   347
    Methods of Entry for Warded Locks   347

Skeleton Keys and Entry Tools   349
Impressioning Techniques for Warded Locks   350
Picking Tools for Warded Mechanisms   351
Special Programmable Keys for Warded Locks   353
Lever Tumbler Locks   353
Trap for False Keys   355
Methods of Attacks Against Lever Locks   355
Belly Decoding with Plasticine or Other Materials   356
False Keys or Key Copies with Wax and Permutating Key
   Machines   357
Early Impressioning Techniques   357
Mapping the Tumblers to Determine Measurement   358
   Mapping the Tumblers with Printer's Ink   359
   Methods of Picking Lever Locks   359
   KGB Programmable Lever Lock Key Set   360
Overlifting Tumblers   360
Decoding Through Belly Reading   362
Opening Letter Locks   363
Mechanical and Arithmetic Attacks and Tryout Keys   363
The Fenby Permutating Key-Cutting Machine   364
Serrated Notches and Security Pins   364
Expanding Bits on Keys   364
Small Keyhole Preventing the Exertion or Use of Force
   from Tools   365
Barrel and Curtain Used to Restrict Access to Internal
   Mechanisms   365
Pressure Against the Bolt   366
The Great Exhibition of 1851, Hobbs, and the Insecurity
   of Locks   366
Lock-Picking Advances in England and America:
   Nineteenth Century   366
Bramah Lock Design   367
Attacks with Explosives   368
Forced Attacks with Special Tools   369
Decoding Lever Locks by Sound   369
Major Crimes Involving Locks During the Nineteenth and
   Twentieth Centuries   370
The Great Train Robbery of 1855   370
The Antwerp Diamond Heist of 2003   370
1950 Brinks Robbery in Boston   370
Attacks on Locks: The Past 100 Years   371
Attacks on Locks: Now and in the Future   373

Chapter 16   An Overview: Vulnerability Analysis in Designs and Testing   379
Primary Components in All Locks   380
Shell or Housing   380
Plug and Keyway   381

Keys or Credentials 381
Shear Line 381
Gates and Sidebars 383
Movable Locking Components 383
Secondary Security Components for Multiple Security
  Layers 384
  Assembly-Retaining Components 384
  Motion Transfer Components for Movement of Bolts, Latches,
    or Blocking Elements 384
  Mechanical Electronic Interface 384
Primary Classification of Attack Types 385
  Traditional Forced Attacks 385
  Hybrid Forced Actions 386
  Covert Attacks 387
  Shear-Line Attacks 387
  Attacks Against Internal Tolerances 387
  Attacks Against Physical Integrity 388
  Decoding Attacks Against Mechanical Credentials 388
  Attacks Against Keys and Bitting 388
  Attacks Against Lock Assembly and Bolt Mechanisms 389
  Attacks Against Systems That Control External Locking
    Elements 389
  Attacks Against Any Openings 389
  Magnetic Fields 389
  Covert Hybrid Attacks Against Mechanical Locking
    Elements 390
  Special Hybrid Attacks to Neutralize Individual Security
    Layers 390
  Covert Forced Hybrid Attacks 391
  Hybrid Attacks Against Detainers 391
  Unintended Consequences 391
    Digital Door Lock Designs 391
    Biometric Access to Gun Safes and Secure Containers 392
    Bumping and Rapping 392
    Bypass of Reset Buttons 392
    Defeating Audit Trails in Electromechanical Locks 392
    Keyway Access to the Latch or Bolt 392
    Nitinol Wire Design Defect in Merchandise Display Case
      Locks 393
    USB Data Port Access in Electronic Locks 393
    Magnetics and Electronic Laptop Locks 393
    Copying Defective Designs 393
    Newton's Laws of Motion 394
    Ratchet Mechanisms and Shims 394
    Use of Plastics in Lock Designs 394
    Vibration and Failure to Use Springs 394

Chapter 17   **Destructive Attacks Against Locks and Related Hardware**   **395**

Tools, Techniques, and Threats from the Application of
  Different Forces   396
  Shearing, Sawing, or Cutting   396
  Drilling   396
  Creating a Shear Line   399
  Drilling and Pulling Attacks on Profile Cylinders   401
  Pounding, Driving, Prying, and Fracturing Materials   403
  Bending   404
  Torsion or Twisting   405
  Torque, Wrenching, Leverage, Jimmying, and Wedging
    Against Components   405
  Opposing Forces Applied Simultaneously: Breaking, Prying,
    Wedging, Peeling, Ripping, and Spreading   406
  Compression and Shearing Force   411
  Impact, Blows, Shock, Hydraulic-Pneumatic Pressure, and
    Compressed Air   411
  Bouncing or Bumping of Locking Components   411
  Battering-Ram Door Hammer   411
  Slam Hammer   412
  Punching   412
  Chisel and Wedging   412
  Application of Temperature Extremes   412
  Chemical Attacks Against Internal Components   414
Basic Tools of Destructive Entry   414

Chapter 18   **Covert Methods of Entry**   **417**
Covert Entry: The Fundamental Premise   418
Primary Points of Vulnerability for All Locks   419
Assessing and Choosing Methods of Attack   420
  Covert-Entry Methods   421
  Shear Line Attacks   423
    Picking   423
  Impressioning   436
    Variable Key-Generation System   438
Magnetic Attacks   440
Processor Reset Attacks   441
Decoding Information from Within the Lock   441
  Audio Frequencies and Sound   442
  Piezo Measurement   442
  Feeling, Friction, and Decoding   442
  Belly Reading and Markings   443
Against Any Openings into the Lock Body with Shims
  and Wires   443

Chapter 19   **Attacks Against Electronic Locks**   **445**
Electronic-Based Locks: Common Design Vulnerabilities
  and Attacks   447

Bumping and Rapping to Move Rotors   447
Attacks Against Electronic Elements Blocking Movement   448
Rotor Manipulation by Application of Energy   449
Piggyback Attacks   450
Replicating the Original Mechanical Key Bitting   451
A Modified Piggyback Attack: Drilling to Create Access
to the Motor   451
Magnetic Fishing and Shim-Wire Movement   452
Direct Electrical Access to the Motor   453
Auto Reset of Relock Exploit   453
Exploiting Reset Functions in Electromechanical Locks   454
Drilling for Rotor Access   454
Drilling to Force the Sidebar to Retract   455
Potential Design Vulnerabilities to Review   455

Chapter 20   **Advanced Attacks Against High-Security Locks**   **459**
Considerations in Developing Attack Strategies, Techniques,
and Tools   460
Unique Design Approaches to Opening Lever and Pin
Tumbler Locks   464
Pin and Cam Systems   464
The Universal Belly Reader   466
Pin-Lock Pin and Cam Systems   466
Systems Based on the Use of Shims   467
The Basic Pin-Lock Decoder   467
Core-Shim Decoder   468
The Medeco BIAXIAL Shim Decoder   469
Material Impressioning System   469
Foil Impressioning System   470
Impressioning Lightbox   471
Plasticine Reading Systems   471
Variable Key-Generation Systems   472
The Universal Pin Tumbler Variable Key System   472
Reusable Variable Key Systems   472

Part V   **Attacks on Key Control and Special Keying Systems**   **475**

Chapter 21   **Attacking Keys and Keying Systems**   **477**
Summary of Attack Strategies Against Keys, Plugs, and
Detainers   478
Intelligence from Locks and Keyways   479
Lock Manufacturer   481
Signature of the Keyway   481
Special Industry Keys and Identification Data   481
Key Codes and Other Data Stamped on Keys   482
The Key's Physical Design   482
The Key's Bitting Data   482
Movable Elements   482
The Number of Pin Tumblers, Discs, or Wafers   483

Correlation Between Physical Key Design and Master
  Key Systems 483
    Depth and Spacing 484
      Decoding Depth and Spacing Information 485
    Manufacturer-Imposed Rules About Bitting and Key Codes 487
    Information Appearing on the Lock Face 487
    Master Keys and Keying Progression 488
    Secondary Locking Systems 488
    Sectional Keyways and Counterfeit Blanks 488
    Maison Keying Systems 488
    Photographing or Scanning Keys for Later Reproduction 488
    Restricted Keyways 489
  Attacks Against Keying Systems 489
    Rights Amplification of Keys and Locks 489
    Recutting a Key to Change the Bitting 490
    Modification of Keyway Warding 490
    Altering Virtual Keyway Systems 490
    Modifying the Secondary Locking System 491
    Inserting an Overlay into a Blank or Cut Key 491
    Converting a Change Key to a Blank Key 491
    Creating a New Shear Line 491
    Replicating or Copying a Target Key 492
    Generating System Keys 492
    Extrapolation of the Top-Level Master Key 493
    Secondary Locking System Decoding 493
    Creating Bump Keys 493
    Decoding Control Keys 493
    Mechanical Bypass 494
    Compromise of Key Control Procedures 495
      Tryout Keys 496
      Exploiting Key-Interchange Issues and Tolerances 496
      Defeating Virtual Keyways 497
      Defeating Ferrous Elements with Magnetic Fields 497
      Incidental Master Keys, Online Key Information, and
        Electronic Credential Cloning 497
  Compromising the Master Key Other than by Extrapolation 498
    Physically Copying, Photographing, or Decoding
      a Master Key 498
    Accessing One or More Cylinders to Decode the Pin
      Segments 498
    Using a Falle Pin-Lock Decoder to Measure Pin Segments
      Using Shim Wires 498
    Falle Pin and Cam Decoder 498
      Shimming the Cylinder with Depth Keys 499
      Visual Inspection of Bitting Values 499
      Viewing Tumblers, Discs, Wafers, or Active Detainers
        with Optical Devices 499

Radiographic Techniques   499
Analyzing Change Keys to Reverse-Engineer the System   499
Top-Level Master Key Extrapolation   500
Extrapolation, Defined   501
The Security Threat   501
Practical Considerations, Variables, and Tactics   501
Information and Intelligence Before an Extrapolation
    Attempt   503
Decoding Options and Logistics   505
Decoding the top-level master key with a Change Key in
    One Session   505
Decoding the top-level master key with a Change Key in
    Multiple Sessions   505
Decoding the top-level master key with All Possible
    Permutations Precut in One or More Sessions   505

**Chapter 22   Advanced Attacks on Key Control: 3D Printers and Special
Software   507**
3D Printing vs. EasyEntrie Milling Machines   510
3D Printer Technology   511
Fused Deposition Modeling Technology   511
Stereolithography Technology   512
Selective Laser Sintering Technology   514
Wax Casting   514
Specialized 3D Software for Keys   514
An Overview of Typical Program Capabilities   515

Chapter 23   Digital Fingerprints of Locks: Electronic Decoding Systems   523
Scanner Tools, Technology, and Physics   524
Primary Patents   526
A Common Transducer   526
Transducer Assembly   527
Reference Software   527
Scanner Designs: Current State-of-the-Art   527
M-SCAN Ultrasonic Lock Decoder and Sound Wave
    Decoder (SWD Version 4): An Overview   528
The Process of Scanning a Lock   531
Scanner Capabilities: A Summary of Required Features   532
Visualization of Scans   533

**Chapter 24   Code-Setting Keys: A Case Study of an Attack on
High-Security Key Control   537**
Background Facts and the Initial Problem   538
An Overview of the Medeco Design   539
Could We Bump Open a Medeco Lock?   540
The Premise That Medeco Locks Could Not Be Bumped Open   541
The Premise That Medeco Locks Could Be Bumped Open   542
Lessons Learned   544

Part VI	**Specific Case Examples**	**545**
Chapter 25	**Case Examples from Part VII Rules**	**547**
	The Introduction of Focused Energy Against Internal Locking Components	549
	A Paper Clip Defeats a Clever Security Enhancement	550
	Defeat of Electronic Credentials	551
	Defeat of an Electronic Access Control Lock Remote Using a Pin	553
	Defeat of the Most Popular Vehicle Anti-Theft Device with a Shim Wire	553
	The Hundred-Million-Dollar Diamond Heist	555
	Vulnerable Design of an Electromechanical Door Lock, and the Murder of Three People	557
	Absence of Evidence of Entry Doesn't Mean a Lock Wasn't Opened	559
	Unknown Tools Specified in Standards Can Produce Invalid Results	559
	Any Opening in a Lock Body or Accessible Component Can Provide a Manipulation Path	560
	Attacks Against Integrated Circuits, Causing Them to Become Unstable	560
	Simple Attacks Against Sophisticated, High-Security, or Complex Locks May Be All That's Required	560
	The Most Popular Bike Lock in the World Opened by a Ballpoint Pen	561
	Axial Locks: Targets for Easy Opening by Bumping and Impressioning	562
	Experts Think High-Security Locks Can't Be Bumped Open	562
	Multiple Security Layers Don't Make a Lock Secure	563
	A Key Isn't Ever What Unlocks a Lock	563
	Attacks on Power Sources Can Affect Electronic Circuits and Cause Locks to Open	564
	Arrogance and a Lack of Imagination Never Works	564
	Small or Uncomplicated Design Changes Can Create New Security Challenges	565
	A 25-Year-Old Embedded Design Defect	565
	Man-in-the-Middle Attacks Can Allow Your Expensive Car to Be Stolen	566
	Hidden or Unknown Security or Design Information About a Device Doesn't Make It Secure	567
	The Most Likely Attack Against an Electronic Lock May Not Be the Most Serious	568
Chapter 26	**Case Examples By Category**	**571**
	Failure to Connect the Dots and Lack of Knowledge About Locks	572
	Failure of Imagination and Engineering Incompetence	574

Failure to Consider or Deal with Hardware Constraints
  or Material Limitations   576
Failure to Understand or Correlate Attack Methods   577
Failure to Consider the Application of Force   578
Failure to Consider Decoding Methods and Attacks   582
Complex Attacks and Security Failures in Designs   586
Attacks on Lock Bodies and Integrity   588
Attacks on Credentials   591
Attacks on Electronic Elements   592
Attacks on Internal Locking Components   593
Attacks on Openings with Shims and Wires   594
Shear Line Attacks   595

Part VII   Design Rules, Axioms, and Principles   597

Chapter 27   Design Rules, Axioms, and Guidelines   599

Epilogue   625

Appendix A   Patents Issued   627

Appendix B   Trademark Listing   629

Index   633

Foreword

The delicate art of security engineering, at its core, is a balancing act. On one side rests the ever-evolving spectrum of innovation: the creation of locks that safeguard our most cherished assets. On the other is the constant challenge to compromise these very inventions—a process as old as time that Marc Weber Tobias insightfully delves into within the pages of this book.

Having served for 19 years as the CTO of dormakaba, one of the world's largest lock manufacturers, I have been at the intersection of innovation and vulnerability. Often, avoidable flaws surfaced, ushering in labor-intensive reparations and tarnishing a reputation painstakingly built over the years. This urgent reminder has always been that in the world of security, there is no room for complacency. From a corporate standpoint, a security failure isn't just a product glitch: it's a liability. The reverberations of such failures can be far-reaching, ranging from reputational harm to potential lawsuits.

Security, I believe, goes beyond mere functionality. It's a philosophy that embraces an understanding of systems and recognizes the complexities woven into the fabric of interconnected technology. Today's digital era intensifies this complexity, urging industry leaders to not just focus on how a system *works* but also understand the myriad ways it can be exploited. This dual vision is vital. At dormakaba, I've tried to instill this approach, advocating for both creators and challengers to scrutinize our products before they reach our customers.

Marc and I have collaborated for over a decade. We've confronted multiple designs, revealing vulnerabilities that escaped our initial engineering discernment. This iterative process, while humbling, has been an indispensable exercise. It has reaffirmed a belief I've always held that security isn't just a technical endeavor but an attitude—an attitude that demands humility, continuous learning, and a touch of paranoia.

As Marc elucidates in this book, an industry-wide disconnect exists: engineers are well equipped with the skills to conceive and implement, but the art of understanding bypass techniques, both elementary and advanced, often remains uncharted. Standards aren't sufficient, as they frequently don't contemplate combining more than one technique to defeat sophisticated systems. This underestimation and lack of imagination of how to compromise supposed security poses significant threats, not just in terms of physical security but also in the realms of reputation and customer trust.

It's an unsettling revelation and one that Marc highlights with meticulous detail. Through an in-depth exploration from the history of lock designs to the nuances of modern-day lock vulnerabilities, this book bridges the gap between proven wisdom and contemporary challenges. For design engineers, risk managers, and even company executives, it provides the guidance and knowledge missing in traditional curricula to tackle real-world security issues.

It's not just a guide but a clarion call to an industry. It's a call to reevaluate, learn, and constantly challenge our understanding of security. I earnestly believe that this book isn't just "good to read" but is a necessary manual for anyone in the realm of security engineering and management.

As our world becomes more connected, the stakes get higher. The chain of security becomes ever more complex and intricate, emphasizing the need for a holistic approach to security engineering.

For the engineers and decision-makers of tomorrow, this book might just be their indispensable compass that points toward a more secure future.

—Andreas Martin Haeberli, Ph.D.

Former CTO, dormakaba

Introduction

Locks and keys, in various forms, have been employed to protect people, places, information, and assets for the past 4,000 years. Although they may outwardly appear simple, their design can be incredibly complex if they're to work properly and securely.

I have been deeply involved in the analysis and design of locks for 40 years and hold many patents on their bypass. Within the last 20 years, the industry has experienced a lock design revolution, partly due to the integration of microprocessors and sophisticated software, especially for access control applications. Improvements in metallurgy, combined with new manufacturing technology, have allowed the development of locks that can better resist criminal attacks. Modern techniques can produce locks with tolerances as high as .002″ and complex designs, yet with all the advances, security is often at risk. Why?

Unfortunately, the industry is still plagued by a fundamental problem in designing locks that must resist ever-developing new vulnerabilities and attacks. That problem partly results from how mechanical engineers are educated in engineering curriculums at universities. Typically, they're taught design theory and *how to make things work*. They aren't taught how to compromise or break their designs or possess the requisite knowledge for "insecurity engineering." This problem has become vastly more complicated by the introduction, integration, and overlay of software-based locking elements, working either alone or in concert with traditional mechanical components.

Electromechanical and electronic locks are slowly changing the landscape in physical security, but they're subject to even more attacks by "lock pickers" and hackers. Technologies such as 3D printing, radio frequency (RF) and electromagnetic pulse (EMP) generators, electronic and mechanical decoders, and various forms of lock bumping, along with the employment of more sophisticated attack vectors, raise the stakes for manufacturers and end users. These problems pervade the industry and highlight the inability of engineers to think "out of the box" to conceive of possible methods of compromise or failure.

Manufacturers' loss of engineering talent through retirement or budget cutbacks has also exacerbated the problem and elevated the urgency of lock security. The loss of seasoned design engineers has largely erased the institutional memory of prior design failures.

What Does This Book Cover?

In the simplest of terms, this book is about what makes a lock or associated hardware "secure" and what can go wrong in the design. In more than one case, the result was the expenditure of millions of dollars on the research and development (R&D) of a high-security lock that was defeated in a few seconds by an 11-year-old kid with virtually no expertise. In my experience consulting for most of the world's largest lock manufacturers, lock designs fail because of a *lack of imagination* on the part of everyone involved in the process. This lack of imagination has had significant and costly ramifications in terms of security failures, legal damages, an inability to meet state and federal standards, and a loss of credibility among customers. Ultimately, it puts consumers at risk, and they usually don't know it. The results are from what I call *insecurity engineering*, which is the inability to design secure locks because of many factors in the education and training of engineers. That is what this book is about.

I started "breaking" things at the age of five years and made a career of discovering and exploiting security and related legal vulnerabilities in locks, safes, and security systems. The locks business is complex, involving liability and compliance issues and engineering requirements. *Tobias on Locks and Insecurity Engineering* analyzes basic lock designs and presents examples of often-catastrophic design failures that sometimes resulted in death and property destruction, compromise of critical information, and millions of dollars in damages.

Who Should Read This Book

Tobias on Locks and Insecurity Engineering is written for design engineers, security and IT professionals, risk managers, government services, law enforcement and intelligence agencies, crime labs, criminal investigators, lawyers, and investigative locksmiths. Even among these professionals, there is a lack of understanding of how to evaluate locks regarding specific security requirements. Relying on industry standards promulgated by Underwriters Laboratories and the Builders Hardware Manufacturers Association (and equivalent organizations overseas) does little to define what *security* means and how to defeat it when considering forced entry, covert entry, and key control issues.

The reader can expect to gain an in-depth insight into lock designs and technology and how to better assess whether specific solutions will meet security requirements for their needs. Detailed information is presented that can help prevent manufacturers from producing insecure locks and assist risk management personnel in reviewing current or proposed systems. For risk management, criminal investigators, and crime laboratories, the information provides a road map showing how locks and security systems can be or may have been compromised by criminals or rogue employees.

Conventions Used in This Book

This book uses certain typographic styles to help you quickly identify important information. In particular, be on the lookout for *italicized text*, which indicates key terms described at length for the first time in a chapter. (Italics are also used for emphasis.)

In addition to these text conventions, you will find the following conventions that highlight segments of text:

NOTE A note indicates information that's useful or interesting, but that's somewhat peripheral to the main text.

TIP A tip provides information that can save you time or frustration and that may not be entirely obvious.

WARNING Warnings describe potential pitfalls or the danger of failing to heed a warning.

SIDEBARS

A sidebar is like a note but longer. The information in a sidebar is useful, but it doesn't fit into the main flow of the text.

Additional Resources

For additional information about locks, please check out the following resources:

- https://Securitylaboratories.org

- `https://lss-dame.com` for detailed videos of the compromise of locks and safes
- `https://zieh-fix.com` for the latest in bypass tools
- Roger G. Johnston, Ph.D., security expert, author of several books on the subject, and editor of the *Journal of Physical Security:* `www.linkedin.com/in/rogergjohnston`
- *High-Security Mechanical Locks: An Encyclopedic Reference*, 2007, by Graham Pulford

For additional information about the leading innovators in the lock-manufacturing industry, please check out the following resources:

- Abloy, Finland: `www.abloy.com/global/en`
- Allegion, Ireland and United States: `https://us.allegion.com/en/index.html`
- ASSA ABLOY, Sweden: `https://assaabloy.com/group/en`
- dormakaba, Germany: `https://dormakaba.com/us-en`
- EVVA, Austria: `https://evva.com/int-en`
- Ikon, Germany: `https://ikon.de/de/en`
- iLOQ, Finland: `https://iloq.com/en`
- Kensington Technology Group, United States: `https://kensington.com`
- Kwikset, United States: `https://kwikset.com`
- Medeco, United States: `https://medeco.com/en`
- Mul-T-Lock, Israel: `https://mul-T-lock.com/global/en/about/mul-T-lock-international`
- SaltoSystems, Spain: `https://saltosystems.com/en`
- Schlage, United States: `https://schlage.com/en/home.html`
- Videx, United States: `https://videx.com`

Finally, the multimedia edition of this book contains extensive video segments and graphics that demonstrate different attack vectors to compromise locks and safes that are referred to in this book. You can find this information at `https://securitylaboratories.org` and `www.wiley.com/go/tobiasonlocks`.

How to Contact the Author

I would appreciate your input, questions, feedback, and information on new tools and bypass techniques! You can find me on Skype, LinkedIn, WhatsApp, Telegram, and Signal. My website is `https://securitylaboratories.org`, and you can email me at mwtobias@securitylaboratories.org or send secure email at mwtobias@protonmail.com.

How to Contact the Publisher

If you believe you've found a mistake in this book, please bring it to our attention by emailing our reader support team at wileysupport@wiley.com with the subject line "Possible Book Errata Submission."

Locks, Safes, and Insecurity Engineering

In this Part, you will be introduced to the concept of insecurity engineering. Locks are often the primary defense for most facilities, so their design is critical for security. Thus, having an understanding of insecurity engineering is vital to every lock manufacturer, risk manager, law enforcement organization, military branch, and government agency. Understanding what insecurity engineering is about is equally important for manufacturers and designers of locks and those who carry out covert operations to gather intelligence by defeating them.

The chapters in Part I provide the foundation to understand why the term *insecurity engineering* was chosen, why it denotes the problems engineers must conceive of, and why they must execute designs that cannot be easily compromised. This Part begins by reviewing the basics of lock designs and then moves on to discuss the critical problems many lock manufacturers experience: a lack of expertise and imagination.

The design of locks is only part of the equation. Testing protocols and vulnerability assessment are coequal parts, and there can be a disconnect with real-world attacks if a failure exists in the assessment process. I, along with my colleagues, have developed a rule by which to measure security. The *3T2R rule* is a way to determine the vulnerability of a lock to attack and its security and legal consequences. This rule is examined in Part I and throughout the rest of the book.

Insecurity Engineering and the Design of Locks

Today's manufacturing technology, software, and hardware design capabilities mean virtually any company can produce a lock if it has the right capital resources. The challenge facing manufacturers, however, is security and the ability to make a lock sufficiently resistant to different forms of attack.

Through my consulting for most of the world's largest lock manufacturers, I've discovered that locks fail for two fundamental yet interrelated reasons:

1. They fail because everyone involved in the process may lack the imagination to anticipate potential and actual security vulnerabilities.

2. They fail due to a lack of engineering expertise about bypass techniques.

This lack of imagination and expertise can have significant and costly ramifications for manufacturers in terms of security failures, legal damages, an inability to meet state and federal standards, and a loss of credibility from their customers. Ultimately, it often places these unaware consumers at risk.

To imagine a vulnerability, it is a prerequisite that you understand and correlate different attack modes and current or proposed designs. My father, a mechanical engineer, encouraged me from the age of five to take things apart, learn how they worked, and figure out how to break them. Before becoming a lawyer, I began my career by discovering and exploiting security and legal vulnerabilities in lock, safe, and security system design. It was during this time that I realized the ramifications of insecurity engineering.

What Is Insecurity Engineering?

In the simplest of terms, *insecurity engineering* is a lack of expertise and understanding of how locks work and the various ways you can make them fail. It creates insecurity, contrary to a lock's *raison d'etre* (i.e., reason to exist). Insecurity engineering results in a failure to "connect the dots" from simple design errors to compound failures, which finally results in the compromise of components that can potentially defeat security. It's an engineer designer's lack of creativity and imagination to consider a "What if?" scenario. Finally, it's the absence of a complete understanding or knowledge of past mistakes in similar designs. Such insights can only be acquired via experience, by working with seasoned engineers and having a full familiarity with what has been designed and patented to remedy past defects or deficiencies that originally created or allowed the vulnerabilities.

Insecurity engineering is also about legal liability and the failure to understand that defective designs ultimately will invite lawsuits and damage awards. If someone is hurt or a company sustains damage in whatever form, it can cost a manufacturer a monetary loss *and* reputational injury. As the name implies, insecurity engineering highlights the need to forecast, discover, and prevent insecure designs from reaching the end user.

This concept, which is discussed more in Chapter 3, ensures that those responsible for the design of locks, safes, and security systems have the requisite expertise to assess a product from many different perspectives, starting with its inception and continuing through analysis and testing by a vulnerability assessment team. *Competent insecurity engineering*, as the term implies, is an absolute prerequisite to successfully developing any security-related product.

Primary Responsibilities of Lock Manufacturers

Let's begin by discussing the primary missions of lock manufacturers. Lock manufacturers are responsible for making products that securely perform their intended function or purpose. I can identify at least nine critical responsibilities for companies that produce locks and related security systems, all based on a foundation of competent insecurity engineering practices and programs. Here are those nine critical responsibilities:

1. Invent or improve on state-of-the-art technology.
2. Develop and continue to analyze and improve on earlier designs.
3. Understand all vulnerabilities and imagine new ones.
4. Apply design expertise to currently manufactured and new products.

5. Protect intellectual property (IP) from infringement.

6. Ensure that IP produced and sold is secure and will not cause injury or harm.

7. Do not produce defective products.

8. Fully understand product liability and its critical importance.

9. Initiate a disclosure program about serious vulnerabilities.

Let's break down these nine responsibilities further.

NOTE For more information on security engineering, check out *Security Engineering, Third Edition,* by Ross Anderson. It's a must-read for Internet technology (IT) professionals, risk managers, and computer engineers and covers system design, emerging technologies, and what can go wrong when system developers don't understand security and vulnerability.

Invent or Improve On State-of-the-Art Technology

Manufacturers should strive to develop, improve, or create new designs to enhance their products, improve overall security, and increase their capability to secure people, facilities, assets, and information. Over the past 200 years, companies have succeeded because they innovated new locking technologies and implemented the latest advancements. The lifeblood of every manufacturer is its creation of IP and the allowance of patents. *Intellectual property* encompasses patents, trademarks, and copyrights and is the foundation of almost every product for every serious lockmaker because patents ensure protection for their work and creativity for 20 years under current patent laws. Customers rely on this protection when they buy *security technology*—a gauge of the state-of-the-art technology in the industry—which is essential for successful product marketing.

Develop and Continue to Analyze and Improve On Earlier Designs

Manufacturers should be vigilant about issues from past and present designs to ensure that they're currently aware of new attacks that could affect the security of their products. Even if a locking system was developed several years ago, if it's currently being sold, any vulnerability can be the basis of a liability. A monitoring system should be set up for every new product, not only for receiving customer feedback but also for discovering or publishing security issues.

Understand All Known Vulnerabilities and Imagine New Ones

A continuous review of products must occur to ensure that a manufacturer's products are secure against current attacks. The Simplex 1000 push-button lock is a perfect example: a mechanical system that was initially patented around 1965 but became the subject of a class action lawsuit in 2010 because it could easily be defeated by a strong magnetic field. Its manufacturer did not review it for or imagine any vulnerabilities, which is critical to securing a lock against attacks.

Apply Expertise to Currently Manufactured and New Products

Manufacturers must maintain and develop an engineering team with the requisite expertise to assess design defects of current and new products in terms of their security. Doing so is imperative to creating locks that can withstand attacks. (You'll find this issue addressed more fully in Chapters 2 and 3).

Protect Intellectual Property (IP) from Infringement

Manufacturers must maintain a corporate policy that stresses the protection of IP in locks and security systems, for the benefit of both the manufacturer and its customers. If patents and trademarks are not constantly monitored for infringement, they will not protect the property's owner or anyone relying on their enforcement. A great example is discussed in Part VI: a large manufacturer held patents for key designs with interactive elements that were reproduced and sold in large quantities in major metropolitan areas by counterfeiters. The manufacturer's inability to protect its IP resulted in economic losses to the manufacturer and many locksmiths and presented security risks to critical customers.

Ensure That IP Produced and Sold Is Secure and Will Not Cause Injury or Harm

From a legal and ethical standpoint, the primary responsibility of a lock manufacturer is to ensure that whatever products it offers for sale are secure and will not harm customers or their facilities due to improper use or the circumvention of security. Any insecurity or harm can potentially damage a manufacturer's credibility, not to mention harming its consumers.

Do Not Produce Defective Products

The term *defective* can be defined in many ways, including design, manufacturing, and warning. In the context of this book, it relates primarily to security vulnerabilities that are present and can or should be predicted. It is imperative that lock manufacturers ensure their products are not defective, to protect the integrity of their companies and products.

Fully Understand Product Liability and Its Critical Importance

Liability considerations must be built into every project and product from its inception until it's sold to its end users. A lock manufacturer's employees should be trained to be sensitive to legal issues that can result in a company's legal liability, which could even extend to its employees. Protocols should be set in place to document in detail every security-related product's development, modifications, and fixes to minimize the company's exposure to lawsuits and damages. Management, in addition to every employee, must be cognizant of the multiple tenets of product liability law and how to guard against tort liability and contract violations while protecting trade secrets, non-disclosure agreements, and confidentiality.

Initiate a Disclosure Program about Serious Vulnerabilities

Once vulnerabilities are discovered and their seriousness is verified, there must be a process to properly disclose all product defects affecting the security of critical customers or even the general public. It is suggested that this process detail warnings about security issues, including those involved with master key systems, key copying, and capabilities to circumvent key control. (Such a process is discussed in more detail in Chapter 2.)

Several years ago, I introduced and promoted the concept of *unethical non-disclosure*, where lock manufacturers were aware of vulnerabilities but failed to disclose them to customers or did nothing to remedy design problems. As a lawyer, I counseled my manufacturing clients to be up front with their customers and the public about their security-related issues. Customers have a right to rely on a manufacturer's expertise in lock design and an expectation to be forewarned about potential or known defects that could place them at risk. It is unethical for a company to fail to disclose or warn its customers about a significant flaw.

Examples of Insecurity Engineering Failures

Throughout this book, I cite insecurity engineering failures that have led to extensive product delays, product recalls, redesign, and significant legal damages. Such failures are more fully described in Part VI, but I summarize a few in this section as a sobering reminder of what can happen when there's a lack of hardware and software design expertise as it applies to lock security.

Locks can be circumvented in several ways. Here are a few examples:

■ *Bumping*: A technique based on the application of force to pin tumblers by a special key, which has caused many security issues for the world's lock manufacturers (see Figure 1-1).

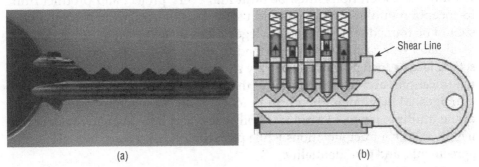

(a)   (b)

Figure 1-1a, 1b: A bump key can be produced from virtually any key blank for a pin tumbler lock by cutting all the bitting to the lowest possible depth. (a) A bump key for Postal Service locks. (b) What happens when the key is forced forward to cause the bottom and top pins to split at the shear line.

■ *Shimming*: A technique in which fine wires are employed to compromise various lock types by exploiting tiny openings that allow the insertion of shims to access critical components.

■ *Impressioning*: A technique in which an impression of a tubular pin tumbler lock is taken with plastic pens to produce a key.

The following examples demonstrate common design errors resulting from engineers failing to consider the basic laws of physics. These errors have cost my clients redesign expenses, product delays, recalls, lawsuits, federal investigations, injuries, and even deaths. Although this example list is not exhaustive, it does include all instances of insecurity engineering failures due to simple attacks that were covert and left no traces.

However, design failures are not limited to the application of the laws of physics. They are also about imagination and the ability to assess each lock component and how these components can be used to cause a compromise. They encompass every aspect of design, from key control to tolerances to the interaction of components. It's about the information derived from how each component works and what can be discovered about the inner working of a lock and, ultimately, the secrets that will enable it to be decoded or opened.

TIP For more about lock-breaking techniques, see Chapter 12. In addition, you'll find multiple detailed lock images and diagrams throughout the book that illustrate critical parts of different lock types and how they work.

The following examples detail the various types of locks and their design errors:

Spring-loaded locking mechanism: Many locks employ springs to retain critical components in place until activated by a key or other credential. Any spring-biased component is subject to potential compromise through the application of force and the laws of physics. Springs control other movable elements that can be subject to such attacks.

One design flaw was exploited by someone using a plastic screwdriver handle to release the locking mechanism of a newly developed laptop lock ready for production. A single strike with the plastic mass (i.e., the handle of the screwdriver) against the locked cylinder released the spring-based internal mechanism and unlocked and released the lock from the computer.

High-security cylinders with side bit milling and a sidebar: As described in Chapter 14, there are numerous techniques to make locks more difficult to compromise. One technique is the addition of what I call side bit milling with a second set of locking pins that interact with the key. The second set of bitting is designed to control more locking tumblers (see Figure 1-2).

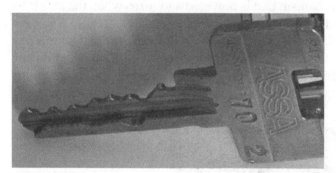

Figure 1-2: A key with side bit milling provides another security layer and can make picking and bumping more complicated.

It was believed that the design of this high-security mechanical lock with a secondary locking system using side bit milling pins would prevent bumping or another type of defeat. When attackers altered the physical design of the milling, I demonstrated that these locks could still be defeated, especially through lock bumping (which is more fully discussed and described in Chapter 18). Bumping, in the simplest of terms, requires using a special key that makes contact with all the pin tumblers in a lock and causes the pins to momentarily move in a way that allows the plug of the lock to turn.

The combination of energy and the modification of the milling was enough to defeat the system easily, even though the engineering team at the lock factory said it was impossible. They required an understanding of how this combination defeated their system.

High-security electronic cylinder: Many locks can be opened by applying force—striking them with hammers, plastic mallets, or other similar tools that can transmit energy to the lock's surface. This energy, in combination with internal components that rely on springs or the lack of springs to control the movement of critical parts, makes the locks vulnerable to this form of attack.

The manufacturer of this popular lock had no idea that the application of energy could easily and quickly defeat its high-security electronic profile cylinder and padlocks sold to foreign governments. This lock manufacturer's engineers had failed to imagine this form of bypass in its design and needed to understand the underlying theory of why their design failed.

Newton's First Law of Motion and electronic cylinders: The First Law of Motion states, "Every object will remain at rest or in uniform motion in a straight line unless compelled to change its state by the action of an external force." Many electronic cylinders rely on a worm gear to advance or retract locking elements when powered after a valid radio-frequency identification (RFID) credential is presented. A worm gear is a small motor that drives a spring or similar mechanism that is powered and turns when the lock is to be opened (or locked) (see Figure 1-3). As we discovered, these devices are subject to a simple form of attack. No one in the industry had connected the dots or realized that in seconds, the First Law of Motion could defeat these mechanisms produced by multiple manufacturers. The vulnerability affected many lock manufacturers because almost all relied on worm gears.

Figure 1-3: A worm gear is controlled by a small motor in electronic locks. The gear is turned when the motor is activated, which causes the gear to advance or retract a locking component.

NOTE RFID is a technology that relies on a tiny passive radio receiver that requires no power. A signal transmitted from the lock energizes the receiver, which responds with a coded signal that validates the credential that energized it. RFID technology is used in thousands of different applications but is particularly well adapted to secure credentials in locks.

Tiny entry points and openings for shims: Many lock designs have small holes or openings that allow for the entrance of fine shim wires to manipulate internal components, making it possible to open the lock. The Kaba InSync is a perfect example: a shim was inserted into the USB data port of this deadbolt cylinder and manipulated to release the locking mechanism (see Figure 1-4).

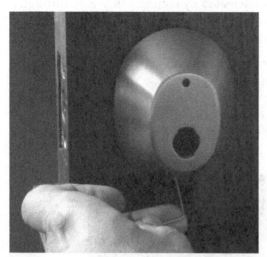

Figure 1-4: The Kaba InSync is a perfect example of a design failure to account for a small opening in the USB data port. This allowed the entry of a paperclip to bypass the release mechanism.

Virtual keyways with an internal sliding element: the *keyway* is the entry point for all mechanical locks. It controls which physical keys can operate the internal locking elements. Lock manufacturers figured out they could also create *virtual keyways*, which, as the name implies, are not equivalent to actual physical keyways. They are designed to simulate traditional keyways that mate with keys.

A clever but flawed concept in a new lock design used a form of virtual keyway. It was based on adding a sliding element to block access to the lock's sidebar until properly positioned by inserting a key. A *sidebar* is a very effective secondary locking system that many manufacturers employ to resist picking and other forms of attack.

In 2002, lock manufacturer Medeco introduced its m3-enhanced version of the BIAXIAL cylinder, in which a sliding element was added that moved laterally by a protrusion on the key's surface. This movement positioned the slider correctly, allowing the sidebar to engage in the plug. However, the team that introduced this concept failed to consider that the slider spacing was constant, regardless of the dimensions of the different slider combinations, and that the required movement of the slider was precisely the diameter of a paper clip (.04"). All that was necessary to defeat this system was the insertion of said clip into the keyway, wedged between the plug body and the edge of the slider.

Electronic credentials and wire in a circuit board feed-through hole: A sophisticated electromechanical cylinder was defeated by fishing a tiny wire through a circuit board's feed-through hole to access and move the blocking rotor, allowing the lock to be opened.

Wafer locks and paper clips: A wafer lock, as described in Chapter 13, is a low- to medium-security mechanism that relies on the use of slidable tumblers, which are moved by the bitting of a key to the shear line, allowing the plug to turn. These locks are easily picked or manipulated (see Figure 1-5). The keys and their bitting can be configured to act on the wafers to move them in one or two directions.

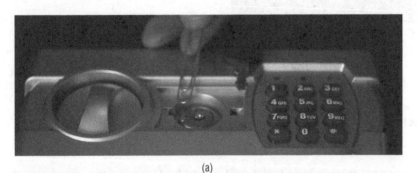

(a)

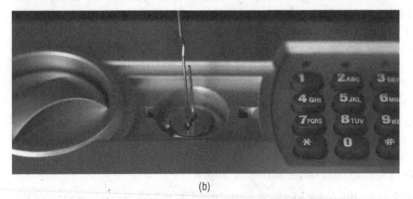

(b)

Figure 1-5a, 5b: Reverse picking of wafer locks is common. (a) A popular gun safe with a wafer bypass lock that can be easily opened with a paper clip. (b) The paper clip is inserted into the keyway, torque is applied, and the paper clip is slowly withdrawn.

Many small in-home safes and other devices employ single- or double-bitted wafer locks. These types of locks can often be easily defeated by inserting a wire, paper clip, or blank key and slowly withdrawing it with torque applied. In a reverse-picking attack, the wafers are trapped in place at the shear line because of the tension applied to the plug as a blank key or pick is withdrawn, one wafer at a time. This lock type is especially dangerous when used in gun-safe designs.

TIP *Single-bitted* means the wafers are moved in one direction. *Double-bitted* means the wafers are moved to the top and bottom of the plug.

Sophisticated push-button access control locks and the insertion of wires, pins, and paper clips: Advanced push-button locks employed by military, government, and commercial facilities can be defeated in many ways with wires, paper clips, and stick pins (see Figure 1-6). Their designers never conceived of simple attacks that could neutralize one or more security layers, notwithstanding the sophisticated electronic card-reading systems featured in the locks.

Figure 1-6: The Kaba 5800 electronic push-button lock could be defeated in six ways. I demonstrated these attacks at DefCon. One serious design failure was demonstrated by the insertion of a pin, wire, or pick tip through an LED mount to ground a contact on the PC board. This sent a remote opening signal to an electric strike at the door.

Vehicle anti-theft device and a shim: Makers of The Club steering wheel locking bar never considered how its ratchet design could be easily compromised in a few seconds with a five-cent piece of wire. Understanding how the locking mechanism worked and using that knowledge to defeat it led to my receiving a patent (U.S. 5,277,042) to fix the problem. The manufacturer's inability to imagine the defeat placed thousands of vehicles at risk of theft. The same security issue applies to handcuffs that can be defeated by circumventing the ratchet mechanism.

Simple key modification and electronic locks: iLOQ (from Finland) produced an award-winning and patented electronic cylinder that required no batteries. The designers of this lock series should have considered the fundamental design of how the lock worked and how design deficiencies allowed the lock to be set in a permanent state of unlocked status once a covert attack was implemented (see Figure 1-7).

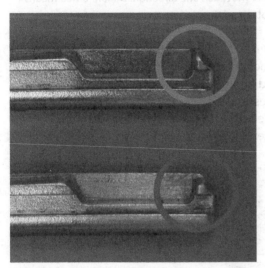

Figure 1-7: A simple modification to a valid key for an iLOQ electronic cylinder could result in it being permanently set with a screwdriver to unlock until reset. The top circle shows a nonmodified key tip. A small amount of material is removed (bottom circle) to defeat the lock's security.

Liquid injections and driver chips in safe and vault locks: The design of electronic locks, especially for safes, often requires an electronic driver chip to control motors or solenoids. Engineers never considered that you could destabilize these chips, causing a reset in critical integrated circuits by altering the impedance around the input contacts on the printed circuit board, which results in an electronic reboot that cycles the motor drives to open.

Wire access through keyways: In many instances, critical components can be reached through an open keyway. Many lock manufacturers have created serious security flaws by not closing and protecting the ends of plugs. A popular fingerprint lock can be opened in seconds by introducing a small wire into the bypass cylinder. This is also the case in file cabinet locks, key-in-knob locks, and even extremely popular locksets in which a release pin could be accessed through the keyway to completely remove the knob that contains the pin tumbler locking core (see Figure 1-8).

Plastic ballpoint pens and tubular locks: A failure to understand impressioning techniques in tubular pin tumbler locks has cost millions of dollars in damages due to faulty lock designs. An engineer's lack of imagination failed to "connect the dots" in the Kryptonite bike lock case. (A more detailed description of this case can be found in Part VI.)

Figure 1-8: Open keyways, as shown in this deadbolt lock, can provide access to wires, shims, and other tools to manipulate a tailpiece.

KRYPTONITE BIKE LOCKS

The Kryptonite bike lock has been recognized as the premiere system for protecting bicycles from theft. The original design was based on the use of a tubular pin tumbler lock, which had a round key that is popular for many applications because of its low cost and simple implementation by manufacturers. The pins were configured in a circle rather than a straight line as in traditional mechanisms. The Kryptonite engineers failed to realize that the pins could be easily impressioned or decoded because they were all accessible simultaneously by an attacker. (The concept of impressioning is explored in Chapter 18.)

In the case of the bike lock, all that was required was a plastic ballpoint pen the same diameter as the opening (i.e., keyway) in the lock. If pressure was applied in a pumping action, the pen barrel deformed to precisely match the bitting values of the key. The failure to understand impressioning, the correlation of the diameter of the keyway to many pens, and the ability to produce a working key led to a recall of hundreds of thousands of locks.

Gun trigger locks and faulty key designs: Gun trigger locks are designed to prevent a pistol from being fired by blocking access to the trigger area by physically covering it. These types of locks are notoriously insecure and inexpensive and are sold mainly to protect access to guns by children. The tolerances between the plug (i.e., where the key is inserted) and the housing are generally poor. The gap created by this tolerance is called the *shear line*. It determines how the key works in the lock. Manufacturers of these locks can save money by stamping rather than individually cutting the keys, so they can be mass produced. In this case, the producer of these locks not only stamped the keys but made the individual cuts almost identical and in a straight line, thus easily circumventing the function of the shear line. It meant every lock the manufacturer sold in the country could be opened by the same key, so a child could purchase a lock for $10 and have a key that would open the lock that was protecting the gun at their residence. Manufacturers producing inexpensive wafer or pin tumbler locks with bitting stamped at nearly the same level for each pin allowed gun locks to be opened with a straight wire or paper clip (see Figure 1-9). Design engineers failed to consider the ability to move all tumblers to the shear line due to their failure to understand the security of one of these mechanisms.

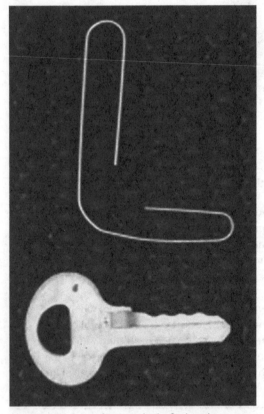

Figure 1-9: Several trigger locks for handguns were produced with stamped keys, all having essentially the same bitting values. A paper clip could lift all the wafers and open the lock in seconds.

Shims as drills in electronic cylinders: Using plastics in electromechanical and electronic cylinders creates serious security issues. In one instance, my security team partner and I used a fine shim wire as a drill bit to create entry holes into the lock face that were almost undetectable and enabled access to critical internal components.

Pin tumbler lock plug: Design engineers for one of the most popular and secure U.S. deadbolt cylinders should have considered what protects a pin tumbler lock from compromise via the keyway. This failure allowed the lock to be bypassed by introducing a small modified screwdriver tip to manipulate the lock's tailpiece element and attack and shear the endcap's retaining screws.

Magnetic fields and ferrous components in locks: Rare earth magnets have been very successful in moving internal components in many locks and electric strikes without a trace (see Figure 1-10). One of the most popular cases involved the Kaba Simplex 1000 mechanical push-button lock, currently used worldwide in banks, airports, pharmacies, government facilities, and many other venues. These prevalent locks could be opened in seconds because a ferrous element was critical to the locking function, and that component could be moved if a strong magnet was placed near the outside of the lock. When that occurred, the lock could be opened in two seconds. All it took to defeat it was an inexpensive magnet (see Figure 1-11).

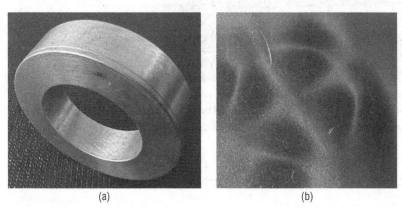

(a)   (b)

Figure 1-10a, 10b: Magnetic fields can move ferrous components within a lock to cause an opening. (a) The devil's ring, developed by Wendt, is the classic attack tool. It is a round metal enclosure with four magnets, as shown in (b) the visa mag film overlay that identifies each magnet.

Magnetic fields were also employed to open electronic cylinders with a small device called a "magnetic devil's ring," originally designed by Addi Wendt in Germany. The devil's ring was simply a round aluminum shell with four magnets placed in a circle to surround the outside portion of a locking cylinder. Rotating caused the lock's internal components to move and open. In my experience, lock design teams consistently forgot about the capability to manipulate ferrous materials with strong fields in locks and electric strikes.

Shims and combination locks: Numerous combination locks for computers and bicycles employ rotary discs that set a combination by the gate position for each number. Many manufacturers fail to consider the tolerances between these discs. Thin strips of metal or shims can be used to probe the individual gates, allowing for easy decoding of the numbers to open the lock.

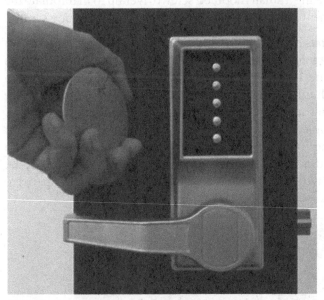

Figure 1-11: The Kaba Simplex 1000 mechanical lock was defeated by a rare earth magnet in seconds because a critical component that controlled unlocking was made of a ferrous material. Moving the round magnet near the lock was all that was required.

Now that we've reviewed the multitude of ways locks can be circumvented, let's consider what I think are the most important design rules when creating a lock's design.

Important Design Rules

> **It ain't what you don't know that gets you into trouble. It's what you know for sure that just isn't so.**
>
> *—Mark Twain*

During my career, I've developed basic engineering rules that apply to locks and security hardware design. (If you wish to rush ahead, a complete listing is provided in Part VII, explaining why each rule is important.) I developed these basic engineering rules to take an alternative look at technical problems and minimize or eliminate the potential vulnerabilities existing in mechanical designs.

Basic engineering rules:

1. *The key never unlocks the lock.* Consider what actually unlocks the lock and how it or its credentials can be spoofed. Look for the path of least resistance to actuate the mechanism to open the lock. In most lock designs, the key controls another part responsible for allowing the lock to open. If the actions of the key can be replicated or simulated, then the key is not essential.

2. *Do not ignore the laws of physics or how they apply to attacks on locks.* One of the best ways I've found to defeat specific locking mechanisms is to rely on Newton's First and Third Laws of Motion. Many engineers do not correlate these principles with the ability to bypass locks and safes. As I note throughout this book, lock bumping is based on the Third Law of Motion: "For every action, there is an equal and opposite reaction" (see Figure 1-12). Bumping became a massive issue for manufacturers due to the vulnerability of most conventional and some high-security locks. It is based on the focused introduction of energy against pin tumblers. To combat this issue, some manufacturers introduced what they call *shock fuses*. These are designed to prevent the effects of bumping and other specific attacks against different parts via shock and vibration. Lock bumping has developed and expanded from its initial application of energy against pin tumbler cylinders to a more sophisticated method of attack for many different mechanisms.

(a)   (b)

Figure 1-12a, 12b: The classic way to describe Newton's Third Law of Motion is with steel free-swinging balls. (a) The four balls are struck, and (b) the ball on the right is moved because of the energy transmitted as an equal reaction. This is the same theory of lock bumping with pin tumblers. When energy is applied to the base of pins by the key, the reaction causes them to move vertically across the shear line.

NEWTON'S LAWS OF MOTION

Sir Isaac Newton was a famous physicist who lived in seventeenth-century England. Most known for his studies of motion and gravity, he developed three laws of motion:

First Law of Motion: An object at rest will remain at rest, while an object in motion will continue in motion with a constant velocity unless acted on by outside forces.

Second Law of Motion: When a force acts on an object, its acceleration is inversely proportional to its mass.

Third Law of Motion: For every action (force) in nature, there is an equal and opposite reaction.

3. *Electrons don't open doors, mechanisms do.* Every lock with mechanical and electronic components that act in concert is vulnerable to attack. The junction of hardware and software must control something that moves, and that interface is always subject to compromise. Only mechanics control bolts and latches, whereas electrons only send signals to movable elements through motors, solenoids, magnetic coils, and so on.

4. *Locks are designed to be tested and attacked by bad guys.* You must assume that any designed lock will be subject to one or more attacks. It is important to try to envision all possible methods of attack against specific mechanisms when designing your lock. Consider every component, even if you assume it's irrelevant to the lock's overall security. Even the most insignificant part can be compromised and cause a cascade of events, resulting in the lock being opened.

5. *Whatever design is secure today certainly will not be tomorrow.* Methods of compromise are constantly evolving and being modified by clever attackers. New materials and tools and past design errors embedded into new locks are constantly being developed and exploited. Do not ever believe that what is secure today will be secure tomorrow.

6. *All security is about liability.* If people or property are injured due to a defective lock's design in a security system, the company that produced it can be held legally responsible.

7. *A lack of imagination in design and testing can lead to security vulnerabilities and failures.* The ability to analyze a mechanism and think about remote failure possibilities is important in lock design when considering a lock's vulnerability.

8. *All exploits ultimately replicate what the key does.* A correct key or code allows a lock's critical locking mechanism to be moved to a locked or unlocked position. Whether it's an actual or simulated key, lock pick, decoder, or special tool, its primary function is to replicate the actions of the key—to move the locking mechanism to an open position. If such a simulation can be accomplished, the lock can be opened without the key.

9. *All secrets in a lock are self-contained.* Whether it is a mechanical, electrome-chanical, or software-based lock, all the "secrets" or puzzle parts are self-contained, assuming that the intelligence running the lock is not networked or stored in the cloud. Locks should be thought of as puzzles that contain a set of secrets. If the secrets are deciphered and understood, then the lock can be opened.

10. *You cannot test against an attack if you have not envisioned the standards for testing.* The standards for testing locks, which are analyzed in Chapter 7, provide testing protocols that specifically include what I refer to as *hybrid attacks* that employ multiple modes and tools. Suppose that engineers do not fully understand what is possible outside the covert and forced-entry standards. In that case, they cannot fully assess vulnerabilities that may not be obvious if the standards are the only metrics. It's impossible to test for all attack types if your standards to test by haven't even conceived of those attack types.

11. *Adversaries can be incredibly resourceful and innovative.* Those planning and researching specific attacks against a lock may know much more than the designers who built the locking mechanism or system. It's often the case that the attackers understand your security and vulnerabilities better than you do. They constantly think about ways to attack, especially by collaborating on the Internet.

12. *Attacks may be low- or high-tech.* When assessing the potential for attacks against a new or current lock design, it's always tempting to think of them as high-tech attacks because simple ones cannot be conceived of. Some very sophisticated locks have been opened by extremely simple means. Locks and their mechanisms may be subject to either high-tech attacks or low-tech attacks that do not involve any technology. Never ignore one for the other.

13. *Design against likely attack vectors, not how secure a lock appears.* It is common for design teams to examine their current or new products and feel they're likely not vulnerable to forms of attack that they understand or can antici-pate. In my experience, it's more important to concentrate on different forms of attack and work backward. Explore every conceivable way that other components and mechanisms could be compromised. Again, think-ing outside the box is critical here because components that may seem to have no connection with security can become highly relevant. In one analysis my colleague and I conducted, the lead representative for a global U.S. company, in response to our claims of insecurity of one of the com-pany's high-security locks, announced to the media that "I see no evidence that a system can be defeated. Therefore, it cannot." He later apologized, as his lock was indeed defeated because he could not conceive of a certain attack as viable.

14. *Suppose you don't believe you can open a lock. In that case, you probably will not be able to.* In my experience in compromising locks and security systems, negative thinking, especially when analyzing and attacking locks, usually leads to failure in such an endeavor because key indicators or paths are either ignored or missed.

15. *IT staff, risk management, security managers, police, crime labs, and locksmiths usually are not experts in finding lock vulnerabilities.* As access control systems migrate to becoming fully electronic, IT must always be involved. They must be able to fully understand system designs from the standpoint of security vulnerabilities. My experience with law enforcement and locksmiths has demonstrated that they need to become experts in discovering or assessing vulnerabilities to comprehend all vulnerabilities. The International Association of Investigative Locksmiths (IAIL) has this as one of their primary goals.

16. *Just because you're intelligent doesn't mean you can think like a bad guy.* Criminals and "bad guys" have different goals in compromising a security system or device. They usually want to gain access, steal assets or information, or sabotage infrastructure. Design engineers are employed to ensure that their products are secure against multiple forms of attack. They have very different motivations than bad guys. Unless they have experience working in law enforcement and interacting with criminals, these engineers cannot understand the thought processes and mentality of a criminal. Thinking like a bad guy requires a great deal of experience and insight into the mindset of someone who would cause harm.

17. *Just because multiple security layers are present doesn't mean all the layers are secure and the system cannot be compromised.* Virtually all high-security locks contain more than one security layer that must be appropriately activated to cause an opening. Although multiple security layers appear to ensure that the lock is more difficult to compromise by covert methods, they also provide an opportunity to do the opposite—create a vulnerability—if they are not designed properly. (Part IV describes many scenarios that allow locks with multiple security layers to be easily bypassed because their designers have yet to consider the possibility of attacks, especially hybrid attacks.)

18. *Insecurity engineering is far different from traditional mechanical or electronic engineering—the goals are entirely different.* Designing a lock requires mechanical engineering, materials science, and electrical or electronic engineering expertise if the system is electromechanical. In contrast, insecurity engineering is a different discipline that requires a thorough understanding of bypass techniques and the ability to project or foresee methods that could circumvent supposedly secure designs.

19. *Security can be viewed as an optimization problem, requiring many complex trade-offs and value judgments.* Designing a secure lock is a complex process involving many disciplines and thought processes that must be considered. Security is not just one factor, and it is not simply the hardware design. It encompasses possible failures, attacks, misuse, production defects, and use cases. There are often design trade-offs based on the complexity of manufacturing, materials availability, security, costs, convenience, human factors, management issues, and the projected user environment. In any project to design or modify a lock design, conflicting needs must be carefully considered and weighed to reach a consensus on the best way to proceed.

20. *Security starts when the project starts, not at the project's end.* If security is not the overriding consideration from the inception to the completion of a project, the result will likely be no security.

21. *Simple design errors can cause larger errors that experts will miss.* In my experience, every aspect of a lock design must be analyzed and assessed for the potential to cause failures in operation or security. The simplest design error can cause a cascading failure between related components, leading to significant manufacturing defects and security vulnerability. My rule of thumb: pay attention to everything and every component and their interrelationships.

22. *A security vulnerability may not be evident because there has been no incident.* In a serious product analysis that I conducted, a design defect that was latent for almost 20 years in the Medeco BIAXIAL pin tumbler lock surfaced in our research; it resulted in the compromise of many high-security cylinders. Do not believe there isn't a defect or vulnerability just because no one has reported a failure. No design is ever perfect.

23. *Sophistication in tech often means vulnerability.* Many believe that sophisticated or new technology means it's better and more secure. Often the opposite is true, because more layers of sophistication can mean more opportunities to defeat any one or more layers.

24. *The belief that all security devices can be defeated can mean none of them will be fixed.* I've often been told that all locks can be defeated with enough time and expertise. That attitude often causes management and design engineers to minimize threats and develop an "it's good enough" attitude in conducting research and development to produce a secure mechanism.

25. *Invest the time and research dollars in eliminating known vulnerabilities before going to market.* Recalls and redesigns are expensive. Unfortunately, management is always in a hurry to introduce new locks to their customers, with the attitude that any security issues are minimal and can be dealt with "down the road." This "down the road" syndrome can result in legal

liability and large damage lawsuits because the design and management teams simply did not want to wait until a product was secure. When analyzing a new lock design with defects, I have often asked management, "Are you willing to bet your company on not fixing a problem before a product release?" Take the time and money to invest in lock research to avoid big liabilities down the road.

26. *Bad guys do not follow the rules, standards, or attack modes*. Criminals, hackers, and attackers do not follow any rules regarding how they work or the techniques they choose to compromise a lock or system. The standards for locks and safes, detailed in Chapter 7, can provide a road map for how locks can be attacked in covert and forced entry mode, considering gaps in what the standards do not protect against. Design engineers must consider novel approaches to compromising their designs.

27. *Arrogance and a lack of knowledge can be the reciprocal of expertise in lock design*. A person who doesn't know they lack expertise can be the most dangerous and destructive to a design team. Many design engineers and managers think they know more about their product and its security than anyone else. This arrogance can result in serious ramifications, including liability and recalls.

28. *Never forget the Dunning–Kruger Effect and the phenomenon that the people who are the least competent in a subject often overestimate their skills*. People can overestimate their abilities, much to the detriment of a design project. Inflated self-perceptions can be fatal in terms of creativity and making errors in judgment about the efficacy of a lock design. David Dunning and Justin Kruger initially conducted a study in 1999. Their research looked at cognitive bias and focused on logical reasoning, grammar, and social skills. In the simplest terms, the Dunning–Kruger effect is the tendency of people with minimal ability in a specific area to offer overly positive reports of their ability. In judging the security of a lock, for example, this can lead to erroneous forms of thinking and conclusions.

Summary

This chapter introduced the premise of *insecurity engineering* and why it is important for every design engineer, product manager, and risk manager to understand. Many lockmakers are engaged in designing hardware that is inherently insecure, and they simply *do not know it*. After many years of working with different manufacturers, it was clear to my team that the simplest way to describe and understand the problem was to label it precisely as what it is: insecurity engineering.

Insecurity Engineering: A Lack of Expertise and Imagination

Around the time of the Great Exhibition in 1851 in London, there was a great deal of publicity about the insecurity of locks and safes. There was also a lot of controversy about the ethics and propriety of publishing methods to compromise security hardware. A.C. Hobbs was the American lock expert who cracked the most secure lock in England; he wrote a classic text on the subject. The following quotes were instructive then and still are, because the same arguments are often made about publishing details of the ways to compromise locks and safes.

> A commercial, and in some respects a social doubt has been started within the last year or two, whether it is right to discuss the security or insecurity of locks openly. Many well-meaning persons suppose that the discussion respecting the means for baffling the supposed safety of locks offers a premium for dishonesty by showing others how to be dishonest. This is a fallacy. Rogues are very keen in their profession and already know much more than we can teach them respecting their several kinds of roguery.
>
> Rogues knew a lot about lock-picking long before locksmiths discussed it, as they have lately done. If a lock, let it have been made in whatever country or by whatever maker, is not so inviolable as it has hitherto been deemed to be, surely it is to the interest of honest persons to know this fact because the dishonest are tolerably certain to apply the knowledge practically. The spread of knowledge is necessary to give fair play to those who might suffer from ignorance.

> It cannot be too earnestly urged that an acquaintance with real facts will, in
> the end, be better for all parties. Some time ago, when the reading public
> was alarmed at being told how London milk is adulterated, timid persons
> deprecated the exposure on the plea that it would give instructions in
> the art of adulterating milk, a vain fear milkmen knew all about it before,
> whether they practiced it or not; and the exposure only taught purchasers
> the necessity of a little scrutiny and caution, leaving them to obey this
> necessity or not, as they pleased.
>
> —*From A. C. Hobbs (Charles Tomlinson, ed.),*
> *Locks and Safes: The Construction of Locks.*
> *Published by Virtue & Co., London, 1853 (revised 1868).*

In most forms, locks are mechanical devices that can appear deceivingly simple even to engineers, unless those engineers are specifically schooled in the multiple complexities of locks. A successful and secure lock design is principally based on materials and their properties and the interaction of internal components. The laws of physics, chemistry, and manufacturing tolerances are all critical elements of insecurity engineering. Although it may appear elementary, the design of a secure lock is complicated, even one that appears to be a "simple" mechanism.

Consider the perfect example of a conventional pin tumbler lock. It has six primary components, all easy to understand: a shell (or housing), a plug, pin tumblers, a keyway, springs and their retainer, and the key and its bitting. I'm often asked what can be so complicated about such a lock and how it works, especially because it was invented more than a century ago when manufacturing processes were rudimentary.

It's easy to understand the fundamental principle of how a *plug* rotates within a *shell* and is stopped from turning by the presence of several *spring-biased pins* that move vertically as the *bitting* of a key lifts each tumbler to a shear line. The concept of a shear line is fundamental to all mechanical locks in some form. A *shear line* defines the gap between the rotating and fixed components of a pin tumbler lock. It's the precise place where all tumblers or detainers must be set by the correct key.

Each of these terms has a subset of complexities, so our "simple" pin tumbler lock is not so simple. The selection of the proper materials, how they self-lubricate to allow movement, the tolerances of components, and how a shear line functions are primary considerations. The design and definition of depth increments that control the number of key combinations and how the keyway is constructed are just a few of relevant considerations by engineers.

Each of these subsets relates directly to security, which must be engineered into every lock component, individually and as cooperating members of a complete mechanism. The mathematics of lock design adds more complexity because *tolerances* define security parameters for all locks. This math involves the size and number of pin tumblers in terms of their diameter and length. It addresses how the bore is produced in the plug and shell and whether each bore is drilled individually or in unison, because the drilling of each hole relates to drill-bit wear, tolerances, and movement. It also involves springs, how they are made, and what pressure they provide within the lock. It includes understanding the concept and math of balanced driver or top pins.

Math also specifies the parameters of key differs and the creation of secure and often complex master key systems, as the number of depth increments directly relates to the ability to exploit tolerances for picking and using *tryout keys*. Tryout keys are specially bitted keys designed to test and exploit the tolerance errors between a lock's plug and shell and the number of depth increments designed into the lock by a manufacturer. Tryout keys are also used to probe a master key system for the correct top-level key. Tolerances define the interaction of the plug, shell, and pins and how they relate to one another. As described in Part IV, tolerance is critical to many recognized methods of compromise of the shear line by picking, impressioning, and decoding.

The function of locks is all about security and the protection of life, property, and information. They must be designed to thwart unauthorized access, consistent with applicable security standards that may apply. Locks are often the first line of defense. A security flaw or failure can result in serious and potentially deadly ramifications.

Lock engineers responsible for conceiving, developing, and executing a new or modified lock design need a deep understanding of the many subjects and disciplines that must be factored into any secure and successful product involving any security hardware. This expertise is essential to meet technical, manufacturing, legal, security, and marketing requirements. A failure in the process can have serious consequences, especially for high-security implementations with an elevated threat level involving critical infrastructure. An insecure product can result in intrusions, sabotage, vandalism, theft of critical and high-value assets, terrorism, unauthorized access to information, identity theft, and interruption of critical essential services. Such failures can often be traced to faulty engineering that is the direct result of inexperience and the lack of training and understanding of the basic concepts of insecurity engineering.

In this chapter, I define several required areas of expertise for design engineers. This knowledge comes from participating in hundreds of cases involving locks and how they were ultimately compromised. It's based on my working with some of the best engineering teams to analyze different lock designs for flaws that can lead to compromise and breaches in the security for which they were created. It's a daunting list of subjects that must be mastered by design- and vulnerability-assessment team members if secure products are to result. Unfortunately, these subjects and concepts are not taught as part of a mechanical engineering curriculum at universities, much to the detriment of the industry.

It is axiomatic that individuals who design locks must understand their history, incremental design advancements, improvements, and current state-of-the-art.

Engineers must differentiate between conventional and high security and the application of standards. More importantly, they must be familiar with prior design defects and failures to avoid repeating those mistakes in new or modified iterations.

They must always remember what security means in a lock. In a perfect world, a lock cannot be opened without the correct key or code. Reality means a lock must be designed to resist covert and forced entry techniques and manipulation, and exactly what constitutes a valid key or credential that will open the lock. This key always depends on the kind of mechanism, secondary locking systems, and security enhancements. Each of these concepts needs to be fully understood.

Lock designs are not just about how they function but also about how and why they are secure. Detailed knowledge about vulnerabilities in different locking concepts and correlating security threats with current or proposed designs or modifications is essential. As detailed in later chapters, *hybrid* attacks employing one or more exploits must be considered because many simple yet successful defeats are a mix of known, imagined, and created techniques. Unless engineers are schooled in the many faces of lock design and bypass techniques, they cannot hope to make products properly and securely.

The history of lock development began 4,000 years ago. How and why a different locking technology slowly improved is extremely instructive, as are the thousands of patents filed for original designs and their upgrades and enhancements. It is obligatory that design engineers study and be thoroughly briefed on how and why individual mechanisms were conceived, how successful they were in the marketplace, and how they were defeated.

I have often counseled engineers that it is not as important to understand *how* a lock is compromised as *why*. The "how" applies to a specific lock, whereas the "why" underscores the essence of the problem and can apply to a class of locks.

Every lock design can teach important lessons, especially considering the next innovation that improves on the last. Understanding the basic types of locking mechanisms discussed in this chapter—their security classifications, their theory of operation, bypass techniques, and limitations is fundamental to a successful lock design because their mechanisms can provide ideas for new combinations of older designs. The important issue is to know what worked, what was unreliable, and what was vulnerable.

Many years ago, my partner and I convinced our client, one of the oldest U.S. lock manufacturers, to alter the design of its lock's sidebar and gate geometry to prevent its locks from being opened by applying torque to the plug. We reached back almost 100 years for the answer, which was the same method employed by Briggs & Stratton in its sidebar locks for vehicles. When we raised the issue with our client's design team, they did not know this lock, how it worked, or why it was so secure. If they had understood why its design applied to solving their serious bypass problem, they could have avoided a great deal of trouble in the marketplace.

An overview of the primary topics that underlie competent insecurity engineering is presented in this chapter. A detailed examination and explanation of the topics relating to bypass are further examined in Part IV.

Basic Lock Types and Components

There are four primary classifications of locks, each of which has unique characteristics and potential security vulnerabilities:

1. Mechanical
2. Electromechanical
3. Electronic
4. Energy harvesting

Currently, traditional mechanical locks dominate the industry, but that will slowly change as users migrate to systems that integrate software control. Electromechanical locks combine some form of mechanical detainers with a secondary locking system, which is usually a tiny motor, worm gear, or solenoid activated by embedded credentials within the key. Electronic cylinders do not rely on internal detainers for locking functions and are controlled by radio-frequency identification (RFID), near-field communication (NFC), or Bluetooth credentials and keys. They can operate in a stand-alone or networked mode. The final category is energy harvesting, where a lock is usually based on using a key to generate electricity to power an internal processor. It contains some form of internal detainers to accomplish locking. It is important to note that each of these primary categories of locking systems has security issues that must be forecasted, considered, and engineered so they cannot be defeated.

Theory of Operation for Each Primary Lock Design Category

Understanding how each type of locking mechanism works, its design limitations, and the development of added security is important because it can translate into introducing improvements in current designs. Implementing a historical perspective of different principles can provide a basis for creating new ideas. At a minimum, engineers should be familiar with these principles: *warded, wafer, lever tumbler, pin tumbler, hybrid, dimple, axial pin tumbler, rotating disc, special sidebar*, and *side bit milling*.

It's crucial for engineers to be able to define the following principles:

- *Warded*: Warded locks were popular hundreds of years ago and spelled the first advancement in mechanical security. A warded lock is based on the use of metal bands that block the rotation of a key until there are corresponding cutouts in the bitting.

- *Wafer*: Wafer locks employ sliding detainers similar to pin tumblers. These popular locks are low-security and easily compromised. They're found in thousands of venues, such as vending machines, control panels, padlocks, and applications that do not require any real measure of security.

- *Level tumbler*: Lever tumbler locks were developed in the 1700s to replace warded mechanisms. Lever locks employ movable "levers" that are pivoted as the key is turned with the correct bitting. They can be found throughout the world and in high-security safes and vaults. They are described in detail later in this book.

- *Pin tumbler*: The original pin tumbler was invented by the Egyptians more than 4,000 years ago. The modern concept was developed by Linus Yale around 1860. The modern pin tumbler lock is the world's most common mechanical security system because it can offer high security against many forms of attack. It is based on at least two movable pin tumblers that block or allow the rotation of a plug within the fixed part of the lock.

- *Hybrid design*: A hybrid lock design means two or more different systems work in combination to offer higher security against methods of entry. Medeco high-security locks are an excellent example. Two distinct systems operate in parallel in the latest M4 designs: standard pin tumblers that must be elevated and then rotated to the correct angle and side bit milling for a second security layer.

- *Dimple*: Dimple locks are a form of pin tumbler lock, but rather than having traditional bitting on the key, they contain holes with various depths that correspond with the length of pins. Dimple locks can be very complex in design, with multiple rows and layers of pins.

- *Axial pin tumbler*: Some locks arrange their pin tumblers in a circle rather than laterally across a key's surface. These lock types are often easier to pick with special tools because all the pins are immediately visible and can be manipulated. Axial locks are very popular in vending applications and offer medium- to high-security protection.

- *Rotating disc*: Rotating disc locks are a form of wafer lock invented in Finland in 1907 by Abloy. They offer medium- to high-security resistance against attacks. Their design is based on multiple discs, which are rotated by the bitting of the key at various angles as the key is turned. Each disc has a slot or gate that must mate with a sidebar. When all the discs are properly aligned, the plug can be turned. Disc locks are very popular in vending machines, parking meters, and gaming applications, such as in casinos to protect slot machines.

- *Special sidebar*: There are many variants of sidebar designs, but they all accomplish the same function: blocking the rotation of a lock's plug until the detainers are properly aligned. Virtually every major lock manufacturer has developed its own sidebar design. One common characteristic is some form of gate on a movable detainer that must be properly entered by the sidebar, regardless of its shape and design.

- ▪ *Side bit milling*: The concept of side bit milling, also known as side bitting, was invented and patented by Bo Widen in Sweden. It provides for a second set of bitting along a different surface of a key. The systems have been implemented by major manufacturers, including Schlage, Assa, and Medeco in its new M4 lock introduced in 2022. Side bitting adds another set of pin tumblers that must be aligned in concert with the primary detainers.

Primary Security Classifications of Locks

Conventional and high-security designations must be understood regarding how they apply to different designs and the distinction between the categories and levels of security. *Conventional locks* are low- to medium-security devices. They are not certified for any specific security rating and are often relatively simple to defeat. Many manufacturers produce conventional mechanisms with some security enhancements but fail to determine their vulnerabilities, placing consumers at risk. Conventional locks can be found in thousands of applications, from simple padlocks to cash registers to residential and business door locks. They are usually inexpensive and do not have the security enhancements offered in high-security hardware. They are often found in hardware and DIY stores. The plastic thin metal keys in Figures 2-1a and 2-1b were produced on a piece of credit card plastic and thin pieces of metal to simulate the bitting values for both conventional and high-security cylinders.

Although all mechanical locks have certain design limitations, conventional cylinders have characteristics that identify their security. For instance, there's usually no audit trail that records when keys are inserted into a lock with the time and date. Adding and deleting keys is relatively simple, but if keys are designed to open more than one lock, each combination must be changed. Most importantly, rights amplification and key simulation can be a security issue and must be considered in any keyway design. If the availability of keys is not restricted, it may be simple to modify other keys or blanks to work in a target lock.

The primary subject area of expertise must include the following:

- ▪ *Covert and forced attacks*: These are forms of attacks against locks that are defined by industry standards in the United States, Europe, and other countries. The primary modes of attack against locks are accomplished covertly and through force. Another mode, a hybrid attack method, combines various kinds of attacks and may not be immediately apparent to investigators. As defined later in this book, covert attacks imply that the technique is not immediately visible or apparent. Forced attacks involve using force to move or alter external or internal components to affect an opening.

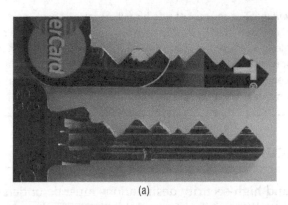

(a)

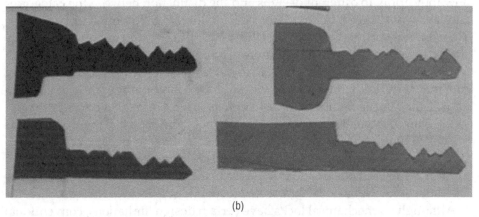

(b)

Figure 2-1a, 1b: Without stringent key control, cut and blank keys can be altered and the bitting values simulated. Keys for both conventional and high-security locks can be simulated in plastic (a) and thin pieces of brass (b).

- *A lack of forensic traces of covert entry*: In certain forms of covert entry, no forensic evidence may be immediately apparent without further investigation. Forensic evidence is usually present in the form of toolmarks, which are created when hard tools are employed to move, alter, or break components, resulting in indications of contact between metal tools and lock surfaces.

- *A lack of intelligence within the mechanism*: Some mechanical locks will not provide you with the intelligence or knowledge of who the user is.

- *Limited key control*: Conventional lock manufacturers often do not restrict the availability of their blank or cut keys, so there's no security against unauthorized copying or key modification. Most low- to medium-security lock producers don't offer any form of restriction on ordering or duplicating their keys. Most high-security lock makers, however, provide several levels of key control to restrict access to blanks and unauthorized ordering of keys.

▪ *An audit trail*: An audit trail provides information for detecting and recording activity involving key usage. Audit trails may also record the attempts at entry with unauthorized keys. They can be found in electronic cylinders.

The design of *high-security* locks requires additional knowledge and skill sets. A detailed grasp of concepts involving covert and forced entry and manipulation forms, adherence to lock standards, and higher levels of key control is required. These types of locks also mandate more sophisticated forms of testing and vulnerability assessment regarding their methods of compromise.

Lock Materials and Their Characteristics

Materials and their characteristics are the fundamental building blocks of any lock design to protect against forced and covert entry and ensure durability and resistance to environmental considerations. Factors such as hardness, brittleness, strength, fracture, flex, and temperature must all be understood and considered when analyzing the possibility of compromising outer and inner materials to access and circumvent locking mechanisms. Following applicable standards and requirements, these materials must also be chosen to resist corrosion, salt spray, moisture, rust, and environmental degradation.

Forced entry is always a challenge because of the available range of hand and power tools to destroy just about any material, given sufficient time. Grinding, pulling, torque, torsion, sawing, drilling, shock, and vibration are all recognized methods of opening locks. There also are other techniques to defeat a mechanism through applying force that may be less obvious or never even conceived.

In one newly designed electronic lock, initial tests were conducted to ensure that applying torque could not compromise the mechanism. An engineer was asked to run these tests. He took a long flathead screwdriver, inserted it in the keyway, and attempted to torque or twist open the lock. He failed. As I later explained to the design team, this type of testing could not identify a possibly serious problem. There were two potential vulnerabilities: the first was to apply torque to break the internal block-to-plug rotation. The other was the more nuanced technique of grinding the internal components into metal filings. The engineer could not imagine the second testing component of simply applying torque.

In this instance, a piece of metal was produced on a computer numerical control (CNC) machine to replicate the original key inserted into the keyway to turn the plug. A CNC is a multi-axis milling machine controlled by a computer for precise cutting of metal. The key was produced from A2 tool steel, which far exceeded the strength of any internal component in the lock. Leverage was applied to this special key with a 9-inch torque bar. The design team believed that applying torque to this key would snap the internal locking components, and it would be the end of the testing. However, that was not the case.

The normal and recognized method to test for torque was insufficient to defeat this or other cylinders. Rather, the key was very slowly and deliberately rocked back and forth after the lubricant WD-40 was squirted into the keyway. It did not take long to pulverize all internal materials and open the lock. This is a perfect example of a failure to understand materials composition, the application of energy, and physics. This discovery resulted in a significant lock redesign to protect against this attack. It is instructive how a failure of knowledge and imagination on the part of those responsible for ensuring that this type of attack would fail could have cost the company monetary damages, delays in manufacturing, and a forced recall.

Electronic locks often employ plastics for internal structures and barriers. These materials can present serious security issues due to their ease of penetration by tiny drills, high-speed rotating shims, and the application of temperature extremes. Although it's common in lock manufacturing to employ materials other than metal, not using internal plastics is preferable.

Standards and Their Criteria

Lock manufacturers must meet certain standards for commercial and high-security mechanisms known as the Underwriters Laboratory (UL) and American National Standards Institute (ANSI)/Builders Hardware Manufacturers Association (BHMA) standards. (Chapter 7 discusses and analyzes several perceived problems with the UL and ANSI/BHMA standards.) Engineers must be cognizant that certain requirements and test procedures do not encompass some bypass methods, especially those involving hybrid attacks. Many locks can be easily defeated by various methods not enumerated within UL 437 or BHMA 156.30 standards. If such omissions are not understood, locks that are certified as compliant may not be, placing consumers at risk.

Security Features and Enhancements

Many enhancements can be added to conventional and high-security locks to enhance their security. Not only should these design changes be understood, but the potential negative ramifications must also be contemplated to ensure that new methods of compromise or vulnerability aren't created. Although many security upgrades are positive, such modifications can also be used *against* the lock. Enhancements can include anti-bumping features, security pins, movable elements, side bit milling, special sidebar designs, more secure keyways, unique gate designs, anti-drill barriers, and the addition of magnetic components.

Magnetics: Theory, Implementation, and Defeat

Magnetic components have gained popularity with lock manufacturers due to their ease of implementation and advanced capabilities. Hackers easily understand magnets, and many of their vulnerabilities are well known. Magnets are accepted as movable elements in keys and as added security layers for internal hardware. They are also embedded in keys to move rotating discs and other detainers. Although using magnetic elements can offer unique opportunities for innovative designs, it also can create security vulnerabilities that can allow decoding capabilities for detainers and permit the movement of internal elements.

Using ferrous materials for any critical component is also problematic because of their sensitivity to strong magnetic fields. One of the most famous cases is documented later in this book and involved the Kaba Simplex 1000 push-button lock, which was defeated in seconds with a rare earth magnet. There are numerous examples of people using strong fields to manipulate critical parts from outside of a lock.

Bypass: Fundamental Expertise Requirements

The bypass of locks and security hardware is a complicated and multifaceted subject that requires theoretical and practical knowledge and expertise. As I note throughout this book, most mechanical engineers do not have the requisite skills to design locks consistently and competently using insecure engineering practices and expertise. Lock manufacturers have no problem producing locks that work. That's not the issue. Making them work securely, with appropriate resistance to different forms of covert, forced, and hybrid attacks, is far different from just being successful at producing a lock that looks good and "works" yet offers minimal protection.

Virtually every lock manufacturer I've worked with has repeatedly made and continues to make variations of the same design mistakes. The result is often the inability to produce a lock that's as defect-free as possible. The following is an outline of the minimum required knowledge and design expertise.

It is impossible to design secure locks without very detailed knowledge of bypass fundamentals and an understanding of general and specialty tools, hybrid attacks, old techniques, and the latest methods of compromise. This is a significant problem in the industry because this kind of knowledge and experience takes many years to acquire and develop. It requires analyzing a design and determining what can go wrong from many perspectives.

The compromise of locks often involves criminal activity. Usually there's a lack of knowledge by crime labs and law enforcement investigators, unless they're part of a special unit operated by major police departments and law enforcement agencies for covert entry. Crime labs don't routinely work on cases that involve locks other than searching for toolmarks in a forced entry. Forensic analysis is almost nonexistent. The Association of Firearm and Toolmark Examiners (AFTE) is the leading organization worldwide for this expertise. Some locksmiths can also be consulted for their expertise, especially if they are members of the International Association of Investigative Locksmiths (IAIL).

It is important to understand specific vulnerabilities of different categories of locks:

- Laws of physics and chemistry and how they apply to open locks and the vulnerability of specific mechanisms
- Traditional and special tools
- Techniques for covert and forced entry
- Mechanical bypass of internal components
- Mechanical bypass of a locking system
- Forensic analysis and evidence of bypass

Mechanical Bypass of Locks and Systems

There are many methods to compromise mechanical and electromechanical locks that may not directly require an attack against the actual locking cylinder. Although the more popular and well-known techniques can involve picking, impressioning, decoding, and bumping, many locks and systems can be defeated through the external manipulation of internal components. These components can be accessed through a keyway or other small openings, including drain holes, pressure-release drains, or data ports.

Unless engineers are schooled in such circumvention methods, they may not perceive various threats that attackers easily execute. Mechanical *bypasses* can include inserting shim wires, straight wires, paper clips, and small pieces of spring steel. Very small magnets can be employed to move components to unlocked positions. A section of spring steel inserted through a keyway can be employed to break retaining screws that hold endcaps, enabling access to a tailpiece. The *tailpiece* and *cam* are found at the back of a plug. Their function is to transmit motion to move a latch, bolt, or other mechanism that unlocks the associated locking hardware. Fine wires can be routed through almost any opening to reach a spring latch that controls locking.

The mechanical bypass also includes the introduction of energy by rapping, vibration, bumping, or strong radio frequency (RF) fields to alter the position of critical components. High-strength magnetic fields, produced by the rare earth metal neodymium, are also useful and can be extremely effective at moving ferrous components that control locking. The employment of strong magnetic fields also includes attacks against electric strikes and solenoids.

Mechanical attacks on worm gears are silent and can result in the locking and unlocking of electronic cylinders, all without creating an audit trail or any evidence of entry. This attack relies on Newton's First Law of Motion and can be extremely effective, often requiring less than one minute to execute. The vulnerability to this compromise must be fully understood because numerous locks integrate worm gears or solenoids into their designs.

Locks are always part of a system because they must control latches, bolts, strikes, or electric switches. These systems are often subject to compromise, obviating the need to attack the lock directly. It is important to be familiar with the most common means of bypassing locking systems, including loiding the latch or bolt with plastic credit cards, special spring-steel loids, flat blades, or under-the-door opening tools to access the knob or lever handle; turning and removing a mortise cylinder if it is loose in the lockset; inserting shims into the lock case on an outward-opening door; removing a key-in-knob assembly using a straight wire or special tool; attacking a defective or worn lockset; and using magnets to move components. Critical parts can also be physically altered by prying a doorframe to provide clearance for an extended deadbolt. Entire doors can be compromised by removing hinge pins using special airbags, small portable hydraulic tools, and jamb spreaders.

> **NOTE** If you've watched much television, you've surely seen someone try the bypass technique of loiding a door lock using a plastic card. In this example, *loiding* a door lock involves inserting a plastic card, such as a credit card, near a door's locking apparatus with the intention of retracting inward-opening retractable latches.

All aspects of the locking system must be assessed for vulnerability because they are all interrelated. A high-security cylinder may be difficult to compromise, but security will be breached if the system it controls isn't secure. The best-designed deadbolt locking system is meaningless if it's subject to compromise by attacking the tailpiece with a tiny screwdriver or other implement.

Brute-Force Attacks

As a rule, burglars and spies do not pick locks except for high-value targets in certain instances. Most often, brute force is applied to gain access. Manufacturers must be conversant with the related systems that protect access, which include doors, doorframes, latches, bolts, and strikes. A full understanding of specifications and standards is necessary to design locks properly and ensure customer protection.

Brute-force entry methods can involve attacks on the locks through destructive means, but more often there is an attack on related systems. Installing secure locks has little bearing on defeating a system if all the other security components offer little protection. Doors are often made of cheap materials, and glass or walls made of drywall can often provide easy access. Even the cheapest lock may be more secure than what it's designed to protect, depending on construction practices.

Traditional Covert Entry

An understanding of, working knowledge of, and practical experience with traditional covert entry methods are essential to secure lock designs. Reading about picking or impressioning a lock is *not* enough; acquiring the practical skills to open locks by various means is necessary due to the many variations in such themes.

The primary methods that must be considered are as follows and are discussed next:

- Picking
- Impressioning
- Decoding
- Bumping
- Hybrid attacks

The extrapolation of the top-level master key (TMK) is another technique and is the process of using a working key for a lock in a master key system to probe all the depth-increment values for each pin tumbler position to derive the master key. This is also a favorite approach for higher-value target attacks because it can be carried out silently. For each method, there are different ways to execute an attack based on the specific lock design.

Picking

The reality is that no mechanical lock is perfect in production because pin stacks or other detainers are often slightly misaligned and not in a perfectly straight line. Even a change of .001" can affect the ability of a lock to be successfully picked.

Picking requires the manipulation of each detainer to simulate the action of the correct key. In a pin tumbler lock, the pins can be targeted individually with a pick, "raked" in rapid succession, or bumped simultaneously. Picking requires skill, and success depends on many variables (as discussed in Part IV).

The procedure to pick a pin tumbler mechanism is to raise and trap each pin at the shear line until there are no further obstructions to plug rotation.

Picking is an orderly process based primarily on the tolerance between the plug and shell and each bore or pin chamber. For design engineers, many variables must be considered. Concepts and terms are essential to understand, including the order of picking, keyway design, and different types of picks and how they are used. Mechanical pick guns, electronic-vibrating pick guns, acoustic picks, signature picks, and "sputnik"-type picks (i.e., picks that can manipulate multiple pins simultaneously) must always be considered due to their ability to compromise certain tumbler configurations.

Certain lock designs are easily compromised with "cross picks" and axial picks that attack multiple pin stacks simultaneously. Cross picks operate with locks that have keyways oriented in multiple rows, often in the form of a cross. Picks for axial pin tumbler locks have wire feelers designed to make contact with each pin tumbler. Other special picking tools can work on telescoping pins. Pick and decode tools can be simple: produce a working key, and open the lock. The Lishi tool is a perfect example because it was designed to decode a lock and then move tiny elements to replicate the decoded key.

There are certain recognized countermeasures to picking. Most important is maintaining high tolerances in manufacturing to minimize misalignment of detainers. Using more pin stacks can increase the difficulty of moving pins to shear lines, which increases the number of available differs. The term "differs" is originally from England and denotes the number of theoretical or actual different key changes or combinations.

A narrow keyway with many wards can make moving a picking tool vertically difficult. Employing pick-resistant security pins such as mushroom, spool, serrated, and micro-milled can also frustrate picking. Applying steel inserts into the pin centers can make acoustic decoding more difficult. The employment of sidebars and side bit milling can also enhance pick resistance, as can the milling of special gate channels within some of the pins—the procedure used in Medeco high-security locks for government and certain commercial use. These special variations are identified as ARX pins.

Impressioning

Impressioning is a technique that allows the "reading" of each pin tumbler or other detainer to determine their measurement to produce a working key. The concept is based on a shear line and when pins, wafers, sliders, or levers are "set" at the gap between plug and shell, or between levers and their gates. In pin tumbler locks, impressioning can occur because pins precisely at the shear line are essentially free-floating and will not attempt to depress material on a blank key during the process. Corresponding marks will not appear on the blank.

Many impressioning systems can produce cut keys. To reduce vulnerability, those designing locks should be conversant with mechanical and electronic systems. Metal foil, lead inserts in key blades, special lever tumbler systems, and reading systems can effectively compromise locks with no trace. There are optical viewing aids, special light-emitting diode (LED) lighting systems, and small video cameras that can be inserted into the keyway or can read a key's surface.

Locks with added security layers such as sidebars, side bit milling, and movable elements can make impressioning more complex because determining when a pin is at a shear line can be blocked by the action of a sidebar.

Decoding

Decoding is a process of covertly determining critical measurements of pin tumblers, levers, wafers, sliders, or other detainers to produce or simulate a working key. In some respects, the procedure can be compared to impressioning, but the techniques to derive the bitting code are quite different in most cases. Some decoders are a combination of a picking tool and a reader. Others are designed to individually measure each tumbler or detainer and produce some form of readout that can be correlated to the bitting of a key. Other more sophisticated tools use electronic measurements to determine bitting values and translate those to key machines or 3D prints.

Conventional cylinders are the easiest to decode because they lack the mechanical complexity of some high-security locks. If there are multiple security layers, decoding may prove difficult. Design engineers must be knowledgeable about the various methods to decode different mechanisms. (These are discussed in more detail in Part IV.) Some of these systems are designed to generate a key matching the decoded value. Sophisticated picking and decoding tools developed by John Falle, Wendt, Madelin, and Vicuna are discussed later in this book.

Those responsible for designing secure locking mechanisms should be familiar with the following decoding techniques and associated hardware, which are defined in greater detail in Parts IV and V:

- Auto-impressioning using metal foil
- Auto-manipulation of components
- Belly reading in lever tumbler locks
- Borescope and optical decoding
- Disassembling a lock and measuring the pins to derive the code
- Electronic decoding that uses piezo probes and audio signatures
- Falle pin lock decoder
- Falle variable key generation system to produce simulated keys
- Manual decoding

- Plasticine reading
- Radioscopy
- Sac probing that measures break points between pins
- Scratch reading of levers
- Shim-wire decoding
- Stack probing that measures the length of the pin stack with a fine wire shim
- Using a special tool that fits in a lock's keyway and probes each pin stack to measure the cut parameters

Originally, the *lock-bumping technique* was confined to opening cylinders with a specially prepared key designed to transmit energy to the base of all bottom pins simultaneously, the idea being to momentarily split the pin segments at the shear line. Although most engineers are familiar with this initial concept, it has morphed into a procedure to target specific components with a burst of energy to cause movement. This enhanced technique is important because it has successfully opened many locks.

The theory underlying bumping is based on Newton's Third Law of Motion, and it constitutes a threat to security when applied to any locking device. Legal issues must be understood because a lock can be bumped open, whereas the manufacturer may claim it's impossible. This idea has often been proven false, so design engineers must understand that their locks can be vulnerable to this form of attack. In the United States, millions of locks can easily be bumped open. Critical infrastructure can be at risk because conventional cylinders often protect it.

WARNING   Lock designers should always follow the 3T2R rule, which is an equation to assess the security of a lock by assessing the time, tools, and training required to make the lock secure. It is discussed in greater detail in Chapter 4.

In making sales and marketing claims, a manufacturer must be certain that they understand the lock's vulnerability and the application of energy caused by bumping its mechanisms. I can attest from firsthand experience that many companies have been surprised that someone can open their high-security locks through a combination of bumping and other techniques. Bumping continues to be a threat because it is often the simplest form of bypass. In my discussion of the 3T2R rule, bumping often poses the greatest threat because of the time, tools, and training needed to accomplish an opening.

The U.S. Postal Service is a prime example. It has millions of post box locks that thieves can bump open. And the threat does not stop there. Private postal rental boxes often have locks that cost about a dollar and are likewise subject to simple attacks, placing mail and personal privacy at risk.

In evaluating their locks against different bumping attacks, engineers must also understand variables that can affect the process, including the number of pins, restricted keyways, the use of security pins, the presence of a sidebar, and what effect these have on the ability to successfully open the lock. They must also understand what locks may not be subject to bumping and whether prior intelligence about the lock is needed to be successful at bumping it. Certain locks, by their design, cannot be bumped open. These include warded, lever, wafer, and disc-wafer mechanisms.

Hybrid Attacks

A *hybrid attack* employs multiple modes to compromise a lock and can target design flaws if not fully imagined and understood. Security standards do not specifically address these attack types and therefore locks aren't thoroughly tested for that vulnerability. One of the problems for design engineers is that these types of attacks may be difficult to conceive of, which is often the result of a lack of understanding about the possible attack scenarios and a lack of ability to imagine or devise how they might be implemented. These attacks must always be factored into the requirement for specific expertise in the different subjects that can impact insecurity engineering. Hybrid attacks are discussed in greater detail in Part IV.

Keys and Keying Systems and Their Design and Compromise

The easiest way to open a lock is with the correct key. What constitutes the "correct key" is not so simple in terms of definition. In a simple lock, one change key is designed to open it; in more complex systems, a lock can be configured to be accessed by the following:

- *Change key*: A key intended to open one or more specific locks. See the simple one-level master key diagram in Figure 2-2.

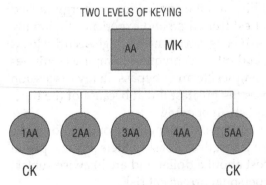

Figure 2-2: Keying systems in larger facilities can be master keyed. The diagram shows one master key and one change level below it that controls Change Keys 1AA-5AA.

- *Master key*: A key that will open a group of locks, which is different from a change key.

- *Simulated key*: A key designed to simulate an actual key. It may be made of plastic, stiff paper, or metal but does not have all the characteristics of the original key.

- *Bump key*: A key that is specially cut and has all of the bitting values for the pin tumblers at their deepest cut.

- *Rights-amplified bitting key*: A key that has been modified to either add or subtract material from the bitting surface so that it will work in a lock for which it was not authorized.

- *Incidental master keys*: One or more keys with a combination of bitting values that will open certain locks in a master key system in which such combinations were not intended.

Key-system designers must understand each of these concepts because in the end analysis, keys open locks, regardless of how they are derived.

Keys combine bitting design, keyway-ward patterns, and special security attributes such as movable elements, unique bitting, and side bit milling. If the keyway is bypassed or the bitting is simulated to equal the depth of the individual detainers, then the lock will open unless a hybrid attack is required. This is especially true in conventional cylinders, where legal protection rarely extends to real-world attacks. If a keyway can be circumvented by a thin piece of metal or plastic, for example, and the bitting values can be replicated, there is no bar to opening the lock with a simulated key.

The concept of *key control* is also highly relevant because it relates to the restricted availability of blanks to produce cut keys. Many years ago, I demonstrated the ability to email images of a high-security key so that it could be duplicated. Access to a target key is often quite simple. Once that occurs, there's little to prevent it from being duplicated, either by code, 3D printing, or hand-cutting a key.

The threat to key control can be substantial because images of keys can be emailed to an outsider for duplication. This is particularly troublesome in corporate and government environments if employees can carry their cell phones, which often have high-resolution cameras that can capture images sufficient for duplication.

Keys can be produced from thin metal strips, plastic sheets, or credit cards. High-security keys with multiple security layers can make replicating keys more difficult but not impossible. Engineers should always consider the design of keyways, as many can be circumvented with extremely thin brass purchased from a hardware store. This material can bypass all the wards, circumventing any security of the keyway.

Rekeyable locks can also pose added security issues, depending on the mechanical scheme employed to accomplish the change of combinations. Some systems, such as the old Fort tubular lock, rotated the key to one of several pin orientations keyed to the *index* or home position when the key was inserted into the lock. This system was popular because it allowed instant changing of the combination for a lock in the system. It was based on changing the order of the bitting of the key. If a cut key was modified, it could be used in any changed combinations. Winfield programmable locks were another classic example where the system could be defeated by changing the maintenance key through vibration.

The following areas of expertise are suggested to properly assess risks from the compromise of key control and keying systems and are discussed in detail in Part V:

- 3D printing and vulnerabilities
- Attacks on key control and the authentication process
- Computation of theoretical and actual combinations (differs) and how this affects the ability to exploit tolerances
- Counterfeit keys and patent infringement
- Cross-keys
- Depth increments and their calculation
- Differs and depth coding: theory and reality
- Direct and indirect key codes
- Disassembly of locks and decoding of master keys
- Incidental master keys
- Information from keys that can provide system intelligence
- Keyway designs and restrictions
- Master key systems and vulnerabilities including extrapolation, incidental master keys, and cross-keying
- Simulation, replication, and duplication of keys
- Tryout keys for extrapolating the top-level master key

Attacks against Shear Lines

Most forms of bypass are *attacks against the shear line*. These may involve common bypass tools such as picks, special tools, and hybrid attacks. In Figure 2-3 a plug from a Medeco lock is shown with the pin tumblers all aligned at the shear line, but the pins are not properly rotated for the sidebar to retract. In this example, the lock cannot be opened.

The following areas of expertise are recommended and described in detail in Part IV:

- Balanced drivers
- Bumping
- Comb picking
- Combination of techniques in hybrid attacks
- Core shimming (e.g., John Falle)
- Electronic signature analysis (e.g., Madelin and Wendt)
- Injection of bearings as a comb-picking technique
- Mechanical bypass
- Pick and form—foil (e.g., John Falle)
- Mechanical and electronic pick guns
- Piezo decoders (e.g., Wendt, Madelin, AT Security)
- Pin and cam (e.g., John Falle)
- Rapping
- Skeleton keys
- Tryout keys
- Vibration techniques

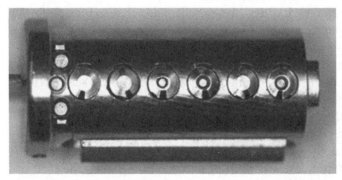

Figure 2-3: Attacking the shear line is the primary method to compromise a lock. A plug and pin tumblers from a Medeco lock are shown, all aligned at the shear line. The plug is prevented from rotating unless the correct key is inserted, aligns all the pins (as shown), and rotates the pins so the sidebar can retract. In this illustration, the pins are not rotated properly, so the sidebar is blocked as a second security layer.

Forensics and Evidence of Entry

Forensic analysis is often important for a manufacturer to determine whether a lock was compromised and how, or to identify a manufacturing defect or failure that could have caused a security vulnerability. Forensics became important to detect bumping because insurance carriers refused to honor claims for mysterious disappearances without signs of entry. There is now a specialty certification for locksmiths who conduct forensic examinations. It is offered by the International Association of Investigative Locksmiths (IAIL), which is part of the Associated Locksmiths of America (ALOA). These locksmiths can assist law enforcement and insurance companies in evaluating claims that involve locks and their possible bypass or attack.

Evidence of Entry

Traditional analysis can involve searching for toolmarks on the lock's exterior and internal components, such as pins, chamber walls, and the areas between pin chambers where no marks should ever appear from the normal use of a keys. A good microscope or a scanning electron microscope (SEM) is preferred for forensic use. One of the best labs in the world is in Mayen, Germany, and is known as Manfred Goth. Insurance companies and law enforcement agencies retain them to identify toolmarks in locks using various sophisticated techniques, including SEM.

Engineering teams must be conversant with forensic techniques that include a component tolerance analysis to ensure that components meet manufacturing specifications. They must identify marks on pins and other detainers, the use of special mechanical and electronic pick guns, and markings consistent with picking tools designed for high-security locks.

Equally as important is the inquiry into whether a lock was bumped open when there are no apparent signs of entry and when a customer complains that perhaps their lock was a defective product. Bumping investigations often show no external evidence, especially if an attacker was competent and the pin stack was conducive to being easily opened. Any assumptions that certain locks cannot be defeated and opened by bumping should largely be ignored, even in the highest-security cylinders.

Questions that must be considered include those surrounding the keyway and blanks and how readily available they are. A fundamental inquiry must be conducted regarding whether it was even possible to bump open the lock and whether it was in a class in which this technique could not open.

Audit Trails

If a manufacturer produces locks with *audit trails*, which are designed to capture the use of keys and openings, the engineering teams must be completely conversant with what the audit trails can record and how they can be circumvented. I was involved in an investigation in which the audit trail for an electronic cylinder could be defeated in certain earlier versions if the lock was bumped open by first removing the battery from the key that powered the internal processor.

In this instance, the audit trail captured the insertion of a key once and then blocked more recordings for one minute to prevent attempts to erase the memory. This setting allowed sufficient time to open the lock without any record. The defeat of an audit record can have serious ramifications both legally and in terms of how it affects employees, labor relations, and criminal investigations. Without evidence of entry, sensitive information and assets can be compromised due to a false sense of security. More importantly, employees may be blamed for access that did not exist, or an individual may be charged with a crime, and evidence of criminal attackers may be lost.

A knowledge base and questions about audit-trail capabilities must include information about the following:

- Potential security vulnerabilities that can be exploited
- How the audit trail can be defeated
- How memory can be overwritten
- Considerations if one security layer is bypassed and the key is disabled from powering the system
- An understanding of when audit trails record data and whether they do so only for entry of the key, not for rotation of the plug
- Whether the lock can be mechanically bumped open by defeating any protective measures
- Considerations of what happens if the battery is removed if the key powers the audit trail
- Anti-defeat mechanisms in the lock
- The delay between reads of the key
- Whether the trail is stored in the key and the lock
- Results when bumping protective measures fail and allow the lock to be opened by bumping or picking
- How many events are recorded before being overwritten
- Whether a programming key is required to access the lock and programming mode when the audit trail is hacked into
- What actions are recorded, including the date/time stamp, action "open attempt," result "granted," and so on
- Whether a new entry is created during each contact between the key and cylinder

- What time parameters can be set that will accept only one entry during a specified window for the same key
- If a parameter can be set, how difficult it is to change

It's crucial for designers to be cognizant of all these issues when dealing with audit trails so they have all the information necessary to form a solid understanding of how a lock is compromised and how they can ensure that it won't be in the future.

The next chapter deals with vulnerability assessment in lock design and what is required of team members and their qualifications. Criteria for the rules for selecting a team, protocols to follow, and how to write reports of findings are topics that are important and detailed so that a lock design can be effectively evaluated.

Vulnerability Assessment in Lock Designs

Lock manufacturers must consider mechanical design and insecurity engineering as coequal elements to create a successful product. One without the other is a virtual guarantee of ultimate failure in the marketplace and a prescription for legal liability, especially in the case of high-security mechanisms. Several aspects must be considered when assessing a lock's performance and success, but the most important is operational reliability and security, because locks must function securely and continue to operate in different conditions. Identification of known and potential vulnerabilities in hardware and software is essential because otherwise, those who rely on the security of hardware will not know or understand whether there is a security problem. Implementing a vulnerability assessment (VA) program involves many factors and relies on expertise, as I outlined previously in Chapter 2.

There are two types of vulnerability assessment:

- One that analyzes a facility's security and how it can be compromised
- One that provides a detailed look at the hardware and software in a locking mechanism

A VA concentrating on a lock requires a different way of thinking and methodology than one that evaluates the risks and vulnerabilities of buildings and internal systems designed to protect people, assets, and information.

When considering a lock's design and the security it provides, such an inquiry must focus on many parameters to discover possible exploits involving the lock. The end goal of any assessment is to determine whether there are weaknesses in the hardware or software that would create one or more methods to open the lock without the proper credentials.

The designation of a separate VA team to test for security flaws is recommended rather than relying on the same engineers responsible for hardware and software development. The VA team's perspective must differ from that of the design team because their primary mission is to protect the product from different forms of attack and minimize any legal liability on the manufacturer's part for security defects in its design.

Their mission must be to objectively analyze a product from its very inception until it's released to the consumer and then to evaluate any post-release vulnerability notifications. The team's mindset and intent should be to attempt to "break" and/or compromise the work of the design team who developed the hardware and software and to identify as many deficiencies as possible.

The problem with many VA teams is that they often don't know what they don't know about specific lock designs and exploitation methods. They may suffer from limitations of requisite knowledge, training, and, most importantly, imagination in formulating possible methods of compromise. Recognizing possible design issues that can lead to the development of exploits is rarely simple or obvious. Therein lies the fundamental problem for all VA team members when they commence an analysis of a new lock or a modification of one that's been in production. Unless they're aware of a problem and know what to look for, they're searching for a vulnerability that may or may not exist. They may be chasing a ghost that can require hundreds of hours of testing, often to prove a negative.

The proper selection of VA team members is critical because to be effective, they must possess certain characteristics that qualify them to figure out what can go wrong with a design and how to make it happen.

Identifying a security vulnerability can be tedious because many elusive issues may not be obvious or may manifest themselves without much testing of various attack theories and scenarios. Developing such theories requires that the VA team fully understands the hardware and asks many questions about "What happens if . . .?" Often, such questions are difficult to formulate, especially if they require some form of hybrid-attack execution or multiple steps to achieve the desired result. Added to the difficulty in identifying security flaws is the knowledge that there's rarely only one design issue that can be exploited to allow a lock to be compromised.

This chapter provides guidance for the VA process and the qualifications required of team members. Principles and techniques that can help a team reach valid conclusions are suggested. The goal of a VA team is to develop criteria to correctly identify relevant problems for consideration by design engineers, risk managers, and corporate decision-makers. This goal allows them to take the appropriate steps to identify and mitigate priority risks.

Vulnerability and Risks

Vulnerability and risks (also known as *threats*) are two distinct issues and should not be confused when developing a VA program for locks. A *vulnerability assessment* is not a *threat assessment*, although one relates to the other. A *vulnerability* is a weakness in the design of a lock or locking system that subjects it to possible exploitation and security breaches. A *risk* relates to the likelihood that such a vulnerability will be exploited to the detriment of the installation or user.

Management decisions must be made regarding a VA program's ultimate goals and objectives, including what constitutes risks in a locking system, what actions will be taken if vulnerabilities are discovered in a design, and what the hierarchy of concerns is insofar as protecting against different attacks. Consideration must also be given to the environments where locks will likely be installed, how to prioritize unacceptable risks, and the likelihood of different forms of attack. These considerations are especially important in a high-security installation where customer expectations for embedded protection are significantly more advanced. Ultimately, a VA must discover and neutralize weaknesses, identify potential attacks, and examine and consider countermeasures.

The VA program should carefully define threats and risks, and a realistic analysis should be provided about the likelihood that vulnerabilities will be exploited, with careful consideration given to the 3T2R rule for the specific locking design. Threats and the risks of security vulnerabilities should always be considered in context because they can be very different, depending on the environment where locks are installed and the expectations regarding the protection they should afford.

Threats can't be assessed unless there's an understanding and analysis of who presents the various threats, their possible motivation and capabilities, and the likelihood of an attack. The VA team should be able to answer the following:

- What do attacks look like?
- Can locks be unintentionally and unknowingly left in an open state without the knowledge of security personnel?
- Can a lock be repeatedly opened and locked without creating an audit trail or evidence of entry?
- Is a lock more likely to be attacked surreptitiously or by force?
- How secure are the keying system and authentication requirements for obtaining duplicate keys or blanks?

Finally, all the components or steps of a *security chain*—which comprises individual critical parts and assemblies—that involve using locks must be considered. Thus their procurement, shipping, storage, installation, inspection, maintenance, and removal; lost or stolen keys and cylinders; and updates, training, employee vetting at all levels, and authentication requests for key replacements are all relevant.

Defining a Vulnerability Assessment Plan

The most important action in developing or modifying a product is defining and implementing a VA plan to identify and properly address all significant flaws and weaknesses to mitigate or eliminate their impact. Sometimes this may be impossible due to the chosen design, but it's important to fully document each potential issue and what steps were taken to lessen any security threat. Such documentation may be highly relevant should legal action ensue against the manufacturer, because it can demonstrate that everything possible was reasonably considered and implemented to deal with all identified vulnerabilities.

Unfortunately, some manufacturers don't conduct VAs, or their VAs are cursory. These manufacturers may not understand the problems that can lead to product failure, recalls, and legal action if they don't conduct such an analysis. A VA failure can lead to a failure in security.

There is often denial or fear on the part of management to acknowledge that threats exist or to take action to mitigate them. This is often due to a lack of experience and imagination regarding even the possibility of potential threats. Sometimes the mindset is that "We're either secure or not secure" or "We've never had a problem." Unfortunately, it rarely works that way, as there are degrees of insecurity. VAs can be detailed, time-consuming, and expensive, but the alternative can be a legal liability nightmare and numerous recalls.

Security in a product's design is a continuum of degrees, and it depends on the VA team's level of expertise to find a vulnerability and decide what to do about it. The security concept and the assessment of how secure a locking mechanism is against attacks must be judged against several primary considerations. For instance:

- What is the target, its value, and its location?
- What is the attacker's sophistication and scoring against the 3T2R rule?
- What is the goal of the attack?
- How is the attacker categorized?
  - Criminal malicious
  - Insider
  - Sabotage

- Terrorist
- Theft (material or information)
- Fraud
- Identity theft
- Other motivation

In many cases, what management or an engineering team *wants* to be true about security vulnerabilities may not be a reality. This can result from their overconfidence, arrogance, wishful thinking, or cognitive dissonance and/or an inability to envision security attacks. It can represent past thinking about a problem, leading to bad outcomes, rationalizations and excuses, and an inability to act. There can also be an inaccurate interpretation of the facts that may cause excuses for why a problem doesn't need to be addressed or remedied. However, denial of vulnerabilities will not make them go away.

Most engineers have trouble thinking like a bad guy, which can be fatal in assessing security. This is because bad guys are largely responsible for defining design problems that create or can lead to security failures. Staff may also be too busy putting out fires to effectively analyze problems other than in a cursory fashion. Management should allow creative and resourceful people to define the problem, especially because most assessments are subjective.

Compounding the problem, many companies rely on standards like Underwriters Laboratories (UL) or American National Standards Institute (ANSI)/ Builders Hardware Manufacturers Association (BHMA) as the ultimate tests and gold standard that define a lock's security. Compliance-based security, unfortunately, rarely identifies security issues. Attacks that aren't foreseen can't be prevented. If not envisioned within the standards, such attacks can't be tested against, predicted, or prevented.

VA Team Selection

In my experience, VA team members must have certain unique traits and characteristics that predict and define an alternative way of thinking compared to traditional engineers, lawyers, accountants, and manufacturing production supervisors. Most important, team members must understand the limits of their knowledge and their ability to recognize possible design defects.

They must realize that preconceived ideas that limit the scope of an inquiry can be detrimental and preclude a valid finding. A mindset that "We know what will work and what will fail" in developing attack modes rarely produces desired or valid results. After extensive testing, the failure of different ideas is normal, but "Failure as an option" isn't an acceptable premise and mindset for developing and finding security vulnerabilities. Team members often don't know precisely what they're looking for, what they will find, or why pursuing a specific train of thought will be relevant when identifying vulnerabilities. That is the nature of looking for security design flaws.

If a team or its members believe that a proposed idea about an attack method will not lead to a successful exploit, then it probably never will. This is because the proper testing and required mental energy to follow through with different attempts of a possible exploit will likely not occur or be present.

I can attest from firsthand experience that not running all the possible iterations of attack scenarios can be deadly in terms of a failure to achieve valid results. Often, the last step in the process yields success, not the first step. Not identifying that "last step" can pose significant risks to a manufacturer and those depending on the represented security of the product. It can also lead to a false sense of security.

Team members must have infinite patience to try various approaches once an attack method is conceived. Lock bumping is a perfect example. Many experiments are required to properly test the design of a new electromechanical cylinder against the application of energy. Each experiment takes a lot of time and involves different variables. In conducting these tests, the VA team must track different response patterns and mechanical feedback from the lock. Once a combination of attacks is determined to be potentially effective, the tests must then be refined to optimize what works to achieve reliability in repetition.

Identifying an exploit and its effectiveness can be complicated. Just because a lock can be opened one time doesn't mean it's a relevant attack. More testing is required because risk and potential vulnerability are always balanced. In the case of bumping, if a lock can be bumped open once out of 100 tries, bumping isn't considered a serious problem. However, if the number of successes increases, then an evaluation must be made regarding what constitutes an acceptable risk. Testing may answer this question, but properly determining what constitutes acceptable security against the specific identified vulnerability depends on the techniques applied by the person performing the testing and the number of variables in the attack.

In one product analysis I conducted that involved bumping attacks, I was required to run many tests before finding that the correct combination would open the lock within a few seconds. It took many hours of experimentation, not knowing whether anything would work. One of the intangible problems with bumping and other attacks is that it can take numerous attempts before the lock is opened, if ever. If the individual performing the testing comes back a few minutes later, the lock may open on the first attempt. Hence, nothing is ever certain until attacks can be successfully repeated with reliability.

Five primary variables are required for any testing against bumping:

1. Key design
2. Design and surface characteristics of the bump hammer
3. Condition and design of the lock

4. Any extra security layers

5. The application of force

In this case, I ran the following tests hundreds of times in varying sequences and leveraged the results against each other before the correct variables were found:

- Bumping the key from different angles against the key head, sides, top, and bottom

- Using a combination of strikes at different angles

- Using different levels of force, with light, moderate, and strong strikes individually or in a sequence

- Lightly tapping the key repeatedly with the bump hammer

- Single strikes or multiple strikes in rapid succession

- Withdrawing the key slightly from the plug before striking or inserting it fully into the keyway

- Withdrawing the key completely from the lock and then reinserting it for each attempt to reset the shock fuse (designed to sense shock and vibration)

- Modifying the key's shoulder to allow it to move forward during the application of force

- Different applications of torque to the plug while bumping

- Different timing of the application of torque, either before, during, or after each strike with the bump hammer

- Determining the proper amount of torque and strike force

I've found that to be an effective team member, each member should demonstrate one or more of the following qualifications:

- *The ability to think both as a group member and individually*: Team members must be able to formulate possible vulnerabilities that may be present in the target mechanism. Individuality and not necessarily conforming to rules can aid in achieving the desired results. Introverts are often preferred.

- *Infinite patience*: Team members must believe that success is attainable when attacking a lock.

- *A testing mentality*: A "one of two possible options" mentality will not work in seeking an exploit. Limiting testing options can yield invalid results. Many attacks are incremental and can require several steps. Each can yield partial results, ultimately leading to a total compromise if executed properly.

- *Fresh and independent thought about a problem*: Each team member must discard any previous perceptions or information about the security or invincibility of a locking mechanism.

- *Creativity*: It doesn't help to set time limits on a team member to force results and creativity or to develop an exploit. Creativity takes serious time and thought. Team members must be able to connect the dots and think "out of the box." The process can't be rushed. Locksmiths may not be good choices due to their lack of creativity in compromising a system.

- *An ability to think intuitively*: A team member must think intuitively about a problem to formulate ideas. Ideas breed ideas, so it's desirable to have individuals on a team who can trigger creative thinking on the part of other team members. This could lead to the discovery of an unimagined exploit.

- *An open mind in terms of design*: If a team member believes there's no problem with a design, then the likelihood is that none will be discovered.

- *A technical and proper psychological mindset*: As a rule, technical people think logically and linearly and have expertise in and understanding of mechanical designs. Simply being intelligent doesn't mean they can think about compromising systems. Formal educational credentials therefore aren't predictors of success as a team member.

- *An ability to think in terms of nuances*: They must be sensitive to subtle clues of potential problems and make reliable observations.

- *Detailed oriented*: They should be more interested in accuracy than speed in work performance.

- *A suspicious mindset*: Team members must be tenacious about tracking potential vulnerabilities. They should be cynical and question even common assumptions.

- *Being a rule-breaker*: They must often question authority, especially when told they can't do something related to a hunt for vulnerability. They shouldn't be binary (black-and-white) thinkers.

- *An understanding of design and security*: In my experience, I never believe what my clients represent about the security of their designs. Even the best engineers are rarely aware of design defects that impact security or will not admit they exist due to management pressure or ego.

- *Have no conflicts of interest*: Ensuring that those on a VA team have no conflicts of interest in promoting the products they're responsible for analyzing is crucial.

- *Ability to analyze complex locks*: They must be able to determine simple solutions and low-tech attacks that are successful.

TIP   Team members should not be "Cassandra" types from Greek mythology. Cassandra was the daughter of King Priam of Troy and predicted that Troy would be destroyed. Cassandra's prophecies were true, but Apollo was mad at her and made it so nobody believed her. So she was not a pessimist, but a true seer.

Finally, it's important to mention that the VA team shouldn't have too many engineers. Having too many engineers on a VA team isn't preferable because they generally don't "get" security. They have a different mindset: one that's solution-oriented and unable to find problems. They simply don't think about malicious attacks—just failures.

The Vulnerability Assessment Process

This process usually begins by assessing what is known about how a locking mechanism works and the obvious potential components or designs that can be exploited. An experienced engineer who has previously been involved in this type of investigation can often spot problems that have been identified with other similar challenges.

Next, a list of possible and known attacks is prepared, and then each attack is prioritized based on the likelihood of its success. Consideration should also be given to amplifying known methods and different iterations of prior attacks. Testing is then assigned to team members, and a detailed matrix of variables for each type of attack is run, which should in part dictate how tests are conducted. The picture in Figure 3-1 is illustrative of the process. My team had absolutely no idea at the beginning of our analysis that four keys would be the result of months of research.

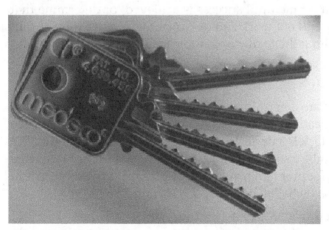

Figure 3-1: Medeco code setting keys were developed and patented as a covert method to pick and bump non-master keyed high-security Medeco locks worldwide. It's a case example of doing a detailed analysis of how a specific locking mechanism works and ignoring statements by the manufacturer and locksmiths that the lock was invulnerable to attack.

An orderly protocol is established that usually adheres to the following logical steps and format:

1. Study the device and figure out how it works, not just how it's supposed to work.

2. Determine whether the security layers accomplish their goals.

3. Determine whether the consumer can easily misuse the device and how the lock is normally used.

4. Consult with locksmiths or end-users who may aid in the assessment.

5. Conduct a preliminary study of the device, and try simple, known attacks.

6. List the most probable attack vectors, and then prioritize them. Remember that testing each idea can be tedious. Patience and optimism are the keys to success. Practicality isn't relevant.

7. Be certain to factor insider attacks into possible vulnerabilities and why.

8. Start testing various ideas. Where you end up will likely not be what is anticipated.

9. Don't solely rely on using AutoCAD or other programs to identify vulnerabilities in components or their interaction. There is no substitute for mechanical "hands-on" testing.

10. Prioritize successful attacks and show how they work, don't work, or partially work and how they can be escalated.

11. Be careful not to focus on one attack because it was successful. There may be others that are equally problematic.

12. Use the Medeco case example of the development of code-setting keys, and take one step at a time until success is achieved, or determine that the proposed attack will not work and document why not. (You can find more information about the Medeco example in Chapter 24 and Part VI.)

13. Test the attacks against the 3T2R rule, and document what the attacks tell and don't tell you.

14. Once vulnerabilities are determined and verified, the team must develop effective countermeasures and test them against attacks. Our Medeco code-setting-keys attack is a perfect example. After developing the ability to "set" each pin tumbler so that it could be picked or bumped, we were granted two patents for programmable security pins to block the procedure of setting all the pins (U.S. Patent No. 7,775,074 and 7,963,135).

15. Attack with modified methods to defeat the countermeasures.

16. Remember that once a problem is discovered and documented, the vulnerability may change in character and require different design iterations to see if the issue is resolved. I spent a full week testing at a Taiwanese factory and had more than 30 iterations of the lock produced by the manufacturer for testing. It resulted in the development of a different way of protecting against bumping and impressioning, for which a patent was granted (U.S. Patent No. 7,441,431).

17. Finally, create a comprehensive VA report.

Insider Threats and Attacks

As part of a VA, *insider threats* and *attacks* must be considered in the context of locks, keys, keying systems, and access control and their potential compromise. Insider attacks can come from employees, service providers, consultants, contractors, vendors, visitors, custodians, secretaries, and retirees who may have unique access. As a class, insiders are often directly involved in attacks or can provide information to outside bad actors. Locks are often the critical element in accomplishing criminal activity. Insiders can access information and intelligence about security systems, locks, and keys. They may also be able to provide copies of keys that can be used for access or are rights-amplified for other locks.

Very careful consideration must be given to the design and security of keys and keying systems. If not designed with these issues in mind, many can be defeated through duplication, simulation, or replication. Photographing a key can defeat an entire system if the image can be decoded or 3D-printed.

Vulnerability Assessment Report

After a vulnerability assessment, a VA report should be provided to the manufacturer's legal counsel and departments of risk management and engineering so they're fully apprised of the assessment's findings and conclusions before releasing a new or modified product for manufacture. This report should detail security strategies, failure consequences, the likelihood of a compromise of products, and resources available to address each identified issue. The report is based on value judgments, experience, and all team members' expertise.

The purpose of a VA is to discover vulnerabilities and attack scenarios and develop design changes and countermeasures against potential compromises. The report should stress that "clearing" an assessment doesn't mean there aren't any vulnerabilities, but simply that they were not identified. Assessments should be routinely conducted because changes may occur in manufacturing, products may be modified, and/or new attacks may be developed. The thought process should be, "Whatever is or appears to be secure today will not be secure tomorrow."

Management should consider a VA like an IQ test: there's no passing or failing grade. However, in all likelihood some attacks were not discovered, so the risk management and engineering departments should always be apprehensive that exploits still exist. From management's perspective, a VA report that identifies previously unknown vulnerabilities should be considered positive, as long as there's proper follow-up.

A VA report can provide detailed information for decision-makers and should address the following topics:

- *How the report was prepared, in addition to the team members involved and their experience*: VA documentation must detail each team member's expertise to lend the report credibility.

- *Known security issues, whether they were fixed, and why or why not*: From a management standpoint, it's important to shield an organization against potential liability should litigation ensue.

- *What is positive and negative about various security layers and levels in each analyzed product, and the recommended fixes*: The report should describe in depth what's positive and negative about each security layer, potential vulnerabilities and exploits, and how each can be remedied.

- *Vulnerabilities and recommendations about countermeasures*: Each discovered vulnerability should be documented with its remedy or countermeasure to ensure that an exploit can't occur.

- *Recommendations regarding any patent filings*: Suggestions that should be pursued to protect any intellectual property that flows from the VA should be detailed in the report.

- *Prioritized recommendations*: Such suggestions should be prioritized based on their probability, liability, security, effectiveness, cost, and customer impact.

- *Results and the priority of action items*: The most urgent issues and how to implement each item effectively should be examined in great detail. Your report should discuss the urgency, effectiveness, and cost of each vulnerability discovered and the notification of those impacted by security issues. The projected time to implement should also be noted. Media considerations and announcements should be planned if relevant.

- *Any legal issues involved and potential liability*: The report must analyze risk, cost-effectiveness, and the probability that identified vulnerabilities should be remedied. This report can mitigate potential liability on a manufacturer's part if litigation ensues based on a defective product.

- *How to educate employees*: A VA report should teach engineering staff to find vulnerabilities and attack methods. Low-level employees should be brought into the VA process, as they often know more than design engineers about specific problems.

- *The result of identified vulnerabilities and attacks*: A realistic review should consider the immediate and long-term potential damage if no action is taken and the minimum changes that would mitigate the security threat. It should detail the risk associated with the discovered vulnerabilities regarding potential loss or harm to end-users. The consequences of security failures should be carefully analyzed and projected.

- *Suggested allocation of resources to risk management*: The job of risk management should be mitigating or eliminating risk, so priorities and using security resources should be addressed.

Finally, the legitimacy of a VA report is sacred. Don't edit, delete, change, or censor any relevant findings in the report. The reports will be discovered if litigation occurs. If derogatory information is edited or deleted, it can certainly assist a plaintiff in any lawsuit.

Suggested Rules, Axioms, Guidelines, and Principles

The following rules, axioms, guidelines, and principles can help identify vulnerabilities as part of an assessment. This list is a synthesis and product of my experiences and those of my colleagues in analyzing hundreds of lock designs and modifications of current products to optimize the VA process and reach successful conclusions:

- *You must examine critical and noncritical components for a component failure analysis.* Any part can become a critical component in defeating a mechanism and may not appear as such in an initial review. This includes movable parts, springs, motors, solenoids, ferrous materials, inertia, coils, mechanical bypass circuits, mechanical overrides, microswitches, drain holes, entry points, data ports, and susceptibility to magnetic principles.

- *Always believe you can defeat a lock.* A positive attitude that a lock can and will be defeated can often ensure ultimate success.

- *An absence of evidence can't be relied on as evidence of an absence of a vulnerability.* A negative rarely proves a negative in terms of finding vulnerabilities. Sometimes, significant defeats are found late in an inquiry, so patience and tenacity are the rules.

- *Analysts rarely know all the tools to open locks.* Many specialized tools, technology, and techniques are available for defeating specific lock mechanisms. This includes general classes of tools that can be adapted to defeat individual security layers within a lock.

- *Just because it can't be conceived of doesn't mean it doesn't exist.* One of the problems of searching for vulnerabilities is the conception of an attack mode. This can occur initially or as an investigation progresses. Most attack vectors aren't initially conceived or would have been solved early in the design process.

- *Crazy ideas in assessing vulnerability can be expanded until they aren't so crazy.* My colleagues and I have had many "crazy" ideas that nobody thought applied to solve a problem. Often, these ideas turned out to be the best solution. Ideas that nobody could imagine would work often turn out to be the unimaginable solution that identifies serious design defects.

- *Creative ideas come from individuals, not groups.* Individual team members generate ideas discussed and analyzed by several team members. It's individuals who are often responsible for the kernel idea.

▪ *Developing and testing exploit scenarios should result in failures that enable understanding of what works and what doesn't.* This is the logical testing process of various potential solutions, especially when a vulnerability has yet to be discovered.

▪ *Don't allow the discovery of possible vulnerabilities to limit other developed attack vectors.* It's important not to limit an inquiry once a vulnerability has been identified. There is usually more to be found, so don't get sidetracked into thinking the product is now secure.

▪ *Don't believe what management tells you about a potential security problem, because they may not know about existing vulnerabilities.* I never believe what design engineers, management, and marketing personnel represent about the security of a product. They often don't understand what is secure and what is subject to compromise.

▪ *Everything we think we know may be wrong.* Many manufacturers and design teams can't believe there's a problem involving a mature product that's been in the marketplace for many years, especially when no issues have been reported.

▪ *Failure to assess vulnerabilities may be because the one making the assessment can't foresee the problem.* This can result from arrogance, inexperience, a lack of knowledge, or a belief that they know everything needed about a specific product.

▪ *"Groupthink" may be counterproductive and doesn't promote creativity about a problem.* General George Patton once observed, "If everyone is thinking alike, then nobody is thinking."

▪ *If you don't believe you can open a lock, you probably won't be able to open it.* As mentioned previously, mental attitude is one of the most important assets in a search for vulnerabilities.

▪ *Just because a lock design has been around for a long time doesn't mean it's secure; there may be embedded security issues that nobody has found.* The Kaba Simplex 1000 push-button lock is a perfect case example. Developed in 1965, it was identified as vulnerable to being opened in seconds by a rare earth magnet in 2009.

▪ *Just because an employee can't compromise a security product means nothing.* Identifying a vulnerability takes special talent and education. Engineering employees rarely possess such attributes unless they have been specially trained.

▪ *You may need to look for vulnerabilities in a device several times before you find some.* This maturation process can take a lot of time and mental energy before one or more vulnerabilities are discovered and exploited. My colleagues and I worked for several years to develop an exploit for a successful magnetic high-security lock. At first the task seemed impossible, but we worked through the problem and ultimately succeeded in decoding this lock, producing simulated keys and other techniques that allowed us to open the lock in seconds.

■ *Simple attacks often work best on sophisticated technology.* Complex or sophisticated technology can create a belief in its security and invincibility to attack. There is often a simple solution to defeat a complicated lock, which can be executed by a person with little skill once shown the method. Always opt for a simple technique rather than developing complicated attacks. Most security issues can be analyzed using common sense. It's the mindset that's important.

■ *The more detailed and structured a security analysis is, often the less careful and imaginative thought has gone into it.* An overly structured protocol for discovering security vulnerabilities can discourage creative thinking because it can limit options to explore in looking for a defeat method.

■ *Don't focus on too few vulnerabilities and attacks, as many more are often missed or never considered.* When a vulnerability is discovered, the team thinks their task is accomplished. Rarely is there only one vulnerability. Finding one method of exploitation often leads to others or modifications in the attack to make it simpler and more effective.

■ *Circular thinking can be deadly in a VA program.* Such thinking relies on the perception that the current security level is acceptable because the potential threat has been defined by the current level of security rather than the threat itself. The failure to find a vulnerability in a product, coupled with the product's success in the marketplace, can lead to the problem of circular thinking and logic.

■ *A team must always focus on a security problem from the attacker's perspective.* Vulnerability should be defined by the likelihood of an attack and consideration of the motivation for such an attack. VA teams should consider what bad actors define as their rationale and then search for breaches in security. Consider what they will attempt to exploit and how they will likely do it.

■ *Adversaries attack using a deliberate, targeted method at points of potential failure, so team members must attempt to identify such weaknesses.* Criminals and insiders are always looking for points of failure in any security system. It's important, especially in locks with multiple security layers, to analyze each layer and attempt to neutralize it independently.

■ *Consider how to stop the attack or defend against each identified point of failure.* Once each point of failure is identified, countermeasures must be developed to protect against an attack on each point of failure or security layer.

■ *Consider the legal ramifications of failing to fix a known security issue.* Whenever a manufacturer is presented with the discovery of a vulnerability, serious consideration must be given to a worst-case scenario. They must ask, "What happens if the problem isn't effectively addressed?" Documentation of the identification of the vulnerability, consideration of remedies, and ultimate action must be developed in the event of subsequent litigation. The best course of action is to fix a problem early rather than later.

■ *From a legal standpoint, you must always consider the security implications of all products, even if they don't appear to have any.* A lock manufacturer must constantly consider the implications of security vulnerabilities and the potential results if they become known by criminals, customers, and the public.

■ *Sometimes, one vulnerability will lead to more serious findings.* The team must never underestimate how the bad guys can exploit vulnerabilities. Finding one way to exploit a lock often leads to others that are even more effective. No vulnerability should be ignored because the manufacturer believes it or its impact is minimal.

■ *Just because no immediate threat exists doesn't mean there's reason to ignore any findings.* Consider the result if the vulnerability becomes public, regardless of how remote its threat is considered. Imagine the result if the problem can't be easily remedied in the field at the customer level.

■ *It's important to reexamine a design after upgrades or changes in a product have occurred.* Any change to a lock's design should prompt a reevaluation of its security, because even small changes can create new vulnerabilities that aren't obvious or apparent.

■ *Be very negative in your belief that no vulnerabilities have been identified.* Always keep looking for vulnerabilities. Don't rely on the fact that none have been found. More often than not, they exist.

■ *In brainstorming different vulnerabilities, don't be quick to discard ideas.* No matter how stupid an idea may appear, every idea could become the key. There's no such thing as a stupid idea to a VA team. Creativity in thinking is a critical issue, and the fastest way to mute it is to berate team members for ideas that may seem improbable or impossible. Crazy ideas may turn out to be the best.

■ *The best ideas often come late in analysis and often occur when all other ideas have been exhausted.* VA is a continuing process that requires much thought and analysis. Sometimes the solution to a problem comes very late in the process.

■ *Be certain you aren't making false assumptions about security features.* There is often a problem with believing that security features and layers accomplish what an engineering team and product literature represent. Assumptions based on facts about a lock's security can result in testing that won't achieve valid results. Care should be taken to establish and verify all assumptions about the effectiveness of security layers or enhancements before possible attack vectors are developed.

- *All ideas should be analyzed, expanded, modified, and combined with other ideas, even hunches.* In my experience, in the hunt for vulnerabilities, we often don't know what we are looking for until we find it.

- *Care must be taken to avoid perceptual blindness, which involves missing obvious things that were not expected to be seen.* Obvious problems can often be overlooked because they were not in our mindset to be discovered. Training and care will help avoid such a problem.

- *Arrogance by design engineers and management about a lock design's security demonstrates ignorance and is a recipe for disaster.* Security arrogance and security ignorance go hand in hand. Many lock manufacturers believe in the maxim that "If it wasn't invented here, it's not good." This philosophy can get a manufacturer into trouble because it assumes that its engineering team knows everything about its product, implying that the team can identify any vulnerability. This mindset has often been proven wrong.

- *Count on finding security vulnerabilities others have missed if you look hard enough.* There is no perfect product, and most locks have one or more exploitable vulnerabilities. The question becomes how relevant and serious such issues are and what can happen if they're exploited.

- *Even high-tech devices can be defeated by low-tech attacks without fully understanding how the device works.* The more sophisticated a lock design is, the more opportunity for vulnerabilities to be embedded in the design. Complexity often breeds vulnerabilities. It remains for a VA team to find each of them.

- *Just because employees—especially engineers—can't compromise a security device often means nothing.* It's about expertise, training, and creativity. A failure to imagine a problem with a design never means it doesn't exist.

- *Just because a lock has been around for a long time doesn't mean it can't be compromised.* It only means there may be security issues that nobody has found. Never rely on the fact that no vulnerabilities have been found in a locking device that's been used for many years. Many locks have embedded design issues that haven't been discovered or exploited. It doesn't mean they don't exist.

- *The value of a target dictates preparation, intelligence, and knowledge by attackers.* When looking for vulnerabilities, the critical question is why the lock and what it protects would be the target of an attack and the likely scenarios for how that would occur.

▪ *There are no long-term secrets*. Nothing can be kept secret for very long, especially targeted products like locks.

▪ *Openness and transparency in a security design is the best policy*. There are no more secrets due to the global flow of information on the Internet. Always assume that everything is known and readily available about any specific lock. The more input is available from users and the public, the better a product will be.

▪ *Just because a team member is intelligent doesn't mean they can think like a bad guy*. It takes a long time to develop the skills essential to a successful vulnerability assessor. The requisite mental tools are often intuitive and require much experience to mature and be useful.

▪ *A failure to connect the dots can have serious or tragic consequences*. The Master of the Titanic, five years before her sinking, made the following statement, "I cannot imagine any condition which could cause a ship to founder. I cannot conceive of any vital disaster happening to this vessel. Modern shipbuilding has gone beyond that." He failed to consider that hitting an iceberg that acted like a sharp knife could tear apart one side of the ship. This failure to connect the dots cost many lives and is representative of how such an engineering failure had serious consequences.

The rules and guidelines I have outlined in this chapter provide varying perspectives on how to think about possible design problems and what creates vulnerabilities. They result from analyzing many supposedly "perfect" concepts and executions of hardware designs that resulted in significant security issues and liability.

The 3T2R Rule for Assessing the Security of a Lock

The 3T2R Rule is my simplified abbreviation and summary of what all security standards specify as to the requirements for conventional and high-security locks, as will be examined in Chapter 7. These standards denote the testing protocols to measure resistance to forced entry, covert entry, key control, endurance, environmental factors, and other criteria for specific security grades and ratings. Standards provide the primary measure of security for most organizations and individual users. Yet they often fail to offer a true picture of whether a lock is secure against various forms of attack.

The standards don't provide an easily understandable method to assess a lock's performance against different attack methods. This can be especially important in terms of the manufacturer's liability for possible deficient or defective designs. However, I have reduced the requirements in the various standards to five keywords:

- Time
- Tools
- Training
- Reliability
- Repeatability

These keywords represent what is relevant regarding the simplicity or difficulty of opening a lock, making it inoperative, or rendering the critical components or security layers neutralized, defeated, or bypassed.

Manufacturers implement and embed mechanisms and components to provide security against varying attacks. This implementation is central to a lock's performance, as measured by its security ratings by the Underwriters Laboratory (UL), American National Standards Institute (ANSI)/Builders Hardware Manufacturers Association (BHMA), VdS, and other standards organizations. Consumers purchase locks based on these standards, and manufacturers give an implied or actual representation that their locks will withstand multiple forms of attack based on the criteria specified within a specific standard. The manufacturer's security analysis is a multifaceted and often complex assessment that encompasses and weighs fundamental questions of liability, standards requirements, buyer and user expectations, and real-world attack scenarios. Manufacturers need an easily understood way to gauge the performance of their products. If litigation is based on a defective product, a judge or jury may have to decide whether a product *is* defective. They will apply some form of the 3T2R rule because it represents the essence of performance, security, and liability questions.

The 3T2R Rule: Metrics, Security, and Liability

It's important to understand the application of standards and the ability to determine the security of a lock, safe, Internet of Things (IoT) device, or access control system against their specifications and requirements. This application can be difficult and may not demonstrate certain vulnerabilities of the item in question. Such an analysis should be easy to translate to a real-world situation, different security environments, and perceived needs for specific users or applications. Security is situational—it may be sufficient for one application and user but not for another.

Security standards often fail to contemplate various forms of attack that can render a lock vulnerable in seconds. Defining the ease or difficulty of such attacks can be summarized and reduced to the five keywords in the 3T2R rule. They can provide a graphic insight into the security and liability issues that may be involved. Compromising a lock within seconds, especially one with a high-security rating, requires little legal or engineering expertise to grasp the potential ramifications. Conversely, that understanding is also relevant if a lock is difficult to open.

Let's now break down the 3T2R rule into a larger discussion.

Time

The first keyword in the 3T2R rule is *time*. How long it takes to open a lock successfully may seem to be a simple and straightforward question.

However, depending on the lock, it can involve multiple factors and often more complex consideration and evaluation.

Security is centered on a time delay to resist or stop unauthorized access to a lock, safe, or security system. Every standard that measures resistance to covert and forced entry, including UL 437 and BHMA/ANSI 156.30 (discussed in Chapter 7), enumerates the minimum times a lock or safe must withstand defined attacks before being compromised. High-security standards generally require resistance to covert entry of at least 10 or 15 minutes, depending on the specific standard. In the simplest of terms, the security of every lock is measured against the time it takes to open it, either physically by brute force or through the covert manipulation of critical locking components.

From both a legal and security perspective, if a lock that has a 10-minute security rating can be opened in 10 seconds without the correct credentials, there's a serious issue, and the device's design may realistically be judged as deficient or defective, and certainly non-compliant with the standard. Part of the problem with the standards can be the limitations of the attack types and methods employed in testing. The designs and security of numerous locks, especially high-security ones, can often be compromised in ways that the manufacturer, risk managers, security officers, and users cannot anticipate. If even the simplest attack methods can be missed by testing labs, there needs to be a way to assess and demonstrate the security of a specific device and a change in the testing protocols.

Time must always be considered in the context of the other two parameters—tools and training—in the equation. Time is a measure of how long the method of attack takes unless the lock can be opened without any tools or training. If an attacker can approach a piece of locking hardware and open it without any keys, tokens, credentials, and/or expertise, no one would argue that the lock fails to offer any measure of protection.

Time encompasses several variables that must be considered when discussing the ability to compromise a lock, safe, or system. Depending on the specific mechanism, time may be computed as a continuous measurement, a cumulative total of separate actions, or in separate segments that are not dependent on one another to accomplish an opening. The computation of time must also consider several different possible operating or attack modes. For example, must a specific segment or portion of an attack be completed before another can begin? Must the attack be carried out in logical order or sequence? Can seemingly unrelated operations within an attack be carried out without effecting a mechanical reset or failure that requires restarting the process, thereby recomputing the time elapsed for the attack? Many such questions require consideration.

Various Time Computations and Attack Vector Examples

The various standards do not adequately address the issue of computing the time to defeat a lock or security component. In certain forms of attack, this can be critical. This issue proved extremely problematic in assessing a lock's resistance to various forms of lock bumping. VA teams must pay particular attention to this parameter because the definition of time in the context of how long it takes to compromise a lock can be critical. Ultimately, assessing attack time is a key parameter, but how that time is computed is equally important.

Continuous Time Measurement: Computing the Total Attack Time

Lock bumping of a pin tumbler mechanism is a perfect example of two methods of time computation: *cumulative* and *stop and start*. There is no required sequence, as each key strike can be considered a separate attack. A bump key is inserted to open a lock, and energy is applied as one or multiple strikes against the head, side, or other parts of the key. If properly designed, the bitting of the key will transmit the energy to the base of each pin tumbler, causing it to move vertically across the shear line. If lock bumping is done properly, the shear line will be open for a few milliseconds, whereby torque can be applied to turn the plug.

This operation is normally carried out in one time frame or sequence. However, sometimes it requires separate attempts. Lock bumping is a random and chaotic attack in the way the tumblers are affected and moved, so many variables within the lock affect the ability to bump it open and the ease of doing so. (These variables are discussed in greater detail in Chapter 17.) The importance of this example is that the attack, which is usually carried out in a few seconds with one or more repeated strikes in a rapid fashion, may require multiple strikes with pauses.

Picking and impressioning would usually be considered in this timing category, although it depends on the design of the lock. Normally, this process is completed in one session, especially if security pins are involved.

> Lock bumping attacks are not uniform. A lock may yield in a few seconds with only a couple of strikes or require multiple strikes over a longer period. Thus the time factor in the 3T2R rule may be misleading in terms of simplicity or complexity. I've opened locks in seconds with one or two strikes. The same lock sometimes cannot be opened or requires repeated attempts at different intervals. Check out this video where I open a door lock in seconds: www.youtube.com/watch?v=6DfPNQJZmM4.

Computing Total Time: Stop and Start an Attack

A lock-bumping attack could also be considered in this category, because each attempt to open the lock can constitute a separate and distinct attack with its timing. Other attacks include decoding a lock with a special tool, such as a John Falle Pin and Cam system, discussed in Chapter 20. This system is based on sensing the pin tumblers binding at the shear line. Other methods include the optical decoder developed for Kwikset locks by LockTech (as discussed in Part IV). Attempting to decode each pin tumbler with optical or sound devices would also be included because such an attack can be carried out over time.

The iLOQ electromechanical lock is an excellent example of this attack type. As discussed in Chapter 3, my colleague and I developed this attack type to compromise a very clever mechanism that required no batteries to drive the electronics portion of the design. This lock is defeated by modifying either a valid key or the primary interface for the tip of the key used to reset the mechanism. The method first requires the modification of the reset mechanism at the outer edge of the keyway. It can be done at any time to preset the internal components for an attack. Once this is accomplished, the ability to access is always present. The manufacturer has made many design changes since this original attack was published in 2011 at DefCon, but the exploit still exists.

Cumulate Total Time: Required Sequential Parts of an Attack in a Specified Order

The attack on the Medeco BIAXIAL and m3 high-security locks is a perfect example. Compromising the lock required several independent steps: producing and using a key with the correct sidebar code, setting the pins to that code, and then picking the lock. These procedures must be executed in the proper sequence to be successful. Each pin tumbler within a Medeco cylinder is rotated to one of three correct angles. In a six-pin lock, there are 729 possible permutations. The correct combination—or, as we named it, the sidebar code—must be properly *set*, or the sidebar cannot retract into the plug once all the pins are aligned at the shear line.

The combination of rotation angles can be set using a key with the correct code or simulated with one of four patented *code-setting keys* that we developed to simulate the 729 codes. Once the pins are properly rotated, they can be conventionally picked to the shear line. This process is a perfect example and can be achieved within about 2 minutes, depending on the bitting pattern. The computation of time depends on all the steps being completed, but this sequence of steps was never contemplated in any high-security lock standard.

Unrelated and Separate Parts of an Attack Conducted with No Time Deadline or Constraints

The extrapolation of a top-level master key (TMK), as discussed in Part V, is the best example of this type of attack and the time it takes to accomplish. The decoding of the top-level master key in a pin tumbler lock that was set up with the Total Position Progression master key system can be carried out at one time or in a series of samplings over an unlimited time frame. This is a simple attack if a *change key* for the system is available to use as a constant. A change key is the lowest-level key designed to open one or more specific locks. The only caveat is if there are multiple master pins in one or more chambers: then the operation becomes even more complex due to the potential for multiple shear lines and keying levels.

In a lock with one bottom pin, one master pin, and one top pin in each chamber, the master key code is extrapolated against the change key code by sampling each chamber and cutting test keys. This procedure can identify all the cuts of the top-level master key through a series of tests and elimination of all but the correct bitting value. The operation can be carried out with as few as three blank keys and requires just a few minutes to perform. The security vulnerability for this system type is the ability to take multiple readings of pin tumbler depths at any time. Each reading is not dependent on another. Using precut keys with known code depths can facilitate the process. In this example, the computation of time to attack a system is irrelevant because of the sampling technique.

Another example of an attack that can be carried out in distinct parts involves an electronic lock with a worm gear controlled by an internal motor. When activated by the proper credentials, this motor is energized to rotate the worm gear, which drives a blocking element and sets it into a locked or unlocked position. This attack and movement of the worm gear can be executed either in steps or all at once. The lock typically has a free-spinning knob that retracts or extends the latch or bolt once the correct credential is authenticated (typically a radio frequency identification [RFID] card). If the knob is rotated at high and low speeds with the proper technique, the worm gear is slowly advanced to a locked or unlocked position without any audit trail or indication of access. Unless the worm gear position resets from using a proper credential, its position will remain at whatever point the gear was left during an attack. Typically, this entire operation can take less than a minute to execute at one time, or it can be done over a longer period.

Time Delay, Security, and Liability

The time to open a lock is one of the three primary criteria to consider in assessing security. It must be measured against the other two elements of the 3T2R rule, but it's often the primary factor in assessing vulnerability. If a lock can be compromised in under 1 minute, the other portions of the rule may not be relevant. Suppose a manufacturer produces a locking device with low time-threshold resistance. In that case, serious liability can result if its compromise results in injury, death, damages, or loss of assets.

Tools

The second *T* in the 3T2R rule is *tools*. The definition of a tool can encompass any implement that can be utilized to open a lock by exploiting mechanical and electronic designs. Although most standards define the types of tools designated for attack testing, an infinite variety of items can be adapted to compromise specific locks and mechanisms. This is the problem with certain standards, even for high-security locks. Attacks in the context of the 3T2R rule fall into two broad categories—*forced* and *covert*—and are often referred to as *destructive* or *nondestructive* entry. A third subcategory is *hybrid attacks*.

Forced Entry

Even the highest-security locks can often be defeated with inexpensive and readily available hand and power tools within a few minutes or even seconds. Grinders, high-speed drill motors, impact drills, portable Dremel tools, and special carbide, boron, and diamond-tipped drill bits can penetrate, cut through, or disintegrate most security barriers and even hard-plate, which is a specially designed barrier material to protect high-security enclosures such as safes and vaults. Modern cutting materials can be extremely effective against almost any metal used in locks. Typically, forced-entry techniques can include using chemicals to alter the molecular structure, tension, compression, pressure, shearing, temperature, and drilling.

According to the various standards, locks with high-security ratings are supposed to withstand attacks for at least 5 minutes. Many do, but different methods and techniques with breaking tools and hybrid attacks can often cause the locks to fail in a shorter period. As noted in Part II of this book, the problem is that the use of certain tools is not defined or specified. Although lock manufacturers often employ the most sophisticated materials that are supposed to resist forced-entry techniques, the reality is that virtually any lock can be defeated with the right tools in a brief time. The importance of tools is critical for the 3T2R rule and its analysis, but it must be considered with the other parameters. *Tools alone do not open a lock.* They must be assessed regarding how long it will take and what training is needed to use such tools.

Covert and Surreptitious Entry

Clandestine attacks are always our priority because they often leave no trace or audit trails and can be the most dangerous security breaches when evidence of entry is important. The government distinguishes *covert* and *surreptitious entry* for sensitive compartmented information facilities (SCIFs), classified containers, areas, and materials. Forensic inspection may not yield any indicia if the method is surreptitious. In contrast, toolmarks or other deformities, fractures, or evidence will ordinarily be present in a covert opening or attempt. Surreptitious entry methods include mechanical, optical, audio, and electronic decoding techniques (discussed in Part IV), and loiding (previously discussed). Covert techniques that leave indications of entry include picking, impressioning, and bumping (depending on the factors that involve the lock's condition and the operative's competence).

The 3T2R rule is a form of threat index that considers any method of attack against a lock. Covert or surreptitious bypass, especially against high-security–rated locks and safes, is a primary concern for lock manufacturers. The prevention, delay, or alert of an attempted or successful nondestructive entry (NDE) into a protected area is a constant threat. It's the reason for designing and integrating defensive mechanisms and multiple security layers. Although locks are designed to resist known attack methods, it is virtually impossible to anticipate every variation or adaptation of different techniques due to individual internal designs. The 3T2R rule often points out covert methods of entry or hybrid attacks that were never contemplated during the design process, known by security officers or risk managers, or even envisioned by vulnerability assessment teams.

My colleagues and I have found that we can employ items with little or no relationship to a lock-defeat tool. *Imagination* and understanding the internal mechanism are often critical for determining what may work to bypass a specific target. For example, I've utilized thin plastic sheets from a report cover as well as Shrinky Dinks®, electrical tape, wires, shims, stiff file folders, carbon paper, small screwdrivers, ice picks, vibrating tools, electric toothbrushes, and many other items to bypass locks. You're only limited by your imagination!

Attack tools need not be from a locksmith shop, supplier, or hardware store. They can come from an international professional defeat tools manufacturer, such as Wendt (Germany), John Falle (United Kingdom), or Madelin (France); American suppliers, including `LockPicks.com`, Brockhage, Lockmasters, or Lockpicks 101; or even Amazon or DIY stores. Office supply centers also have tools and materials that can be useful in compromising locks.

When considering the 3T2R rule, you must understand that there's a distinction between the tools, who uses them, and whether they're for forced or covert entry. Sophisticated and professional entry tools designed specifically for opening identified locks by law enforcement, government, and intelligence agencies are restricted and originate primarily from Wendt, Lockmasters, Madelin, and Falle. Independent sources produce and distribute specialized tools throughout the world. Certain systems, often unknown to lock manufacturers, will be examined in greater detail in Part IV.

The next category of tools includes those available to locksmiths, locksport, and nonprofessional lock pickers. Common hand and cordless tools found at Home Depot, Lowe's, Ace Hardware, and similar outlets may be equally useful and easiest to obtain or modify. Finally, office supply stores like Staples and Office Depot are among my favorite venues. They have an incredible array of items that can be adapted to accomplish simple and effective openings, especially with hybrid attacks on multiple security layers in a lock. The compromise of Kryptonite bike locks and most axial pin tumbler mechanisms began at an office supply store that sold ballpoint pens and magnets and a grocery store that sold toilet paper rolls!

One of the benefits of the 3T2R rule is that any tool is acceptable to test and compromise the security of a lock. The reasonableness of such a choice is relevant to the lock type, the venue, the attack mode, the ability to carry or conceal the tool, and the likelihood of discovery up to and during the attack process. The selection and use of one or more tools or implements is part of the overall security analysis in conjunction with the other parameters of the formula.

Hybrid Attacks and the 3T2R Rule

A hybrid attack relies on a combination of steps to bypass a lock and is discussed at great length in Parts IV and VI. A hybrid approach that contemplates multiple operations is often required when several security layers must be neutralized or certain internal components are not immediately accessible. Hybrid attacks may also require covert and forced manipulation of components. Such attacks can employ many nontraditional sequences and techniques that often are not obvious. They require a careful target analysis, a clear understanding of mechanical and electronic design, and, most important, imagination.

> **WARNING**   It's important to realize that testing within many standards does *not* adequately contemplate nontraditional hybrid methods or the sequences of steps necessary to neutralize critical locking components. Complicating the problem for security analysts is a failure to identify relevant or critical components. These mechanisms may not appear directly connected with the ability to bypass a mechanism or can be overlooked or thought irrelevant or unconnected with a security vulnerability. Even more troublesome is the ability to bypass the lock by altering or modifying an internal component that does not appear related to security.

In one case, my team neutralized the primary design element of a highly sophisticated magnetic lock. We employed a hybrid attack that allowed us to create a second set of gates in combination with a correctly bitted key. It enabled the highest-security lock in government and intelligence services to be quickly opened without any external trace. This is one of several hybrid attacks we developed that ultimately required a significant redesign by the manufacturer. Several years later, a patent was issued in the United States to prevent a different attack against the same lock (Vornbrock U.S. Patent No. 10,563,426 B2).

In my experience, hybrid forms of compromise can be extremely effective. The problem for designers and VA teams is that such attacks can take many forms and may require developing or adapting specialized tools or implements. They are sometimes logical yet unimaginable, especially in combination with traditional tools and other modes of attack.

It is impossible to offer a comprehensive list of hybrid attacks because each can be unique, depending on the design of the target mechanism. It is only necessary to provide an overview in this chapter to aid in understanding how the concept of hybrid attacks fits into the 3T2R assessment of security. More detailed information is provided later in Part IV.

Examples of hybrid attacks that can defeat the security of a lock can include the following:

- Achieving direct rotor access on internal motors with shims after drilling a small access hole
- Altering primary credentials, followed by a forced form of attack
- Changing primary physical locking components
- Combining correct mechanical key bitting with a bypass of electronic credentials
- Completing a bypass of primary security elements by physically altering their characteristics to create additional shear lines, gates, or paths to allow sidebars, levers, or other blocking elements to act as if they're part of the intended design
- Covertly manipulating and then forcing components
- Creating a modified original key from another system
- Causing minute openings to allow access to critical components by shim wires
- Developing an attack against an opening
- Drilling fine holes to directly fish wires to power leads to the internal motor
- Employing a secondary key or credential to set or neutralize a primary locking element
- Exploiting an optional feature that allows a lock to be opened by completely bypassing all security mechanisms
- Forcing the movement of components, followed by nondestructively manipulating components to alter their state or cause critical locking elements to move in an unintended way
- Pressuring multiple internal components in a specific sequence and then nondestructively manipulating other components
- Injecting steel bearings to lift pin tumblers across the shear line
- Inserting material into the keyway to move wafers or pins and then applying torque
- Injecting silicone or other material to simulate internal elements that can then be manipulated
- Introducing shim wires into openings to manipulate components before they can be moved

- Jiggling an improperly bitted key and applying torque
- Moving critical locking components beyond their normal position or limits to bypass or create unintended shear lines
- Relocating or setting locking elements to a position where they're subject to vibration or shock to create or bypass a shear line
- Neutralizing a sidebar with a fine shim wire
- Nondestructively neutralizing a primary and secondary security layer and then manipulating the primary obstruction to open the lock
- Simulating credentials on a lock's key to eliminate an audit trail
- Faking a primary credential and then forcing a second security layer
- Simulating, replicating, or exploiting mechanical and electronic credentials
- Trapping a relocker to circumvent its action
- Using bumping and vibration to move internal components and defeat relockers
- Utilizing magnetized wires to fish internal components to a different position
- Employing magnetic fields to alter or move critical locking components
- Applying one valid credential and simulating another in multilayer security levels
- Piggybacking from a simulated mechanical key and using valid credentials from another key
- Applying shims to route around internal components to reach direct locking mechanisms
- Incorporating vibration and picking to alter the position of wafers or pin tumblers
- Simulating the mechanical portion and using shims or specially prepared credentials to bypass the electronics within an integrated locking system that combines mechanical and electronic credentials

Tool Assessment and the 3T2R Rule: Simple, Complex, or Special Designs

When selecting your tools, remember to assess your selection by thinking about the 3T2R rule. Remember the concept that virtually anything can be a tool when assessing a lock's security. Its defeat is vitally important, so do not limit your perspective when imagining or designing a method or procedure to compromise security. You must ask yourself, can a specific item be a "tool" to open a lock or neutralize its security layers? At a minimum, the following issues must be considered with regard to assessing an operation and in analyzing the use of any specific item, tool, or set of tools that could constitute a threat within the meaning of the 3T2R equation:

- What is the size of the tool or tools?
- How heavy is each tool?
- Are your tools easy to conceal, or can they be camouflaged to appear to be something other than bypass tools?
- Are your chosen tools portable?
- Can your tools be carried by hand?
- Will using the tool(s) make noise or draw attention?
- Will you need light or darkness for the tool's use?
- Do the tools require power to operate?
- Are the tools readily available?
- How expensive are the tools?
- Are multiple tools required for the bypass procedure?
- Are multiple tools or components required for the tool's operation?
- Can one operative perform the opening operation, or are more people required in the operation?
- Can the tools be easily damaged or broken when in use?
- Are the tools restricted as to who can purchase or possess them?
- Are there any records for purchasing the tools or audit trails that will identify the buyer?
- Are there commercially available tools specially designed for the target lock?
- What estimated time may be required to accomplish the lock's entry or compromise?
- Can the lock be opened and a key produced during the same process?
- Can pieces of a tool break or remain in the lock?
- Can the tool damage internal lock components?
- Do the tools leave any traces during or after use?
- Will toolmarks be visible for inspection?
- Will traces of the tool remain and be present in a forensic examination?
- In contemplating criminal statutes for possession of burglary tools, does the item have an arguably legal use or legitimate purpose if an operative is caught using it or in possession of it?
- Are there any serial numbers or identifying information located on the tool if it's left at the scene?

- What is the cost of the tool or system?
- Is any advanced intelligence or information required about the target lock before selecting or using a specific tool?
- Are tool accessories required, such as lights, video monitors, acoustic devices, or optical viewing equipment?
- Is the tool universal for a class of locks?
- Are several different tools available for a target lock?
- Are there export controls for the tools or systems?
- Can the tools or their components be 3D printed?
- Can the tools be easily reproduced without special processes?
- Can anyone buy the tools, or is access restricted to the government or locksmiths?
- Is there a black-market availability for the tools, or are there knockoffs?
- Does using the tools violate any laws, such as the Digital Millennium Copyright Act (DMCA) or 18 USC 1029, 1030 (unauthorized computer access)?

Training

Training is the third leg of the 3T2R rule. It encompasses the overall learning necessary to carry out a successful bypass and any specialized skills that may be required. Some attacks, such as bumping, entail little or no training or understanding of the underlying principles of compromising specific mechanisms. Other attacks involve significant training and the development of precise skills.

Many professional and specialty tools have been developed to attack a broad range of high-security mechanical and electromechanical locking systems. These instruments decode, pick, manipulate, impression, measure, or simulate critical locking components. These systems, which cost thousands of dollars, are only sold to the government or intelligence agencies. Some are so complicated that a few days to several weeks of personal instruction is required to become proficient in their usage. John Falle, Wendt, Lockmasters, and Madelin are world famous for designing and manufacturing opening systems for the highest-security locks. Attacks on such locks would be considered state-of-the-art.

Many other tools available to the locksmith, amateur, and locksport sectors are primarily for conventional locks and require far less skill to employ. They are also less expensive. Hundreds of dealers and Internet sales outlets offer tools to open various locking-mechanism categories. The Lishi tools, produced in China and sold everywhere, are a prime example. This series of inexpensive decoders is designed for automobiles and other locks and allows for the rapid decoding of tumbler or wafer codes and then replication of keys to open the target lock.

They are recognized worldwide for their simplicity of operation, low cost, and capabilities to decode and open many different locks.

Whether the target is a complex high-security lock or a relatively simple mechanism, the required training to effectively use a bypass tool is critical to the 3T2R rule and the assessment of the lock design's security. If tools are complicated and exact, the security rating of a lock will be higher. If simple tools can compromise security, the lock can be gauged as less secure or even defective in design. In evaluating the tool component in relation to training of the security formula, many questions must be considered:

- Are special keyways, bitting values, or inserts required to pick, decode, or impression a target lock?
- Have lock manufacturers enhanced their design to prevent or obstruct using a specific tool or technique?
- Have internal tolerances or mechanical changes been implemented in a target lock to frustrate the use of a tool or render its use less reliable?

Tools must also be analyzed in terms of required training. The following questions are relevant to the expertise required:

- Who can use the tools?
- Is the tool's operation complicated?
- Are the tools difficult to operate?
- What training is required to use the tools to open the lock?
- Are multiple steps required to use the tool(s)?
- How much training is required to become proficient?
- Are there any training videos on the Internet that demonstrate the tool's use and will allow someone with little formal training to reproduce or use it?
- Does the tool require the extrapolation of minute measurements and skill?
- Is manual dexterity necessary to use the tool?
- Are skills required to correlate feeling and probing of internal components and mechanical and tactile feedback from the lock?
- Can anyone accomplish the opening procedure?
- Are covert entry experts required to use specialized tools?
- Is the ability to mentally image what is happening inside a lock necessary to evaluate mechanical feedback from a bypass tool?
- Are multiple security layers involved that must be neutralized and bypassed?
- Is there any outward indication that the lock's design has been modified or updated to frustrate the use of commercial tools?

Reliability of the Exploit

The *R* in the 3T2R equation represents *reliability*. Although many locks can be opened with various bypass tools and attack techniques, the issue is always attack reliability. A lock with a design deficiency or defect can often be compromised through mechanical manipulation, brute force, or the application of energy such as bumping, vibration, magnetic fields, or other attacks. Some locks, for example, can be bumped open once after 50 or more strikes. Does this constitute reliability and potential liability? The ability to *randomly* open a lock indicates that certain aspects of its mechanical or electronic design can be exploited to compromise its security. Still, it does not mean the attack can be judged as reliable in the ability to open the lock *consistently*. I've encountered hundreds of locks, including some of the best high-security mechanisms, that could be opened without any specificity or pattern to replicate the attack. To be considered reliable, the opening of a lock must occur consistently and predictably. Only then is the attack useful and practical in the context of a covert or forced entry.

Mechanical locks rely on the interaction of moving components. Anything that moves must yield information about its parts, location, and interactive tolerances and clues about its exploit or compromise. Given the right convergence of factors, most locks can be opened unpredictably. The problem for lock designers is that many variables must align to make the lock's components susceptible to a certain form of attack. This is precisely the problem in complete and competent vulnerability testing that produces valid and usable information about the security of the product. As stated, a full consideration of the variables in a design measured against different and often-imaginative forms of attack equates to valid testing for reliable exploits.

Repeatability of the Exploit

The last part of the equation is *repeatability*. If a lock's exploits are not repeatable, they are far less relevant regarding security and exposure to legal liability for defective products.

To assess a lock's overall security against potential exploits that have been demonstrated to be possible, these attacks must be repeatable. The repeatability of a lock's opening method is essential to assess its security. The fact that a lock can be opened one or more times in a way that the manufacturer did not anticipate does not mean it's defective, deficient in design, or even insecure. The relevant question is one of repeatability versus time. If I discover an exploit or weakness in a design that allows me to open a lock once within a few seconds or even a few minutes, that may constitute a security threat. However, if the method of attack or exploit is difficult to cause to occur and is unpredictable, it can be said not to be repeatable. The criteria of reliability and repeatability must be considered together. Such an assessment is important because it relates to liability, mandatory recalls, notification of customers of risk, and routine upgrades and enhancements to current designs.

Overall Security Assessment and the 3T2R Rule and Numerical Scoring

The 3T2R rule summarizes the criteria for locks to be rated for security against an attack. This rule encompasses the critical elements for standards, which apply to different types of testing that are supposed to assure a user of a certain level of protection against defined methods of attack. It should be clear that the five components of the 3T2R rule must be considered both individually *and* as they relate to each other. Lock manufacturers aren't particularly impressed if someone says they can open their highest-security locks through an innovative or novel attack. In my experience, clients routinely receive these reports from white-hat hackers (i.e., legitimate security researchers), locksmiths, locksport groups, and even criminals.

If the attack was never considered or anticipated during the product's design and testing before its release, it gets more attention. In my investigation of many such client claims, especially where demonstrations are sent via video without the author's identification, the recipient must consider many variables. Such communications are often coupled with subtle publicity threats if payment is not made for the information.

A manufacturer utilizes the 3T2R rule, at least initially, to determine whether the security threat is indeed real and how to deal with it effectively, ethically, and legally. Such decisions should not be made in haste or during a crisis but should be well thought through and planned, with policies and procedures in place. Chapter 9 provides a road map to assessing claims of defective products and security vulnerabilities.

I recommend an arbitrary scale of 1 to 5, where 1 is the lowest and 5 is the highest level of security for each criterion. A lock with a low score can indicate serious security issues and potential liability for legal damages. Conversely, a high score for each or most of the components in the formula can indicate a secure lock and no liability for its defeat. An analysis of the scoring must also be considered in the context of the environment where the lock will be installed and the security requirement.

A lock that is simple to open and requires little or no training or special tools is at the low end of the scale if the process to defeat its security is reliable and repeatable. Conversely, a lock that takes a lot of time, the use of expensive or special tools, and significant skills or training can be said to be secure. This is especially true if the exploit is not easily repeatable because it is unreliable.

Security Ratings for Simple or Complex Attacks: Case Examples

The following cases are good examples of locks and their 3T2R ratings. For some locks, low scores indicate simplicity in an attack; others have higher scores that identify them as secure:

- *Lock bumping of conventional pin tumbler locks*: Bumping of conventional pin tumbler locks yields a low-security score for all five parameters because relatively little skill is required, the tool consists of the proper key cut to the lowest bitting values for each chamber, and the time to open a lock can be a few seconds. If key blanks are readily available and easy to cut, not much more is needed to open this class of locks.

  Although there are variables, many locks can be easily opened, so bumping provides an example of a simple attack. Many conventional pin tumbler mechanisms are not secure against this method. Therefore, they would receive a very low 3T2R score, depending on the availability of keys that can be modified to all deep cuts, the lock's condition, and other factors.

- *Bumping Medeco and other high-security pin tumbler locks*: The concept of bumping is the same here, but the difficulty of bumping many high-security locks differs greatly from the previous example. Medeco makes some of the best high-security pin tumbler and sidebar locks in the United States and throughout many parts of the world. A key with the correct sidebar code must be obtained or simulated to successfully open this lock The key must be properly cut to the correct depths to create a bump key, and then the appropriate force and torque must be applied with the right timing to split the pins and not disturb the sidebar position. I have demonstrated how some of these locks can be opened in less than 30 seconds, but a lot of training and tools are necessary. If the proper technique is applied, the locks will open.

  My team has also succeeded in opening other high-security cylinders with similar results. They also require properly modified blanks to create bump keys, training, and time. The attack's reliability depends on the operator's expertise, so the 3T2R security rating would be relatively high.

- *Picking Medeco high-security locks*: Many conventional pin tumbler wafer, and lever locks can be relatively easy to pick, yielding a low 3T2R score. This depends on many factors, including security pins and other enhancements. Medeco locks are different and require time, tools, and training to open successfully. These locks were considered virtually unpickable for 40 years and had the highest security score. In 2008, my colleague and I published a detailed account of how the locks could be opened, sometimes in seconds. Notwithstanding our analysis, the locks would still have a very high security score because the technique to open them by picking requires special *code-setting keys* to set the sidebar combination, which meant unique tools are involved. Training is essential to determine the proper code format to align the pin tumblers to the correct rotation angles. The slider in the m3 version has to be aligned separately, so it is a complex attack that takes a significant amount of time in most cases and a high level of training for picking and setting pins. Depending on the sidebar code, the exploit's reliability can vary because multiple sidebar codes must be simulated. These locks would carry a high 3T2R rating.

- *Opening Kwikset programmable locks*: Kwikset makes one of the most popular consumer locks in the United States, Canada, and South America. It is based on six sliders that interface with pin tumblers that contact the key's bitting. The system is programmable, so the relationship between the pins and the sliders can be instantly altered to change the combination. Earlier lock versions demonstrated that the sliders could be physically altered by applying torque and inserting part of a blank key into the keyway. The attack could then be carried out with a screwdriver and Vise-Grips and was simple, but then the design was radically changed to prevent this technique. Before the lock was upgraded, it was graded as extremely simple to compromise and essentially failed the 3T2R test.

- *Opening Kryptonite bicycle locks*: Kryptonite bike locks used to be the most popular security devices for securing bicycles in the United States. They employed an axial pin tumbler lock with seven pins. As previously noted, the design engineers failed to connect the dots in considering security against bike theft: they did not consider many issues directly impacting the ability to open these locks in seconds with a plastic ballpoint pen. These locks failed the 3T2R test and cost the manufacturer millions of dollars because no one analyzed how easy it would be to open one of the locks with simple tools, no training, and a few seconds.

- *Opening iLOQ electromechanical cylinders*: iLOQ, which is analyzed in Part VI, produces a sophisticated electromechanical locking system that requires no batteries. The internal mechanism can be altered externally by removing some material from the reset lever, which is designed to interact with the key as it's withdrawn. If this critical part is ground down with a Dremel tool, the lock can be set to open without the correct credential. This attack type is a multistep approach and thus would be classified as moderate security because tools and training are required to execute it. Another similar attack on this lock involves modifying the tip of the key, which accomplishes the same result.

The next chapter examines the nexus between security and liability, because they are inextricably linked. All security is about liability, and failure to understand this maxim by design engineers, management, and vulnerability assessment teams can result in significant risk to lock manufacturers. I discuss legally actionable issues and conduct to avoid.

Next up, Part II presents important legal and regulatory considerations, as well as preplanning for notifications of alleged design defects in products that have already been released into the market. Every aspect of the lock industry is complex, from design, manufacturing, marketing, and service to support. There can be legal consequences for errors at every stage of the process. Complex warranty issues, trademark and patent protections, and meeting design standards are critical to a product's success, and they protect manufacturers, distributors, and dealers from liability for product defects and misrepresentations about security. Most important, consumers have many legal rights tied to virtually anything they purchase and rely on. This is even more important in security products. Although all lock manufacturers have legal counsel that protects intellectual property, much of that information may not reach design engineers and customer support staff. These issues are discussed in greater detail in Part II.

Legal and Regulatory Issues in Locks, Safes, and Security Systems

Part II examines legal and regulatory issues inextricably linked to the design, manufacture, and testing of mechanical, electronic, and electromechanical locks. These topics involve intellectual property protection, patents, and compliance with industry standards, which are important because they can affect every lock manufacturer regarding their liability and the security of their products. Unfortunately, the engineering curriculum at most universities rarely includes these topics, so graduates do not understand the nexus between the law, security, liability, and design defects.

This Part also defines a protocol for action when a manufacturer is notified of a design issue that can cause the compromise of a lock or security system. When such reports are received, management's decisions about what actions to take are critical and must be considered well before an event even occurs.

Finally, legal and security issues can flow from the design, defeat, and circumvention of key systems. Any facility with numerous locks installed can be subject to compromise by an attack on a keying system design. Risk managers often are not aware of vulnerabilities in the design of certain keying systems.

Some readers may feel that the chapters in Part II do not apply to them because the topics are outside the scope of their responsibilities or job description. The issues raised in these chapters, however, are relevant to anyone responsible for designing, analyzing, testing, supporting, or marketing locks and security systems. Locks and their manufacturing are complex and based on technical, legal, and security issues. Deficiencies in their designs can have many significant ramifications that can be expensive, affect compliance with standards, and trigger recalls. The chapters in this Part are intended to provide a basic understanding of what can happen when things go wrong and are pertinent to anyone involved in any part of the process.

CHAPTER 5

Security Is All About Liability

After directing a school of engineering's security engineering laboratory at a major university for many years, I can attest firsthand that many schools' curriculums do not teach, or even contemplate, the subject of liability as it applies to project development. Mechanical and electrical engineers often have no understanding of the issues involved. This lack of understanding can cost them significant damages if they fail to consider the potential security vulnerabilities of their designs from the very inception to the finished product.

Avoiding Legal Issues

After involvement in many cases of product analysis for defective and security-deficient designs, I have compiled a summary of actions and underlying legal theories that can give rise to liability by companies, their employees, and their representatives. Product liability law, discussed in Chapter 6, has developed over many centuries to define activities that can be legally actionable. Identifying the more recognizable forms of conduct will hopefully alert those involved in product design, testing, and the vetting process about what they must do to minimize or alleviate potential legal issues and exposure. (For more information, see the discussion in Chapter 9 regarding the different actions that may be taken in response to a notification of a security vulnerability in a released product.)

Design Defects and Other Actions as the Basis of Product Liability

A design defect in a manufactured product is usually the basis of product liability law. The question of what constitutes a defect can sometimes be difficult to determine, especially for lock manufacturers, due to the complexities of some of their products. A defect can originate from a mistake in the production process. There could be a deviation from the manufacturer's specifications. Even more troublesome, the specifications could fail to assess potential security vulnerabilities. A defect calls into question the competence of the engineers who conceived, designed, and developed a product, and it can challenge the integrity of the entire process. If a successful lawsuit is filed, a judicial ruling regarding a defective product is a statement that the manufacturer's product line is defective.

Virtually all courts assess claims that a product is defective based on one of two standards or a combination thereof. Manufacturers must be able to answer these questions: Does the design meet the safety expectations of users? What is the risk-benefit analysis if the safety or security vulnerability exceeds the resulting costs to minimize or eliminate it?

Lock manufacturers must be concerned about and focus on three primary forms of defect in creating, producing, and marketing their products:

- Manufacturing
- Design
- Warning

Any failure in these critical areas can be costly regarding product changes and modifications, recalls, and liability.

Design Defect Liability

This issue has two components: liability for a design defect and liability for knowingly selling a product with a defect. The legal question is whether a seller, with full knowledge that its products have a security vulnerability, would be negligent in selling such a product. The definition of a defective product in the context of a lock can be tricky, especially if it is a high-security mechanism. As discussed throughout this text and more particularly in the previous chapter on the 3T2R rule, the question is always whether a lock design is defective because it can be bypassed and whether that vulnerability was foreseeable by the manufacturer.

A manufacturer may have constructive knowledge of the foreseeability of a security vulnerability in a product. The relevant questions to ask include the following:

- Did the manufacturer act unreasonably in developing, producing, or marketing a defective product?

- With the manufacturer's expertise, should it have been able to determine there was, or could have been, an exploit based on its design?

- The courts have adopted the Reasonable Man test for such cases. Would a reasonable man, with full knowledge of all the properties and dangers, continue to market the product?

- Did the product's utility or, in the case of a lock, design and security enhancements outweigh the potential to be bypassed and create a security threat?

How to Define Defectiveness

Certain assumptions can be made to define a defective product:

- Did the manufacturer know of the product's defects or dangerous conditions?

- Was the manufacturer negligent in placing the product on the market or supplying it to another party?

- Should the manufacturer have known that a specific product's design created, or was likely to create, a security vulnerability that, if disclosed, the consumer would not accept?

- When advised of the product's defect, what did the manufacturer do?

- Would the manufacturer or seller be negligent if they sold the product, knowing the risks involved?

- Could the manufacturer be strictly liable if it continued to market a product in the same condition in which it was sold to a customer with knowledge of potentially dangerous consequences?

A manufacturer can be liable for selling a defective product if the result harms the buyer or a third party. The following actions can arise in the product's conception, design, development, prototyping, production, sale, and marketing.

Fraud and Misrepresentation

A misrepresentation of a material fact in statements or advertising by a manufacturer or its agents or representatives can provide grounds for liability. The classic tort was *deceit* or *fraud*. It required a showing of knowledge by a defendant that he or she knew the matter being represented was false and that the representation was intended to mislead. Under common law, the elements included a representation, its falsity, its materiality, the speaker's knowledge of its falsity, the hearer's ignorance of the truth, an intent that the recipient will act on and in reliance of the misrepresentation, the justifiability of reliance on the misrepresentation, and resulting harm due to that reliance.

The action of *fraudulent misrepresentation* can be traced to Old English law in the *Writ of Deceit,* which dates back to 1201, and Roman law and the concept of *dolus*. The relevant questions in any fraud case are whether the speaker knew the matter represented to be false, whether it was intended to mislead another, and if the plaintiff had a right to rely on the false representations. The representation must be of an existing fact. To support a claim of fraudulent misrepresentation, the plaintiff (or someone acting on the plaintiff's behalf) must learn about and act in reliance of the misrepresentation.

How does this rule apply to lock manufacturers? Suppose they, their dealers, distribution centers, or locksmiths make false statements about the security of a lock or piece of hardware, and someone is harmed because of those representations or statements. In that case, any party that misrepresents the product and its capabilities might be liable for damages. Lock bumping is a perfect example. Many high-security lock manufacturers have claimed their locks were "bump proof." In many cases, they were not. Consumers believed the lock's dealers, representatives, and lockmakers, and they purchased expensive locks for protection in reliance of such statements. Burglaries resulted due to the ease of opening many locks with bumping attacks. Many locksmiths did not believe bumping was a threat; they said this to their customers, partly because manufacturers made such statements and allowed their dealers to do the same.

False Representations

Statements and assertions about a product can be expressed through the seller's affirmative communications and actions, or the nature of the transaction may imply them. If these statements and assertions are false and cause harm, they can be legally actionable. The rule is, don't make statements unless serious and competent testing has been performed to validate your claims or denial of facts, especially about the security or insecurity of a lock or other piece of hardware.

Failure to Warn of a Dangerous Condition

Many readers have likely heard about the following example of the failure to warn of a dangerous condition. A customer of McDonald's, Mrs. Liebeck (the plaintiff), bought a cup of coffee, apparently at the drive-up window. She did not know, nor was she warned, that the temperature of the liquid was between 180 and 190 degrees Fahrenheit. She placed the coffee cup between her legs to remove the plastic lid and spilled the hot coffee, causing third-degree burns to her body. The company settled the lawsuit for under a million dollars. McDonald's should have warned its customers of the dangers of the high temperature of the coffee they served and the potential for injury.

Failure to Foresee Product Use and Subsequent Liability

A manufacturer must foresee and design for the reasonable use of its products. Liability only extends to such *foreseeability*. This is an elastic term, and some courts have held that manufacturers should be able to foresee certain product uses that may not be immediately apparent. Liability usually extends only to foreseeable plaintiffs and not to those injured by a product considered outside of the orbit of risk. The question then arises about a lock manufacturer that produces a defective product that ultimately harms a third party due to its design. Should the manufacturer foresee abuses of its products that could create a security vulnerability? That situation is precisely why a competent product vetting team is required: expertise in design analysis is essential to determine the foreseeability of risks that are not immediately apparent. Lock manufacturers hold themselves as experts, so they should be able to foresee less obvious uses and attempts to circumvent designs that might not be obvious to an average consumer.

A perfect example is the alleged compromise of a lock in an apartment complex. The lock's design was known to be deficient, if not defective, and many locksmiths and criminals knew about the vulnerability. I lectured on this vulnerability and demonstrated how the locks could be opened in seconds by applying torque to the plug after inserting a piece of broken key that raised the wafers to a neutral position. A security guard watched the videos of my lecture and figured out how to open the lock that was installed on one of the apartments he was tasked to protect. In 2015, he opened the apartment's locks and raped and killed the young female tenant.

The lock manufacturer, building owners, and security firms were all sued. The question was one of liability for the acts of a third-party actor (i.e., the security guard). Did the killer's conduct intervene on a set of risks created by the lock company's sale of an easily opened and arguably defective product? Did such conduct distance the seller or manufacturer from the plaintiff's harm? Was the lock company's defect so legally remote that the defect was not the proximate cause of the plaintiff's harm? As stated, the question is whether the third-party conduct is so significant, compared to the product's defect, that it lessens the role and significance of the defect.

Post-Sale Failure to Warn

Perhaps a lock manufacturer has sold a product and then determines there's a defect that might create a security vulnerability. When should the manufacturer warn customers, and when does it incur liability if it fails to do so? The test is whether a reasonable person in the seller's position would provide a warning. There likely would be liability if the seller knew, or reasonably should have known, that the product posed a substantial risk of harm to persons or property. The critical question is to whom the warning should be provided, assuming that the manufacturer knows who the average consumer is and that they are likely to be unaware of the risk.

The other critical question is whether the risk of harm is sufficiently great to justify the burden of issuing a warning. As discussed in Chapter 9, many factors enter into the issuance of a warning and to whom. If the defect is serious, that decision must be made with a full understanding of the problem and the potential result.

Post-Sale Duty to Remedy a Defect or Recall

Is a lock manufacturer under a duty to remedy a defect or recall a product already in the marketplace? This can be a complicated decision based on many considerations, as discussed in Chapter 9. Suppose the public is aware of the issue. That can complicate the decision, especially if there is a large market penetration, or it can be the basis of a potential class-action lawsuit. If the company has fixed the problem, it might constitute an admission that there was a problem; and if there is existing litigation, it might be more difficult to defend.

Many issues can flow from a defective security product sold to consumers. New litigation may be spawned. Advantages might be created for competitors. Sales can drop and regulatory agencies can become involved, depending on the product rating, triggering a Consumer Product Safety Commission (CPSC) recall. Such a recall resulted from defects in gun safes that could be jiggled open by a child. A failure to remedy a problem can also result in an award of punitive damages. See *Riggins v. Stack-On Products Co.*, U.S. District Court, Northern District of Illinois, Case 12-cv-5886, in which I was co-counsel in a federal class action lawsuit against a large gun safe manufacturer.

A manufacturer can get into trouble for the following actions in connection with a failure to remedy a defective product:

- Failure to issue a post-sale warning
- Refusal to repair a defective design
- Failure to accept engineering staff recommendations on how to remedy a serious defect, especially if it can be shown that it can be dealt with simply or inexpensively
- Failure to study how to minimize or eliminate a recurring design issue that was known or believed to have been injuring customers or that placed them at risk
- Failure to stop selling a product that was causing injuries to customers

Failure to Disclose or Warn of a Known Defect

Manufacturers must warn consumers of hidden product dangers and provide information on how products can be safely used. A product that doesn't carry such information can be deemed defective. Injuries from warning defects can subject a manufacturer to liability if harm results. This legal doctrine stems back to Roman sales law, where a seller aware of hidden defects was guilty of fraud for a failure to disclose any hidden flaws to the buyer.

In American law, it wasn't until the 1900s that a duty to warn developed, which contained two segments: *warning* and *instruction*. My rule about warnings, in general, is predicated on the view that when a consumer is informed about product dangers or security vulnerabilities and methods of safe use, they will use that information for self-protection. The informed consumer may choose not to buy or use a product, which is a marketing problem for the manufacturer. The user or consumer should be entitled to choose whether the product's utility or benefits justify exposing them to the risks of harm.

A plaintiff must prove that the product's warning was inadequate, or a defective warning claim will likely fail. The question is one of adequacy to warn. The rule normally holds that the warning:

- Must provide complete disclosure of the existence and extent of the risk involved.

- Must be designed so it can reasonably be expected to attract the consumer's attention.

- Must be understandable and provide a fair indication of the specific risks involved with, or inherent in, the product.

- Must be worded strongly enough to convey the magnitude of the risk.

This is especially important for lock manufacturers when a design issue allows a lock to be opened rapidly or easily. A 3T2R rule analysis should guide you in such situations. If the lockmaker underrates the risk, this can be very costly if losses occur to customers because the vulnerability was not properly disclosed. Conversely, suppose experts determine that the vulnerability can be dealt with in normal product upgrades and isn't serious. In that case, customers should know exactly the risks involved, especially in highly secure venues.

Failure to Design Away Known Defects or Dangers

A manufacturer can be liable based on a failure to adopt design solutions or fixes for a substantial security vulnerability, apparent by a simple and economical or easy fix. If a manufacturer refuses to implement a design change or improvement, it's often strong evidence of their indifference to customer security. The critical issue is simplicity and expense. For lock manufacturers, it appears to be a simple question: are they liable for refusing to implement security fixes that they know would make their locks more secure? It's also important for the manufacturer to have the technical and security competence to understand security and design problems. If a manufacturer produces its products with a flagrant disregard for consumer safety, it may be held accountable. In one case, a high-voltage transformer in a color television set was prone to catch fire. It would have cost one dollar to fix, but the company refused. Liability followed.

Misconduct in Marketing

If a manufacturer engages in misconduct in its marketing, this might constitute liability if it disregards the consumer rights of reasonable safety and security. A consideration of the following issues should serve as guidelines:

- The magnitude of the product danger and how it could be reduced
- The practice and economic feasibility of reducing the dangers to acceptable levels
- A manufacturer's awareness of the hazards
- Why the manufacturer failed to act, and for how long
- How long it took the manufacturer to discover or reduce the problem
- How much danger was created by the manufacturer's refusal to act

Tortious Misrepresentation about a Product

If a manufacturer's representative or its agents communicate false or misleading information to another about a competitive product, it can give rise to legal action and damages. The issue is the *communication* of materially false information about a product to a person who was harmed by the reliance on the truth of the communications. In this instance, claims do not require an actual defect in the product but only false words.

If a locksmith who's a dealer for a manufacturer makes false statements about the security of a lock or piece of hardware, for example, and those statements convince a customer to purchase a different lock or system, liability can be attached. Manufacturers should include strict contractual language in any dealer agreement that notifies any distributor, dealer, locksmith, agents, or employees of the legal necessity not to overstate information about the inability to compromise the security of the locks they sell or misstate security vulnerabilities about other competing products without solid confirmation about those vulnerabilities.

Failure to Adhere to Industry Standards, Cutting Corners, or Falsifying Test Results

One of the traditional definitions of negligence is a failure to exercise ordinary care. It is assumed that most manufacturers will act prudently and balance the costs and benefits to others and themselves. Negligence can be found in people failing to conform to customer levels of care. The test, which equates to industry standards, is whether a manufacturer acted unreasonably in developing, producing, or marketing a defective product. However, such a failure to adhere to industry standards isn't definitive evidence of the reasonableness of conduct. Conformance with, or violation of, applicable customary standards is evident but is rarely conclusive as to the exercise of due care.

The importance of customs or standards relates to the foreseeability of risk. A plaintiff will seek to introduce specific evidence regarding foreseeability and the magnitude of risk. This showing will be coupled with evidence of whether the risk was hidden and the feasibility and cost-effectiveness of ways to avoid it. If you're a manufacturer, you will try to demonstrate the opposite: that the risk was open, obvious, impracticable, and costly to eliminate.

The standards organizations discussed in Chapter 7, including the Underwriters Laboratory (UL) and American National Standards Institute (ANSI)/Builders Hardware Manufacturers Association (BHMA), work with manufacturers to ensure that they represent an industry consensus on a balance between security, safety, and practicality.

Negligence in Design or Manufacture, or Failure to Provide Adequate Warnings or Instructions

A manufacturer is liable for a broad range of negligent actions in connection with manufacturing or marketing a product if they fail to disclose or warn of known security vulnerabilities and warnings regarding the use of their product that would cause harm to the buyer.

Failure to Implement a Risk-Utility Test in Product Design

If a product has a security vulnerability or defect that can cause harm, a manufacturer must demonstrate that it has considered the issue and examined alternative designs that would have reduced or eliminated the risk. This means an evaluation was conducted, which determined that the ultimate product configuration was the best in terms of security and the reduction of risk.

Failure to Consider Alternative Designs

A manufacturer should consider alternative designs in a security product to ensure that any discovered vulnerabilities have been thoroughly evaluated and the best remedy for such a defect has been implemented. Companies can be found liable for a failure to explore other designs that would have mitigated the threat that placed consumers at risk.

Malfunctions and Liability

A product that's defective *and* malfunctions can lead to legal liability. A manufacturer must be vigilant and carefully document all reports of malfunctions to determine their cause, remedy the problem, and avoid legal issues. The legal doctrine of malfunction holds that proof of a defect can be inferred and established by circumstantial evidence showing that a product failure occurred in normal use, which suggested a defect.

It is unnecessary to show that a specific defect caused the failure if the evidence demonstrates an inference that there likely was a defect. In the context of lock designs, an inference can be drawn that the product is defective if there are multiple reports of security vulnerabilities or failures. A manufacturer must keep up with trade journals, locksmith reports, bypass-tool manufacturers' catalogs, and product offerings to be certain that any information disseminated about the bypass of their security hardware is acted on before it can ultimately form the basis for costly litigation.

A manufacturer must meet the three following criteria to prove potential liability if malfunctions are reported:

- The product malfunctioned or failed.
- The malfunction occurred during proper use.
- The product had not been altered, abused, or misused in a way that likely caused the failure.

Flagrant Disregard of Consumer Safety

A manufacturer can be liable in rare cases where it is guilty of the following for intentionally disregarding the rights of consumers:

- Flagrantly disregarding consumer safety
- Fraudulently marketing unsafe products
- Selling a product known to have a serious hidden hazard without disclosure to consumers

Failure to Exercise Due Care in Manufacturing

A manufacturer can be liable for negligence at *any* stage in producing a product, including design, manufacturing, and marketing. To establish liability, a plaintiff must prove the following five factors:

1. The seller owed a duty to the plaintiff.
2. The seller breached that duty.
3. This breach of duty was the cause of the plaintiff's injury.

4. That cause was the proximate cause of the injury.

5. Damages for the harm suffered are recoverable in negligence.

Manufacturers have a duty of reasonable care to protect foreseeable victims from foreseeable risks of harm. In American courts, the rule was discussed in *Winterbottom v. Wright, MacPherson v. Buick,* and other cases.

Failure of a Manufacturer to Exercise Reasonable Care in Product Concept and Formulation

A manufacturer must consider and meet the following guidelines in product development:

- Determine the product's foreseeable uses and abuses.
- Select the proper materials and components for use within a finished product.
- Consider the product's expected uses.
- Test the product's prototypes to duplicate the harshest environments and uses that can be expected

Defective Product or Improper Consumer Use

A defense to a defective product claim is that the injured party used the product improperly or that something else caused the harm. Was the product defectively produced or marked, or falsely described? Could the consumer's use have been foreseeable by the manufacturer? Many of my lock manufacturing clients claim that there's no liability if a product is improperly used and that such a premise extends to anyone who attempts to circumvent the security of their locks by any method, including bumping, picking, decoding, and other bypass techniques. This premise, however, is not correct.

Summary of Specific Actions that Can Trigger Liability and Legal Issues

The following is a summary of legal and marketing hazards that should be considered by engineering and marketing management teams to ensure that the proper procedures are in place to limit exposure to lawsuits and adverse media:

- Breach of or a failure to honor a warranty
- Designs that the manufacturer should have known were vulnerable to attack and compromise based on the manufacturer's experience, competitive product analysis, or industry reports
- Flaws or defects in a manufacturer's products

Engineering and marketing management teams must also ensure that the proper procedures are in place to mitigate liability by dealing with the following issues:

- To make sure the design engineers possess proper expertise in security products
- To adhere to laws and regulations involving data protection
- To analyze similar competitive products for security vulnerabilities that might translate to design deficiencies
- To be conversant with current techniques to circumvent classes of hardware or software in mechanical or electronic locks
- To conduct a competent VA of a product *before* and *after* its release
- To consider my 3T2R rule
- To contemplate simple attacks on hardware or a manufacturer's systems
- To define a policy about the disclosure (or nondisclosure) of discovered security vulnerabilities to shield the company from liability
- To define a specific policy about handling a recall and notification of critical customers when a defect is discovered that poses or can pose a serious security vulnerability
- To disclose significant vulnerabilities to customers about the various kinds of key systems and credentials

Failure to Discourage a Culture of Arrogance in Engineering and Design

In my experience, design teams often believe they know more about their products and how they will perform than anyone else, especially someone outside the company. They are often wrong, and the results can be costly regarding redesign, time delays, tooling costs, and marketing pressures. "Not invented here" is a dangerous and bad doctrine that too many lock manufacturers adhere to. Design teams must avoid the following actions:

- Failure to document alleged security vulnerabilities in products to defend against potential litigation
- Failure to document and test various bypass methods and tools that are designed to attack a manufacturer's hardware and software
- Failure to enforce patent rights and infringement of intellectual property for the protection of dealers and distributors, especially involving key control
- Failure to establish guidelines for the protection of computers and records from theft and hacking for a manufacturing facility, dealers, distributors, and locksmiths

- Failure to fully understand bypass methods as outlined in this text
- Failure to have in place a plan for dealing with reports of security vulnerabilities in products
- Failure to implement and comply with personally identifiable identification (PII) protection requirements
- Failure to employ and document alternative design methods to mitigate potential or known security vulnerabilities
- Failure to enact different methods of testing for vulnerabilities
- Failure to effectuate media- and information-handling guidelines
- Failure to investigate reports of vulnerabilities in locks, either as to their overall integrity or as to the defeat of one or more security layers or components
- Failure to make design changes in components that are vulnerable, to mitigate security risks
- Failure to present information to customers about the limits of key and credential control for specific products
- Failure to properly design keying systems in buildings to prevent the decoding of top-level master keys in locks in public areas
- Failure to protect critical information for keying systems
- Failure to defend key control procedures in high-security locks
- Failure to guard keys or credentials from unauthorized duplication or counterfeiting techniques that can jeopardize the security of customer facilities and place at risk competing locksmiths who represent the same manufacturer
- Failure to shield locksmiths with registered keyways from counterfeits sold by other locksmiths
- Failure to safeguard the company's intellectual property (IP) physically and legally against compromise and infringement
- Failure to pursue information about vulnerabilities in locks and safes produced by any manufacturer that are similar in nature to products that the manufacturer produces
- Failure to remedy known security issues
- Failure to research and consider social media and other public vulnerability disclosures of products of the manufacturer and competitors
- Failure to understand 3D-printing technology and how it applies to the security of specific products

- Failure to understand and be current on attack vectors that involve specific designs of the manufacturer
- Failure to warn about resetting default keys and codes
- Failure to advise customers of known or potential security defects or vulnerabilities in a timely manner, including:
  - Making and publishing statements about specific security protections in locks and safes without the proper testing to confirm such claims
  - Making claims about a product's security that employees or agents should have known were false or misleading
  - Knowingly making claims of product security that are false
  - Making inaccurate statements about the inability to duplicate, simulate, or replicate keys or credentials
  - Advertising the security of a product in a misrepresented way. One example is a major high-security lock manufacturer that claimed its locks were the "ultimate in security." Their locks, however, could be easily picked.

The next chapter explores the nexus between legal liability and insecurity engineering and the ramifications of improper or defective product design.

Legal Liability and Insecurity Engineering

My fundamental premise is that *all security is about liability*. If harm results from defective or deficient designs, someone must pay as recompense for injury or loss. This axiom is true *unless* the harm is caused by actions of a federal or state government agency. These entities normally can't be held liable under the common law doctrine of *sovereign immunity*: "The King can do no wrong." In certain circumstances, however, the government can waive its immunity and agree to accept liability.

Based on various theories of liability discussed in this chapter, manufacturers, suppliers, designers, wholesalers, and any person or entity that may cause harm to another can be liable for civil remedies and monetary damages. In certain instances, such liability can also extend to criminal sanctions. Different legal theories of liability are directly applicable and highly relevant to lock and safe manufacturers. They may also apply to Internet of Things (IoT) security devices and systems and virtually any product related to security or safety and protecting people, property, and information. Locksmiths, security consultants, architects, installers, maintenance technicians, marketing representatives, software engineers, and customer service agents can all be held responsible. Essentially, anyone who has any contact with a security-related system or its users can find themselves a defendant in an action relating to a design failure that impacts security and causes harm.

In today's litigious environment, especially in the United States, lawyers are actively looking to file lawsuits, especially class actions, against lock manufacturers whose designs were the proximate cause of someone suffering damages or injury or, even worse, death. Liability can also extend to manufacturers for false or misleading representations or statements in specifications, product brochures, advertising, warranties, and contracts. Companies can also be held responsible for the actions of their technical service representatives, sales personnel, or even dealers who make statements about the security of their products.

I investigated locks that could be easily and quickly opened by applying torque to the keyway with a screwdriver. Several phone calls were made to customer service (all of which were recorded) to document the lock manufacturer's employee claims. Many of them made false and misleading statements about the security of their locks. It did not matter whether the speakers knew what they said about the defective designs was false or whether they were making statements to protect their employer. The designs allowing the locks to be opened were defective, and the manufacturer could be held liable for such false representations.

In another case, my colleagues and I placed multiple calls to locksmiths and distribution centers that sold one of the most popular mechanical push-button locks in the United States. These locks were installed in thousands of government, commercial, and residential venues and could be opened quickly with a strong magnetic field. We developed evidence that dealers, sales representatives, locksmiths, and the manufacturer directly or impliedly misstated the vulnerability and, in many cases, denied that it even existed. The company ultimately settled a major class-action lawsuit for its design.

Development of Product Liability Law

The development of product liability law has its roots in Rome and later in England. It's highly relevant to every engineer and manufacturer who designs, produces, and sells locks, safes, and related hardware. The concepts and basic tenets of contract law, negligence, tort, and strict liability are explored and summarized in this chapter to facilitate an overall understanding of the basic legal doctrines and how to minimize the risk of litigation. Product liability is an extremely complex legal area, with different criteria for assessing who is liable for what. Although they depend on case precedent in different state and federal jurisdictions, the basic principles and rules are essentially the same.

It's important to understand what can go wrong and avoid the often-costly consequences of a failure to implement procedures and controls to avoid liability. Even more important is to initiate a vulnerability assessment (VA) program from the very inception of a project. This analysis and assessment are needed to document the due diligence review of potential design deficiencies and risks and show how they were anticipated and mitigated. A manufacturer must produce non-defective products. A breach of this duty can lead to legal liability.

Product liability law, from ancient Rome to medieval England and American law in the nineteenth and early twentieth centuries, was primarily about defective food and drink or cases involving physical flaws or defects. The question mainly revolved around whether the product had a flaw created by the manufacturer and whether it caused a plaintiff harm or injury. A manufacturer will likely contest and possibly litigate a case for a flawed physical product if they believe the following conditions exist:

- The product was not defective.
- Even if there was a defect, the injury was the result of something other than the defect.
- Even if the defect caused harm, someone or something other than the manufacturer created or caused the defect after the product left the factory.
- The claim for damages is unreasonable.

Criminal, Civil, and Criminal Law

Often, there is confusion about the relationship between criminal, civil, and tort law. *Criminal law* is designed to punish and deter conduct. The principal purpose of *civil law* is to deal with contractual rights, compensate injured persons for wrongfully inflicted harm, and provide a judicial remedy. *Tort law* provides for redress and liability for negligence and other forms of conduct by actors who produce or sell products that can cause harm, danger, injury, or product failure. Tort law is the basis for manufacturing defects in product liability claims, including unreasonable conduct.

Overview: Origins of Legal Liability for Product Designs

The concepts of moral and legal responsibility of makers, buyers, users, and third parties for harm caused by a product originated thousands of years ago. The customs and laws that have developed are complex and often vary for each jurisdiction. They can bring civil, criminal, and statutory case law and precedents into play. A possible liability assessment against a defendant for improper actions can involve multiple factors relating to causality, the reasonableness of design, compliance with standards, customs, and many often-complex defenses.

Tracing the development of product liability law from ancient Rome to the present offers a perspective on how society viewed and dealt with the role of merchants, manufacturers, and users of products and the attempt to define legal responsibilities for each. Their obligations and duties to each other regarding product defects, statements and representations about known and unknown defects, product quality, and fitness for intended purpose have developed and evolved over thousands of years. Legal liability, strict liability, warranty, negligence, privity of contract, and tort law have changed as technology developed and society became more industrialized and reliant on more complex technology and designs.

For manufacturers, it's imperative to understand what can constitute a defective product and the liability they can incur for deficiencies or failures in design, manufacturing, and marketing. Even in medieval times, the simple rule was that one is responsible for what they make and sell; there's always a potential for liability if things go wrong. As the law evolved, certain obligations and protections arose for those who purchased a product, used it, or were injured. The important point is that every engineer is responsible for properly designing a product, understanding that rarely is anything defect-free.

It's helpful to consider critical milestones in the law as it developed to insulate manufacturers and protect buyers and third parties from dangers that a product may present. Significant cases dealt with failures to hold accountable those who cause harm by creating and selling products. How we progressed from the ancient concepts of liability and "buyer beware" to the current state of the law is best understood by examining the cases that formed the basis of modern product liability law.

Ancient Roman Law and the Twelve Tables

The laws relating to product liability originated in 449 B.C. in the Twelve Tables, considered the foundation of Roman law. The *Twelve Tables*, a consolidation of earlier traditions into a more formalized compilation, enumerates the rights and duties of Roman citizens and was the basis of Roman law for a thousand years. The Tables itemized the definitions of private rights and procedures, including transactions between individuals and merchants.

The original civil law principle was *caveat emptor*: "Let the buyer beware." The seller wasn't liable for any defects in goods unless the parties agreed to such terms. Between 300 and 200 B.C., principles of seller responsibility for certain transactions began to emerge. Product liability for a defective product found little protection under the laws of torts. A *tort* is a wrongful act that involves the infringement of a right not under the contract that leads to civil liability. It's defined as a civil wrong that causes someone to suffer a loss or harm and a commensurate legal liability against the person who commits the act.

The Emergence of a Standard of Care and an Extra-High Standard

The concept of a *standard of care*, which means conduct that would be considered reasonable against those who produce goods offered to other parties, began to develop for sellers. The *extra-high standard* for sellers in Roman law may be the origin of the modern doctrine that states, "A product seller is bound to exercise care at the level of an expert in the field" and appears in U.S. product liability law in both negligence and strict liability. By the sixth century A.D., sellers were held responsible for certain losses from failing to exercise a higher standard of care. It was meticulous and severe: "Negligence due to the absence of the greatest care is a failure to observe such diligence as a good man of business or a very prudent man would exercise."

This concept is important to all manufacturers, especially those of locks and safes, for their representations of their products' security.

Manufacturers are held to the standard of knowledge of an expert in their field. A famous Roman jurist stated, "Want of skill is reckoned as negligence." Concomitantly, a person or manufacturer who held themselves out as an expert was deemed culpably negligent if they failed to use such skill. The victim's contributory negligence offset a finding of liability in negligence in Roman law. Express and false misstatements by one to another about a product were considered and known as *fraud*. This doctrine also broadly included a failure to disclose to the buyer latent defects that the seller knew a product to possess.

A seller was also responsible for the failure of a product to conform to express promises of quality. Thus began the developing law of *implied warranty of quality*, which can be thought of as an understood but not specifically stated representation of the quality of the product. It's similar to the modern concept of strict liability for selling a defective product. Around 367 B.C., the law evolved that states, "All sellers of all sorts of things are liable for defects."

In the early sixth century, there was a codification of Roman law developed until that point. It was called the Code of Justinian. It established the following basic implied warranty of quality that was applied to the sale of goods: all sellers of all sorts of things are liable for defects. Thus, this was the beginning of strict liability wherein the knowledge of a defect by the seller was *not* a shield for liability. At the same time, the knowledge of obvious defects discoverable by a buyer was their responsibility. Damages in Roman law were tied to the basis of liability. For example, establishing fraud on the seller's part, including failing to disclose a latent defect known to the seller, would entitle the buyer to recover fully.

Now, let's fast-forward to England in the thirteenth century. Saint Thomas Aquinas outlined the basis of obligations consistent with Roman law, shaping 700 years of Catholic doctrine. According to Aquinas, the seller was bound to disclose a product's secret flaws. It was a sin and fraud to sell a product containing a latent defect known to the seller and not to the buyer, and it meant the sale was void. If the seller was unaware of the defect, the sale was *not* a sin, but the seller was obligated to return any excess price attributable to the defect to the buyer.

In England, early common law developed the theory and doctrine of *caveat emptor:* buyers had the duty to protect themselves from obvious defects. This was extended against hidden defects and was the law for 200 years until 1810, when the courts shifted this rule to the opposite doctrine of *implied warranty of quality*. The seller impliedly warranted that its products did not contain any defects and were reasonably fit for the ordinary use of such goods.

The Sale of Goods Act in 1893 established an *implied warranty of fitness* for a particular purpose, which became a separate and independent implied warranty. It was distinct from the *implied warranty of merchantability*, which included the concept that the goods were fit for their ordinary purpose. The rule was that a seller should be liable, as a matter of law, rather than the buyer having to rely on intent and knowledge regarding product defects.

Caveat emptor is a Latin term meaning "Let the buyer beware." It was a legal concept that equated to "sold as is" and made the buyer responsible for the risk assumption of product failure or defects. The doctrine continued to be judicially accepted into the twentieth century. The courts initially ruled that the sale of products for an acceptable price communicated an implied warranty that what was sold was free from defects, whether known or unknown, by the seller. This was essentially an implied quality warranty and was put into the U.S. Sales Act of 1906, which was patterned after the English Sales of Goods Act.

In 1804, the chancellor of New York decided that caveat emptor applied to latent defects. Later in the century, the Supreme Court issued an opinion summarizing the American view of the doctrine in *Barnard v. Kellogg* (77 U.S. 383, 1870). This case related to the sale of commodities and personal property in the absence of an express warranty, assuming the buyer had an opportunity to inspect the commodity. The ruling was that the seller was not guilty of fraud, nor was the manufacturer or grower of the article he sold.

Privity of Contract: The Case of Winterbottom v. Wright

Another major development in English product liability law was in the nineteenth century when the concept of *privity of contract* was established in connection with negligence claims. It could shield remote sellers from liability for defects in the products they sold.

In 1842, the landmark case of *Winterbottom v. Wright* was tried and subsequently decided in 1846 by an English court. The controversy involved the legal concept of *privity of contract* and whether a mail coach driver (i.e., Winterbottom) had a cause of action for negligence against Wright for injuries he suffered when the coach collapsed and overturned while being driven by Winterbottom. Wright had a contract with the postmaster general to keep the coach safe. Winterbottom had no contractual relationship with Wright; thus, he had no *privity of contract*, which meant he had no direct legal relationship with the defendant. Winterbottom claimed in his lawsuit that Wright "negligently conducted himself and so utterly disregarded his aforesaid contract and so wholly and negligently failed to perform his duty on his behalf." The ruling was for the defendant.

Lord Abinger held that to allow such claims would open "arbitrary an infamy of actions unless we confine the operation of such contracts as this to the parties who entered into them the most absurd and outrageous consequences, to which I can see no limit would ensue." This decision was important because a party injured by a defective product had no legal cause of action against those parties to the contract. Even though Wright did not maintain the coach, Winterbottom had no privity with Wright and, thus, no obligation to Winterbottom.

In 1932, England finally abolished the defense of privity of contract in negligence claims in *Donoghue v. Stevenson*. In that case, a plaintiff was sickened by the decomposed remains of a snail in a bottle of ginger beer purchased by a friend. The House of Lords abandoned the legal bar against negligence actions through the privity of contract. This decision would subsequently apply principles of circumstantial evidence to assist in proving product liability cases. The rule would ultimately be overturned in the United States as well.

Privity of Contract and Avoidance of Liability by Manufacturers: Implied Warranty Claims

Manufacturers soon realized they could sell their businesses to third parties and avoid their liability for product defects. Consumers ended up with little recourse because they had to deal with the seller or retailer and had no *privity of contract* with the manufacturer, which meant producers had no liability under a theory of implied warranties of merchantability. Initially, the courts ruled that damages could not be recovered without a direct relationship between buyer and seller. Sales contracts stated that a manufacturer was only liable for a product that failed under the theory of implied warranty of merchantability that the goods were reasonably fit for their intended purpose and for which they were purchased. Auto manufacturers dodged responsibility other than for the replacement of parts that they found to be defective.

Privity was first used as a defense of implied warranty cases by manufacturers in defective food cases. Ultimately, the defense was argued to protect remote sellers in implied warranty cases from human food to animal food and products for intimate bodily use. In the 1950s, the courts allowed nonprivity recovery to durable goods litigation.

In 1960, the landmark case of *Hemmingsen v. Bloomfield Motors, Inc.* (161 A.2s 69) was decided in an implied warranty lawsuit that involved a defective car design. This case was important because it signaled the end of the privity defense in product liability claims under an implied warranty of merchantability. The car manufacturer had denied liability for injuries suffered by the driver in an accident because it relied on the theory of privity of contract between buyer and seller. Chrysler did not sell the car to the Henningsens, so the car manufacturer claimed it wasn't liable.

In 1955 the plaintiff, Mr. Henningsen, purchased a new Plymouth from the dealership Bloomfield Motors. Subsequently, the car was being driven by Mrs. Henningsen when it veered off the road and smashed into a brick wall. The driver reported that the steering wheel suddenly spun in her hands after she heard a loud noise from under the hood. The car had been driven less than 500 miles. Both Mr. and Mrs. Henningsen sued the dealership and Chrysler. The car manufacturer claimed it was not liable other than for the replacement of defective parts because it had no contractual relationship with the buyer. The defendants initially paid for medical bills. Chrysler then claimed the buyer was told that the warranty was limited to replacing parts. The lower courts ruled that the passenger could not sue because he had no privity of contract with the car manufacturer or Bloomfield Motors.

This case set the stage for *strict liability* in such actions. The theory of recovery claimed there was an implied *warranty of merchantability* of the car. The court permitted a nonpurchaser to sue the manufacturer despite two fundamental principles of liability in warranty law: disclaimer by the defendant in the contract and privity.

The justice who wrote the opinion for the New Jersey Supreme Court stated, "We see no rational doctrinal basis for differentiating between a fly and a bottle of beverage and a defective automobile. The unwholesome beverage may bring illness to one person, the defective car with its great potentiality for harm to the driver, occupants, and others demand even less adherence to the narrow barrier of privity."

This case marked the virtual disintegration of the privity defense. The courts then established a privity exception to not only implied but also express warranties. The result was that consumers could recover for false advertising statements in warranties. The courts reasoned that the warranties went indirectly to the purchaser despite an absence of privity of contract.

Defective Products: What Are They, and Why Are They Important?

Defectiveness in a product is at the core of modern product liability law everywhere. A claim must elicit proof that an unreasonable hazard in the product caused the injury; something was wrong with the design. The reality is that any product can be dangerous in some form for certain uses. The fundamental principle of modern product liability law is that a manufacturer is liable for the harm caused by defects in the products they sell. The legal challenge is often determining how a defect occurs and its precise definition.

This can be especially true in the world of locks and safes, as noted in the discussion about the 3T2R Rule. These "unreasonable hazards" are identified as security vulnerabilities and are often a result of the laws of physics and chemistry. In some products, there's simply no way to avoid such threats. Locks are a unique category; if a manufacturer does not foresee and deal with such issues, the manufacturer can be held liable. In the normal course of product use, the buyer rather than the supplier is responsible for avoiding injury. For lock manufacturers, the security of their devices can vary and may not create an expected result. Part of the challenge for lock manufacturers is to foresee and imagine how users may misuse a product to their detriment.

To be judged defective, an excessive or unwarranted danger must be created before the risk of loss, damage, or injury is passed to the seller. Product defects can take many different forms, but there are three primary recognized classifications:

- *Manufacturing flaws*: Physical irregularities during the process of production.

- *Design flaws*: Inadequacies and vulnerabilities that are at the core of product engineering or conception and could be avoided by a different or altered design.

- *Insufficient warnings*: Such warnings include the dangers to the consumer in marketing statements and misrepresentation about the product; they can also form the basis of liability but don't directly relate to a defect.

For example, a manufacturer can get into trouble and be held accountable for producing a defective product due to different failures in the processing or use of raw materials. Evidence could be adduced against a manufacturer for negligence or improper procedures, so care should be exercised in the following areas:

- Raw materials or compounds that contain physical flaws

- Production where a product can become damaged or contaminated

- Mistakes in assembly

- Improper finishing that causes potential hazards

- Dangerous flaws in packaging or containers

Failures in any part of the process can result in serious consequences. The most important rule for a lock manufacturer is this: "You are responsible for what you make and sell." Each of these three defect classifications involves some form of breakdown that can affect the end user or third parties.

Manufacturing Defects

Manufacturing defects are generally unplanned, although I have been involved in cases where I discovered product defects in electronic devices. When I discussed the design with one of the largest radio manufacturers in the world, it responded that it was aware of the problem *before* running the assembly line. The manufacturer intentionally released a defective product because, in the company's view, it was less expensive to deal with any returns and litigation than to resolve the issue properly. Depending on the severity of a defect, this is a common response to minor issues and is more fully discussed in Chapter 9.

A *manufacturing defect* means the product differs from the intended design and can create a hazard, risk, or injury. Production mistakes, flaws, machining, tolerance, or calibration errors are usually unintended. Such defects may encompass a conceptual error in the design that did not anticipate one or more risks that could have been minimized or eliminated. Even if all possible care was exercised, a manufacturing defect can still expose the producer to liability. Such a defect can also mean a product may not perform as represented or that it varies from specifications. Sometimes a design defect can be elusive and difficult to identify and may not manifest itself reliably, highlighting the need for competent and robust vulnerability testing.

Design Defects

Design defects manifest in virtually every product; it's inevitable and built into the process. They're inherent in the creative process despite the best efforts by the team that creates the design's initial ideas and concepts. Design defects can cause unreasonable risks and vulnerabilities. The problem with design defects is that it's likely they will be cloned or replicated in every product.

Although identifying a manufacturing defect can be relatively simple, defining a defective design can often be difficult and complex, especially in the world of locks and safes. The assessment of a design defect may require the expertise of mechanical, chemical, and materials engineers, chemists, physicists, and other experts to determine whether a product is defective and whether it caused an alleged injury. Experts will want to know how the product was made, how it was supposed to operate, how it malfunctioned or otherwise created a vulnerability, and—perhaps most importantly—how it could have been made differently to avoid the threat or risk.

A manufacturing defect normally fails in a production process when the product or component deviates from the specifications of an intended design. An allegation that a product is defective in its design goes to the heart of the specifications and the failure of design engineers to consider and implement protective measures against known or potential security vulnerabilities. Stated more simply, a manufacturing defect is a mistake. A *design defect* is often a conceptual failure of what the product should accomplish and protect against. It's frequently an indictment of the competence and quality of an engineering group and a company's management in developing its standards. A design defect claim attacks the integrity of the entire production process; a judicial negligence determination can be deadly to a company. A manufacturer can be held liable for defective design under several theories of liability.

Warning and Marketing Defects

A *warning defect* can be described as the absence of enough information about a hazard or vulnerability to avoid it. The issue is a failure to properly tell people how to use a product safely with notice of risks. It's also about marketing and sales information that promises more than could be delivered. The rule is that a manufacturer must exercise reasonable care to instruct how to use a product safely and to warn of any hidden dangers.

Suppose a manufacturer creates a product with known or potential security vulnerabilities. In that case, there should be disclosures and warnings to the consumer or purchaser about their origin, how they can be exploited, and how to avoid them. The relevant questions to consider are whether the dangers or defects are excessive, whether the defect has been reasonably removed, and whether it caused an alleged injury. Unfortunately, many defects are hidden, so a manufacturer should provide information about their nature and how to minimize any impact. Not only must these warnings be adequate, but their content and the way they're communicated to users should be adequate as well. VA teams must decide whether such warnings should be placed directly on the product or in the provided literature or instruction manuals. In a product liability class-action suit involving gun safes in which I was co-counsel, the settlement required that the defendants place conspicuous warnings on the outside packaging and directly on the safes to warn about how children could easily open them.

There is generally no duty to warn of obvious product vulnerabilities or hazards that are well known because it's argued that there's no reason to tell a consumer what they already know. The duty to warn comes into play when discussing hidden or inherent defects. A product isn't defective for obvious risks. A manufacturer may be obligated to warn of a risk they can reasonably foresee in the state-of-the-art when they sell the product. There's also a duty to warn even in the case of the *abuse* of a product.

To prove negligence or a negligent failure to provide adequate warnings or instructions, five criteria must be established:

1. The seller owed a duty to the plaintiff.
2. The seller breached that duty.
3. The breach of duty was the cause, in fact, of the plaintiff's injury.
4. The cause was a proximate cause of the injury.
5. The harm to be recoverable lies in negligence.

Post-Sale Issues and Duty to Warn

It's generally the rule that a manufacturer isn't liable for normal product deterioration that may ultimately result in a hazard unless such an issue is foreseeable, creates a serious risk, and renders the product defective. This doesn't relieve a manufacturer from a *post-sale duty* to provide reasonable warnings when a significant problem is discovered after the sale. In most states, the rule is that if a manufacturer could not reasonably perceive a risk when the product was sold, it may not be held liable. The rationale is that the product isn't defective.

In some cases, there can be a post-sale duty to warn, repair, or recall a product if defects are discovered after it has been sold and is in use. Often, a vulnerability in locks and security devices is discovered that had not previously been found and was not foreseeable by the manufacturer. Circumstances can change unexpectedly or dangerously due to advances in state-of-the-art attacks or consumer uses.

A manufacturer or seller can be liable for compensatory and punitive damages if it fails to take reasonable steps to protect a consumer from danger after discovering a defect. These duties are a requirement to warn consumers to allow them to mitigate the risk or a duty to repair, retrofit, or recall a product. In many jurisdictions, rulings have held that a seller must warn when a reasonable seller in the same position would do so. Four criteria provide guidelines in such cases:

1. The seller knows or should have known there's a substantial risk of harm to persons or property.

2. Consumers can be identified to be reasonably assured of receiving a warning and who would likely be unaware of the threat.

3. A warning can be effectively communicated to those at risk, and they can act on it.

4. The risk of harm is sufficient to justify the difficulties and cost of providing such notice.

Exemption from Warnings: Sophisticated Users

Lock manufacturers may not have to provide warnings about potential security hazards and vulnerabilities to two classes of purchasers and end users because they're deemed to already know about the risks. Two doctrines in the law address this issue: the *Sophisticated User Doctrine* and the *Bulk Supplier Doctrine*. The Bulk Supplier Doctrine is irrelevant to our discussion as it applies primarily to liquids, sand, and chemicals and relates to how a product is sold and its nature.

Under the Sophisticated User Doctrine, the theory essentially exempts a manufacturer from the requirement to warn because of the buyer's expertise.

They're assumed to know that the vulnerability or hazard could cause them harm. The commonsense rule is that there's no duty to warn of obvious dangers that are commonly known.

The purpose of warnings is to provide relevant information about risks and vulnerabilities that a consumer may not be aware of so they may choose not to purchase the product to avoid risk. The Sophisticated User Doctrine isn't absolute and may not shield a manufacturer from liability if the warnings are insufficient to address specific risks or vulnerabilities that a buyer with only general knowledge of risks may not know about.

Lock manufacturers must notify buyers of certain bypass techniques that may defeat their security, especially in special keying systems involving high-security locks. This may include top-level master key decoding, sophisticated bumping techniques and bypass methods, hybrid attacks (as discussed in Part IV), and key replication when a manufacturer has made representations that copying or replicating keys is impossible.

High-security locks are supplied to many commercial and government institutions where it may be assumed that the risk managers or security directors are conversant with bypass techniques and vulnerabilities that may obviate the necessity of warnings. In my experience, this often isn't the case. I have been directly involved in many investigations and instances where supposedly knowledgeable key individuals were responsible for making buying and implementation decisions for various locking and security systems. These individuals had no information or understanding of many methods to defeat the systems they were purchasing, and the lock manufacturers did not brief them on critical information that might have altered their perception of the security of what they were buying or installing.

Warranty of Merchantability, Defective Products, and Negligence

A manufacturer can be deemed *negligent* if it produces a defective product. That recognition of negligence can result from a breach of a *warranty of merchantability*, which renders the product unsuitable or unfit for its intended and ordinary use. In the legal sense, *unfit for ordinary use* means the same thing as *defective*. Strict liability in tort is based on the sale of a defective product.

Designers and manufacturers of locks and safes, especially high-security ones, imply and hold themselves as experts in the field due to the nature of their work and the products they produce. Suppose a product defect or significant security vulnerability results in a major upgrade, recall, or litigation. In that case, the manufacturer will likely have to testify, and their depositions will be taken to adduce evidence to prove or disprove negligence or a breach of warranty.

Chapter 2 discusses the requisite skills and expertise for designers and members of engineering and manufacturing teams who must provide documentation about a wide array of issues relating to every aspect of a product, from design and materials to testing, production, and quality control.

The evidence in a product liability case will help a trial of fact (either judge or jury) decide whether a product was defective and whether such a defect caused an injury or loss. An expert witness may be required for either the defense or the plaintiff to express an *opinion* of defectiveness and causation. Special requirements are required to be qualified as an expert, as initially outlined in the landmark case *Frye v. United States* (293 F. 1013, D.C. Cir. 1923) by the Supreme Court and discussed in Chapter 2.

Employees of a lock manufacturer may be called as fact witnesses, testifying to all aspects of product production. Design engineers and VA team members should be competent to offer evidence about the following:

- The design and production of a product
- How the product was supposed to function
- Issues about how the product did or did not function as designed
- How and why a product's security layers were or were not compromised
- How the product's design or components may or may not have created a security vulnerability
- Whether a product's part or system could have been designed differently to minimize or eliminate the defect
- Whether the failure to implement an alternative design made the product less reasonably safe

The Repair Doctrine: Liability for Subsequent Product Upgrades

A manufacturer may be concerned about the legal ramifications of implementing subsequent remedial measures in a deficient or defective product design because it fears that such changes may be a tacit admission of guilt, which could be used against the manufacturer by a plaintiff in litigation. The *Repair Doctrine* was an outgrowth of the common law designed to deal with this issue. That a manufacturer implemented changes to a product's design isn't dispositive either way: it doesn't establish that a product was or wasn't defective.

In 1982, the U.S. Supreme Court announced the doctrine in *Columbia & Puget Sound Railroad Company v. Hawthorne* (144 US 202, 1982). This case involved a sawmill and an employee injured by an allegedly unsafe and defective machine. The court held that post-accident repair evidence was incompetent and that "taking a precaution against the future is not to be construed as an admission of responsibility for the past." In most jurisdictions, the Repair Doctrine applies to lawsuits involving product liability and bars evidence of safety improvements to prove negligence and effectiveness. The exception to the rule is where a defendant manufacturer asserts that the change or upgrade was impractical at the time.

Negligence vs. Privity of Contract

Industrialization in America in the 1800s saw a change in the business models that split the manufacturing and retailing functions, insulating manufacturers from direct liability to consumers. U.S. law borrowed from England the *privity of contract* precedent and defense established by *Winterbottom v. Wright*. It was a barrier to holding manufacturers liable for injuries from defective products. Winterbottom prohibited negligence actions against a producer of products that had no privity of contract with the plaintiff. The privity defense's result was to promote nascent industries' development. Then came the MacPherson case.

MacPherson v. Buick Motor Car Company

MacPherson originated from a small village near Saratoga Springs, New York. He bought a new Buick Runabout from the local dealer in July 1911. While he was driving a sick neighbor to the hospital, the wooden spokes of his Buick's left rear wheel failed, causing the wheel to collapse. The car careened out of control and into a ditch and pinned him under the axle.

The Buick dealer couldn't afford to reimburse MacPherson for his damage claim, so he sued the Buick Motor Company and challenged the Privity of Contract Doctrine. The jury in the original court case brought a verdict of $5,000. Buick appealed to the New York Court of Appeals, which also upheld the verdict. Judge Benjamin Cardozo (who later was appointed to the Supreme Court) held that the imminent danger rule "is not limited to poisons, explosives, and other products that in the normal operation are implements of destruction." The importance of the ruling was that if a manufacturer produced something with such a foreseeably dangerous nature, irrespective of contract, the manufacturer of this thing of danger is under a duty to make it carefully. The rule for a manufacturer was then "if the nature of a thing is such that it's reasonably certain to place life and limb in peril when negligently made, it's then a thing of danger. Its *nature* gives warning of the consequences to be expected."

Buick knew the wheels might fail. The ruling was important because it held that if the manufacturer knew of a potentially dangerous condition, it was obligated to warn consumers of it. This was the beginning of negligence and strict liability in the law. If you manufacture a product that can harm people, there's an extra layer of due diligence.

The court repudiated the privity defense in negligence claims, making irrelevant contract relationships between sellers and end users by the law of torts. As Judge Cardozo stated, "We have put aside the notion that the duty to safeguard life and limb, when the consequences of negligence may be foreseen, grows out of contracts and nothing else. We have put the source of the obligation where it ought to be. We have put its source in the law."

What is important for a manufacturer to understand is the legal premise as stated in the opinion that "The law of obligations towards other persons was imposed on every person, regardless of consent, as distinguished from the law of contracts, which enforces private agreements, which people consequently undertake."

Today, the MacPherson rule applies to nonpurchasers, bystanders, nonmanufacturers, suppliers, repairmen, and anyone encountering a product. Another landmark ruling in California in 1963, *Greenman v. Yuba Power Products Inc.* (377 P.2d 897), declared that manufacturers of defective products should be strictly liable in tort to persons injured by such products, irrespective of any contractual limitations, including warranties.

Product liability is central to U.S. law. Litigation and prevention should figure prominently by every manufacturer because thousands of lawsuits are filed annually. As I have noted in this book, negligence can occur at any design, manufacturing, or marketing stage.

Strict Liability vs. Negligence

There is often confusion between strict liability and negligence and the legal responsibility for each. Simply put, negligence can be said to be a fault-based liability where someone did something improperly that caused an injury. In contrast, *strict liability* means a manufacturer or supplier is responsible for harm caused by a defect in a product, regardless of fault.

Strict Liability

The concept of strict liability supersedes contractual obligations or due diligence. Liability doesn't matter if a manufacturer produces something with serious risks. Strict liability took hold in the early 1900s in the food and pharmaceuticals business. Historically, it was based on deceit in ancient Rome, from the principles of sales law and warranty.

Strict liability is based on "no fault"; liability is assessed regardless of fault. Liability is based on the *product*, not the conduct of the manufacturer. Once a defect is proven, negligence is inferred as a manufacturer's failure to detect or remove a defect. A finding of strict liability is almost always based on some form of underlying negligence.

Who Can Sue for a Defective Product? Horizontal and Vertical Privity

A manufacturer must always consider who has the standing to sue if they produce and sell a defective product. There are two concepts, *horizontal* and *vertical* privity, which are both important and based on implied warranty under theories of contract. These concepts are relevant because they can define who can be sued by nonpurchasers, sometimes quite remotely, and who has no privity of contract with the seller or manufacturer.

Horizontal privity applies to nonpurchasers extending horizontally away from the original purchaser in a diminishing connection order. This can include family members, guests, employees, or bystanders. For lock manufacturers, it may include occupants of a building or dwelling who are ostensibly protected by security products. This class of potential plaintiffs attempts to stand in the purchaser's shoes to obtain whatever legal benefits originally flowed to the purchaser by some form of the contractual relationship.

In the context of producers of locks and safes, *vertical privity* encompasses the extension of liability and claims of warranty to everyone in a vertical or direct line from the manufacturer to the distributor, sales agent, locksmith, installer, and any remote individual or entity downstream from the seller who attempts to claim the benefits of a warranty and who has been injured.

The Malfunction Doctrine and a Defective Product

In certain cases, proving that a product defect caused an injury is unnecessary. The *Malfunction Doctrine* provides that an injured plaintiff can establish proof by showing that the product failed in normal use, suggesting a defect. Thus, the defect can be inferred by circumstantial evidence under the following conditions: a malfunction occurred during proper use, and no alterations or misuse could have caused the malfunction that occurred. The importance of this doctrine for lock manufacturers is that a plaintiff doesn't have to establish that a specific defect caused the injury or vulnerability. Why is this relevant? If a lock can be opened but exactly why it happens isn't understood, a manufacturer may claim they aren't liable under the 3T2R Rule. A good example is lock bumping. Most manufacturers were not aware of the vulnerability. Burglaries occurred because the locks were bumped open, even high-security locks. A manufacturer could claim the lock was not defective because there was no way it could be opened. The manufacturers did not understand how or why, so they tried to avoid liability. Still, if a security vulnerability is created, the manufacturer may be liable if the vulnerability is repeatable and reliable.

Failure to Implement an Alternative Design and Proof of Possibility

Suppose a product has a known or potential defect or vulnerability. In that case, it's incumbent upon the manufacturer to explore all alternative designs under some form of cost-benefit and risk-utility analysis, because this is the essence of design defectiveness. If litigation ensues, design engineers and management will examine whether a certain design wasn't considered or why it wasn't adopted. This is important in determining whether the risk of injury or vulnerability might have been mitigated if a feasible alternative had been implemented.

Every lock manufacturer should carefully document all such inquiries so that, if necessary, evidence can be adduced of due diligence in the design and testing of the product. Every alternative design should be documented to determine whether it could have been integrated and the issues, both positive and negative, they might have encountered by doing so.

Risk-Utility Analysis of an Alternative Product Design

Several considerations exist in the risk-utility analysis for a product, either under development or already in production. They're important, especially if injuries or security breaches have occurred or are likely to occur. Considerations include:

- The cost of an alternative design feature or modification, including the costs associated with the adoption of some or all products.

- Any loss of utility, security, or usefulness that a design change could cause.

- Any new security vulnerabilities that such design changes may create. This is particularly important for lock manufacturers because even changes that appear to be minor can have major security implications.

Many years ago, a client made what appeared to be a minor change in a computer cable lock to fix a lock-bumping vulnerability. The manufacturer caused a serious problem in its "simple" fix that not only didn't lessen the security issue from bumping with a ballpoint pen but also allowed the entire cable assembly to be easily removed from the lock body, permitting the laptop to be stolen in seconds. Simple changes are rarely simple in terms of security.

- The cost of adopting or implementing an alternative design or feature in a new product or one that is already being produced.

- Loss of functionality or usefulness that might be caused by adopting a different design.

- Any new security concerns or vulnerabilities that might be created or exacerbated by new designs.

- Balancing implementing alternative designs and benefits and a consideration of whether such actions would be worth the risks.

- Feasibility of implementing design changes.

- Whether the alternative design is a reasonable choice among all available design considerations.

- Whether it's reasonable for the manufacturer to adopt or implement a different or alternative design when the product has already been designed and produced.

- Whether the design's alternative proposed by a plaintiff in litigation is technologically and commercially practical.

- Whether the design alternative is considered state-of-the-art.

- Whether the design alternative is commercially practicable. This consideration must consider profitability and the availability of materials and components.

- Whether the design change would be acceptable to consumers.

- Whether all significant disadvantages have been considered.

Knowingly Selling a Defective Product

Can a manufacturer knowingly sell a defective product? Although that may appear to be a simple question, the answer can be complicated and not so obvious. This is especially true in the world of locks and safes because the definition of *defective* must often consider multiple criteria. This topic is also discussed in Chapter 9 because a manufacturer may have legal and moral responsibilities when notified of a potential product defect.

As noted, a lock manufacturer is a security expert either by direct representation or inference, requiring that the manufacturer understands and knows all the foreseeable risks associated with the design of any product it produces. The manufacturer is said to have *constructive knowledge* of such risks, defined as knowledge and understanding imputed to the manufacturer because it was responsible for the design. Suppose it's determined that a product is, or may be, deficient or defective. In that case, a manufacturer must assess and answer several questions, which will likely result in legal liability. Such questions include:

- Has the manufacturer been notified or alerted about the security vulnerabilities? If so, would it be considered negligent to continue selling the product without making necessary changes to mitigate possible damages?

- If changes are required, are they minimal, and could they be considered simply an upgrade?

- What actions were taken to assess the severity of the vulnerabilities?

- Would the degree of risk caused by the defect outweigh making changes in the design or recalling the product?

- Would the manufacturer be negligent in selling the product, knowing of the defect or vulnerability?

- Would the manufacturer, with knowledge of the defect or vulnerability, be considered as acting unreasonably and negligently toward a purchaser who was adversely affected or injured?

User Misconduct Defenses

A manufacturer must discover or forecast potential misuse or abuse of its products, as I previously discussed in Chapter 4. Lock manufacturers must understand and have complete knowledge of how their product works and try to imagine how the product can be used in a manner that's not normally anticipated or expected. Determining how a consumer will abuse a product in normal use and guarding against such eventualities can be difficult but is essential.

The Consumer Product Safety Commission has reported that over two-thirds of injuries related to consumer products have nothing to do with the product's design. Rather, they relate to its misuse or abuse. Although misuse by a user may mitigate or relieve a manufacturer from liability, design engineers must imagine how the product design can be circumvented or bypassed.

In our investigation of Medeco's design of high-security locks in 2007, my colleague and I figured out how to engineer four keys that would allow us to pick or bump open all their non-master keyed locks worldwide. Could that misuse have been anticipated? The answer involved an analysis of several design criteria in that high-security lock. With enough imagination and knowledge by the design engineers, it might have been possible but not likely. Would Medeco have been legally responsible if a defeat of its design resulted in losses? Probably not, but it's a good example of the necessity of a thorough analysis of designs and a project of "what could go wrong" with a particular design. Although our deconstruction of the security of the Medeco BIAXIAL lock was complicated, the defeat of the m3 (a later model) with a paper clip was not. The manufacturer should have forecasted that defeat and made changes to the original product rather than waiting for the next generation to fix the problem.

If a purchaser or user of a lock or security system isn't aware of how it can be compromised, then ordinarily they can't assume the risk of a security vulnerability and would not be liable to anyone for damages that might occur based on the defect. Lock manufacturers should be careful in their warranty claims related to implied merchantability warranties. This requires a product to be fit for its ordinary purposes, which are reasonably foreseeable.

In the case of locks, especially high-security locks, a design team must have the requisite expertise to be knowledgeable about various current and prior bypass techniques. They must be able to assess and imagine possible attacks and misuse of a product to defeat its security. Although an implied warranty doesn't usually extend to abnormal or unforeseeable misuse by the user or another individual, the question about locks is what constitutes "abnormal."

Liability for Misuse of a Product

Is a lock manufacturer liable for product failures if there's misuse or alteration by a user or third party? As noted in this text, this question is sometimes difficult to answer easily. My fundamental rule is that locks are *designed* to be attacked, manipulated, and misused by criminals and bad actors to defeat the lock's security and to open them. Security locks are installed to prevent or block unauthorized access, so what constitutes "misuse" is open to question. Is inserting a pick and tension tool to manipulate pin tumblers or other internal components a misuse of the lock? Would using a simple decoder, probing each detainer to determine its individual length to produce a key, be considered misuse? I have never believed that such examples constitute misuse. My lock-manufacturing clients often disagree, stating that when third parties deliberately put products to unfair and possibly criminal uses, the question is whether such actions are *intervening* events.

Was the ability to compromise a lock due to a defect in design, or was it inherent in the type of mechanism? Lock bumping isn't the direct result of a defect in pin tumbler locks but rather a built-in problem that has existed since Linus Yale invented his design. The critical question is whether the type of "intervention" was a reasonably foreseeable consequence of the product's design or alleged defect or whether the manufacturer could not reasonably anticipate the exploitation of an inherent design parameter.

A manufacturer may avoid liability if the product was defectively designed and a user's behavior caused an injury. The fundamental question is whether a lock manufacturer is responsible for an injury to the plaintiff through the improper use of its products and by whom. The simple rule is this: product misuse will most often bar recovery altogether if it's *unforeseeable*, considering the manufacturer's expertise and whether it should have anticipated the misuse and guarded against it through different protective mechanisms in its design. Products can't be designed to be perfectly safe or secure for every intended or unintended use. The laws surrounding product misuse and alteration, however, can provide limitations on liability.

The relevant concept for a manufacturer is *unforeseen* in terms of unintended uses, misuses, or alterations accomplished to defeat its primary function or, in the case of locks, its security. I have presented significant examples of hybrid attacks against locks. Whether these qualify as legitimate abuse or alterations is open to discussion and analysis. The legal question is whether the manufacturer should have foreseen or been aware of the potential for such misuse or alteration.

A manufacturer must implement reasonable designs to mitigate product uses or misuses that they reasonably could foresee. Although third-party misuse can raise legal principles of intervening or superseding causation that can bar liability, this only occurs if the misuse is unforeseeable. Comparative negligence rules and responsibility may also come into play to reduce liability, depending on the action of plaintiffs.

Suppose a use or misuse isn't reasonably foreseeable. In that case, a manufacturer has zero responsibility to protect against it, but the duty to anticipate harm can extend to product misuse or use in a way for which it was not designed, built, or sold.

State-of-the-Art or Defective?

Design defectiveness can be actionable under product liability law, but only if it was not reasonably foreseeable. Generally, if a manufacturer implements the state-of-the-art in the design it can shield them from liability. If the defect could have been foreseen by the manufacturer and it was not remedied and resulting dangers could have been prevented, there can be liability. Thus, in most cases, foreseeability limits the responsibility for defective products. That doesn't mean a state-of-the-art design can't have flaws and/or be defective, especially in lock and safe designs. I have often analyzed such state-of-the-art designs and found serious but not immediately evident flaws that opened the locks and compromised security in seconds.

The legal premise for courts to assess liability on manufacturers is that vulnerabilities were not knowable or unable to be prevented when the products were designed and sold. Manufacturers consider state-of-the-art legal issues regarding the foreseeability of risk and then implement a design that reduces the potential for vulnerabilities. They often refer to customs and practices in the industry when doing so. The ultimate and best in existing technology includes all knowledge bases relevant to security issues at the time, regardless of their source. It's anticipated that the source of such information can come from government, industrial, or academic institutions and, even more importantly, from competitors.

Different courts have summarized the meaning of *state-of-the-art* as a defense in product liability cases like these:

- The best technology reasonably available at the time.
- The dangerous nature of the product wasn't known and couldn't reasonably be discovered at the time the product was placed into the stream of commerce.
- Technical, mechanical, and scientific knowledge of manufacturing, designing, testing, or labeling for the same or similar products that were in existence and reasonably foreseeable for use at the time of manufacture.
- The existing technological expertise and scientific knowledge relevant to a particular industry when the product was designed.

State-of-the-art defense evidence has one of three procedural effects:

1. To establish an affirmative defense
2. To create a rebuttable presumption of nondefectiveness or non-negligence
3. To provide evidence that a product wasn't defective or that a manufacturer or other supplier wasn't negligent

Manufacturers should also consider a second type of defense relating to the state-of-the-art: the feasibility of adopting designs that would fix a problem or reduce or eliminate risk. Many potential issues are involved in taking corrective action: Who should bear the costs, risks, and benefits of changes brought on by newer technology? Are there risks that a manufacturer can't control? Are all risks discoverable, knowable, or avoidable in the meaning of state-of-the-art?

Often, the liability question in state-of-the-art designs revolves around risks that can't be controlled. It also becomes a question of warnings to consumers. Dangers can be unknown or unforeseen before a lock is sold. Such was the case with the Simplex 1000 lock, discussed in Part IV, involving magnetic attacks. The original design was patented in 1965. In 2009, I published several reports about how these incredibly popular mechanical push-button locks could be opened in two seconds with a rare earth magnet. The manufacturer was unaware of the issue and failed to understand how the design could be compromised if one critical component could be moved, as that component was subject to strong magnetic fields.

When the lock was originally developed and sold, it was the newest programmable access-control system design. The company did not issue warnings for about six months after the problem was known to some locksmiths and government agencies, thus placing many secure facilities at risk. In this instance, during testing, the manufacturer should have considered using a strong magnetic field to compromise the one component controlling how the lock functioned. In this case, the designers were unaware of the problem, even though government agencies were very aware of the vulnerability for many years and used it to their advantage for covert entry teams.

Another famous case in our industry involved using the magnetic ring developed by Addi Wendt in Germany. Mechatronic lock manufacturers had no idea, nor had they ever thought about using a series of rotating magnets to open their locks without any trace in seconds. Manufacturers can be held responsible for a failure to discover and avoid or mitigate security vulnerabilities under the principles of negligence or strict liability. The question of responsibility for a failure to warn consumers becomes much more complicated.

An allegation of negligence is usually at the heart of state-of-the-art claims and defenses. These are often predicated on a manufacturer's ability to understand, foresee, and prevent security vulnerabilities. The questions for a lock manufacturer must include:

- Was the risk foreseeable, did the manufacturer consider modifying its design to eliminate risk, and did the manufacturer have a duty to warn of an unavoidable risk?
- Does the product provide the safety that a person is likely to expect?
- To what use could the product be expected to be put?
- How was the product presented to the purchaser?

The safest rule is this: the design of a product and its warnings need only be as safe as reasonably possible under the prevailing state-of-the-art.

Manufacturers Are Experts

A fundamental principle in product liability law is that a manufacturer is held to the standard of care of an expert in their field. The reasoning is that the manufacturer was involved in the design, production, and marketing of its products. A lock manufacturer is considered a security expert on how its product protects against foreseeable threats. Expertise is measured against other reasonable manufacturers for the specific product type, which confers a duty to be aware of a particular product's foreseeable use environment.

Established lock manufacturers are often the real experts in their field, although they can also make serious mistakes in design and manufacturing. The problem is for the smaller and newer entrants into the field, who are held to the same standard of knowledge and responsibility, which they may be unable to meet. The lock design and manufacturing business is complex, both technically and legally, as is the security design business. Many start-ups may have good ideas but, in my experience, don't have the experience and understanding of complicated security issues to produce a product that doesn't place customers at risk.

Reasonable Foreseeability

A lock manufacturer is liable for reasonably foreseeable threats, considering their expertise in security engineering. Suppose a security threat posed by its design or product is outside of what can be considered reasonable foreseeability. In that case, the manufacturer can't be faulted for failing to take steps to avert a risk or to protect one who is harmed.

Constructive Knowledge of Risk

A manufacturer may not be able to challenge the foreseeability of a risk or whether a victim of a manufacturer in the same position, acting reasonably, should have foreseen the risk. A court can imply or construct "the knowledge based on a reasonable foreseeability of the risk." The reasonableness test has three components:

1. The foreseeability of the risk of harm from a product.
2. The foreseeability of the use to which the product was put.
3. The plaintiff must be one who can be seen as foreseeably placed at risk by the manufacturer's negligence.

Due Care in Manufacturing

Mistakes are inevitable in the manufacture of a product. Such mistakes can cause harm to consumers and others who may be foreseeably placed at risk. In every step of the process, due care is required, so a manufacturer must be cautious in all aspects of production and preparation of a product for commercial distribution.

Due Care in Design

The exercise of due care in developing a new product design is critical to prevent vulnerabilities in the product. *Due care* in this context means a thorough analysis of all components to ensure that they can't be compromised, either individually or in concert with each other. A VA team should participate in any design from its inception because a manufacturer can be held liable for defects that can be traced to an original design.

Industry Standards and Proof of Negligence

Industry organizations for locks and safes develop standards often relied on by courts in negligence and defective product cases to gauge an industry consensus and the most appropriate balancing of security, safety, and practicality. The relevant organizations in the United States are the American National Standards Institute (ANSI), American Standards Association (ASA), Underwriters Laboratory (UL), and Builders Hardware Manufacturers Association (BHMA).

A manufacturer can be liable for negligence when it fails to exercise reasonable care for a plaintiff's safety or security. The test is whether the manufacturer was unreasonable in developing, producing, or marketing a defective product. Such conduct is expected and can form the basis of an industry standard and custom. Negligence can be considered as the failure to exercise "ordinary" care. One can assume that most manufacturers will usually act sensibly and prudently. They will balance the costs and benefits to others as well as themselves. A failure to conform to the customary level of care constitutes negligence because industry practice and custom can be important in establishing conduct, but not conclusive.

Evidence of a failure to abide by an industry standard of care or noncompliance is often admissible to the question of due care. This assumes that the standard is relevant to the dangerous or security aspect of the product.

Elements of Proof by a Manufacturer

Plaintiffs and defendant manufacturers will seek to develop and introduce specific elements of proof to establish their cases. Here are a few examples:

- The risk was remote.
- The risk was open and obvious.
- The defect was impracticable and costly to mitigate or remove.

Elements of Proof by a Plaintiff

Plaintiffs will also seek to develop and introduce specific elements of proof. Here are some examples:

- Evidence of applicable standards and customs to demonstrate the foreseeability of the risk
- Cost feasibility, utility, and acceptability of the security or safety measure that should have been implemented or adopted

- The foreseeability and magnitude of the risk
- The hidden nature of the risk
- The cost, utility, and feasibility of avoiding the risk

Negligence has usually been the basis of recovery in cases during most of the twentieth century. In most states, the manufacturer's fault is usually the basis of recovery in a negligence action. The *negligence cause of action* is still the theory of recovery in product liability litigation. As I've mentioned, it's important to understand that negligence can occur at any stage of design, manufacturing, or marketing.

The basis is negligent design, negligence in the manufacturer, or negligent failure to provide adequate warnings or instructions. A plaintiff must establish the following:

- The seller owed a duty to the plaintiff.
- The seller breached that duty.
- The breach of duty was the cause, in fact, of the plaintiff's injury.
- The cause was a proximate cause of the injury.
- Damages for the harm suffered are recoverable in negligence. The plaintiff has the burden to prove each element of the negligence cause of action.

Liability for Nonmanufacturers and Retailers

In certain cases, a nonmanufacturer or retailer can be held strictly liable for injuries from a defective product. Thus, a locksmith, lock shop, architect, or contractor could be liable for selling or supplying a lock or security system that posed a significant security threat they were unaware of. Still, due to their status as having security expertise, they should have known of the threat. This rule only applies if these parties substantially participated in the product's design. Otherwise, no liability should be attached. The following entities can't be held responsible for defective products they provide or sell: parent corporations, trademark holders, and franchisers (unless they have substantial control over product safety) and successor corporations (unless there is a fraudulent attempt to avoid liability).

Fraudulent or False Misrepresentation

Assertions about a product may be expressed through the sellers' affirmative communications, or the nature of the sales transaction may imply them. If a lock manufacturer materially misstates the security attributes of its products, there can be legal liability for such claims and damage awards for injuries suffered as a proximate cause. The threshold question is whether the user was justified in relying on the statements of the manufacturer, seller, installer, or locksmith. The criteria that must be considered include whether the representations were material and the precision or vagueness of the statements. Was the statement one of fact or opinion? How was the statement made—for example, publicly on television or in an owner's manual? Should the buyer have suspected the statements were not to be relied on, and could other sources of information have been checked to confirm the accuracy of the information? Was any information available on a Google or YouTube search?

The next chapter examines the applicable and relevant industry standards in detail. In the United States, the important criteria for forced and covert entry are defined in UL 437 and ANSI/BHMA 156.30. These set the benchmarks for security ratings and performance for locks. Unfortunately, they don't allow for a thorough examination of potential security threats.

Standards for Locks and Safes

Virtually any product or equipment in an industrial society is designed to meet the recognized standards. This is especially true for locks, safes, and all related security hardware. These standards are developed by different industries to create and define products and to protect consumers, commercial enterprises, and government agencies from numerous threats and risks. These can cause property damage, economic loss, personal injury, or death. Insurers rely on these standards and compliance by customers to minimize their potential exposure to unnecessary liability. The rationale for the standards organizations is based on the premise that most consumers or organizations have limited or no ability to conduct independent testing to determine the suitability, safety, quality, reliability, endurance, function, and fitness for an intended purpose of the security of products or devices they purchase, use, or install.

Without standards or the capability to conduct independent testing, it would be impossible for consumers to know what they're buying or whether it will meet their specific use-case needs. Interoperability, functionality, and security are critical and essential in our technical world. Communication systems, security hardware, transport, packaging, infrastructure, and most everything technology-based are guided and governed by standards that can impact almost all global trade. Standards increase commerce and foster consumer confidence. Any manufacturer that supplies its locks and safes to the public must be concerned with creating products that meet certain standards.

All high-security locks are developed and rated to meet defined levels of protection and deterrence against various identified and established threats. Many countries develop their own standards, and some adopt them from other jurisdictions. The global market means locks from many countries may be present locally, especially in less well-developed regions, where the standards become even more important. Government agencies, military organizations, financial institutions, medical facilities, and critical infrastructure must decide what they need and what products will meet their specific requirements. Without the standards, this would be impossible, placing everyone at risk.

There is a standard for everything we use or do in life. Whether it is the tire-pressure monitoring systems in our cars; the design of credit cards, cell phones, or seat belts; or the airplanes we fly in, every piece of technology in a system and any subsystem is based on standards. Nothing would work reliably, correctly, safely, or conveniently without them.

In this chapter, I explore the requirements of various lock standards that U.S. organizations have defined. More importantly, perceived problems with certain standards and testing methods are presented, along with basic rules and maxims that should serve as a guide and discourage an absolute reliance on or adherence to testing protocols as the "gold standard."

For security engineers, standards are important in developing, testing, and vulnerability analysis for locks and safes. Many buyers mandate meeting defined standards because it is their assurance or belief that such hardware will meet their requirements. In my experience, this may not be the case, which is why it's even more important for manufacturers and users of high-security locks to understand what the standards do not address and the liability that may flow from attacks that aren't anticipated by such standards. I have been involved in hundreds of cases where a lock, especially a high-security lock, met all the standards but could be opened in a few seconds with little expertise and no specialized tools. This reality continues to plague lock designers and manufacturers and standards organizations.

As a member of the Underwriters Laboratory (UL) Standards Technical Panel for Locks and Safes for many years, I have a simple answer to this conundrum is: "If it can be opened within a specified time, regardless of the tools or techniques employed or the expertise of the attacker, the lock should not be certified for its high-security rating." The process to adopt new standards by UL and the Builders Hardware Manufacturers Association (BHMA) is based on a consensus of manufacturers, security experts, insurers, consumers, trade organizations, and other interested groups. The adoption procedure can be cumbersome and, in my view, either overly restrictive or too broad, to the extent that the standards are reduced to the lowest common denominator and may not yield the intended result.

Rather than classifying a lock's security in terms of time and perceived threat, the standards often attempt to define each technique or category of attack. Suppose the method employed by a criminal to open a lock doesn't precisely fit a standard. In that case, these organizations deny any responsibility, saying that the standard doesn't address the issue and needs to be modified.

As a result of research conducted by myself and my colleagues in both the United States and Europe, we can demonstrate that in some cases, UL, BHMA, VdS, and other organizations certify locks that may not be secure for their intended purpose or environment. I have advocated that UL and BHMA re-examine their testing protocols to ensure that what the consumer believes they're installing as a rated lock with a specified level of security is the case. The 2020 BHMA 156.30 standard revision reflected some of the changes my colleagues and I proposed, but many areas still need to be closely examined. This high-security lock standard must specify testing protocols that ensure significant resistance to forced and covert attacks.

Engineers, risk managers, and others responsible for making decisions based on the standards should understand that they don't cover every current and future attacks. The reality is that they can never anticipate or protect against every threat. None of the cited standards are perfect. They're simply a starting point and often the best practices that the industry can offer for its locks and safes. Some manufacturers test in extensive labs and go far beyond what the standards mandate. One example is Assa Abloy and its Sargent factory facility in New Haven, Connecticut, which the company has developed; it uses testing protocols that far exceed what BHMA and UL require. However, such testing still doesn't contemplate many attack vectors that can cause Sargent locks to be opened quickly and reliably.

Toward the end of this chapter, I attempt to provide a comprehensive list of areas not adequately covered by the UL 437 and BHMA 156.30 and 156.5 standards. This list should guide product analysis and vulnerability testing because it's an inventory of what can be exploited to compromise high-security locks that likely weren't tested before certification.

Basic Rules and Axioms Relating to Standards

Standards should be considered guidelines and not absolute assurance that compliance or "meeting the standard" equates to protection against the risks specified and tested against. In analyzing locks, many variables and nonprecise definitions exist in testing protocols. This is especially true for tests involving covert or surreptitious attacks. A manufacturer must determine whether the prescriptions in a standard should cause additional examination to assess product performance and, more importantly, protection against real-world threats and attacks. The reality is that a standard can't cover every eventuality or often-subtle variable encountered, especially in covert-entry testing.

I have developed several "axioms" that should be considered in assessing the relevance or relationship of testing protocols to real-world threats. The question is whether meeting specific standards is a valid representation of security and protection for a lock or safe that "passes" such a standard. A complete list of these rules and axioms can be found in Part VII, but here's a summary:

- *Standards are often outdated and may not reflect current attack technology.* Many standards haven't been reviewed or revised for at least five years. Lock-defeat technology is constantly evolving, as is new lock design. The standards simply don't keep pace with methods of covert and forced entry and updates in technology, such as 3D printing and piezo-electric measurement and decoding tools.

- *Standards can't be easily and timely updated.* Bypass techniques and defeats may be developed against locks that have received a high-security rating. Those locks would not be able to meet the same requirements if they were subsequently tested. The standards likely would not reflect the current state-of-the-art in attack techniques without an update in testing protocols, and no expedited process would allow for this to occur. This means locks currently in production and/or sold may be vulnerable to attacks not tested for at their certification date. This calls into question the validity of the security rating and the consumer's reliance on it, unless their testing facility accesses the latest in bypass technology and advances in lock designs.

- *Just because a lock receives a high-security rating doesn't mean it's secure.* Design engineers should never consider that a lock meeting a standard's requirements is prima facia evidence that it can't be easily compromised. In my experience, this simply isn't the case.

- *Standards don't mandate certain tests that should be conducted to determine bypass capabilities.* Attacks ranging from simple to more subtle or sophisticated are often omitted from test protocols. They should not be.

- *Analysts rarely know all the tools that can compromise some high-security locks.* Some specialized tools and techniques may not be known to test personnel, especially those available to government agencies and hackers. Tests that should be conducted often aren't, which can provide a false assurance of security.

- *Analysts are prevented from using all the available tools.* The standards specify the type of commercially available hand tools employed to run the certification tests, which limits the ability to properly determine a lock's security. If a valid analysis and result are to be rendered, design teams should be able to utilize all available tools and methods to ensure that the locks they produce are immune to common attacks, especially for high-value targets.

▪ *Testing personnel are precluded from using their imagination and creativity in determining a lock's security under testing.* The standards limit the testing methods and tools. In my experience, creativity is required to exploit possible design defects that can allow a lock to be opened. There is no incentive for test personnel to be creative.

▪ *Locks can be certified as passing all tests to comply with the standard but still be opened in seconds.* In my experience, the fact that a lock can be certified as complying with all testing requirements doesn't mean it is secure against nontraditional attacks and those that locksmiths haven't envisioned.

▪ *Prior certification as complying with a standard means nothing.* Attack vectors are constantly evolving and being discovered. The fact that a lock has passed all testing requirements in the past isn't determinative that the mechanism is secure today. Test personnel may not be aware of the methods of bypassing a specific lock. As cited in a case example discussed in Part VI, neither industry personnel nor covert-entry specialists were aware of the use of *code-setting keys*: a set of four specially designed keys that I patented to allow picking and bumping and to circumvent the security in perhaps the highest-security-rated lock in America. This lock hadn't been easily or successfully compromised for over 40 years, yet my colleagues and I could open some of these locks in under 30 seconds. The lock's certification under UL 437 and BHMA 156.30 meant nothing in that case, which involved the Medeco BIAXIAL and m3. The latest version, the M4, mitigates many of these threats.

▪ *Patents mean nothing in regard to a lock's security testing.* The fact that a lock is patented has no relationship to its ability to withstand various attack methods cited by standards organizations. The U.S. Patent Office and other patent offices don't test for security based on the patent application and disclosures. Design engineers should never rely on the fact that their products have received prior patents to guarantee security, especially if their product modifications have been implemented to extend a patent's life.

▪ *Bad guys don't follow standards.* Criminals don't carry a copy of standards when attempting to compromise locks and safes, nor are they restricted to the methods enumerated in the applicable standards. Conversely, they may rely on what was *not tested* in a standard to determine what will allow them to quickly bypass a lock or safe.

▪ *Standards are often too general and may be oversimplified.* This generalization and oversimplification is often done to satisfy stakeholders in the original committees who wrote and adopted the standards. Many detailed and important tests may be omitted or minimized to satisfy lock manufacturers and interest groups. This was particularly evident in my interaction with the California Department of Justice and its forensic laboratory when gun lock and safety standards were drafted. Although these standards established the baseline for many other jurisdictions in the United States, they have proven to be flawed. I demonstrated easy methods of compromise to the U.S. Department of Justice (DOJ) and in a federal lawsuit in 2012 against the largest gun safe manufacturer in the United States.

▪ *Standards don't cover all vulnerabilities in locks being tested.* Prescribed testing procedures often provide a narrow framework and rarely encompass many serious vulnerabilities that should be contemplated. The criteria enumerated in the standards are defined by each standards organization and its members (industry and other stakeholders).

▪ *Security standards may not be good enough for the anticipated use of the locks and safes for a specified rating.* A standard may only require minimal testing, whereas a more rigorous examination may be necessary to meet a specified safety rating.

▪ *No incentive exists for examiners in the standards organization to find design flaws.* In the United States, many standards testing laboratories aren't encouraged to discover compromise methods outside the tests defined by the applicable standards. Incentives should exist for employees who find vulnerabilities during testing, even if such issues fall outside the enumerated protocols.

▪ *Just because a testing lab reports that a lock is secure doesn't mean it is.* This was evidenced by various laboratories finding that certain high-security cylinders couldn't be bumped open. However, they were wrong: it was shown that several locks with high-security ratings could be opened within seconds using bumping attacks.

▪ *Standards are often unrealistic in their specification of attack tools and methods for forced entry.* Like fire departments and search-and-rescue organizations, criminals have various sophisticated attack tools. The U.S. standards limit the size and tool types that can be used for testing, which provides a false impression of security and can expose users to liability or losses.

▪ *Reliance on a "certified Associated Locksmiths of America (ALOA) locksmith" as an approved test examiner for picking, bumping, and other covert entries may not yield valid results.* Many locksmiths aren't experts or adept at picking locks, especially high-security ones. Usually, their primary job is to sell, install, and maintain security systems and related hardware unless they have developed specialties. Specifications that require locksmith certifications to be qualified as experts are often misleading. I have met and worked with non-locksmiths, hackers, lock-sports enthusiasts, and even kids who are far more competent at opening certain types of cylinders than many locksmiths I know. The requirement of an ALOA-certified locksmith is a good starting point, but it is by no means a guarantee of results.

▪ *Standards for high-security locks don't anticipate many hybrid attacks.* My colleagues and I have developed many hybrid attacks, as described in Part IV, that are outside any enumerated protocols. They involve a combination of specialized keys, tools, and processes, some of which are easily created or produced.

▪ *Compliance with high-security standards may not be a shield for defective-product liability claims.* Lock companies have asserted that they "meet the standards" and are thus immune from liability. The reality is that a lock may be compromised by means that are untested in a standard and may not even be contemplated by locksmiths. The standards may not shield a manufacturer from product liability in such cases.

U.S. Standards Organizations

Two primary standards organizations in the United States assess and rate the security of locks and safes: the Underwriters Laboratory (UL) and the Builders Hardware Manufacturers Association (BHMA). A third group, the American National Standards Institute (ANSI), also develops standards and works with BHMA to create standards. In this section, I discuss all of them.

Underwriters Laboratory

Many standards organizations were originally founded to protect insurance companies. UL, the most famous in the United States, was established in 1894 to test emerging technologies and devices and define safety and security standards. Standard technical panels (STPs) have been created to review and advise on each particular standard. Two STPs relevant to any discussion about locks and safes are STP 0140 and STP 0437. For reference, their applicable standard numbers are provided for further research.

STP 0140 reviews and revises the standards that rate burglary-resistant safes, vaults, automatic teller systems, and night depositories. STP oversees seven standards:

1. UL 140 standards for relocking devices for safes and vaults
2. UL 291 standards for automatic teller machines
3. UL 608 standards for burglary-resistant vault doors and modular panels
4. UL 680 standards for emergency vault ventilation
5. UL 687 standards for burglary-resistant safes
6. UL 771 standards for night depositories
7. UL 786 standards for key-locked safes

STP 0437 oversees the standards for burglary-resistant locks and locking mechanisms. The critical standard for our analysis is UL 437. This STP is responsible for five standards:

1. UL 437 standards for key locks
2. UL 768 standards for combination locks
3. UL 887 standards for delayed-action time locks
4. UL 1034 standards for burglary-resistant electric-locking mechanisms
5. UL 2058 standards for electronic locks

Builders Hardware Manufacturers Association

BHMA is a collaborative group of manufacturers representing the builders' hardware industry for residential and commercial products. It's the only organization accredited by ANSI, a private nonprofit organization that collaborates with BHMA to develop, review, and revise locks and related hardware standards. They work with various government and industry groups to develop and coordinate voluntary standards and solutions for national and global priorities.

The BHMA standards that are important for any discussion about locks are the 156 series, which addresses performance criteria for deadbolts and locksets. There are two pertinent standards:

1. BHMA/ANSI 156.30 standard for high-security cylinders
2. BHMA 156.5 standard for auxiliary bored and mortise locks, rim locks, cylinders, and push-button mechanisms

American Society for Testing and Materials

Organized in 1898, the American Society for Testing and Materials (ASTM) is one of the leading international standards-developing organizations and aims to provide voluntary standards to improve product quality and safety and facilitate trade through global standardization. This internationally recognized organization has created six classifications relating to manufacturing involving testing, materials classifications, and operation. Its criteria and standards cover test methods, specifications, classification, practice, guidance, and terminology.

Description and Analysis of U.S. Lock Standards: UL and BHMA

The primary elements and requirements of the UL 437 and BHMA 156.30 and 156.5 standards are identified in these standards, and their perceived deficiencies relate to the security ratings of high-security locks. Many manufacturers also conduct their testing according to the standards and, as a result, are confident about their products' security. Meeting the standards is only part of ensuring that locks that purport to resist covert and forced attacks actually do so.

The UL requirements apply to door locks, locking cylinders, security container key locks, and two-key locks, such as in safe deposit boxes. The BHMA 156.30 standard is also directed at pin tumbler designs but doesn't exclude other locking mechanisms (such as wafer and lever tumbler mechanisms). UL 437 was last updated in 2017 and BHMA 156.30 in 2020. The BHMA 156.5 standards provide for operational tests that aren't covered in 156.30.

Design engineers must understand that neither the UL 437 standard nor the BHMA standards address what I refer to as "real-world testing" issues. Certain rated locks can be bypassed faster than these standards provide for forced and covert entry.

UL 437: The Commercial Security Standard

The UL 437 standard is *not* a high-security standard but rather what I would call a "higher-security" commercial standard; nowhere does its language directly refer to high-security locking mechanisms. It is perhaps one step above BHMA 156.5 in its requirements and refers to UL 437 as part of its language. BHMA/ANSI 156.5 applies primarily to a conventional pin tumbler mechanism and associated locking hardware. The confusion stems from the fact that the requirements of UL 437 are contained and referenced in both BHMA 156.30 and 156.5. These two BHMA standards can be thought of as operating in parallel, depending on the hardware involved.

UL 437 Definitions and Test Requirements

Understanding the basic requirements of the standards provides insight into the protection levels these locks are supposed to afford, how some of them can be compromised, and why the ability to do so can be catastrophic. The UL standard refers to door locks and locking cylinders. A *door lock* is defined as a rim or mortise-type locking assembly. A *locking cylinder* is used in door locks, alarm control switches, alarm shunt switches, utility locks, and similar devices. Our focus here is primarily on door locks because they mandate higher protection.

The UL 437 standard addresses six principal areas of testing:

1. *Corrosion resistance (in Section 7)*: These requirements specify the construction materials that a manufacturer can use to ensure corrosion resistance. They include brass, bronze, stainless steel, and other noncorrosive materials.

2. *Key changes and differences (Section 8)*: The standard specifies the key changes and differs for a lock with pin tumblers, wheels, levers, and wafers and the number of depth increments the manufacturer assigns. In a six-pin tumbler lock with six depth increments per tumbler, the total number of differs is 46,656 (or 6^6).

3. *Endurance testing (Section 10)*: This area of the standard specifies endurance testing for at least 10,000 full operational cycles for a traditional cylinder and 50 complete cycles for an interchangeable core or programmable lock.

4. *Attack-resistance testing (Section 11)*: This is the most relevant portion of the standard for high-security lock designers and is also the most problematic because of the often intangible variables in attack methods. It is referenced in the BHMA high-security standard 156.30.

5. *General requirements (Section 11.1)*: This section specifies that an attack shall not open a lock with certain classes of tools and methods. It allows multiple testing methods to be applied and different forms of testing if the construction of the lock so mandates.

6. *Tools (Section 11.2)*: This section specifies the various types of tools that can be used. The standard limits testing to certain types of tools, which I submit doesn't consider the many methods of attack available:

   a. Tools may include hand tools, chisels, screwdrivers over 15 inches long, hammers with a three-pound head weight, jaw-gripping wrenches, and pliers.

   b. Portable electric tools include electrically operated vibrating needles and high-speed handheld drills that operate at 5,000 rpm maximum, have no greater than a 3/8-inch chuck size, and use high-speed drill bits limited to 1/4-inch.

   c. Puller mechanisms must be either a slam-hammer type with a maximum head weight of three pounds or a screw type.

   d. Picking tools are common for standard patterns and are commercially available, designed for use on a particular make or design of the key lock, including custom-designed bump keys. I submit that this is insufficient for proper testing because there are many special picks that can facilitate the opening of many locks.

7. *Polymeric materials tests (Section 13)*: This section refers to the testing of materials that can be considered plastics. Because they're embedded in many locks, this is an important criterion. Polymeric materials aren't plastics and have different characteristics relevant to lock testing. Polymers that aren't petrochemical-based aren't considered plastics.

Plastic is a certain type of polymer that encompasses long chains of polymers. A polymer is made up of uniform molecules that are smaller than plastic molecules.

Several important distinctions between polymers and plastic, primarily in tensile and impact strength, must be considered:

a. *Tensile strength* depends on the material's crystal structure and refers to the maximum strength a material can support before a fracture occurs when it's stretched. It is all about the crystal structure and whether it's compact and may be more ductile, thus having a higher strength.

b. Another criterion is *hardness*, which is highly relevant to the materials with which locks are made. Hardness is the property of a material to resist deformation. Plastics are normally harder than polymers.

c. *Impact strength* is another important property. It is the ability to resist fracture from a sudden applied load or shock, which could be induced during a forced attack by a slam-hammer, for example.

Polymeric testing can take many forms and is critical for life cycle and endurance. These tests include impact, tensile, thermal, thickness, friction, and rheology assessment (a measure of deformation under stress from different forces).

Attack-Resistance Times for Door Locks (Section 11.5)

The following discussion details the time that locks must remain intact. Security is all about time delay to defend against an attack, so how long a lock can resist different forms of attack is highly relevant and directly relates to its physical security. This is why time is the first component in the 3T2R rule, as discussed throughout this book:

■ *Covert entry*: Locks shall not open in under 10 minutes against picking, impressioning, and lock bumping.

■ *Lock bumping*: Commercially available or specially designed bump keys can be used. The lock must not be opened in less than 10 minutes. This portion of UL 437 is referred to and incorporated in the BHMA 156.30

high-security standard, but only after several years of disagreement between the industry and parties interested in the standards formation process.

▪ *Forced entry*: The sequence for forced-entry tests is irrelevant, nor are there many methods to apply. Samples may be tested for several techniques, or a new specimen may be utilized for each procedure. A lock shall not open in less than 5 minutes against the following types of forced entry attacks:

  ▪ *Forcing*: By forcing a lock, you're attempting to open it by applying rotary forces, using the test tools in the keyway, exposed parts of the cylinder, and lock assembly.

  ▪ *Drilling*: A drill and drill bits can be employed to drill the plug, any exposed part of the lock, or parts of the lock assembly. Drilling tests include using different size bits such as 1/8, 3/16, and 1/4 of an inch. Tests may include reaming the material in the keyway and from the plug so that the pins or tumblers can be exposed or removed from their location for access to the tailpiece or cam. Drilling by attacking the shear line and creating a new one may also be accomplished.

  ▪ *Sawing*: A saw can cut critical lock parts, including the plug body, lock bolt, or other parts.

  ▪ *Prying*: Specified tools can be utilized to pry the lock bolt away from the strike opening on a doorframe or assembly. This may also be defined as "jimmying" the door.

  ▪ *Pulling*: Locks can be opened by pulling the plug, the lock's body, the bolt, or other critical components.

  ▪ *Driving*: Driving of the plug, body, lock bolt, or other critical parts is involved in this attack type.

  ▪ *Other methods*: Other methods that involve small hand tools may be employed.

BHMA/ANSI 156.30 High-Security Standard

The BHMA, in conjunction with the ANSI, developed two primary standards related to locks: 156.5 (for conventional auxiliary locks and cylinders) and 156.30 (for high-security locks). Unlike UL, independent laboratories and lock manufacturers conduct compliance testing for the BHMA/ANSI standards.

The BHMA 156.30 standard defines tests for mechanical, electromechanical, and electronic high-security locks. The included performance-based requirements encompass keys, credentials, movable detainers, electronic-control devices, a lock's tailpiece or cam, and electronic output ports.

There are three tenets of high security: protection against forced entry, protection against surreptitious/covert entry, and key control. All three criteria must be met for a lock to be rated for high-security implementation. In contrast, a close examination of the UL 437 standard reveals that only two criteria are present; key control is neither addressed nor required.

The BHMA 156.30 standard requires that a lock must resist the defined forced-entry attempts for 5 minutes and surreptitious attacks for a minimum of 10 or 15 minutes (depending on the security level).

Three critical sections are enumerated in 156.30:

1. *Section 5*: Key control

2. *Section 6*: Destructive testing

3. *Section 7*: Surreptitious entry resistance tests

Section 5: Key Control

Three levels of key control are specified in the BHMA standard, and they relate to the availability of blanks, legal patent protection, and factory control of blank and cut keys. This standard addresses mechanical keys, electronic access-control system credentials, audit trails, and time-zoning capabilities. It is intended to prevent or limit the availability of blanks, keys, cut keys, or credentials by unauthorized individuals. The standard requires 500,000, 1 million, or 10 million theoretical changes (*differs*).

Visual key control, cylinder identification, and direct-bitting coding aren't allowed for high-security cylinders. Any markings on locks and keys that provide information about the system are prohibited. The rationale is that if any information is provided on any lock part or key, that data can be decoded to possibly provide insight into how the system has been programmed and the way in which master keys have been defined and their hierarchy established. If enough keys are compared, it's possible to produce change keys and master keys to defeat an entire system. It's especially critical to never stamp keys with direct code numbers that specifically identify the bitting values for individual keys.

In the lowest security level (C), blank keys aren't commercially available from a source other than the factory or authorized agent. Internal controls must be set in place to ensure that the manufacturer properly controls key blanks and their distribution.

The intermediate security level (B) adds the requirement to protect blanks through patents, copyright, and other legal constraints and remedies.

The highest security level (A) of key control considers the requirements for the lower two levels. It specifies that the factory can only cut keys on valid authorization of the designated individual at the user's location. There are equivalent requirements for electronic credentials, including audit-trail and time-zoning options.

Section 6: Destructive Testing

Destructive testing for forced-entry methods encompasses four categories under this standard and defines three security levels (A, B, C). A is the highest level. Under this test, plugs in mechanical or electronic cylinders are evaluated for their resistance to pulling, impact, torque, and drilling. Locks must not yield to these forms of force for a minimum of 5 minutes. The pull test also requires a special screw to be inserted into the keyway and force applied to break the plug or gain access to other critical mechanisms.

Drill Resistance

Cylinders are tested against drilling with bits up to 3/8 inch in diameter, with a rotation speed of up to 900 rpm for up to 5 minutes. The plug must not be able to be turned after the tests.

Key Changes

The standard specifies three levels of security associated with key changes and requires 500,000, 1 million, or 10 million theoretical changes.

Section 7: Surreptitious-Entry Resistance

To receive a high-security rating, there are five test criteria and three security levels for surreptitious-entry-resistance testing. The criteria relate to key changes and differs (tolerance between depth increments), mechanical bitting, allowable differences between two adjacent depths (MACS2), and pick and manipulation resistance. MACS stands for maximum adjacent cut specifications. It defines the maximum allowable physical distance between adjacent cuts so the key will work properly when inserted into the keyway. The requirements in this portion of the standard also ensure the inability to identify the dimensions of pins by a visual inspection or with probes, shims, or another manual measurement tool.

Manipulation and Mechanical Pick Resistance

There are two classifications in this protocol: decoding and pick resistance. Locks must resist picking and decoding attacks for at least 10 minutes (as specified in UL 437) for the lower two security levels and at least 15 minutes for the highest security level (A). This standard classifies lock bumping as a subset of pick resistance and relies on the reference in UL 437 for its definition and requirements that a lock shall withstand a bumping attack for a minimum of 10 minutes.

Decoding

This requirement relates to determining the correct key's bitting values by visually observing the pin tumblers through the keyway or other openings in the cylinder face. The standard contemplates that the manufacturer won't define or alter the value of any pin tumbler or detainer so that its value can be differentiated from any other in the lock. Typically, pins may be color-coded by their length. This isn't permitted under the standard.

In higher-level classifications, the effectiveness of shims, probes, and other manual measuring tools must be minimized. In the highest security classification, the effectiveness of electronic measuring tools must be considered. These include piezo measurement devices that compute the length of pin tumblers electronically.

> **NOTE**   Piezo measurement devices use ultrasonic sound waves to "ping" and measure each pin to determine its length. The resulting data, which can be almost instantly derived, can lead to the production of the bitting codes of hundreds of different locks and manufacturers' products. These devices are discussed further in Part IV.

Pick Resistance

Pick resistance addresses three critical issues: security pins, paracentric keyways, and balanced or graduated drivers or top pins (to prevent the use of comb picks). The standard also identifies certain forms of attacks for electronic locks, including electrostatic discharge, overvoltage, magnetic fields, and conductive liquids.

The BHMA 156.30 standard requires that at least two security pins be placed in the lock to increase resistance to picking. Paracentric keyways are keyways that are physically designed to restrict the vertical movement of picks within a keyway. They do so by placing wards in the keyway that cross the centerline to block the movement of any manipulation tool. Finally, the standard also requires that the length of each pin stack (i.e., bottom pin, top pin, and spring) be at least one depth increment longer than the overall length of the chamber to prevent comb picking. As explained in Part IV, comb picking is a method to force all of the bottom pins upward into the upper chamber to create another shear line. Many manufacturers are unfamiliar with the concept, which can lead to an extremely simple way to bypass a pin tumbler lock. I have used this technique to bypass some of the highest-security locks because the manufacturer did not compute the overall length of the bottom and top pins to prevent both pins from being forced into the upper chambers.

The lock must resist picking for up to 15 minutes, depending on the security level.

Attacks on Electronic Cylinders

Electromechanical and electronic locks are growing in popularity in many parts of the world. Appropriate testing parameters are required to ensure that they are secure against many attack forms. I submit, based on personal experience in circumventing several electronic-based systems, that the current standards may not address these concerns and that added testing protocols are needed, including against forms of hybrid attacks and shim insertion to reach critical components:

- *Electrostatic discharge (ESD) and magnetic tests*: The standard requires electrostatic discharge, overvoltage, and magnetic-field testing to ensure that the lock can't be opened within specified parameters.

- *Conductive liquid testing*: The lock shall be tested against the insertion of a liquid to affect the internal electronics. It must remain locked for a minimum of 15 minutes to meet the standard.

- *Rapping test*: The lock mustn't be subject to rapping with a correct key but not having the correct electronic credential.

- *Mechanical security tolerance test*: The lock must be tested with keys bitted for one tumbler and one depth increment above and below its proper depth coding to be considered up to standard. This is a test that is equivalent to protection against tryout keys.

BHMA 156.5 Cylinders and Input Devices for Locks

This standard can be considered the companion to 156.30 because it specifies operational and security requirements for mechanical cylinders, electrified input devices, and push-button mechanisms. It defines three grade qualifications and incorporates security requirements defined in UL 437 and high-security protections in 156.30. BHMA 156.5 tests against operational cycle tests, cylinder plug pulling, plug torque, and key strength. It also requires an analysis of UL 437 drilling and picking.

Operational Tests Before and After Cycle Tests

Operational testing ensures that a lock can be opened and locked before and after testing is accomplished. The purpose is to ensure that multiple operations don't affect how the lock works, pursuant to its specifications:

- *Force to insert a key into the keyway and retract it*: 3 to 5 pounds of force (lbf)
- *Torque to rotate the cylinder plug*: 18 to 36 ounce-force inches (ozf-in), depending on the grade
- *Force to insert key after cycle test*: 5 to 10 lbf
- *Force to extract key*: 6 to 10 lbf
- *Torque to rotate cylinder plug*: For all Grade 1, 13 lb-in

Cycle Test

Cycle testing is just what the name implies: the number of operations performed against a lock to ensure it continues to work. Grades 1 and 1A require that a lock operate properly after being opened and locked 40,000 times. Grade 2 is half that number, and Grade 3 only requires 10,000 operations or cycles to pass:

Grades 1 and 1A: 40,000. Grade 2: 20,000. Grade 3: 10,000

Strength Tests

Strength testing measures how strong the lock is and how resistant it is to the application of force. Measurements are defined as pound-feet (lbf) and pound-inches (lb-in):

- *Cylinder body or housing tension*: Grade 1: 3,600 lbf. Grade 2: 2,500 lbf. Grade 3: 1,000 lbf
- *Cylinder or housing torque*: Grade 1: 120 lbf-ft. Grade 2: 80 lbf-ft. Grade 3: 40 lbf-ft
- *Plug pulling*: Grades 1 and 1A: 500 lbf. Grade 2: 300 lbf. Grade 3: 250 lbf
- *Plug torque*: Grades 1 and 1A 300 lbf-in. Grade 2: 150 lbf-in. Grade 3: 120 lbf-in
- *Drilling and picking*: UL 437 and Grade 1 requirements
- *Input device pulling*: Grade 1: 2,500 lbf. Grade 2: 1,000 lbf. and Grade 3: 500 lbf
- *Input device torque tests*: Grades 1 and 1A: 300 lbf-in. Grade 2: 150 lbf-in. Grade 3: 120 lbf
- Key (credential) strength test
- Key freefall strength test
- Key water resistance test

Electrified Input Devices

The standard provides operational tests to measure the force to extract a key or credentials from a keyway and torque to rotate the plug within a cylinder. It also specifies cycle tests for rotating and inserting input devices.

Security tests for electrified input devices include tests for the following:

- Overvoltage
- ESD immunity
- Wrong code entered

Deficiencies in the UL 437, BHMA 156.30, and 156.5 Standards

Neither UL nor BHMA addresses the problem of mechanical bypass if the attack doesn't directly involve picking, bumping, or manipulating detainers; nor do they anticipate hybrid attacks. This is a real-world problem because certain relatively simple techniques can circumvent one or more levels of security for Grade 1 (BHMA 156.5) and high-security cylinders. The use of wires, shims, magnetic fields, and other techniques must be more thoroughly addressed in the standards.

The scope of any standard should clearly state that it may not encompass all attack vectors and may not reflect the current state-of-the-art in compromise methods. It should also disclaim any liability and indicate that locks that have received a high-security rating may not meet the requirements subsequently if they are tested after a new attack is discovered or developed.

UL 437 Failures to Identify Vulnerabilities and Issues in Testing Protocols

I submit that there are significant deficiencies in the UL 437 standard that allow locks to be rated under the current protocols but don't anticipate or protect against certain forced and covert entry methods. All high-security locks advertise the UL rating as a representation to the public of their protections. UL 437 isn't a high-security standard but rather a higher level of attack resistance.

The standard fails to allow for methods employed by criminals who may utilize advanced techniques or a combination of methods that may not have been contemplated by those who drafted the test protocols and resistance levels. The standard essentially excludes all others by defining specific tests and tools that must be employed. However, criminals don't follow the rules established in the

UL protocols; they just open locks, containers, vaults, and strong rooms. Many issues regarding lock design and testing protocols are simply not addressed in UL 437.

Why neither UL nor BHMA define security levels in terms of time and expertise can't be understood and is illogical. For example, if there were three security levels, and the commensurate resistance in terms of time and expertise were defined, it shouldn't make any difference how the attack occurred. The relevant issue is whether the lock or hardware is compromised.

To reiterate, lock designs and testing protocols are simply not covered in UL 437. This point was graphically demonstrated in a New York bank burglary where more than $700,000 was stolen by thieves who compromised a strong room rated to require a minimum of 30 minutes to make a small hole in the wall. During their endeavor, the thieves started a fire to which the New York Fire Department (NYFD) responded. It took NYFD exactly 4 minutes to cut a large hole in the strong room wall that UL had certified to be resistant to attack for substantially longer.

In another case, New Jersey CitySafe experts verified similar results. In that case, the high-security vault in a large jewelry store in Manhattan was attacked, and burglars easily penetrated the walls. It turned out that wood, rather than steel, was employed as the barrier material to save money during construction. Unfortunately, bugs had gotten into the wood and essentially eaten the material, so after a few years there was nothing but sawdust to act as a barrier against thieves.

Key Control

Key control protects keys and key blanks from access, duplication, and replication. This protection must encompass mechanical, legal, and tactical considerations. See the landmark cases of *Best v. Ilco* (1995) regarding the protection of keyway design patents, *Chicago Lock v. Fanberg* (1982), and *Medeco v. Swiderek* (1981) concerning the ownership of key codes discussed in Parts III and V. Almost any mechanical key can be compromised for high-security locks. Patent protection won't prevent the illegal duplication or replication of keys but may restrict the ability of an unauthorized supplier to make such blanks available commercially or otherwise.

Pick, Bumping, and Impressioning Resistance

Picking, bumping, and impressioning techniques are considered in the UL standard. Special decoders, picks, electromechanical pick guns, borescopes, and other tools are omitted. UL 437 allows for picking tools designed for a specific lock, however.

The UL standard doesn't define *picking* but states that "any technique can be used to align the detainers." It limits such tools to those commercially available and provides that an ALOA-certified locksmith of 5 years must conduct the tests. This definition is flawed, however, because it doesn't contemplate special picking tools that may not be commercially available to locksmiths but may be purchased by government agents and through unauthorized supply channels. Many tools described in Part IV for bypassing high-security locks are neither commercially available nor known to the locksmith community. But the locks the locksmiths can defeat are installed to protect those very same government and commercial facilities. This standard appears to apply only to attacks where the intruder may have limited sophistication or access to specialized picking tools. In many cases, my colleagues and I have designed our own tools to circumvent a specific lock that we are analyzing.

One example is a tool that can be purchased to bypass three different generations of Mul-T-Lock UL-rated cylinders. Many locksmiths weren't aware of the availability of this pick, which allows for the bypass of UL-certified cylinders within a minute or two. Suppose those conducting covert-entry resistance tests are unaware of its existence as well. In that case, they're certifying locks that can be bypassed in well under the minimum times specified in the standard. In either event, a serious problem exists because the UL 437 certification represents to the consumer and the security community that these locks will be impervious or highly resistant to picking for 10 minutes.

Complex Forms of Picking

It is unclear whether the UL standard addresses advanced and complex picking forms, even though the language states "any method to manipulate the detainers." To pick a Medeco lock, for example, it's required that one completes certain preliminary steps regarding the rotation angles that constitute the sidebar code. It's unclear whether this picking mode would be included in UL 437 because it can involve advanced picking forms with keys specially created for Medeco cylinders. The language of UL 437 never contemplated this technique because the Medeco attack requires four special keys. Whether this particular method of attack constitutes the form of picking defined in the standard is important because many Medeco BIAXIAL and m3 cylinders can be reliably and rapidly picked if the correct procedures are followed. This lock is perhaps the most popular high-security lock in the United States and is UL-certified. The failure of the standard to address this hybrid method of attack is significant.

The standard also doesn't address the compromise of interchangeable core cylinders. They can be bumped and picked to the control shear line and the core removed. If the key code for the control key can be decoded, the entire system can be compromised.

Expertise Level of Those Performing Tests

In certain cases, the attacker is expected to possess special training and expertise in bypassing a particular lock type. High-security cylinders are specified for their increased tolerances, workmanship quality, materials, and resistance to forced and covert entry. They're designed to protect high-value and critical targets. Suppose a facility is selected for attack by experienced criminals, saboteurs, or spies. In that case, they'll likely possess the required expertise to open the locks if a vulnerability can be exploited. The facility protection officer often selects locking hardware based largely on its UL or BHMA/ANSI security rating. This rating guarantees that it will significantly resist various forced and covert entry methods that may be anticipated in an attack. But in many cases, this isn't true.

ALOA certification doesn't ensure the competence required to attack a specific lock. In my experience, the UL 437 certification only indicates quality and security. Some methods of compromising cylinders detailed later in this text require little expertise or training once the bypass concept is understood. Others, however, require more proficiency. The significant issue for UL is whether it intends its standard to apply to expert attacks. If so, it should rewrite UL 437 to ensure that it protects against real threats and that the individuals who conduct the tests are qualified.

I submit and have publicly suggested that if lock manufacturers utilized the expertise of some of the sports lock-picking groups, such as members of The Open Organization of Lock Pickers (Toool) in the Netherlands and those who present at DefCon, they might more thoroughly understand the potential security vulnerabilities of their locks and be able to rectify them before the public is placed at risk.

Forced-Entry Resistance

The UL standard specifies the tools that can be employed to test for forced-entry resistance. Several forced attacks have been developed to access certain high-security cylinders within seconds. These locks are rated as compliant with UL 437. Such techniques are examined in subsequent chapters and can result in the complete bypass of all levels of security for certain locks.

Reliance on UL Standards: No Liability

UL assumes no liability whatsoever for reliance on its standards and clearly states that it has employed its best efforts to test cylinders at the time of certification. Still, it can't be responsible for any detriment from deploying certified locks. Protocols are only based on state-of-the-art judgment when the standard was approved. Fair enough, but UL 437 doesn't consider new attack methods like those developed for Medeco and other high-security locks. Periodic UL reviews to ensure that current production locks are complying don't solve the problem posed by new compromise methods unless the standards are routinely updated through the STP review process.

Bump Keys

The industry now recognizes that bump keys seriously threaten conventional and high-security locks. Any standard must adequately address different expertise levels of attack. A "standard" bump key will *never* open any high-security cylinder that contains any form of a sidebar. If a bumping standard is only defined in terms of conventional bump keys, it simply won't address the real issue.

This problem was highlighted in 2006 (and the extensive media attention that resulted from disclosures) in reports about the vulnerability of pin tumbler locks from lock bumping in Europe and the United States. I published a detailed technical and legal analysis of bumping in 2006. UL 437 was finally updated in 2015 to include tests for bumping.

In addition, an ASTM standard was developed over 10 years ago and should be integrated in UL 437 and BHMA 156.30. It has never happened because industry representatives decided not to adopt it. The standard provided for "professional locksmiths" to test five locks, with each of three locksmiths using both a "pull" and "push" bump key. (See Part IV for a more detailed analysis of bump keys' design, construction, and use for specific attacks.)

ASTM testing standard F883-09, Section 9.6, defines the grades, each requiring 20 bump attempts by each locksmith, 10 with each type of key for 60 bump attempts to attain a grade. If all 60 attempts are unsuccessful, the lock passes that specific grade. Bumping is a real threat to both conventional and high-security mechanisms. The problem with defining a standard for such an attack is that many variables are involved in opening a lock, including the attacker's expertise, the condition and age of the lock, and the type of bump key employed. These issues are discussed more thoroughly in Part IV.

Decoding Attacks

UL 437 is silent about attacks based on decoding internal components and developing intelligence from the information derived from such techniques. Certain lock characteristics can be observed without disassembly, and the information that results can often be used to circumvent the lock's security. The BHMA/ANSI 156.30 standard addresses this issue on a very basic level but doesn't go far enough. The UL standard is essentially silent regarding protecting the lock from such attacks.

Key Control and 3D-Printed Keys

UL 437 is also silent regarding any issues related to key control; for this reason, it doesn't constitute a high-security standard. It doesn't address the ability to compromise high-security locks by copying, replicating, or simulating patent-protected keys, although this topic is in the BHMA 156.30 standard to a limited extent. Key control is one of three primary criteria defining a high-security lock because the ability to compromise legally protected keys can be critical in certain forms of attack, including bumping, picking, and extrapolating the top-level master key.

Testing Deficiencies in the BHMA 156.30 Standard

Even the 2020 release of the latest BHMA 156.30 standard fails to consider more sophisticated forms of attack that would be expected to occur against high-security cylinders. The standard specifies the types of tests that will be performed but fails to address methods and techniques (as with UL) that allow many high-security-rated cylinders and systems to be bypassed, sometimes within seconds. Manufacturers may be unaware of such bypass techniques, may ignore them, may know about them and misrepresent the security ramifications to customers, or may simply be unable to make changes in the mechanical design to prevent bypass. The public is misled and at risk if the standard doesn't address such circumvention methods.

The following sections about testing deficiencies are included here so that design engineers and VA teams can target them to confirm that such attacks are contemplated and dealt with in current and future designs.

Forced Entry

The 156.30 standard defines certain tests to resist the application of force on lock bodies and plugs. These tests involve using torque, slam-hammers, and drilling and inserting special screws to pull or break plugs apart. However, the standard should approve using specialized carbide-, boron-, titanium-, tungsten-, cobalt-, or titanium nitride-coated or diamond-tipped drill bits for testing anti-drill lock features. The standard should specify that drills designed to penetrate hard steels and alloys specifically can be used, as well as high-speed drills and specified drill-motor power ratings.

The standard should address the following forced-entry issues that are presently not covered, described, or contemplated:

- *Access to critical components through the keyway*: My colleagues and I have successfully attacked many locks through the keyway by releasing the mechanisms controlled by the tailpiece or removing the entire plug assembly by accessing retaining pins.

- *Access to the tailpiece through the keyway*: If the keyway is open-ended, this can be a simple operation. If the end of the keyway is open, the tailpiece may be subject to manipulation directly. If closed, I've found it simple to punch through some endcaps.

- *Unprotected endcap fasteners*: This is especially important if the endcap's screws can be easily sheared by inserting a steel shim into the keyway's end and then applying repeated hammer blows. If the screws can be broken loose, access to the critical mechanism the endcap controls can be achieved, as was the case with the Medeco Maxum high-security deadbolt. Once the two endcap screws were sheared, a small screwdriver was inserted through the keyway to manipulate the tailpiece and open the lock.

- *Milling of special steel keys with A2 tool steel or 4140 or equivalent to replicate and bypass the keyway wards*: If extreme torque is applied, it may destroy the internal locking elements.

- *Lack of consideration for reverse-picking the lock once the endcap and tailpiece screws have been neutralized*: During reverse lock picking, a pull pressure is applied to the plug, and then the lock is picked to set the pins at the shear line. Once all the pins are set, the plug can be fully removed, and a screwdriver can be utilized to control the mechanism that releases the deadbolt or latch. This attack is discussed in Part VI and involved the Medeco Maxum deadbolt cylinder.

- *No protection against drilling through areas not protected by anti-drill pins to access critical locking components*: This is not even considered. Drill pins are placed at critical points to protect against drilling the shear line or sidebar. It is often possible to bypass such pins with shims where no protection is provided because the design team never considered a threat.

- *Access to critical internal areas by drilling through plastic*: Plastic is often used for internal parts, especially in electronic cylinders. It can be a target for inserting shims to manipulate critical internal locking components.

Mechanical Bypass of Locking Mechanisms

The Medeco Maxum deadbolt is listed as meeting Grade 1 (in 156.5) and is supplied with a high-security cylinder. The cylinder and deadbolt hardware could be bypassed in about 30 seconds, yet the consumer believed both had been tested to the 156.30 standard's requirements. The lock was redesigned once the problem was presented to Medeco in 2007.

The standard fails to test for certain methods to bypass locking mechanisms mechanically by force as well as hybrid attacks. Most engineers fail to consider the first rule in designing a cylinder and related components: *The key never unlocks the lock; it merely actuates the mechanism that controls the bolt, latch, or other devices.* Many locks and their sophisticated security features can be easily bypassed through mechanical means with or without force. The case example in Part VI describing the Medeco Maxum deadbolt is a perfect example. Thirty seconds, a piece of spring steel, and a two-dollar screwdriver were all that was needed to circumvent that mechanism, which was and is considered the best deadbolt for commercial and residential use in the United States.

Audit Trail for Electronic Locks

An audit trail should record every time the lock is opened. In many cases, there are methods to unlock the mechanism without recording an audit trail because the software that controls the blocking element is bypassed. The standard simply isn't sufficient to record valid and invalid or unsuccessful attempts.

Keys and Key Control

The standard fails to address the simulation of keys. It speaks about the physical protection and control of key blanks but doesn't address real-world attacks. The ability to replicate or simulate restricted keys can be critical to advanced bumping and picking attacks and the copying of keys that are supposed to be secure.

The standard is intended to prevent or limit the availability of blanks, keys, cut keys, or credentials by unauthorized individuals. However, it should specify that the generation, replication, simulation, or duplication of keys should be prevented or made difficult. There is no reference to producing 3D-printed blanks and cut keys in the standard. The capability to produce blanks from different materials, including thin brass that bypasses wards within the keyway or plastic that can reproduce the bitting pattern of the correct key, is also not addressed. There's also no provision for key control to prevent attacks against locks via the following:

- Hybrid attacks against mechanical mortise cylinders using plastic keys with a correct bitting combination and keyway modification to change their geometry to bypass a sidebar
- Hybrid attacks against electromechanical locks using plastic or thin metal keys to bypass secondary locking systems such as sidebars

- Hybrid attacks against keys with side bit milling and other secondary security layers by splitting the protective mechanisms to neutralize each layer separately

- Bypass of interactive movable elements within key blades using shims, wires, and even paper clips

- Using universal key-generation systems to create bitting patterns from extremely thin metal sheets that have been precut to allow for the rapid creation of any bitting depth for any keyway

- Exploit tolerances between depth increments by bumping a key with bitting depths above or below the target pin length

- Using actual key changes and duplicate or invalid bitting patterns in determining the actual versus theoretical differs

- Using plastic bitting inserts on restricted key blanks, especially those involving dimple locks

- Higher technical security controls for unsecure key cards issued by the manufacturer, to prevent ordering restricted keys to be cut

- Hybrid attacks utilizing correctly bitted keys in electromechanical cylinders, coupled with wires and shims, to access blocking elements

- Hybrid attacks applying torque to a plug to exploit weaknesses in detainers by inserting portions of a key blade to move the detainers to their most vulnerable position where there's minimal blocking of rotation of the plug

Decoding

The decoding reference isn't specific enough to encompass certain forms of intelligence gathering about internal components within a lock. A sidebar lock can provide several indications as to the pin tumbler position and the sidebar code. In addition, there are many methods and tools to decipher information about the bitting pattern of a key or measurement of pin tumblers, wafers, or discs. These sources of data can be derived and categorized by access to the cylinder internally and from the cylinder without disassembly.

The standard does address decoding resistance in terms of limiting information gathering about the correct key dimensions via visual inspection through the keyway or other openings using manual or electronic measuring. Specifications presently refer to the gathering of information about the color, length, and dimensions of detainers. The standard should also include data about the angles of pin tumblers (if applicable) or other locking components and their shape, the location of gates and sidebars, and other critical information that allows the lock to be opened in less than 10 or 15 minutes.

Data From Within the Lock

The standard should address the following issues:

- Shims and wires measuring the length of pins, gate positions, and distance to the shear line
- The use of a borescope, otoscope, ophthalmoscope, or other optical decoding method in terms of lock security
- Visual inspection from outside the keyway
- Specially designed decoding tools using wire probes, special key blanks, cameras, ultrasonics, piezo crystals, and decoding systems to determine the shear-line set position
- Impressioning materials
- Sound to determine pin length
- Pin and cam decoders to determine when pins are at the shear line
- Feeler keys
- Detection of true and false gates and any patterns that can yield information about the correct bitting depth to pick or generate a key
- Pick/decoder combination tools that can open the lock and then produce the bitting values to reproduce the key
- Electronic decoding circuits that can read codes from within the lock, including devices such as computers with programs designed to decrypt internal algorithms and opening devices that have been designed to immediately determine the unlock codes for locks and safes

Data From Sources Outside the Cylinder

Critical information can be obtained from sources other than those within the lock. The following can enable the decoding of a system and the production of keys that will match or replicate bitting values for detainers:

- Visual observation and decoding of keys, bitting, and the first two or three pins through the keyway
- Visual observation with a borescope to determine wafer and slider positions
- The ability to decode master key systems from a sufficient sample of change keys
- The ability to disassemble the lock and decode the bitting code
- Access to bitting lists
- Using sound amplification devices to listen to pin tumblers, levers, or wafers setting at the shear line

Pick Resistance

There are several picking techniques that the standard doesn't properly address or identify and that my colleagues and I have successfully employed to open the highest-security cylinders. Design engineers must ensure that their products can't be compromised by methods that are unknown to testing personnel, including the following:

- Impressioning techniques
- Using the laws of physics to bypass electronic locks based on the movement of a worm gear
- Inserting shims into any opening
- Using electronic measurement tools, as well as the new generation of piezo decoders
- Using audio to determine pin tumbler lengths
- Using vibration to move detainers to the correct position
- Using special mechanical and electronic vibration and bumping picks
- Using electromechanical picks
- Bypassing the shear line using core shim decoding tools (described in Part IV)
- Preventing access to critical locking elements with shims via cylinder openings or through data ports or small manufacturing or weep holes to allow moisture drainage
- Overlifting of pin tumblers

For example, the standard only requires that a minimum of one pin stack be set to exceed the overall bore length. In this event, it would be simple to defeat such a system by overlifting all the other pins with a comb pick or injecting ball bearings and then picking the remaining pin. The standard should require that all pins be "balanced" to prevent this method of compromise.

Exploit of Internal Tolerances

The standard fails to examine the ability to exploit internal tolerances to circumvent the depth-increment requirement in Section 7.4. This was one of the critical design deficiencies in the older Medeco cylinder that allowed the exploitation of the bottom pins' rotational tolerance to compromise the system. The failure to adequately address this issue should invalidate any high-security rating of any cylinder wherein such tolerances can be exploited. The standard only identifies the depth-increment tolerance of conventional pin tumblers and doesn't consider side millings or pin rotation that control sidebars. See the case example in Part VI about the code-setting keys used to exploit rotational tolerance in Medeco cylinders.

Electronic Attacks and Testing

Several attacks can be implemented to circumvent and compromise electronic-based locking systems. These modes of attack should be addressed in any high-security standard. I've listed four critical methods that my colleagues have successfully employed:

- *Attacks using electromagnetic pulse (EMP) and radio-frequency (RF) energy should be incorporated.* The standard only addresses ESD and over-voltage attacks and protection. The use of an EMP or RF generator has been shown to be successful against many electronic circuits.

- *Protect printed circuit-board runs from external access.* The standard doesn't address protections against exposed printed circuit-board elements that control local and remote openings or system resets. The manufacturer should prevent access to the electronics that can trigger such events. (In the case examples in Part VI, I demonstrate how I short-circuited the contacts on a commercial and government push-button lock in a few seconds with a straight pin.)

- *Protect all critical integrated circuits (ICs) with potting compounds.* ICs can be destabilized by injecting certain liquids and causing a system reset.

- *Protect access to power leads to motor drives in an electronic cylinder.* All direct and indirect access points to motor drives must be protected to prevent the routing of external power from activating such circuits or motors.

Tools Commercially Available to Locksmiths

The standard should allow for using *any* lockpicking and decoding tools available to anyone, whether through a locksmith distributor, Internet vendor, or another source. This includes picks, feeler picks, decoders, special key blanks, insertable video cameras with special keys, vibrating tools, and combination pick and decoder tools produced by Lishi, Wendt, John Falle, and Lockmasters. Any design should be concerned with resisting attack by such tools, which should be considered critical data based on which the security of a lock is designed. The standard should also refer to data-collection techniques, including electronic, mechanical, optical, shim wire decoding, audio or acoustic, piezo, and impressioning techniques.

Bumping and Rapping Resistance

As discussed, numerous locks are subject to bumping and rapping to move internal components to an unlocked state. Rapping is the application of energy to the *body* of a lock, whereas bumping is focused on channeling the force to the bottom pin tumblers.

Certain designs have implemented *shock fuses* or similar mechanical devices that sense a certain level of energy from bumping or rapping and prevent or block the plug's movement until the fuse is reset. The standard addresses rapping resistance with a correctly bitted key but not with an invalid electronic credential and shock application to the lock body or through the key. It doesn't consider an electronic lock that relies on only an electronic credential and a mechanical key whose only purpose is to turn the plug once the electronic code is verified. I've had considerable success opening such locks because most, if not all, rely on some form of blocking rotor that can move freely. This is also true with various high-security padlocks in which a design error allowed the rotor to be vibrated or rapped into an unlocked position. The standard should clarify its requirements for such designs and occurrences.

Both the BHMA 156.30 and 156.5 standards refer to bumping, but the requirements and established grades of protection don't provide a realistic or valid test or any assurance that any lock grade under the standard offers the stated protection. As noted in Part IV, bumping is a very nonpredictable and often chaotic method of attack due to the laws of physics and its many variables and methodology. Based on my experience and that of my colleagues, a high-security cylinder may be opened by one strike or by many, or it may never open.

Recommendations for a High-Security Standard

I offer the following recommendations for a high-security standard specifying that cylinders offer security against a range of current and potential future attacks, with the understanding that no standard can ever anticipate every challenge:

- Add another level in 156.30 or create an entirely new standard addressing advanced attacks.
- Define what *high-security* means and should mean in a standard, and consider increased threat-level and attack techniques for high-value targets.
- Eliminate the requirement that only ALOA-registered locksmiths are competent to test locks.
- Create a standard that states, regarding covert entry, that if the lock can be opened in 10 or 15 minutes without any damage, regardless of the tools or techniques, it doesn't pass.

- Don't limit the standard to commercially available tools.

- Incorporate mechanical bypass of any kind into the standard.

- Incorporate bumping as a subset of picking.

- Contemplate any hybrid technique with hand-carried tools that can accomplish a forced opening within 5 minutes.

- Don't limit the kinds of tests or types of tools, at least for the highest security standard.

- Incorporate key control criteria that define both organizational and security standards to restrict not only the availability of blanks but also the ability to replicate or simulate them easily.

- Convey the fact that patents don't guarantee the security of keys; they create civil remedies to prohibit copying or manufacturing them.

- Address the issue of the EasyEntrie and other milling machines regarding the duplication, replication, or simulation of blanks.

- Address 3D-printing technology and the ability to integrate high-resolution scanners.

- Address self-service key kiosks, and distinguish non-high-security blanks and key control from consumer-level blanks.

The next chapter analyzes the protection of intellectual property. Lock manufacturers protect their IP with patents, trademarks, and copyrights, but in the case of patents, these only provide limited protection against infringement through civil remedies. Patents may grant exclusive use of inventions and new locks, but they don't prevent criminals from circumventing the security of locks through the unauthorized production of keys or the use of decoding and bypass tools. Remedies for lock manufacturers and actions that can create legal problems are also discussed.

Patents, Security, and the Protection of Intellectual Property

A *patent* is a legal right granted by the federal government to an inventor as compensation for an innovation that benefits society. This right is given for a limited period and grants the holder the legal means to control an invention and its use for up to 20 years. In its simplest legal terms, it's a license to litigate to protect the intellectual property (IP) contained in a patent grant.

High-security lock manufacturers file for patent protection to secure their intellectual property rights and guarantee their inventions a monopoly for a maximum of 20 years. Patents can carve out a space in the industry for new or modified designs and block others from adopting or copying identical or equivalent mechanical or electronic innovations. Patents are essential for designing and manufacturing locks, safes, and related hardware due to the often high investment in engineering, research, development, and manufacturing. Valid patents are often a prerequisite for customers when security is critical.

The life of a patented product is often considered when facility risk managers and security officers consider installing or upgrading a system, due to the costs involved. Patents can offer assurances of legal protection, especially involving key control if restricted blanks with movable or interactive elements or unique security layers are at issue. The ability to legally limit access to blanks and prevent or deter duplication, replication, or simulation of keys can be critical and a compelling reason to upgrade locks to newer designs and technology. Customers view new patents as important because they note current technology and guard against potential infringement by hackers, criminals, and even locksmiths. Such actions can affect a facility's security if a lock manufacturer doesn't vigorously protect its intellectual property and, in turn, customers.

> I directed a major counterfeiting investigation in the United States and Taiwan involving a manufacturer that was producing and importing hundreds of thousands of key blanks that infringed critical patents. Ultimately, the manufacturer refused to prosecute offenders, which left its customers and locksmiths at risk. The manufacturer's failure to act could subject it to liability and lawsuits by major installations due to the created vulnerabilities.

Although every lock manufacturer employs patent counsel, a basic understanding of U.S. patent law's primary tenets and principles is necessary for everyone on a design team due to their potential to compromise early designs and the manufacturer's legal ability to obtain and protect a patent. This chapter isn't intended as a detailed treatise on patent law but rather as an overview of critical issues regarding the requirements for securing and enforcing patents. This knowledge is especially important for those tasked with conceiving new products or modifying existing designs because of the complexities of creating IP that doesn't infringe on other patented products.

Carving out a unique space in the industry requires understanding patent criteria and having a close relationship with competent patent counsel during every process step. A failure to thoroughly understand the intricacies of similar patented designs and claims when analyzing a slightly different invention can invite infringement litigation by other patent holders. Harry C. Miller, a prolific inventor and one of the giants in the U.S. lock industry, aptly observed that very little was new in lock and safe designs, only new combinations of older technology. This observation should be a caution to engineers, as they risk infringing on designs protected by patents or implementing designs that could be considered prior art.

In 2010, I analyzed and tested a new lock design developed to facilitate an instant key-change capability, which was the subject of a patent-infringement lawsuit by Kwikset against Schlage. In 2007, Kwikset was instrumental in bringing to the U.S. and Canadian markets a lock that incorporated SmartKey, which allowed instant rekeying to a different bitting combination. The Schlage lock was named SecureKey. Kwikset alleged false advertising and the infringement of two U.S. patents: 7,213,429, "Re-keyable Lock Assembly," issued on 8 May 2007; and 7,434,431, "Keying System and Method," issued in 2008.

The Schlage design was similar enough to Kwikset that the company was ultimately forced to withdraw its product from the market. This was a very expensive lesson for Schlage in terms of legal costs, bad publicity, and manufacturing and advertising expenses that could have been avoided. If the Schlage design team had worked more closely with patent counsel to understand exactly how the Schlage design could be seen as potentially infringing on the patented Kwikset mechanism, litigation could certainly have been avoided.

Patents and Their Relationship to the Security of an Invention

The federal statutes that set forth the rules and requirements for patents can be found in Title 35 of the United States Code. The United States Patent and Trademark Office (USPTO) in 35 U.S.C. 101 follows three primary threshold criteria for any invention to meet the requirements for patentability:

- Uniqueness
- Novelty
- Nonobviousness

Design engineers and the public often fail to understand that patents have no direct connection with security; nor does a patent examiner assess the security of an invention when determining whether the application meets statutory requirements for issuance.

Whether an applied-for design, machine, or process is "secure" or enhances security is irrelevant regarding patentability. The underlying designs disclosed and described in a patent application are considered in the context of the basic three requirements for patent issuance. In 2003, I was involved in the new patent of a sidebar and an interlocking sliding component in a mechanical lock that provided security. Whether the design could be easily defeated was not in the scope of the review. It would not be considered *unless* the patent was to improve on a prior design where a security vulnerability could be demonstrated and one or more of the claims was to fix or exploit a problem that formed the basis for the new patent. In this case, inserting a paper clip into the keyway could easily and instantly defeat the slider mechanism.

One of the best examples is the series of patents issued for defeating a widely recognized high-security lock produced by Medeco in the United States. My colleague and I filed patents for the process and mechanical keys that allowed these locks to be picked or bumped open, often in seconds. In contrast to the previously cited example involving the sidebar and slider design, the claims in the patents in this case described the security vulnerabilities that had been discovered and how the described inventions exploited them.

There have been many instances where bypass tools have been patented for similar inventions. Still, in most cases, the patent office doesn't consider a claimed invention's underlying security or insecurity. This fundamental premise is often misunderstood by consumers and risk managers who rely on patents to guarantee security. My rule here applies: *Just because something is patented doesn't mean it's secure.* Although claims in a utility patent may describe how the invention improves or enhances security and why it's unique, the examiner doesn't directly rule or offer an opinion as to the actual security of the claims in the context of the invention. Whether the design of a movable element, sidebar, or side bit milling enhances a lock's security is generally not in the purview of the patent process, nor does the patent office have the capability to verify such claims.

Modifications to Existing Patented Products and Security

Lock manufacturers are constantly filing for new patents and design modifications to extend their products' patent protection periods. This is done for both commercial and security reasons. Buyers want to be assured of the latest technology to protect their facilities, employees, assets, and information. Most high-security lock makers strive to improve their products' security, enhance performance, and correct defects found in prior designs. The market continually demands next-generation iterations, so the desire to innovate and invent often places undue pressure on manufacturers and engineers to upgrade their locks. The problem with this scenario is that it's expensive and can lead to decisions driven by marketing departments and sales rather than solid engineering, vulnerability analysis, and testing. The result can be costly and include recalls, security breaches, bad publicity, loss of certifications, and legal liability.

In my experience, design teams must carefully consider any modification of a current design, whether for security, newer options, product enhancement, or simply a new patent filing. Any addition or design change must be carefully analyzed to ensure that there is no direct or indirect impact on security. Such changes can be very subtle and not obvious until discovered by hackers, criminals, or competitors.

History, Origins, Chronology, and Rationale for Patent Laws

The rationale for developing patent law stems from an individual's natural right to enjoy a proprietary interest in their inventions. The patent systems are designed to protect inventions, encourage individuals to invent technology, and stimulate advancements for the benefit of society. In return for patent protection, the law requires full disclosure of the technology protected by the patent so that others can learn from what the patent teaches, which encourages inventors to refine, produce, and market more advanced technology.

Patent law originated in Medieval Europe, where the first known legislation was the Venetian Patent Statute of 19 March 1474 by the Republic of Venice. These codified laws established the concept of IP and recognized the importance of protecting the rights of inventors. The Venetian statute required that the invention be new, useful, and reduced to practice. It granted a 10-year term of protection.

By the seventeenth century, many European countries had enacted patent legislation. The *English Statute of Monopolies*, an act of Parliament, was passed in 1624. It was the first set of statutes that defined patent law. The monarch issued *letters of patent* to confer monopolies over certain industries to skilled craftsmen. Intended to bolster England's economy and promote innovation, the act was seen as landmark legislation to transform England's economy from a feudal to a capitalist one. The act was in effect until the United Kingdom subscribed to the European Patent Convention in 1977, which created a unified patent system.

The statute was copied in various forms by the U.S. colonies to grant monopolies "for such new invention as shall be judged profitable for the country and for such times the general court shall judge meet." By 1787, many states were granting patents. The founding of America and Jeffersonian democracy occurred through the Constitutional Convention in Philadelphia. Patents and copyrights are a form of state-granted monopoly and were included by Alexander Hamilton in the Constitution, even though Jefferson vehemently opposed any form of monopoly. The Constitutional Convention delegates unanimously drafted Article I, Section 8, Clause 8, which held that Congress should have the power "To promote the Progress of Science and useful Arts, by securing for limited Times to Authors and Inventors the exclusive Right to their respective Writings and Discoveries."

The first Congress enacted the first "federal" patent statute, which was signed into law on 10 April 1790 by George Washington. It created a board called the Commissioners for the Promotion of the Useful Arts. This board aimed to "decide whether the invention or discovery was sufficiently useful and important" to deserve a patent. The U.S. patent laws were finally codified in 1952 and became Title 35 of the United States Code.

Relevant International Patent Treaties

There have been five significant conventions and agreements between countries that affect IP rights for inventors in signatory states and provide a basis for the filing of patents. These treaties set the foundation for recognizing patents, copyrights, and trademark rights in many countries, including the United States. One such agreement, the Budapest Treaty (Budapest Treaty on the International Recognition of the Deposit of Microorganisms for Patent Procedure), was signed in 1977 and provided for the establishment of an international depository of microorganisms that could serve as the depository of biological material for patentability in all signatory countries. I'll discuss a few of the others next.

Paris Convention for the Protection of Industrial Property

An international convention in Paris in 1883 was the first major action to help IP creators ensure that their work was protected in other countries. This convention dealt with patents, trademarks, industrial designs, service marks, trade names, and utility models. The original signatories were Belgium, Brazil, France, Guatemala, Italy, the Netherlands, Portugal, El Salvador, Serbia, Spain, and Switzerland. Today there are more than 178 contracting member countries, which means it's one of the most widely adopted treaties in the world.

The convention was a significant step forward in the move to protect IP and had three primary provisions:

- *National treatment*: Regarding industrial property, each state must grant the same protection to the nationals of all contracting states as it grants to its citizens.

- *Right of priority*: For utility patents, a right is provided for filing a standard application in a contracting state. For 12 months from the filing date, an application can be filed in any other contracting state. Priority is given as if it had been filed in the applicant's home jurisdiction. The importance of this provision, even today, is that an applicant seeking protection in multiple countries is *not* required to file all their applications simultaneously but has up to 12 months to file in the countries in which they seek protection.

- *Common rules among contracting states*: Several common rules were defined that all contracting states are required to follow. A patent for the same invention obtains equal protection but is treated as independent for each state. This means any action regarding any patent does not affect or bind any other state, so if a patent is challenged, refused, or terminated, it has no impact on any other state authority. The rules also provide that the inventor has the right to be identified in a patent and that, in certain cases, patents can be judged abandoned if they aren't used.

Patent Cooperation Treaty

In 1970, the Patent Cooperation Treaty (PCT) was signed by 35 countries and open to any country that signed the Paris Convention. The PCT established a centralized filing system and standard application formats, making it simpler for U.S. companies to file foreign patent applications and reducing costs.

TRIPS Agreement: Trade-Related Aspects of Intellectual Property

This 1996 agreement is the most comprehensive IP agreement enacted between countries. It addresses copyright, trademarks, industrial designs, patents, layouts and designs of integrated circuits, trade secrets, and test data. The agreement has three main features:

- *Standards*: TRIPS establishes minimum standards for each member state and requires them to adhere to the Paris and Berne conventions, which became obligations under TRIPS.

- *Enforcement*: The convention requires that all contracting states agree to allow enforcement actions to prevent infringement and enact remedies that will deter acts of infringement. The provisions outline procedures that shall be fair, equitable, and not unreasonably costly or delayed.

- *Dispute resolution*: The agreement specifies the procedures to follow in the case of a dispute between the contracting countries.

Overview: Current U.S. Patent Law

Patent law in the United States is exclusively governed by federal law based on the Patent Act of 1952. It allows inventors to obtain patents on processes, machines, and manufacture, in addition to compositions of new, nonobvious, and useful matter.

In 1982, a federal court reorganization under the Federal Court Improvement Action established the Court of Appeals for the Federal Circuit. All appeals from USPTO decisions are required to go to the Federal Circuit and then to the Supreme Court for further appeal. This court has 12 active federal and senior judges, usually sitting as a three-judge panel.

In 1999, the American Inventors Protection Act became law. This act has many provisions to protect inventors and to put the PTO on a sound business footing based on performance. It's permitted to run like an efficient business, which means a lot of autonomy in management.

Key provisions of the law include the following:

- *Inventors' rights*: This provision helps protect inventors from the deceptive practices of promotional companies. Materially false or fraudulent statements are subject to damages.

- *Patent and trademark fees*: Certain filing, reissue, and initial maintenance fees were modified and reduced. The PTO also had to report to Congress about the changing fee structures to encourage filing by inventors.

- *Defense against charges of patent infringement*: A defense was established for good faith actions by patentees who reduced the subject matter of their invention to practice at least one year before the effective filing date and who could commercially use the subject matter before the filing date.

- *Patent term guarantee*: A term of patents and extensions can be obtained for USPTO activities that interfere with the issuance of a patent due to interference proceedings, secrecy orders, and appellate reviews. Usually, at least a grant of 17 years is provided for diligent applicants.

- *Domestic publication of foreign-filed patent applications*: This portion of the act allows for the publication of patent applications 18 months after filing, with certain exceptions, including a certification that the application has not been and will not be filed in a foreign country.

The Definition of an Invention

Under U.S. law, an *invention* is a "technological advancement that is useful, new, and is not obvious to a person with ordinary skill in the field of technology." Inventions can include a machine, device, method, or process and can even be a new composition or use of an old technology.

Types of Patents

The USPTO issues three patent categories: utility, design, and plant.

Utility Patents

A *utility patent* is the primary type of patent filed by lock manufacturers and is based on technological advances and innovation. This kind of patent relates to how a device operates or is produced or a process for achieving something that has utility.

The subject of a utility patent must result from human activity. Utility patents cover many categories of inventions:

- Manufactured articles
- A machine
- A composition of matter
- A process for making or doing a task or method
- A combination of things
- A new use for an old invention that becomes a process

Design Patents

In contrast to a utility patent, a *design patent* under Sections 171–173 relates to a new and original ornamental shape or surface treatment for an article of manufacture. It's distinguished from a utility patent because it *can't* have utility. A design patent can be copied for unrelated articles or products and must *not* infringe on another design patent. The critical distinction from a utility patent is that it must be primarily ornamental rather than functional. For lock designers, this is important for creating keyways, heads, and distinctive key shapes. Note that key shapes can also be trademarked. Vachette Locks in France is a perfect example. Assa Abloy registered the V Vachette logo and key head with three distinctive colors with the European Union Trademark Information. The open "V" design identifies Vachette everywhere.

Plant Patents

Although not applicable to lock design, a plant patent covers the characteristics of new plants created by grafting or cuttings. A new variety of a plant can also be issued a utility patent.

Patent Rights and Their Value

A patent can be an extremely valuable IP right. Patents can be sold or licensed for royalties or other benefits and can also be employed to block or prevent anyone from utilizing an invention. They're a limited legal right up to 20 years from the filing date. Although the U.S. patent law does grant very specific rights, those rights don't come without peril, as many of my manufacturing clients have learned. Enforcing patent rights can be extremely expensive and sometimes risky.

Specific and critical patent rights can include (or limit) the following:

■ Granting an individual or organization sole control over patented technology.

■ Unlimited subjectability to any other individual or entity who may own a "dominant" patent and superior rights relating to the same subject matter.

■ The right to ask a court to stop another from potential infringement may be subject to someone's higher right because there's no *absolute* right to do anything with an invention. The right conferred by a patent only applies to preventing someone else from using, manufacturing, selling, licensing, or exploiting what is precisely covered in the patent claims.

■ The granting of a patent provides the inventors with the right to exclude all others from manufacturing, selling, making, using, offering for sale, or importing into the U.S. the patented invention. For injunctive relief and monetary damages, suits may be filed against infringers in federal district court.

Filing and Obtaining a Patent in the United States

U.S. patent applications are filed with the USPTO and must contain a complete specification that can be understood without requiring experimentation by skilled artisans. The filed application is said to be "prosecuted" at the patent office and is known as the patent "instrument." The subject matter that can form the basis of a utility patent is considered "useful arts." It relates to someone who "invents or discovers any new and useful process, machine, manufacture, or any composition of matter or any new or useful improvement thereof."

There are two classes of patent applications: provisional and nonprovisional. *Provisional applications* are filed to timestamp an invention to secure priority until the formal *nonprovisional* application is filed. Complete disclosure of an invention is required in a provisional application to establish such a time priority. Let's break these classes down further.

Provisional Applications

The rationale for filing a provisional application includes numerous advantages:

- It's good for one year.
- A patent can't be granted from this filing. It's simply a way to disclose an invention in contemplation for filing a nonprovisional formal application.
- The invention described in the application is kept secret for a limited period, regardless of whether it's followed up with a nonprovisional application.
- It must be followed with the nonprovisional application within one year.
- It allows time to add claims and refine an invention before a nonprovisional application is filed.
- The application is initially less expensive than a formal, nonprovisional application.
- It can be less detailed than a nonprovisional application.
- It allows for filing multiple related applications within one year, especially if it's for making changes, updates, or improvements.
- It establishes a record of the invention.

Nonprovisional Applications

A *nonprovisional application* is a formal, detailed, and complete instrument to file for a patent. It must contain all the required components to be considered for examination. This application type is the most expensive and direct way to secure a patent. It's important to note that claims and improvements can't be added once this application is filed. Anyone concerned about disclosing an invention in an application should request a nonpublication application. Otherwise, competitors are placed on notice as to filings.

Critical Steps to Take Before Filing a Nonprovisional Application

Note that much of what is described in this section became less important after 2013, when the "first to file" rule was introduced into the U.S. patent law. However, I still recommend these practices.

When any IP is contemplated, researched, and developed, it's vital to document all aspects of the invention's progress, from initial conception to reduction to practice. Very detailed notes should be contained in a bound notebook in ink, and drawings should be kept proving who conceived the invention first, along with who worked on it and when. Inventive activities must be carefully documented and corroborated to provide sufficient evidence of conception, reduction to practice, and diligence, especially when two separate inventors make the same claims. The motive for this requirement is to prevent fraud and subsequent challenges.

The "first to file" requirement places a premium on early filing and is a good reason to submit a provisional application.

It's important to develop documentation that will provide evidence of the date of first conception and, when reduced to practice, submit a disclosure document to be filed with the USPTO. This documentation will be stored for two years and can be referred to in a formal filing for up to two years. Note that this isn't an official filing, but some "patent help" companies may falsely advertise this procedure as official.

The patent process usually begins with filing a provisional application, which timestamps the invention and allows one more year to file the formal nonprovisional instrument. The post office can date-stamp notes to confirm when mailing the application is completed. Always remember that the goal is a legally admissible document.

Specific Legal Filing Requirements

There are certain primary requirements for filing an application, including these:

- The applicant must include the inventor and possibly the employer.
- The invention must have been conceived by the listed inventor or inventors.
- The applicant must be the first to file in the United States. Several years ago, the law was that the first to invent took priority, but that requirement was changed to promote technological advancements and force early disclosures.

- The inventor can't obtain a foreign patent before filing a U.S. application. The exception is if the foreign application was filed one year or less *before* the U.S. application.

- An invention can be abandoned by failure to pursue a patent because of an unduly long period before filing. Placing the invention for sale can also invalidate a patent application.

Proper Naming and Identification of the Inventor

Legal steps must be taken from the beginning to protect the IP rights of creation and ownership. Nondisclosure agreements (NDAs) and the assignment of IP rights should always be set in place for employees and individuals involved in developing or tweaking prototypes or models. This is extremely important for manufacturers because every design engineer or employee who has anything to do with the development of the invention and who provides advice or suggestions may have legal rights as a contributor.

A sworn declaration must be filed with the application to identify each person who conceived the invention, including those involved in developing or refining prototypes or models. This is very important, especially for manufacturers, because any contributor can have rights equal to those of everyone involved in the creation process. Note that there's a difference between ownership of an invention and contributions.

Only the actual inventor can apply for a patent. Thus, no patent can be issued if an individual "derived" the invention from another person. Manufacturers must be extremely careful to ensure that no person or employee gives an idea or conception to another who then claims to be the inventor to apply.

Companies should routinely require their employees to transfer their IP rights, usually during the hiring process. Anyone involved in the creation process, including outside consultants, must agree to assign their rights to the company. It is a good idea for any employee handbook to address these issues and specify that failure to comply can result in termination.

Companies should verify with their counsel the following forms and practices to protect IP, which include not only patents but also copyrights and trademarks that may involve input from anyone who has contributed to the creation process:

- *Employment agreements*: All agreements should include IP assignments and NDAs.

- *Shop right*: This right under the patent statutes protects the company and allows it to use an invention if any part of it was created with company facilities.

- *Partnership agreement*: Either formal or informal, this agreement creates a legal relationship and partnership in which the IP belongs to everyone who has a similar interest in the business arrangement.

- *Government assistance*: If any federal monies, grants, or funding are involved in developing a project, the United States may be entitled to IP rights and profits.

- *Former employees*: A former employee who refuses to cooperate and assign IP rights can be troublesome, so all legal documents must be completed to avoid a legal controversy. For example, I was involved in a triple homicide case in which the killer claimed rights to a patent developed by one of his victims. His sole motivation was revenge because he wasn't credited for developing IP rights in a project. Although this was an extreme case, it's a good example of what can go wrong.

Primary Parts of a Patent Application

A patent application has two major parts or divisions: specification and claims. The specification contains three parts: enablement, written description, and best mode. The claims are the most significant part of the patent instrument because they define the invention for purposes of patent law. Let's break these down further.

Specification

A *specification* is a detailed description of the invention and how it's to be practiced and is accompanied by detailed drawings when needed. The requirement is that the language is specific enough to allow a skilled person to practice the invention. The specification includes a title, abstract, and detailed textual description of the invention. Known as *enablement*, this enables those skilled in the art to *practice* the invention without undue experimentation. The *best mode* sets forth the most advantageous implementation of the disclosed technology.

Claims

Claims can be viewed as the area of technology carved out by the patent exclusive to the inventor. Each claim specifies a different area or scope and provides a boundary of legal coverage. Claims are often thought of as either a *product* or a *process*. Products refer to tangible things, whereas a process contemplates the steps or acts to achieve a specific result.

Processes can be subdivided into two types: *methods of using* and *making*. These distinctions can be relevant to lock manufacturers and designers to increase legal protection. The invention can also be *both* a product and a process. A perfect example is the case of the patents I received for the design of four code-setting keys (i.e., the product) that allowed Medeco's high-security locks to be opened (i.e., the process) by picking or bumping.

The claims define what the patent holder can prevent anyone else from doing. The primary rule in drafting claims is that the shorter and less specific, the better, because they can be easier to litigate in the case of infringement. A broad claim can afford more coverage. Those responsible for designing a new lock or modifying one that has already been patented should be very careful to identify every relevant possibility in drafting claims. These claims are the basis for protecting what is patented and what another manufacturer may design in the future, which could conflict with specific claims.

Properly drafting claims can be critical in any subsequent patent-infringement action. The language must accomplish three functions:

1. Properly capture the inventor's actual contribution to the art.

2. Avoid any subject matter within the prior art.

3. Most importantly, anticipate future embodiments that other inventors might employ.

The following four areas of the application are also important:

Abstract: This is a summary of the patent and provides an overview of its importance.

Field of invention: This part denotes the area of technology that is involved.

Background: This part provides the reason and rationale for the invention.

Description of the preferred embodiment: At least one example of how the invention can be practiced must be defined in this part.

Primary Statutory Criteria for the Issuance of a Patent

In the United States, there are three primary statutory criteria for patent issuance: utility, novelty, and nonobviousness. Let's break these criteria down.

Utility

Utility, the first criterion for issuance of a patent, means practical usefulness. Does the invention have any real-world use? Whether the invention works isn't relevant in most cases, but rather that it achieves a pragmatic result. The real question is whether the invention is credible to persons of ordinary art skill and whether it has at least one lawful use.

Novelty

The second criterion, *novelty*, is a prerequisite and at the core of the patent system. An invention must create something new and not be currently existing technology. Novelty as a bar to patentability requires that one piece of prior art (i.e., patent publication, known product, machine, and so on) discloses all claim elements. This is a relatively low bar to overcome because it requires an identity between the claimed invention and the single piece of prior art, which is unlikely because two people will not come up with the same solution.

The novelty concept requires an invention to be innovative and not duplicative of current technology. The idea is to advance the state-of-the-art. The test requires an original method to solve a defined problem. The critical issue for novelty is *prior art* in such a consideration. The application can be denied if there is prior art or references to its prior use, publications, or patents in the machine or process that includes all the basic tenets of the invention. Once prior art has been cited or identified in an application, the examiner must decide whether it *anticipated* the claimed invention. An invention will be found to be novel *unless* a single element of a claim discloses every element found in the prior art, enabling one skilled in the art to produce the anticipated invention.

Nonobviousness

This definition is slightly more nuanced and describes something not immediately apparent to one skilled in the art when the invention was conceived. *Nonobviousness* means the claimed invention isn't "obvious" (legally), given something known in the prior art. It doesn't require an exact identity between the claimed invention and prior art. The USPTO takes the position that the claimed invention is an obvious modification of some prior art (e.g., the invention is made bigger to achieve greater strength) or isn't an obvious combination of two more things in the prior art (e.g., a patent has all elements of the invention but one and then takes the missing element from another prior art and combines with it).

This can be a very difficult test to overcome because there must be a difference between the invention and any prior art, which can't be obvious to a person with ordinary skill in the field of the invention. The question is always the definition of what constitutes "ordinary skill in the field." One way to look at the definition is to ask if the invention offers a solution to a problem by "teaching away from the prior art." The test of nonobviousness is the high bar to patentability. The real question for an examiner is whether the invention differs sufficiently from the state-of-the-art to be worthy of a patent.

Patent Life and Validity

This provision dictates the potential term or life of an invention. *Utility* patents are valid for 20 years from the first filing of a nonprovisional application or priority claim. *Design and plant* patents protect for 15 years. In certain circumstances, patent terms can be extended if the government delays the review. There is a caveat that lock manufacturers should always remember, though: a patent can be ruled invalid by a court, recalled by the USPTO, canceled for the nonpayment of maintenance fees, or transferred to the public by the patent owner. Competitors can always file a challenge to the validity of a patent.

Manufacturers must receive competent analysis and review of their patents before initiating any enforcement or infringement action due to the potential to lose the protection of patent claims, especially on critical designs and products. I've been involved in infringement investigations where major manufacturers were reticent to proceed against locksmiths and other infringers for fear that a challenge would be filed. Patent litigation can be extremely expensive to enforce rights without a guaranteed result.

After a patent expires, anyone can use the patent's claims for any purpose. Thus the inventor can't prevent anyone from using the invention. This is highly relevant for lock manufacturers because once their protection expires, the design of locks and keys that are claimed can be copied and produced by anyone. This is especially important for issues of key control where key designs, keyways, and special features such as interactive elements are present. Medeco is a perfect example. Its m3 and M4 generations incorporated clever movable elements and side bit milling to make duplication difficult. Assa, Mul-T-Lock, Kaba, and other high-security lock manufacturers rely on their patents to protect their mechanisms and customers. If they're infringed on during the patent's life, it's incumbent on the patent owners to pursue the infringers to protect their legal rights and those of their customers. A failure to do so could subject the manufacturer to liability, especially for representations as to the security of their key control, which may not be accurate.

What Patent Rights Do Not Cover or Allow

Patent rights have limits, and it is important to understand them. Although an owner can sue anyone who infringes on their invention, there may be instances where one is prohibited from exercising the rights granted by the USPTO. For example, an inventor received a design patent for a complex key-blank design that combined several different warding patterns to accommodate restricted keyways. Warding patterns are the protrusions and indentations on the sides of keys that mate with corresponding wards in a keyway. In one specific case, the design patent provided for multiple ward patterns on one key, which allowed one key blank to copy keys intended for different restricted keyways. These special counterfeit blanks were referred to as "master keys" by offending locksmiths who cut keys they were unauthorized to make.

The design patent holder then produced a counterfeit key blank incorporating a *movable element* protected by a utility patent. The legitimate key-blank manufacturer was barred from incorporating the "master key" multiple wardings on its keys, and the design patent holder was prevented from legally producing its blanks with the movable element, so both grantees could prevent the other from utilizing each patent. The manufacturer of counterfeit key blanks agreed to stop producing the multiple-ward pattern keys as the case progressed. However, the lock manufacturer was still prevented from issuing keys that could work with different restricted keyways. This is a prime example of patent holders with different rights blocking each other from utilizing the others' claims.

Another demonstrative case involved an Austrian high-security lock maker. It received many patents for its cylinders. An American inventor figured out a way to circumvent the security of this very popular mechanism and filed for a patent to fix the problem that presented a vulnerability to the manufacturer. A patent was filed and granted for the fix, which the lock manufacturer was barred from implementing because the patent holder for the remedy wanted to sell or license the right to do so. Many of these cases occur in the world of lock manufacturing: companies must always be alert to the potential for hackers, locksmiths, or others to figure out how to modify or improve their locking mechanisms and then essentially hold them hostage for a fee, or to block the company from correcting a security vulnerability.

Invalidation of a Patent Application: The Concept of Prior Art and Nondisclosure of Inventions

Prior art is the essence of the nonobviousness and novelty criteria requirement for filing a patent. The surest way to invalidate a patent application is to disclose the invention *before* filing a formal application. Generally, any evidence of prior art or disclosure can cause a patent application to be denied, but this isn't absolute. Unless information about an invention was intentionally concealed and there was no way to discover it, a patent will not be granted if any public disclosure is located within certain periods, generally within one year before the filing by the inventor. Understanding and adhering to strict nondisclosure policies regarding any information about an invention before filing a patent is critical to any inventor or manufacturer that wishes to protect its intellectual property.

The following actions must be avoided because they can identify areas that can be adjudged as prior art and disclosure:

- *No prior art before the invention*: Any knowledge, possession of an invention, or information can be considered prior art if it occurred more than one year before filing. Any disclosure of the invention by the inventor more than one year before the application's filing date is considered prior art and is likely fatal to the application or a patent if it was erroneously issued. Any disclosure by anyone else before the application's filing is prior art and likely also fatal to the application.

- *Prior art can come from any source*: Any information, including documents, books, technical papers, PowerPoint presentations, lectures, or other publications, can be fatal to an application or, if discovered later, will invalidate a patent granted to an inventor. Any publication describing the invention, regardless of the media or location, can invalidate an application based on prior art if it occurred more than one year before the patent application date in the United States.

- *The invention can't be described in another patent or published patent application*: A patent application published in the United States before the date of the invention can be disqualifying. The "critical date" is one year before the filing date; any sale in the United States, publication, or other act will invalidate a patent filing. Design engineers should be especially careful not to discuss the inventions or projects they are working on with third parties, because this action can act as a bar to filing a patent.

- *Inventor publication of information or use*: If an inventor publishes any information or sells or shows the invention, they must file a patent within one year of that date or forfeit their rights.

- *The invention has been abandoned*: If abandoned, the invention can't be granted a patent. This means the inventor intentionally surrendered the invention to the public.

I was involved in an interesting European case involving a piezo decoder for government use in opening locks. A covert-entry tool manufacturer in France researched and produced a sophisticated tool for almost 10 years before a patent was discovered in England for the same technology application. The English patent holder did not have a claim against the French company for infringement because the technique was being sold and appeared in certain advertising materials that were circulated to mostly government buyers and vendors. In this case, the interesting twist was that the tool was government-restricted, It posed a very interesting legal question of whether such restricted publication constituted prior art and invalidated the British patent. The French manufacturer continued to market its decoder without fear of being sued for infringement.

- *The invention can't be in the public domain or used in the United States more than one year before an application for a patent*: The inventor can't have made or used the invention described in the claims more than one year before filing. Disclosure by anyone else before filing prevents patenting. There is an exception, however: experimentation will *not* invalidate the patent. Therefore, NDAs and confidentiality agreements are prerequisites for anyone working on any potential IP.

- *Any information or action anywhere*: The present patent law doesn't recognize borders when determining what is and isn't prior art.

- *Anything outside the field of the invention but equivalent to it*: Any information outside the analogous field of the invention that may have been researched or likely to have been researched during the invention's development could invalidate the application. Note, however, that applications are normally published 18 months after filing, which discloses the invention even if that application isn't successful in obtaining a patent. The publication makes trade-secret protection impossible. Nonpublication of the application can be requested if no foreign patent protection is applied.

- *My rule on publication or disclosure*: Discussing or disclosing *anything* about the invention with a third party could invalidate it. Remember, the patent examiner can access millions of documents, including published applications and expired, abandoned, or canceled patents, which can prove that an invention is neither new nor nonobvious.

Filing for a Patent to Protect IP: Pros and Cons

Pursuing a patent filing can be expensive and very time-consuming. Many considerations determine the wisdom and advantages of filing or deciding not to file. Let's break them down.

Advantages of Filing an Application

There are several advantages to filing a patent application:

- A patent can afford a greater scope or range of protection.
- It can be a method to protect against competition and infringement, and infringement suits can be extremely costly for infringers.
- An IP portfolio is a valuable business asset, especially for companies that want to raise capital.

Reasons Not to File an Application

Patent laws are based on full disclosure so that others may understand the technology and advance the state of such technology with additional innovations. There are many reasons *not* to file for patent protection:

- *Disclosure of secret information that must be contained in a patent application*: Note that an application can be marked secret, providing 18 months of nonpublication. Not doing so can give competitors advance knowledge of product development and ideas about to how to carve out noninfringing areas. It can also create the basis for challenging an application.

- *Legal costs can be significant*: Legal costs can be high due to rejections by the examiner and litigation to appeal adverse office actions and multiple amendments to applications.

- *Time delay in filing the nonprovisional application and processing time*: Initial office action usually takes about two years, but that's only the beginning. Most filings are initially rejected, which means more time and legal fees.

- *Patent protection only extends up to 20 years from the earliest filing date*: Consideration should be given to the value and life of the patent. Other alternatives, such as using trade secrets, may be a better option for short-term protection. Depending on trade secrets to protect IP can be risky, especially if someone else learns of or discovers the invention on their own. Nothing prevents the discoverer from filing a fraudulent patent application and then litigating to prevent the original creator from using their invention. Only the inventor can file for patent protection. Otherwise, it's fraud.

I always recommend filing a provisional application as soon as possible for any IP creation because it's a good insurance policy. Note that if other competing applications covering the same invention are filed, nobody knows for at least 18 months.

Many of my clients have decided not to file patents because they don't want to disclose trade secrets or pay maintenance fees to the Patent Office. These fees can become very expensive, especially for a large patent portfolio.

Patent Searches and Tools

Patent searches for the state-of-the-art, title, and infringement may be conducted in many databases through www.patents.google.com and via the USPTO website at www.uspto.gov. To search for IP when contemplating filing a patent for prior art or infringement, the following categories can and should be researched: any prior patents or filings that include expired, abandoned, published, or canceled applications. Keyword searches can be very effective, especially under the patent holder's name, assignee, and company.

Patent Classification System

All patents are classified to define the technical field of an invention. The most popular systems are the *International Patent Classification* (IPC) and the *Cooperative Patent Classification* (CPC). These systems are designed for examiners in patent offices to assign categories, making it easier to research patents and disclosures for inventions and technology. Codes are assigned to facilitate searches in different languages. The category for searching locks is Class 70 and can be found at `www.uspto.gov/web/patents/classification/uspc070/sched070.htm`.

The master USPTO public search page can be found at `www.uspto.gov/patft`. Detailed subdefinitions can be found at `www.uspto.gov/web/patents/classification/uspc070/defs070.htm`. Class 70/394, which categorizes lock picking and other attacks, is particularly interesting to search.

Note that the most significant benefit of class searching is that not all patents use the same terms for elements, and this can limit the effectiveness of searching by keywords only.

Patent Infringement

Section 271 of Title 35 defines acts of infringement as "whoever without authority makes, uses, offers to sell, or sells any patented invention, in the United States or imports into the United States any patented invention during the term of the patent therefor, infringes the patent."

Issued patents enjoy the presumption of validity, although they may be challenged. Infringers can assert that the patent is invalid or can't be enforced on several grounds, per 35 U.S.C. 282. This is one of the hazards for patentees in pursuing infringers.

Liability for patent infringement can be extremely costly for infringers, if proven. Conversely, alleging infringement without sufficient evidence can expose anyone making such a claim to liability. Before making such allegations, an expert opinion must be obtained, or it can constitute prima facia evidence of reckless behavior or intentional harassment. The statute of limitations for infringement is six years: patentees must litigate claimed acts within that time, or such actions will be barred.

Summary of Criteria That Constitute Infringement

The following key points summarize the requirements that constitute infringement:

- The device or process includes all the elements or substantial equivalent in any of the patent claims.
- The product doesn't have to infringe on all the claims—just one.
- The scope of a claim must be determined through an interpretation of its language.
- There must be a substantial similarity of function, method, and results between the patent claim and the infringement.
- Every component in a certain identified claim must be literally or equivalently present in the accused device or process.

Direct Infringement

A patent grants the right to exclude all others from making, using, selling, offering for sale, or importing the patented invention. Liability can extend for doing any one of these actions. The law prohibits *behavior* regarding the invention; the infringer's intent is largely irrelevant. The patent claims are relevant as they're compared to the technology that is the subject of infringement.

Note that the rights conferred by a U.S. patent are only protected in the United States. If foreign coverage is required, applications must be filed in specific jurisdictions. If the acts of infringement don't precisely meet the language of a claim but are substantially equivalent, the courts have ruled that the *doctrine of equivalents* applies: it states that infringement that can be said to be equivalent to the claims is essentially the same as infringing the claims. The doctrine was developed to prevent competitors from introducing insubstantial modifications to a patented device. However, there are limitations and constraints to applying it, depending on the language of the patent, what may be considered prior art, and what is claimed.

Indirect or Dependent Infringement

Anyone who encourages, aids, or abets the unauthorized practice of a patented invention is liable for infringement, even if they used the technology themselves. There are subsets of indirect infringement: *contributory infringement* and *active inducement* to infringe. Courts have ruled that active inducement may require intent and at least constructive knowledge of infringement. The following is highly relevant to lock manufacturers: if all or a substantial portion of patented components are shipped outside of the United States to be assembled into a product reintroduced in this country, such acts will be considered an infringement.

Defenses to Infringement Actions

A defendant can take several defenses in an infringement lawsuit. They relate to enforceability rather than the validity of a patent. The risk to a patentee is that if the defendant prevails, it serves as a license to implement the patented technology without risk. For this reason, lock manufacturers may hesitate to initiate infringement actions, especially if they aren't certain their patents will withstand such defenses. I ran into this issue in a major infringement investigation for a company with a significant market share for its patented key with interactive elements. The infringers figured out a way to slightly modify such a design. Although it infringed on the original patent, my client was concerned enough about losing a challenge that it decided not to litigate. If my client had lost such a legal battle, not only would it have been incredibly expensive in terms of legal fees, but they also would have lost their advantage in the marketplace for their design of high-security locks.

Defenses include the following:

- *Laches and estoppel*: The *doctrine of laches* holds that an inordinate delay by a patentee in enforcing its rights may bar it from doing so. The flip side of this premise is *estoppel*, which states that if a patent holder indicated to an infringer that they didn't intend to enforce their rights, they may be barred from doing so. If the infringer relied on and believed such representations, the infringer will not and can't be held liable.

- *Shop rights*: If an employee has been granted a patent while working for their employer, this employee may not be liable for infringement for using such an invention. The requirements for this doctrine to apply include evidence that the employee conceived of the invention during working hours, reduced the invention to practice while using tools and equipment of their employer, and incorporated the invention into the employer's facilities. These cases often arise when an employee leaves, files a patent, and then sues their former employer.

- *Misuses*: The defense of misuse occurs when the patent holder exploits the patent and its claims to exceed its scope with an anticompetitive effect.

Other defenses are beyond the scope of this discussion. They include the reverse doctrine of equivalence, experimental use, file wrapper, prosecution history, public dedication, and sovereign immunity.

Civil and Criminal Remedies for Infringement

In contrast to copyright and trademark violations, there are civil and criminal penalties for IP infringement, although Congress hasn't made patent infringement a crime. Electronic locks, safes, and security systems that rely on embedded hardware and software to ensure or enhance their security can be subject to multiple forms of compromise. These types of attacks aren't covered by patent laws but by federal criminal anti-hacking statutes, copyright laws, and the Digital Millennium Copyright Act (discussed in Part IV).

Specific remedies for patent infringement include reasonable royalties, lost profits, provisional rights, enhanced damages, attorney fees, and marking. The listed remedies are important for patent holders to enforce their rights against infringers:

- *Injunctions*: Permanent injunctions can be granted to plaintiffs that prevail in an infringement claim. They will be valid until the patent's expiration date. A temporary injunction may also be granted based on four criteria: the probability of success on the merits, irreparable harm to the patentee, a balance of hardship between the parties, and the public interest.

- *Damages*: Monetary damages are allowed by the patent statutes for infringement. Criteria for damages is "adequate to compensate for the infringement but in no case less than a reasonable royalty for the use made of the invention." The test to assess damages is often based on lost profits. The statute of limitations provides that a patentee can look back six years before filing a complaint or counterclaim for infringement. If "reasonable royalties" are to be awarded, the test the courts apply is a hypothetical licensing agreement. A patentee can also collect up to triple damages in cases of infringement where there are exceptional circumstances.

- *Lost profits*: The patent owner must show that, except for the infringer, it would have made the sales produced by the infringer. Another test examines several factors to determine whether the patentee could produce the product and if there was a demonstrable demand for it and no noninfringing equivalent available.

- *Marking*: Marking goods with the word *patent* or *pat* and the number puts the world on notice of a patent. The term *Patent pending* has no real legal significance and may indicate that a patent application has been filed. Until a patent is issued, no legal protection is afforded.

The next chapter discusses possible plans of action in the event that a lock manufacturer is notified about an alleged defect or security flaw in a product. It's imperative that a lock company contemplate the courses of action and reduce them to writing before action is required.

Notification of Defects in Product Design

Issues inevitably manifest in all products once consumers run the ultimate suitability tests for the intended purpose in their real-world environments and applications. In my experience, this especially holds true for locks and related security hardware. It's virtually impossible for a manufacturer and its vulnerability assessment (VA) team to identify every potential issue related to product manufacturing, design, warning information, and misuse. The end user eventually provides that feedback. Unfortunately, in today's environment, hackers, criminals, lock researchers, lock sports groups, security lecturers, and even extortionists can all interact with lock manufacturers.

After introducing a product and its sale, a manufacturer may discover or become aware of hazards or previously unforeseeable security vulnerabilities. This can be due to state-of-the-art technology advances that permit the discovery of an exploit or defect. It can also be caused by consumers using or implementing the product in an unexpected or unanticipated way. Locks are a special category because the ability to compromise them is always advancing. Methods to decode, manipulate, pick, or bypass current or newly developed locking mechanisms are inherent in the business, and many manufacturers simply aren't conversant with the latest bypass and attack methods. The following two examples illustrate this problem for manufacturers.

In England and France, piezo decoders were developed to measure the length of pin tumblers rapidly and covertly and then translate that information to a key machine or 3D program that produced bitted keys. Such technology was far beyond the comprehension of most lock manufacturers. It was developed by Madelin, a French company specializing in covert-entry tools. Madelin spent more than a million dollars on research and produced a handheld device that could probe a lock and produce a key. It was virtually unknown outside of the government.

My second example involves using strong magnetic fields to open push-button locks. The design engineers of these locks never considered using rare earth magnets to move an internal critical component and cause a lock to open in two seconds.

Many lock manufacturers solicit input from security researchers and hackers and pay for their information. The advantage is that these manufacturers can often improve their product designs and discover deficiencies through this solicitation. The negative side is that if a significant vulnerability is found, hackers know the company will often pay large sums and may offer consulting agreements with nondisclosure agreements (NDAs) to ensure their confidentiality.

In the past 30 years, I've been involved in numerous incidents that my colleagues and I have created in the industry. In these cases, there was a security engineering failure where the net result produced and released a defective/deficient product that cost my clients or other target companies significant damage and extremely negative publicity. Often, technical information wasn't shared between companies, and their security designs were jealously guarded, even within large international manufacturers. This guarding of information led to design defects being discovered by external sources.

The most important issue for manufacturers is to plan ahead for such an eventuality. Acting in a crisis environment rarely yields a good result, especially if the media is involved or aware of a problem with a major company. I developed protocols for my clients to use as a template for a standard action plan when there's a notification about an alleged product defect. Certain legal, ethical, and moral practices can be involved. Having a plan of action ahead of time is much more prudent than dealing with urgent issues without the proper ability to work through a problem. This chapter presents a suggested way to analyze defect notifications and deal with the issues that may (or may not) be involved.

Primary Rules and Questions

The following primary rules and questions can help a company's management and decision-makers act properly, prudently, and expediently when receiving a notification about defective or deficient products:

1. Don't panic or make statements to the media until the problems and what to do about them are understood. Consult your predesignated plan of action for risk assessment and actions.

2. Caution every company employee not to make any false or misleading statements about the issue to anyone.

3. Consult with a company expert or a consultant who has dealt with defect notifications in other cases. This may include legal counsel who has conducted investigations, or it may require a qualified engineer with experience to assess security engineering issues.

4. Assign one individual to deal with media inquiries. That person should be conversant with journalists and social media and have technical knowledge. They should understand the legal jeopardy of releasing too much information until a coordinated response has been carefully drafted and vetted. Never misstate information that's provided to any media representative. Don't let the company's legal officer draft a response, at least initially, until all the facts are understood.

> In one case my colleague and I investigated and documented, we were able to trigger the legal counsel of a major lock manufacturer to issue a detailed denial letter defining the different modes of attack that we could demonstrate on a sophisticated electronic access-control lock used commercially and by government agencies. We discovered multiple methods to compromise the lock and its underlying systems and presented our findings to a large audience at DefCon. As a result, the manufacturer denied all the issues we discovered and detailed its denials in a written series of statements. We then published each denial as part of a devastating PowerPoint presentation.

5. Don't issue any written statement to critical customers until all the ramifications of such a statement can be analyzed.

> I received an urgent call from a client about a problem with restricted keyways sold to a major U.S. facility. The risk-management director could have keys duplicated by a local lock shop, which, according to the manufacturer's statements made to the customer, was impossible. My client wanted me to generate a letter to the customer saying that this matter was under investigation and they would be notified when the client understood more about the issue. The problem with this approach was that the customer believed the lock manufacturer had known about the issue and failed to make a full and honest disclosure. My advice was not to send any written letter but rather to meet in person to explain the limits of key control and defuse potential litigation.

6. Assess all the information, and determine whether a defect exists and its origin. Be sure to ask the following questions to ensure that you have all the necessary information:

   ▪ Is it the materials or manufacturing?

   ▪ Is it a design problem?

   ▪ Is it an issue about providing sufficient consumer information?

7. Consider the interests of all the affected users, depending on the perceived seriousness of the problem and potential or operational threats. Be sure to ask these questions:

   ▪ Would it be better to do nothing to remedy the problem?

   ▪ Would notifying customers of a significant problem lead the manufacturer to additional exposure and negative publicity or legal action?

   ▪ Would any disclosure of the problem alert hackers and criminals so that they could replicate it to the customers' detriment?

   ▪ How much should be disclosed to the media and consumers about the problem's nature and how the manufacturer will deal with it?

   ▪ Does the issue arise from product misuse?

   ▪ Has prior information been known about this, or has a similar problem occurred?

   ▪ Have any fixes been implemented previously for the same problem?

   ▪ Who in the company is most familiar with the product and its potential defect?

   ▪ Does the communication from the informant provide any indication of special knowledge about the product, its design, or production procedures?

   ▪ Does the defect notification suggest that the informant may be an insider?

   ▪ Is the lock mechanical, electromechanical, or electronic?

   ▪ Can you attempt to replicate the attack? If so, can you determine the likely causes and remedies?

   ▪ If an attack involved any software-based lock, is encryption of internal data involved?

   ▪ Was hacking of the software involved, and if so, do certain federal statutes come into play?

   ▪ Do your customer contracts require notification if a defect or potential security vulnerability is discovered?

8. Try to identify the source of the information supplied. If it's anonymous or the individual won't disclose their identity, this can complicate your analysis and response and raise cautionary flags.

9. Decide which people should be warned and what categories they should be warned about, as these both raise important questions of duty and

adequacy. The selection of the proper groups to warn raises several questions:

- Whom should the warning protect?
- Who can best accomplish that protection?
- What type of warning will provide the most reliable notification of those affected?
- When a manufacturer has a duty to protect, who has the right to be protected?

Even when a manufacturer sells its products to intermediaries, it normally should provide warnings and instructions about product hazards directly to users and consumers if there's a reasonable way to do so. When users and consumers rely on others for protection, warnings should be given to those other persons in addition to or, if appropriate, instead of warnings to users and consumers.

10. Don't rush to fix a problem before it's fully understood. There's often an impetus to remedy a design defect as soon as possible. Unless the issue is thoroughly analyzed, immediate remedies can complicate the original problem, thus requiring yet more changes. For example, I initiated a case that involved defectively designed laptop cable locks. The manufacturer, an industry leader, made changes to reduce the vulnerability of bypassing the tubular lock. In doing so, it made the lock easier to open in a totally unanticipated manner, which required yet another version of the lock to be introduced.

11. How the complaint was received is important. Know whether a trace can be made to determine where the complaint was initiated. See if you can validate the informational source and determine whether the information was obtained first-hand from the informant. Discover whether they developed the information alone or if others were involved.

12. As a corporate requirement, don't deal with anonymous informants in any NDA or contractual relationship or to pay for information. Be sure to answer the following:

- Can contact be maintained with the source of the information?
- What is the technical expertise of the source of the information? Is the source knowledgeable about locks, or does an intermediary appear to be involved?
- Does the information notification involve high-security locks that government facilities utilize, and if so, should law enforcement be involved?

- What locks and models are affected?
- Is the defect or vulnerability in a common platform across multiple companies or lock designs? If so, the seriousness of the defect may be amplified.
- If a video or photographs of an exploit are provided, determine the following preliminary information, if possible:
  - Has the lock been altered?
  - What version and manufacturing date are shown?
  - How did the informant secure the lock samples, especially if they're restricted?
  - Is the lock an original, a knockoff, or counterfeit?
  - Can any special markings, product numbers, or serial numbers be identified?
  - Have this video and/or images been posted on social media or provided to the news media?
  - Has the video been edited?
  - If the video shows an exploit to open the lock, has the video's time been compressed?
  - How long does the exploit take?
  - Does the video pose a threat?
  - Has the vulnerability been assessed against the 3T2R Rule?
  - Is the time shown to open the lock longer than that required by any applicable covert-entry standard?

13. If the informant produces a video with a threat to make it public, does the video positively show the lock's security? Always consider the possibility of initiating litigation for libel or slander by asking these questions:

- How significant is the problem?
- How many customers or facilities are affected?
- When was the lock first introduced?
- What market size can be affected if the defect is validated?
- Do patents still protect the lock?
- What's the possible motive for the defect disclosure to the lock manufacturer? Is it . . .
  - A legitimate concern from a customer?
  - A warning from a security researcher?
  - Identification of an operational problem by an end user?

- From a disgruntled employee?
- An extortion attempt?
- From a competitor?
- A vendetta against another employee on the design team?
- How many people are aware of the alleged issue?
- Has every employee aware of the problem signed an NDA to prevent disclosure?
- Did the demonstration of the vulnerability or the methodology required to execute the attack involve a violation of the Digital Millenium Copyright Act (DMCA)?
- Can a patent be filed to remedy the defect, and if so, should one be filed without delay?
- Has the informant produced a bypass tool to exploit the defect further, and how well does the tool function?
  - Can such a tool, or the process of how it works, be patented?
  - Is such a tool being offered for sale or threatened to be offered?

Internal Notifications

When a lock maker is notified about a potential problem, many people at the management level come into play and should be immediately involved, including those in the following departments:

- Legal affairs
- Insurance
- Engineering and design
- Research and development
- Product management
- Distributors and distribution facilities
- End users and critical customers
- Tech support
- Customer service
- Media
- Production
- Quality control
- Public relations

- Compliance
- Standards certification
- Marketing
- Customer service centers
- Locksmiths

Assessing the Scope of the Issue or Problem

It's imperative that once a potential product defect has been discovered, an assessment be conducted that answers the following:

- Who is involved?
- Who is affected?
- How many customers are affected?
- What are the security risks to those customers?
- Should the company publicly admit to the problem to warn customers?
- Is there a contractual requirement to warn customers?
- Who needs to be warned?
- Which geographical areas are affected?
- What exactly is the problem?
- What systems are affected?
- What components are most at risk: internal mechanisms of the lock or credentials (mechanical and/or electronic)?
- Where are the affected locks utilized?
- Are the company's audit capabilities affected?
- Are there potential regulatory or standards compliance issues?
- What are the possible consequences and the probability of not correcting the issue?
- Which production lots are affected?
- If the replacement of locks is warranted, how would that be accomplished?
- What mechanics of a replacement or recall of locks would be involved?
- What would be the potential economics of a replacement or recall?
- What are the priorities for action and the time frame?
- When can the problem be fixed, and when can the corrected product be supplied?

Action Items and Priority

When a notification is received about a possible product defect or vulnerability, it's important to initiate certain procedures to ascertain exactly what the problem may be and who should be involved, both initially and as the issue is more fully understood. The following potential action items should be carried out, depending on the apparent seriousness of the subject matter of the notification:

- Preliminary analysis
- Immediate action
- Production impact
- Reporting and confirmation
- Comprehensive analysis
- Corrective action list
- Long-term preventative actions
- Process management locally/group-wide

Design Defects and Liability Considerations

Depending on the nature and severity of a defect, especially in locks, a manufacturer can be liable for products that aren't as represented or that cause physical or economic injury. (This topic is discussed more fully in Chapter 6.) When one is notified about a potential problem, one must always consider certain legal issues *before* any action is taken once the "problem" is defined as a defect or something less that requires a modification in design and upgrade. Any actions taken to remedy a defect may allow for the potential that such action can be used as evidence of negligence by the manufacturer.

A problem's severity dictates corporate actions, as I note later in the section about the protocol for handling such events. Once a product is available in the marketplace, a manufacturer has two basic options: attempt to warn consumers who own or use the product, or take a more drastic measure and initiate a recall. There are problems with both alternatives. A warning may be an option if the alleged defect isn't serious enough to require a recall. However, warnings have their perils. Notifying consumers and end users can also alert criminals to a problem. In today's Internet world, even stating a vulnerability will give rise to hackers, lock-sports enthusiasts, and criminals trying to determine the problem and then publish and exploit it.

Caution must be exercised in any disclosure of the problem's precise nature. It's a delicate balance. Disclosing too little can be as troublesome as describing the problem in too much detail. Either way, both your customers and your facilities can be placed at risk.

Consideration must be given to the possibility of initiating an upgrade. The timing and costs of doing so are important. You must balance the risk of not doing anything versus improving the product's security or safety with the foreseeable dangers of both actions. If the foreseeable risk stems from an occasional flaw, that's a lower-level priority. Conversely, if the foreseeable risks from a manufacturing flaw are more significant, courts may require a manufacturer to use considerable resources to prevent, minimize, or eliminate such issues during production.

A critical question for management is the likelihood that the defect, once confirmed, can cause some form of injury to a plaintiff. In modern product-liability litigation, the injured party must prove that a product was defective, that the product contained the defect when it left the defendant's control, and that the defect proximately caused the harm. As noted in Chapter 6, if the exact cause of a product malfunction can't be determined, the legal doctrine of *res ipsa loquitur* can allow a jury to *infer* a manufacturer's negligence when circumstances suggest that a product was negligently designed or manufactured.

It's to be expected that the longer a product is in the marketplace, the more is learned about product deficiencies and defects in design and the best way to enhance its performance. This natural product evolution is important regarding the admissibility of evidence that the product was improved to minimize or eliminate security risks. Conversely, if a product is known to have caused injury or security vulnerabilities, that's also relevant in the event of litigation.

Any responsible manufacturer must take steps to upgrade and enhance its products to improve safety and security and provide additional warnings or instructions to cover the improper use of applications that can create extra vulnerabilities. It's axiomatic that improvements and modifications will be seen as an acknowledgment that the benefits of improvements exceed their cost in implementation. Always consider that evidence of product enhancement may suggest or confirm that before an improvement modification, the product was indeed defective, and the changes potentially indicated some form of negligence on the manufacturer's part.

As noted in the discussion of the Repair Doctrine in Chapter 6, fixing a problem can dissuade a manufacturer from remedying an issue because it may be seen as an admission of liability. Courts have generally assumed that evidence of a defendant's post-incident repairs will be barred from introduction in an action for negligence.

Compensatory and Punitive Damages

A manufacturer or other seller that fails to take reasonable steps to protect consumers from harm after discovering that a product is defective may subject itself to liability for compensatory damages and, in certain cases, punitive damages. Post-sale discovery of dangerous defects can require a duty to warn, repair, retrofit, or recall, minimizing or eliminating risk. Some of the latest law holds that a product seller has a post-sale duty to warn when a reasonable seller in the same circumstances would do so. Damages can be awarded for failing to issue post-sale warnings and refusing to repair a defective design. Likewise, liability can occur when a company refuses to accept engineering recommendations for ways to remedy a significant defect simply and inexpensively.

Manufacturers must document their efforts to analyze how to eliminate a recurring design problem when they know it causes a security vulnerability for their customers. If the design defect is serious, they may be advised to stop selling the product.

Failure to Take Any Substantive Steps

Once a product has been sold, efforts to remedy a discovered defect usually are at least inconvenient, generally expensive, and otherwise very damaging to both the manufacturing enterprise and its responsible employees. The problem is that manufacturers are most likely to initially ignore and later deny certain developing security problems. They often do this well past the point at which ordinary prudence, good morals, and common sense dictate that post-sale steps be taken to protect the consumer.

Post-Sale Duty to Warn or Recall

Most often, manufacturers and other sellers discover defects in their products only *after* those products have been sold and put into use. After a sale, for example, a manufacturer may discover a hazard or vulnerability that had not previously been foreseeable, perhaps because consumers used the product in an unexpectedly dangerous way.

Does a manufacturer have a duty to remedy product defects in the marketplace? Consider the question regarding locks. What's considered a dangerous defect, and when does the manufacturer have a duty to warn? Once the public discovers that a manufacturer has improved the security or safety of a product line, the manufacturer may encounter many problems. Its management team should carefully consider the following potential ramifications of actions after a notification is received:

- Existing litigation may be rendered more difficult to defend.
- New litigation may be stimulated.
- Competitors may be advantaged.
- Product demand may fall.
- A regulatory safety agency may be prompted to investigate the problem and ultimately order a recall.

The Protocol for the Notification of Defects in Locks

Many years ago, I organized a meeting in Stockholm with lawyers, design engineers, compliance officers, manufacturing and production supervisors, and marketing representatives from different lock manufacturers. The purpose was to establish and map out an action plan when a notification was received about a security deficiency or defect that could place a facility, user, or customers at risk. Such notifications aren't unusual for high-security lock makers and are to be expected because they're targeted by hackers, lock-sports enthusiasts, and sometimes extortionists.

The conference resulted in a structured, relatively simple protocol following my 3T2R Rule on evaluating risks and what actions to take in response. We considered threat-level criteria, communications requirements, and specific actions. *Communications* and defined *actions* were classed into two categories: mandatory and optional. We determined that once the threat level was assessed, specific optional or mandatory actions should be dictated. This protocol allows a reasoned approach to evaluating whether a problem exists, who is affected, and what to do about it.

The protocol has served as a model for many of my clients about what to do when they're notified about a problem, especially when it's serious and can affect many customers, facilities, and products that utilize the same technology platform across different companies. Following a defined procedure can save time, money, and bad media exposure and deter litigation for a wide range of potential legal actions.

Threat-Level Criteria

The threat-level criteria determined at the conference followed the 3T2R definitions: tools required, time required, training, repeatability of the method to open the lock, and reliability of doing so. Five distinct levels were established: no threat, minimal, moderate, serious, and severe, with a numeric ranking of 0–4. Those levels are listed next, along with the criteria for each.

Threat Level 0: No Threat

- *Tools required*: None
- *Time required*: Greater than 10 minutes
- *Training required*: None
- *Repeatability of the method*: Minimum of 10 samples
- *Reliability of the method*: None

Threat Level 1: Minimal

- *Tools required*: Expensive, sophisticated, lock-specific, restricted access
- *Time required*: 7–10 minutes
- *Training required*: Complicated, detailed, prior knowledge or intelligence; lock specific; restricted availability
- *Repeatability of the method*: 15%
- *Reliability of the method*: Random, nonpredictable

Threat Level 2: Moderate

- *Tools required*: Any two of the four criteria in Threat Level 1
- *Time required*: 5–7 minutes
- *Training required*: Minimal; any two of the five criteria in Threat Level 1
- *Repeatability of the method*: 30%
- *Reliability of the method*: Rare

Threat Lever 3: Serious

- *Tools required*: Any two of the three criteria from the Threat Level 4
- *Time required*: 2–5 minutes
- *Training required*: Any two of the five criteria from Threat Level 4
- *Repeatability of the method*: 50%
- *Reliability of the method*: Often

Threat Level 4: Severe

- *Tools required*: Simple, cheap, readily available
- *Time required*: Less than 2 minutes
- *Training required*: Easy, quick, no prior knowledge or intelligence, general application, readily available
- *Repeatability of the method*: 75%
- *Reliability of the method*: Almost always highly reliable

Communications and Actions on Notification of a Defect

It's important to define specific lines of communication and action requirements based on the different threat levels. Levels 3, 4, and 5 may require the involvement of a task force (e.g., product management, research and development, operations, legal, marketing, and sales). Higher managerial levels, such as division and group management, should carefully consider the levels of publicity, the potential impact of the problem, and the legal ramifications. Communications and actions may be optional or mandatory for Threat Levels 3, 4, and 5. Here are the criteria for the managerial levels according to the issue's threat level:

Threat Level 1: Minimal

- *Communications*: Research and Development and the product manager, feedback to the source. Inform those who initiated the complaint or initially received the notification.

- *Action*: Investigation and documentation; no redesign requirements.

Threat Level 2: Moderate

- *Communications*: Those in Level 1, as well as legal and local management.

- *Action*: No immediate action may be required as the problem can likely be fixed as part of normal development and upgrades

Threat Level 3: Serious

- *Communications*: Criteria include the prior two levels plus divisional management. Depending on the circumstances, it may be optional to include group management, sales management, customer service, tech services, the sales force, distribution, media, and critical customers.

- *Action*: Mandatory actions can include immediate design or production review and preparing internal talking points and possible media response. Optional actions may include implementing design or production changes and stopping production or sales internally or at the supplier level.

Threat Level 4: Severe

- *Communications*: Mandatory and includes all the actions of previous threat levels and communication with group management. Optional actions may include communication with end users, insurance carriers, and members of the previous three threat levels.

- *Action*: Actions include all those found in the previous threat levels. Mandatory actions include design and production changes, halting sales and production, a product recall, and an independent vulnerability analysis.

Special Cases: Consulting Agreements, Nondisclosure Agreements, and Extortion Attempts

When a manufacturer is presented with verifiable evidence of a significant defect in one of its locks or safes, it must take the report seriously. This is certainly true in the United States, where lawyers are looking for class-action cases to file, especially if the security vulnerability is easily understood and can result in significant losses or harm to customers. The problem becomes even more intense when high-security locks are involved.

Once an issue is confirmed by a lock maker, and depending on the assessment of severity as noted in the protocol, many questions must be asked and answered about the classification of the defect's type, how it can have occurred, whether it should have been discovered, and how it can be remedied.

The decision about how to act can be complicated and, if the defect is severe, fraught with legal issues. In my experience with many such cases, my rules are simple: tell the truth, precisely figure out the problem, and get out in front of it as soon as possible. If a press conference is warranted, call one once you know all the facts, and be prepared to answer relevant questions. Remember, anything said to any media representative can be used for or against you in litigation.

Once notified about a problem, my clients are often inclined to limit their exposure and damages by engaging hackers or security researchers in a consulting agreement with an appropriate NDA to minimize the potential for publication. Careful consideration must be given to communicating with these individuals, especially if they insist on remaining anonymous. If an NDA is entered into with hackers (or others), certain preliminary questions must be raised:

- Identification of the person executing the agreement
- Payment terms and the ability to track payments to bank accounts
- The likelihood that the information will be kept confidential
- The likelihood that the information has already been disclosed to others
- The ability to enforce the NDA in the event of a breach
- The effect of sanctions if the NDA is violated
- Duration of the NDA
- What precisely is covered in the NDA document
- What information is prevented from disclosure, and by whom
- What information can be used by either party in the NDA
- Whether the NDA is unilateral (i.e., one-way flow of information) or bilateral (i.e., information flows in both directions), meaning any information disclosed by either party to the other can or can't be used by either

An NDA, if not carefully drafted, can be fraught with peril because it may prevent a manufacturer from using any information to fix or remedy a problem disclosed by a hacker or one attempting extortion. If the documents state that irreparable harm and injury would result from disclosure, serious problems can arise, as I experienced in a case where there was a fatal design defect in a lock made by a dominant player in the industry. The NDA didn't allow for the use of any information by the manufacturer or researcher and specified significant damages for using any information provided by either party. Because the manufacturer was a public company, it couldn't allow a defective product to continue to be sold. So, the company fixed it, violating the NDA because it used the information it provided, of which the company was not previously aware. The company would have been subject to serious damages for breaching the document.

There are many dangers in dealing with hackers or those threatening public exposure unless payment is received. Unless they and their information can be vetted, they may be able to extract information from a lock manufacturer and then use it against the company, either in litigation or on social media. Carefully consider the potential for all communications between the company and someone reporting an alleged defect. Representatives may inadvertently make admissions and disclosures that would be harmful if published. Any offer of remuneration or payments for information, an NDA, or moving forward with other actions can likewise prompt others to make similar demands and may constitute admissions against interest.

Possible Extortion Attempts

Many of my lock manufacturing clients have had direct or subtle threats of exposure of alleged defects if some form of compensation isn't received in consideration of nonpublication or nondisclosure. Such situations require expertise in criminal investigation and prosecution to develop evidence to protect the company.

The normal scenario is that a lock manufacturer is contacted about what is alleged to be a critical design defect that will affect the security of many users and facilities. Such attempts become more important and potentially harmful to manufacturers as the market penetration of the identified products and the manufacturer's reputation increase.

Threatening any form of disclosure or other action can constitute extortion, which is a crime in virtually every state and federal jurisdiction. The principal element of extortion is attempting to obtain money or other things of value by force or threat. State laws deal with many forms of extortion, and federal criminal statutes in the United States prohibit certain forms of activity. If high-security locks or systems are involved, regardless of venue or jurisdiction, a manufacturer should consider advising law enforcement and national security agencies about the potential threat. They have resources that aren't available in the private sector. In jurisdictions that prohibit one-party recordings of interviews and undercover operations, law enforcement can conduct such scenarios.

In the United States, 10 states prohibit secret recordings unless all parties consent (two-party jurisdictions), unlike one-party states, where only one person in a conversation consents. Recordings and undercover wires can constitute the best evidence, as I can attest from many successful cases I have worked on.

Under the U.S. federal criminal system, extortion attempts can involve several federal statutes, include making threats to publish harmful information, using interstate communications to transmit a threat, and possessing the proceeds of any such crime. The specific federal statutes include the following:

- *Blackmail (18 U.S.C. 873)*: Threats of informing, or as a consideration for not informing, against violating any laws of the United States, unless demands or receiving any money or valuable thing occurs.

- *Interstate communications (18 U.S.C. 875(d)*: Whoever, with intent to extort from any person, firm, association, or corporation, any money or other thing of value, transmits in interstate or foreign commerce any communication containing any threat to injure the property or reputation of the addressee or of another or the reputation of a deceased person or any threat to accuse the addressee or any other person of a crime.

- *Mailing threatening communications (18 U.S.C. 876d)*: Whoever, with intent to extort from any person any money or other thing of value, knowingly so deposits or causes to be delivered, as aforesaid, any communication, with or without a name or designating mark subscribed to it, addressed to any other person and containing any threat to injure the property or reputation of the addressee or another, or the reputation of a deceased person, or any threat to accuse the addressee or any other person of a crime.

- *Mailing threatening communications from a foreign country (18 U.S.C. 877)*: Whoever knowingly deposits in any post office or authorized depository for mail matter of any foreign country any communication addressed to any person within the United States, to have such communication delivered by the post office establishment of such foreign country to the Postal Service and by it delivered to such addressee in the United States, and as a result, thereof such communication is delivered by the post office establishment of such foreign country to the Postal Service and by it delivered to the address to which it's directed in the United States.

  Whoever, with intent to extort from any person any money or other thing of value, knowingly so deposits as aforesaid, any communication, for the purpose aforesaid, containing any threat to injure the property or reputation of the addressee or of another, or the reputation of a deceased person, or any threat to accuse the addressee or any other person of a crime.

▪ *Receiving the proceeds of extortion (18 U.S.C. 880)*: A person who receives, possesses, conceals, or disposes any money or other property obtained from the commission of any offense under this chapter.

Other criminal remedies may be available, including violation of the DMCA and unlawful access to a computing device.

Civil Remedies

Civil remedies may also come into play when it isn't feasible to prosecute for criminal extortion. Most states and many foreign jurisdictions have causes of action for libel, slander, tortious interference with business and contractual relationships, and business disparagement. If it develops that an insider provided information to a third party to facilitate the scheme, trade secret laws, violation of nondisclosure agreements, and violation of the terms of employment agreements may be available for use.

Other remedies can include a temporary injunction prohibiting publication, although such an action can be perilous. I was involved with a case at DefCon where some engineering students had figured out how to defraud the metro transit system in a major U.S. city and other venues worldwide where the same systems were in operation. I counseled these students to go on the offensive and hold a press conference, even though a federal judge had issued a temporary injunction against them giving their presentation. Ultimately, the judge lifted the order, and the students worked as consultants for the company. (Check out www.cnet.com/news/privacy/judge-orders-halt-to-defcon-speech-on-subway-card-hacking.)

Any time a company receives a communication notifying them about a product defect, their legal counsel should be alerted to consider the potential that the notification will escalate into an extortion attempt. Initially, it may not appear that the objective is for the informant to receive compensation, but that depends on the sophistication of the informant and the seriousness of the threat to the company. Threats can be extremely subtle, especially if the informant is knowledgeable about actions that constitute crimes.

Acts that may constitute a crime can include the following:

▪ Threats to publish or a notification that an individual is preparing an article about the defect

▪ A request for a comment about an article regarding the alleged defect used to send the message that information will be made public, with the hope that the company will attempt to persuade the writer not to publish

- Contacting risk managers or security directors in companies that utilize the product, advising them of the security vulnerability so they will then communicate with the manufacturer about the problem to apply pressure on them
- Threats to make the defect public and to demonstrate how to defeat the locking system
- Threats to register domain names that describe the problem and company
- Threats to give a presentation, such as at DefCon or a hacking convention, that makes public the attack details so they can be replicated
- Threats to write an article on social media or in legitimate news media
- Threats to file for a patent to remedy the problem, thus preventing the manufacturer from doing so
- Offers to work for the company as a consultant to fix the alleged problem
- Threats to file a lawsuit, especially a class action, on behalf of all consumers
- Threats to notify facilities that utilize the alleged defective product
- Threats to file complaints with certifying agencies, challenging security classifications or ratings, such as Underwriters Laboratories, ANSI/BHMA, and VdS (Europe)

Suppose the locks subject to a complaint involve critical infrastructure. In that case, law enforcement should be notified if the defect can be confirmed as one that can create a security vulnerability or public threat. The FBI InfraGard group may also be contacted, because their primary responsibility in every field office is to provide a liaison between federal law enforcement and the private sector. This group of public and private security professionals issues timely bulletins outlining threats and holds local and online training seminars.

If there's a possibility that the actions of third parties will escalate into a possible criminal offense, the following actions, as a minimum, should be taken:

- Document all contacts and communications.
- Save all written communications and attempt to determine the metadata about where emails or text messages originated.
- Record all conversations if you are in a one-party jurisdiction for covert recordings. Or obtain permission from law enforcement to record, without the other parties' consent, any communications with any party making a notification.
- Meet with the informant if possible, and have a second party present as a witness.
- Obtain photographs and video (if possible) of any meetings.
- Seek out samples of the affected locks to demonstrate their vulnerability.

Ask for details from the informant about the following:

- What they expect or want for providing information
- The time frame for their demands
- How they expect to be paid
- What amount they're demanding
- Positive identification of both the informant and the involved products
- Their past employment and expertise in locks and security
- How they discovered and documented the problem

Ask for proof of their discovery, including the following:

- Submission to the company of locks that were analyzed and defeated
- Verification of the lock's manufacture date and current models
- Whether patents have been applied for to remedy the problem
- A request for a demonstration of the exploit live and in person

Developing evidence for a criminal extortion case can be complex and time-consuming and often requires expertise and a lot of patience from a possible victim. Still, the basic tenets of the scheme are always the same: employ a threat of exposure, publicity, legal action, patent filing, or other conduct that would be detrimental to the company and its reputation. If possible, the manufacturer should "engineer" the one making the notification to turn it into a direct threat: "If you don't pay me, I will cause you trouble or economic injury." Doing so can take time to draw the individual out. If the goal is money, the longer the communications occur, the more incessant their demands become. By "engineering," I mean using time, psychology, and future "carrots" of money or other things of value to lure the one attempting extortion into identifying themselves and their location, and gathering critical evidence for a criminal prosecution.

These operations require expertise in investigative and evidence-gathering techniques and a full understanding of the elements that constitute different offenses. Having been involved in investigating and prosecuting many such cases, I can confirm that most lock manufacturers don't have such in-house expertise unless they have internal security officers or legal counsel with law-enforcement and prosecutorial experience in such matters.

Many of my clients abhor publicity in such cases. I've always advocated that preventing future attempts is of prime importance. Major lock manufacturers need to send a message that all remedies will be pursued in the event of extortionate threats. This may require filing criminal charges and civil actions against anyone involved.

Insider Threats as Part of a Scheme

The possibility should always be considered that an insider is communicating with a third party about a vulnerability and trying to obtain payment without being identified. In my world, this means everyone can be a suspect in the event of a report of a serious design defect. Consider the following employees as having the potential to be involved in a scheme to obtain something of value from the company:

- A current or former employee with a grievance or vendetta against the company.
- A member of organized labor wanting to cause trouble.
- A hacker who gained access to critical information and is using it to their advantage.
- A vendor with access to design information.
- Someone with advanced knowledge about a defective design that wasn't remedied.
- An aggrieved employee who believes they weren't given enough attention after reporting a design issue.
- Someone aggrieved who feels they didn't receive recognition for their work on a product design or patent filing. In Part VI, I describe a case I investigated that involved an individual who killed three people in a family because he didn't receive the proper credit in a patent filing by one of the victims.

In the next chapter, I examine legal and security issues and potential liability in keying systems and key control. High-security lock manufacturers, either directly or by inference, represent that their keys and keying systems are protected, will maintain certain levels of security, and will resist replication, duplication, and simulation of keys for their locks and master key systems. This may not be the case, especially as described in Chapter 22, involving 3D printing software and technology. I describe cases that I investigated in the United States and overseas where elements of patent, trademark, and copyright law intersected with key blanks and counterfeiting, costing my clients the loss of significant revenue and creating serious security vulnerability issues for their customers.

Legal and Security Issues in Keying Systems

Mechanical and electromechanical locks are designed around their primary credentials: keys. Depending on the internal active locking elements, keys can take many forms based on the security of the locking system. Fundamentally, all keys perform the same function: to properly actuate some form of movable detainer that allows the plug to turn once the correct bitting combination is presented.

Lock manufacturers have sought to devise infinite ways to vary the design of keys to enhance security, maintain key control, and prevent or resist unauthorized duplication. Key control is relevant in high-security locks because of Underwriters Laboratory (UL) and American National Standards Institute (ANSI)/ Builders Hardware Manufacturers Association (BHMA) standards (described further in Chapter 7). Intricate and clever iterations of keyways, wards, bitting patterns, virtual keyways, interactive elements, movable elements, laser tracks, dimples, and magnetics have all been patented and are prevalent in many of today's locks. Electromechanical locks are becoming more popular due to the added access options and security they can provide. Regardless of whether encrypted elements are incorporated into keys, the same issue always exists: the security of the mechanical portion of the credential.

Because keys are essential to unlock a mechanism, much technology has been developed in the industry to meet various customer needs. Every commercial facility may have different design and operational requirements for master key systems. Variance in defining depth increments, which translates to the number of possible differences or combinations that can be available for a specific application and keying system, is also critical.

Certain legal and security requirements and ramifications are associated with any system that uses keys. The fundamental problem with mechanical keys is 3D printing technology. Initially, 3D software was adopted to generate and defeat the security of mechanical keys; its capabilities to attack many levels of key control have increased, as discussed in Chapter 22. Some of the major lock manufacturers were shocked that even their highest-security keys could be easily compromised by 3D methods, in combination with other techniques, as was shown at a DefCon conference.

Two MIT engineering students at this conference demonstrated the ease with which they compromised the Schlage Primus side bit milling that was the principal security for every one of the manufacturer's patented locks on campus. Schlage wanted to sue for patent infringement and obtain injunctions. I explained the problem to the company's lawyers and engineers: technology had caught up with their little piece of metal!

This chapter examines the legal aspects of mechanical and electromechanical locks and their keys. Manufacturers can have responsibilities and liability toward their customers in conjunction with the performance of the integration between the internal locking mechanisms and the design of their keys. Vulnerabilities and potential system deficiencies can lead to significant consequences because they can also place facilities and users at risk. In Chapter 22, attacks on keys and special keying systems are described.

How Manufacturers and Locksmiths Can Be Liable for Damages

Three critical players are responsible for key control: manufacturers, locksmiths, and end users. In most cases, locksmiths are the most important and vulnerable. They're the gatekeepers for many systems, the most vulnerable to attack, and the least equipped to deal with security issues.

Locksmiths are usually the people who plan and order a system in conjunction with the local facility. They're responsible for receiving cylinders and keys, both cut and blanks. They're the installers responsible for keying, rekeying, cutting keys, and adding cylinders to a system. They often store blank keys for customers, and, perhaps most critically, they keep keying charts and system records. They also verify employees' authority to order cut and master keys.

If a locksmith and their facility aren't secure, they can be liable for a breach that can damage their customers. Lock shops store the components of many of their customers' systems. They also have direct access to manufacturers and their databases via data links. Their computers may not be secure, especially in mobile service vans.

Specifically, a locksmith can be held responsible for a failure to implement the proper controls relating to the following:

- *Data security*: Includes customer data, backups, storage, access, transmission, deletion, updating, audit trails, remote access security, defining what is personal identifying information (PII), and media-handling controls.

- *Physical security*: Encompasses a secure physical location, inventory, locks, keys, data, databases, records storage safe, access to secure areas, protection against natural disasters, and secure work areas not accessible by customers.

- *Employee vetting*: Involves employees' background, criminal history, access levels, audits, defining responsibilities, and nondisclosure agreements (NDAs).

- *Compliance*: Comprises all legal and contractual requirements, applicable legislation, and intellectual property rights.

False or Misleading Advertising About Security and Key Control

Lock manufacturers are constantly racing to develop new products to compete in a marketplace with hundreds of players worldwide. Marketing departments drive sales and revenue, so there's always an impetus to introduce new locks with changes in key designs to entice customers into upgrading or replacing their current systems. This race costs companies millions of dollars to compete in selling their products.

New patents must also be filed to assure customers of the most current state-of-the-art technology and security protection to stay competitive. In my experience with the marketing teams of many of the largest lock manufacturers in the world, they often overstate the security of their products. They can force products to market before they have been thoroughly vetted for security vulnerabilities. This is especially true for high-security locks that must meet certain standards. Often, the marketing teams don't understand all the security ramifications of newly incorporated or updated designs.

Statements about key control and resistance to forms of covert entry can be troublesome because they're often misleading or even wrong. In 2006, my colleague and I presented information at DefCon demonstrating how most pin tumbler locks could be opened in seconds with a plastic mallet and a bump key, rendering about 95 percent of the conventional pin tumbler locks in America vulnerable. The Medeco high-security locks marketing team saw this as a huge opportunity to sell their cylinders due to the national media focus on the security issue.

The news media worldwide published and aired stories about lock bumping and its dangers to security. Because it was so demonstrative on video, it caught the attention of almost everyone using locks. Medeco announced to the media that its locks were bump-proof. It was wrong, however, and in 2007, we demonstrated, again at DefCon, that a 12-year-old girl could bump open the highest-security cylinders. High-security locks were at risk of bumping, but that didn't stop many manufacturers from claiming they were resistant or impervious to the technique.

This is precisely how a company can get into trouble. If customers rely on statements involving security and a loss occurs, the manufacturer can be held liable. Claims of being bump-proof, 3D copy-proof, pick-proof, impossible to decode, and similar representations can lead to class-action lawsuits.

A claim of being "the ultimate in security" was a highly misleading statement by one of the leaders in the industry. The reality was that its locks, admittedly a high-security design, could be picked, often in less than two minutes. The problem was that the manufacturer was unaware of a $200 tool made in China and didn't believe its locks could be picked. Today, sophisticated and inexpensive tools can pick and decode many conventional and high-security locks. They require little skill and are available to anyone. Some of these are described in Chapter 18.

My colleagues and I have analyzed many conventional and high-security locks represented as secure. Complex keys, multiple bitting layers, movable elements, and unique keyways all contribute to the appearance of security. The reality is that many keys and their locks can be compromised, notwithstanding the representations of the manufacturer, and potentially to the detriment of the end users. My rule is that the mechanical portion of any key, even if it has an electronic element, can be replicated. It's just a question of the time and expertise required and the sophistication of the attack.

Like the manufacturer, a locksmith can get into trouble for making false or misleading statements regarding the security of what they sell. They can also be liable for videos that are false or materially misstate security facts.

Key Control Procedures by Manufacturers

To comply with applicable standards from ANSI/BHMA in the United States, every high-security lock manufacturer must provide one or more levels of *key control*. This term connotes several components regarding physical control: the ability to obtain blank keys, order cut keys from the manufacturer for a specific system, and have an approved locksmith duplicate keys provided by a customer. Three levels of physical key control are discussed in Chapter 7. The applicable standards recognize the correlation between the ability to obtain blanks or cut keys and restrictions on who can order or receive keys. This is the essence of key control. There's also *organizational key control,* which defines who has access to what areas and individual locks.

Lock manufacturers implement key control schemes using plastic credit-type cards, usually with magnetic stripes, barcodes, or radio frequency identification (RFID) technology. These cards either contain the bitting code for the specific lock and key or require the card's insertion into a key machine to download the codes directly from the manufacturer to facilitate tracking and an audit trail.

My colleagues and I have conducted many undercover investigations involving locksmiths who completely disregarded the contractual requirements of the lock manufacturers they represent. These locksmiths have cut keys that are supposedly restricted. We found that selling duplicate keys is more important to many locksmiths than abiding by their contracts, much to the detriment of their customers. Such conduct is legally actionable.

How Locksmiths and Key-Duplicating Shops Can Defeat Key Control Schemes

Locksmiths are the main gatekeepers of key control because they're most often responsible for duplicating keys, especially restricted ones. Virtually all manufacturers establish levels of restriction for their high-security cylinders and their keys. These restrictions are based on the BHMA 156.30 standard in the United States. Although some manufacturers conduct routine audits to ensure compliance, locksmiths often violate these requirements and duplicate keys without verifying the proper authority from the customer to do so. These actions can seriously impact facility security and subject the offending locksmith to damages for breach of contract. In many of our investigations, keys were cut on counterfeit blanks, which can also lead to patent infringement lawsuits if the counterfeit blanks are still protected by patents.

There are many ways that key control procedures and physical protections can be circumvented and violated. The following issues should be considered by a manufacturer when establishing policies to protect their customers and their intellectual property in patents and trademarks:

- The authenticating cards can be easily counterfeited.
- There is widespread violation of policies established by the lock companies.
- The locksmiths offer a pretense of requiring authentication from anyone who wants keys duplicated but then cuts them without any authorization. They charge more for doing so.
- There is no industry uniformity in how cards are designed or protected.
- The standards don't establish any security criteria for the cards.

▪ Locksmiths may provide the actual direct key codes to the customer for future reference and duplication.

▪ There is no legal requirement to comply with factory mandates, only contractual requirements, which many locksmiths ignore.

▪ Locksmiths may cut keys on counterfeit or knockoff blanks.

▪ Locksmiths may cut keys on counterfeit blanks that contain multiple keyways.

▪ Locksmiths don't need the key card to cut a key; all they need to do is decode the key bitting and then enter the code.

▪ Lock manufacturers may be lax about contract enforcement.

▪ Locksmiths cut keys on patent-expired blanks for restricted keyways.

▪ "Do Not Duplicate" warnings legally mean nothing, and many locksmiths ignore the warning.

▪ Lock manufacturers fail to establish a licensing agreement that controls all blanks they sell to their dealers, which requires them to *only* cut keys on those blanks and not to violate any key control policy of the company.

When lock manufacturers do not vigorously enforce their key control procedures and allow their dealers to cut keys for customers without appropriate authorization, they invite lawsuits from other locksmiths and critical customers. Every time a restricted key is cut for an unauthorized individual, it can place a facility at risk. It likely can give rise to a lawsuit for fraud or misrepresentation if sales representatives tell the customer that restricted keys are protected against improper copying.

Cutting Keys on Counterfeit, Knockoff, or Legally Restricted Blanks

Certain popular U.S. lock companies have been targeted by overseas manufacturers to produce counterfeit blanks that replicate their keyways and patented interactive elements. In one investigation I led, almost 400,000 counterfeits flooded the country that, years later, can still be found in many lock shops and hardware stores in major cities. In our inquiry, many locksmiths cut keys on blanks that combined several keyways and illegally circumvented valid patents. Combine this practice with a willingness to violate contractual relations with manufacturers, and the result is complete abrogation of key control.

Several legal issues can result from such practice, including patent infringement lawsuits, violation of contracts and resulting damages, and litigation by affected customers. Replicating certain government blanks is also illegal for obvious reasons.

Legal Restrictions

Department of Defense (DoD) blanks and those employed by the U.S. Postal Service have been designated as restricted. It's illegal to sell, manufacture, or duplicate the blanks, and they aren't readily available in the marketplace. However, they've been sold on eBay and other sites as surplus from military bases overseas.

Patent Infringement

Every time a locksmith or hardware store cuts a key on a counterfeit blank, they're infringing on the patent right of the lock manufacturer, assuming the patent for the knockoff key is still valid. In our investigations, locksmiths knew precisely what they were doing but opted to make more money by supplying counterfeit blanks to the consumer. With undercover videos, such cases are easy to prove. Most locksmiths won't engage in this practice, but many do, especially in large cities. Their national trade organization, Associated Locksmiths of America (ALOA), has specific ethical guidelines for members that prohibit the cutting of keys without the proper authorization.

One interesting exception doesn't prevent cutting a restricted key into sections and then putting it back together to create a different combination. In 1976, the case *Medeco Security Lock, Inc. vs. Lock Technology Corp. 75 CIV 0963* was decided in the Federal District Court of New York. Although the case was settled, the Court held that patent protection did not extend to creating a decoding tool based on reassembling key sections that had already been purchased.

Contract Violation by Dealers

Some contracts with lock companies assess up to a $25,000 fine for each violation of using nonoriginal blanks and not requiring adherence to key control procedures. Most high-security lockmakers require adherence to rules about the requirements for verification of an authenticated user before keys can be cut. Many provide significant penalties for violating these rules, as outlined in dealer contracts. Penalties can include fines and termination of the right to represent a specific company and access to restricted blanks.

Voiding of Warranty

A consumer or facility is at risk if they use counterfeit blanks because any warranties the manufacturer offers will likely be inoperative. This also means if the locks malfunction, they probably will not be covered by the warranty. This issue must be stressed to large customers concerned about service and warranty coverage.

Potential Violation of City Ordinances

In certain jurisdictions, such as New York City, cutting keys and acting as a locksmith without a license or violating ordinances can bring civil and criminal penalties and the loss of a license. Cutting keys on counterfeit blanks can be grounds for enforcement action.

Identification of Counterfeit Blanks by Customers

Consumers can't usually distinguish between factory originals and knockoffs or counterfeits. Makers of these blanks rarely duplicate trademarks or logos because doing so is criminal. The key heads are usually blank and often a different color than the factory originals. Lock manufacturers should clarify to customers that they must use original keys and that all warranties will be void if non-original equipment manufacturer (OEM) parts are substituted.

Patent-Expired Blanks

For 20 years after the patent filing date, key-blank manufacturers can replicate and supply blanks without any legal liability for infringement. There's no legal protection, and any facility with a patent-expired system can't be assured of significant key control. This is one reason lock manufacturers continually update their designs: so a patent continuously protects their keyways and keys. Keyways are rarely patented, but interactive or movable elements described in a utility patent are protected. Even though patents expire, some high-security lock manufacturers make it a practice to continue auditing lock shops for using non-OEM keys. Medeco, for example, is known throughout the industry in the United States for aggressively enforcing its key blanks, even when patents have long since expired. Its policy of protecting its keys has been a model for the industry.

Keyway Restrictions Are Often Easily Circumvented

Lock manufacturers worldwide have developed millions of different keyways. This means there are many similar keyways between manufacturers, which can often be easily adapted to fit different locks for which they're not intended. Customers should be advised about the likelihood that nonoriginal blanks may be utilized or modified to circumvent key control for a system. It's also advantageous for high-security lockmakers to explain to end users the lengths a company has gone to ensure that its keys aren't subject to similar blanks, including installing interactive elements to discourage such practices.

Desktop milling machines, CNC, EasyEntrie, and sophisticated key-copying machines are available to locksmiths and anyone who wants to buy them. The ability to modify or mill a blank is relatively easy. Any mechanical key can be replicated, even with interactive elements. The only reliable control usually involves integrating electronic elements that are properly designed and encrypted.

Compromise of Physical Key Control: Duplication, Simulation, and Replication of Credentials

The primary goal of any key control scheme is to prevent access to blanks and the corresponding ability to cut them for a specific bitting combination. It also provides for legal sanctions against manufacturing, producing, or copying any key protected by a valid patent.

There is an infinite variety of mechanical iterations to protect keys from being copied, replicated, and simulated, and many patents have been granted to enhance security against these threats. In my experience, the problem with most of these designs is that they can be defeated; it's just a question of time and expertise. The keys, no matter how complex, are still small pieces of metal unless they contain embedded electronics, and even then, they can often be circumvented.

Manufacturers and their customers need to understand and, in some cases, be briefed on the simplicity or difficulty of defeating key controls they thought were in place to protect their facilities against access via unauthorized keys. A failure to conduct such briefings thoroughly and accurately can lead to legal liability for damages in the event of a breach, because lock manufacturers rarely discuss such subjects with their users or disclose defeat techniques. This discussion must begin with a simple analysis of what constitutes a mechanical key.

In any form, a key is designed to mate with interactive detainers within a lock, such as pin tumblers, rotating discs, wafers, or levers. A key consists of bitting—the portion that lifts, rotates, or moves critical locking elements to the correct position. Keys must also have protrusions, channels, or other methods to create keyways that match the warding pattern in the lock's plug. There are millions of different keyways and key profiles. This is how one manufacturer controls what keys can enter specific plugs and block all other keys from use. Keyways can be subdivided into sections to facilitate access control and master-key systems. Virtual keyways can also be created that simulate the actions of ward patterns.

The third component in high-security keys is secondary or multiple security layers that can make key duplication and other forms of attack more difficult. These security layers consist primarily of movable elements: interactive mechanisms that mate with pins or other elements within the lock. To work properly, they require cooperation between key elements and those in the lock's core.

To obtain new patents, manufacturers are constantly inventing innovative measures to protect their keys from compromise. The problem is, there are many ways to defeat these systems, depending on the specific designs, but they all have certain characteristics in common. Suppose a lock employs two, three, or even four security layers. In that case, the task may seem more difficult but certainly is not impossible, regardless of how complex the key appears.

Key control can be compromised using many techniques, which can be subdivided into the following primary categories:

- Duplication
- Simulation
- Visual decoding of keys
- Replication
- Decoding
- Impressioning
- Rights amplification of restricted keys and virtual keyways
- Inadequate number of differs
- Maximum adjacent cut specification (MACS)
- Extrapolation of top-level master keys
- Creation of bump keys and lock bumping
- Analysis of multiple keys in a system to derive a pattern or sequence of bitting
- Analysis of many keys in a positional master keying system to derive the composite master key code

Duplication

There are many ways to *duplicate* a key, the easiest of which is with a key machine. Today's hardware is sophisticated, and many key cutters are miniature milling or computer numerical control (CNC) systems. They can be programmed for hundreds of different locks and thousands of blanks. They're software-based and can cut conventional keys as well as dimple, laser-track, double-sided, tubular, angled-cut, and many other configurations.

Sophisticated Computerized Key Machines

Many companies offer computer-based machines, some with incredible capabilities. The major players are HPC, Ilco, JMA, Keyline, and top-of-the-line Silca.

Silca produces some of the most sophisticated key machines in the world, including the Triax and Futura Pro. It also has a factory in Italy that makes many blank keys for lock manufacturers worldwide and offers keys when the patents have expired.

Not only is this new generation of machines programmable and able to cut almost any key, but many also automatically decode keys for bitting values, depth, and spacing, which is important if the bitting is worn so it doesn't match factory standards. Some manufacturers have also implemented restrictions on which keys and codes can be duplicated, according to agreements with lock manufacturers to protect against patent infringement.

Milling Machines

Milling machines like the EasyEntrie and Keyway King allow blanks to be modified or created. The *EasyEntrie*, discussed in Chapters 18 and 21, is a milling machine produced in Germany for locksmiths. It was developed because lock shops can't keep blanks for all of the millions of different profiles in Europe. The machine won't reproduce the bitting; it only replicates the warding pattern on one of several special blanks. The machine's output still needs to be cut on a traditional key machine. The problem for lock manufacturers trying to maintain key control is that the EasyEntrie can replicate virtually any conventional profile unless it contains movable elements.

The government version of this machine allows it to be used with Adobe Photoshop editing software to modify any portion of the blank to fit the keyway. This includes adding undercuts such as those used by Schlage Everest. The machine can't replicate side bit milling, as employed by Assa and Medeco in their latest M4 lock designs. It also can't replicate laser tracks or dimple patterns.

The Keyway King is another milling machine and lathe that can modify or generate any profile. Its capabilities differ from those of the EasyEntrie in that it doesn't sample a target blank for duplication—it can create it.

3D Printers and Key Machines

Several 3D printers and key-cutting machines combine large databases of key profiles and the ability to translate scanned or programmed information into working keys for specific locks. A leading French company, Madelin, has produced one of the best law-enforcement 3D programs to store, generate, and modify thousands of profiles and print keys with the proper bitting code. U.S. Lockmasters produces a lock decoder that translates its information into a 3D-printed key. AT Security, also in France, has the most sophisticated program for generating thousands of profiles. The software and several different key-blank examples are discussed in Chapter 22.

The risk to key control and high-security facilities from 3D technology is the ability to generate a properly bitted key or a hybrid key carrier, which can allow the insertion of movable elements that may be difficult to print. 3D technology can also allow the generation of separate secondary security layers that replicate the actions of the key. Two pieces of material are produced to compromise side bit milling and the mechanical credentials in electromechanical keys and locks. Essentially, the functionality of a complex key is split into individual components to be inserted into the keyway.

Simulation

Simulating a key means fooling the lock's internal components that the correct credential has been inserted and properly mated with all the primary and secondary security layers to allow the plug to turn. Mechanical locks don't have any intelligence, so if the key parameters are correct, the lock will open. What the simulated key looks like, and whether it is inserted as one piece of metal or plastic or split into two or more pieces, is irrelevant as long as the composite result matches all the individual requirements for each security layer.

The simulation of a key requires an analysis of each of its components: warding, bitting, and secondary security layers, including sliders, side bit milling, laser tracks, edge tracks, angled bitting, ball bearings, magnetic pins, movable elements, double bitting, or odd bitting shapes.

The important aspect and risk to a system regarding simulating its keys isn't what the target key looks like but how it works. Suppose each of its security layers can be simulated as they enter and cooperate with internal components in a lock. In that case, a simulated credential may appear very different than the original key. Security officers, risk managers, and law enforcement should be vigilant about people possessing keys who may be obtaining unauthorized access to areas or specific locks. If a suspect is encountered, their keys should be forensically examined for criteria matching a key that will open a lock.

Visual Decoding of Keys

Visual decoding means looking at a cut key and deriving the direct bitting code. Sometimes no special measurement tools are required; just as often, a visual inspection can yield the necessary information to cut a key with a machine or handheld device. Although some expertise is required to identify different depth increments and assigned values, the process is often not difficult. The ability to visually decode rests on the complexity of the bitting. Thus, the process can be imprecise in a Keso, Kaba, or Mul-T-Lock dimple lock with many drill points and depths. In contrast, it can be relatively simple to decode many high-security cylinders and derive their bitting combinations. A lock manufacturer must be conversant with the ability to visually decode its locks and provide an honest assessment to its customers of the security risks inherent in its keying and bitting schemes.

Keys can be visually decoded in a few seconds by a trained person. Conventional locks are especially prone to compromise by such techniques, so high-security locks are recommended for any level of required key control. Unless the bitting is complex, such as in a dimple lock or a lock that contains varying bitting angles, it won't prevent someone from decoding it and generating a key. Inexpensive calipers and handheld decoding tools are also available. Keys are inserted into the small device, and the bitting value is displayed on a card for that specific lock. Keys can be photographed or scanned to read the bitting values, and an image can be sent to an online 3D print facility to generate a key in metal or plastic.

Most conventional keys can be easily decoded because the coded depth and spacing information are online and readily available. The number of depth increments can make the task of visual decoding simple or more difficult. Kwikset keys have only six depth increments and are easily decoded without reference to outside data. Medeco high-security keys likewise have six depths and one of three angles for each chamber position. These angles are easily identified, as are the depths, so even some high-security keys can be easily reverse-engineered. However, the task may be more complicated if special key machines are required to replicate complex bitting patterns or angles.

Variable Key-Generation Systems

John Falle developed a variable key-generation system many years ago to allow the simulation of keys by creating a series of stainless-steel sheets with scoring for individual depth increments on a blank to be cut with scissors. These sheets were designed for different depth and spacing values to be universal for pin tumbler locks. The metal was very thin so it wouldn't be blocked by any ward pattern in a keyway. All that was required to create a key was knowing the depth for each cut.

A variation of this technique was a series of magnetic individual bitting segments that could be combined to form a key to be inserted into a plug. This system was employed in a decoder, discussed later in the decoding section.

Dimple Key Simulation and Overlay Bitting Insert

A key may look incredibly complex, and security managers may believe it will be difficult to decode or simulate. In many cases, this isn't exactly true. Two examples are illustrative: Keso and Mul-T-Lock. Both companies produce dimple high-security locks. Mul-T-Lock is an Israeli company that developed the pin-within-pin concept: it provides for an outer and inner telescoping pin for each chamber, together with elements that move between opposite surfaces of the key blade. Keso is a Swiss company with incredibly complex bitting designs that make visual decoding difficult. Simulating keys can defeat both of these key control systems. In one case, my colleague and I developed a nylon overlay with the bitting values that could be inserted laterally in the key blade. That way, a restricted keyway wasn't an obstacle to simulating a key. The blade could be reused as a carrier and easily 3D printed, or an original key could be milled for the insert.

Replication

Falle and others have also developed systems to piece together a key from individual sections having the correct bitting values for a specific lock and manufacturer. All that is required is to join the segments to form a key.

3D printing systems are also perfectly suited to this task. Segments or entire keys can be printed easily for different keyways. In one case I was involved with, a student could derive all the control key codes for the Best removable-core system and generate 12 keys to remove virtually any core on a large campus. When I discussed this vulnerability with senior law enforcement in the university's police department, they were unaware of the risks in the interchangeable core (IC) systems and the ability to print or generate keys that could be used to gain or sabotage access to an area. The control keys for these systems are equivalent to master keys, only more dangerous because they allow the core of the lock to be removed and replaced, thereby creating a potential lockout condition.

Decoding

There are many methods to decode the bitting values in almost all forms of locks and their internal detainers. Wafer, tubular, pin tumbler, disc, and lever locks are all subject to key compromise through decoding, either visually, with depth keys, or with specially designed decoders such as those developed by John Falle, Madelin, and Lishi. (For more information on this subject, check out Part IV.)

Key systems and their keys can be decoded and reproduced with specialized decoding tools that pick and decode the bitting values, allowing a key to be generated by a key cutter, mechanical reproduction with bitting segments, or 3D-printed individual segments.

Impressioning

Impressioning is a nondestructive covert technique that can be carried out in multiple steps at different times. The ability to compromise a key control system and obtain the impression of the internal detainers of a lock is based on many factors, but obtaining or simulating blank keys is critical. When considering the implementation of a specific type of high-security cylinder, several issues must be discussed with the manufacturer:

- Does the lock design allow any impressioning to produce a key?
- Can the lock be easily decoded, facilitating the use of the resulting information to create a key with a code-cutting machine?
- Can the lock be decoded by a piezo decoder produced by Madelin or C.O.F.E.D. and then translated into a key machine–generated duplicate?
- Are the lock type and the key system included in the Madelin, C.O.F.E.D., or AT Security database for 3D generation?
- Are special cuts, angles, depths, or other unique parameters required to produce a working key?
- What is the difficulty in obtaining blank keys and enforcing key control procedures?
- Are similar blanks available that can be modified for impressioning?
- What's the complexity of the bitting surfaces and the difficulty of impressioning?
- Do the types of security layers make impressioning more difficult or time-consuming?
- How difficult is it to replicate and cut the individual bitting surface?
- Is a special key machine required, or is a handheld one available?
- Is there a tool to decode the lock and replicate the bitting without physically cutting a blank (such as the Lishi tool)?
- How much expertise is required to impression the target lock and key?
- How much time is required to accurately impression the lock and produce a key?
- Are unique or costly tools required to impression and produce a working key?
- Are online videos available that demonstrate how to impress a specific lock being considered for installation or upgrade?
- Can key bitting be accurately cut by hand?

Rights Amplification

Rights amplification is altering or modifying a cut key in a key control system to make it work in locks with different bitting values. It's a favorite technique for insider attacks and should be carefully considered in the policies of organizational key control. The ability to obtain and alter keys can be critical, especially where it's difficult to obtain or simulate blanks. Deleted or unused keys can be modified to alter the bitting.

Inadequate Number of Differs

One of the security metrics for key control is the number of theoretical and actual differs or different key combinations available for a cylinder. This is especially important in master key systems, assuming that master keying is even available. Security may be at risk if a manufacturer offers fewer than 100,000 key changes. Some inexpensive consumer locks offer far fewer combinations. Depending on the security requirements, this should be a red flag, especially if no secondary layers of security are incorporated in keys.

The type of active-locking detainer is also important, and customers should be briefed on how the locks work and their limitations. Kwikset is one of the most popular consumer brands in the United States, but it can't offer high-security cylinders or traditional master keying capabilities. Its SmartKey allows instant combination-change capabilities for keys but limits the number of differs. Thus, its theoretical number of combinations for a five-pin lock with six depth increments is 6^5. The number of key changes may be much smaller, depending on the tolerances achieved in manufacturing.

If tolerances between the plug and shell allow for $+/-1$ or 1.5" depth increments, then the number of keys that can open a lock is significantly fewer. This is how tryout keys were developed for General Motors (GM) sidebar cylinders in the auto industry. The theoretical number of keys for all GM vehicles was about 4,096 4^6 (four depth increments and six wafers). The number of keys required to open every GM car in the country was really 64 because the tolerance between cuts was a half-depth increment.

The result of too few differs and poor tolerances can lead to unauthorized access to locks. Key jiggling and feel-picking are the results, especially with worn bitting surfaces or tumblers. This can be particularly critical in complex master keying systems. See Part IV for a more thorough discussion.

Pinning Restrictions and Maximum Adjacent Cut Specifications

A manufacturer must also apprise its customers if there are pinning restrictions that may limit the number of available combinations. Medeco BIAXIAL locks are a perfect example. The design of its pin tumblers and chisel point prohibits certain combinations between what Medeco refers to as fore and aft pins because of how the pins contact the bitting surface of the key. Its codebook restricts certain combinations, but if not followed, the result can be keys opening locks they are not intended to open. MACS may also restrict the number of available combinations. Each manufacturer limits the depth of adjacent cuts due to mechanical limitations, so this must be considered to ensure reliable operation between the key and internal mechanism. These issues may be irrelevant in conventional cylinders but are important in high-security systems.

Extrapolation of Top-Level Master Keys

As described in Part V, the extrapolation of top-level master keys can seriously threaten any master key system that employs total position progression sequencing. The process is covert and only requires the availability of blank keys or keys that can be modified to test the different bitting combinations. A manufacturer should be questioned about the capability to compromise its system with this technique and how it's guarded against.

Defeat of Virtual Keyways

Many lock manufacturers implement virtual keyways to enhance the number of differs available in a system. Although they may be identified as security enhancements and bars to the compromise of key control, they can often be easily defeated. These schemes can take many forms, including edge bitting, dimples, laser tracks, placement of movable elements in different positions on the key blade, undercuts, and indented secondary bitting patterns on multiple key surfaces. Although all these layers may appear secure, they only add a bit of complexity to defeating the security of the physical key.

The 2003 release of the Medeco m3 is a perfect example. Adding a slider in the cylinder corresponding to physical steps on the key was clever and unique; its real function was to create a form of additional sub-keyway. Unless the protruding step on the key matched the position of the internal slider, the lock could not be opened. Even if the primary characteristics of the key were correctly matched to the warding of the plug, that didn't allow the key to function properly because the slider wasn't moved to the correct position to allow the sidebar to engage.

In earlier releases, this design was very simple to defeat, even though it appeared to add significant security. The m3 and similar virtual keyways deter locksmiths from importing or cutting keys on these blanks due to the multiple combinations required to keep them in inventory. Any manufacturer that implements virtual keyways should be questioned about how difficult they would be to defeat, thereby compromising key control based on these designs.

Creation of Bump Keys and Lock Bumping

Most conventional locks can be easily bumped open, which is the rationale for purchasing rated high-security cylinders for added security. See Chapter 13 for a more thorough discussion of the distinguishing features of the different types of locking systems.

High-security locks are less susceptible to attacks by lock bumping, but it's often still possible. The ability to open these locks largely depends on access to blank keys or the use of keys modified to produce a bump key. If keys of the same keyway are available, they can be altered and cut down to all the deepest cuts. Bumping can be significantly more difficult if there are secondary security layers, such as side bit milling or rotation of pin tumblers. However, my colleagues and I have analyzed many high-security locks and found that quite a few can be bumped open. Even the implementation of rotating pins, side bit milling, telescoping pins, movable or interactive elements, and other measures may not prevent the practice. Manufacturers should be questioned about their test procedures and results against bumping in any locking system being purchased or installed.

Legal Issues in Master Key Systems

Unlike certain government and military installations, most large facilities implement master key (MK) systems. Although they may promote organizational control, they're inherently less secure than systems where locks only have a change key and can't be accessed any other way.

Security officers, if they're unaware of the nuances of master key systems, must be briefed and confirm that they understand the risks of implementing a system unless effective secondary security layers are in place. The vulnerabilities of an master key system can be critical. Essentially, there's no forensic trail in a system that has been compromised by extrapolation, and all locks on the system can be affected and at risk. Defeating the security of an master key system isn't high-tech, and it doesn't take any real expertise to accomplish: only blank keys or keys that have been lost or deleted from a system and a way to cut them. Even more troublesome, an attack can occur when the pin stack can be sampled in stages—one pin tumbler at a time—until the correct code is derived.

A failure to explain the potential security issues, limitations, and tradeoffs when master key systems are implemented can lead to legal liability in the event of a serious breach. Although these systems facilitate organizational key control, they also offer serious methods of compromise of the locks in such systems. master keys are convenient for ease of access but are inherently not as secure as locks set up with individual change keys only.

Suppose adherence to *total position progression* master keying schemes is followed. These systems can be decoded unless secondary security layers are implemented, including sectional keyways, sliders (Medeco m3), different system sidebar codes, and other enhancements.

Manufacturers should specify to customers how their master keys are derived and the system tolerances, and then explain any system limitations or vulnerabilities, especially in relation to depth increments and cross-keying issues. Unintended master keys are a security vulnerability, particularly on large or complex master key systems. Incidental keys are a problem in most keying systems that create a matrix of key combinations and virtual shear lines due to how levels or master keying are derived. From a security standpoint, unintended combinations allow unforeseen keys to open locks and can be a security risk.

The most common concerns and security vulnerabilities include the following:

- The number of theoretical versus actual available key combinations.
- Tolerance between plug and shell and the measurement of each depth increment. This relates to key jiggling, feel picking, and the development of tryout keys wherein one key can be manipulated into a lock that isn't supposed to open with that bitting code. If the tolerances aren't precise and the depth increments aren't sufficiently deep, it may be easy to utilize a key by manipulating it to open a lock that isn't coded for that key.
- Failure to meet UL 437 and BHMA 156.30 standards.
- Whether the system is engineered from one or more keys to determine the master key coding.
- An ability to extrapolate the top-level master key (TMK) if key blanks are available.
- Whether locks on the master key system are accessible to the public.

A good example of an master key system's lock being accessible to the public is the public restroom at BHMA offices. This lock was a high-security cylinder on the master key system. The problem was that the key given out to the public had the correct side bit milling code and keyway so that the master key could be derived through extrapolation, or the cylinder could be removed and decoded.

- Lost master keys and how to deal with the resulting security issue.
- Reduced pick resistance. Double pinning (i.e., a master pin and bottom pin in one or more chambers) can make it easier to pick the lock.
- Unwanted cross-keying, key interchange, or incidental master keys from the same or other systems that can open more locks than intended.
- Unauthorized rights amplification.
- Electronic access-control systems that have bypass cylinders, which can be easily compromised.
- The ability for a change key to be modified to work as a master key.
- Physical integrity and monitoring of cylinders to protect against disassembly and decoding.
- Whether a change key, or any key in the system, can be easily converted to a blank key.
- Whether virtual keyway schemes, such as Schlage Everest, can be easily circumvented.

- Whether keys or cylinders contain magnetic material and can be easily decoded with visa mag, a Gauss meter, a Hall effect probe, or another method.

- Whether keys can be photographed and easily decoded, or a 3D replica can be produced.

- Whether restricted blanks with secondary security layers can be dissected and reconfigured to a working key to allow unauthorized access.

- Whether computerized key-duplicating machines, such as KeyMe and those used by DIY stores, can replicate or duplicate keys.

Extrapolation of Top-Level Master Keys

A failure to warn facility managers of apartment complexes and risk managers in buildings about the ability to compromise master key systems can present a serious liability in the event of a compromise. If conventional locks are employed that can be easily decoded for the top-level master keys, everyone in such a facility can be at risk.

High-security locks with effective key control and secondary security layers can mitigate the dangers of a procedure to decode top-level master keys. Still, managers must be briefed about the security and legal vulnerabilities involved. Unless keys are designed with safeguards that prevent modification, replicating or duplicating of keys can be employed to decode the master key system, and every mastered lock on a master key can be decoded covertly. This threat primarily applies in a system based on the *total position progression system*, which is the most popular in the United States for pin tumbler locks. If this system is employed for coding all cylinders in a system, it can be relatively simple to determine how individual keys and master key codes were originally derived if enough samples of keys can be obtained and compared.

Systems Protected by Side Bit Milling and Sidebar Codes

Side bit milling is employed on several high-security key designs, including Assa Abloy, Medeco M4, certain Assa series, and Schlage Primus. Bo Widen, one of the world's most famous engineers and lock designers, was responsible for creating side bit milling as a second security layer. Although it's very effective in preventing copying, it's not difficult to replicate with modern key-cutting machines, milling and CNC systems, and 3D printing.

For risk managers and security officers, the way manufacturers assign side bit milling codes to dealers and locksmiths is problematic. A locksmith may purchase one or more unique codes for all their customers. If another customer purchases locks from the same vendor, they have keys with the same side coding. Keys can be cut on different bitting codes and then cut down, or positions can be rights-amplified and built up for the desired combination.

All Medeco high-security cylinders employ what I defined as sidebar codes in the book *Open in Thirty Seconds*. In a six-pin lock, Medeco provides 729 different possible combinations of angles. The pins within the lock are both elevated and rotated, which is the genius of the lock's design. If the pin tumblers aren't lifted to the shear line *and* rotated to the correct angle, which can be –20, 0, or +20 degrees, the lock won't open because a sidebar will be blocked from retracting into the plug. Six pins, with one of three possible rotations, mean 3^6 combinations. Like keys with side bit milling codes assigned by the factory, sidebar codes are also set up by the factory or locksmith and are often the only ones for a system. If a person has blanks or keys that can be modified, having the correct sidebar code enables part of the system's security to be compromised.

Analysis of Multiple Keys in a System to Derive a Pattern or Sequence of Bitting

Suppose a keying system for master keys is sequenced predictably, and it's possible to compare several keys to decode bitting values. In that case, the master key or other change keys can be deciphered. Manufacturers should be questioned about how the bitting codes were developed to ensure that they can't be reverse-engineered and keys produced for specific areas or locks. This can be precisely the problem with a system set up using total position progression keying.

Analysis of Many Keys in a Positional Master Keying System to Derive the Composite Master Key Code

A positional master key system was developed by Sargent Keso many years ago. High-security dimple-lock manufacturers employ it in certain current Keso and other cylinders. These systems can be compromised with sufficient samples of different decoded bitting values because the master key is a *composite* of all the individual change keys in a system.

Security Policies for Organizational Key Control

Organizational key control involves planning a system that defines and controls access to specific areas and locks. It's also the procedure to control and account for all keys in a system and includes currently valid keys and those taken out of service, not returned by terminated employees, or lost. It's important to account for all keys because of the potential to rights simplify the bitting values or sectional keyways to access locks without proper authorization. When planning your organizational key control, the following questions should be asked:

- How are keys tracked in a system?
- What is the procedure for destroying keys removed from service?

- Can the bitting surface be easily altered or modified?
- What tools are required to recut keys removed from service?
- Does the keying system provide for special depth cuts not used for changing keys to prevent rights amplification for master keys?
- How difficult would it be to add height to the bitting surface in one or more positions?
- Can keys be easily modified to create bump keys?
- Can the system be compromised by using a key with the correct sidebar code or side bit milling and altering the bitting?
- Can a sophisticated attack be conducted using a key with the correct side bit milling or sidebar code in combination with a picking tool?
- Can a key with the correct sidebar code be employed to set the position of the pin tumblers and then conventionally pick the lock?
- What is the procedure if master keys are lost, stolen, or not returned by employees? Must the system be rekeyed?
- Is the system protected against extrapolation by a master ring such as was introduced by Corbin more than 75 years ago?
- Who is responsible for controlling key blanks in the organization?
- Who keeps keying records and code lists?

Organizational key control must also encompass the security protections implemented by a manufacturer. A customer must be certain to receive assurances from the manufacturer in writing that the following aspects of key control are properly addressed and secured:

- Access to manufacturer's computers that contain critical customer information
- Database of coding of keys and code lists
- Inventory control
- Identification of customers in a database and protection of that information
- The security of shipments of keys and locks
- Reordering of blanks, locks, and cut keys, including master keys
- Whether the company enforces its intellectual property (IP) to stop the counterfeiting of its keys

Chapter 11 presents a brief history of lock design and development. This provides the foundation of modern locking systems and the many iterations and improvements required to reach the current state-of-the-art. I explore the different primary locking systems and their vulnerabilities from early Egypt until the present.

Basic Designs and Technologies for Mechanical and Electronic Locks

One of the recognized pioneers of high-security lock designs in the twentieth century once told me there is nothing new in locks, only a recombination of past ideas. Part III thus examines the history of lock mechanisms. Almost all the current designs in mechanical locks can be traced to those invented hundreds or even thousands of years ago. Understanding the present designs requires an appreciation of how lock design has evolved and the inventiveness and creativity that is the foundation for current lock designs.

The brief history of locking mechanisms presented here includes a dictionary of industry definitions to help you understand the material in some of the later chapters. The focus is on modern high-security locks and how the old and new systems merged into the current state-of-the-art.

A Brief History of Lock Design and Development

Our ancestors have needed to protect their belongings since the beginning of civilization, and this became more pronounced as they gathered more valuable possessions. The answer for their physical security was locks, initially in primitive forms. You can find references to these early locks, along with evidence about locks and keys from more than 4,000 years ago. Such references can even be found in the Bible. What developed over the following 40 centuries has provided the foundation and principles of modern locking technology. It's been an amazing journey of inventiveness and innovation, from the most primitive measures to secure a door to our current high-technology locks and safes. Today's products utilize sophisticated hardware and software designs, coupled with the science of physics, chemistry, and metallurgy, to produce secure locks and safes that can be highly resistant to all attacks.

The development of modern locks is fascinating and reflects the incredible creativity of thousands of artisans who searched for and invented solutions to the problem of securing people and their possessions and abodes. Consider that 4,000 years ago, locks were very different from those we have today. Different mechanical systems have been conceived and painstakingly developed to make locking devices more adaptable to users' requirements and resistant to all attacks.

The long history of lock-design evolution includes the challenges that criminals have posed for lock makers and locksmiths. Today's manufacturers continue to search for more sophisticated lock designs. The primary innovations and developments of various lock designs are covered in this chapter. It provides a historical perspective and serves as a guide for engineers about how various approaches to locking technologies came to be and their relevance to current and contemplated designs.

For centuries, craftsmen have faced essentially the same problems in locking hardware; only the materials and technology have changed. Looking back at some of these problems can be instructive and can provide different ideas for their solutions.

Much of this chapter's material is taken from my treatise *Locks, Safes, and Security: An International Police Reference*, Second Edition. More detailed information and images appear in that work.

From Blacksmiths to Locksmiths: The Development of the Technology of Locks

Locksmithing, which originated in blacksmithing, is one of the oldest trades. Blacksmiths worked in Egypt, Babylon, Assyria, and China long before the Great Pyramids were built. For 4,000 years, their primary mission was to conceive of, design, and construct ways to protect humans and their possessions and then protect those devices and systems against thieves and methods to circumvent such protections.

Locksmithing developed customs and traditions, which emanated from Medieval *guilds*. These groups were the supreme masters of this craft; the penalty for defiance was expulsion and the loss of the right to make a living as a locksmith.

The locksmith trade became a father-to-son enterprise and continued as such until the end of the eighteenth century, which is one reason lock designs failed to progress technologically. Lockmaking had to wait until the Industrial Revolution for the ability to manufacture and mass-produce commercially viable products.

Although much of the world awakened to science, art, and engineering, locksmiths concentrated on trick locks and fancy devices. False keyholes and wards, along with many security-superfluous designs, were the order of the day. During the Renaissance, the *lever tumbler* was the only significant innovation. Lever tumbler locks, as described later in this chapter, were based on a new design that employed movable flat pieces of metal called *levers*, which had a cutout or gate that allowed a protrusion (called a *fence*) to enter once the action of a key properly aligned the lever. This was a revolutionary design and an improvement in security.

In the United States, the tradition and rules of the guilds never took hold. Rather, locksmiths in America took advantage of the period's available technology, precision, and security. The two preeminent locksmiths and inventors were Yale and Sargent. As factories were established, the locksmithing craft was divided into two segments: lockmakers and lock repairmen. Today, locksmiths' work is relegated to repair, installation, and maintenance rather than manufacture.

The capabilities, efficiency, and professionalism of locksmiths and their industry were significantly advanced by several inventions and innovations in applicable technology. A *key-duplicating machine* was invented by Henry Gussman in 1909. This device ended the time-consuming and tedious cutting of keys by hand. Next, the *code machine* was introduced in 1926 by the Independent Lock Company and gave locksmiths new capabilities and economic benefits, especially in creating master key (MK) systems.

Many pioneers helped to advance locksmithing in America and Europe and added to the state-of-the-art in terms of its capabilities to provide security and service. Major trade groups, including the Associated Locksmiths of America (ALOA), the American Society for Industrial Security (ASIS), the Safe and Vault Technicians Association (SAVTA), and the European Locksmith Federation, have continued the profession. With modern techniques, scientific tools, and continuing education, the locksmith profession has progressed from a small handcraft to guilds to a flourishing service industry.

It's hard to imagine that over 4,000 years ago, there were no locks or technology to protect people or their abodes or assets, except perhaps ropes hooked to doors in Greece! That was the beginning; and over the next 40 centuries, thousands of craftsmen, blacksmiths, locksmiths, inventors, and manufacturers created an incredible array of modern locks, safes, technology, and systems to keep us safe and secure. This chapter documents these primary advances, from ropes and wooden beams that secured doors to sophisticated locking mechanisms. All these advances are built on individual ideas, concepts, and often brilliant flashes of creativity that form the basis of all the locking systems we rely on today.

The First Locking Systems

Four thousand years ago, the Greeks originally devised locks based on intricately tied knots made from rope. Their purpose was to detect if anyone tried to open them (see Figure 11-1). The theory was that only the owner could determine the proper method of unknotting. Once doors or other barriers were employed, the question was how to fasten such movable obstructions. All basic locking systems face the same primary problem today: preventing someone or something from moving against a fixed enclosure or object.

Figure 11-1: An early Greek door lock. Access to move the bolt was through the door.

Initially there were no latches, bolts, or other devices as we know them today. Long wooden or metal planks on the inside of doors created a barrier to movement, representing primitive bolt work. To release this obstruction, a rope or cord was inserted from outside the door that could be pulled to raise the blocking member. Then the rudimentary lock designers utilized a massive bolt with a large sickle-shaped key. The key consisted of a semicircular blade measuring a foot or more in diameter and a long handle that tapered to a blunt point.

The design of Greek keys suffered from a very serious problem: there were too few varying patterns, which allowed primitive skeleton keys to replicate the curvature and length of a specific key. Interestingly, this is the same problem that existed when warded locks became popular in hotels and other locales: the position of the wards could easily be located, decoded, and bypassed. The requirement for the number of combinations or differs for a locking system can be found in the UL 437 and BHMA Standards today. The Greeks are credited with the concept of an inside-locking mechanism: they placed the bolt system on the inside of the door and provided access to manipulate it from the outside through a keyhole.

> **NOTE**   One Egyptian artisan made an image of a lock on a fresco in a palace near the ancient city of Nineveh. Over 4,000 years old, that image appeared to reflect Egyptian lock design, which provided the idea for the modern pin tumbler mechanism invented by Linus Yale. It consisted of movable pegs and used a long key with protruding pins.

The Egyptians, Greeks, and Romans devised the first wooden locks with movable pins, which were the precursors that Linus Yale improved on in 1860. Each civilization did so independently of the others. These locks consisted of a post affixed to a door that interacted with a sliding horizontal bolt that entered the post, much like the modern latch, bolt, edge-bore, and strike plate.

The Greeks and Egyptians developed various implementations of movable pins. In the Greek design, the key moved the pins into position to allow the release of a bolt by hand movement. The Egyptians employed a key to withdraw the bolt. This bolt had several openings or bores designed to be filled with movable pins. The system was locked or unlocked using a large wooden key resembling a toothbrush with pegs matching the holes and pins. To open the lock, the key was inserted and lifted, which caused the pins to move, thus allowing the bolt to be moved. In modern terms, this mechanism contains a *shear line*.

In the final primitive adaptation, a spring was added to the bolt works on the inside surface of the door, which spread against the sides of its enclosure. The *key* compressed the spring and allowed the bolt to be moved. The early implementation consisted of a crossbeam bolt to secure a door. It was likely hollow, requiring a hidden vertical locking pin to restrict lateral movement. This pin was accessed by a key with protruding pegs.

The Original Egyptian Pin Tumbler Design

Egyptian craftsmen conceived one of the fundamental principles of modern lock design: the pin tumbler. Ultimately, their innovation led to the Linus Yale lock. The early design, as shown in Figures 11-2 and 11-3, was based on the premise that movable pins had to be lifted to the correct level by a primitive key. This movement allowed the bolt to move to a locked or unlocked position if the pins (or pegs) were set to the proper level. Later iterations used the concept of a shear line and a double-detainer theory of locking, where the pegs, pins, or levers must be lifted to precisely the correct position. *Double detainer* means there is only one correct position for movable elements that must be positioned by the key to form a shear line (i.e., the minute gap between pin tumblers or the gate where the fence aligns). Virtually every modern lock relies on some form of the shear line, because a movable bolt or latching mechanism must act against a fixed portion to be released or engaged.

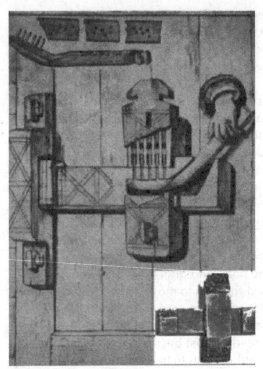

Figures 11-2: An Egyptian pin tumbler lock mounted on the inside of a door, with a key inserted from outside.

Figures 11-3: The original pin tumbler lock design replica from the British Museum collection

The design of the key for the Egyptian lock could be two to three feet long, with vertical wooden pegs placed to match the pins within the lock in both position and length. The concept of a pin tumbler mechanism, although primitive, was widely imitated in many different parts of the world. The original lock, as shown in Figure 11-4, comprised three primary parts, just like the modern equivalent.

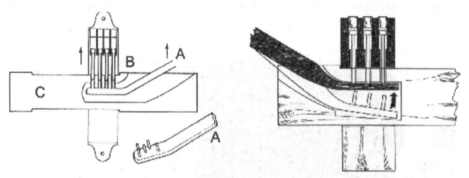

Figure 11-4: The Egyptian lock had three primary components: the key (A), the pin tumblers (B), and the lock body (C).

Early Roman Locks and the Introduction of Wards

The Romans took the best of Egyptian and Greek ingenuity and produced locks that were considered far more sophisticated. They recognized the defects in the earlier designs and the security vulnerabilities inherent in such simple mechanisms. They moved from wooden parts to metal and included smaller keyholes and more intricate keys.

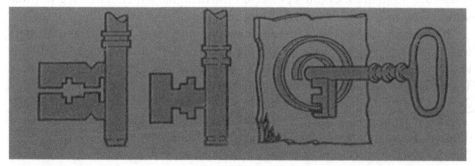

Figure 11-5: The warded lock relied on circular obstructions or bands to block the rotation of the key.

One of their true innovations was the introduction of *wards*, shown in Figure 11-5. These were a logical extension from the early design of key shapes made to prevent entry into a lock. The concept was to place blocking elements that prevented all but the matching key from entering and being able to rotate or control the movement of the bolt or latch. If a series of obstructions could be placed in the path of turning a key, the lock could be far more secure. The secret was to create spaces in the key that could pass the internal obstructions in the lock body (see Figure 11-6). Wards added an entirely new dimension to security.

Figure 11-6: An early warded lock.

Improvements in design continued, which made the keyway and ward patterns more complicated and intricate. When this wasn't sufficient, multiple locks were installed. The keys were often ornate and complex in their design. Smaller was better for both keyholes and keys. The Romans realized that the design of their keyholes, combined with warding patterns, made their locks more difficult to manipulate by picking. Although the actual origin of the warded lock is obscure, Roman locksmiths perfected the designs, which remained popular until the middle of the nineteenth century.

The concept of wards is embedded in every modern lock design as a primary means of providing security by barring entry of all but the proper key blank. Figures 11-7, 11-8, and 11-9 show early warded locks, keys, and mechanisms. They can also ensure different key combinations for each manufacturer and distinguish one lockmaker from another.

In modern locks, wards are formed by broaching: side grooves that create different keyways are matched with a mirror image of metal wards in the lock. *Broaching* is the process of creating these patterns with specially cut hardened steel dies that are rammed into the plug and cut the ward patterns. A solid piece of metal is initially broached and forms the plug. The plug is usually made from brass or nickel-silver stock. The process creates longitudinal protrusions along the length of the keyway and is designed to mirror those obstructions in the key. Keyways, which are the outgrowth of simple wards, provide the first access barrier to the internal locking mechanism.

Figure 11-7: An early warded lock and key.

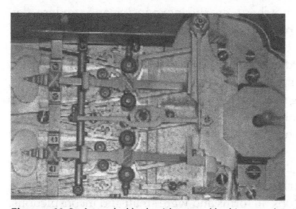

Figures 11-8: A warded lock with several locking mechanisms

Figures 11-9: A complex warded key.

In the original warded locks, the wards were more primitive and often took the form of a complex of metal blocks that had to be traversed for the key to move or turn. The design of the valid key was such that cutouts were embedded to allow passage of the various wards, which were placed in various hidden positions within the lock. That was their secret and thus their security: the number and locations of many different wards.

Although the concept was novel, it wasn't secure against manipulation, impressioning, and picking. The idea was that the internal wards would stop all but the proper key from turning an internal component, thereby actuating the latch or bolt. If there wasn't a corresponding cutout at every point in the key where a blocking ward was positioned, the key was physically prevented from moving. In many locks, finding the location of the wards was obfuscated by artistic and intricate designs, including multiple false keyways. The problem was that their fundamental principle and "security secret" were always the same: you must find the wards within the lock and then fashion a key that would circumvent them.

Even today, some very old hotels still have warded locks for guest rooms. *Skeleton keys* can be easily fashioned to bypass all the wards, allowing the key to move the bolt to an unlocked position. A similar design is present in many inexpensive padlocks. Every kid used to have a Master padlock for a locker or bicycle. Their flat keys with notches were the inexpensive and modern-day equivalent of warded locks. I produced skeleton keys that would open all of them by stripping away all the bitting on both sides of the key blanks to "pass" all the wards. Virtually all warded locks could be defeated similarly.

The Romans also developed spring-loaded bolts in their locking mechanisms, which obviated gravity-locking problems. The spring-biased bolts required less than a 360-degree rotation to unlock—a significant advancement in lock design. Examples were discovered in the ruins of Pompeii long after the volcano froze the community in 64 A.D.

Padlocks were the logical evolution from fixed mechanisms. Originally developed and enhanced by the early Chinese, they were popularized and made practical by the Romans. Keys took all forms and were small and inconspicuous. They can be seen as the link between primitive devices and the development of the modern lock.

Lock Designs in the Middle Ages: The Introduction of the Lever Tumbler

After the fall of the Roman Empire, locksmithing flourished during the Middle Ages. Craftsmen continued to improve on the warded lock designs, adding complexity and producing works of art. Security became more urgent in the days of castles and knights, robber barons, and monasteries that contained books and manuscripts of great learning from ancient days. It focused an impetus on more sophisticated lock designs.

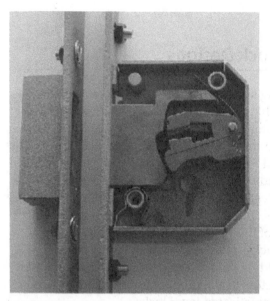

Figure 11-10: An example of a lever tumbler lock with multiple levers.

The concept of wards and the warded lock had limited capabilities and design life because the principle was based on a single premise: blocking elements to inhibit movement of all but the correct key with matching ward cutouts. Try as the locksmiths might, there simply was no place for added improvements except more complexity based on the same fundamental limitations. From the Romans until the end of the eighteenth century, security in locks was based on fixed obstructions, elaborate keyholes, fine slits, and intricate keys. No other method existed to make locks more secure. Toward the end of the seventeenth century, locks were based on the pushing and sliding of keys and bolts. That concept gave way to mechanical turning to actuate bolt mechanisms where keys rotated around a fixed pin or slid through a keyway.

Warded locks had been designed as far as possible, but it wasn't enough. Recognizing this inherent limitation, locksmiths and manufacturers devised the next refinement: the *lever tumbler,* as shown in Figure 11-10. That security capability was innovative and unique and has survived for the past 200 years.

Lever tumbler locks introduced movable locking components (i.e., levers) that pivoted or were raised by the key's bitting. The distinguishing feature was one or more gates in each lever. The function of each gate was to allow or block the movement of a fence or protrusion that interacted with the gate. This was the genius of the basic lever lock design: a system whereby the key bitting corresponded to different gate positions on one or more levers. Unless all the levers were properly lifted and aligned, a slidable bolt could not be moved by the action of the key.

Advancements in Lever Lock Designs

The development of a secure locking system that employed lever tumblers was conceived in several stages by notable pioneers in the industry, many of whom worked in and around Wolverhampton, England. That area was about 130 miles northwest of London and home to most lock designers and factories. Is this 200-year-old lever lock relevant to design engineers today? Each technological advance has led to more security and laid the foundation for modern-day locks. Shear lines, movable bolts, false gates, traps and mechanical-picking detection, multiple gates, rotating mechanisms, and the idea of a fence-gate relationship to accomplish locking are all products of this genre in lock design and development.

Modern safe locks with wheel packs, gates, and drop-in fences can be traced to the original lever lock designs. Sliding bolts with multiple shear lines, double-detainer locking systems, and detectors to alert about an attempted entry demonstrated the evolution of more sophisticated lever locks.

Although Linus Yale took a different path in his modification of the Egyptian pin tumbler, his invention around 1860 utilized several fundamental principles that were taken from the lever lock: double pins that blocked movement and rotation of the key that actuated critical internal components and moved them across one or more shear lines. Lever locks also made possible modern-day master keying capabilities by creating multiple gates or shear lines.

Robert Barron, Joseph Bramah, Charles Chubb, Parsons, Robert Newell, Alfred Hobbs, Tucker and Reeves, and Linus Yale were notable inventors and pioneers who devised and introduced security enhancements to the basic lever tumbler mechanism.

Robert Barron: Double-Acting Lever Tumbler

Major innovations in the lever lock are said to have begun with Robert Barron in 1778. The *double-acting lever tumbler* was the most significant development of this era. Originally the lever was a form of catch, which, until raised by the key, held the bolt immovable. The first lever locks required the key to lift a single spring from a notch in the bolt and force the bolt forward once released. This principle was employed in Banbury wooden locks.

Barron made a square-cut notch that he called a gate. This gate was combined with a stump that was part of the lever and projected into the gate. It blocked the bolt from moving until the key lifted all the levers when the stumps cleared the gates and allowed the bolt to slide into a locked or unlocked position.

The genius of the invention was that if any of the stumps were in the wrong position (either too high or too low), the bolt could not move. This is the principle of double-detainer locking, and it added a new security dimension that was lacking in warded mechanisms. The combination of a stump (i.e., fence), key bitting, and interaction with individual gates meant each lever was independently secured against improper alignment by a key that didn't lift each lever to the precise height or position. This same operating principle is one of the fundamental design parameters in locks today, whether in a lever, pin tumbler, disc, or wafer. Each active locking component provides security against manipulation or using a key not properly bitted for a specific lock.

Skeleton keys defeated the security of the warded lock because there was only one real-locking parameter. In contrast, applying one and then multiple levers eliminated this kind of vulnerability. It was also believed that an *impression* of the lever interaction in the Barron design couldn't be used to determine precise mechanical details to circumvent it. As might be expected, that belief was short-lived.

The next 200 years saw many improvements and enhancements to the original Barron square-cut gate and pivoting-lever design. The idea of allowing the key to raise and pivot the position of each lever independently so that all the gates aligned in some form remains a fundamental precept in modern locking technology. Today's high-security safe locks have seven or more levers and can be incredibly difficult to pick and decode.

The Bramah Lock: No Direct Contact Between the Key and Bolt Mechanism

Joseph Bramah was one of England's most famous inventors and lock makers. In 1784, he devised and received the first patent for a system where the key controlled a series of sliders that allowed the bolt to move (see Figure 11-11). The key was shaped like a tube with longitudinal slots, forming a new kind of bitting. This allowed for a very small key with much higher security than had previously been possible.

When the key was inserted into the lock, the internal sliders aligned with each protrusion or bitting of the key so that all the individual sliders were positioned at a shear line. This mechanism was the forerunner to the modern axial pin tumbler lock invented by the Chicago Lock Company for vending and other industries. Today, the Ace Lock and many similar designs are popular for alarm locks, computer-cable locks, elevator control, and other applications.

The invincibility of the Bramah lock lasted for more than half a century until an American locksmith named Alfred C. Hobbs figured out how to open it at

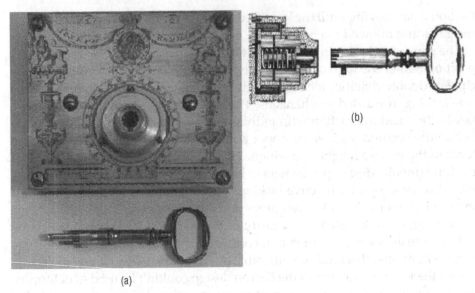

Figure 11-11a, 11b: The original Bramah lock and tubular key.

London's Great Exhibition in 1851. The "pick-proof" lock was displayed at the Bramah lock shop at 124 Piccadilly. The Great Exhibition was a world event and the catalyst for subsequent lock designs and improvements. Many of the latest locks were on display, demonstrating the highest security available from many manufacturers.

Bramah was the most prominent and well-known manufacturer and offered a reward to anyone who could open its invincible design. Alfred Hobbs did this by visiting the Bramah shop for a few minutes at a time for about 16 days. Hobbs then produced a key to open the lock and won the reward.

I interviewed a descendant of Bramah in London at the lock company. I was shown the exact model of the original lock that supposedly hadn't been compromised until Hobbs made the key that opened it. It was relatively simple for me to decode because of my familiarity with a unique design introduced by the Chicago Lock company, called the Tubar. This adaptation of the Bramah design consisted of two rows of four-pin tumblers on a unique key. When inserted into the horizontal keyway, the different bitting cuts moved individual sliders, so their gates allowed a sidebar to engage. Hobbs figured out how to impression the lock to determine when each slider was at the shear line.

The House of Chubb and the Detector Lock

Charles Chubb was a famous inventor who founded his company in 1818 after the commercial success of his Detector lever lock, which was patented that same year (see Figure 11-12). Chubb and his brother opened a lock factory in Wolverhampton to produce and market the lock. Ultimately, Chubb became one of the world's most respected names in locks and safes.

Figure 11-12: The Chubb lever locks with a detector above the levers.

The Chubb Detector was a new type of Lever Lock mechanism and an immediate commercial success. It had a slightly different lever design than was offered in the Barron lock. In this iteration the gates formed part of each lever, rather than part of the bolt as in Barron's design. This modification remains intact in locks today.

The Detector lock became popular because it could alert the owner and disable further operation if any attempt was made to manipulate or pick the lock or use the wrong key to lift a lever. Chubb also introduced an internal *curtain* that surrounded the keyhole and revolved around the key, making picking virtually impossible.

Parsons Balanced Lever Lock

In previous designs, the key bitting acted on the opposite end of the lever from the pivot point. Parsons (Figure 11-13) improved on this approach by creating a lever tumbler that made contact at its center or middle. The design was such that if any lever was raised too high with a false key, it was caught by the bolt and immobilized. Parsons made his lock with seven levers, providing functionality like that of the Detector lock.

Newell Parautoptic Lock

In 1841, Robert Newell of New York demonstrated his Parautoptic lock at the Great Exhibition. The word *parautoptic* was taken from the Greek meaning "concealed from view." The design made accessing the working parts through the keyhole almost impossible. Newell accomplished this by employing a double set of levers, with one acting in sequence on the other. A rotating plate blocked

Figure 11-13: The Parsons balanced lever lock.

the tumblers from view, making picking virtually impossible. Another innovation was changing the keys' bitting combination by altering their positions. This was accomplished by providing 15 different interchangeable segments.

The Newell design provided the origin and impetus for instant rekeying, popular today in several systems, including Winfield, Kwikset SmartKey, and InstaKey. The system was also adopted by Sargent and Greenleaf in their key-changeable programmable combination locks, including their 8077 and 8088 series padlocks, for high-security government installations. Developed in the 1950s, these locks were thought impossible to manipulate or decode. Subsequently that was proven false, and they were removed from service when it was determined that they could be compromised with shims and certain decoding techniques.

Hobbs Protector Lock

Alfred Hobbs, the famous American locksmith who succeeded in opening the Bramah lock and the six-lever Chubb Detector lock during the London Great Exhibition in 1851, also invented and manufactured the Protector lock, which he touted as unpickable. Interestingly, Theodor Kromer of Prussia invented and patented a similar design in 1874 and started a safe lock company that was recognized globally for its security and precision designs. His locks competed with those from Bramah and Chubb but were designed for mass production, making them commercially successful. For more than 150 years, the name Kromer was associated with the highest-security lock designs available. Subsequently, Kaba-Mas (a Swiss company) acquired Kromer and Mauer, both manufacturers of high-security safe locks. See Figure 11-14 for a high-security mechanism.

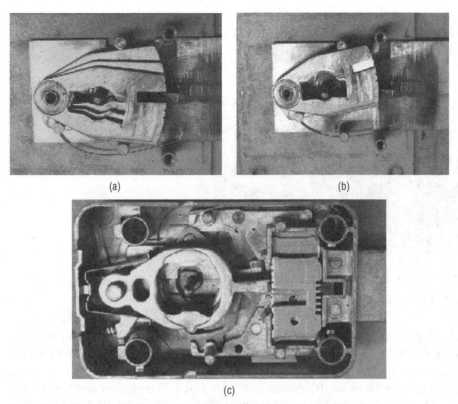

(a)

(b)

(c)

Figures 11-14a–14c: Lever locks can offer high security and pick resistance, depending on the number of levers. The photographs show all levers aligned with the fence (a) and misaligned (b) A complex high-security lever lock is also shown (c).

Hobbs understood that locks could be opened by employing a set of "false keys" to probe, test, and exploit internal lock tolerances, much like the modern-day tryout keys discussed in Part IV. He opened many locks by applying pressure on the bolt while moving each lever with a pick. In 1851 he created a more secure locking system, the Protector, which worked by transferring pressure between the bolt and tumblers to a fixed pin. Although Hobbs claimed his design couldn't be defeated, it was defeated in 1854 by a Chubb locksmith. To quote one of my many maxims for design engineers, "What can't be opened today will be opened tomorrow." It was as true then as it is now. In the world of locks, no design is truly secure.

Tucker and Reeves Safeguard Lock

A design similar to the Chubb lock was introduced in 1853 by Tucker and Reeves. But this lock was unique because it had four levers forming a wheel, mounted on a central pin and then enclosed in a moveable barrel. This barrel formed the keyhole, which was offset from the key. It was impossible to insert a pick tool to reach any levers. To further increase pick resistance, the inventors required that the key turn the movable barrel before the stump on the bolt could enter the gate.

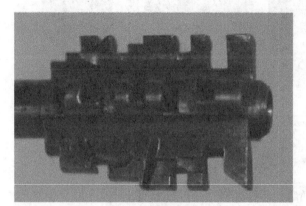

Figure 11-15: Time locks for safes and vaults.

Developments in combination locks were also ongoing while the lever tumbler designs continued to progress. In 1831 a Scottish inventor, William Rutherford, modified a clock mechanism and integrated it with a combination lock to create a time lock for a bank vault, shown in Figure 11-15. The system worked with a disc containing a notched gate driven by a clock mechanism. A stop plate was placed at the lock's rear, which prevented the bolt's operation until the disc arrived at a specific position controlled by the timing mechanism. Modern time locks are similar, although many are now electronic. Before the introduction of time locks, combination locks didn't provide any security against robberies and kidnapping of bank employees forced to open safes at gunpoint.

Time locks vastly increased the security of safes and vaults and were popularized by James Sargent in 1865. As a result of his improved designs, combination locks became widely accepted in the United States as a valid means to secure bank holdings.

Yale Pin Tumbler Lock

Linus Yale, Jr. was an inventor and manufacturer living in Connecticut. His father, Linus Yale, Sr., was also an inventor and a producer of bank locks. Yale Sr. developed the first version of the modern pin tumbler lock in 1844, and his son refined it around 1860 (U.S. Patent 48,475). For the next eight years, Yale Jr. conceived and produced refinements for this lock, which is still the most popular mechanism today.

This lock provided thousands of key combinations, unlike its predecessor from Egypt 4,000 years earlier (see Figures 11-16 and 11-17). Yale utilized a small, flat steel key with bittings aligned with internal movable pin tumblers that were spring-biased. Each chamber contained at least two pins and a spring, which, when lifted to the shear line, allowed the plug to turn. A tolerance of .02″ ensured that the plug couldn't be turned if one or more pins were above or below the shear line.

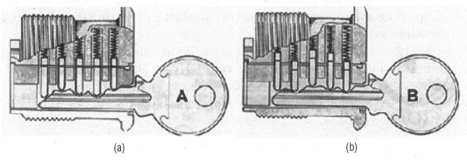

(a) (b)

Figure 11-16a, 16b: The original Yale pin tumbler design. The correctly bitted key (a) moves all the pins to the shear line. The key in (b) is the incorrect bitting.

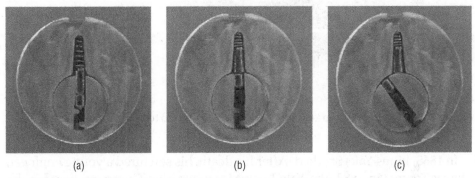

(a) (b) (c)

Figures 11-17a–17c: These three locks demonstrate the locking principle of the Yale pin tumbler. (a) shows the plug blocked from rotation because the top pin is entering the lower chamber in the plug. (b) shows the pins at shear line, so the plug can turn. (c) shows the plug turned because the top and bottom pins, as shown in (b) are at shear line.

(a) (b)

Figure 11-18a, 18b: A modern pin tumbler lock with a sidebar for added security. This is a Medeco six-pin lock.

The Yale lock made possible the mass production and implementation of a secure locking system at an affordable price. It allowed for complex keying systems, such as master keys, Maison keying, and construction master keying. The lock was ultimately produced in many different iterations and formats. There are thousands of versions of this mechanism globally in many sizes and configurations (see Figure 11-18).

As described in Part IV, this lock type is subject to numerous attack methods, including picking with a bump key (see Figure 11-19). This serious security vulnerability must be recognized even in high-security locks. Many manufacturers have attempted to inhibit the ability to bypass their locks using this technique, but with limited success.

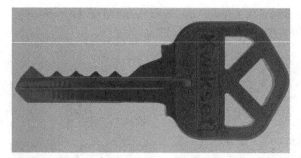

Figure 11-19: A modern bump key is designed to bounce all pin tumblers simultaneously.

In 1868, Linus Yale, Sr., died. After his death, his son hired a young engineer, Henry Towne; in 1883, the Yale Lock Manufacturing Company became the Yale and Towne Manufacturing Company. It's now known as Eaton, Yale, and Towne, Inc.

Disc Tumbler Lock

The disc tumbler lock is described and analyzed in Chapter 14 of this book. The original design was introduced in 1907 in Finland and is still popular in many configurations. It can provide a high level of security, depending on the number of discs and their internal tolerances. The disc tumbler lock can be found in many applications, including vending, alarm control, padlocks, door locks, computers, slot machines, and parking meters.

The design requires that each disc has one or more gates rotated to the proper position when a key is inserted. When all the discs are properly aligned so the gates are lined up, a sidebar can retract so the key can turn the plug.

As originally conceived in the lever locks designed by Barron and others, the gate and fence combination remains the primary locking principle for disc locks. Within the lever mechanism, keys and their bitting are flat pieces of metal that are inserted in the keyhole and act against the levers in a lever stack. They must raise the levers to properly align their gates, so that a fence or stump attached to the bolt can slide to a locked or unlocked position. The bittings are two-dimensional on the lever key, meaning the cuts vary according to their vertical depths.

The Abloy disc lock relies on the same principle to the extent that the key raises each lever to a shear line. However, the disc key has actual angled cuts individually set at varying angles when the key is originally produced. These angled cuts correspond with the required rotation travel of the discs. Rather than flat levers with gates, the Abloy lock has round discs with slots or gates that interact with a sidebar. The principle can be seen as similar: the fence in the lever lock was exchanged for a sidebar in the disc lock, but functionally, both systems create a fence-gate relationship to control the plug's rotation or the movement of a bolt.

The bitting of the semicylindrical key consists of a series of different cuts of varying angles, which correspond to the rotational relationship of each disc and its gate. The discs are all free-floating; there are no springs to return them to a home position as there are in the wafer tumbler lock.

The original Abloy Classic lock contained a series of discs with gates ranging from a semicircle (180 degrees) to a three-quarter circle (270 degrees). The key is initially inserted and rotated 90 degrees. The bitting on the key corresponds to the complementary angles of the gates on each disc. Continuing to rotate the key picks up each of the discs and moves them until the gates are aligned. Rotating the key in the opposite direction resets the sidebar and scrambles all the discs.

Disc tumbler locks are immune to harsh environments and are suitable for outdoor applications where weather may be an operational factor. Power, railroad, and other utility applications find these locks in wide use because temperature, water, dust, and other artifacts rarely affect their operation.

Wafer Tumbler Lock

The modern disc, flat, or plate-wafer tumbler lock was patented in the United States by Philo Felter in 1868 (U.S. Patent 167,088) and Hiram Shepardson in 1870 (U.S. Patent 99,013; see Figures 11-20 and 11-21). The mechanisms have wide acceptance today in many low- to medium-security applications, ranging from padlocks and vending machines to desk locks to key switches, display cases, cash registers, and thousands of other applications.

Keys were single- and double-bitted; they were referred to as *feather keys* because they were so light in contrast with heavy lever lock keys. Many inventors introduced different designs with single- and double-bitted keys. In 1924, Briggs and Stratton filed for a patent for a five-wafer single-bitted wafer lock installed in a Hupp motor car for its ignition lock. Although there are numerous

Figure 11-20a, 20b: A six-wafer lock. The wafers aren't properly aligned (a) All the wafers are at the shear line (b) and the plug is free to turn.

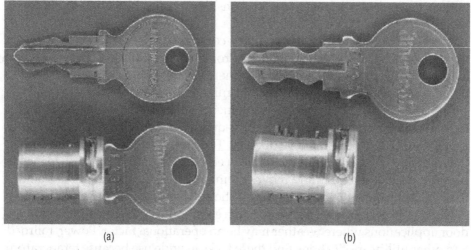

Figure 11-21a, 21b: A double-sided wafer lock. Each side of the key acts on alternate wafers.

configurations for wafer tumbler locks, they generally share the same operational principles and design characteristics.

The primary components are a shell, a plug with individual slots or chambers, flat wafers, and springs for each wafer to force them into a "home" and locked position. As with virtually all other locks, a shear line is created precisely at the plug's surface, either on one side (i.e., single-bitted key) or on both surfaces (i.e., double-bitted key). The function of the bitting is to lift the wafers to the shear line. If these wafers are under- or overlifted, the plug's rotation is blocked in much the same fashion as a pin tumbler lock, except there's no double-detainer locking because the wafer is a single piece of metal.

Each wafer has a square slot where the key runs once inserted into the keyway. The wafers are spring-biased, which forces them to protrude above or below the shear line to accomplish rotation blocking. In a double-bitted lock, the wafers alternate in their orientation to the shear lines, so locking occurs because wafers protrude vertically on both surfaces of the plug when no key is present or a key with the wrong bitting combination is present.

Most wafer locks offer low to medium security with poor tolerance. However, some advanced designs employ triple bitting for added resistance against picking and decoding. Wafer locks are inexpensive to produce and come in many sizes, making them simple to install for many applications. One drawback of the wafer design is the ease of picking and visually decoding the position of the wafers, which can then be translated to producing a key.

I led a major investigation and litigation involving the design of gun safes, during which I demonstrated that many single- and double-bitted locks, which were supposed to secure the enclosures, could be rapidly opened by reverse picking with a paper clip and applying slight torque as the clip was withdrawn. A class-action lawsuit in federal court in Chicago cost the manufacturer millions of dollars because its engineers failed to understand the security vulnerabilities in the design of its locks and the ease with which even a child could compromise its containers with shims, shock, vibration, and plastic straws. It's a classic case of a failure to imagine the consequences of mechanical configurations that appeared secure but were not.

Sidebar Locks: Briggs & Stratton

As described in Chapter 14, the sidebar lock was introduced in the United States in 1935 after being patented by J.W. Fitz Gerald (U.S. Patent 1,965,336). It was first employed in General Motors (GM) cars. It utilized wafer tumblers with a radically different design than that of traditional wafers: a sidebar was introduced as the primary method to block the plug's rotation until the correct key was inserted. The sidebar provided indirect access to the shear line by the key bitting. Each of the six flat wafers had a side cut that allowed a sidebar to retract once all the wafers were properly aligned. The sidebar, rather than the actual wafer, formed the obstruction to rotation. The locks remained impossible to bypass for almost 50 years and are considered the logical advancement from Abloy's 1907 disc tumbler design.

Advancements in the Past 50 Years

In the past 50 years, there have been improvements in designs, combinations of technologies, the introduction of electronics and software, and the development of sophisticated metals and production techniques that would have been unimaginable to our ancestors. A survey of the current state-of-the-art is presented in Chapter 13 and summarized here. Perhaps the most relevant lesson from this history is that although designs have advanced, the basic principles have not changed markedly, nor have design modifications successfully minimized certain security vulnerabilities.

All mechanical, electromechanical, and electronic locks must include and integrate moving elements. Whether those elements are controlled by a key, an electronic token, radio frequency identification (RFID), near field communications (NFC), or some other authentication method equivalent to the bitting of a key, the same attack methods continue to be a threat. The world of locks has changed, but their principles and vulnerabilities are the same. And in the migration toward the Internet of Things (IoT) and software-based systems, the ability to circumvent security has shifted to different methods. However, attacks on the hardware-software interface continue: integrating hardware and software is still a threat.

Many years ago, I interviewed the KGB's station chief for Riga, Latvia. He was responsible for breaking into homes and businesses to install electronic surveillance and surreptitiously search for evidence to help the state. The Soviet Union had a sophisticated factory to develop and produce devices to open all locks, including those on cars, to support their intelligence services. He brought many such tool samples to show me how they worked. We would consider them innovative, but primitive compared to what is available today.

One of the issues I discussed with him was what he thought about modern picking, impressioning, and decoding tools. He answered, "The principles have not changed, only the sophistication of the tools. Fifty years later, they still work the same way."

My colleagues and I have been incredibly fortunate to work with the industry's best lock manufacturers, design engineers, and inventive minds. Unfortunately, I am reminded that they often fail to understand how we got here in terms of innovations in locking technology and are unable to recognize nuances in designs and their associated failures and threats. Every new lock design can be said to be based on a prior security vulnerability or failure. The patent offices of many countries contain the best evidence of the evolution of locks and security vulnerabilities. Most patents are filed to enhance the technology of locks and remedy real or perceived problems with the prior art. Understanding history is essential in lock design, or we are bound to repeat past design errors and mistakes (and often do).

In Chapter 12, the most common industry definitions and jargon are presented to assist in understanding the materials throughout this book. Many terms are unique to the lock and security sectors and are also defined in the UL and BHMA Standards.

Industry Definitions

Some design engineers and security experts have a detailed understanding of how locks and safes work at the mechanical and electronic component levels. Most risk managers, IT professionals, and even members of a vulnerability assessment (VA) team may not. Locks and how they work are taken for granted by most, and often, this question is asked: "What is so complicated about inserting a key into a lock to open it?" The reality is that the design of locks and the interaction of their components can be exceedingly complicated. Their tolerances are often maintained to a couple thousandths of an inch, so making everything secure and working properly can be challenging.

The industry has developed many specialized terms (or jargon) to describe and identify critical parts and functions for the thousands of locks and subsystems worldwide. These terms are understood by mechanical and electrical engineers and others involved in the complex world of locks. Standardized terminology is important for manufacturing, testing, vulnerability assessment, marketing, sales, maintenance, installation, and customer support. The agreed-on definitions of terms are also important for global standards organizations so that when a security, environmental, or endurance rating is specified, it means the same thing to end users, risk managers, and compliance officers, regardless of venue. This is especially true for high-security ratings, where protecting property, people, lives, dangerous goods, and information can be critical.

This book uses terminology to identify, explain, and enhance understanding of concepts, designs, and technology embedded in locks and safes. Even more importantly, the interaction of common components can, and often does, result in actual or potential security vulnerabilities. Everyone needs to be on the same page as they describe and identify the distinct parts of a lock and how they function.

Some terms and associated diagrams specifically refer to mechanisms, tools, processes, or techniques described to specific security failures of certain types of locks or attack vectors. Some of the material in this chapter is taken from *Open in Thirty Seconds* and *LSS+ The Multimedia Edition of Locks, Safes, and Security."* (The author wrote both works.)

Terminology

Associated Locksmiths of America (ALOA): This is the largest locksmith trade group in the United States. Due to an organizational change it now encompasses several related groups, including the Safe and Vault Technicians Association (SAVTA). The technical name is now the ALOA Security Professionals Association.

American National Standards Institute (ANSI): This organization, in conjunction with the Builders Hardware Manufacturers Association (BHMA), was responsible for drafting the high-security lock standard BHMA/ANSI 156.30 in the United States.

Arc ring: A metal ring, also called a *circlip*, that has open ends and can be sprung into place to retain a plug within the shell of a lock.

Axial pin tumbler lock: This is a pin tumbler mechanism in which the pins are positioned in a circle. (See *tubular pin tumbler lock*.) The Figure 12-1 shows both a lock and a key.

Figure 12-1a, 1b: Tubular pin tumbler lock and key. The key is (b), lock is (a).

Balanced driver: The concept of balanced drivers or top pins is important due to the ability to attack pin tumbler locks by creating different shear lines. Many manufacturers fail to consider the ability to circumvent the security of this type of locking mechanism if a policy of ensuring the computation of balanced drivers isn't adhered to in *any* pin tumbler design. (See *pin stack*, in addition to the discussion of different attack vectors in Part IV.)

A pin tumbler lock typically has two primary pins: the top and bottom tumblers. There may also be master pins that are inserts between the top and bottom pins to accomplish master keying. (See *master pin* or *master wafer* [the older terminology is now out of favor.])

Why are balanced drivers required, and how can they create a security vulnerability if not implemented properly? The answer is simple: each pin chamber has a finite dimension, which holds the springs and all pins. The total length of all the pins must be considered to ensure that they can move up, down, and across the shear line, based on the bitting combination of the key coded for a particular lock. If the total length of the pin stack is too short or too long, the system can be easily compromised, and the lock may not work properly.

The concept of balanced drivers requires that the top pin length is varied for each chamber and is based on the measurement of the bottom pin so their overall length is correct for each chamber. The function of the balanced driver, also called a compensation driver or *graduated driver*, is to make the overall pin stack length constant between chambers.

BIAXIAL lock: BIAXIAL is the name of the second generation of Medeco technology, which was introduced in the 1980s. It featured a redesigned bottom tumbler that allowed the tip of the pin to rest in one of two distinct positions on the bitting surface of the key. Medeco invented the technology to elevate and rotate each pin tumbler for high-security applications. Figure 12-2 shows how each pin is rotated to one of three angles. (See the discussion in Chapter 14 to compare different high-security lock designs.)

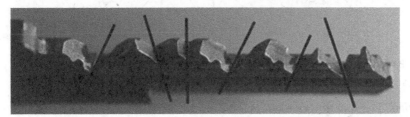

Figure 12-2: A Medeco BIAXIAL key showing fore and aft cuts with different rotations.

Binary cut key: A key that allows for only two bitting depths for each position: a cut or no-cut. (The Winfield lock is an example discussed in Part VI as an illustrative case.)

Bitting: The portion of the key that contains depth and space information that corresponds to wards, wafers, levers, or pin tumblers. The bitting interacts with the internal locking components and is contained and created in the key's blade. The term also refers to the numbers that represent the physical dimensions of the actual cuts and can describe the code combination of the key. Each manufacturer devises its coding scheme based on many factors, including the chamber dimensions that determine the overall pin stack length, the number of defined depth increments, and the length of each bottom pin. Modern key cutters are often computer-controlled systems programmed with depth and spacing data for all major manufacturers, so inputting a specific key code generates a properly bitted key on the correct blank.

Thousands of variables must be considered. The bitting for a Medeco key, an axial pin tumbler lock, an Abloy disc lock, and a conventional pin tumbler cylinder are all different. Still, the concept is the same: the variations on the interactive surface of a key raise or move those components to a shear line.

Bitting depth and measurement: The depth of a cut made in the bitting, or the blade portion of a key, is measured from the bottom to the root of the cut. Figure 12-3 shows various bitting depths, the parts of a pin tumbler lock, and how they're coded and measured.

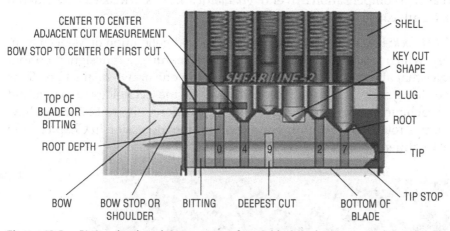

Figure 12-3:   Bitting depth and measurement for a Schlage lock.

Bitting position: The location of a cut related to the shoulder or tip of the key.

Blade of the key: The portion of the key that contains the bitting surface. The bottom of the blade is opposite its surface, which is cut. The top of the blade is the surface on which cuts are made. Almost any part of the blade can form a portion of the bitting area, although bitting is confined to the upper half of the blade. The depth of a cut is measured from the root to the bottom of the blade, although in some instances a manufacturer may choose to compute it from the root to a register groove.

Blank or blank key: A key that has not been cut.

Bolt: A lock's active external locking component that secures the moving member to which it's affixed. There are several distinct types of bolts, including the auxiliary dead latch, deadbolt, latch bolt, and deadlocking latch bolt. A flush-mounted bolt is designed to equal the door's surface and not protrude from it. A mortised bolt is installed in a pocket in the door.

Bottom of the blade: In a single-bitted key, the blade portion opposite the cut edge. *Single-bitted* means only one set of cuts interacts with the internal locking components.

Bottom pin: Any tumbler that makes physical contact with the bitting. Its shape may be cylindrical, conical, ball, or chisel-pointed at the contact end. (See the definitions for *pin tumbler lock* and *shear line*.

Builders Hardware Manufacturers Association (BHMA): The trade organization representing most lock manufacturers in the United States and responsible for developing and implementing security and quality standards for locking hardware.

Bumping: Technique that uses a specially cut key to activate all the bottom pins within a pin tumbler lock. When energy is applied to the bump key, it causes the pins to jump across the shear line. Virtually all conventional pin tumbler locks and some high-security cylinders can be opened with this technique. (See Part IV for a more detailed discussion.)

Bump key: A special key with all the bittings cut to the lowest level.

Cam: The tailpiece, thrower piece, or tongue attached to the end of a rotating plug that's used as the locking mechanism's actuator. (This definition relates to the Medeco Maxum deadbolt bypass described in Part VI.)

Chamber: Any opening, hole, or cavity in the shell and the lock plug containing pin tumblers and springs. In a five-pin tumbler lock, there are five individual chambers.

Change key: The lowest individual level of keying. A lock may have a change key and several levels of master keys (MKs). The term also refers to a special key with combination locks to alter the relationship between the gates and drive pins in each disc in the wheel pack.

Chisel point: The geometry of each bottom pin in a Medeco cylinder is formed as a chisel point to properly interact with the angles of the bitting. The relationship between the chisel point and the true gate of each pin determines its rotation angle.

Code: A record of the bitting that corresponds to a particular key. A "code-cut key" is produced from such information rather than a physical copy of the original key. Most computer-controlled key machines allow the input of specific codes to produce the key automatically.

Code-original key: A code-cut key that conforms to the lock manufacturer's specifications. Note that the factory direct reading code may appear on the key head and correlate to each cut's depths, from tip to shoulder.

Code-setting key: Code-setting keys were developed to pick and bump Medeco high-security locks. The author patented four keys to defeat the security of certain Medeco cylinders in 2008.

Control key: A key used for the sole purpose of installing or removing an interchangeable or removable core from the shell of a lock. The bitting of the key that releases the control lug (and the core) is referred to as the control cut(s). The compromise of interchangeable core (IC) locks can present a significant security vulnerability and is discussed in Part V of this book.

Core: All components in a lock (i.e., plug, all pins, plug retainer, and springs). (See *shell*.)

Cross-combinations and key interchange: If multiple shear lines are created in a pin tumbler, wafer, disc, lever, or combination lock, then keys with different code combinations can open the lock. Especially in a master key system, cross-combinations can be a serious problem and create a security vulnerability because many different keys can open a lock. These are also referred to as incidental master keys or combinations. Why is this important? If cross-combinations aren't planned for and properly controlled, they can allow unauthorized access to one or more locks in a system.

> I was involved in a case involving three high-rise buildings in which tenants could enter offices with keys not intended for those locks. Critical information could be accessed because of an improper system design. In one building, a halfway house for prison inmates, residents were entering rooms and stealing property because the lock manufacturer didn't prevent key interchange and jiggling to overcome internal tolerances in the locks.

Cross-keying: Either an intentional (i.e., controlled or intended) action or a system keying error (i.e., uncontrolled cross-keying) that is caused or created by setting the combination of a master keyed cylinder to create one or more virtual shear lines to allow more than one key to operate the lock. Uncontrolled cross-keys may allow unintended or unauthorized keys to open one or more locks. They can also permit two or more different keys grouped under higher-level keys to operate one cylinder. When a lock is master keyed, many virtual shear lines are created because multiple pins are placed in each pin stack. Each added pin creates another shear line. In a six-pin lock with a lower pin and master pin, there are 64 (2^6) combinations.

Cut angle: The measurement of the combined angles created by cutting a key, expressed in degrees.

Cut root: The base or bottom of a key cut.

Cut root shape: The shape of the bottom of a key cut. In the case of a lever tumbler lock, the cut root shape is flat with 90-degree corners. The shape is usually curved or angled in a pin tumbler lock. The root has a specific shape that may be flat, radiused, or a perfect "V."

Cylinder: A self-contained lock assembly that consists of the plug, shell, tumblers, springs, plug retainer, cam, and tailpiece. The portion surrounding the plug is called the *cylinder body* or *shell*. The cylinder *plug* contains the keyway and bottom pins and is inserted into the cylinder body. See Figure 12-4 for the critical parts of a pin tumbler lock.

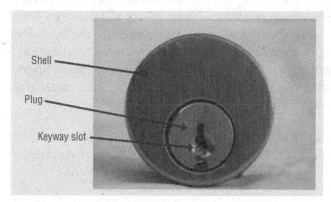

Figure 12-4: The critical components of a pin tumbler lock.

Cylinder body: The portion of a lock that surrounds and contains the plug and the tumbler mechanism. The cylinder body is sometimes called a *shell*.

Cylinder guard: A protective assembly for the exposed portions of a cylinder to resist wrenching, cutting, pulling, or prying.

Cylinder plug: A cylinder portion containing movable locking elements, which are rotated when the correct key or credential is inserted.

Deadbolt: Usually a square-shaped bolt that extends into the strike or recess of the doorframe, is locked into place, and can't be retracted due to end pressure. See Figure 12-5. The design in one high-security cylinder was compromised by shearing the endcap screws, which allowed access to the tailpiece with a small screwdriver. Attention should be paid to affixing the plug to connecting components to prevent simple attacks.

Figure 12-5:   Deadbolt cylinder.

Decode: A process to ascertain the bitting or combination of a key or keys that fit a lock by physical measurement or extrapolation with specialized tools or procedures. Decoding is accomplished without disassembling the cylinder. Many methods exist to decode the bitting in a lock and produce a working key. Decoding tools are described in Part IV and may consist of shim wires, calipers, pin-and-cam systems, Lishi tools, borescopes, impressioning, and visual and electronic decoding methods.

DefCon: The annual conference held in Las Vegas for IT professionals, government agents, security experts, and hackers. Lectures on diverse topics that relate to cyber and physical security are presented during the three-day event.

Depth increments: Every manufacturer must calculate and establish the total number of theoretical combinations or differs for each lock. This is the primary criterion that determines how many different key codes are available in a system. The greater the number of distinct codes, the more secure the system is against keys from other locks opening unauthorized or unintended cylinders.

The bottom pin length can be divided into segments or increments in a pin tumbler lock, often measured in .015″ or .023″ differs. These segments are then translated into numeric values so a locksmith or factory can cut "keys by code" using these numbers. The diagram in Figure 12-3 shows the correlation between key codes and depth increments for a Schlage lock. Specific rules govern depth and spacing between pins to ensure that keys work properly. Why is this an important concept? If the depth increments are too close together, there is the possibility that keys cut to one code will open locks for a different combination. The tolerance between plug and shell at the shear line is critical, especially when analyzing the potential for attacks using tryout keys, giggle keys, signatures, and rake picks, as discussed in Part IV.

Depth key set: A set of reference keys for a specific lock that provides complete depth and spacing measurements. A key can be duplicated from such a reference. Each key in the set is cut so that all bitting positions are the same, with the proper spacing between positions. Typically, one key is cut for each depth.

Depth and space values: The center-to-center measurements between pin chambers and the number of depth increments established for a specific lock design.

Differs and differing: Differing originated in England and refers to the designated change key that fits a lock. It also describes the number of combinations and change keys that can theoretically open the same lock. The number of wards, levers, pins, and discs, along with the design of the keyway and tolerances, determine differs. Each lock manufacturer establishes several variables contributing to the total number of differs.

Although the number is mathematically based, it isn't absolute. Differing is also affected by the method of cutting a key. The number of combinations may be increased through complex lock design, such as magnetic and mechanical locking action or standard pin tumblers combined with a sidebar. I prefer the term *differs* to denote combinations in this text, although other terms are accepted. The theoretical number of key changes or combinations may exceed the number of usable differs.

Dimple key: A key in which the cuts are produced by drilling holes and removing material from the bitting surface. Mul-T-Lock introduced dimple keys in Israel. (See the discussion in Part V to analyze issues involving bypass and the limited number of different or key permutations.)

Direct code: A direct code corresponds precisely to the bitting pattern of the key. The code designates a bitting depth for each chamber that correlates directly with the measurement of each pin or active locking component. (See *code*.)

Double-bitted key: A key cut on two surfaces, usually opposite each other. These surfaces activate the internal mechanism of the lock. A *double-cut* key differs from a double-bitted key because the cuts appear on the key's blade in the same bitting space, not opposite each other. The Medeco BIAXIAL uses double cuts for master keying and complex systems.

Double cutting: This technique was utilized to compromise Medeco's high-security locks by adding extra cuts on the surface of a key. Medeco BIAXIAL pin designs were especially vulnerable to this attack because the key blade surface could be cut in two distinct spots for one bitting position.

The concept of double-cut keys was introduced with the BIAXIAL and refers to the division of the bitting for each chamber into two parts (before and after). The technique allows the creation of twice the bitting codes in the same space normally occupying the original Medeco key.

Double-detainer locking theory: In a pin tumbler lock, the genius of Linus Yale was his invention of double-detainer locking. This meant pin tumblers in the design blocked the rotation of the plug if the bottom pins protruded above the shear line or the top pins entered the plug below the shear line. If even one pin was below or above the shear line, even by a few thousandths of an inch, the plug was prevented from turning, and the cylinder remained locked. The term also applies to lever tumbler locks.

Driver pin: The top portion of the pin stack in a pin tumbler lock. It's biased directly by its spring (i.e., driver spring). In a chamber with only two pins, it provides for double-detainer locking of the plug. The preferred nomenclature today is *top pin*.

Effective changes: There is always a difference between effective key changes and theoretical changes. Manufacturers always reduce the number based on technical considerations. (See *differs*.)

Electrostatic discharge (ESD): A transfer of high-voltage electric energy or charge between two bodies of different electrostatic potential. The discharge may be by direct contact or in proximity. A stun gun is a source of ESD. Electronic locks are tested against ESD.

Endcap and tailpiece: Component that affixes and links the plug to the latch, bolt, or actuating mechanism to transmit a turning motion when the proper key is inserted. If not executed properly, a security vulnerability can be created between the plug, endcap retaining mechanism, and tailpiece interface. (See the discussion of the compromise of the Medeco Maxum high-security deadbolt in Part VI.)

Extrapolation of a top-level master key (TMK): I first used this term to describe the process of decoding a pin tumbler lock top-level master key by probing the specific length of each bottom pin. This is accomplished using a key that fits any cylinder in a master keyed system. The process can be carried out covertly and doesn't require disassembling any lock. (It's described in more detail in Part V.)

Feel-picking: A lock bypass method requiring that each tumbler, wafer, or lever is manipulated or raised with a curved or similar pick tool or a key that is moved back and forth in the lock with tension applied. Feel-picking is the traditional method of lock manipulation and is contrasted with rake-picking and other methods.

Fence: This term applies to lever locks but can apply to the sidebar, combination, and other mechanisms. It denotes a projecting component designed to prevent the movement of a critical locking part unless proper alignment occurs between a corresponding fence and gate. Each rotating wheel in a wheel pack has a gate in a combination lock. When all the wheels are properly aligned the fence can enter all the gates, and the entire wheel pack can be turned to effect retraction of the bolt. The EVVA MCS magnetic code system, analyzed in Part III, relies on eight magnetized rotors, each with one or more gates that must be properly aligned with individual fences for the lock to open.

Graduated driver: Top pins of different lengths that compensate for the overall length of the pin stack to make the total length constant. (See *balanced driver*.)

Grand master key: A key that operates locks in several series, all with their group master key.

High-security lock: A lock designed to offer a greater degree of resistance to surreptitious and forced-entry methods, including picking, impressioning, key duplication, drilling, and decoding. The criteria for high-security locks are established by standards organizations worldwide and contain requirements for controlling and accessing blank keys.

Impression system: A technique to produce keys for certain locks without removing the mechanism. The process determines the position and depth of cuts corresponding to the tumblers, levers, discs, wards, or wafers. Another form of impressioning involves copying keys with wax, clay, or metal impressions.

Indirect code: All keys are defined by their bitting codes. Manufacturers can establish direct or indirect code schemes. Direct-reading codes correspond to the actual bitting depth increments for a specific key. An indirect code translates to a set of numbers or letters with no mathematical relationship to the bitting.

Interchangeable core: A locking system that allows the rapid interchange of the entire lock assembly. All the components (i.e., plug, shell, pins, springs, and retainers) are self-contained in the core, which can be easily removed with a control key. The term *removable core* can also describe this mechanism. ICs can be supplied in a mortise, rim, or key-in-knob configuration. The IC is available in two standard formats: small (SFIC) and large. The best-known system was invented by Frank Best 100 years ago. Best Lock Company leads the industry today by supplying this locking system. Understanding IC locks is important because all major manufacturers supply them to their customers, and they can suffer from a common security vulnerability: decoding and production of a control key. The entire system can be compromised once a control key is generated (if all the locks have the same keyway). A control key allows the plug to be instantly removed and switched for another one with a different key combination.

Jamb: The vertical portion of a door or window frame.

Key gauge: A mechanical or electronic device that can measure the individual depths of a bitting pattern and provide precise information about depth coding. A key micrometer or similar tool is used for this function. Wendt produces a "key checker" to verify alternative blanks. The Medeco key decoder is an example of a simple tool to derive a specific key's depth, spacing, pin position, and angle. There are also electronic decoders using highly effective lasers.

Keyhole: The opening in a lock that allows key entry. It can also refer to a keyway but is more generic to a warded lock.

Key milling: The grooves, wards, or bullets along the side of the key. The term can also denote the alteration or modification of a key blank to enter a restricted keyway or one that is different than intended by the blank manufacturer.

Key picking: Means of jiggling open a lock by moving a key back and forth across the wafers, discs, or tumblers, much like a rake pick. Maison-keyed locks are especially vulnerable to key picking because of the multiple virtual shear lines that must be created to allow access to all tenants. Key manipulation also defines a key designed to open one lock, which may be manipulated or jiggled to open another. This can occur due to wear of the lock components or key or from using master pins that are too thin. (Key picking and manipulation are discussed in Part IV.)

Keying symbols: Standardized alphanumeric symbols to define keying systems. (The key symbols are enumerated in Part V.)

Key interchange: Depending on the selection of bitting and sidebar codes, a key designed to open one lock may open one or more unintended locks. For example, are certain conflicts inherent in the Medeco BIAXIAL systems because of the chisel-point design of the pins? Although statistically this vulnerability is remote, it's nonetheless relevant in critical or high-value targets. Key interchange can also be referred to as pin interchange.

Keying levels: An master key system is divided into access hierarchies that begin with the individual change key. The standard keying levels are individual keys, keyed alike, keyed differently, and master keys.

Keyway: The opening in a plug into which the key is inserted, shown in Figure 12-6. A keyway provides a certain measure of security in most modern locks, based on the placement of *wards* to block the entrance of all but the correct key. Keyway is a relatively modern term; earlier references used the word *keyhole*. Keyways can be a critical security component in any lock. They block access to critical locking components to all but intended keys with the correct warding and can make picking extremely difficult, depending on their design. Risk managers and security officers should be alert to blank keys with similar warding patterns. They can often be easily modified to replace or replicate keys for a high-security facility, thus defeating key control measures.

Figure 12-6: A keyway.

Loading: A technique to bypass a latch or bolt by inserting a shim or thin, flexible material between the moveable locking component and strike or frame.

m3 Medeco cylinder: The third generation of Medeco high-security technology. It differs from the BIAXIAL in that it includes a slider element for enhanced key control. (The latest version is the M4, described in Part III.)

Maximum adjacent cut specification (MACS): The maximum allowable depth of adjacent cuts in single- and double-bitted and dimple locks that can be made without interference to each other (see Figure 12-7). MACS is an integral factor that must be considered, especially in a master key system. Each manufacturer defines the MACS specification and will physically prevent a key from being improperly cut.

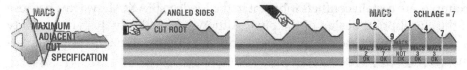

Figure 12-7:   Maximum adjacent cut specifications. The difference between a 9 cut and a 2 cut, as shown in the diagram, will prevent the key from operating properly.

Master key: A key that operates two or more locks with different change keys. Simple to complicated master key systems can be designed so that one or more master keys can operate one or many groups of cylinders. A system is said to be *master keyed* when individuals change keys, and one common key can operate a group of locks. The top-level master key (TMK) is the highest keying level. The top-level master key usually opens all locks in the system.

Master pin: Originally, this was referred to as a *master wafer*. The build-up pin is used to create a different virtual shear line. In America, there is typically just one master pin (or master wafer) in one or more chambers. This practice is different in Europe, where master keying can be accomplished by adding multiple pin layers to create multiple shear lines.

Mechanical bypass: A technique encompassing the use of nontraditional means to circumvent the internal security of a mechanical lock by direct actuation of the bolt mechanism. The process can be accomplished in various modes and depends on design deficiencies in the target lock. Methods include magnetics, shim wires, stiff wire probes, forced air, vibration, shock, temperature extremes, radio frequency energy, electrostatic discharge, and directed energy attacks.

Medeco high-security cylinder: The Medeco cylinder relies on a *sidebar* design to provide a second layer of security. Figure 12-8 shows a diagram of a complete cylinder and a plug with six-pin tumblers aligned so the sidebar legs can enter the pins. This allows the sidebar to retract and permits the rotation of the plug. Note the three anti-drill pins at the front of the plug to prevent direct access to the shear line by attackers.

Mortised cylinder: A pin tumbler cylinder affixed to a locking assembly that has been inset into a door. The cylinder is screwed into the assembly and held in position by a set screw. Figure 12-9 shows a conventional mortise cylinder cutaway. Note the integrated tailpiece at the end of the plug.

Movable detainers: Critical locking components such as pin tumblers, wafers, or levers. The correct key must move them into the correct position to allow the plug or bolt to move or rotate.

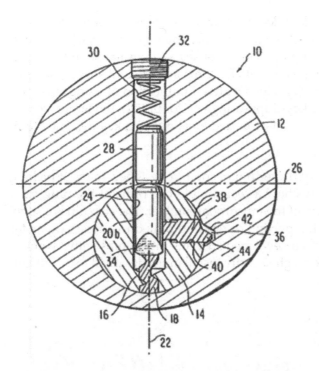

(a)

Figure 12-8a, 8b: Medeco sidebar lock. In (a) the operation of the sidebar is shown in the Medeco patent diagram.

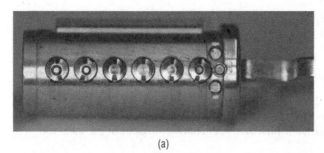

Figure 12-9:   In a pin tumbler cylinder, all pins aren't aligned at the shear line (left image). The proper key moves all pins to shear line (right image).

Multisection blank: A key blank milled to allow entry into more than one keyway in a multiplex keying system. This blank will not enter all keyways, however. A multiplex keying system integrates a series of key sections to expand a master key system. Bittings can be repeated with locks having different keyway sections without compromising security. The negative ramification of using such systems is that if a locksmith or key-duplicating vendor utilizes the wrong keying level blank, the system can be compromised by allowing a key designed to fit one lock to open another.

Mushroom tumbler: A security driver pin or top pin designed to resist picking attempts. Figure 12-10 shows how a security pin can prevent the plug from turning. A spool pin is a form of the mushroom tumbler. The step pin is a spool or mushroom tumbler with a portion of one end milled to a lesser diameter than the opposing end. Medeco developed specially milled pins with advanced resistance Xtended (ARX) for high-security installations designed to be difficult to pick or decode.

Figure 12-10:   A pin tumbler cylinder with a mushroom tumbler trapped at the shear line.

Paracentric keyway: The keyway in a pin tumbler lock with wards on either side that protrude past the centerline of the plug (see Figure 12-11). Paracentric keyways can be much more difficult to pick and are required in high-security locks.

Figure 12-11:   A paracentric keyway.

Picking: The action of opening a lock by manipulating the internal components to simulate using the correct key. A *pick* is an implement utilized to manipulate active locking components. (Many different pick shapes are described in Part IV.)

Pin stack: All the tumblers in one chamber. The pin stack height is the total combined length of all pins in one chamber. It's highly relevant in certain forms of bypass, which are discussed in Part IV.

Pin tumbler lock: A lock originally invented by the Egyptians that utilizes moving pins to prevent the rotation of a round plug by all but the correct key. Conventional pin tumbler mechanisms are the most popular type of lock in the world and contain five primary components: shell, plug, bottom pins, top pins, and springs. Other locks contain additional components to enhance security. Often, their distinguishing feature is a sidebar that provides a second layer of security. (See *sidebar lock*.)

Plug: The round central part of a lock that contains the keyway and is rotated by the key to operate the mechanism. It's sometimes called a *core*. The preferred term is *plug*.

Rap or rapping of a lock: A process to cause a lock to be opened by applying directed energy to a key or lock. This may occur by applying tension and shock to a specially prepared key or a padlock's lock body or shackle release mechanism.

Removable core cylinder: A complete locking assembly designed to be removed and replaced with a control key. (See *interchangeable core*.)

Restricted keyway: A special profile designed for limited use by one or more customers.

Rim cylinder: A cylinder utilized for surface mounting.

Security pins: Special pins inserted in a pin tumbler lock to make picking more difficult. There are many forms, including mushroom, serrated, and spool. They're required for a UL 437 certification. Their function is to be trapped at a shear line to prevent the plug from turning.

Shear line: The space between the plug and shell of a lock that makes it possible for active locking components to secure or release rotation or movement of the plug. Figure 12-12 shows a shear line and how it functions.

Shell: The nonmoving portion of a lock that contains all the internal moving parts. It's also referred to as the *cylinder*.

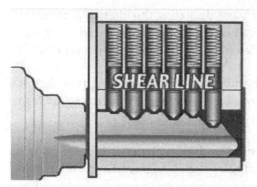

Figure 12-12:   Pins at the shear line in a conventional pin tumbler lock.

Sidebar: A component in the plug of a high-security lock. Its function is to block rotation unless the key properly activates it. In the Medeco cylinder, the sidebar interacts with the gates of each bottom pin with its legs. It prevents the rotation of the plug when it's locked into the longitudinal channel in the shell, shown in Figure 12-13a at (36).

Sidebar lock: A lock incorporating a secondary locking mechanism that appears in both disc and pin tumbler mechanisms. A separate spring-biased projection blocks the plug's rotation until all tumblers are properly aligned. The sidebar was originally developed by Briggs & Stratton for automobiles and was introduced in 1935. It's implemented by many manufacturers worldwide as a recognized security layer, especially for wafers, pin tumblers, and disc locks. It's also employed in locks that offer instant key-change capabilities, such as the Kwikset SmartKey system.

Standards for sidebar locks are promulgated by government and private agencies in every industrialized country. A complete listing can be found in the *National Resources for Global Standards*. `www.consortiuminfo.org/metalibrary/nssn-a-national-resource-for-global-resources`

Strike: The mortised or surfaced-mounted metal plate installed as part of the doorframe to allow receipt of the bolt when it's projected. A strike box can be utilized as an enclosure formed by the strike to surround and protect the bolt. An armored strike is reinforced to strengthen the frame to which it's applied.

Tailpiece or connecting bar: A component that projects from the back of a rim, bored lock cylinder, push-button mechanism, or key-in-knob lock to transmit rotational motion to the bolt.

Theoretical key changes: The total number of mathematically possible individual key (i.e., bitting) combinations for a particular lock.

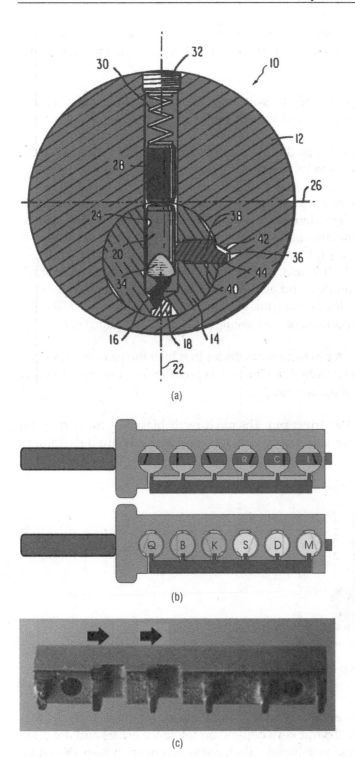

(a)

(b)

(c)

Figures 12-13a–13c: (a) The lock diagram in the original patent, (b) A sidebar blocked by the pins (top) and one aligned (bottom). (c) The sidebar of the m3 has two gates (shown by arrows) that must align with the protruding tabs of the slider.

Triple-bit key: A conventional key cut on three sides or surfaces. It appears that the original patent (2030837) for a triple-bitted lock was granted to George Full in 1936.

Tip position of bottom pin: Where the bottom pin contacts the bitting surface of the key. That position is identified as the root.

Top-level master key (TMK): The defined key bitting that opens multiple locks and levels below the top level. Generally, it opens all locks in a system.

Tolerance: The deviation or variance from an actual dimension or standard. Lock manufacturers specify the difference between a theoretical specification and the actual measurement. Chamber bores, for example, are theoretically all drilled in a straight line. There is a slight variance in their positions due to drill fatigue, movement, and wear. In this text, *high tolerance* refers to an extremely small deviation between theoretical and actual measurement. Tolerance errors contribute to the ability to pick or manipulate a lock. A certain amount of tolerance must exist in every mechanism, or the moving parts can't act against each other.

Tubular pin tumbler lock: A pin tumbler cylinder in which the pins are mounted in a circle rather than a straight line. The lock is popular for vending and other control panels. (See *axial pin tumbler lock*.)

Top pin: Also known as the driver pin. The pin directly biased by the spring and that abuts master pins or lower pins. The top pins or drivers (old definition) block rotation of the plug.

Figure 12-14: The top pins protrude above the shear line.

Tryout key: One or more keys designed to manipulate the tumblers, wafers, discs, or levers to open a lock. Tryout keys depend on tolerance errors and are often cut between normal depth increments. (Their use is described in Parts IV and V.)

Underwriters Laboratories (UL): One of the primary standards organizations in the United States responsible for rating the security of locks. It publishes the UL 437 Standard.

Virtual shear line: A shear line created by inserting more than one bottom pin in a chamber. When the bitting raises the pin stack, the pins "break" at more than one position relative to the physical shear line; in contrast, interchangeable core and master ring locks contain two physical shear lines.

Wafer lock: A lower-security cylinder in which movable detainers are raised to the shear line by the key bitting. Locks can be single-bitted, dual-bitted, or triple-bitted.

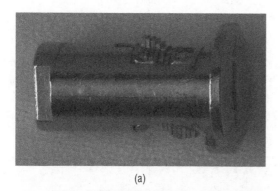

(a)

(b)

Figure 12-15a, 15b: (a) A double-bitted wafer tumbler lock common in vending machines. (b) shows examples of double bitted keys.

Chapter 13 traces the history and design of modern locking mechanisms and the merging of old and new technologies. It's important because it provides a timeline of technological advancements in the development of locks.

13

Modern Locking Mechanisms: A Merging of Old and New Technology

The past 20 years have witnessed significant seismic changes in the lock industry and the concept of keys globally. This change has been driven by the world's connectivity and smartphone advances. In 2023, it's estimated that there will be 50 billion connected devices, and more than half of the global population will be connected through the Internet. For many, especially in the 16–30 age group, life revolves around their portable devices.

How we live, work, function, and use facilities, buildings, residences, and cars has changed. The digital shift affects every way of life, significantly impacting security, safety, compliance, and energy conservation.

The COVID-19 pandemic was largely responsible for the accelerated shift in utilizing buildings and space. It forced a different way of thinking about building safety and how people work, reside, and shop. Remote work has also driven the need for more sophisticated credentials and management.

The tech giants are changing how people live, operate, and function. Amazon, Google, Apple, and Samsung base their visions on their smartphone designs as identity management tools. The storage of credit cards for making purchases, driver's licenses and passports for identity, health certifications, and many other daily life functions that are merged into one device are forcing the lock industry to adapt from a traditional, purely mechanical environment to a digital world where convenience, safety, security, and a simpler life are possible. The major lock manufacturers embrace this vision mainly because they simply have no choice.

Twenty years ago, a typical office or building required mechanical locks for master key (MK) systems and access controls. Today there are many connected products, Internet of Things (IoT)-enabled control, environmental systems, green energy efficiency, and far better space utilization for residences, offices, recreation, and retail sales.

The residential world has witnessed faster change than the commercial sector, with a massive shift in thinking in this regard. Building owners compete to sell/use space and add services like laundry rooms, gyms, and meeting spaces. They have demanded solutions to obtaining and issuing access credentials for tenants and service providers. Owners require more versatility in their remote access and management. Single-family and multi-family units are the fastest-growing product segment. For example, digital door locks are now incredibly popular.

This digital evolution has driven a radical change in how lock manufacturers develop products and operate because the global population is changing how they live, work, and function. Today, about one-third of the revenue for major lock manufacturers is derived from nonmechanical digital solutions.

Smaller companies have merged or been purchased by international conglomerates such as Assa Abloy, Allegion, and dormakaba. Venture capital groups have also begun to acquire manufacturers, which has resulted in enhanced research and development (R&D) capabilities and often information sharing that can affect and mitigate insecurity engineering issues. This has created the impetus for developing electronic and keyless entry platforms in multiple companies' products under the same corporate umbrella. Shared technology can be smart and afford customers access to the latest access-control and lock designs in many countries. This consolidation will continue, as will the entry by allied disciplines such as the smartphone and IoT sectors. It encompasses lock manufacturers and wholesale distribution centers that serve the locksmith and security sectors.

For certain companies, lock technology has rapidly advanced to a new state-of-the-art level. It's enhanced the capabilities and security of mechanical, electronic-based, and fully electronic designs. The integration of microprocessors and encryption in locking and control functions is now sophisticated and mature in many, but not all, products. Advances in production techniques, materials, 3D printing, and computer-aided design (CAD) systems, and the ability of engineers with little to no mechanical lock design expertise to develop software, mean any company can enter the market and produce locks. The problem is the development of secure products. From firsthand experience, I know there are a lot of low-cost, poor-quality products that appear secure to the consumer but aren't.

Virtually any company with sufficient capital can design and manufacture a lock. Companies can make claims about security that may not be true or are overstated, and they can sell their wares online and through commercial distribution channels. The market has been flooded with substandard hardware, often from overseas. Unfortunately, most consumers rarely understand the differences between mature and properly engineered locks and systems and those that aren't.

Developing secure mechanical or software-based locking systems is expensive and calls for knowledge, skill, and proficiency. The business is complex and requires engineering, manufacturing, support, and legal expertise. Many companies don't have the technical competence and funding or choose to take shortcuts to save on R&D and other costs. The result can be locks and locking systems that are vulnerable to attack.

The public popularity of home-automation systems is causing a shift away from traditional mechanical locks to more convenient forms of credentials that obviate the need for traditional keys. The move to adopt electronic-based systems is also increasing in government and industry due to enhanced security and options for access control and multisystem management capabilities.

Locks were always considered a local commodity because locksmiths were required to sell, install, and service them. That's changing as consumers demand more options, convenience, and the global availability of locks on the Internet. The public generally has little understanding of security, especially in terms of lock design, unless they work with expert advisors, trained locksmiths, and high-security locks. Driven by the globalization of locks and how they are marketed, consumers also want to upgrade to newer systems. Google, Samsung, Apple, Amazon, and many DIY stores now sell locks to a worldwide audience. For complex systems, local locksmiths are the experts on the ground and the foot soldiers for the lock manufacturers. They are essential to the migration to digital security.

The blurring of traditional functionality and design between conventional and high-security locks has occurred rapidly because of advances by cell phone manufacturers and wireless technology such as Bluetooth and near-field communications (NFC). Consumers often trade classic, recognized security metrics in mechanical and electronic locks for convenience and access-control options in newer technology that may result in vulnerabilities. Locks and their functions can still be classified as mechanical, electromechanical, and electronic. But now, locking systems take many hybrid forms that would have been unimagined in research labs and only dreamed of by manufacturers 20 years ago. More importantly, large manufacturers are developing ecosystems that incorporate all the elements for access, security, remote control, and management of these systems.

Alternate technology relying on contactless smartcards and wireless connections is replacing traditional credentials. Home-automation systems that employ authentication with voice response and the ability to use artificial intelligence allow users to control alarm systems and environmental interfaces that monitor and operate heating and air conditioning, building access control, and various appliances and their functions. The IoT world is gaining traction for security and remote control of everything related to living and working spaces. Unlocking doors is now just a small part of the broader concept of system control and integrated ecosystems with digital credentials.

Battery technology has improved to allow electronic-based locks to function for years on one cell and to power internal software, ensuring that the proper credential is submitted to open a locking device or system. Abloy and iLOQ, two Finnish companies, pioneered energy harvesting to eliminate the need for batteries in their electromechanical and electronic locks and keys. Companies have also figured out how to exploit NFC designs in smartphones to power locks and thereby eliminate internal batteries, which is ecofriendly and reduces maintenance and battery replacement costs.

Authentication using fingerprints, facial or voice recognition, and retinal scans is no longer science fiction. Even in smartphones, authentication using integrated facial recognition and fingerprints is demanded by consumers to protect the data in their devices. This authentication type is preferred, as it's viewed as being a more secure credential to open doors, buy things, and even start cars.

Although the industry has progressed in developing locking systems, these ostensibly sophisticated designs can pose new security threats in bypass, hacking, and engineering failures. As pointed out throughout this book, rarely is anything completely secure. The incredible advances in the technology of locks and access-control systems don't mean all innovations should change the basic rules of how locking systems are developed in favor of implementing the latest advances.

The rapid changes in the security industry require that design engineers be conversant with the current forms of bypass and defeat of systems. They must understand and implement the latest methods to thoroughly vet new systems before they implement them. As locks become more reliant on software and hardware integration for their security, the risks to consumers escalate in terms of potential vulnerability.

In this chapter, examples of the current state of lock technology are surveyed, focusing on design security and representing what's available in the marketplace. Many of the locks and techniques discussed aren't new but mature. They have survived for years due to their solid engineering, design reliability, and proven security. I present an overview of the different modern locking systems, again with an accent on vulnerabilities, because many of these fundamental designs form the basis for new products, albeit with modifications and alterations. If there are vulnerabilities, they will be embedded in newer systems unless they're fully understood and dealt with effectively.

This discussion is a preface and lays the groundwork, in Part IV, for the detailed analysis of traditional and advanced attack techniques for today's technology and provides a guide for design engineers for tomorrow's products. In my world, locks still must perform certain basic functions, regardless of how sophisticated their mechanical and electronic credentials appear. The basic modes of defeating current designs are often simple and always exploit a lack of knowledge and imagination in those who conceive and implement the hardware described in this chapter.

The discussion of the currently available technology is divided into categories of locking systems: conventional, high security, electromechanical, electronic, and energy harvesting. Keys still open locks, but the definition of what constitutes a key and how keys work has been radically altered. No longer a traditional piece of metal, a key can also be a combination of bitting and electronics or pure electronic software-based or wireless credentials.

Traditional keys can be purely mechanical and require direct interaction between internal locking components and parts of the key. They can also talk to locks via a wireless link. Everything is changing for credentials, but keys, in whatever form, must still perform the same basic function: cause something mechanical to move to accomplish physical locking or unlocking. And that basic fact must always be the starting point in assessing the security and functionality of any lock by a design team. Regardless of the technology, the primary rule for security still applies: the key never unlocks the lock; it actuates the mechanism that allows unlocking.

The transition from mechanical to digital systems will take time, but it's occurring at an accelerated pace. Keyless solutions, mobile access, and the evolution of ecosystems for access control and facilities management are growing, especially due to the green revolution. The goal is to make things simpler. Lock manufacturers are implementing this revolution.

Conventional Mechanical Locks

Conventional locks, as a class, aren't intended for high-security applications. As noted in Chapter 7, specific criteria are assigned to a high-security rating to distinguish mechanisms that cannot meet the Underwriter Laboratories (UL) and American National Standards Institute (ANSI)/Builders Hardware Manufacturers Association (BHMA) standards. Conventional locks can have certain security enhancements but are less expensive and easier to defeat in forced and covert attacks. These locks are primarily available through retail distribution channels, some lock shops, and the Internet.

Many variations can be classified as conventional locks with mechanical credentials (keys). Wafer, disc, and pin tumbler locks are the most recognized variations. There are also hybrid mechanical locks that combine more than one system, including both pin tumblers and some form of movable element or special pin configuration. Some advanced designs can also be found in high-security locks and meet the standards.

Physical locking systems are most venues' first line of security and defense. In most parts of the world, some form of pin tumbler locks protect facilities and internal access. Design engineers, risk managers, security officers, and IT professionals must understand how locks work, what makes them secure, current attack types, and available iterations.

It's also incumbent on them to understand how the standards for rating locks are important in their environments, especially when high-value targets or critical infrastructure are involved. Meeting standards by a lock manufacturer may not tell the whole story about security and limitations of protection against knowledgeable criminals and attackers. In my experience, many locks, including those with a high-security rating, are subject to compromise, sometimes in seconds, even by non-experts. It's essential to understand what's in the marketplace, the attributes of each system type, and what's available.

Many organizations don't have the expertise to properly evaluate the locks and security systems they purchase from manufacturers. They rely on statements from marketing and technical representatives about security and key control, which may not be accurate. High tech doesn't mean real security, nor do patents guarantee protection. Many design engineers and salespeople don't know about certain vulnerabilities in what they sell and the inherent limitations of current devices. Two very important rules to remember are that insecurity means liability, and what is secure today will not be secure tomorrow.

Wafer Tumbler Locks

A *wafer lock* can be classed as a conventional mechanism. Almost all traditional use of wafers doesn't involve high-security applications. They're the least expensive and most common lock type worldwide. They can be found in thousands of applications, including gaming, vending, cabinets and showcases, gun locks, safes with bypass locks, cash boxes, elevators, key switches, electric panels, lockers, padlocks, alarm control, desks and furniture, computer locks, and many low-level security uses. The traditional wafer lock design hasn't changed radically in the past 100 years, although variations in some designs have vastly improved.

Most wafer locks are simple in concept and can be produced in single-bitted, double-bitted, and triple-bitted configurations, normally with five wafers. However, some may have up to 13 wafters in a special wafer pack, typically found in vending applications. A shear line is created around a rotating plug, and the wafers must be properly aligned to permit turning movement. The original patent in the United States was issued around 1868 to Philo Felter. Three years earlier, Linus Yale introduced his pin tumbler lock design. By 1878, Yale had purchased several companies that produced wafer locks. In 1915, Briggs & Stratton began offering a wafer tumbler lock for the ignition switches in cars. They gained wider acceptance when they introduced the wafer tumbler with a sidebar in 1935, because the sidebar provided another security layer against common methods of attack. It set the stage for the implementation of this method of protecting many forms of locks, including wafers, discs, and pin tumblers. The development of the sidebar was the impetus 40 years later for one of the most successful pin tumbler adaptations in the United States and worldwide: the Medeco rotating tumbler and sidebar system.

In most versions, wafer locks mimic pin tumblers in that detainers must be moved to a shear line. The wafers are normally spring-biased like their pin tumbler counterparts. A famous wafer lock design by Winfield didn't employ springs to keep its sliders (i.e., a form of a wafer) in place, resulting in a simple attack that could be carried out in seconds and placing many hotel rooms at risk worldwide. I developed this attack vector, notwithstanding the popularity of this programmable lock and its patents. The case is discussed in Part VI.

Any manufacturer contemplating using wafer tumbler locks, especially in protecting access control systems in buildings, apartment complexes, and mechanical or electronic door locks with bypass cylinders, must fully understand the limited security provided. Some vendors are tempted to reduce costs by providing inexpensive wafer locks in their products. However, they fail to understand or consider the security and legal ramifications that can allow the underlying systems to be easily compromised.

To save costs, keys for some of these locks may be stamped rather than cut for each bitting position, resulting in almost no differences in depth increments. This can create a vulnerability to *shimming*, where a thin metal blade is inserted and the tumblers are lifted to a shear line. Legal liability can be attached to a manufacturer that installs such locks into its products or to a facility that relies on the protection these locks offer if a serious security issue presents itself.

It should always be considered that using these locks on access control systems can provide a gateway to enter an area or facility or the ability to reprogram mechanical or electronic push-button locks or safes. Inexpensive alternatives to traditional wafer tumbler designs offer a much higher level of pick resistance and key control.

A traditional wafer lock's design has the following limitations and security characteristics:

- Inexpensive to produce.
- Low tolerances between components.
- Low to medium security.
- Lack of key control.
- Subject to the application of torque to force open or break.
- Easily picked and vibrated open.
- Subject to key jiggling and preconfigured tryout keys.

- Single and double-bitted keyways can be easily reverse-picked with paper clips and shims, trapping each wafer at the shear line.
- Cannot be bumped open.
- Can be visually decoded from the outside of the lock.
- Offer a limited number of differs.
- Can be master keyed using split wafers and dual-contact points.
- Keys may be available on the Internet for many common cam locks.

Hybrid Wafer Lock Designs with Sidebars

Certain manufacturers have cleverly modified the traditional wafer lock design to incorporate higher-security enhancements, with many variations bearing little resemblance to the original wafer tumbler mechanism. Two leading producers, *Kwikset SmartKey* and *EVVA 3KS* and *4KS*, employ what can be described as modified wafers or sliders.

Kwikset SmartKey

The Kwikset SmartKey shown in Figure 13-1 is a user-programmable lock that utilizes a form of slider. It has two sets of meshing wafers that allow the shear line to be adjusted to fit any bitting values of a key. This allows the consumer to instantly change the key combination.

When a special pin is inserted into the programming slot to the left of the keyway and depressed, it causes the wafers to separate and change their relative position and height, as their gates are aligned to allow the sidebar to enter. The slot to the wafer's left is the true gate position for the sidebar. The correct bitting of the key moves each wafer into alignment with the sidebar. The wafer in the right image has been bent through torque application on the plug. Before a new sidebar design was created, this defect allowed the lock to be opened in seconds when a screwdriver was inserted into the keyway and twisted.

EVVA 3KS

The EVVA (Austrian) 3KS (and upgraded 4KS) (Figure 13-2) is a multitrack key that controls two sets of sliders that interface with sidebars. Sliders are moved to the correct gate position by the multiple-depth horizontal channels in the key. Each slider has at least one true and several false gates. When the key interacts with each slider as it traverses the keyway, the sliders on different levels are moved to their correct positions by pickup pins that control how each slider is moved. When all the sliders are properly positioned, the gates are aligned so the sidebars can retract into the plug.

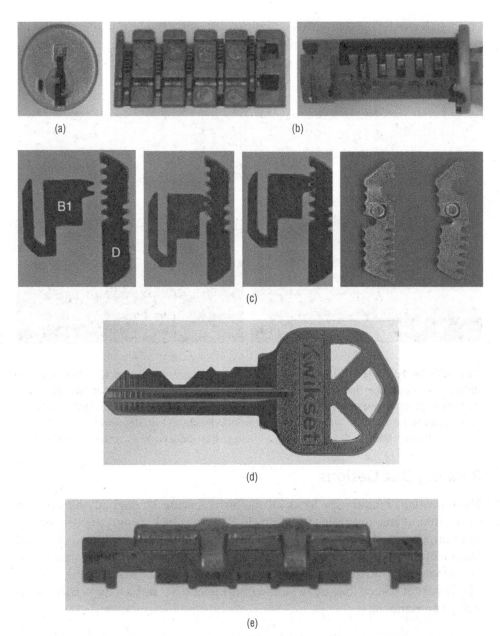

Figures 13-1a–1e: (a) The cylinder, (b) the sidebar rack, (c) movable sliders, (d) a properly bitted key, and (e) the sidebar. The Kwikset SmartKey is based on the use of five wafers that mesh with the tumblers that contact the key bitting.

The name 3KS means "three curved systems," which describes the multiple tracks on the key. The lock is virtually maintenance-free because it has no springs. It can be picked with some difficulty using the John Falle tool developed many years ago, but it's still quite secure, although it may not qualify for a high-security rating.

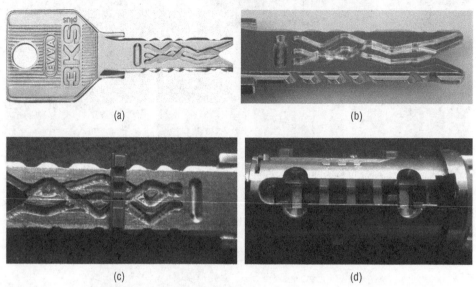

Figures 13-2a–2d: The EVVA 3KS (and later 4KS) is a multichannel laser track lock that moves sliders to align at a shear line so their protrusions can enter the gates of a sidebar. Multiple track levels interact with the sliders. Note the false gates on the slider. The false gates don't have the same depth as the true gate. (a) and (b) show the track detail. (c) illustrates how the sliders interact with the tracks. (d) shows all sliders aligned so the sidebar is free to retract into the plug.

Rotating Disc Designs

There are many rotating disc locks, all of which replicate the original Abloy design from Finland (see examples in Figure 13-3). These lock designs are extremely popular, especially in vending applications, padlocks, and door locks, and feature up to 13 discs and a sidebar. The discs can be considered more sophisticated wafers, with gates for creating a shear line and a corresponding sidebar. The key rotates each disc by its angled bitting and scrambles the setting of all wafers on removal.

Pin Tumbler Locks

Pin tumbler locks, originally invented by Linus Yale around 1860, are the primary locking devices in the United States. They can be produced in unlimited configurations, with the number of tumblers normally ranging from three to seven. The basic locking theory is employed in conventional and high-security locks, as described in Chapter 14. Because of their versatility and popularity, many factors come into play if design engineers contemplate their use. The basic concept remains constant with all the innovations: pins that block rotation, and a shear line.

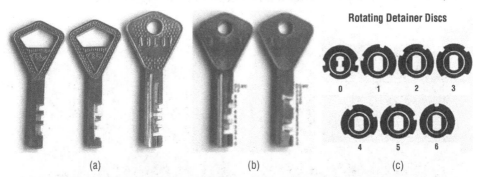

Rotating Detainer Discs

(a)   (b)   (c)

Figure 13-3a–3c: Abloy Classic standard 9-disc key, Classic 11-disc key, and Profile 14-disc key (a) and keys for (b) an Abloy 10-disc lock and (c) a 14-disc lock. Each bitting portion picks up and rotates a different disc. Many disc designs, sizes, and gate positions have multiple gates. The key bitting picks them up as it's rotated.

Courtesy of Han Fey.

Conventional pin tumbler locks can be identified as those that don't contain any security enhancements but have only the most basic components. They have limited protection and don't possess multiple security layers to frustrate known forced and covert attack methods. An example of a popular pin tumbler cylinder is produced by Schlage, one of the country's oldest and most respected lock manufacturers. Its five-pin lock can be considered a traditional version because it has limited security features compared to its high-security counterparts. The pin tumbler mechanism is the backbone of physical locking security in many countries because it's recognized for its versatility in implementation to meet different locking requirements.

Many manufacturers in the United States and overseas offer similar systems with varying levels of quality in materials, tolerances, security enhancements, and costs (see Figure 13-4). These locks are best known for residence and business applications on doors. They are typically available in five-, six-, or seven-pin tumbler configurations and a maximum of 1,000,000 or more theoretical key combinations. The higher-quality locks can include protection against forced entry and are typically offered in brass, nickel silver, Zamak (zinc and alloying elements of aluminum, magnesium, and copper), and metal injection molding (MiM).

Components and Fundamental Operating Principles of a Conventional Pin Tumbler Lock

The fundamental principle of all pin tumbler locks is based on the *double-detainer theory* of locking and creating a shear line: the physical breakpoint between the rotating plug and fixed body (i.e., shell). In virtually every kind of lock, whether wafer, lever tumbler, pin tumbler, sidebar, rotating disc, or magnetic, some form of shear line is provided to allow critical components to be turned (or moved) when the correct key or credential is presented. See Figure 13-5.

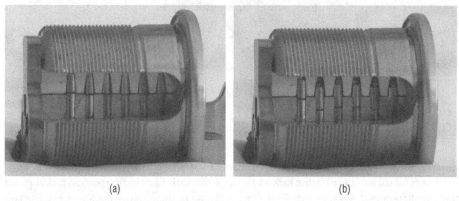

(a)   (b)

Figure 13-4a, 4b: A conventional pin tumbler lock. (a) shows all pins at the shear line, thus allowing the plug to be turned using the correct key. (b) the pins are not aligned so the lock will not open.

(a)   (b)

Figure 13-5a, 5b: Creating a shear line places a gap between the plug and shell, as shown in the six-pin lock. In (a) the pins are aligned at a shear line, and the plug is free to turn. In (b) two pin tumblers protrude from the plug into the shell, thereby blocking it from turning.

A conventional pin tumbler lock has six primary parts: plug, shell, springs, top pins, bottom pins, retaining mechanism (to keep each pin stack in place), and screws or clips to link the plug to the tailpiece or cam. The plug, which contains the keyway and bottom pins, is free to rotate when all lower pins are at the shear line, thereby actuating a tailpiece or cam, which controls the actual locking mechanism. The shell holds the top pins and springs. The function of the springs is to provide a bias to each pin so the pins aren't free-floating. Pins not under tension can present a serious vulnerability to vibration attacks, as demonstrated in the Winfield lock case in Part VI.

A pin tumbler in each bore or chamber is moved across the shear line by the bitting of the key. The proper operation of every pin tumbler mechanism allows each top pin to rest below the shear line in an idle-locked state. Depending on the bitting values, pins are moved below or above the shear line when an incorrect key is inserted. When this occurs, the plug can't turn because there are one or more obstructions to rotation.

When the correct key bitting is presented, each pin can be elevated precisely to the shear line: the top pin is completely within the shell, and the bottom pin is completely in the plug. No part of any pin is entering above or below the shear line. If any tumbler extends even .003″ above or below this breakpoint, the lock cannot open. This tolerance depends on the lock manufacturer, the cylinder's quality, and how it was produced.

The purpose of the keyway (Figure 13-6) is to limit the universe of keys that can enter and is based on a matching of wards within the plug that corresponds with channels or indentations on the key's surface. In higher-security locks, paracentric keyways are employed to make picking more difficult.

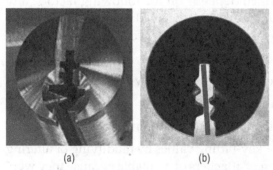

(a)   (b)

Figures 13-6a, 6b: Paracentric keyways can make picking difficult because the wards cross the center line of the keyway. In (a) wards would make picking difficult. In (b) the line shows a clear path for the vertical movement of a pick.

Security Vulnerabilities of Conventional (and Some High-Security) Pin Tumbler Locks

Almost all conventional and high-security pin tumbler locks can be subject to defeat by covert and forced methods of entry. Design engineers and vulnerability assessment (VA) teams must understand and consider these during R&D before releasing a modified or new product. Because new techniques are continually being conceived of by criminals, hackers, locksmiths, and sports lock-picking groups, the descriptions of attack modes found in Part IV are not exhaustive, especially when considering hybrid methods that combine two or more techniques.

Bumping and bump keys (see Figure 13-7) threaten all pin tumbler locks, even those with high-security ratings. Keys are readily available from many Internet sources and can be easily produced. Conventional locks, especially Kwikset and

Schlage, are particularly vulnerable because of the popularity of their keyways. Blanks can be obtained from Amazon and every DIY store.

Depending on how such locks are configured and the security designed into the mechanism, the order of threat levels can vary from very simple to complex. Conventional pin tumbler locks often suffer from the following vulnerabilities:

- Poor plug-shell tolerances
- Ability to overlift pins to create another shear line by comb-picking
- Inferior materials that make the locking elements subject to methods of forced entry
- Use of hollow, rather than solid pin tumblers
- No intelligence in the lock or keys and no capability for an audit trail
- Nonexistent or minimal key control and the ability to simulate, replicate, and duplicate most keys, which depends on the following factors: any legal protection for blanks and keyways, the availability of blanks for a targeted keyway, and the ease of cutting keys by code or by hand
- No security for lost, stolen, or deleted keys
- Can be subject to key-interchange issues based on low-tolerance components
- No evidence of a breach or unauthorized opening
- A limited number of depth increments for each pin chamber
- The amplification of rights of key-bitting values by modifying or altering keys that are in the possession of attackers or available because they were lost, canceled, or deleted from a system but not physically destroyed
- Bypass of the lock through mechanical means, including picking, impressioning, decoding, bumping, and extrapolation of master keys
- Accessibility for shim wires and other tools to manipulate critical components or gain access through the end of the keyway or plastic housings
- Visual decoding of internal components
- Reverse picking by shearing the retaining screws between the plug and cam and tailpiece and then applying reverse tension against the pins and manipulating them in the correct order of picking so they set at the shear line
- Drilling to create a shear line
- Key jiggling or the use of preconfigured signature keys, picks, or tryout keys to exploit low tolerances between plug and shell
- Ease of lock bumping
- Extrapolation of master keys

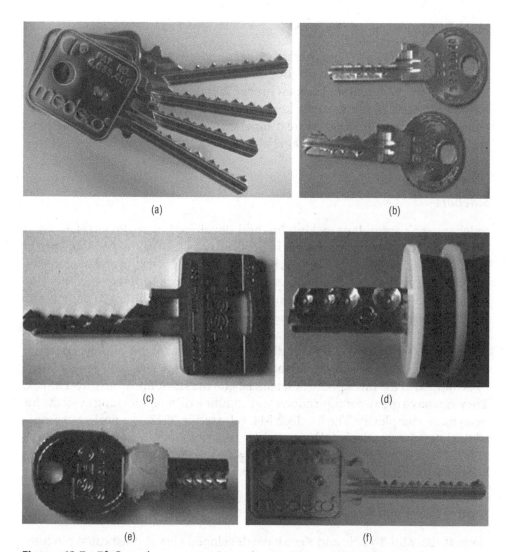

(a)

(b)

(c)

(d)

(e)

(f)

Figures 13-7a–7f: Bump keys are a persistent threat to pin tumbler mechanisms. Shown are (a) and (b) bump keys for conventional locks, (c) side bit milling, (e) a dimple lock with (d) a movable element, and (f) the code-setting keys for bumping Medeco BIAXIAL locks. The rubber spacer on the dimple key creates a gap between the face of the plug and the bitting of the key. Lower-security dimple locks that contain no movable elements in the key are especially vulnerable to bumping.

- Vulnerabilities associated with the use of vibration, magnetic fields, shims, and energy shock
- Ability to decode the control key in a removable core system
- Mechanical bypass of critical components that may be simple

Hybrid Mechanical Designs

Some pin tumbler locks incorporate sidebar and other security enhancements to elevate their protection without qualifying for a UL 437 or ANSI/BHMA high-security designation. Locks with combinations of different mechanical attributes are intended to make key duplication and certain forms of covert entry more difficult. Examples are dimples, axial pin tumblers, magnetic pins, split sidebars, laser tracks, movable elements in the key, and side bit milling with secondary finger pins.

Sidebars

Sidebars are a secondary locking method developed over 100 years ago and discussed in Chapter 14, comparing high-security locks. They're popular, even in inexpensive conventional cylinders, because they make picking and other forms of defeat more difficult. Some locks have two sidebars for increased security. Whatever the configuration, sidebars act as a mechanical buffer to deny direct feedback between internal components. That derived information is critical to picking, decoding, impressioning, and other bypass forms.

Traditional shear lines allow for direct manipulation of pin tumblers or other detainers and provide better information and response when each element "sets" or is trapped at the breakpoint. Sidebars isolate the shear line from direct attack. They can have many configurations and combine different locking systems for even more complexity. The Medeco M4, released in 2022, is a perfect example of the latest integration of the secondary security layer in conjunction with a sidebar. The M4 employs side bit milling and the rotation of pin tumblers to control the sidebar, making covert attacks more difficult.

Dimple Locks and Telescoping Pins

dormakaba, Mul-T-Lock, and Keso have developed very sophisticated pin tumbler locks based on dimple design (see Figures 13-8 and 13-9). Multiple drill points, angles, and depths form the bitting surface of a key. These locks can offer high-security solutions but can also be subject to simple impressioning techniques. John Falle developed a system using metal foil about .060″ pressed against a predrilled key carrier to match the dimple pattern corresponding with the location of all tumblers within the lock. The foil key is inserted, and pressure is exerted in different orientations. When this action is properly applied, the foil is depressed to the exact length of each pin and provides a working key.

Mul-T-Lock (from Israel) pioneered the dimple lock with telescoping pins or pin-within-pin technology. See Figure 13-10. Each tumbler has an outer pin containing a smaller inner pin. Both must be raised to the shear line by the complex bitting of the key. Telescoping pins have two contact points: the outer pin and the inner pin. An interactive pin, or laser track for sliders, and a second "alpha spring" at the key tip may also be present to add security against covert entry and key duplication methods.

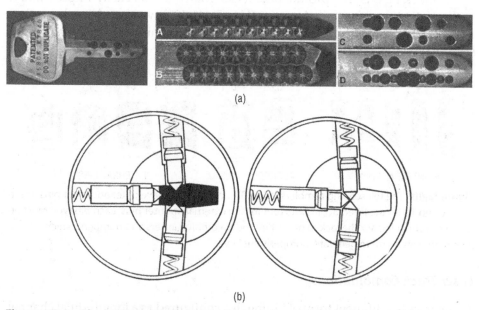

(a)

(b)

Figures 13-8a, 8b: (a) (A) and (B) The original Sargent Keso featured three rows of pin tumblers in reversible key positional master key systems that provided security against traditional means of extrapolation. (C) Mul-T-Lock is one of the leading manufacturers of dimple keys in many different configurations, from low to high security. (b) shows the interaction of pins into the individual drill point positions.

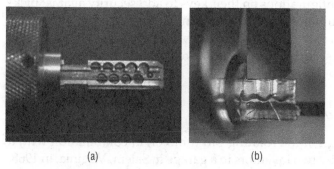

(a)   (b)

Figures 13-9a, 9b: Many dimple locks are susceptible to impressioning with metal foil. John Falle developed this system, comprising a key carrier (a) that precisely matches the location of the pins and is overlaid with foil (b).

Axial Pin Tumblers

Axial pin tumbler locks are popular for computer protection, vending applications, switch locks, parking meters, alarm switches, elevators, and other installations. They are available in many configurations, from very low to high security, and offer reprogrammability options. See Figure 13-11. Axial locks, or tubular pin tumblers, are subject to many forms of compromise; the best known is the attack against Kryptonite bike locks. Many can be easily impressioned with plastic tubes and foil. A patent (U.S. 7,441,431) was issued to the author to make this lock less vulnerable to impressioning. This mechanism has high-security versions; the best known is the Ace lock.

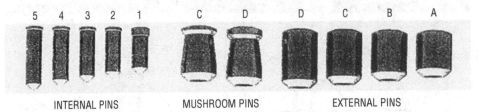

INTERNAL PINS   MUSHROOM PINS   EXTERNAL PINS

Figure 13-10: The telescoping tumblers in Mul-T-Lock cylinders have outer and inner pins. There are five depths for the internal pins and four for the external or outer pins. Each pin type must be raised to a shear line for the lock to open. Key codes combine letters and numbers, which locksmiths can utilize to generate a properly cut key.

Laser-Track Combinations

A *laser track* is a different form of bitting. It's configured as a longitudinal channel across the surface of a key blade rather than traditional bitting that lifts individual wafers or pin tumblers. The tracks are designed to move the wafers or sliders within the plug, often to mate with a sidebar (see Figure 13-12).

Many manufacturers have integrated laser tracks with pin tumbler dimple cuts, wafers, or other configurations on their keys to add security against picking and key copying. Automotive systems began adding wafers controlled by laser tracks many years ago. They are also a favorite for imported locks and those that are very low security because they are inexpensive to produce yet appear secure.

Rotating Pin Tumblers and Sidebars

The revolutionary design of the rotating pin tumbler, in combination with a sidebar, was developed by two inventors in a garage in Salem, Virginia, in 1968. These individuals changed the definition of high-security locks in the United States by inventing a cylinder with pins required to be elevated to a shear line.

The pins were rotated to one of three positions by the angled bitting of the key (see Figure 13-13). Unlike a conventional pin tumbler design, this one created a traditional shear line and a secondary locking system with the implementation of a sidebar. This invention led to the design of many high-security innovations and, ultimately, to electrotechnical cylinders branded as the Assa Abloy CLIQ.

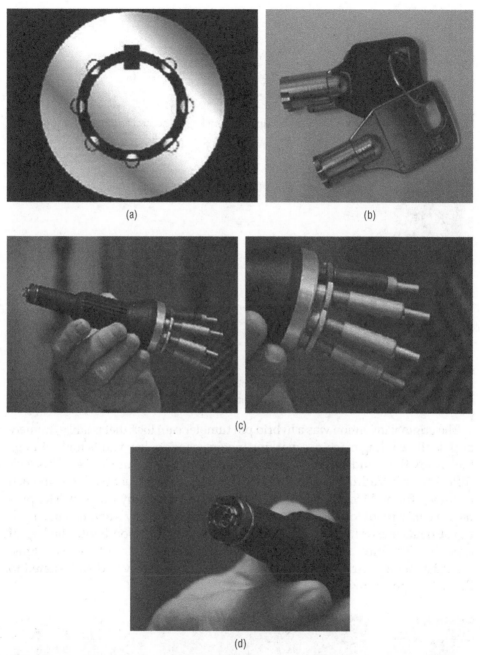

(a)

(b)

(c)

(d)

Figure 13-11a–11d: Axial pin tumbler locks are based on the pin tumbler principle and haven't changed in the past century. They are often easy to pick with tools that manipulate all tumblers simultaneously. Peterson designed such a pick. (a) and (b) show a typical seven-pin lock and tubular key. (c) and (d) show a special picking tool.

Figure 13-12: A laser track is milled into many different keys to control another security layer of sliders or discs interacting with a sidebar.

Figure 13-13: Medeco developed the rotating pin tumbler design. The photograph shows the pin with a chisel point, which is twisted by the bitting on the key to one of three angles.

The original invention was a hybrid pin tumbler cam lock that is still extremely popular in vending machines, parking meters, gaming, key vaults for buildings (i.e., Knox Box), and switch control applications (see Figure 13-14). This lock differs from a traditional pin tumbler that requires at least two pins in each chamber. In the Medeco cam lock, each chamber has only one pin. The pins have a chisel point to allow proper rotation against the key's angled cuts. Each pin also has one or more holes precisely placed to correspond with the legs of a sidebar. The pins are rotated and lifted, as with the later Medeco designs. A sidebar with protruding legs enters each hole when elevated and rotated to the correct position.

(a)   (b)   (c)

Figures 13-14a–14c: (a) The Original Medeco cam lock design with (c) a single-pin tumbler in each chamber. Note the chisel points that mate with the key bitting to rotate to the correct position so the legs of the sidebar can enter the holes. (b) The key rotates the pins so that the fence can enter each hole from the sidebar.

Magnetic Fields and Rotating Discs

EVVA developed the Magnetic Code System (MCS) over 30 years ago (see Figure 13-15). The lock is still popular in high-security installations requiring large, complex master key systems. The design relies on eight individual magnetic rotors that are actuated by corresponding magnets embedded in the key's surface. Other locks employ magnets to move detainers to shear lines, such as Miwa (from Japan). Other manufacturers, such as Mul-T-Lock, have embedded movable magnetic elements to make key duplication more difficult.

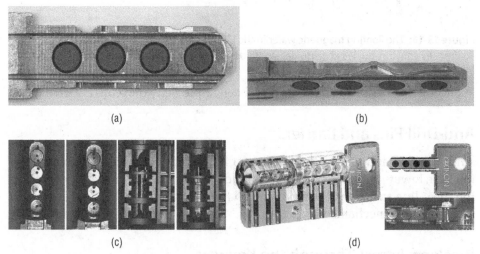

(a)   (b)

(c)   (d)

Figure 13-15a–15d: The EVVA MCS was developed many years ago but is still favored by government and intelligence agencies and for large master key systems. The MCS uses four rare earth magnetic pellets (a) embedded in a key and encoded on surfaces with different magnetic orientations. They control eight rotors (c) inside the lock that the individual magnetic fields move to align their gates with two sidebars. The key also controls seven sliders (b) with the bitting that runs the length of the top of the key. A diagram of the locking mechanism is shown in (d).

EVVA introduced its Acura 44 system (Figure 13-16) incorporating a floating magnetic element in the key that mates with a corresponding element in the lock. This system isn't designed for high-security applications but rather to make key copying more difficult, especially with 3D printing.

Security Enhancements to Conventional Locks

Conventional locks don't typically offer significant security enhancements that approach those found in high-security-rated cylinders. One notable exception may be the Kwikset SmartKey's pick and bump resistance. Those features weren't designed into the lock when the concept was developed but were an unintended marketing and security advantage.

Figure 13-16: The floating magnetic wafer in the EVVA Acura 44 can provide added protection against key copying, but it's trivial to defeat. It's designed for key control.

Several security improvements have been implemented in conventional locks.

Anti-Drill Pins and Barriers

Anti-drill pins and plates are common for high-security locks but aren't usually found in lower-grade conventional cylinders. Their purpose is to block access to the shear line and critical components that would allow defeating the primary security of the mechanism.

Blocking Access Through the Keyway

Some of the better conventional cylinders close the end of the keyway to prevent access to critical components. Even in higher-security locks, some manufacturers leave the keyways open where the plug is connected to a tailpiece or cam. Depending on the design of the locking system and associated hardware, this can provide an entry point for shims, screwdrivers, and other implements to manipulate elements that can control locking. It can also allow an attack on the screws that secure the part that links the plug to the cam and tailpiece.

Anti-Bumping Pins

Intense media publicity after 2006 has caused almost every lock manufacturer to explore ways to restrict the ability to bump open cylinders. Master Lock began implementing a special pin to prevent bypass by bumping. However, it could be easily defeated if the attacker knew its placement and how to circumvent it. Other manufacturers have tried similar techniques with limited success. All pin tumbler locks have an inherent design problem if they rely on spring-biased movable pins in each chamber. The theory of bumping is based on Newton's Third Law of Motion: for every action, there is an equal and opposite reaction.

Security Pins and False Gates or Notches

Security pins are placed in one or more chambers to make picking more difficult (see Figures 13-17 and 13-18). Medeco developed special tumblers for government installations to prevent attackers' picking and decoding the length of pins using acoustics, sound injection, or measurement by piezo decoders. Security pins take many forms and are known as mushroom tumblers, spools, serrated, or ARX pins (Medeco). They are designed to be trapped at the shear line when torque is applied during the picking process. This prevents the plug from rotating or falsely indicating a pin setting. Security pins do not prevent lock bumping or effectively address the inherent insecurity of basic pin tumbler mechanisms. I hold two U.S. patents (7,775,074 and 7,963,135 B1) for designing security pins to prevent bypassing Medeco high-security locks.

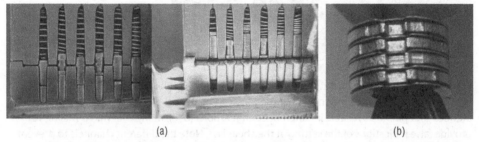

(a)   (b)

Figure 13-17a, 17b: (a) is a six-pin tumbler lock with different security pins and false notches to catch at the shear line when torque is applied. (b) shows an Abloy Disc Classic. The #3 disc shows the true and false gates to catch the sidebar in a rotating disc. It's the same theory for both types of mechanisms.

Bitting Design

Bitting is the material on the key's surface that contacts internal detainers and other components inside the lock. The function of bitting is to move critical elements to an unlocked state. Variation in bitting is a primary means to add security to a locking mechanism and enhance the ability to restrict key copying. Differences in the geometry, bitting thickness, and height; embedding movable elements, magnets, ball bearings, and laser tracks; and other alterations can add security to conventional and high-security mechanisms. EVVA secured a patent for the tip design of the key so that it must interact with the internal mechanism in the plug before rotation can occur.

Some bitting can be very complex, making traditional copy techniques difficult. With the advent and sophistication of 3D printing, producing a key that can't be copied becomes extremely difficult, especially if a hybrid approach is employed. Adding side bit milling and undercuts, as in the Assa Abloy, Schlage, and Medeco, can significantly add to key control and security. Some locks and keys employ multiple bitting systems, such as the EVVA 3KS, Acura 44, and Mul-T-Lock MT5 and MT5+. Mul-T-Lock added a laser track to control sliders and a single or double spring-loaded movable element at the tip of the key. Other manufacturers have invented protrusions, special notches, indentations, and transponders. Unfortunately, even with added enhancements, the conventional pin tumbler lock still has the same basic security limitations (see Figures 13-20 and 13-21).

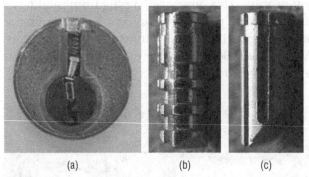

(a)   (b)   (c)

Figures 13-18a–18c: This pin tumbler cylinder (a) graphically illustrates how the mushroom pin (i.e., top pin) is trapped at the shear line. The plug can be turned only slightly during picking. Medeco ARX pins are available in different configurations (b–c), many with micro-milling to provide false indications of the setting at the shear line. Note the different channels to prevent types of attacks by probing.

High-Security Mechanical Locks

High-security locks are produced to more exact technical specifications than conventional cylinders. Special enhancements increase resistance to different destructive and covert compromise forms. As noted in Chapter 7, locks are tested against many forms of attack, including drilling, jimmying, picking, prying, forcing, impressioning, driving the lock cylinder, sawing, and pulling.

The mechanisms in high-security cylinders normally contain two or more security layers to frustrate attacks and provide more secure key control. As demonstrated in Chapter 14, comparing high-security locks provides insight into different design philosophies. High-security locks are theoretically more resistant to forced entry and covert methods.

Many high-security cylinders can be bumped open, but more expertise may be required. A key for a conventional lock won't bump open a high-security mechanism without added information and expertise in either picking or bumping techniques for the specific lock.

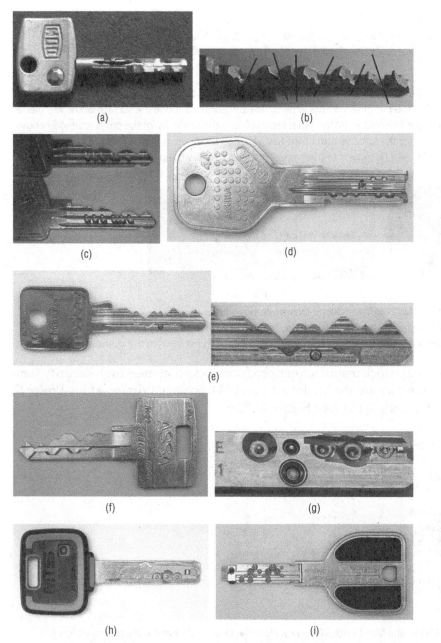

(a)

(b)

(c)

(d)

(e)

(f)

(g)

(h)

(i)

Figures 13-19a–19i: Different bitting designs include (a) DOM Diamant, (b) Medeco m3 showing angled cuts, (c) Medeco M4 with side bit milling and movable element, and (g) Mul-T-Lock with pin-within-pin technology and a movable element. Mul-T-Lock requires the two components and surfaces of its telescoping pins to be elevated by the bitting at two different contact points. Vachette (i) has a complex dimple design. The EVVA Acura 44 is also shown (d) with the magnetic element and angled bitting. The Mul-T-Lock (h) has a special alpha spring for added key control at the tip. The Assa Twin (f) features side bit milling and conventional pin tumblers. The EVVA (c) is the older model DPS with added virtual keyway bitting.

(a)	(b)

Figures 13-20a, 20b: Many manufacturers have adopted the Mul-T-Lock interactive pin concept after their original patents expired. The pin is forced above the surface of the key blade once the key is inserted. In (a) the pin is recessed into the blade. In (b) the pin is extended above the surface after the full insertion of the key. The interactive pin mates with another element in the lock that must be moved to the correct position to allow the plug to turn.

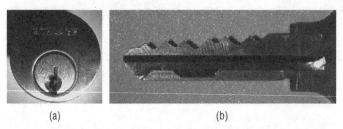

(a)	(b)

Figures 13-21a, 21b: The Schlage Everest employs an undercut (a) as an additional key control method. It can easily be defeated with a shim inserted along the key's side. (b) shows the undercut on the side of the key that controls an internal check-pin in the cylinder.

Every major lock manufacturer produces locks that meet high-security standards. Examples are the Medeco m3 and M4, Schlage Primus, Abloy Protec II, and Mul-T-Lock MT5+ (see Figure 13-22).

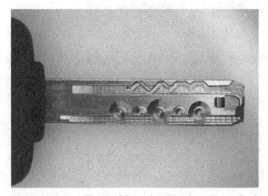

Figure 13-22: The Mul-T-Lock MT5+ key. Note the laser track that moves sliding wafers in combination with pin-within-pin tumblers. The tip of the key also features a movable element that must be depressed by corresponding elements in the lock.

Attributes of High-Security Locks

A comparison of high-security locks and their designs is presented in Chapter 14. Their primary attributes, in contrast to conventional locks discussed in this chapter, are significant and must also meet the requirements of ANSI/BHMA 156.30 and UL 437 standards, analyzed in Chapter 7:

- Multiple security layers
- More than one point of failure
- Each security layer is independent
- Security layers that operate in parallel, all of which must be circumvented to open the lock
- Difficult to bypass each layer
- Difficult to derive intelligence about a layer
- Difficult to simulate, replicate, or duplicate the action of the key
- Increased resistance to covert and forced entry

Software- and Hardware-Based Keys, Locks, and Access Control

Three distinct and interrelated technologies can be identified as state-of-the-art and integrate mechanical and digital locking systems: key-based digital cylinders, wireless door locks, and access control. Lock manufacturers offer electromechanical, electronic, and wireless systems in different designs to accomplish essentially the same result: the employment of some form of digital rather than purely mechanical credential to accomplish locking and unlocking functions. A combination or mixture of mechanical keys, electronic elements, wireless components, and energy-harvesting systems can provide power in the current production environment. Systems are designed to be backward compatible to allow the use of older mechanical cylinders with newer digital technology.

Key-Based Digital Cylinders

In traditional nondigital systems, a lock relies on some form of credential, a key, that contains a physical representation of a code (bitting). It interreacts with internal detainers such as pin tumblers, discs, and sidebars. Key-based digital cylinders employ some form of key that contains traditional mechanical bitting, an embedded electronic identifier, or a purely electronic credential. In a digital-based system, there is, at least in part, reliance on software and encryption algorithms rather than older-style hardware to accomplish traditional locking.

Key-based digital systems also have common elements, just like their traditional counterparts. These include a key or simulated key, an encrypted element that contains a unique identifier of a specific key code; a microprocessor (often in the key and the lock); a mechanical blocking element that accomplishes physical control of the latch, bolt, or other elements; and a source to power elements in the key and the lock. The internal processor inside the lock communicates with the key and ultimately issues commands to some form of motor or solenoid to move the blocking element to change locking states. When this occurs, the mechanical locking hardware is allowed to be activated by the key.

Examples of the latest digital cylinders include the Assa Abloy CLIQ and eCLIQ, and similar designs offered by many leading manufacturers including dormakaba, Allegion, EVVA, iLOQ, and SaltoSystems.

Assa Abloy CLIQ

In the late 1990s, companies began to develop electromechanical locks that relied on a bitted key in combination with an electronic credential (see Figure 13-23). Ikon (Germany) introduced one of the first profile cylinders with advanced security and programming options, including an audit trail. The CLIQ became one of the premier designs that offered enhanced key control for facilities and combined the security of a mechanical sidebar with an encrypted element to validate the key.

In these locks, mechanical security relies on the key bitting controlling wafers, discs, pin tumblers, or sliders. Electronic security is based on embedded memory in the key. It operates in parallel and normally communicates through a contact along the blade's surface, in the key head, or inductively to a corresponding contact within the lock housing. Several versions of the CLIQ are offered by different Assa Abloy companies that incorporate unique mechanical bitting designs and the shared CLIQ electronic platform.

Some digital-based cylinders can be subject to certain attack techniques to bypass the bitted portion of the key and defeat the processor-controlled blocking element. I have found many vulnerabilities in different investigations of these types of systems. They are stand-alone cylinders or can be networked.

Assa Abloy eCLIQ

The next generation of CLIQ is eCLIQ, shown in Figure 13-24. It's a lock designed with an electronic primary credential and a simulated mechanical key to transmit turning motion to control a cam or other actuating mechanism. Different Assa Abloy companies worldwide have marketed the technology platform, including Abloy, Ikon, Medeco, and Mul-T-Lock. In 2021, Assa Abloy announced the addition of energy harvesting in the key head to power 60 different lock versions. The system will be called Spark and will be backward compatible with almost all the eCLIQ platforms.

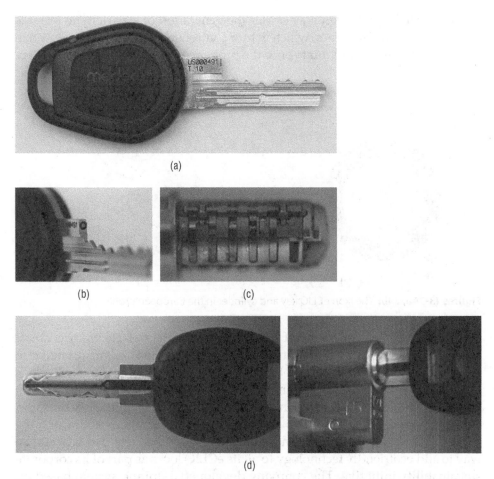

(a)

(b)   (c)

(d)

Figures 13-23a–23d: The Assa Abloy CLIQ (c and d) and the Medeco X4 use the same platform but have different configurations. The CLIQ employs a double-bitted wafer lock and sidebar for mechanical security. Medeco has a standard pin tumbler lock and electronic element. Both employ an encrypted chip in the key for authentication. Note the contact in the key head in the Medeco (a and b).

Energy-Harvesting Locks

Energy harvesting is part of the future of electromechanical lock design, whereas batteries have previously been required to power either the key or the lock. Almost all systems that employ some form of software control to authenticate credentials are dependent on internal power. The development of energy-harvesting technology was a natural evolution in the lock industry due to concerns about battery cost, life, maintenance, and disposal. In these systems, the key's movement through the keyway causes the generation of electricity to provide power to internal electronics, which in turn control mechanical components that allow keys to unlock and rotate once the proper credential has been presented.

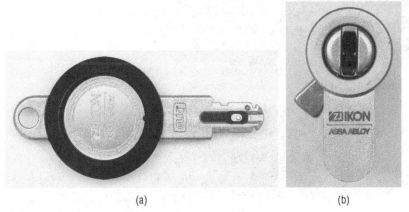

(a)   (b)

Figures 13-24a, 24b: The Ikon eCLIQ key and cylinder in the European profile.

There are only so many ways of generating electricity in an electromechanical lock because some form of motion involving the key must be transformed into usable energy. The recognized method is a tiny generator embedded in the lock or key. Abloy chose this design in its Pulse configuration. A slightly different design by iLOQ has a dual-function generator motor, but the principle is the same.

The Abloy and iLOQ systems are activated as the key moves through the keyway, which winds up the generator. Assa Abloy then decided it needed a way to add ecofriendly technology to all its eCLIQ locks as part of its corporate sustainability initiative. The company developed a unique system based on generating power in the key rather than internally in the lock. A tiny generator is positioned in the key head. This required a modification of the design of the eCLIQ key to include a slidable spring-biased element that contacts the face of the lock and retracts as the key moves forward, thus turning the generator. Assa Abloy branded this system Spark.

iLOQ

The iLOQ key, shown in Figures 13-25 and 13-26, is universal and mechanically identical for every lock. Each key has an embedded chip with an electronic serial number. As the key moves in the keyway and is validated, the generator changes its state to a motor that causes a critical component to move. A single-pin tumbler can be lifted by the key's tip, which then permits the plug's rotation. Once the key is withdrawn, its tip resets the entire mechanism. As noted in one of the case examples in Part VI, earlier designs of this lock presented some serious vulnerabilities for attackers. Later designs resolved the problems. Those issues should be instructive to any manufacturer that attempts to design an energy-harvesting approach to lock designs, because the problems were serious and allowed locks to be circumvented.

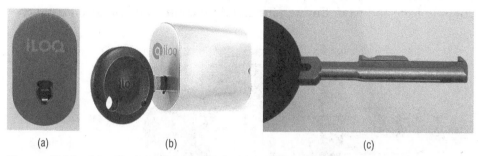

(a)   (b)   (c)

Figures 13-25a–25c: The iLOQ key is universal for these cylinders. Only the electronic serial number embedded in the key head is individualized for each system.

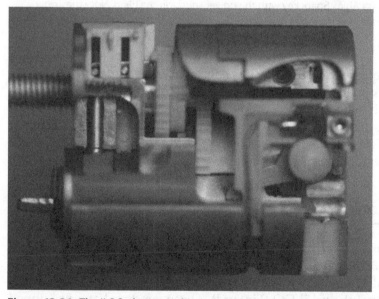

Figure 13-26: The iLOQ electromechanical mechanism. The key enters on the right side, winds up, and then releases the generator to power the internal processor to validate the key. Once authenticated, the generator becomes a motor and moves the arms (upper left) to lift the single pin, letting the key turn and actuate the tailpiece. As the key is withdrawn, it resets the entire mechanism.

Abloy Pulse, eCLIQ, and Spark

Abloy spent years developing its Pulse system and later eCLIQ and Spark (Figure 13-27) to eliminate the need for batteries in these locks. They're like the iLOQ in the way they generate electricity. The locks are part of a fully developed ecosystem that mates electronic and self-powered cylinders and padlocks. It's a wireless access system requiring no batteries or external power. Locks can communicate and work through the cloud for control and programmability.

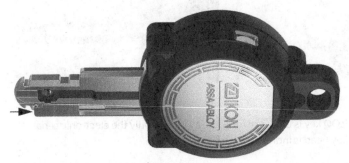

Figure 13-27: The Assa Abloy Spark key with the power source in the head. Note the arrow (lower left) that indicates the sliding arm, which drives the generator as the face of the lock plug pushes the slider.

The insertion of a key causes a tiny mechanism to generate power. Once fully inserted, the lock analyzes the encrypted credential in the key and either validates or rejects it in about 1 second. Mechanical security is assured using the sidebar locking scheme for which Abloy is famous. This system is particularly well suited for high-traffic multi-user sites, where the ability to change or delete keys and their permissions is important.

Electronic Locks

Many manufacturers offer fully electronic cylinders, usually in a European profile (see Figure 13-28). Leading companies are Assa Abloy (global), dormakaba (Switzerland), Allegion (United States), EVVA (Austria), Videx (United States), SaltoSystems (Spain), and iLOQ (Finland). These vendors have developed networked and stand-alone systems that present encrypted credentials using radio frequency identification (RFID), NFC, and other wireless technology, including Bluetooth.

Figure 13-28: Many vendors offer RFID-based electronic locking systems. Shown is the completely self-contained EVVA European profile cylinder. After you tap the proper credential on the face of the lock and turn the knob, an internal motor clutch enables the link between the knob and the actuating tab.

Hybrid Electronic Locks with Biometric or Wireless Authentication

A class of locks contains mechanical bypass cylinders and biometrics or keypads for authentication, shown in Figure 13-29 and 13-20. Kwikset, one of the leading lock manufacturers in North and South America, has introduced a series of locks that use fingerprints to authenticate the user. They also contain a bypass cylinder in case codes are lost or electronics fail. These locks can also be controlled and monitored remotely. Similar locks rely on entering a personal identification number (PIN) code through a digital keypad, often containing a bypass cylinder. Schlage is one of the dominant suppliers in the industry.

Kwikset KEVO

Kwikset introduced the KEVO (Figure 13-31) deadbolt cylinder that communicates with its application on iOS or Android. This lock senses an impedance change when the cylinder face is touched for entry. It authenticates through a smartphone via Bluetooth. It also has a SmartKey bypass cylinder. The lock can be accessed remotely through a supplied gateway, which allows opening and closing, adding and deleting authorized users, and an audit trail. The lock is smart enough to sense the handling of the door and whether the person attempting to enter is outside or inside the facility. The lock also determines and alarms if the deadbolt doesn't properly extend or retract. Different light-emitting diode (LED) ring colors indicate the lock status. The KEVO is one of many locks that are now offered to consumers. Most of the designs interface with deadbolt cylinders.

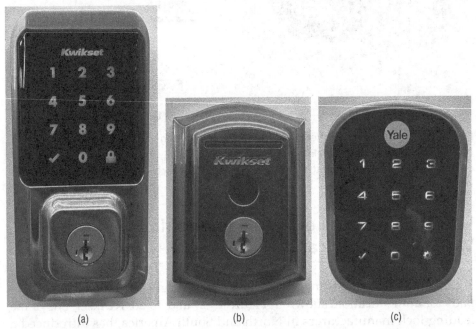

(a)   (b)   (c)

Figures 13-29a–29c: Three examples of electromechanical and electronic consumer-grade digital locks. The industry is moving toward digital keypads and fingerprint readers. The Kwikset SmartKey locks also feature a bypass cylinder that's instantly programmable for the key change. All these locks have Internet connectivity for remote control, monitoring, and programming for guest keys.

Wireless Door Locks, Access Control, and Authentication

Many leading manufacturers with a global presence are now offering wireless solutions for keyless and mobile cloud-based access and management applications, including Assa Abloy, dormakaba, and SaltoSystems. Products and platforms such as Aperio (Assa Abloy), Cumulus (Abloy), Data-On-Card (Salto), and AirKey (EVVA) are designed to meet requirements for access control for virtually any application. Many companies offer the integration of mechanical, electromechanical, and electronic hardware; almost everything today is through the cloud. Manufacturers have integrated their security expertise into digital solutions for secure management applications. Keyless access, including mobile keys, padlocks, and controllers, are all standard offerings.

Figure 13-30: The Schlage electromechanical lock with bypass cylinder is a popular consumer access control device. The bypass cylinder is easily defeated: in an investigation involving a triple homicide, we determined six different ways to open this lock.

Keyless smart padlocks that use Bluetooth or NFC for outside environments are IP68-rated and available for specialized markets. Two companies, iLOQ and EVVA, produce a padlock that requires no batteries but relies on NFC for power from a smartphone. These locks, especially suitable for the utility industry, can report events in an audit trail and be tracked in the cloud.

Wireless systems are versatile and well suited to cash-in-transit monitoring, construction site access control for subcontractors, parcel delivery and package tracking, office space control, postal deliveries, cargo containers, and many other requirements for simple to sophisticated control. In earlier systems, electronic access control was limited to perimeter protection. The state-of-the-art systems are now IP-enabled and combine WiFi and real-time wireless to extend the capability of a system, improve the safety and security of facilities, and increase the efficiency and productivity of employees. Wireless systems can offer most of the benefits of wired systems for a reduced cost. Today's modern systems can avoid hardwired cabling to secure any access point. Eliminating mechanical keys is becoming desirable to offer enhanced permissions and real-time monitoring and management.

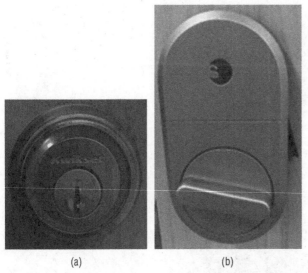

(a)   (b)

Figure 13-31a, 31b: Kwikset KEVO indicates a different status with color LEDs when the face of the lock is touched. Also shown is a very popular wireless access lock by August that requires a smartphone application or remote access through the Internet to operate.

Home security systems are largely running on wireless networks due to the difficulty in hardwiring trips and sensors. Most alarm devices employ one-way transmission, which means they aren't truly supervised for malfunction or detecting an event. Many systems can be jammed or defeated with denial-of-service (DoS) attacks, radio frequency (RF) energy, or electromagnetic pulses (EMPs), rendering them incapable of sensing an alarm event. Although lock manufacturers are implementing wireless communications for their access-control systems and devices, those designing these systems must understand the limitations of wireless and the built-in vulnerabilities it brings. Virtually every system that's based on the use of a wireless protocol can be defeated or jammed.

Hotels now utilize Bluetooth authentication for direct room entry by guests using their phones. This technology was developed by Assa Abloy Hospitality, dormakaba, SaltoSystems, and other smaller companies. A reader and RFID or magnetic stripe cards are added to the lock to provide wireless access. Auto manufacturers are beginning to implement smartphone access for cars to replace traditional transponder keys.

Locks are also embedding sophisticated authentication schemes, as disclosed in a 2020 U.S. patent application (2020/0300002 A1) by Lexmark International. The patent describes several methods to protect keys and locks from cloning attacks. They include premagnetized flakes that are measured by an internal magnetometer of their magnetic fields and their three-dimensional orientation. The patent also describes using a light beam and how it's transmitted through the key. A patent was also issued to the author to measure the differences in porosity of 3D-printed holes in a key (U.S. 11,629,525).

Selecting Conventional or High-Security Locks

Those responsible for the decision to purchase and implement conventional, high-security, or a mix of systems should consider the following issues:

- That the selected locks meet ANSI/BHMA 156.30 requirements for forced and covert entry if high security is required
- An independent analysis, if possible, of the proposed lock system to ensure that hybrid methods of bypass will not defeat any of its components
- Research to verify information on the Internet about bypass techniques and how they apply to the proposed system
- Consultation with security experts in covert entry to analyze the proposed system for vulnerabilities
- Confirmation that key blanks are restricted and not generally available to the public if in a mechanical system
- Verification that key blanks cannot be easily duplicated, cloned, simulated, or replicated if key control is important
- Ensuring that change keys cannot be easily converted to the top-level master key if a master key system is ordered
- Verification of key control procedures in place by the manufacturer and whether the manufacturer enforces its intellectual property (IP)
- Verification that a system's compatibility and security are maintained and there's no degrading of security if there is a mix of conventional and high-security cylinders

In the next chapter, several high-security locks are compared to illustrate various design philosophies and the application of locking technologies that make these mechanisms more secure.

A Comparison of High-Security Lock Designs

Much of the material in this chapter is based on research that appeared in my book *Open in Thirty Seconds: Cracking One of the Most Secure Locks in America*, published in 2008 by Pinehill Press.

An examination of several different engineering approaches to high-security lock designs by Medeco, Assa, Schlage Primus, and EVVA Magnetic Code System (MCS) is presented in this chapter. These locks were chosen because they incorporate unique characteristics and have been graded by standards organizations for their ability to thwart compromise or make it more difficult than their conventional, consumer-level counterparts.

The importance of this discussion for security engineers and risk managers is twofold. It provides insight into different mechanical designs that have proven effective and secure. The chosen systems have common elements that form the basis of most modern high-security (and some conventional) locks but combine and implement their mechanisms in unusual ways.

The application of security layers and secondary locking systems should be instructive in designing new locks or modifying current products. Studying the most popular designs provides a better understanding of what works and what is vulnerable or invites compromise. Engineers responsible for implementing or integrating different locking systems must fully understand how they work and what can go wrong to improve future designs.

The common element in each of the chosen locks is a secondary locking element that uses some form of a *sidebar* in combination with side bit milling. All but the EVVA Magnetic Code System (MCS) employ pin tumblers in different forms as the primary security layer. Although each lock has a high-security rating, all of their systems can be defeated by various attacks, some much more complicated and sophisticated than others. Remember, virtually all locks can be compromised, given enough time, specialized tools, and training, but certain designs make the task much more difficult and complex. Time delay and complexity are what security engineering is all about. The locks discussed in this chapter represent some of the most secure implementations of mechanical security layers and present a model of what high-security mechanisms should accomplish.

As noted in Chapter 6, the improper or insecure design of locks and safes can have real-world consequences in terms of liability, compromise of secure facilities, and, most importantly, injury or the loss of life to those who rely on their ability to protect. Lock manufacturers have a legal and moral duty to produce secure products, especially when those products carry high-security ratings. I've personally been involved in many criminal investigations where locks were compromised. The result: people or organizations suffered losses, or victims were injured, attacked, or even murdered by intruders.

In my experience, even a minor or insignificant design deficiency or failure can escalate, resulting in serious consequences. To that end, an insight into various high-security designs is presented here in the hope that past security engineering mistakes can be minimized or not repeated; the analysis of these locks can provide ideas that may not have been considered, whether such designs may be either good or bad.

Criteria for Judging a Lock's Security

In Chapter 16, I attempt to define the relevant criteria for what is important in assessing the protection of a high-security locking mechanism. Such a list must always be dynamic and adaptive because each manufacturer defines what constitutes security differently based on the specific mechanical and electronic design it has incorporated. The converse of such attributes defines insecurity in terms of real and potential vulnerabilities and evolving attacks. The approaches to high-security lock designs in this chapter by some of the world's leading manufacturers reflect an understanding of that "real world" of defenses against multiple attack vectors, as discussed in Part IV. In my experience, a manufacturer should never be content or complacent until it believes it has identified all vulnerabilities, because that will rarely happen, if ever. As I've noted, "Whatever is secure today will not be tomorrow."

All the locks described in this chapter have been defeated through covert attacks by myself and my colleagues. The question is not *how* but *how difficult* it is to accomplish one or more of those attacks. Virtually any lock can be compromised based on my 3T2R Rule, discussed in Chapter 4. Given enough *time, tools,* and *training,* a lock or system can be defeated, assuming the exploits are *repeatable* and *reliable.* The reality is that attacks can be made exceedingly difficult with certain hardware designs and security enhancements. The locks discussed in this chapter demonstrate some state-of-the-art mechanical lock designs. The security measurement for a lock against a surreptitious attack centers around time delay. In Chapter 18, I present a more detailed analysis of the locks discussed in this chapter.

Sidebars and Secondary Locking Systems

Sidebars are among the most popular methods to add security to a mechanical lock. They can take many forms in various mechanisms, including combination locks for safes and vaults, pin tumblers, and disc locks. All rely on creating a shear line that indirectly blocks something that must move to a locked or unlocked state. Thousands of years ago, the Chinese invented puzzle locks based on a series of wheels with letters or symbols that had to be turned to display the correct code. Moving the wheels aligned a gate or indentation on each wheel that would allow a movable form of primitive padlock shackle to be released. The design was an early sidebar.

Modern combination locks rely on this basic principle: They have three or more wheels, each with a gate. When the wheels are properly aligned, a horizontal bar must simultaneously drop into all the gates. Inexpensive bike and computer cable locks are based on the same principle but offer far less security. The concept is the same, however.

In 1907, the Abloy disc lock was invented (Patent 1,514,318), and its fundamental premise is evident in most of the Abloy locks currently in production. Rotating discs with one or more gates are turned at different angles by the correct key until they're all properly aligned so that a sidebar can drop into the channel, allowing the plug to turn with the key. A photograph of a disc lock is shown in Figure 14-1.

Figure 14-1: An Abloy disc lock shows the sidebar (a) and two gates (b) The key must rotate every disc to align all the gates so the sidebar can drop.

The concept was commercially implemented in 1934 in the Briggs & Stratton automobile lock in America, based on the J.S. Fitz Gerald patent (1,965,336). It was a six-wafer design that incorporated a metal blocking bar. Its "V" shape formed a fence that entered gates in each movable wafer. When aligned (i.e., raised to the correct position by the key's bittings), the sidebar could retract, and the plug could rotate. This design was highly resistant to picking, which is why it was so popular and has remained so since its introduction. The square gate sidebar design was successfully implemented in the Kwikset SmartKey programmable locks almost 85 years later to increase the torque resistance of its sliders. This was the preferred method to open the rekeyable cylinder.

In 1970, the Medeco lock company was formed and introduced its rotating tumbler design using a sidebar in a pin tumbler lock. Since the debut of the original Medeco product and the increased popularity of various sidebar implementations, many other manufacturers, including Assa, Schlage, and dormakaba, have followed Medeco's lead with innovative designs. There are hundreds of different concept adaptations, yet every sidebar performs the same function. It's a second indirect layer of security that prevents the plug from rotating until the obstruction can be removed by the operation of the correct key.

Some inexpensive locks also employ sidebars because they can make picking, bumping, and other forms of bypass much more difficult, if not impossible. Even Kwikset, known for its overall lack of security until 2012, introduced a reprogrammable sidebar lock in 2008 that couldn't be bumped and was highly resistant to picking. Today, the company is one of the leaders in the U.S. consumer lock market.

Understanding sidebar designs in various locking systems is important to avoid creating security vulnerabilities. The Schlage Primus, Assa, Medeco, and EVVA locks provide excellent examples of successful and secure use of sidebar concepts.

Side Bit Milling and Sidebars

Sidebars are only part of the "security puzzle" in a mechanical or electromechanical locking mechanism. They're often combined with other elements to create multiple security layers that are more difficult to compromise by picking, decoding, impressioning, or manipulation. *Side bit milling* creates added bittings that interact with and control another set of modified pin tumblers, often called *finger pins* or *side pins*. A side bit milling series often appears adjacent to the primary bittings and is usually cut into the side of the blade at the factory. Many manufacturers have implemented multiple bittings, including Assa, Schlage, Medeco, Yale, Dom, and EVVA (4,638,651; 4,377,082; 4,434,631). There's a commonality in designing high-security locks with side bit milling, especially by Assa and Schlage. This isn't a coincidence, as one of the leading engineers in the world, Swede Bo Widen, created and patented the Schlage Primus and several of the Assa designs.

Side bit millings offer many advantages to traditional key-bitting designs incorporating sidebars. They can be configured with many variables to heighten the security of any sidebar-based locking system. Side bit milling is often high precision and can provide, as in the case of Schlage and Assa, virtual keyways and the ability to tightly control the distribution of blank keys to specified locksmiths or customers. Examples in this chapter detail the differences in implementing traditional sidebars.

Assa Twin, V10, and Similar Sidebar Designs

Although the security of the Medeco, Assa, Schlage, and EVVA designs are based on the use of sidebars, each of their approaches is radically different. Assa has produced many different locks with advanced sidebar designs that have matured through several generations with side bit milling. They're all based on the Bo Widen concept that was originally patented in 1980 and 1988 (4,756,177; 4,815,307; 5,067,335; 5,640,865; 5,715,717; 5,809,816; 5,845,525; 6,134,929; 4,393,673).

The Assa V10 implementation of side bit milling provides many options for the pins to contact the finger pins, as shown in Figure 14-2.

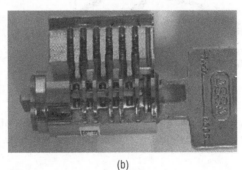

(a)   (b)

Figure 14-2a, 2b: The side pins appear on the left side of the keyway in the Assa V10 (a) The cutaway view (b) shows the action of the sidebar and the conventional pin tumblers at the shear line. Courtesy Han Fey.

Introduced around 1980, the Assa Twin is a lock with six traditional pin tumblers and five secondary pins (i.e., side pins) controlled by side bit millings on the left of the key's surface. The pin tumblers and a set of finger pins are separately elevated by contact with the side millings on one face of the key, providing an extremely high-security cylinder. Pick and manipulation resistance is assured because both sets of independent tumblers must be raised to their respective shear lines for the plug to rotate.

Unique Finger Pin Design

Each finger pin is elevated to one of five positions, and every pin has four false gates and one true gate. Note that *every side pin is identical*. The genius of this design is the mating of the finger pins derived from the key's side bit milling code to the sidebar code assigned to the locksmith, geographic location, or system. This bitting pattern must match the factory-preassigned sidebar coding and ridge pattern for the specific series of locks. The factory normally preprograms every key for a system of locks with the same side bit milling pattern. Although the sidebar coding shown in Figures 14-3 and 14-4 allows the manufacturer to implement key control of blanks, it also can provide a vehicle to defeat a system if there is access to blank or cut keys from a locksmith assigned the same coding.

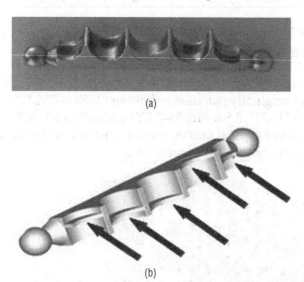

(a)

(b)

Figures 14-3a, 3b: The unique sidebar (a) has five ridges capable of mating to five depth increments. The arrows (b) show the five different individual depths.

About 3,125 separate sidebar permutations are available in the Assa "sidebar universe." This number is based on five finger pins, each with five depth increments; thus, $5^5 = 3,125$ theoretical differs. Not all finger-pin positions are available for all depth cuts, and according to Assa, there are only 1,402 useable differs per sidebar side. (The sidebar can be reversed in a cylinder for another 1,402 codes.) This means a unique sidebar code can be realistically assigned to each system of locks, thereby making key interchange virtually impossible.

Side Pins: Two Contact Points

In 1996 the Twin was updated to the Twin V10. In the original Assa design, the finger pin was centered within the root of the side milling for each pin. In the

V10, as shown in Figure 14-5, the finger pin contacts either the left or right side of the milling for each position, thereby allowing greater complexity in master keying. This modification also offered the option for multiple sidebar codes to be created under one top-level master key, a capability similar to that of the Medeco BIAXIAL and m3.

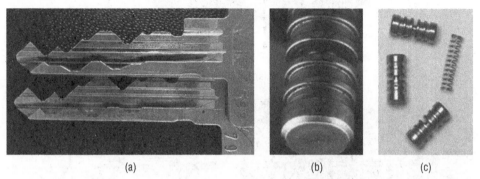

| (a) | (b) | (c) |

Figures 14-4a–4c: The design of the finger pins is unique and identical. Keys for the V10 show the primary and secondary bitting.

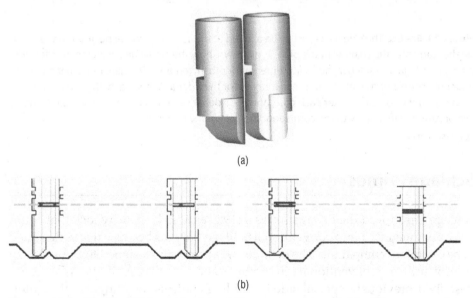

(a)

(b)

Figures 14-5a, 5b: The V10 introduced the ability to contact the side bit milling at two points for increased keying capabilities.

Sidebar Interaction with Side Pins

In the Assa design, the sidebar must properly interact with each of the side pins for it to retract into the plug. This interaction provides a higher level of security against certain attacks (see Figure 14-6).

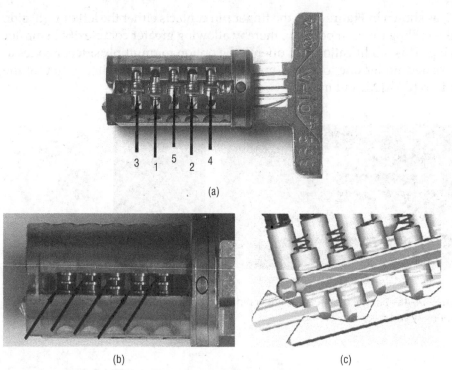

Figure 14-6a–6c: The side pins must all be aligned at the same horizontal position so the sidebar can enter the channel in the plug. The arrows show the actual depth increments for side pin coding. In (a) the sidebar shows five different depth increments. The gate placement in each finger pin corresponds with the depth increment for the sidebar. When each finger pin is raised properly (b) the fence can enter each gate, and the sidebar can retract. The Assa sidebar (c) has five protrusions to mate with the corresponding gate in the finger pin.

Courtesy Han Fey.

Schlage Primus

Schlage introduced the Primus series in 1989 as a high-security lock that could be easily integrated into conventional Schlage systems because it was designed to be backward compatible. The cylinder was primarily designed to facilitate key control, utilizing conventional pin tumblers and a sidebar. As in the Assa design described previously, special side bit milling controls the "fingers" that interface with the sidebar. The Primus employs side pins differently than Assa, but the use of a secondary security layer is similar between the two manufacturers.

The Primus is a pin tumbler lock with a second line of five finger pins that control the operation of a sidebar, as shown in Figure 14-7. These secondary tumblers are located on the side of the keyway and toward the bottom of the plug. The millings superimposed on the blank are produced at the factory for each locksmith or customer. The locksmith can only cut the standard bitting portion of the key, and the factory maintains close control of the secondary key differs.

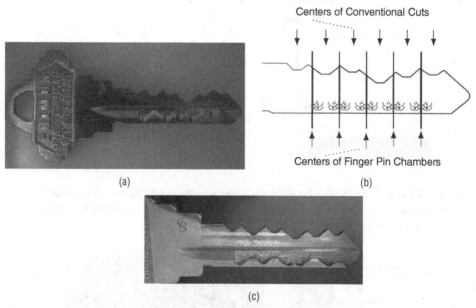

(a)   (b)

(c)

Figures 14-7a–7c: The Schlage Primus has five finger pins and seven positions to control the sidebar. (a) and (c) show two different side bit milling arrays. (b) shows the placement of the finger pins.

Primus keys will work with conventional Schlage plugs; however, the converse isn't true. This allows high-security locks to be integrated into a conventional system without disruption. Conventional keys can't be cut to fit Primus cylinders.

Schlage introduced a modification of the Primus concept based on the Bo Widen patents (4,715,717; 4,756,177; 4,815,307; 5,809,816) in 1998.

Primus Sidebar and Finger Pin Design

Whereas the Assa Twin 6000 and V10 have identical side pins, the Primus has different pin shapes based on their seven-depth increments. The pins interact with the side bit milling differently by entering the ridges. Unlike Assa's approach, where the pins *rest* on the side bit milling edges, the Primus pins enter the angled bitting to be *lifted* and *rotated*. This is shown in Figures 14-8 and 14-9.

The key is unique in this system. It has an undercut profile groove at one surface and a corresponding profile tongue with a downward-projecting end that fills the key's undercut portion on insertion into the keyway. There are two versions of the Primus: the model 20-500 series that UL 437 listed and the unlisted model 20-700 series. The listed version contains hardened anti-drill rods.

There is a significant difference in how the finger pins in the Assa and Primus designs control the sidebar. Whereas the Assa sidebar can have individual ridges or gates at five different defined levels to determine its code, the Primus sidebar has uniform gates at *all five* finger pin positions. All sidebars for Primus cylinders have the same configuration and are interchangeable.

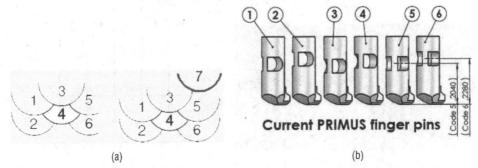

(a)   (b)

Figures 14-8a, 8b: The Primus finger pins have seven gate combinations. The design was upgraded from the original six gate positions. (a) shows original and updated configuration, which added an extra position (7).

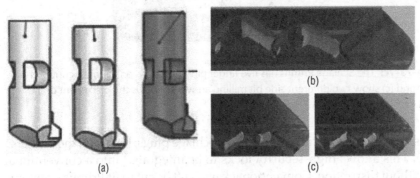

(a)   (c)

Figures 14-9a–9c: The side bit milling on a Schlage Primus key controls the elevation and rotation of the finger pins.

There is only one fence-gate for each of the finger pins. This pocket forms a fence when the pin is in the correct position. It must be elevated and rotated precisely to mate with the corresponding gate in the Primus sidebar at the same horizontal position. The Primus finger pins have one of three rotations and four actual depth increments.

Medeco Rotating Tumbler Sidebar Design

The introduction of the Medeco high-security lock with its unique rotating tumbler caused a revolution in U.S. lock design. Medeco was founded in a garage in Salem, Virginia, in 1968 and became a multimillion-dollar company that is part of the Assa Abloy group. One of its inventors was Roy Spain, who initially received a patent for a sidebar lock in 1963 (3,080,744) that employed a form of movable wafer. This was followed in 1970 by a patent assigned to Medeco. Spain and his partner, Oliver, were granted the first patent for their revolutionary design that involved using a sidebar (3,499,303) in concert with traditional pin tumblers. The original Medeco lock was based on one set of bottom pins with holes to accept the sidebar protruding legs. When each pin tumbler was raised and rotated to the correct position, the sidebar could retract, and the plug could be turned to the unlocked position.

The initial patent described a new and innovative locking technique (4,723,427; 3,722,240). It relied on the traditional double-detainer principle first invented by Linus Yale and introduced the rotating or twisting tumbler theory.

Medeco went on to develop its original pin tumbler sidebar lock that was the outgrowth of the 1970 patent. In 1985, it introduced the BIAXIAL, a new form of bottom pin tumbler with a chisel point that allowed it to rotate as the key was inserted (4,635,455). In 2005, Medeco updated its BIAXIAL to incorporate a third security layer to block the action of the sidebar until the correct key was inserted (6,477,875 and 6,945,082). In 2021, the M4 cylinder was introduced, which implemented side bit milling to replace the m3 slider.

The Medeco BIAXIAL sidebar design requires angular bitting to rotate the chisel point of each bottom pin to one of three positions that are offset by 20 degrees. The lines drawn in the different tumbler positions shown in Figure 14-2 indicate different angle rotations of each position and its letter designation as the fore or aft position. Figure 14-10 shows a plug with the pins rotated to the proper angles for the sidebar to retract.

Figure 14-10: All the bottom pins must be properly aligned for the sidebar to retract into the plug. This photograph shows each gate in alignment with the legs of the sidebar. (top image) and the key with angled cuts that properly positioned the pins.

There are now several generations of Medeco security technology for mechanical cylinders: original, BIAXIAL (1985), m3 (2003), and M4 (2021).

Original Medeco Designs

The initial Spain patent was premised on the standard pin tumbler lock, which required that all conventional pins be raised to a shear line so the plug could turn. However, that's where all similarities to the original Yale pin tumbler design ended. The Medeco inventors, in effect, created a second shear line by integrating a sidebar mechanism into the plug that had to be retracted so that rotation could occur.

The sidebar is a spring-biased bar with protruding legs corresponding to slots or channels on each bottom tumbler's side. The design's security is based on the mating between the sidebar legs and these channels. The vertical channel in each pin allows the sidebar leg to enter when the pin is properly positioned by rotation. The interaction of the angled cuts on the key bitting and the chisel-shaped tips of the bottom pins causes this movement.

Medeco BIAXIAL

In 1985, a new patent was issued for certain modifications to the original Spain pin tumbler configuration, referred to as the BIAXIAL. This patent claimed an alteration of the tumbler and key bitting design that affected the position where the chisel point of each lower tumbler came to rest on the key's bitting surface. (BIAXIAL refers to the ability to effectively double the bitting positions and theoretical differences for the new lock compared to the original Medeco design.) There are six rotation positions assigned as fore and aft angles. These are identified as Q, B, and K for fore angles and S, D, and M for aft angles. The diagrams in Figures 14-11 and 14-12 show the pin position for fore and aft positions. The designation of *fore* denotes pin positions before the center of the cut of the key. *Aft* means past the center position.

The new patent accomplished two primary functions: it kept the legal protection alive for another 20 years and introduced a lock with complex keying abilities that surpassed the original design.

Whereas in the original Medeco lock (see Figure 14-13) the chisel points centered in the root of each cut, the BIAXIAL was designed to cause each pin to rest at one of two different positions along the bitting surface, as shown in Figure 14-14. This allowed for extremely complex master keying and more combinations for a given keyway. The BIAXIAL pinning scheme incorporates three variables to increase the number of differs: depth of cut, rotation of tumbler, and position of tumbler-bitting interface.

Medeco m3

The Medeco m3 system (6,477,875) was introduced in 2003 and theoretically adds another level of security to the BIAXIAL design. The manufacturer added a step and a sliding element to the key blade. This design added a physical block to the movement of the sidebar until the slider was properly aligned with the key step and the pins were rotated to their proper angles. This novel design created other unintended security problems that allowed the slider to be aligned with a simple attack. Medeco subsequently rectified the problem with varying step lengths, shown in Figures 14-15 and 14-16.

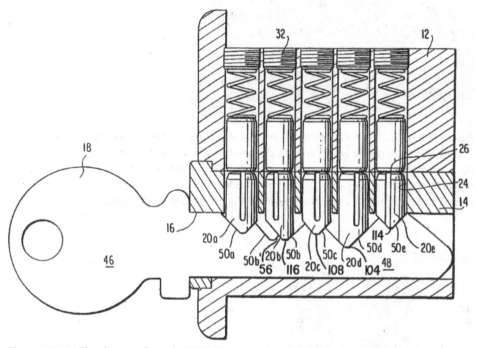

Figure 14-11: The diagram from the BIAXIAL patent shows the cylinder design with five pin tumblers. Note that each pin can be in either the aft (i.e., after the center of the cut) or the fore (i.e., before the center of the cut) bitting position. The gap between 26 and 24 represents the shear line.

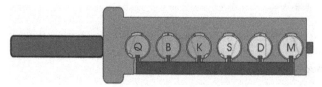

Figure 14-12: A diagram of each angle rotation with the sidebar's legs.

The defeat of one of the layers of security in the Medeco m3 demonstrates the dangers of modifying a lock design to extend the life of patents. Although the slider did enhance key control by creating virtual keyways with the step on the side of the key, it also created many vulnerabilities. Figure 14-17 graphically demonstrates the necessity for design engineers to analyze any modification in the design of a lock and new patent to ensure that security vulnerabilities aren't created or overlooked.

Figure 14-13: This Medeco cutaway of a BIAXIAL shows the critical components. The bottom pins are aligned at the shear line, and the sidebar is retracted. The plug is slightly turned. Arrow (1) indicates the shear line between the plug and shell, and arrow (2) is the sidebar. The legs are shown by arrow (3) as they enter the true gates shown by arrow (4). Note that the sidebar is pressed directly against the bottom pins, and the legs have entered the gates.

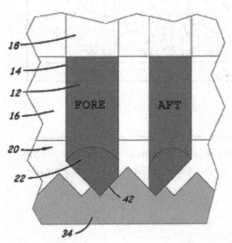

Figure 14-14: This diagram shows the position of the fore and aft pin for the key bitting. The diagram is taken from the BIAXIAL patent. Note the design of the chisel point (22) as it interacts against the ramp (42) and the blade of the key (34).

The primary differences between the BIAXIAL and m3 are the internal slider (and corresponding fixed protrusion on the key), the keyway widening to accommodate the slider, and the sidebar's modification to mate with the two protruding slider tabs. The sliding element was added to the BIAXIAL to provide for complex keying requirements and to extend the patent protection of the original BIAXIAL design. To allow for the introduction of a slider, the keyway was widened by approximately .007"; the key for the m3 is thicker than that of the BIAXIAL. This allowed for the development of different forced and covert entry methods that exploited this additional width of the m3 keyway. The design of the m3 appeared to provide enhanced security and key control for Medeco customers, but in fact opened the door to serious bypass issues. See Figure 14-18.

Figure 14-15: The Medeco m3 incorporated different length steps (a) on the side of the BIAXIAL blank. Arrow (b) indicates where the internal slider interacts with the step. When inserted, the key moves the slider to one of 26 positions.

(a)   (b)

Figure 14-16a, 14b: Cutaway of the Medeco m3 showing how the sidebar and slider are integrated. In (a) the black arrow indicates that the slider is out of alignment with the sidebar. The arrow points to the two gates cut into the sidebar and must align with the slider tabs. The white arrow in (b) shows the slider tabs in alignment with the sidebar gates.

The original slider design was flawed from a security perspective. Although one of the patent claims related to enhanced security, the patent's real purpose was to extend the BIAXIAL patent life and provide added key control options. The bypass of the slider is trivial because all sliders originally had the same geometry and overall length. Engineers should look at the m3 and note that even a clever adaptation to modify a lock design and allow for filing new patents can have serious and negative unintended consequences. In this case, the m3 could be easily bypassed with a simple paper clip.

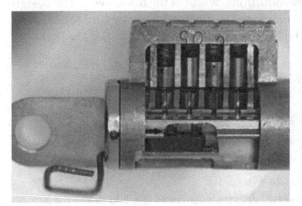

Figure 14-17: This photograph shows the m3 slider in alignment with the sidebar gates. Note that a wire clip has offset the slider to the proper position, approximately .040" from the face of the plug.

Figure 14-18: This m3 cutaway shows four critical components. Arrow (1) shows the slider properly aligned with the sidebar indicated by arrow (3). Arrow (2) shows the sidebar leg that will enter the true gate (4).

Medeco M4: The Latest Adaptation of Side Bit Milling

Medeco released an updated version of its high-security cylinder in 2021, almost 20 years after the m3 was launched. The design is unique because it combines Medeco's iconic twisting pin tumbler with side bit milling on the key's surface. It's a third security layer, much like Assa, Schlage, and other manufacturers have implemented. What is unique is the combination of three distinct actions using the side bit milling in concert with an interactive pin in the key blade. This floating pin must be moved into position to raise one of the side bit milling tumblers to the sidebar shear line, which occurs as the key is inserted fully into the plug. Figure 14-19 shows the side bit milling on the key.

Figure 14-19: The Medeco M4 key vertical perspective shows the side bit milling as an added layer (lower right).

The M4 abandoned the m3 slider, recognizing that it was a method of enhanced key control rather than an actual and effective security layer. The movable element, which is a pin embedded within the key's side surface, must be laterally moved to control the vertical movement of one of the side pins. As with many other locks, the interactive component moves and controls another element. If it isn't activated, the lock can't be opened. What is different in this design is how the interactive pin is controlled (see Figure 14-20).

Figure 14-20: The M4 key with primary and side bit milling. The interactive pin is shown in the third bitting position from the key's bow (left side). Internal wards move it in the keyway.

In most locks, such an element is actuated by a matching spring-loaded pin in the lock's shell. It interacts with the pin to make it protrude from the key's blade into the plug. In the M4, part of the warding in the keyway performs this function. This design that implements an interactive movable element in conjunction with the side bit milling was never anticipated by designers of the original side bit milling mechanisms that form the basis of the Assa and Schlage designs.

Four side pins must be raised to the shear line so their gates align with the sidebar to allow it to retract. Before that can occur, the interactive pin must contact one of the side pins to raise it to the shear line; otherwise, the sidebar remains a block to the plug's rotation.

Although side bit millings are nothing new or unique in high-security key systems, how Medeco implemented this design provides engineers with ideas for locking systems not covered by patents. This mechanism instructs how different implementations of a recognized design can be achieved. The results of the modifications in the evolution of this Medeco cylinder are enhanced key control and increased difficulty in 3D key replication, picking, and bumping (see Figure 14-21).

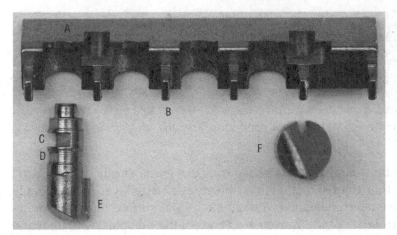

Figure 14-21: The sidebar for the M4, together with one of the side pins. (a) is the fence for the true gate, (b) is the leg of the sidebar that interacts with the bottom set of pin tumblers controlled by the primary bitting, (c) is the true gate of the side pin, (d) is a false gate, (e) is the contact point for the side pin to the side bit milling, and (f) is a top view of the primary pin tumbler and its gate.

EVVA Magnetic Code System (MCS)

Magnets and magnetic fields have been employed in lock designs for more than 100 years in various forms, including as interactive elements, embedded magnets within keys to control corresponding moving elements in the lock (4,333,327; 2,121,301), and magnetic fields to control locking elements to make them highly resistant to attack, including with external fields (8,074,479). Figure 14-22 shows the MCS key with its four rare earth magnetic pellets embedded in the key.

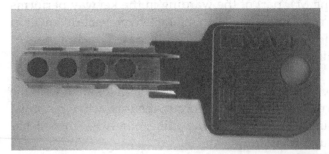

Figure 14-22: The EVVA MCS key contains four rare earth magnets that are magnetized on both sides of the blank with different north-south orientations at 45-degree angles.

Using magnets and magnetic fields in lock designs to enhance security offers many opportunities for innovation due to their availability in unlimited configurations and materials. The EVVA deployment of rare earth pellets in a key created a unique way to create and control fence-gate relationships as a primary means of securing the plug's rotation. Other manufacturers have implemented magnets as interactive movable elements and to enhance key control to prevent copying.

One extremely clever and secure use of magnetic fields was developed by a small lock manufacturer, YeboTech, in South Africa. Its design of an inexpensive electromechanical system is based on movable elements configured in a manner that frustrates most methods of attack (8,074,479 B2). When I met with the inventor, Dr. David Harley, in Cape Town, the design's security and uniqueness were obvious. The application of laws of physics to frustrate the introduction of strong magnetic fields to attack the mechanism was highly effective. It can be instructive to any manufacturer wanting to explore using magnets to create security layers. It's another example of how physics can play a vital role in lock design.

Although magnets can create added security layers, they're also vulnerable to attack. My caveat: there are many ways to defeat a lock (or even an electric strike on a door) that utilizes magnets or magnetic fields. In 2010, a class action was filed against Kaba for its Simplex lock design, which can be found in widespread use. Millions of locks were found to be vulnerable to a simple attack by a rare earth magnet, as discussed in Parts II and IV.

I always believed the most effective way to add a magnetic security layer to a mechanical lock was to cause two separately magnetized elements (as sliders controlled by the bitting of a key) to move and be forced together in a way that would make it impossible to defeat the lock picking or other mechanical manipulation.

If two elements having the same polarization, which normally would repel each other, could together create a narrowly defined gate for a matching sidebar to enter, the security of such a lock would be difficult to compromise. I was granted a patent for such a design, which required two opposing fields in a vertically sliding element to be brought together to form a gate and shear line (8,997,538).

I believe the other option to produce a secure magnetic lock and key is to follow the tact that EVVA pursued in the MCS. EVVA replicated the actions of a traditional combination lock but with the equivalent of eight wheels in a wheel pack, as opposed to the typical three or four wheels and corresponding gates. It traded the actions of turning a dial to move the individual wheels for magnetically controlled rotors that could be manipulated by the magnetic fields in individual embedded magnets in the key.

Magnetic lock designs can be divided into six primary categories:

1. Magnetized pin tumblers designed to attract or repel each other

2. Blocking elements to attract or repel

3. Ball bearings or elements that move based on the manipulation of a magnetic field

4. Angled pins with magnetized tips controlled by the position of a magnet in the key

5. Rotating magnets that control a sidebar, either laterally or radially

6. Magnetized cards that control magnetic pins in a matrix

The EVVA MCS high-security mechanism was developed as a cooperative project between the manufacturer in Vienna and the engineering departments of two universities in Austria more than 30 years ago. The lock is still considered unique and is a favorite for high-security installations, especially for government services and major facilities that require large and complex master key systems. It features four embedded neodymium rare earth magnets in the key on two surfaces and lateral tracks across the top and bottom surfaces of the key blade that control seven sliding wafers. The keys are difficult to copy with 3D printing technology.

See Part IV for a discussion of attack vectors against magnetic locks, including the MCS, and how Eastern Bloc intelligence services attempted to develop methods to open earlier lock versions. The original MCS was a target for clandestine services, as I learned in a detailed briefing in the Czech Republic by the country's leading expert responsible for devising and producing tools and techniques to compromise such systems. Figure 14-23 shows how the gates and sidebar interact with the turning of the individual rotors.

(a)   (b)

Figures 14-23a, 23b: The arrow in (a) denotes the sidebar sliding fence assembly placement that mates with gate G1. The markings G1–G4 in (b) show the rotors on one side of the lock, which match one surface of the key. Arrow G2 indicates center pivot points for each rotor. These are retained in position by a cover plate.

Within the lock, two sets of four corresponding rotors interact with the magnets embedded in both key surfaces. Each rotor has a gate that must be properly aligned for the sidebar tabs to enter. Each rotor pivots around a center point and is turned by the action of the magnetic field in the key.

One of the unique characteristics of the MCS is the ability to magnetize the rare earth magnetic pellets in the key on both sides by fields that are spaced at 45 degrees, allowing for eight different variables for each magnet (see Figure 14-24).

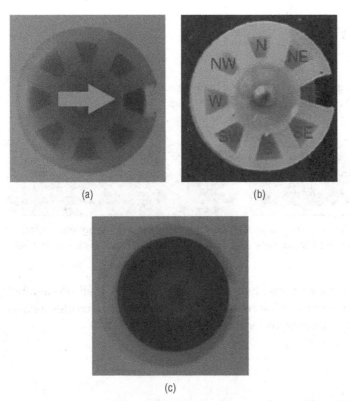

(a)

(b)

(c)

Figures 14-24a–24c: This series of photographs shows the EVVA MCS's four rotors controlled by the key's embedded magnets (a) They control eight corresponding rotors, which must be aligned for the sidebar to enter (b) When that occurs, the two sidebars with their fence can enter their respective gates, permitting the plug to turn. (c) shows the reverse side of the rotor.

Unlike locks made by Medeco, Assa, and Schlage, this lock has unlimited master keying capabilities and individual key differences. Its main attribute is its high resistance to covert manipulation or violation of its key security or control. This lock is one of the best models for what high-security cylinders should represent with the integration of magnetic elements.

Unlike any other traditional mechanical key, the MCS is more difficult to replicate because of the embedded magnets. They can only be encoded at the factory with proprietary techniques that are virtually impossible to duplicate. Even if magnetic pellets can be obtained to make a composite key, the likelihood of proper indexing and creating dual magnetic fields is extremely remote, considering that each magnet has 64 different field pairs (see Figure 14-25).

Visa mag is a useful tool for finding magnetic fields in keys. It displays the position but not the polarity of any magnetic flux. In Figure 14-26, the magnetic divisions of an MCS magnetic pellet are shown.

Figures 14-25: This photograph shows the top and bottom profile of the MCS key. Note the tracks that control seven sliders as a second method of locking.

Figures 14-26: Magnetic film overlay (visa mag) shows the permutations in magnetic coding for two different MCS keys and their magnets. Each face of each magnet can be sliced into 1/8th segments.

The next chapter discusses a brief history of different attack methods against the primary classification of locking mechanisms. Chapter 15 provides a basis for understanding later designs and vulnerabilities.

Design and Insecure Engineering
of Locks

Locks are essentially security puzzles. Ideally, from an attacker's perspective, it may not be known whether a target lock can be compromised or opened, or whether it contains any inherent design flaws or vulnerabilities. If the lock is securing a high-value target in a high-security environment, it's common for those intent on opening the lock to research how that lock works and engage in reverse engineering. This same methodology and process must also be conducted by those responsible for ensuring that lock's security. Part IV covers attack methodology in detail, beginning with an examination of how different defeats were developed as new locking mechanisms were invented.

Design failures can lead to insecurity, with real consequences that might remain unknown for years, or they may be discovered by hackers, lock enthusiasts, locksmiths, criminals, government agencies, or engineers, often with serious security and legal outcomes. Because it is important to identify and understand all possible points of vulnerability and probable attack methods, this Part presents a detailed examination of the basic parts of mechanical locks that can be inherently vulnerable. This discussion is followed by a comprehensive summary of the potential defeats of conventional, high-security, electromechanical, and electronic locks. Sophisticated methods to assess possible weaknesses in lock designs are also examined, which can provide engineers with a starting point for examining what can go wrong or be exploited and how to reverse engineer those products.

Virtually all conventional locks, and some high-security cylinders and their associated systems, can be compromised by employing one or more of the techniques outlined in the following chapters. To understand the complexities, modes, and variations of forced and covert bypass of a locking mechanism, it is essential to be fully conversant with the classifications of attack methods and how they can be carried out. Chapter 20 examines these enhanced attack principles and provides a detailed compilation of the methods forming the basis for some of the most sophisticated tool designs for compromising conventional and high-security locking systems. Many of these well-known techniques are relied on by government agencies worldwide for covert operations, in some cases of the highest order.

For design engineers, the chapters in Part IV may be the most critical due to the ramifications of deficient and defective hardware and software. Diverse attack techniques are covered in this Part, including impressioning, picking, bumping, shimming, and special decoders, in addition to the oft-overlooked hybrid attacks. The compromise of multiple security layers within mechanical locks using magnetics, vibration, shock, sound, and related techniques is also reviewed, in addition to how and when they can be employed.

Finally, this Part discusses different attack vectors, especially those that involve sophisticated picking and decoding tools relevant to lock manufacturers that supply systems for high-security facilities and government agencies.

Very specialized tool designers produce systems for defeating many such locks. Although bypassing these systems can require more expertise, their vulnerability is still based on traditional mechanical components. Falle, Wendt, Madelin, and Miller are known throughout the global lock industry for their creativity and problem-solving for covert-entry government teams and the tools they manufactured.

Attacks Against Locks: Then and Now

From the beginning of time, locks and locking systems have been designed to protect people, assets, structures, and buildings against unwanted intruders and access. Whenever a new lock is introduced, it's axiomatic that different attack methods will be developed by criminals, locksmiths, governments, competing manufacturers, and, more recently, hackers to defeat and compromise security. It started with the Egyptian pin tumbler when the challenge was to devise a method to simulate its primitive key and to fool the lock into recognizing it as a valid credential.

The history of lock development and the invention of different mechanisms closely coincided with methods of compromise and the required tools and expertise to accomplish the task. The need for security increased with the focus on locks and safes as primary protection methods. The sophistication and technology of bypass tools and procedures closely tracked the locks as they were introduced.

Each primary classification of locking mechanism, from warded to lever tumbler to discs and pin tumblers, prompted inventive minds to devise methods to defeat each succeeding design. Whenever an attack became known, the manufacturers would respond with improvements, which were subsequently defeated and rendered insecure.

Attackers always had the same goals: to open the lock or safe and, most often, steal the protected contents. They may have accomplished their task with brute force and specialized breaking tools or more covertly to minimize or eliminate any trace of entry or damage to the lock. The methods and tools were initially simple because the lock designs weren't sophisticated from a security perspective. That changed as manufacturers introduced more advanced mechanisms to stay ahead of the criminals. It didn't matter. There was always a way in, and clever, inventive people always figured it out.

The world began to pay much more attention to lock designs and their failure to offer protection due to the Great Exhibition in London in 1851, which about six million people attended. The best locks of the day were on display for all to see. The inventors touted them as offering "perfect security." There was great interest from the public and heightened media attention because of robberies and major thefts. Among the principal answers for protection were locks and safes.

To increase publicity and interest in the Exhibition, a substantial reward was offered to anyone who could open the famous Bramah lock. One of the original inventor's descendants told me, "It was incomprehensible that anyone could devise a method to open the lock recognized worldwide as one of the most secure."

A famous American locksmith, Alfred C. Hobbs, visited the London Bramah lock shop to accept the challenge. The lock was advertised and known as being impenetrable for almost 70 years. Bramah would pay a reward of 200 guineas to anyone able to open it. It took Hobbs 21 days to produce a key and collect the large reward.

That result began the race to invent new higher-security locks. This was due to the recognition by manufacturers and the public that current designs could be defeated, notwithstanding manufacturers' representations to the contrary. Hobbs and Brahma attracted significant media attention, and the contest was known as the Great Controversy.

The history of lock making is a story of continued enhancements with the elusive goal of producing a lock that could not be picked, decoded, bypassed, or opened with false keys. It's about how criminals responded to improved lock designs, from the early Egyptian pin tumbler to the high-security locks of today. Each time a new lock was introduced, the criminals demonstrated an equal ability for cleverness, innovation, and technical expertise.

In my experience, not much has changed in the competition between manufacturers and those who would compromise the security of whatever was invented and produced. Regardless of the expertise of the design teams, even for the most respected manufacturers of today, there's always a way to bypass their locks' security. Often, the more sophisticated the designs are, the more vulnerable they are to attack.

This chapter is about basic locking mechanisms and some compromise methods, from the earliest mechanical designs to the present state-of-the-art designs. Although a discussion of ancient Egyptian, warded, and lever locks may not seem relevant, it provides insight into current designs, attack techniques, and the evolution of vulnerabilities of locks and safes.

One of the primary references was published around the time of the Great Exhibition, edited by C. Tomlinson, Esq., lecturer of physical science at King's College, London. It's a fascinating read about different attack strategies against the latest lock designs thought to be "absolutely secure." It's titled *Locks and Safes: The Construction of Locks* and was compiled from the papers of A. C. Hobbs, Esq., of New York.

I met with a former KGB bureau chief in 2010 in Lithuania. We discussed entry techniques before 1991, primarily to compromise locks installed in Eastern European and Communist bloc countries. These tools were developed by his Russian agents and the special factories tasked to design and produce the technology needed to break into businesses, homes, and cars. He proudly showed me many different instruments from his collection. These instruments were usually used in covert operations to conduct searches or plant bugs. I have included some of them in this chapter.

He was familiar with older techniques for opening locks and the more modern tools in use after the collapse of the Soviet Union. He assessed that not much was different today in solving the problems of opening different locks, other than how tools were produced and their construction and materials. Their underlying operation and tool design theories were largely the same because the locks and how they work haven't materially changed. The history in Hobbs's book reinforced his thoughts. Many of the techniques and devices employed to open locks today are based on principles that were developed and implemented hundreds of years ago.

Regardless of the design and primary mechanical-locking mechanisms, these basic components must be circumvented or neutralized: keys, keyways, shear lines (in whatever form), moving parts, and the exploit of tolerances. Only the methods to defeat these elements have changed by introducing more sophisticated manufacturing techniques and miniaturization in tool design.

All locks are puzzles that contain one or more secrets defining and controlling how they can be opened. Starting with the early Egyptian and Greek locks, the job of burglars has been to discover their secrets and how to exploit and circumvent them.

Egyptian tumblers, warded, lever, Yale pin tumblers, and letter (i.e., combination) locks were all thought to be the most secure of the day. Their mechanical attributes are worthy of analysis because they all introduced radical security enhancements. Each iteration necessitated the development of different attack modes, which usually focused on duplicating false keys, decoding the information from internal components, impressioning to derive bitting codes, and running permutations of key bittings to find the right combination.

Different methods of forced and covert entry and the requisite tools are surveyed in this chapter and illustrated with different bypass tools and examples of major crimes that involved the compromise of locks and safes. This discussion lays the foundation for understanding modern conventional, advanced, and hybrid methods of attack that are examined in later chapters. Going back thousands of years in lock designs is instructive because many early techniques, sometimes with slight modification, are equally applicable today. They can still form the basis of certain current attacks and are often simple, effective, and overlooked by design engineers.

This chapter focuses on insecurity engineering issues that can create a path to circumvent even the most sophisticated locks currently available. An introduction and an understanding of some early methods to manipulate, impression, and decode mechanisms can and should offer an awareness of successful attack techniques. Many may be unknown by design engineers or not understood or translated in the context of current designs.

Paraphrasing Winston Churchill, "Those who fail to learn from history are doomed to repeat it." That can be true in insecurity engineering: if a mechanism is developed like those of the past, it's likely vulnerable to earlier attacks. Unfortunately, there is far too little institutional memory about bypass techniques and their history in the lock industry today.

A historical perspective on attacks can offer new avenues of investigation into the proper design and assessment of the vulnerability of proposed or current designs. Sometimes, very simplistic methods of attack that defeated even the most respected mechanisms hundreds of years ago can be employed against our best locks today.

The Origins of the Pin Tumbler Lock and Attacks on Its Security

The original Egyptian pin tumbler differs from what Linus Yale invented in 1860. Still, it was the genesis for the idea and set the groundwork for drastic changes in lock designs thousands of years later. The Egyptian mechanism was attacked by housebreakers and criminals almost from its inception, and an offshoot of some of those methods of compromise is in use today, which is why they are important to understand.

This mechanism's security relied on a series of wooden pegs that protrude from the lock's body to the movable element, whose function was to block or allow movement of the obstruction that secured the door. A wooden key with protruding pins can perform the same function as the bitting of today's pin tumbler keys. It's inserted into the main lock body to raise the pegs above what can be considered a shear line. When correctly elevated, the "bolt" can be released and slid to an open or locked state. The photographs in Figure 15-1 show how the lock works.

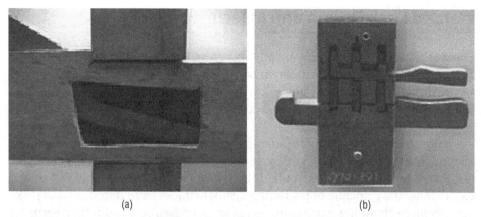

(a)   (b)

Figure 15-1a, 1b: Examples of early versions of the Egyptian lock. (a) shows a key partially inserted into the lock. (b) has key lifting tumblers so the major portion of the lock can move.

Creating an accurate false key required an attacker to ascertain the number of protruding top pegs and their positions. That information mirrored the key and indicated which pegs had to be lifted for the bolt to move freely. Although this operation was very different from the locks of today, there are obvious similarities in the information that must be decoded to defeat the lock's security. This is similar to a case I investigated that involved magnetic barium ferrite cards for access control systems.

That case is documented later in this book and required the determination of three critical pieces of lock information and subsequent actions to produce a working keycard. To create a valid credential (the equivalent of a false key for the Egyptian lock), the number of internal pins needed to be determined to move them into position properly. This was important because the pins in the Egyptian tumbler (and modern magnetic card lock) kept the movable platen or bolt in place. The positions of the pins was equally important. In the ancient tumbler lock, the pegs on the key had to match where the pins in the lock's body were positioned to elevate them to their correct height. In the card lock, the polarity of magnetic pins was the equivalent of the wooden pegs from 4,000 years ago.

To determine the secrets—how many pins and their location would provide the information necessary to pick the lock or create a false key?—a special magnetic field visualization material called *visa mag* was employed in the card lock. The equivalent of decoding the Egyptian lock was carbon deposits from a flame or wax placed on a "blank key." It was then inserted through the equivalent of a keyway and pressed upward against the pinholes to read the individual chambers for each peg. Those impressions presented a guide for constructing a false key. The lock could also be picked easily by moving each pin vertically until it was caught and the bolt advanced or retracted.

Warded Lock Design and Insecurity

The warded lock was a significant advance from the original Egyptian pin tumbler regarding security, but its premise was flawed. It was touted as the most secure due to the often intricate design of the keys, false keyholes, multiple and sometimes angled bolts, hidden and complicated keyways, and different ward shapes and positions.

The security of these enhancements turned out to be an illusion, as simple methods of attack were developed by thieves to defeat them. The public perception was that complicated keys and multiple bolts ensured a secure locking mechanism. Its fundamental principle of protecting against attacks from decoding and picking was more about the artistic creation of keys, chests, and vaults than security.

The lock operation principle was innovative and clever, based on blocking a key's rotation with internal circular metal bands called *wards*. Unless a key had the proper bitting or corresponding cutouts to pass the wards, turning the key was impossible, and thus the bolt could not be accessed or moved. The interaction of the key bitting and wards is illustrated in Figures 15-2, 15-3, and 15-4.

(a)   (b)

(c)

Figures 15-2a–2c: Early examples of Roman warded keys show the intricacy and complexity of the ward patterns.

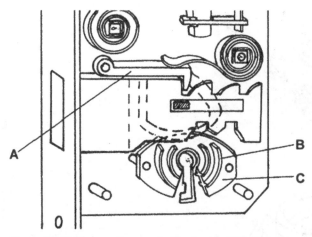

Figure 15-3: The mortise-warded lock can still be found in older hotels worldwide. In the diagrams, (A) maintains spring pressure on the bolt. (B) and (C) are wards that correspond with the bullets and pattern in the keys. This typical warded lock has only one locking lever and may be opened with a hook or metal pick.

Courtesy Munich Reinsurance, Munich and British Museum, London.

Multiple Bolts for Warded Locks

Lock manufacturers decided that implementing multiple bolts would markedly increase their security. Bolts were designed to extend from many directions, making forced entry more difficult. Unfortunately, additional bolts didn't enhance security against covert entry from picking, key duplication, and impressioning.

A major Israeli manufacturer, Mul-T-Lock, developed strong doors with vertical and horizontal bolt works during the twentieth century. Although the doors were secure, the locks could still be picked or impressioned, and there was a security problem like that of the warded lock. The bolt works made the doors more secure, but not the locks, because one key could still act on all bolts simultaneously. In 1824, Mr. Duce constructed a four-bolt lock with four distinct individual locking mechanisms, meaning the locks had to be opened with the same key but in sequence rather than all at once.

Methods of Entry for Warded Locks

The original warded locks were vulnerable to attack using false keys, skeleton keys, and special bypass tools. Many years later, unique variable keying systems were created that simulated various bitting combinations. All these methods were successful and required minimal skill to execute. The techniques are instructive when considering current lock designs because manufacturers tend to implement enhancements and more complex key designs and mechanisms to frustrate picking and other entry forms like their forerunners.

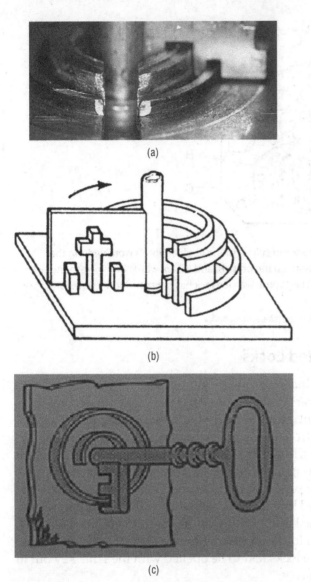

(a)

(b)

(c)

Figure 15-4a-4c: A side view showing the interaction of the key bitting and wards (a, b). The bitting matches and clears the wards so the key can turn. The warded lock is limited to only a few key variations. (c) shows a straight-on view of how the key passes the wards.

Several lock manufacturers add apparent complexity to their cylinder and key designs that can seem much more secure than they are. Adding enhancements to create virtual keyways is a favorite, but the locks can be easily defeated.

Unless possible exploits are carefully analyzed, they are often subject to compromise like the older warded and lever lock designs. The Medeco m3 slider concept discussed in Chapter 14 was a perfect example. Although it was a clever update to the original BIAXIAL lock design and patent, its security was flawed due to the relative ease with which it could be circumvented with a simple paper clip. That system was primarily designed to create multiple virtual keyways, although it was also supposed to increase security against attack. The concept of virtual keyways was implemented in various forms by other companies, including the approach taken by EVVA in some of its keying systems. The important issue to consider is what potential vulnerabilities are created by adding the equivalent of wards or blocking elements. Virtual keyways increase the complexity of keying systems and their capabilities to handle such requirements. The keys in Figure 15-5 show approaches to creating these kinds of keyways.

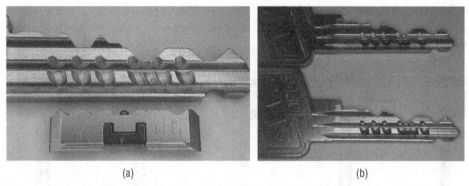

(a)   (b)

Figures 15-5a, 5b: The two keys shown in the image for the EVVA DPI reveal a set of dimple cuts that mate with a sidebar insert, which must retract into the plug to allow rotation. Some manufacturers don't implement a divided element, so if the dimples are removed by grinding, the sidebar will not catch and allow the plug to turn. Different dimple configurations can create different virtual keyways. (a) and (b) create multiple sub-keyways.

Skeleton Keys and Entry Tools

Regardless of the number of wards and the keys' corresponding complex design, they can all be bypassed with *skeleton* or master keys. Each key can appear differently with varied bitting designs. Although they can't be interchanged to open a specific lock, their mechanisms are vulnerable to simple attack methods against the bolt. Some master key systems for today's pin tumbler locks can be defeated by decoding cylinders with a change key and extrapolating the top-level master key. There's no mechanical equivalent to the older skeleton key, but generating a master key isn't much more complicated. Figures 15-6 and 15-7 show warded skeleton keys with different bitting combinations.

What the bitting of the skeleton key has in common with the others may be easily explained. Wherever there is solid metal in all the individual key bitting, there must (or may) be solid metal in the corresponding part of the skeleton key. Any place bitting material is absent in any change keys, there must also be a lack of bitting in the corresponding part of the skeleton key. The relevant and operable portion of the key is the tip and leading edge of the bitting.

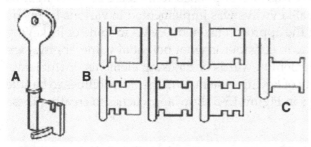

Figure 15-6: (B) shows six individual warded keys with different bitting patterns corresponding to unique ward placement shown for one key in (A) Skeleton key (C) will bypass the ward patterns for all six keys.

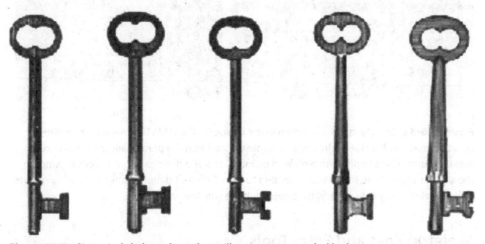

Figure 15-7: Six typical skeleton keys that will open many warded locks.

Impressioning Techniques for Warded Locks

Ironically, the fundamental concept of warded locks couldn't have been more perfectly designed for impressioning techniques. This is because wards consist of circular arcs of metal arranged to require a key with the corresponding bitting to pass each band. Even the most complex ward patterns can be easily decoded through impressioning because the wards will mark a blank key when the bitting encounters them.

Warded locks can be easily impressioned to determine the position of each blocking element. The procedure is to insert a blank key that properly fits in the keyhole. The blank is coated with wax, soap, or a carbon residue from a flame and then pressed against the wards. Whenever the material meets an obstruction, a mark is produced. Then the material is removed from the blank key with a small file, drill, saw, or chisel. Repetition of this process may be required if complex wards aren't encountered on the first attempted key rotation. When there are no more marks, the key turns and moves the bolt.

The principle of impressioning hasn't markedly changed in the past 4,000 years. It's as relevant for consideration by design engineers today as it was for the Egyptian warded and lever locks. The interaction of any internal moving part can yield information from which a key can often be produced. Different keys for warded locks that are impressioned are shown in Figures 15-8 and 15-9.

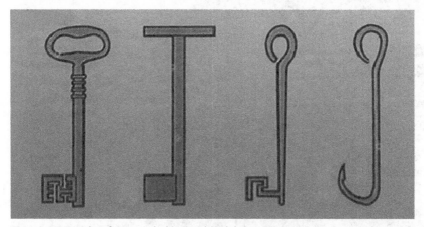

Figure 15-8: A key for a warded lock, a blank key, an impressioned equivalent to the bitted key, and a skewer tool to bypass the wards and access the bolt.

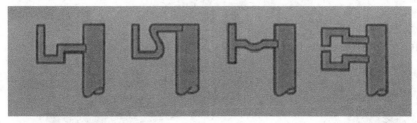

Figure 15-9: A warded lock that was impressioned to produce a working key. At right is the properly bitted key to open the lock.

Picking Tools for Warded Mechanisms

Warded locks were subject to many bypass methods with some tools. Once the design's simplicity was understood, regardless of hidden keyways and multiple wards, their compromise was simple and inevitable. Burglars found that one of the easiest ways to open these locks was with a tool called a *twirl*. It was a piece of bent steel wire fashioned into a *sweep* to allow it to reach around the wards instead of passing through them. This tool design prevented the twirl from being obstructed by internal wards and provided direct access to the bolt. Many tools were developed to bypass warded locks, some of which are shown in Figure 15-10.

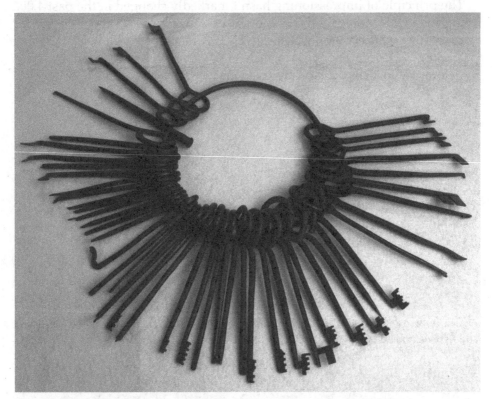

Figure 15-10: Tools to bypass warded locks.

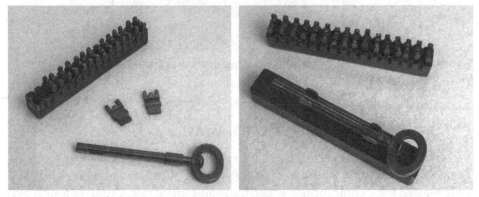

Figure 15-11: A set of old picking tools and skeleton keys for warded locks used by the KGB.

Special Programmable Keys for Warded Locks

The KGB developed different tools to pick and open warded locks encountered in Eastern Europe. Their kits contained a sample of interchangeable bittings to bypass many locks, as shown in Figure 15-11. The interchangeable bits allowed an attacker to simulate many different kinds of locks that might be encountered in field operations.

Lever Tumbler Locks

It's unknown who first developed the lever tumbler concept, but it was designed due to the understanding that warded locks weren't secure. There is a reference to this mechanism in a British patent in 1819 and the French treatise *Art du Serurier* in 1767. When and where it was introduced isn't particularly important, however. It signified a change in locking mechanisms and concepts because there was a recognition that the warded lock could be easily compromised and a radical change was needed in lock design. The diagrams and photographs in Figures 15-12 and 15-13 show the design and construction of a basic lever lock and how it works.

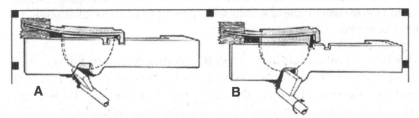

Figure 15-12: Simplified diagram of a lever tumbler lock. In (A), the key is blocked from turning by the presence of a tumbler. In (B), the key can rotate.

In the most basic configuration, lever tumbler locks have a bolt that slides to a locked or unlocked position and is retained in place by one or more tumblers. In Figure 15-12, the key is blocked from acting on the bolt because of a tumbler that prevents the rotation of the key (A). In (B), the tumbler is lifted by the bitting of the key, so there is no obstruction to the movement of the bolt.

Figure 15-13 shows a modern Canada postal service lock and a Chubb Detector from over 200 years ago. There is little difference in the designs. The Chubb was unique because it trapped tumblers if they were overlifted by someone attempting to pick the lock.

This mechanism's security is based on the alignment between a fence that is part of the bolt and several lever tumblers. Each tumbler is lifted to its correct position by bitting on the key. When all are properly aligned, the bolt is free to slide.

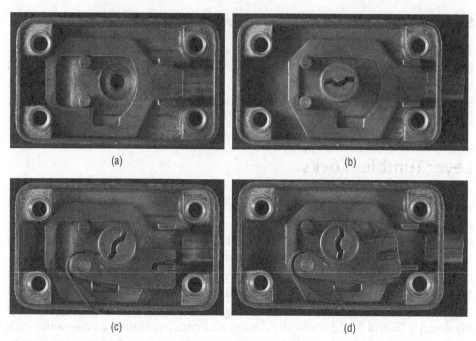

Figures 15-13a-13d: Canada postal locks (a) show the bolt without a keyway, (b) with a keyway, and (c) with one lever tumbler in an unlocked position. Note that the fence has entered the gate of the tumbler to allow the bolt to slide to an unlocked position. (d) Several tumblers aren't properly aligned, so the fence can't enter the gates.

There were two critical defects in the lever lock principle that could be considered fatal to its security. Direct access through the keyhole by picking tools was a serious problem. Repeated trials of false keys produced from wax impressions of the true key would ultimately allow the false key to open the lock.

The original lever tumbler lock could be easily picked because the tumblers could be raised to a height to allow opening. They didn't limit how high the levers could be raised. Why is this concept of overlifting active elements important for today's lock design? The corollary between lever and pin tumblers is relevant because several lock manufacturers produce pin tumblers that can be defeated similarly by overlifting.

I've encountered current lock designs that ignore this requirement or don't understand the concept of balanced drivers. Many design engineers are unaware of the bypass techniques that allow a second shear line to be created by overlifting all the bottom pins. It is, in theory, the same problem as with the original lever tumbler locks—they were vulnerable to bypassing their basic security. The practice of attacking pin tumbler cylinders with this technique is discussed in Chapter 18.

In 1778, another famous lock inventor, Robert Barron, introduced a double-acting lever tumbler to address this security issue. His design established a limit on the height a tumbler could raise. It was achieved by making the bolt immovable if the tumbler was raised too much or too little in comparison to the position of the gates. Another modification was the introduction of multiple tumblers and a refined bolt design that featured upper and lower gates, which would catch the stump and prevent movement. The Barron lock had two improvements: two tumblers instead of one, each with double rather than single action.

Barron further modified his design by reversing the actions of the bolt and stump. He engineered the stump on the bolt and the opening in the tumblers. This arrangement allowed a stump on the tumbler to pass through an opening or a stump on the bolt to pass through an opening on the tumbler. In some ways, it isn't difficult to imagine that the inventors of the Medeco rotating tumbler in 1968 may have considered the Barron design. The positioning of the gates with the movement of the stump, driven by the bittings of the key, has some mechanical parallels to rotating pins with sidebar channels.

Trap for False Keys

Some locks were designed to trap a false or counterfeit key copy by causing movable wards to be thrown to prevent the key from being turned back or withdrawn. In such an event, the false key was held permanently and could only be released by destroying the entire mechanism. The lock was never popular due to the forced attack required if the wrong key was used intentionally or accidentally.

Methods of Attacks Against Lever Locks

Many methods were developed to attack lever tumbler locks, some of which are still in use today in many countries that continue to install these mechanisms. This is especially true for high-security applications. Picking, impressioning, decoding, and "ringing the numbers" were favorites. This technique contemplated generating all the possible permutations (numbers) that could open the lock.

Much attention was focused on different impressioning methods due to the unique construction of lever tumblers, their bellies, and the bolts' configuration. Many techniques developed 200 years ago are still as valid today as when they were first conceived and perfected. Originally, carbon generated from a lighted taper could cause the production of marks between movable elements and the bitting of a blank key. Later, many different mediums were employed, including soap, wax, lead, foil, tape, wooden keys, and soft materials. Silicone is often the preferred material for making an impression of a key to produce a copy, as shown in Figure 15-14.

John Falle developed a self-impressioning system for lever locks that employs a specially designed key with a movable pin corresponding to each lever tumbler.

Each pin is set in a bore with a nylon filament and provides sufficient resistance to allow movement only when forced against an immovable lever not aligned with a gate. The system, in theory, resembles a shim pick-impressioning tool for axial pin tumbler locks, wherein the moveable pins replace the position of the tines as pressure is applied in a pumping action. The system is described in more detail in Chapter 20.

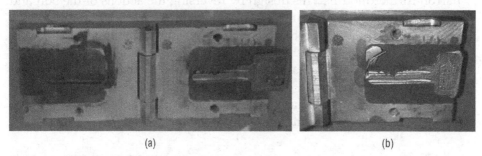

(a)   (b)

Figure 15-14a, 14b: A copy of the key (a) was impressioned in silicone-type material in a special clamshell that was pressed together after removing the key. Low-temperature metal was poured into the mold, producing a key (b). This was one of the casting techniques developed by locksmiths and burglars hundreds of years ago to obtain exact information about a key and to replicate it.

Belly Decoding with Plasticine or Other Materials

Martin Newton (UK) developed an improved plasticine key impressioning kit for lever locks based on techniques developed 200 years prior. The material was utilized to produce an imprint of the levers' bellies so they could be decoded and a key produced. Critical issues were determined from this attack: material transfer from the plasticine to the levers and the user's key, and difficulty in interpreting the marks. If done properly, the system is as valid today as it was hundreds of years ago. The photographs in Figure 15-15 show the application of plasticine to indicate tumbler markings.

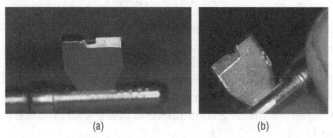

(a)   (b)

Figures 15-15a, 15b: Plasticine is painted (a) on the blade of the lever tumbler key that contacts each of the bellies. The material is then removed based on contact (b).

False Keys or Key Copies with Wax and Permutating Key Machines

If a burglar obtained access to a valid key, an impression or copy could be made that would defeat the security of the internal locking mechanisms. There is no difference between this scenario and many of today's keying systems with the advent of 3D copying, even though many keys contain levels of copy protection. To combat the problem of false keys, the tolerance on better locks was tightened to require much more accurate impressions to be produced from the original key.

Design changes were implemented in lever locks to cause levers to be stationary while the stump entered the gate. The tolerances between the stump and gating were such that even a minute error in the impression or lifting of any levers was enough to prevent an opening. Higher tolerances weren't the only solution.

In comparing the true and false keys, it could be determined whether the copy had been made with no knowledge about the lock's construction or whether the key had been made from a wax impression or other information. The owner was then better positioned to decide whether to replace the lock with a different key combination.

One way to combat the problem of false keys was to use keys with moveable bits to scramble the code so that someone with key access wouldn't know the true combination. The problem with this scheme was that to be effective, the tumbler combination in the lock also had to be altered, which necessitated removal from the door. Interestingly, Fort and other companies developed programmable keying systems that use different sequentially programmed keys, all of which can open the lock. The Fort tubular mechanism had seven different keys with the same sequence of combinations; only the keys were rotated around the plug. Once the Fort system was understood, it was easily defeated.

Many years ago, a clever copying system, shown in Figure 15-16, was developed to replicate the bitting on keys for lever locks. Single- or double-bitted keys were no problem. A series of fine shims were depressed against the target key. A duplicate could then be generated from this precise outline.

Another design feature in early locks was to separate the bitting from the stem when inserted into the lock or safe. This scheme made it impossible to try multiple passes with the false bit. The labor to fabricate a false key was lost because the bit could be tried only once.

Early Impressioning Techniques

There were two different forms of impressioning: One involves making a cast or direct copy of an imprint of the target key in a material like soap or clay, and the other required placing materials on the surface of a blank key and bellies of the levers to produce indications of contact. These could be translated into bitting positions and depths to produce a working key.

Figure 15-16: A tool to precisely measure and replicate the bitting of different keys is still used today. A series of metal shims are pressed against the key.

Modern techniques employ metal foil, Velcro, plastic tape, and similar flexible mediums. William Martin invented a blank key with a lead overlay for impressioning (U.S. 4,817,406). The lead was depressed due to the pressure from the tumblers at the shear line. John Falle then developed a system that utilized foil on a key carrier designed for the specific lock (see Figure 15-17). (The process is more fully discussed in Chapter 20.)

Mapping the Tumblers to Determine Measurement

A method was developed in America to derive the measurement of lever tumblers by injecting material into the lock. The process required first oiling the inside and then inserting two pieces of India rubber to limit the amount of dispersal. Then a combination of glue and molasses in a heated state was injected from a force pump and chilled quickly.

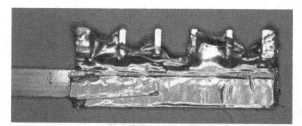

Figure 15-17: The John Falle foil system is superior to the earlier Martin lead key but based on the same principle. The proper carrier is covered with metal foil and inserted into the keyway to obtain a depression for each pin position.

This mixture was extremely elastic but retained the form and position of the lower side of the bellies of the levers. A thin-bladed instrument cut the resulting cast out of the lock. A key could then be made from the impression that was accurate enough to open the lock. This process was effective with the best lever locks. In Part VI, I describe a case that involved silicone as a casting material for reproducing keys and injection into locks to create interface components to produce gears and other critical elements. In later iterations of lever locks, the bellies were made uniform so this impression technique would fail.

Mapping the Tumblers with Printer's Ink

With a special instrument that was designed for the process, a small amount of printer's ink or other suitable material could be deposited on the tumblers so that when a valid key was inserted, the ink was distributed along the tumblers' edge at distances corresponding to their heights that matched the key's bitting. After this process, the lock had to be accessed again. A wooden key bit could be cut to match the curvature of the tumblers and covered with paper. This was inserted into the keyhole.

The instrument was then pressed against the tumblers to take an impression from the ink, showing the form of the key previously employed to open the lock. This is another application of an older method of using carbon residue from smoke to obtain markings corresponding to the tumblers.

Methods of Picking Lever Locks

Two picking methods were developed after the introduction of the lever tumbler lock. These were picking by pressure (i.e., the tentative method) and picking by the arithmetic process, otherwise known as "ringing the changes."

The tentative method required that the type of tool shown in Figure 15-18 be inserted to apply constant pressure against the bolt, while a second tool was inserted to manipulate each lever to align the gates with the stump or fence.

When this occurred, the bolt was shot to the unlocked position. This technique was the impetus for the development of the two-in-one pick.

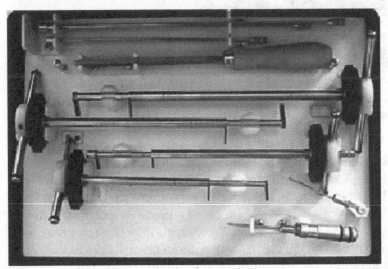

Figure 15-18: The two-in-one tool was developed to pick lever locks using the tentative method of applying tension to the bolt while manipulating each lever to clear the gate. This set shows different sizes of picks. The two-part pick has a dual function: to place pressure on the bolt and raise each lever tumbler.

KGB Programmable Lever Lock Key Set

The KGB produced a pick set to generate different bitting patterns for lever locks and their keys. This system allowed field operatives to work on different locks they might encounter in covert operations. The system shown in Figure 15-19 was effective in opening lever locks.

Overlifting Tumblers

The overlifting of tumblers continued to be a problem, just like the failure to employ balanced drivers in the later pin tumbler lock designs. Beginning in 1824, Chubb patented his famous detector that employed double-acting detainers and a unique mechanism to signal when any tumbler was overlifted during the picking process. Six separate and distinct tumblers had to be raised to a very specific position—not too high or too low—to allow the bolt to pass. A detector was incorporated that trapped the tumblers the next time a valid key was used if picking or using a false key was attempted. A diagram of the system is shown in Figure 15-20.

Figure 15-19: The KGB developed a clever variable-key-generation system for lever locks based on selecting different bitting values to match the levers.

CHUBB'S LOCK

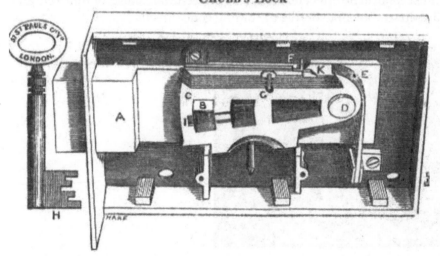

Figure 15-20: Chubb detector lock, circa 1837, and a diagram of its operation, circa 1850. If the levers were overlifted, they were caught and locked into position to alert the owner. Note the different bolt and gate designs. In (c), (K) and (F) form the detector mechanism. (K) is the catch on the back of the lever, and (F) is the end of the horizontal detector spring. (H) is the correctly bitted key, and (A) is the sliding bolt. (B) is the stump that must pass through the gating on the levers (C).

Courtesy of Wikimedia Commons.

Once the detector was set, it had to be released by the property owner. The true key was inserted and partially turned in reverse, restoring the detector to its home position. The true key then operated in the normal fashion. A valid key could never overlift any tumbler or trigger the detector.

After a single trial of a counterfeit key bit, the bit fell through the lock and inside the door. This feature had an added advantage: the owner would know of the attempted attack and could see how close the counterfeit was to the original key.

Although this issue occurred almost 200 years ago, it should provide caution for engineers today. Often, there's one critical component that, if bypassed, will allow the lock to open. I've often been told it would be impossible to do so because a lock is protected against pressure, movement, or manipulation. However, such protections often lead to added vulnerabilities once attackers know their interaction with other components.

Decoding Through Belly Reading

An early design defect in lever locks created the capability to read the bellies of the levers when at rest because they replicated precisely the same arrangements as the bitting of the key. In Figure 15-21, different belly positions are shown. This issue is also present in modern wafer locks, allowing them to be decoded visually or with feeler tools to determine the depth of each cut. Lock design teams must confirm no direct relationship between wafer, disc, or tumblers and the ability to read them to derive the bitting code directly.

Figure 15-21: The bellies of the levers can be decoded because they replicate the key's bitting when they are at rest. In this five-lever lock, note the different belly positions.

The earliest methods to decode lever locks employed a lighted taper inserted into the keyway to smoke the bottoms of the bellies with a carbon deposit.

Marks were then transferred to a blank key to determine the positions and measurements for creating a decoded key. Another popular method was to insert a small mirror attached to a wire that could be viewed with a strong, focused lamp. Unfortunately, the usual method to prevent decoding was to alter the forms of the bellies, which greatly reduced the lock's security. This vulnerability of visually decoding belly positions was partially solved by Hobbs when he enlarged the back part of the gating of each tumbler.

Bramah had a better idea, however. He determined that this problem was best solved using sliders rather than pivoting tumblers. He understood that regardless of the lock's complexity, if access could be gained through the keyhole, a key could be fabricated or the lock could be picked. Bramah is responsible for inventing what could be considered a high-security lock in its time.

Opening Letter Locks

Letter or combination locks with multiple rotating wheels or rings with symbols or numbers were popular almost 2,000 years ago in China. They resembled bike locks and computer locks sold today. They were designed for padlocks and were easily circumvented. A wire was inserted into the lock body, which forced the retaining springs apart, and the mechanism was opened.

Putting tension on the shackle was also developed in the eighteenth century and remains a bypass. The probing of the gates of each rotating ring was also a favorite. All the rings were rotated until the correct combination was derived, usually by applying end pressure to the shackle, which then identified the binding of each gate on the associated fence that blocked movement until all gates were aligned. This was an early determination of the order of picking, which is identical to the principle of picking locks today. The concept exploits the tolerance differences between each gate and fence or between the pin tumblers and shear line.

Lock makers today who produce small multiwheel combination locks for laptop computers and similar applications should ensure that shims can't be inserted between wheel spaces to probe gate locations and derive the combination.

Mechanical and Arithmetic Attacks and Tryout Keys

Around the time of the Great Exhibition, a distinction was developed between mechanical and arithmetic attacks against locks, classified as picking forms. *Mechanical* attacks required manipulating internal components with picks and devices to apply tension to the bolt, levers, or pin tumblers (after the Yale lock was introduced). *Arithmetic* attacks involved the generation of different bitting combinations and were referred to as "ringing the changes." This process became possible and effective once Fenby invented the permutating key machine. It was a precursor of modern key cutters; some are software-based multi-axis milling machines. Depending on the manufacturer, key machines today can generate specific profiles and cut the bitting for any key code.

The Fenby Permutating Key-Cutting Machine

Automated key machines were invented to facilitate the production of multiple key copies. They were also employed to make counterfeit key duplicates more easily because accuracy was vastly improved in comparison to wax impressions and hand cutting. Their other benefit was the capability to generate all permutations for a specific lock to determine the correct bitting combination. This involved generating every combination until the right sequence was determined.

This practice of "ringing the changes" could be considered a precursor to tryout keys but with a slightly different approach. In the mid-1800s, the practice required using lever lock keys equal to the number of combinations, or with changeable bitting, so that each combination could be tested. If the lock featured high-tolerance gates, attempts to exploit tolerance errors in the gate position likely would fail.

The concept of tryout keys involves exploiting tolerance errors for movable detainers. Tryout keys are employed to determine the bitting code for a specific lock and can provide a shortcut to opening with a special set of keys. Different combinations of depth increments are generated that will work, even though they aren't the exact depth for each lever or pin bitting. They were extremely popular early on for car locks in America: 64 keys would open all General Motors vehicles until the locking systems were updated.

Serrated Notches and Security Pins

One enhancement to security in lever locks was the addition of false notches and serrations on both the bolt and gates of levers. That principle relied on tension being applied to the bolt, which caused the serrations to lock into each other and prevent movement. This is the same technique employed today in pin tumbler locks to make picking difficult. The bottom pins can be configured as mushroom or serrated tumblers to catch at the shear line during the picking process. They were an outgrowth of the lever lock designs that resulted from the ease of manipulating the levers to find the location and height of the gates.

Expanding Bits on Keys

One interesting design of keys for lever locks was the expansion or enlargement of bits in the bitting. An eccentric plate drew out the bits as the key was turned.

When acting on the tumblers, they protruded farther from the key as it entered the keyhole, meaning the key was larger when inserted than originally.

Added to this security was a powerful spring that locked the mechanism if a false key was inserted. This advance was the precursor to implementing modern locks with movable key components. These elements, biased by corresponding pins inside the lock body, must be acted on to allow the key to rotate properly. Elements are sometimes spring-loaded, ball bearings, or magnetic. The theory that originated with the lever tumbler lock was to create a system that was difficult to pick or manipulate because the key's insertion changed its geometry and measurements concerning how it acted on internal locking elements. Movable elements or key bits were only active when the key cooperated with the locking elements in the lock.

Small Keyhole Preventing the Exertion or Use of Force from Tools

Small openings in locks were designed to prevent the application of force from tools. One of the favorite methods to open lever locks was the introduction of explosives. The effect of concussion was prevented by reducing the size of any entry point into the lock. This also was true for the attempt to use force to move internal components.

Barrel and Curtain Used to Restrict Access to Internal Mechanisms

One of the most successful security enhancements was the introduction of the *barrel and curtain*. A circular metal shield was attached to the barrel of the keyhole, which revolved around the drill pin. If any instrument was introduced to pick the tumblers, the curtain immediately closed and blocked the keyhole. The effect prevented the introduction of any combination of instruments to affect an opening. The idea was that the barrel could keep any tool confined to a very small space. This limited the tool's expansion or manipulation and prevented tools from working together. The barrel and curtain were invented separately, but until an 1846 patent, they hadn't been employed together. Interestingly, they were ineffective individually, but together they were a significant security enhancement.

The problem with this design was that the key couldn't work the internal mechanism without direct access. The reality was that any instrument passing in the same space as the key could also access the locking components. Employing the tentative method of applying tension and manipulating tumblers through an open keyhole, any lock can be picked.

Pressure Against the Bolt

An initial security problem with lever locks was the capability of inserting a strong wire or piece of metal into the lock to put pressure against the stump on the bolt, which allowed the binding of each lever gate against the fence. Even in modern lock designs, this is always a concern because if critical components can be directly addressed, there is usually a way to manipulate them to cause an opening.

Hobbs introduced the movable stump to defeat picking by the tentative method of applying pressure to the bolt, causing binding between the stump and the lever. It was a great advance in lock making, but of course, with the modification of the moveable stump came another problem. Although picking was made more difficult, the small parts could not withstand any amount of stress applied to force back the bolt. As is true today, every security modification or enhancement can cause other unforeseen problems.

The Great Exhibition of 1851, Hobbs, and the Insecurity of Locks

Mr. Hobbs stated that the principle on which the picking of locks depends is that:

> **Whenever the parts of a lock which come in contact with the key are affected by any pressure applied to the bolt or to that portion of the lock by which the bolt is withdrawn, in such a manner as to indicate the points of resistance to the withdrawal of the bolt, such a lock can be picked. The first step is to produce the requisite pressure.**

The Great Exhibition provided the forum for Alfred Hobbs to show lock makers and the public how insecure all the locks of the era were. Everyone believed that the lever tumbler offered true security against picking and other forms of attack.

Hobbs had all the facts and fully understood the design limitations of the current locking systems. He also was an expert at picking, employing the tentative method. He declared to a group of scientists at the Crystal Palace (the venue for the Exhibition) in 1851 "that all the locks made in this country up to that date admitted of being very easily picked." He then began operating on one of the Chubb six-lever detector locks, which he opened in a few minutes.

Lock-Picking Advances in England and America: Nineteenth Century

After 1851, attention was focused on techniques for opening locks. Locksmiths in America appear to have been far advanced: lock picking had been analyzed and developed as a science in lock manufacturing. It was clear that lock making and lock breaking went hand in hand because of the heightened concern about security.

When Hobbs showed up in London in 1851, it was a wide-open field for his expertise. All his assertions about the insecurity of locks and the principles of lock manipulation were proven. Even though the "discovery" of the tentative method of lock picking had been known in England, nobody understood the process. It was clear that virtually every lock presently manufactured had no real security because of the technique of applying pressure against the bolt. The security achieved by the presence of six lever tumblers meant nothing against this method of attack.

American locksmiths learned how to pick locks because they understood the interaction of pressure and movement on levers or pin tumblers. They figured out how a shear line, in whatever form, was vulnerable to applying torque and lifting detainers.

Linus Yale revolutionized the security capabilities of mechanical locks by incorporating the original pin tumbler idea from the Egyptians with the action of a cylinder developed by Bramah. The result was a lock that had a small footprint and was adaptable to any security requirement. It was recognized that it provided attack resistance superior to that of the lever tumbler designs. Once the Yale lock gained acceptance, it became the standard in America for security, as is true today.

In England, locksmiths used the two-in-one pick to lift lever tumblers and apply pressure against the bolt. If done properly, this process allowed the stump (or fence) to move through the gates so the bolt could be retracted. The two-in-one pick wasn't suitable for open pin tumbler mechanisms.

A different technique was developed for picking Yale locks. An instrument (i.e., pick) was designed to fit between the pins to move them. Another tool was attached that provided pressure on the plug (i.e., tension wrench). When applied in the correct rotation direction, the pins could become trapped (at that time, this was called the "joint") between the inner plug and outer shell of the lock (i.e., shear line). When all the pins were "set," the plug could turn. This technique was the same as applied to the Bramah lock with its sliders, ultimately allowing Hobbs to open it. Once this principle was understood and mastered by locksmiths in England and America, it didn't matter how many pins were installed to frustrate picking. Even locks with 40 pins could still be opened.

Bramah Lock Design

The Bramah lock design introduced a radically different type of keyway and tumbler system that proved more difficult to copy and pick. Interestingly, the Bramah design has eerie similarities with current axial pin tumbler lock designs employed in computer locks, particularly the Kryptonite bicycle lock in 2004. The earlier version of this attack involved the use of quills from feathers. They were fashioned as keys to open the Bramah in much the same way as the tubular locks were opened with the plastic shaft of a ballpoint pen having the same diameter as the keyway. The quill and the pen worked well to replicate the key's bitting. The Bramah lock is shown in Figure 15-22.

Figure 15-22: The Bramah lock with sliders is still one of the highest-security locks today.

Bramah was recognized as one of his era's most ingenious craftsmen, manufacturers, and lock designers. As noted earlier, his lock hadn't been successfully picked or otherwise compromised in more than 60 years. The design's importance was the introduction of the radial-acting slider-tumbler, which meant the sliders were configured around a radius or circular keyway. This was a departure from the Yale design, where the lock had a flat key with pin tumblers in a straight line. The Bramah also was the precursor to the invention of the sidebar, which first appeared commercially in the United States in 1935 in the Briggs & Stratton automobile lock and was later introduced by Medeco in 1968.

Keys for the traditional pin tumbler and lever locks were flat and relatively easily copied. In contrast, the keys for the Bramah were round in design, which meant they could be more difficult to replicate because the tumblers were configured in a circle. Although providing a false key was more difficult, the process was not insurmountable.

Attacks with Explosives

A favorite method of attack against locks and iron safes was to inject gunpowder or guncotton into keyholes and open chambers through the keyhole. Before design changes, safes and locks yielded to the forces exerted by detonation.

Only sufficient space was allowed for components required for locking, thus preventing anyone from placing a large quantity of material in the lock or safe. A charge of gunpowder inserted into the keyhole would only blow out at the orifice without damaging the lock.

Forced Attacks with Special Tools

Locks and safes could be forcefully opened with tools such as steel wedges, steel-pointed pinching bars, and drills. This was the case until safe-door design improved with the advent of rabbets, which made it impossible to get any wedge to drive between the door and the frame so they could be opened. *Rabbets* were a step-shaped groove along the inside edge of the door casing to increase the resistance to the insertion of tools to pry the door from the housing. The term originated in old French and meant recess into a wall.

The Chatwood safe made the door rabbets in cross-section curvilinear so that even if a wedge could be driven forward, it would also have to be curved. As a result, the wedge broke into short bits close to the entry point.

Decoding Lever Locks by Sound

Some lever locks could be opened by listening to the interaction of the movement of the tumblers and the use of shallow false notches in the stud rings. In certain locks there were only one or two notches, and the cessation of sound caused by the slight interaction of the T-piece when it arrived at the notch could indicate the proper depths. The interruption or lack of audio feedback caused by shallow notches remedied the vulnerability. Similar tactics have been employed in modern locks to determine when pin tumblers are at the shear line and to decode the correct depth increment for each pin to code-cut a key that will open the lock. Medeco implements steel pin inserts in some of its high-security tumblers to reduce the vulnerability from audio pinging to determine pin length.

When assessing lock designs, care must be taken to ensure that audio feedback can't be created with internal components to provide information about true and false gates or shear lines. An acoustic lock pick is shown in Figure 15-23 that improves feedback during picking.

Figure 15-23: An acoustic lock pick with an embedded microphone for listening when the pins are set at the shear line.

Major Crimes Involving Locks During the Nineteenth and Twentieth Centuries

Several extraordinary crimes have called into question the security of locks in banking, valuables transport, storage of jewels, and other facilities where the highest level of security was expected to protect against burglaries.

The Great Train Robbery of 1855

In a daring theft, about 200 pounds of gold were stolen from a shipment aboard the South Eastern railway from London to Paris. It was a well-planned attack involving acquiring key copies for four different lever tumbler locks, considered the most secure of the day. The thieves methodically worked their plan to obtain keys for the different locks over seven successive tries. They gained access to the containers where the bullion was stored and replaced the exact weight of the gold in lead. For security, all shipments were weighed before transit and on delivery. The weights were the same. Unfortunately, when the safes were opened, they were found to contain only lead. The complicated plot to obtain access to original keys to produce impressions was one of the primary reasons the public expressed concern for the security of the locks.

The Antwerp Diamond Heist of 2003

Seven career criminals planned the crime for over two years and stole over $100 million worth of stones from Antwerp, the world's diamond capital. The loot was never recovered, but the thieves were caught and prosecuted. The burglars compromised many security levels in the supposedly impenetrable Diamond Exchange, including locks, safes, alarm systems, cameras, and video systems. When I visited the crime scene with the chief of the diamond squad, it was clear that the crime could be repeated due to the deficiencies in security hardware and procedures. It's a case study of a lack of imagination by the building management, an understanding of inventive criminals, and the failure of multiple locks and protective systems. You can find my lecture about the theft at www.securitylaboratories.org/wp-content/uploads/2020/06/ANTWERP-THEFT.pdf.

1950 Brinks Robbery in Boston

Brinks, founded in 1859, is one of the best-known armored car companies in the United States. On the evening of January 17, 1950, a Brinks armored car facility in Boston was robbed by five career criminals. It was called the crime of the century.

All the criminals were armed and wore masks, disguises, and gloves to make identification or finding forensic or fingerprint evidence impossible. The thieves bound the employees and began gathering bills, taking over $1.2 million dollars in cash and another $1.5 million in checks and other securities in a few minutes. It was the largest robbery in the United States at that time.

The loot was stored in a counting room on the second floor of the Brinks building behind several locked doors. How the thieves got into the building and got easy access through the facility was a mystery for several years.

The FBI and other law enforcement agencies conducted an intensive investigation. It took almost six years to solve the crime, although the first arrests were made about six months after the robbery. On January 11, 1956, 11 criminals were indicted and subsequently convicted. Only $57,000 of the stolen money was ever recovered.

What is interesting and relevant about this crime and investigation was how the thieves obtained access to the Brinks facility. Five locks were secretly removed one at a time over several months and taken to a nearby lock shop to have keys produced. The locks could be easily picked, as was demonstrated by one of the detectives on the investigation. This reinforces the requirement for any business entity to install high-security locks with key-copy protection.

Attacks on Locks: The Past 100 Years

The development of bypass tools and techniques during the past century combines traditional and new mechanical concepts and the integration of electronics and sophisticated software. Some interesting designs deserve mention and are examined more fully in later chapters. Most of the covert-entry tools are mechanical, although some rely on software databases for each lock that's the subject of an attack. Many tools are designed for locksmiths; some have government-only restricted availability and are often export-controlled for shipments to certain countries. Many tools are simple yet effective in design because they don't have to be complicated to be functional. My favorites are those developed by Lishi, Wendt, John Falle, Madelin, and Lockmasters. The KGB was responsible for creating many unique tools, as shown in Figures 15-24, 15-25, 15-26, and 15-28. The Sputnik tool, while not designed by the KGB, was useful in picking pin tumbler locks because it allowed access to all pins simultaneously (see Figure 15-29).

Different decoding systems were developed for locks based on the use of magnetic rotors. This lock, by Nykustukas, was decoded and could be opened by the tool developed by the KGB.

Figure 15-27 shows a sample of locksmith and government tools developed over the past 100 years. The picks and decoders by master locksmith Aldo Silvera are particularly interesting. Silvera, the Justice Ministry expert in France, designed and constructed the tools shown. He told me he designed his custom tools to open locks and safes.

Figure 15-24: These KGB tools were designed to simulate different keys for locks with multiple rows of tumblers.

Figure 15-25: A KGB pin tumbler lock decoder to probe each tumbler and the length of the bottom pin. This was the forerunner to the John Falle early pin decoder.

Hundreds of tools are available through public distribution channels, including Amazon, Lockmasters, Wendt (zieh-fix.com), and Brockhage (lockpicks.com). Information about lock picking is everywhere and no longer considered as secret as in times past. The intrigue by the public and sports lock-picking groups has increased due to the fascination with security and the locks designed to protect it.

(a)

(b)

Figure 15-26a, 26b: A Soviet Nykustukas magnetic padlock from the 1980s (a) The KGB devised this decoder (b) to determine the polarity and placement of magnetic discs. My colleague and I used the same technology to decode magnetic card locks and the EVVA MCS high-security lock and produce a working key.

Attacks on Locks: Now and in the Future

The security enhancements during the past few hundred years involved warded and lever locks and the early pin tumbler designs. As security technology advanced with manufacturing techniques, so did sophistication in attacking newer designs and mechanisms. The chapters in Part IV present a detailed analysis of those responsible for creating and producing secure systems more resistant to new forms of compromise. One of the most clever tool designers during the past 10 years is Li in China, who conceived the Lishi pick and decoder shown in Figure 15-30. It's one of the easiest systems to use on many different locks.

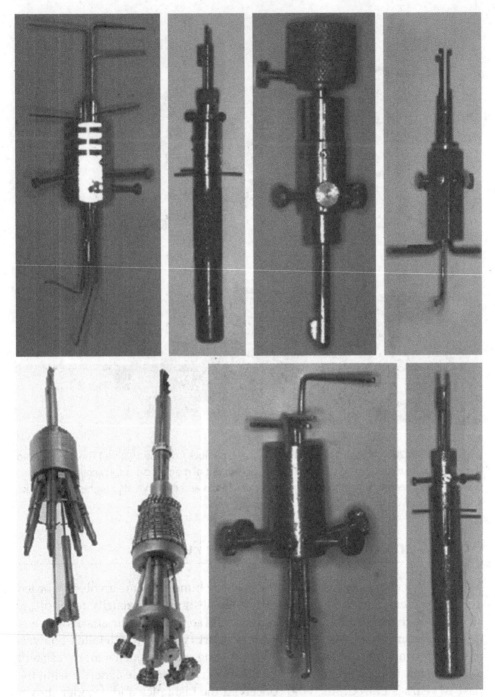

Figure 15-27: These tools were designed and made by hand by Aldo Silvera, a famous Parisian locksmith who worked for the Justice Ministry in forensic lock cases. They opened various complex French locks.

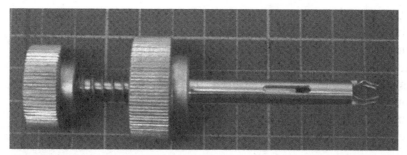

Figure 15-28: This is a cross pick for locks with multiple rows of pin tumblers. It works like the earlier KGB version but can't decode the lock.

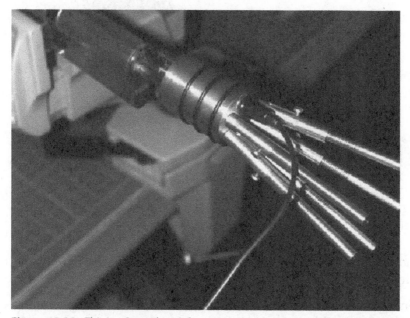

Figure 15-29: This is a Sputnik pick for pin tumbler locks. It can manipulate all the pins at once and is more efficient at picking. Adjustable set screws control individual probe wires to pick each pin. (More information is provided about this tool in Chapter 20.)

Many changes have occurred since the Great Exhibition and the inventiveness of Chubb, Bramah, Barron, Yale, and other legends and geniuses in the quest for "perfect security" in locks. Although the reader by now surely understands that in both mechanical and electronic systems, there is no such thing as perfect security, every major lock manufacturer continues to strive for that objective.

The remaining chapters in Parts IV and V describe different methods and techniques for compromising locks, keys, keying systems, and access-control technologies and why they are vulnerable. The pioneers of Wolverhampton, England, and America in lock design and defeat methods would be amazed and pleased that the ideas and techniques they conceived and developed hundreds of years ago have laid the foundation for many modern attacks. It's because the principal concepts of locks, their interaction with keys, and how they work have not materially changed. The internal components may appear different from the original systems but aren't so different in fundamental principles. Still, as noted previously, it's always something that moves that is enabled and driven by the correct key and some form of shear line that causes the lock to open. Those are the constants that provide the basis for successfully attacking locks.

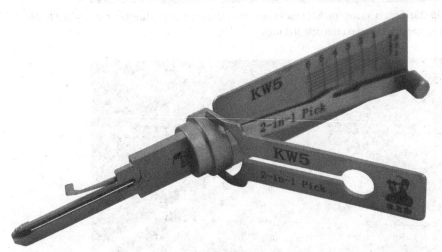

Figure 15-30: This Lishi combined pick and decoder tool is one of the latest available. It's made for many different locks, including motor vehicle locks, and is easy to use and very functional.

The technology and science of attacks on the locks of today and tomorrow include the following:

- 3D printing capabilities for replicating any mechanical key and generating the proper bitting codes
- Using rare earth magnets and strong magnetic fields to affect and move ferrous internal locking elements and systems
- Employing RF energy and electromagnetic pulse radiation to affect electronic locking systems
- Measuring internal components, including pin tumblers and lever tumblers, with piezoelectric and ultrasonic emitters and receivers
- Introducing miniature video cameras and fiberoptic links into locks to view and read the interaction of detainers and shear lines
- Generating the precise bitting codes for keys and mechanical credentials from electronic decoding systems that use piezo and acoustic measurements and to translate those credentials into cut keys

- The sophisticated employment of shim and memory wire to reach critical internal-locking components and access minute open spaces created during the manufacturing process

- Using new materials to impression the movement of mechanical components

- Developing combined pick and decoding systems to both decode and open mechanical locks and produce a working key

- Creating variable-key-generation systems to replicate and duplicate key profiles and bitting codes for any mechanical lock and its credentials

- Using specialized picking tools that can act on multiple detainers at one time

- Developing sophisticated keys that can act on pin tumblers and secondary locking elements, such as side bit milling, through the introduction of focused energy to create modern bump keys to defeat many high-security mechanical locks

- Injecting conductive liquids into electronic locks to defeat or destabilize software-based control circuits and processors

- Simple and sophisticated DoS attacks to defeat security and locking systems based on many forms of radio transmission of credentials, including Bluetooth and other protocols

- Injecting materials into a mechanical pin tumbler lock to create new shear lines and defeat balanced driver top pins

- Man-in-the-middle attacks to spoof credentials and software that control locking in electronic systems

- Using lasers and electronic measuring techniques to plot minute changes in wheel packs and mechanical elements

- Employing sophisticated optical viewing and decoding systems to look inside locks to determine measurements of the internal detainers

- Using focused shock and vibration to move internal components

- Using ultrasonics to map and measure internal locking components

The starting point for the vulnerability assessment in lock designs and testing is presented in Chapter 16. This material can provide ideas for looking at and identifying potential deficiencies or defects in designs. It's often difficult to know where to begin in this process. The overview in the next chapter offers some guidance.

An Overview: Vulnerability Analysis in Designs and Testing

This chapter examines threshold vulnerability considerations in the initial design and analysis of locking mechanisms and hardware. It defines the primary components that can be at risk and attacked. The tools and methods utilized in lock defeats are described in subsequent chapters. This material should provide fundamental design considerations to mitigate potential mechanical, electro-mechanical, and electronic lock design weaknesses.

Attacks against a locking system's components, elements, security layers, and type of mechanism will dictate the required tools and techniques. The material in Part IV is organized into conventional attacks, high-security locks, hybrid attacks, and advanced compromise methods. The topics are arranged and based on the primary components found in virtually every lock. Attacks on electromechanical and electronic locks are examined in a separate chapter because they normally require different methods.

The attacks are described in their primary classifications and ordered by forced, covert, hybrid, and advanced methods. Each of these categories is subdivided by vulnerability and analyzed in detail. All the variables in the methods of attack are presented for each classification. This offers a comprehensive checklist for design teams and law enforcement to reverse-engineer current or proposed systems for security deficiencies. Some distinctions are blurred or cross into multiple classes because many attacks involve the vulnerability of more than one component or technique.

Primary Components in All Locks

Every locking mechanism that relies on the movement of internal physical components to create a locked or unlocked condition relies on certain basic elements, regardless of whether the configuration is mechanical, electromechanical, or electronic. All locks control something that must move, normally a latch, bolt, or blocking mechanism. Some credential, usually a key, is the reciprocal element that allows that movement. Thus, these components can all be critical in analyzing possible vulnerabilities. Whether alone or in combination, this can result in the compromise of the basic design and a breach of its security. Regardless of the tool's simplicity or complexity or the attack technique or method, virtually every lock can be compromised by manipulating, modifying, or defeating one or more of these primary components, because they are fundamental and essential in every lock design.

The potential vulnerability of these primary categories of components may be obvious and doesn't require any explanation of rationale. Although you might think the compromise of one or more of these elements is straightforward and is understood by every design engineer, I can attest from hundreds of cases that this is often untrue. It's correct that each primary component alone can be subverted, but what isn't obvious is how that can occur. Often, combining attacks on more than one of these elements can lead to a complete security compromise. Recognizing that combination and designing around it is what insecurity engineering is about.

Shell or Housing

In pin tumbler mechanisms, the shell or housing contains all the moving parts, including plugs, pin tumblers, springs, retaining clips, chamber-sealing strips or set screws, tailpiece, cams, and secondary security layers. Within a lever lock is the case: cover, bolt, levers, and post or keyway. As described in Chapters 18 and 20, there are many ways to compromise the shell, the housing, or the relationship between the plug and shell to expose or provide access to internal parts. Attacks to pull or twist the plug by applying force or breaking retaining screws that hold cylinders in place are favorites of thieves, and there are many versions of tools to do so. Attacks on set screws for mortise cylinders are another tactic to allow the lock's removal from the door. Doing this can provide direct access to manipulate the bolt mechanism. An attack against the breakpoint between the plug and shell provides yet another means to compromise a cylinder.

Driving all the pin tumblers upward into their top chambers with enough force can sometimes cause the staked retaining strip to release. If this occurs, pins can be moved above the shear line, allowing the plug to turn. Another favorite is direct access through the keyway to the tailpiece or other mechanisms. Many commercial tools for popular locks offer such access. Even higher-quality locksets employ spring-loaded pins to release the core in a key-in-knob assembly. These pins can often be released directly through the keyway.

Plug and Keyway

Plugs and keyways are subject to attack because they are almost always exposed unless security covers like the *Geminy* are employed. Drumm developed these high-security secondary shields in Germany to control access to keyways and resist enhanced forced physical attacks such as pulling, drilling, sawing, and beating with a hammer. These shields also protect against the insertion of glue, gum, jamming substances, wood, or other materials that could otherwise be placed in a keyway.

Unless extra protection and barriers are used in high-security locks, cylinders are vulnerable to drilling attacks to neutralize shear lines, sidebars, and sliders and provide access to critical internal components. The design of some keyways also permits an alteration of their geometry to bypass secondary security layers.

Keys or Credentials

The duplication, simulation, and replication of credentials continue to be problems for lock manufacturers, as noted in Part V. Mechanical locks rely on keys that are simply pieces of metal, fashioned with many enhancements that ostensibly make them more difficult to copy or counterfeit. The reality is that, especially with the advent of 3D printing technology and specialized software, mechanical keys will always be vulnerable unless they contain electronic elements for higher levels of authentication. Combining technologies in electromechanical locks can provide more security, but it isn't guaranteed.

The trend is toward using radio frequency (RF)-based access as a more secure credential, such as Bluetooth, near-field communication (NFC), radio frequency identification (RFID), Wi-Fi, Zigbee, and Z-Wave. Unfortunately, most formats can be hacked, spoofed, or subject to a denial-of-service (DoS) attack. RF-based credentials will continue to mature and will, to a greater extent, replace mechanical keys.

Mechanical credentials in the form of bitting can be manipulated or spoofed. This was demonstrated in high-security dimple locks when a nylon insert was placed over the key's bitting portion, allowing the use of a restricted blank as a carrier and the exchange of different bitting surfaces to open target locks. This technique allowed one blank to open many different cylinders.

Shear Line

In any form, a shear line is the most-targeted component of any lock. It's subject to manipulation through picking, impressioning, bumping, decoding, and other techniques. Attacks on the shear line are as old as locks, dating back to the Egyptians 4,000 years ago. A shear line is manifested in a physical hardware design and is a theoretical concept that forms the basis of every modern mechanical lock. All shear lines control the movement of rotating or sliding elements, usually with the insertion or mating of valid mechanical credentials. In conventional locks, if moving elements can be positioned at the shear line, by whatever means, the lock will open. The primary purpose of a shear-line attack is to create a gap between the plug and shell or equivalent hardware in different locking mechanisms. If a gap can be created, which constitutes a breakpoint where the plug and shell meet, turning or moving the plug without resistance is possible.

A pin tumbler mechanism creates one or more shear lines when all the detainers (i.e., pins) are precisely at the breakpoint between the plug and the shell. The easiest way to accomplish this is by picking each pin by individual manipulation, by raking, or by mechanical or electric pick guns. Unless security pins are implemented, the process can be relatively easy. If multiple security layers are part of a design, the process becomes more difficult because secondary shear lines are created.

Many manufacturers have implemented some form of security pin tumbler, but Medeco may be the best known for its Advance Resistance X-tended (ARX) design. This pin has many variations to frustrate picking, bumping, and decoding. Even though these pins provide a high level of security, they aren't immune to bumping and picking. Two patents (U.S. 7,775,074 and 7,963,135) were granted for modifying them to increase their security against more advanced attack methods.

Shear lines can be created by drilling, a common form of attack. A small bit is forced through the plug across the plug-shell breakpoint. Regardless of the positions of the tumblers, a new shear line is created to override where the normal shear line appears. A less-known technique is to freeze the top pins by inserting a blank key. This action physically splits the pins, with the bottom portion dropping into the plug. When this occurs, there is nothing to prevent the plug from rotating.

The geometry of the keyway can also be physically altered to change the relationship between a sidebar and the shear line. (See the following section, "Gates and Sidebars.") This technique can be effective against mortise cylinders that contain secondary security components such as sidebars.

Shear lines can also be created in a pin tumbler design by injecting ball bearings into the upper chambers. Some manufacturers don't implement balanced drivers to prevent the overlifting of bottom pins. Although the normal bypass process uses the comb pick, my colleague and I developed a more sophisticated approach that involved delivering and injecting bearings to create another set of virtual pins and a new shear line. This procedure proved highly effective in attacking dimple locks.

The tolerances between the shell and the plug at the shear line can affect the lock's security against key interchange, tryout keys, key jiggling, and vibration. The efficacy of a shear line is all about tolerance. If too much of a gap exists, the lock can be easily picked, impressioned, or decoded. If the gap is too small, the lock won't function properly. The outer geometry of the plug and tops of the bottom pin tumblers can also reduce the gap and increase the lock's security.

Gates and Sidebars

The relationship between pin tumblers, gates, and the shear line can be altered by applying torque to the plug. In one example, when sliders are lifted to the correct position with a precut blank key, the contact between the sidebar and gates changes. This allows the plug to turn because the sliders no longer create a physical block. A second example involves a mortise cylinder with a sidebar. The pin tumblers and sidebar lock the plug in place. If the proper bitting combination is known, it can be simulated with a thin piece of plastic and torque applied to the keyway's base. If done properly, the action against the keyway changes the relationship between the sidebar and plug, and the lock can be opened. In this instance, the sidebar becomes irrelevant to the lock's security.

The design of some locks requires rotating magnetic rotors with one or more gates that interact with sidebars. The lock can be opened when all the rotors are moved to their correct position, either with magnets in the corresponding key or by other means. If the rotors are constructed of nylon or another softer material, it was found that new gates could be created by deforming the rotors with the application of force with any key. The lock manufacturer never anticipated this action, creating a significant security vulnerability until the problem was fixed.

Movable Locking Components

Within the design of mechanical locks are movable detainers. They may be pins, rotors, discs, wafers, wheels, or magnetic elements. They keep the plug or other components from moving without the proper credentials. If their position or shape is moved or altered, such an action can affect when and how locking occurs. A perfect example of insecurity engineering occurred with the older iLOQ electromagnetic lock design discussed in Part VI. If a small portion of the reset mechanism at the front of the keyway is removed, this lock can open when an invalid key is inserted. This design issue was subsequently remedied, but there remains a threat to older cylinders still in service. In the original design, it was never anticipated that a simple external action could block the entire system.

Secondary Security Components for Multiple Security Layers

An attack against secondary security layers is always a concern. In high-security locks, the sidebars, side bit milling, sliders, and movable elements provide the physical characteristics that create part of the high-security rating. If these can be altered, moved, or bypassed, the overall security of the mechanism is threatened.

Assembly-Retaining Components

External attacks on retaining screws or clips that bind the plug to the lock body are a prime target. The "C" clip or similar arrangement at the end of the plug can often be removed or warped by force. In a serious case involving a popular high-security deadbolt, the two retaining screws that bound the endcap to the plug were sheared through force. A small screwdriver that had been modified was inserted into the keyway to where the tailpiece abutted the end of the plug. It was simple to push that piece away from the back of the plug and rotate it, thus controlling the bolt.

In older key-in-knob designs, it was possible to remove the entire lock assembly from the knob by inserting a special tool that was commercially available. A piece of spring steel was compressed to affect an opening. It was a simple and very effective attack and remains so to this day. Care must be exercised when designing any component that can control the disassembly of a lock because it can be the primary and simplest method of attack.

Motion Transfer Components for Movement of Bolts, Latches, or Blocking Elements

One of my favorite maxims is, "The key never unlocks the lock." Although this may seem counterintuitive, it's true, because in most cases, the key allows the actual mechanism to do the unlocking. If it's possible to go directly to that mechanism, the key is unnecessary. One of the best demonstrations of this principle is the example in the previous section of shearing the retaining screws in a high-security deadbolt. Once the endcap was physically disconnected from the plug, it was a simple action to directly transmit motion to the tailpiece, which was the driver for the bolt-actuation mechanism. Any time a direct connection can be established to transmit motion, the security of a lock can be defeated.

Mechanical Electronic Interface

The design of virtually every lock is based on the premise that one or more components must move to affect opening or locking. In electronic and electromechanical locks, the interface between the digital credentials and the mechanical portion is most vulnerable. My colleagues and I always attack this interface because the encryption and digital security layers are irrelevant compared to the physical layers. If direct access can be obtained to what must be moved, then every electronic security enhancement has little importance.

The attack on a very sophisticated electromechanical cylinder was a prime example. The lock's security was the bitting of a mechanical key in combination with an electronic credential. The lock's encrypted portion drove a rotor that acted as a block to the plug's rotation. The correct key with the right credential was required for the lock to open. The lock could be opened if the rotor could be moved to simulate the correct credential action within the key. A design error in the lock allowed the insertion of a very thin shim wire through a feedthrough hole in the printed circuit board to directly access the rotor. The lock was defeated by attacking the hardware–software interface.

Primary Classification of Attack Types

The previous sections defined potential vulnerabilities of the primary components in all mechanical locks. This section identifies the methods of attack for mechanical locks. It provides an overview of potential vulnerabilities and additional areas of inquiry and testing for new designs, upgrades, and current products. This comprehensive summary examines each form of attack and delineates them as forced, covert, hybrid, or advanced. Depending on the methods employed, forced attacks can involve destructive and nondestructive entry. In some attacks, damage may occur to external parts, internal components, or both.

Traditional Forced Attacks

Force is the mode for most attacks against locks and related systems, such as doors, glass, bolts, and strikes. Intruders often perform them with no special skills. The rule is that any lock is vulnerable with enough force, time, and tools. These types of entries are most often directed at cylinders and bolts. There are many basic techniques for such attacks, including prying, sawing, punching, drilling, pulling, and wrenching. Burglars rarely pick locks or employ the more sophisticated methods of entry that require special tools and techniques. It's much simpler to break or smash barriers to entry.

All forced attacks aim to physically manipulate, move, break, disable, alter, or destroy locking mechanisms so they can be opened without using a key or correct credential. The standards define traditional or common forced attacks in UL 437 and ANSI/BHMA 156.30, but they don't directly address hybrid methods that employ multiple modes or a combination of techniques. "Normal" methods use various tools: mainly drills, grinders, axes, hammers, slam hammers, and implements to apply torque and wrenching.

Very specialized tools are available online and from locksmith suppliers. They offer an incredible array, not only to open locks because of lost or broken keys or mechanical malfunctions, but also for search and rescue, fire brigades, and forced entries for law enforcement operations. Several vendors offer a full line of equipment for defeating locks by the application of force, as well as lock picks and many covert entry tools. A description of relevant equipment can be found in Chapter 17.

Forced attacks may not be obvious from a cursory inspection and can require a forensic analysis, depending on the methods employed. Most of the time, there are visible indications such as tool marks, material deformation or removal, scratches, dents, and marring of surfaces. Other more apparent indications can be the inoperability of components, obvious external damage, missing or broken parts, and distortion and destruction of keyways. If drills are employed, holes and missing materials are usually obvious. What is observable depends on the mode of attack. The problem for the lock owner is that with some techniques it may not be immediately apparent that an attack has occurred and may or may not affect the operation of the lock. Discovery may only occur after an attempt with the use of a valid key.

Hybrid Forced Actions

Some attacks are hybrid, combining one or more techniques to compromise a locking mechanism. They are usually characterized by force combined with a nondestructive method, like a shim wire, magnetics, partial key blank, or other modes that leave no trace. These can be far more difficult for vulnerability assessment teams and design engineers to assess or envision. They often require a detailed analysis of the mechanical interactions in the lock to determine what may be vulnerable.

In many cases, those responsible for the design cannot imagine a critical component being accessed during an attack, so they disregard the possibility.

Hybrid forced attacks are generally not enumerated by standards organizations other than in a generic description or definition. In my experience, imagination is the critical element in analyzing the security of a lock against hybrid attacks because of the number of possible variables that can be involved. Two examples illustrate this issue. A reprogrammable lock that employed sliders to change the relationship between bitting values could be circumvented by introducing a partially cut blank key and applying torque to the plug. This action altered the mechanical relationship of the sliders and sidebar by significantly warping the slider shape. It wasn't immediately apparent, and the original key could still work when the lock was reset.

In another example, a high-security deadbolt could be easily and successfully attacked by driving a spring steel shim through the keyway to break the screws that retained the cam. Once this occurred, the tailpiece could be manipulated to move the bolt. The attack was discoverable if the lock was disassembled. Two elements were required to defeat security in both examples: force and a second nondestructive component.

Covert Attacks

In the context of nondestructive attacks, two terms are important: covert and surreptitious. *Surreptitious attacks* are most often performed by skilled individuals whose task is to compromise locks without their actions being apparent or obvious and to leave no trace. *Covert attacks* are similar in nature to those that are surreptitious, but they can often leave some indication that such an event occurred. Both forms of attack can leave forensic traces, but they are easier to discover when they are covert.

The concept of *surreptitious* connotes a secret attack against a lock: for example, when agents compromise a foreign embassy by opening critical locks or safes. No trace of such an entry must be observable or evident in such an instance. Our government is most concerned with surreptitious rather than forced entry. It needs to know whether high-security targets, containers, restricted areas, or information was accessed rather than whether a breach or compromise occurred. Physical evidence of a breach can indicate entry, but a serious security problem can exist in its absence.

A covert attack has no such requirements. Normally, these methods use keys to circumvent or manipulate barriers, shimming, and certain hybrid techniques. There is less concern about evidence of compromise or manipulation of a lock. There are several types of covert attacks, depending on whether any force is applied to locking components. These are identified in the broad categories of covert, covert hybrid, and surreptitious hybrid.

Shear-Line Attacks

Shear lines can be the most vulnerable component to attack because the security of virtually every lock is based on the physical concept of some form of breakpoint between moving parts that control locking. As described in the chapters in Part IV about bypass tools, many different systems, both simple and advanced, for a bypass relate directly to the compromise of a shear line and include picking, decoding, and impressioning locks. Any device that can manipulate or move pin tumblers or other detainers to simulate the actions of a valid key or credential can be employed in a shear-line attack.

Attacks Against Internal Tolerances

Attacks that exploit internal tolerances between moving components can involve picking, impressioning, shimming, and forms of tryout keys. The attack is usually aimed at a key interchange, jiggling, and vibration attacks and using keys with bitting values different than pin tumblers or other detainers. Tolerances can directly affect the ability to "set" pins at the shear line and to employ sophisticated decoders that rely on extremely thin shim wires to probe each pin chamber. Maintaining close tolerances in manufacturing is expensive. Cheaper locks don't offer the same clearance level between components, thus making them more vulnerable to different attack forms.

Attacks Against Physical Integrity

Attacks against a lock's physical integrity can involve removing or destroying components that allow access to those parts, which can result in unlocking. Some cylinders combine metal and plastic for outer barriers as a first line of defense. In the newer electromechanical and electronic locks, the use of plastic is common. Such designs can invite attacks because of their vulnerability to small drills, shims, and temperature. One smart lock has a mechanical bypass cylinder, Bluetooth wireless access, and a plastic outer face that protects the electronics. A patent (U.S. 10,443,267) was issued for an integrity sensor that monitored the cylinder cover for intrusion and a break in the material. If the cylinder cover was fractured or removed, it could permit access to certain critical components.

Another example is an electronic lock compromised by injecting a lubricant through the keyway slot and applying extreme torque with a specially prepared steel blank key and a long bar for leverage in a back-and-forth motion. The internal parts of the lock could then be ground down to tiny pieces of metal. There was no outward indication, but the lock was destroyed.

Decoding Attacks Against Mechanical Credentials

Locksmiths invented decoding systems hundreds of years ago, beginning with warded locks and lever tumbler mechanisms. Today, many approaches allow internal components to be measured both mechanically and electronically. Decoding systems can provide detailed information about modern pin tumblers, lever tumblers, and other detainer forms that may normally be encountered. This information can be obtained through optical viewing with borescopes that have a probe with a diameter of 0.6 mm or less. Shim wires can be employed to measure the length of pins physically. Tiny video cameras can be inserted into locks. Pick and decode tools can manipulate tumblers to shear lines and then act as keys for repeated use or to generate a working bitted key. There are laser measurement tools to decode physical keys and provide the bitting codes.

Attacks Against Keys and Bitting

There are many possible attacks against keys, their bitting, and any movable elements, which are described in further detail in Part V. This is especially true with the advent of advanced 3D printing software and the use of innovative types of secondary locking systems that may combine sidebar controls with side bit milling and magnetics.

Attacks Against Lock Assembly and Bolt Mechanisms

An analysis must involve any part that could provide access to a critical component that might result in a system's defeat. In one example, the plug in a pin tumbler cylinder had an open end with a very thin barrier designed to block tailpiece access. It could be easily penetrated with a sharp piece of spring steel or a blank key modified at its tip. The key was slammed forward with enough force to penetrate the metal barrier. Once this occurred, the tailpiece could be directly manipulated to retract the bolt or latch.

Attacks Against Systems That Control External Locking Elements

Some locks are designed to control external doors, gates, barriers, and electric strikes. These options can be vulnerable to defeat if not properly integrated into the hardware design. In one design-failure example, an advanced access-control system for commercial and government facilities contained a keypad, card reader, and bypass cylinder in the lever handle that functioned in the event of an electronics failure. An LED status light located immediately above the keypad was encased in a silicone or rubber grommet. Immediately behind the indicator was the printed circuit run that could trigger any remote device when taken to a ground. The circuit board could easily be accessed with a pin that pierced the grommet.

Attacks Against Any Openings

Any lock body, face, plug, or keyway opening can provide access to manipulate critical components by inserting tiny shims. They can be fashioned to virtually any shape and routed through a mechanism to reach internal parts. Nitinol (NiTi) is a nickel-titanium alloy with enhanced elasticity and shape-memory properties that can be made into custom shims. It can be configured to retain and return to its programmed structure even if bent or deformed during its route into a lock body.

Magnetic Fields

Magnetic fields are a valuable aid in the bypass tool arsenal. They can be employed to manipulate ferrous components and as a fishing wire to reach internal parts. The availability of high-power rare earth magnets has led to serious legal liability cases for lock manufacturers, resulting in cylinder recalls.

Attacks using magnetic fields are often misunderstood, and design engineers frequently ignore their potential.

One famous instance involved a company that designed and produced a popular mechanical push-button lock, originally patented about 1965. The critical component was subject to a magnetic field, which meant it could be moved if a nearby magnet was strong enough. Thousands of locks were affected worldwide in commercial, private, and government facilities. As a result, the company had to issue an upgrade to a nonferrous part.

Wendt originally produced its magnetic ring in Germany. It consisted of a round aluminum case, several inches in diameter, with embedded magnets. When this ring was placed on the outside of an electronic lock and rotated, it caused the internal mechanism to move, resulting in a covert opening.

Covert Hybrid Attacks Against Mechanical Locking Elements

There is a class of attacks against mechanical locking elements that aren't readily apparent and require a combination of modes to accomplish. They are identified as *covert hybrids*. Attacks against the older Kwikset locks are a perfect example. Before the design was upgraded, these cylinders could be easily opened by applying torque to the plug while inserting a partially cut blank key to raise all the sliders and allow the sidebar to enter their gates. These attacks weren't visible without the lock's disassembly and allowed the lock to continue functioning with the correct key.

Many locks can be compromised by attacks that involve multiple techniques in the correct sequence. Designers must consider "what if" a series of actions was applied to different components to cause something critical to fail.

Special Hybrid Attacks to Neutralize Individual Security Layers

Most high-security cylinders have secondary security layers, making bypassing significantly more difficult. These enhancements include sidebars, side bit milling, interactive movable elements, magnets, sliders, and other systems that add security against credential duplication, simulation, and replication. Protection against picking, decoding, impressioning, and other more sophisticated attack methods requires employing hybrid techniques to neutralize these layers, which can be accomplished in different ways but usually requires splitting functions and attacking each separately. Thus, in a lock with side bit milling, an attack required the primary bitting to be replicated or simulated on a key and the side bit milling to be reproduced as a separate insert. When the two elements were employed simultaneously, the lock could be opened.

The important consideration about neutralizing multiple security layers is to focus on each element as a separate and distinct challenge and fashion the required credential accordingly. The neutralization of individual security layers is always about simulating a valid key or credential, because mechanical locks have no intelligence and can't determine whether valid or simulated credentials are employed.

Covert Forced Hybrid Attacks

A class of covert attacks that can be considered hybrid attacks require an element of force. These are some of the most difficult for design engineers to forecast due to the combination of different elements. One example is the attack cited on an older high-security deadbolt system, where the plug endcap retainer screws were sheared by exerting force through the plug to break them. This attack wasn't externally visible and was never contemplated by more than one manufacturer.

Hybrid Attacks Against Detainers

The actions of detainers can be neutralized by various methods that are not apparent and may leave no forensic trace. An example is the John Falle attack on lever tumbler locks, which required that a post with the proper diameter be drilled with holes in the same place to match each lever tumbler. Pieces of nylon fishing line were then inserted into each hole to secure steel pins that replaced the bitting on a key. With the application of vibration and pressure, the pins depressed on each lever until each was at the shear line. A perfect key was then produced through this unique impressioning process.

Unintended Consequences

Any time a lock's design is modified or altered or a new design is implemented, *unintended consequences* can make it easier to bypass the security of the locking mechanism. This can become a significant problem for a manufacturer due to potential liability, recalls, and degradation in its reputation. The problem can occur with any design, lock, container, or system. A summary of a few cases my colleagues and I have investigated is presented here to demonstrate the magnitude of the issue and why an underlying understanding of bypass techniques is so important. This knowledge must be coupled with unrestricted imagination on the part of the design team to explore what can go wrong and how to prevent it.

Digital Door Lock Designs

Foreign residential digital door locks are popular, especially in Asian markets. Although they appear sophisticated and come with many options, including digital touch displays, bypass keys, and voice prompts, simple defeats are often missed by the engineers who create these designs. They include inserting shims through openings to reach unlocking mechanisms, running direct power to motor drives controlling the latches, and directly connecting to wiring harnesses. Other more serious problems allow the removal of digital displays to directly access the motor-control circuit.

Biometric Access to Gun Safes and Secure Containers

Fingerprint readers are popular with gun safe manufacturers and other secure containers because they give a high-tech appearance that connotes added security. In many instances, it's possible to forcibly depress the readers into the container's body, granting direct access to bolt mechanisms. The readers are enclosed in plastic holders and snap-fit to the container door because doing so is less expensive. They also aren't secure.

Bumping and Rapping

Any time parts are spring-biased, they are subject to attacks that use shock, vibration, rapping, and bumping. This is especially true when solenoids block bolt movement in small containers. Solenoids aren't secure and can be quickly circumvented by shock to the container. This can have tragic results with gun safes, if children figure out how to access them.

Bypass of Reset Buttons

Many small safes have programming reset buttons to clear and enter new access codes. It's often simple to slide a shim between the safe body and door to press the button while the safe is locked, causing a reset and allowing a new password to be entered.

Defeating Audit Trails in Electromechanical Locks

The design of many electromechanical locks requires a battery in the key head to power the internal electronics of both the key and the lock. Care must taken to ensure that the lock cannot be bumped open when the electronics are disabled and that no audit trail exists.

Keyway Access to the Latch or Bolt

In some cylinders, direct access can be obtained by running a wire or shim through the end of an open keyway to manipulate the latch's control mechanism. In a case involving a biometric lock featuring a fingerprint reader, it was simple to insert a paper clip through the keyway to release the latch and then activate the lever handle. That same design defect was also present in an access-control lock and allowed the bypass of a high-security cylinder in the actuating lever controlling the bolt. Inserting a wire through the keyway was simpler and faster than entering a PIN code.

Nitinol Wire Design Defect in Merchandise Display Case Locks

A clever lock produced by InVue is utilized worldwide in retail sales and relies on NiTi wire for part of its security. When the introduction of current activates the wire, it heats up and changes its shape. This causes the wire to move and release the security latch retaining the locking device. The design also allowed the introduction of a shim wire to lift the NiTi wire, performing the same release function. The defect puts every display area at risk of theft of merchandise protected by these devices.

USB Data Port Access in Electronic Locks

Some electronic locks have programming ports for USB or other connectors. The design team who conceived some of these locks never considered someone feeding fine shims alongside the ports to reach critical release mechanisms. This vulnerability is described in Part VI for the Kaba InSync lock.

Magnetics and Electronic Laptop Locks

One of the leading laptop lock suppliers had a prototype produced that relied on a smartphone to unlock and release the mechanism from the protected computer. The company failed to understand the security issues in making a secure mechanical release mechanism. The design had at least three significant vulnerabilities that my colleagues and I discovered and exploited. First, a thief could insert a shim through the lock opening to release the latch directly. Second, a strong magnetic field could be employed to accomplish the same result. Third, this prototype was susceptible to rapping and vibration that caused critical components to move and release the actuating mechanism.

Copying Defective Designs

Some foreign manufacturers try to duplicate successful designs and circumvent patents so they can produce knockoff products less expensively. This practice is common in the lock industry. It's also a high-risk endeavor if the underlying designs haven't been fully vetted. In one investigation, a foreign lock company in Canada copied a defective deadbolt design and incorporated serious security flaws because its design engineers did not consider possible vulnerabilities. Read my article in Forbes that described the problem: www.forbes.com/sites/marcwebertobias/2011/08/22/a-medeco-knockoff-lock-you-can-open-with-a-3-screwdriver/?sh=2165b8273310.

Newton's Laws of Motion

Unfortunately, Sir Isaac Newton couldn't consult with lock manufacturers to educate them about how his Laws of Motion applied to their designs. His First and Third Laws directly relate to the ability to open many locks by applying force, shock, and vibration. Lock bumping is based on Newton's work, even though the pin tumbler was invented hundreds of years after his death. In one case, a high-security government padlock produced by a major manufacturer could be easily opened by rapping it with a wooden mallet. It was a serious security flaw.

Ratchet Mechanisms and Shims

Ratchet mechanisms are simple to design and produce and can be found in many security products. They can be very simple to defeat with shims, as was the case for a popular antitheft device for cars called "The Club." Handcuff locking systems also employ ratchet mechanisms.

Use of Plastics in Lock Designs

Plastic is a favorite material for internal parts and some outer controls and knobs in access-control systems. However, plastics can create serious security vulnerabilities because they are easily penetrated with tiny drill bits, high-speed shim wires, and temperature extremes. There are many cases where a lock was defeated because direct access was obtained to actuating mechanisms and electrical circuits controlling motors and worm gears. Although plastic is an inexpensive alternative to stronger and more expensive materials, it ordinarily does not provide significant security.

Vibration and Failure to Use Springs

Some locks don't use springs to bias their detainers. This can allow certain designs to be vibrated into an unlocked state. This design flaw was found in a popular hotel lock that protected millions of rooms worldwide. The lock's mechanism was based on using sliders to provide for key programmability. The sliders could all be moved to one position and then vibrated open in seconds, or the key's combination could be changed to lock out guests or maintenance staff.

The next chapter explores methods of entry against locks that employ force. Many tools and techniques are available for simple defeats of locks, their internal components, and associated protective hardware.

CHAPTER 17

Destructive Attacks Against Locks and Related Hardware

The organization of this chapter is based on the same outline of vulnerabilities presented in Chapter 16, but specific destructive forced attacks and tools are discussed in greater detail. *Conventional locks* are those that don't contain security enhancements and protections as specified by applicable standards for high-security ratings. *High-security locks* are designed to resist forced-entry attempts, internal component manipulation, key control, and the defeat of credentials. The attacks described in the following pages apply equally to conventional and high-security locks. The differences lie in the level of resistance that manufacturers incorporate into their cylinder designs.

Understanding how attacks can be executed and what components may be at risk is important. Conventional cylinders are subject to a wider array of defeats by direct and hybrid approaches than those with high-security ratings. Such attacks can be carried out with simple, sophisticated, or specialty tools from commercial sources, Internet vendors, and locksmith suppliers. Some tools and systems are configured for specific lock types or designed to target a particular manufacturer and cylinder. High-security cylinders are more difficult to compromise, but the methods to do so are almost identical.

It's important to understand how certain tools work and their physical characteristics. In my experience, many design team members have never seen or used any or most of the tools that can defeat the security of the locks they conceive and manufacture. Unless they understand how to defeat a mechanism and the underlying principles of physics and chemistry, they can't hope to design anything that isn't vulnerable. A comprehensive listing of common tools appears at the end of this chapter.

Tools, Techniques, and Threats from the Application of Different Forces

This chapter describes many tools and techniques that use force to accomplish a destructive entry. In such attacks, there's always forensic evidence in the form of internal and external damage, which is often visible without lock disassembly. Methods to compromise conventional and high-security locks can involve hybrid attacks combined with direct force.

What constitutes a "tool "can be difficult to define because many common implements can be used for such purposes. Applying force to a lock can take many forms, so a mechanism's design must consider the potential for different methods that may not be addressed in testing standards. It's always a question of what components would be vulnerable to different methods to assess their sufficiency to resist such attacks. Forced-entry methods are about the laws of physics and chemistry because all such attacks are against materials that comprise locking components. Suppose the physical characteristics of these materials can be overcome or exceeded by the direct application of energy. In that case, critical parts can be made to fail or be altered in such a way as to permit unlocking.

The following discussion identifies the forces that various tools can apply. Most implements are readily available to burglars, law enforcement, and search and rescue teams. Other than explosives, none have restricted access.

Shearing, Sawing, or Cutting

A favored entry method is to shear or cut the barrier or protective material. This can be accomplished in many ways, including driving, cutting, sawing, filing, and grinding. Shearing and cutting forces are based on pressure between two edges, much like scissors. Successful attacks against cylinders have employed a back-and-forth torque movement with a piece of metal inserted into the plug to replicate a key. The goal is to grind internal components to neutralize them so they no longer present an obstacle to rotation. This method can be very effective in certain mechanisms, especially designs in which a sidebar constitutes the primary block against plug movement.

Drilling

Drilling is often the most effective method to compromise a lock. A drill bit is an extremely complex device engineered to cut various materials based on their hardness rating. Drill bits can contain carbon steel, cobalt, chromium, tungsten, and diamond. Locks and locking devices have been protected from drilling using various barrier materials, although these protections are uncommon in conventional cylinders. Blocking materials against drills can include anti-drill pins, free-rotating hardened discs, ball bearings, and steel inserts ahead of critical components such as shear lines and sidebars. Anti-drill hardened steel pins can prevent access to critical areas, including the shear line and sidebar, as shown in Figure 17-1.

Figure 17-1: These Medeco m3 plugs contain anti-drill pins made of hardened steel to prevent access to critical areas, including the shear line and sidebar. Anti-drill pins are standard in virtually all high-security cylinders and some conventional locks.

Since the introduction of the first drills at the end of the nineteenth century, many engineering advances have produced improvements in metallurgy, speed, pressure, operating temperatures, and the ability to penetrate different barriers. Standard high-speed drills are typically tipped with special materials. They are utilized to make precise holes in pin tumbler locks by creating a new shear line, providing an insertion point for a shim, or allowing the complete removal of the plug. The photographs in Figure 17-2 are of pin tumbler locks drilled by various tools to provide access to or obliterate certain components.

Pin tumbler locks can be drilled to destroy pins and plugs or create shear lines. In Figure 17-3, an end mill destroys the shear line and plugs on profile cylinders in about 1 minute. A large drill bit almost the same diameter as the plug can remove all the material. A hole through the face of the lock cylinder is effective for destroying tumblers or drivers and allowing the operation of the mechanism through direct access. Holes can also be made above and below some cylinders to allow manipulation of the bolt works. These attack forms must be considered in choosing the proper materials to deter the use of force against a cylinder.

Battery-powered tools are particularly troublesome when their target is a lock. In Figure 17-4, a portable grinder was used to attack an EVVA lock.

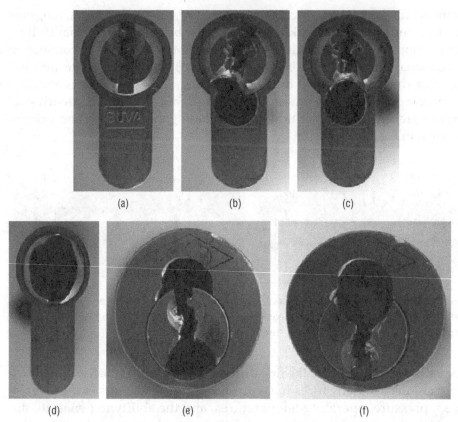

(a)   (b)   (c)

(d)   (e)   (f)

Figures 17-2a–2f: These photographs show the results of drilling a standard profile (a) and mortise cylinder (e, f) with an end mill and power tool, as demonstrated by Paul Crouwel, an expert locksmith and safe technician in Holland. In (b) and (c), the plug is drilled at the shear line. (d) shows the entire plug removed.

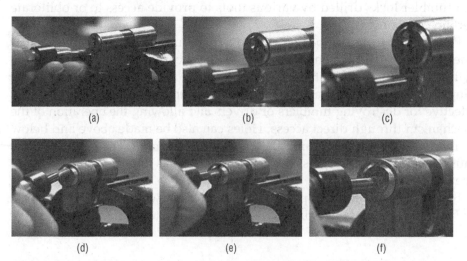

(a)   (b)   (c)

(d)   (e)   (f)

Figures 17-3a–3f: This sequence shows the use of an end mill in drilling the shear line (a–c) and the plug (d–f). This technique can be used when picking or impressioning isn't possible.

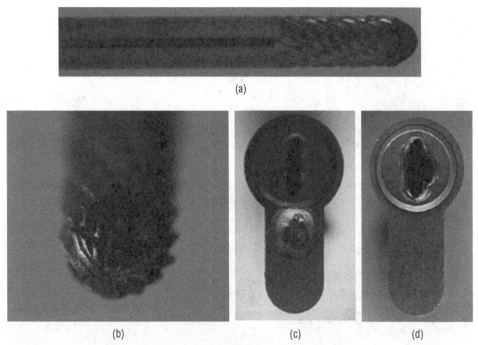

(a)

(b)   (c)   (d)

Figures 17-4a–4d: Portable battery-powered grinders can drive end mills to attack cylinders. Shown is an example of a cutting tip by Wendt (a, b). Anti-drill pins can protect a shear line from a drill attack, as shown in the EVVA 3KS profile cylinder (c, d). It thwarted any attempt to use a drill or burr to compromise the plug.

Creating a Shear Line

Three primary methods use a drill against a cylinder to affect a bypass. The face of the cylinder can be penetrated immediately below the top of the plug with a bit 3/16″ or smaller. It's placed above the centerline of the keyway so it's even with the plug's circumference to create a new shear line. The bit must be run across all pin chambers. The placement of the drill bit in Figure 17-5 is the normal location to compromise the shear line.

Another variation of this procedure requires that a key blank be inserted before drilling to engage all the lower pins and then raise them to their highest point in the plug. This places all the top pins above the plug or at the shear line. A drill is inserted just above the shear line, creating a new breakpoint. The key is removed once the cylinder has been penetrated and all pins severed. The plug can then be rotated. This technique, shown in Figure 17-6, is less known and can be more difficult to accomplish.

A third method, shown in Figure 17-7, relies on a very fine hole drilled precisely at the shear line, extending to the first pin chamber. A shim is inserted and fed through each breakpoint between pins as they are raised with a pick. This is the exact reverse procedure for shimming a lock from the rear of the plug.

Figures 17-5a–5c: The placement of a drill bit to drill across the shear line to eliminate any obstruction to rotation. The correct point is chosen (b), the hole is drilled (a), and the plug is turned (c).

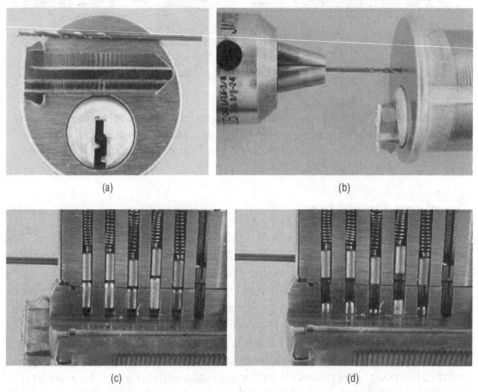

Figures 17-6a–6d: A blank key (a) is inserted before drilling to raise all top pins to a position at or above the shear line. Then a drill bit is run across all the chambers (b) The blank is removed (c) and the pins can fall into the lower chamber (d) The plug can now be turned.

A similar method was described in U.S. Patent 5,987,946. This technique was attempted in a triple homicide case in Canada in 2015, where I determined how entry was attempted after disassembling the lock at the Calgary crime lab.

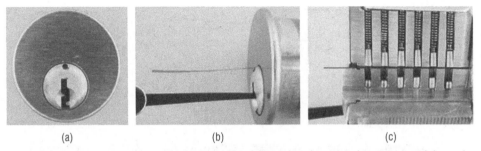

(a)   (b)   (c)

Figures 17-7a–7c: A new shear line is created by drilling the plug (a) A shim is inserted through a small hole drilled as far as the first pin chamber. Each pin is picked to the shear line, and the shim is forced forward (b) The line indicates the shim, showing how the top pins are split from the lower pins, allowing the plug to rotate (c) In such attacks, the hole may be repaired, and an examination of the internal plug may be required. A pick raises each pin from the front to the back of the plug.

Removable-core locks can be attacked similarly by drilling the control-locking lug that retains the core. Once that block is removed, nothing prevents the core from being pulled forward, as shown in Figure 17-8.

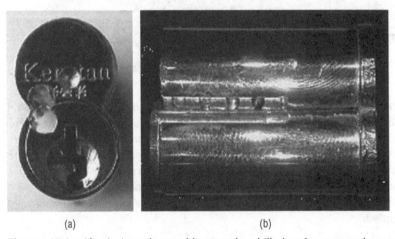

(a)   (b)

Figures 17-8a, 8b: An interchangeable-core plug drilled so the core can be removed.

Drilling and Pulling Attacks on Profile Cylinders

Profile cylinders are the standard footprint of locks in many parts of the world outside North America. Their design and construction are often subject to attack. Many specialized tools are available to force the cylinders to break apart, sever the retaining screws between dual cylinders, or forcibly remove the plug. Even for conventional cylinders, most manufacturers implement some form of protection against these tools and methods. Pulling tools are shown in Figure 17-9. They are quite effective and allow rapid removal of cylinder components.

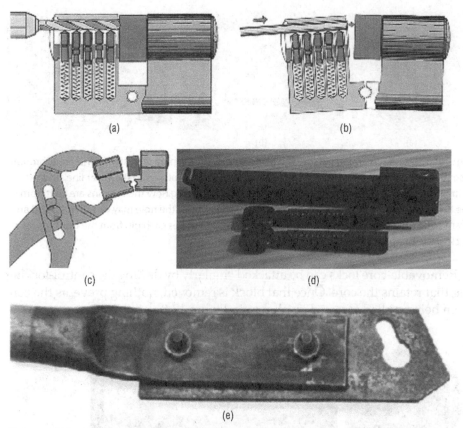

(a)

(b)

(c)

(d)

(e)

Figures 17-9a–9e: A profile cylinder may be removed by drilling through the plug (a) inserting a steel rod, and applying downward pressure (b) This causes the shell to split, releasing one-half of the assembly (c) The retaining screw between cylinders is broken, so force can be exerted to drive the part of the lock to break the link and remove it. An example of a breaking tool is shown; force is applied to snap the link where the mounting screw is anchored. (d) is a profile cylinder breaking tool that is designed to snap the link screw between the two portions of the cylinder. (e) is a different form of simple breaker tools that fits over the profile cylinder and allows downward pressure to be applied.

Courtesy Munich Reinsurance Co.

Another technique taps a special metal screw into the plug and then uses a dent puller or slam hammer to remove it violently. This technique is shown in Figure 17-10. The nose-puller jig can also remove the plug after the screw is inserted and reverse torque is applied. It works because the pulling force exceeds the material's tensile strength in the lock. A steady force is required to pull the lock apart. The theory of this attack is the reverse of that described in other chapters, in which a special key is inserted into the keyway and extreme torque is applied to grind down the internal components.

Special extraction tensile puller tools are available to apply thousands of pounds of reverse torque to remove a plug or cylinder from its housing, as shown in

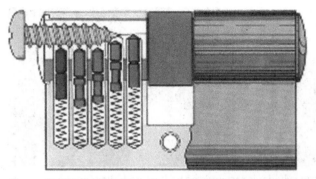

Figure 17-10: A special metal screw can pull a plug or cylinder. It's tapped into the keyway; then a sharp counterforce is exerted to rip the assembly loose.

Courtesy Munich Reinsurance, Munich.

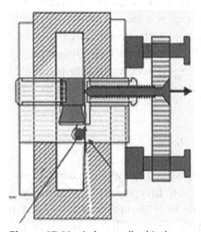

Figure 17-11: A dent puller kit that contains all the implements necessary to remove most cylinders from their mountings. This is accomplished by introducing a tapped metal screw into the keyway. A counterforce is exerted with a long-threaded bolt against a fixed platform.

Figure 17-11. Other tools enable pulling, tilting, and bending movement. They are also known as *profile-breaker* tools. The underlying theory of operation relies on exerting a pulling force that exceeds the tensile strength of the material to which the tool is attached. Like a slam hammer, the dent puller requires that a metal screw be tapped into the target device. However, unlike the slam hammer, slow and steady force is applied, rather than a violent shock, to accomplish the removal.

Pounding, Driving, Prying, and Fracturing Materials

Poorly designed hardware is often subject to attacks from pounding, driving, prying, and fracturing of components, as shown in the photograph in Figure 17-12 from a burglary that the Illinois crime lab investigated. Engineering teams must test for many common weaknesses in much of the locking hardware in use today.

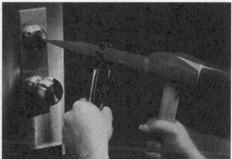

Figure 17-12: The mounting for the cylinder is cast and can be fractured, allowing the lock's removal.

A prying load can be applied to a protruding deadbolt cylinder housing with a modified hoof nipper, which is a tool that can apply extreme forces to protruding elements on a lock as an attack tool. A hoof nipper is a steel tool employed to trim horses' hooves. The tool is offered in different lengths and sizes up to about 15 inches. It looks similar to pliers, but the tip has sharp cutting edges.

The nipper is ground to create a wider opening to accommodate the lock's larger diameter. A chisel and hammer can effectively get access behind a dead-bolt strike plate as another mode of attack.

Bending

A material that can be repeatedly bent can be fatigued to cause a fracture, allow-ing a bypass of its function. Jamb spreaders illustrate this problem in aluminum doors and frames. They can be bent to allow the bolt to pass and then return to its normal shape. A bending force can be applied with a long pipe over the knob or handle for leverage, as shown in Figure 17-13. Several thousand inch-pounds of torque can be exerted.

A bending load can be applied by slipping a length of pipe over the knob or through the handle. A bar or a pair of levers can also apply a bending or a tension load to a padlock shackle or other fastener.

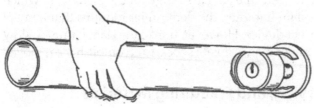

Figure 17-13: A long pipe provides sufficient leverage to apply torque to break internal components.

Torsion or Twisting

With a flathead screwdriver inserted in the keyway, a torque as great as 600 inch pounds can be applied using an adjustable wrench. In many lock designs, torsion or twisting force can be applied to break the plug. Figure 17-14 shows a tool made for applying torque. Wendt and others produce a customized tool made of hardened steel designed for a specific keyway. Extreme torque can destroy the plug.

Figure 17-14: Wendt developed a tool to apply extreme torque to a cylinder and plug.

Torque, Wrenching, Leverage, Jimmying, and Wedging Against Components

Any tool that can amplify torque can be employed to break and remove locks from their mountings and compromise their physical structure. Channel-lock pliers, a cylinder wrench, or a pipe wrench can be very effective. A plumber's tool can provide extreme leverage with a chain linked to a mechanism that holds a pipe. It's placed around the lock, and torque is applied. The chains will self-tighten and shear the lock from its housing or anchor. These tools generally adjust to the lock; the cylinder is twisted and turned. The result is that set screws are sheared or broken, or the cylinder is ripped out of the jamb.

Another form of this tool can remove guard rings from cylinder locks. A pipe with a diameter large enough to fit over the guard ring and cylinder is tightened with a bolt through its center. A rod is utilized to twist the end, thereby providing sufficient leverage to release the lock. Torque can also shear set screws that retain a mortise cylinder. A clever device is a jeweler's watch-face-removal tool, shown in Figure 17-15. It's affixed to the protruding cylinder and twisted. Several fingers are tightened around the cylinder's lip to engage it. When the rotational force is applied, the set screw shears.

Torque can be directly applied to internal components within a lock to alter or destroy their structure. If a hardened steel simulated key is inserted through a keyway and torque is properly applied, with enough back-and-forth motion, many locks can be forced to open. This is especially true where sidebars are the primary locking elements. An analysis of the materials responsible for blocking plug rotation must be conducted to determine whether their physical characteristics can be overcome by exceeding their tensile strength.

(a)   (b)   (c)

Figure 17-15a–15c: Torque is applied to the cylinder until the set screw is sheared and the lock can be removed.

Certain dimple locks can be subject to the shearing of pins when force is applied to the plug. In Figure 17-16, in one popular lock, the mechanism's security could be compromised by turning the plug with a key inserted and forcing it in one direction. Pins were sheared and broken, which allowed the plug to be turned.

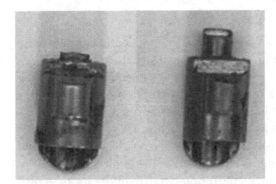

Figure 17-16: Tumblers from a dimple lock. In this instance, the tips of the pins could be sheared. Pins were sheared with minimal torque applied to the plug.

Opposing Forces Applied Simultaneously: Breaking, Prying, Wedging, Peeling, Ripping, and Spreading

Force can be applied in opposing directions simultaneously to pry or wedge components from their positions and gain access to critical locking elements. Another technique, peeling or ripping, is employed to remove metal laminations from safes and vaults. This method relies on a wedge, which is used to attack the construction of many locks. This allows force to be exerted between different metal layers in different directions to separate them and create a gap between surfaces. Various tools have been employed for centuries, as shown in Figures 17-17 and 17-18.

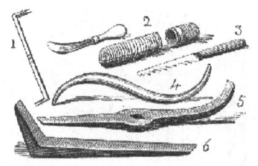

Figure 17-17: This tool collection from the Chubb archives was used more than 200 years ago for breaking. 1, 4, 5, and 6 are prybars; 2 is a slip knife for shimming doors, and 3 is a small saw for cutting bolts.

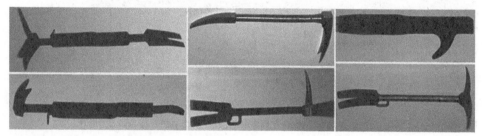

Figure 17-18: Iowa American produces several prybars for specific applications. Their length, weight, and configuration of claws and hooks vary.

Sigma Security (UK) is a leading supplier of forced-entry tools for law enforcement agencies, SWAT teams, and Special Action Services. Some of their prybars and systems are shown to penetrate virtually any barrier in Figures 17-19, 17-20, and 17-21. I spent time at Sigma to watch as different doors and locks were compromised in a few seconds.

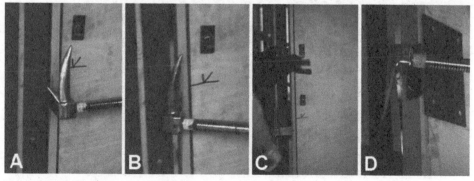

Figure 17-19: The Sigma Hooligan separates the door from its jamb. The wedge is inserted (A) and driven (B) into the gap between the door and frame. Rotational torque is then applied (C) to force the door to pivot outward (D).

Courtesy of Sigma.

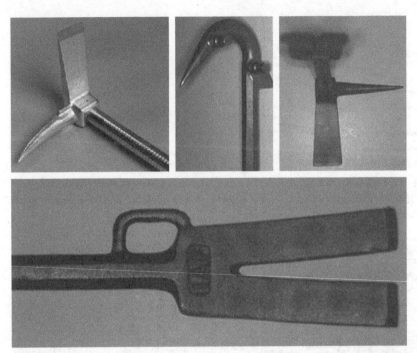

Figure 17-20: Four different attack tools for prying, wedging, peeling, and ripping.

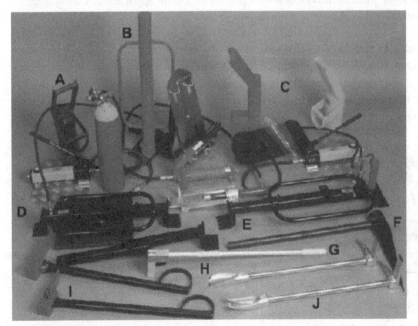

Figure 17-21: (A) Sumo single-man ram, (B) two-man Enforcer ram, (C) Firecracker single-man ram, (D) Blower two-man hydraulic/pneumatic ram, (E) hydraulic ram, (F) duckbill, (G) hinge puller, (H) Highway Hooligan prybar designed to cut heavy gauge metals and composites, (I) tapered blade ripping tools (with and without ratchet), and (J) Hooligan prybar for levering and puncturing.

Courtesy of Sigma.

Jamb spreading and peeling is another variant of the application of opposing forces. This is a technique to withdraw or displace the strike casing far enough for the bolt to clear the obstruction that blocks its movement.

Most bolt systems can be bypassed if a large enough gap is created between the lock and strike, eliminating the obstruction to the door's movement. Although crowbars, prybars, and wedges may be utilized, several hydraulic jamb spreaders are available. They can compromise almost any doorframe with little effort. The force can be applied between two jambs to spread and overcome them by deflection of the length of the bolt throw. This technique is shown in Figures 17-22 and 17-23.

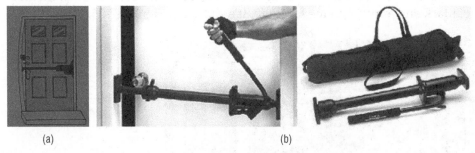

(a)   (b)

Figures 17-22a, 22b: The principle of jamb spreading is to exert force against two different surfaces to warp a door frame to allow the bolt to pass. (a) shows a spreader, and (b) is a spreader kit.

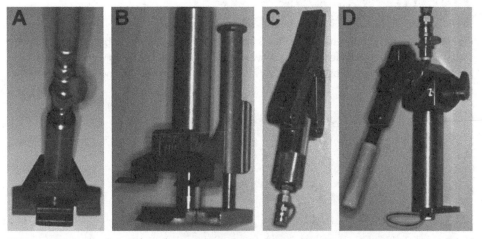

Figures 17-23: The Omni hydraulic jamb spreader is a simple and effective handheld tool for widening doorframes to provide clearance for the bolt. In (A), it's placed in position and extended between the sides of the frame. Several thousand pounds of force can be exerted with the hydraulic mechanism. The unit can be easily carried by one man (B). (C) and (D) show other forms of spreaders.
Courtesy of B-Safe Company.

Using a hydraulic car jack with wood blocks effectively spreads a jamb. One such device develops 4,000 pounds of pressure without damaging the door frame. This spreader type won't work on heavy metal frames, however. A brace, a bit, and a keyhole saw can cut an access hole in a door.

Compressed hydraulic fluids or air pressure are developed by pumping and can be used to open a door in a few seconds. This spreader type can develop 8,000–10,000 pounds of force.

The K-Tool from Iowa American Company, shown in Figure 17-24, provides another means to remove a rim or mortise cylinder from its housing. This device is constructed as a slotted box with an extremely sharp wedge. Its design causes it to be vertically locked onto the cylinder so that a prybar or duckbill can be utilized to rip it loose from the door or frame. The duckbill tool is another method to attack and apply extreme leverage. It's shown in Figure 17-25.

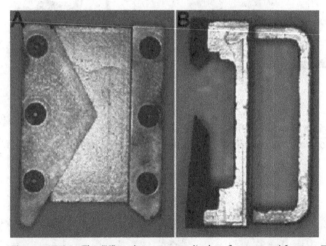

Figure 17-24: The "K" tool removes cylinders from metal frames. The assembly (A) is placed over the lip of the mortised cylinder, forced downward, and then ripped outward with a duckbill lever. The angled wedge grabs the lock body and provides a firm hold. An end view of the tool is shown in (B).

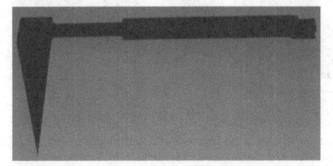

Figure 17-25: Another form of wedge that employs leverage to create energy from a graduated angle on impact. The duckbill tool is primarily used to compromise padlocks and cylinders and is configured as an L-shaped crowbar. Compromising a lock by applying two opposing forces to a shackle or other component employs wedging.

Compression and Shearing Force

Some materials and components can be subjected to extreme compression to alter or destroy their structure. Wire or bolt cutters, shears, and similar tools can compress materials to reduce their strength. Compression or shear force can cause critical locking components to fail.

Impact, Blows, Shock, Hydraulic-Pneumatic Pressure, and Compressed Air

Safes, vaults, security devices, and barrier materials can be bypassed or destroyed when subjected to impacts or blows caused by direct contact or concussion. In first-generation safes after the Industrial Revolution, it was a favorite practice to strike the metal sheets with a heavy hammer, causing deformation so the metal pulled away from the rivets. A lever or axe would be utilized to peel the face. In the same way, blows can compromise a deadbolt locking arrangement. A well-known technique is to place a bar at the top of a bolt and then apply a downward force with a sledgehammer. The action generally releases the bolt from its housing.

Sigma produces a unique forced-entry tool that utilizes compressed air to generate 10,000 pounds of pressure against a fixed object such as a door. The system comprises compressed air, a mounting frame, and a specially designed rubber bag. The system is designed to be attached to a metal doorframe. The bag is placed between the door and a reinforcement plate and inflates in milliseconds. It then forces anything occupying the same space to move.

Bouncing or Bumping of Locking Components

Inferior-quality padlocks can often be compromised by applying shock to the shackle assembly using a rubber or wooden mallet. This causes the locking dog (the internal component that retains the shackle) to retract, releasing the shackle. Working on the same theory, impact pick guns, both mechanical and electronic, are used to bypass pin tumbler locks. Applying shock to the walls of small safes that employ spring-loaded bolts and solenoids with sufficient energy can cause the bolts to retract momentarily.

Battering-Ram Door Hammer

Law enforcement, military, security services, and rescue teams have developed one- and two-man battering-ram door hammers to effect rapid entry. A great deal of force can be generated through weight, physical design, and impact velocity. Generally, these tools are made of steel, contain concrete, and can deliver up to 14,000 pounds of pressure. One such device, manufactured by Sigma (UK), offers eight times the force of a 14-pound sledgehammer. It can open almost any door in seconds. In use, the ram is placed to hit a door on either the hinged or the locked side. It is extremely destructive because of its tremendous capability to deliver focused energy.

Slam Hammer

The slam hammer resembles a dent puller and can exert a magnified pulling force to remove plugs, locks, safe dials, and other fixed components. The tool is simple in design and relies on force multiplication by creating momentum with a heavy sliding mass. The energy created by sliding the mass away from the target object is transferred to that target object. The theory is based on Newton's Third Law of Motion.

The tool comprises a long pipe with a collar that is free to move over its entire length. The tool's tip is designed to retain a metal screw that is tapped into the component to be removed. The round collar is heavy and slightly larger in diameter than the guide pipe. The collar's weight, the guide's length, and the speed with which the collar is withdrawn determine the force applied to the lock.

In operation, the front end of the slam hammer is attached to the component to be removed with a self-tapping metal screw. The collar is moved to the device's tip and then violently slides backward. The counterforce or momentum generated when the collar stops at the guide's end is transmitted to the lock or component. A slam hammer can remove safe dials, cylinders, and other fixed objects. A movable weight is employed to increase the pulling forces greatly.

Punching

Force may be delivered through punching using a sharp-pointed rod, punch, spike, piercer, awl, or other cylindrical object. This is a popular technique used to bypass bolt mechanisms and locks in safes. The punch is placed in a position to dislodge the lock by forcing the spindle forward. Shock, created by repeated blows with a hammer, generally removes a lock case or bolt.

Chisel and Wedging

A chisel with a sharp point is a favorite tool for bypassing hinges. In practice, the tool spreads the leaves and breaks loose a piece of the hinge. The sharp wedge is inserted, and the hinge is pried loose from the door. Sigma produces a special tool to remove hinges. It's slid over the hinge assembly and the hinge is pried loose at an angle. Hinge pins can also be removed with a sharp chisel.

Application of Temperature Extremes

Applying high and low temperature extremes to surface materials can affect the molecular structure of components and allow them to be compromised. It can cause a change in density, loss of temper, weakening, or distortion. Temperature changes can also soften, cause brittleness, and shatter, melt, or vaporize barrier material. A portable propane or oxygen-acetylene torch can easily cut a door lock or padlock shackle. These tools can achieve temperatures up to 6,000 °F. Figure 17-26 shows a portable briefcase-size thermic lance produced by Broco that can generate 10,000 °F instantly and cut through any material. I employed one of these

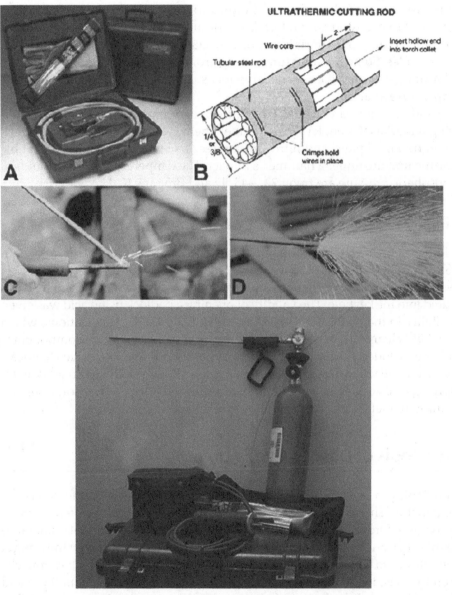

Figure 17-26: The Broco portable thermic lance will penetrate virtually any material. The system is contained within a small carrying case (A). The ultra-thermic cutting rods (B) comprise a steel tube with a copper sheath containing a wire bundle. The rod is ignited (C) with the voltage supplied by a car battery. Once a spark is generated, oxygen is fed through the rod (D).

systems to cut the bars in a cell door at our state penitentiary in a few seconds and to make a hole through granite blocks.

Certain chemicals can induce an exothermic reaction to generate heat. Thermite can develop high temperatures to melt barrier materials. Heat applications can be localized or targeted to a more general area.

Introducing extremely low temperatures can also change the molecular structure of materials. Freon and liquid nitrogen have been successfully employed to make barrier materials brittle and subject to fracture on impact. The supercooling of materials can be especially effective for bypassing padlock shackles. Some manufacturers add chrome and nickel or other materials as hardening agents. Less expensive locks can be more vulnerable to low-temperature attacks.

Liquid nitrogen can be applied at a freezing temperature of −320 °F, shattering materials. Freon, R134a, and other chemicals can have the same effect. Liquid freon, propane, and nitrogen can freeze a lock and make it susceptible to brittle fracture under a hammer's impact. The temperatures of the liquids at atmospheric pressure are freon 22, −45 °F; and propane (C_3H_8), −48 °F.

Chemical Attacks Against Internal Components

Acid has been utilized to soften or dissolve critical components in a lock. In 1985, a patent (U.S. 4,512,165) was granted to LaGard for its LK1200 padlock. The patent describes a system that permanently locks the mechanism if acid is poured into the keyhole. The validity of opening a padlock using acid was given credibility in the HSP MIL-P-43607 and MIL-DTL-43607 specifications, which note that "chemicals, capable of softening or dissolving critical components" could be included during the forced entry test. Acids and corrosive chemicals have been utilized to destroy barrier materials. Although difficult to work with, applying acids can effectively neutralize security devices. Many solutions can eat through metals, plastics, ceramics, and glass.

Basic Tools of Destructive Entry

Many tools can be employed to breach a lock, locking system, safe, or critical components. The selection of a tool dictates the application of different levels and types of force that can be applied. When assessing the potential vulnerabilities of a lock and related hardware, reviewing these tools and how they might be employed to break, modify, alter, or create a path for a hybrid attack must be carefully considered. No lock is immune to a successful attack from these and other exotic tools. It's always a function of time, determination, and an ability to exploit the characteristics and physical limits of construction materials and the capabilities of tools to exceed those limits. The following is a basic list of the tools you can use:

- Bolt cutters
- Battering ram (one- and two-man operation)
- Axe
- Channel-lock pliers
- Chisel
- Compressed air system (produces up to 10,000 pounds of pressure)
- Crowbar
- Cylinder wrench
- Dent pullers
- Disc cutters
- Drift punch
- Drill rigs, including vacuum, magnetic, and attachable systems
- Drills made of or coated with carbon, chromium, tungsten, boron, diamond, or carbides
- Dremel tools for removing material from outside surfaces of locks
- Duckbill wedge tool
- Glass cutter and fracture tool
- Grinding wheels and grinders
- Hinge-removal tool to shear the sides of a door hinge
- Hole saw
- Jamb spreaders, bumper jacks, and hydraulic spreaders by Iowa American and Sigma
- Jimmies in various lengths
- K-Tool for shearing and removing locks from metal frames
- Levers and long bars for leverage
- Lifting tools (such as Hydra-force for doors and heavy objects) up to 60 tons
- Nail-puller
- Piercer
- Pipe wrench
- Plug pullers with special screws
- Profile cylinder-removal tool

- Prybars for leveraging, puncturing, and cutting
- Pulling tools, including slam hammers, dent pullers, and nose pullers
- Punches, ice picks, chisels, awls
- Rams, including hydraulic and pneumatic
- Ripping tools, including tapered blades with and without ratchets
- Saws
- Screws (metal) for dent pullers
- Shove knives
- Slam hammers
- Sledgehammers and dead hammers
- Spring punches for fracturing glass
- Torches and thermic lances
- Wedges
- Wrenches, including plumbers' wrenches

Covert methods of entry are described in the next chapter. They can be difficult to detect and are especially problematic for government agencies if classified information is compromised. Many entry methods leave little or no forensic trace, making investigation by crime labs more difficult.

Covert Methods of Entry

Locks are primarily designed to resist, deter, or prevent covert and forced attacks that can compromise their security. Understanding the different techniques to attack conventional and high-security locks is essential for anyone designing or testing locking mechanisms. It is axiomatic that to produce a secure lock, one must know the techniques to defeat it. The challenge is always in the specific details, as many methods exist to bypass the individual components and subsystems identified in this chapter.

Finding and remedying a possible locking mechanism's insecurity in either current or proposed designs can be complicated and often involves multiple steps or techniques. It is often unknown whether a design can be compromised and whether the lock can be covertly opened. Discovering a design flaw or vulnerability and its remedy is always the goal. That result can be elusive, especially if there's a mindset that all flaws have been identified or don't exist.

Design failures leading to insecurity have real consequences. They can be unknown for many years in a product's life, only to be discovered by accident or by hackers, locksmiths, or criminals. In my experience, countless initial insecurity engineering failures have led to recalls and lawsuits and required major modifications, which proved very expensive. Every major manufacturer has experienced serious engineering and liability issues with the design of their conventional and high-security locks.

Most of these problems could have been avoided if the proper product analysis and vetting had been conducted *during* the design and prerelease phase rather than later. No one is immune, so it's important to be completely conversant with the bypass techniques described in this chapter and the advanced scenarios discussed in Chapter 20. These attack vulnerabilities must be considered and tested against any lock design. Design issues with electromechanical and electronic locks are analyzed in Chapter 19.

Covert Entry: The Fundamental Premise

Covert entry methods are premised on the nondestructive compromise of certain critical components within a lock, whether mechanical, electromechanical, or electronic. These methods and techniques are all based on attacks that don't involve the direct use of force or that don't cause damage. Certain hybrid techniques may combine different attack vectors that employ some aspect of force as part of the technique.

In many attacks, the application of force is incidental to the result. It may not be a significant component of accomplishing the objective of compromising critical components. However, the definition of *covert* or *nondestructive* entry signifies no visible signs that a lock was breached or opened.

As noted in this book, there's a further subdivision of terms for covert and surreptitious methods particular to government specifications. It's vital to know whether a lock or protective system that protects classified areas or materials has been compromised. In *covert* scenarios, attacks aren't obvious but are discoverable. In *surreptitious* entries, attacks may not be discoverable, which can pose serious security issues for government agencies or contractors.

This chapter identifies and summarizes traditional nondestructive methods of entry. Virtually all the techniques rely on manipulating components internally or from external sources to cause critical locking elements to move to a different state: locked or unlocked. Vulnerability to covert-entry attacks can be further exacerbated if a lock contains audit-trail capabilities bypassed by such methods. Security, liability, compliance, and protective issues can be serious when this occurs. In earlier designs of electromechanical locks, this problem resulted from an ability to bump open a mechanism if the power supply was removed before an attack or a magnetic field was employed to move components without a trace. Most such design issues involving the storage of access information have been resolved, but not all of them.

High-security locks often contain multiple security layers to protect against covert manipulation and forced attacks. The difficulty in defeating each layer and the security provided by these additional measures must be assessed. Some can present significant obstacles, whereas others can be relatively simple to bypass.

An important issue for design teams is the possibility that locking mechanisms and their functions can be defeated without leaving any forensic or visible traces.

This can occur in many ways, and the configuration of components, elements, and security layers dictates the tools and techniques employed. Whether it's a conventional, high-security, or hybrid design, the lock type may not matter. This can also be the case with electromechanical and electronic mechanisms, because even with more sophisticated systems that rely on an electronic credential, something must move to create a locked or unlocked state. The junction between electronic and mechanical elements is always the vulnerable point and should be the focus of any vulnerability assessment (VA). This becomes even more complex and problematic when machine learning is built into locking systems.

The fundamental issue is discovering any method that can allow a lock to be opened without evidence of damage to internal components. It's important to assess how difficult an attack is to execute in terms of tools, training, and expertise. Finally, what is the likelihood of success in a short time frame, and is such an attack consistent with the lock's security rating and the consumer's expectations? These fundamental questions and the premise of nondestructive entry relate to the first design rule and commensurate question: what opens the lock? It's often not the key, because the key only actuates the mechanism that allows the lock to be opened. If direct access can be achieved, the key isn't required.

Primary Points of Vulnerability for All Locks

The same points of attack and component failure can be the targets of destructive entry. They can also be vulnerable to covert compromise of locking mechanisms, although different methods are employed to accomplish nondestructive defeats. For covert-entry and VA teams, the first considerations are how these critical elements may be circumvented and how to identify which elements are the most likely to be exploited. Each of these categories has the potential to be a weak link in a design:

- Internal tolerances
- Keys and bitting
- Keys or credentials
- Mechanical credentials
- Magnetic fields
- Physical integrity
- Assembly-retaining components
- Decoding attacks
- Gates and sidebars
- Mechanical electronic interfaces

- Motion transfer components that move bolts or latches, or block elements
- Movable locking components, including pins, rotors, discs, wafers, wheels, wards, and magnets
- Neutralization of each security layer which can provide a weak link in the overall security of the device
- Openings into lock bodies
- Plugs and keyways
- Processors
- Secondary components for multiple security layers
- Shear lines
- Shells or housing
- Critical locking elements
- Lock assemblies and bolt mechanisms
- Systems controlling external locking elements
- Sidebars and side pins

Assessing and Choosing Methods of Attack

Determining the best (or most likely) methods to successfully open a lock depends on many factors. The most relevant issues are presented next, and then the most important techniques are outlined. Initial questions must include the following:

- What is the type of lock, manufacturer, vintage, and security rating?
- What information is known about the mechanism?
- What specific mechanism unlocks the lock?
- Is there any public information about defeating this lock type?
- What are the known bypass methods?
- Are there any special security enhancements to overcome?
- Are blank keys available for impressioning or extrapolation?
- Is a paracentric keyway in use that makes picking more difficult?
- Is the keyway open-ended?
- Is it possible to exploit any available opening to access critical components?
- Is it possible to reach locking components with shim wires?
- Can detainers be manipulated by picking or key jiggling?
- Are there possible methods of bumping, vibration, or rapping?

- Can extrapolation techniques be used to derive the top-level master key?
- Is key control compromised by duplicating, replicating, or simulating physical credentials?
- Is any amplification of rights of physical credentials occurring?
- Are different attacks combined to compromise critical locking elements?
- Can internal components be viewed externally to derive intelligence, allowing keys to be produced?
- Can internal elements be defeated through the keyway?
- Can detainer values be decoded?
- Can focused energy be applied to move critical components?
- Is it possible to decode the bitting or other critical information?
- Can internal elements be observed, measured, or decoded from outside the lock?
- Are specialized tools available or designed to compromise the target lock?
- Is the lock or its data contained in any database for electronic decoders (discussed in Chapter 23) to determine the bitting values of internal detainers?

Covert-Entry Methods

Many traditional methods exist to open conventional and high-security locks covertly and nondestructively. There are also techniques to bypass the more sophisticated cylinders using advanced methods and tools developed by experts such as John Falle, Wendt, Madelin, and Lockmasters and others specializing in producing tools primarily for government services.

Certain information must be gathered for any operation involving high-security locks and facilities to disclose their vulnerabilities and possibly facilitate a successful, nondestructive entry. This kind of information is important to both those who attack specific systems and those who design them to resist such attacks. Virtually all conventional locks, high-security cylinders, and associated systems can be compromised by targeting one or more potentially vulnerable elements.

Preliminary questions about circumventing the security of a specific lock or system must address the following issues:

- Have all relevant patents been researched, including tools produced to defeat the lock?
- Is there any external access for a bypass to circumvent internal mechanisms?
- Can the plug endcap be compromised, allowing access to the cam and tailpiece, which control other elements that must be moved?

- If a removable core lock is the target, can the control key be decoded?
- If the lock utilizes a sidebar or side bit milling, can the code be determined to simulate or replicate it?
- What components are viewable from outside the lock?
- Can the lock be bumped open with traditional or hybrid techniques?
- Is it possible to introduce instruments into the lock to avoid direct contact with locking mechanisms?
- How many detainers are blocking plug rotation?
- Are there multiple security layers, and if so, what are they?
- Does the lock contain multiple physical shear lines that can be attacked? (This includes interchangeable core cylinders, locks produced by Corbin with a normal shear line, and a second sleeve surrounding the plug to prevent cross-combination of pin tumblers.)
- How complex is the keyway, and does it make moving instruments in the lock more difficult?
- Is there direct access to locking elements?
- Is it possible to disassemble the lock to determine critical information about how it works or bitting values?
- Does the key make direct contact with the blocking elements?
- Can information about the coding of bitting values be derived from analyzing different keys in a system?
- Are there openings, access points, holes, or paths to insert shim wires to move critical components?
- Can you impression internal components to derive bitting values?
- Can voltages be induced to affect the operation of motors or other electronic components?
- Are there any ferrous components that make the lock subject to strong magnetic fields?
- Are any components sensitive to radio frequency (RF) energy from transmitters or electromagnetic pulse (EMP) devices?
- Are components subject to shock, vibration, bumping, or rapping attempts to cause them to move? (This includes using solenoids and unbalanced wheels in combination locks and non-spring-biased detainers.)
- Can any noncritical mechanisms be accessed through the keyway or other opening, including a key-in-knob assembly, to remove or circumvent critical parts, bolts, or latches?

- Are there similar designs in different locks that might instruct how to defeat them?

- Can all springs be determined to be functional, providing the proper bias to prevent improper manipulation of detainers by vibration?

- What are the internal tolerances of critical components, and can poor tolerances lead to simple bypass techniques and tryout or jiggle keys?

- Is public information available about the target lock and system?

Shear Line Attacks

Compromise of the shear line can take many forms for most locks, particularly pin tumblers. Almost every locking function is connected to the operation of the shear line because it controls the plug's rotation. If the plug can't be turned with the correct key, the motion can't be transmitted to a cam, tailpiece, or other interconnection that interfaces with bolts, latches, switches, or other mechanisms that unlock the lock.

The shear line is the physical breakpoint between the plug and shell in a pin tumbler lock. It permits free rotation of the plug when all the pins are precisely at that breakpoint. In a shear-line attack, the goal is to move all the pins or detainers to the point at which the plug can be turned. There are many ways to accomplish this, but regardless of the method, the result is the same.

The effort can be more complicated if multiple layers of security include sidebars, side bit milling, security pins, and interactive elements that cooperate between the key and lock.

The most recognized techniques for bypassing the security of mechanical locks involve the shear line. They include using the correctly bitted key, picking, bumping, jiggling, impressioning, and exploiting tolerances with tryout keys. More sophisticated attacks are described in Chapter 20. They can involve measuring the length of bottom pins with shim wires and special mechanical and electronic decoders. Some devices can determine mechanically when pins are precisely "set" at the shear line.

Picking

Lockpicking is a generic term that can have many meanings but always identifies techniques to raise pins, levers, or other detainers to a shear line to mimic the actions of a key with the correct bitting. The result of all picking is to replicate the key's actions so the plug can be turned. How that is accomplished can take many forms. Picking is just one attack on a shear line, but impressioning, decoding, bumping, and other techniques are equally important. They're all predicated on the compromise of the shear line.

The theory underlying picking is to trap each pin at a shear line and maintain its position with torque until all pins are properly positioned. As noted in other chapters, there are many obstacles to picking where *security pins* have been inserted. They falsely indicate that a pin has been set when trapped *between* the plug and shell. When this occurs, the pins *appear to be* at the shear line, but they aren't, and it's impossible to rotate the plug. Many systems in addition to security pins have been implemented to frustrate picking. All of them must be circumvented and overcome simultaneously if the lock is to be opened. This subject is discussed more fully in Chapter 14, which describes high-security locks and their enhancements to make picking and other forms of attack more difficult. Typical pick sets to defeat security are shown in Figure 18-1.

The lock's tolerance is also a crucial factor. Poor tolerances between the plug and shell can make a lock much easier to pick or susceptible to tryout or jiggle keys. The springs' condition is also important. If they're broken or compressed or have lost their temper, the lock may be difficult to open.

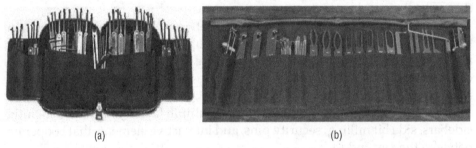

(a)   (b)

Figure 18-1a, 1b: A locksmith commercial pick set (a), and the John Falle professional set (b).

Traditional techniques with a manual picking tool are the most common picking methods. There are wide varieties and designs of picks to manipulate each pin individually or by *raking*, which requires that a special pick be moved across the pins simultaneously and rapidly while tension is applied to the plug. The process requires applying the correct amount of torque via a tension wrench inserted into the keyway and operated simultaneously with the pick. As expected, many tension wrenches are available for various keyway designs. Different picks are shown in Figures 18-2 and 18-3. They're used to move different types of pins or detainers.

Lock picks come in many different forms. They primarily consist of curved, diamond, half-diamond, single- and double-ball, and other shapes.

John Falle produces a set of professional torque wrenches that provide enhanced plug control during picking. These tools contact the keyway at two points and apply tension along the plug's centerline, reducing the problem of binding and obstruction of the keyway. The wrench can be adjusted to fit almost any lock. Falle also produced a special pick set for pin tumblers and lever locks. Tension

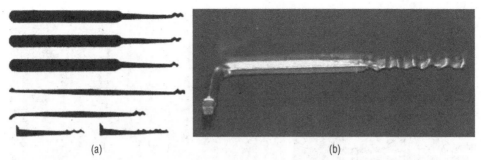

Figures 18-2a, 2b: Rake picks (a) can take many forms. They're designed to manipulate multiple pins at once. A modified Allen wrench (b) was used to break into the key cabinet at the Diamond Exchange in Antwerp in 2003.

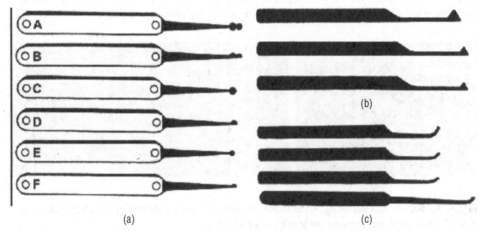

Figures 18-3a–3c: Ball picks are available in several configurations. (a) shows various picks: (A) double ball, (B) double half ball, (C) large single ball, (D) half ball, (E) small ball, (F) small half ball. The picks in (b) are of different diamond shapes, and (c) shows curved picks.

wrenches are shown in Figure 18-4. Depending on the internal design of the lock, different wrenches can optimize the feedback from pins and make picking more effective.

Signature picks have been introduced to replicate various bitting patterns. These picks can be jiggled in a keyway to create multiple combinations. Two different signature picks are shown in Figure 18-5. They can prove highly effective at opening some pin tumbler and wafer locks.

Mechanical pick guns, shown in Figure 18-6, are popular because they replicate the action of a bump key and are often used because they require less expertise. There are also many versions of snap-pick (or similar) designs, but they all work on the principle that energy is applied to the base of one or more pins, which causes the bottom and top pins to split for an instant. With the proper timing and the application of tension, all the top pins are separated at the shear line.

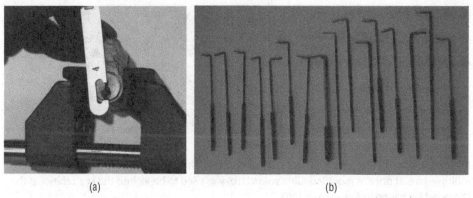

(a)   (b)

Figures 18-4a, 4b: The John Falle tension wrenches (a) are unique. They facilitate applying even torque to the top and bottom of the plug while providing the most access to the keyway for the pick. Standard tension wrenches are shown in (b) in different configurations, primarily for locksmiths.

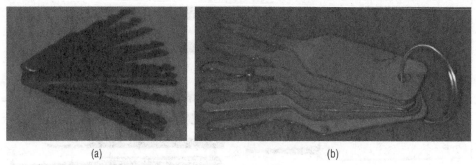

(a)   (b)

Figure 18-5a, 5b: Rocker picks can facilitate the raking of pins and simulating different bitting patterns. Two different versions are shown in (a) and (b).

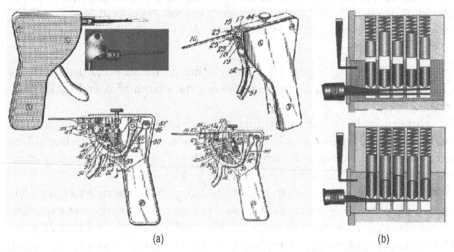

(a)   (b)

Figures 18-6a, 6b: One of the patent diagrams for the original mechanical pick guns for pin tumbler locks (a) The pin tumbler lock (b) shows how the pick gun works against the base of all pin tumblers.

Electromechanical pick guns are extremely effective, especially for locks containing security pins. Wendt produces a custom tool with special tips for bumping different pin designs, shown in Figure 18-7. The intensity and travel of the tip can be adjusted. These devices can open difficult-to-pick locks, sometimes in seconds.

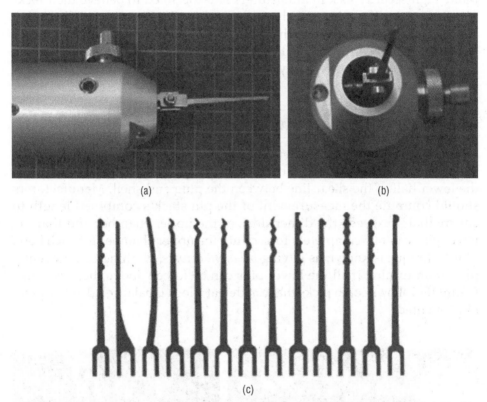

(a)   (b)

(c)

Figures 18-7a–7c: Electronic pick guns generate vibration at the pick tip. The smaller ring in (a) can adjust the vibration. There is an adjustment in (b) for the intensity and tip travel. The tip is placed parallel to the bottom pin tumblers to energize them. Wendt has constructed different tips with varying tumbler designs especially for bumping (c).

As described in Chapter 23, electronic decoding systems primarily for government use can measure the length of each pin or lever and provide that data to produce a working key. They're available from Wendt and Madelin and are extremely versatile. These decoders work on hundreds of profiles and contain precise databases of locks and keys. Every lock design team should understand these tools to determine the efficacy of security pins and other protective measures.

Bumping

Lock bumping is an automated form of picking. Based on Newton's Third Law of Motion, a bump key is designed to contact all pins simultaneously and raise them to a shear line. This technique can circumvent certain security pins and is generally not hampered by paracentric keyways that can make picking difficult. Many high-security lock manufacturers have been led to believe their locks were resistant to bumping, which wasn't the case. The techniques of bumping are described in more detail in Chapter 15. It's incumbent on assessment teams to be thoroughly conversant with and have expertise in this type of bypass, because even the highest-security locks can be vulnerable to the application of force to detainers.

Comb Picks and Balanced Driver Attacks

Pin tumbler locks must contain at least two pins in each chamber: a top pin and a bottom pin. When raised to the correct height, the lower pins constitute the lower half of the shear line between the plug and shell. Manufacturers should compute the measurement of the pin stack's combined length to ensure that it exceeds the dimensions of the upper chamber and that the lower pins can't be completely forced into the upper chamber for each bore. This technique is known as having *balanced drivers*. Nothing can prevent a plug from turning if all the lower pins can be forced above the shear line. Figure 18-8 shows comb picks that can defeat a lock if balanced drivers aren't implemented.

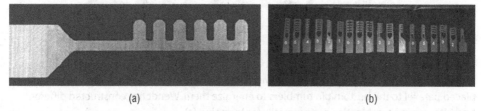

(a)   (b)

Figures 18-8a, 8b: The John Falle comb pick set (b) is designed to work with many pin tumbler cylinders. The fingers that protrude from the comb (a) can be adjusted with various tools in the kit to match the precise positions of tumblers in a target lock.

A new shear line can be created with a comb pick if balanced drivers aren't employed. There are tines for each chamber that push each bottom pin upward to clear the radius of the plug. If the comb pick can act on each bottom pin, a new shear line is created, and nothing prevents the plug from rotating. The original patent for a comb pick is shown in Figure 18-9. Note that all bottom pins are forced into the top chambers.

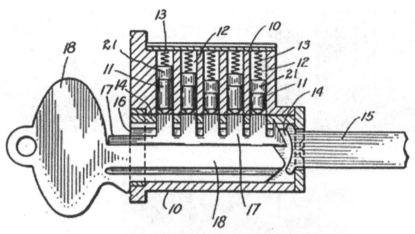

Figure 18-9: The comb pick described in U.S. Patent 2,064,818. A comb pick creates a new shear line by lifting the lower tumblers above the plug and into the shell. It's inserted below the bottom pins and forced upward by a specially cut key blank.

Using a comb pick is a common way to defeat poorly designed or inferior-quality locks. My colleague and I demonstrated another more sophisticated approach to create a shear line: injecting ball bearings into the shell through each chamber in the plug. Nothing can prevent the plug from rotating if bearings can be injected with a special syringe and forced into the shell. Using comb picks and this advanced technique is undetectable but can stop the correct key from working because the bitting values have changed. The process compresses and damages the springs in the upper chamber, but it can be highly effective.

Simultaneous Chamber Picks

Special picking tools can access and manipulate several pins simultaneously or sequentially, as shown in Figures 18-10 and 18-11. One is the Sputnik, which works on profile cylinders. The other is an axial pin tumbler pick, which was designed and patented by Peterson, allowing each pin to be picked sequentially. Many such tools have been designed to move pins to shear lines. It's easier to manipulate the pins in a paracentric keyway, and tension can be maintained, especially in the case of security pins.

Reverse Picking with a Key Blank

In normal picking of a cylinder, tension is applied to the plug either counter-clockwise or clockwise as part of the requirement to trap pins at the shear line until they're all elevated to the correct height. At least three other methods exist to bind tumblers with tension and pin movement. The most common for locksmiths is to employ a blank key to attempt to trap the pins, one at a time,

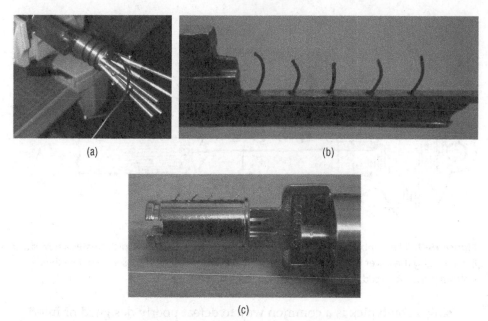

(a)　　　　　　　　　　　　　　　　　(b)

(c)

Figures 18-10a–10c: The Sputnik tool can pick pin tumbler cylinders by extending individual wires to contact each pin. (a) shows the tool with multiple-pin chamber controls. In (b) wires that control each pin protrude from the special key once inside the lock. (c) shows a plug with wires extended for each bottom pin tumbler.

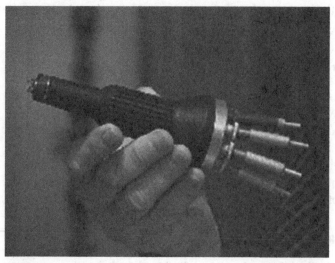

Figure 18-11: The Peterson decoder is for axial pin tumbler locks and can manipulate all the pins at the same time.

beginning at the back of the plug. With tension applied, the key is fully inserted and then slowly removed, hopefully causing each pin to bind at the shear line as it drops from its elevated position. This technique can work, depending on several factors, especially in low-tolerance mechanisms. With the proper torque, the pins catch at the shear line, one by one, and remain in that position. If all the tumblers are bound properly, the plug can be turned. This procedure is quite effective with wafer tumbler locks.

Reverse Picking with a Key Blank, a Hole, and a Drill Bit

This is a forced-entry attack with a key blank, as described in Chapter 17. It requires drilling a very small hole above a lock's normal shear line after inserting a blank key. The key's blade then causes all the pins to be elevated to a position at or above the shear line. The drill bit severs each of the pins. The blank key can then be released, resulting in the bottom pins dropping into the keyway. When this occurs, the plug is free to rotate.

Reverse Picking the Medeco Deadbolt

This method is described in Chapters 17 and 24 and Part VI case examples about unanticipated forced attacks. It can be employed against a deadbolt lock when the retaining screws are sheared, breaking loose the endcap from the plug. Once no further link exists between the plug and shell, forward torque is applied to pick the lock toward the operator rather than turning it to the right or left.

Modification of Side Bit Milling

Side bit milling is popular for adding another security layer in mostly high-security locks and can effectively prevent bumping. It is generally not compromised in bumping attacks because the secondary pins cause sidebars to misalign with pins when the bump key is forced forward. To overcome this, the milling is physically modified to accommodate the slight movement required by the key. If a bump key is produced, sidebar locks can be opened with the correct sidebar milling or simulation. In Figure 18-12, an Assa key with side bit milling has been modified to open the lock.

Amplification of Rights

In the amplification of rights, the credentials presented to a shear line must elevate the pin tumblers to the precise position for the plug to rotate, even though the original key may not have the correct bitting. Attacks on keying systems can circumvent how the key interacts by modifying the bitting values of the key through a process known as *rights simplification*. This involves using a key *not*

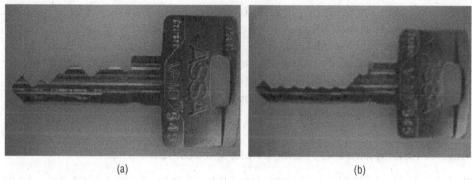

(a)   (b)

Figures 18-12a, 12b: (a) shows an Assa V10 normal bitted key before modification of the side bit milling dimensions. (b) is a bump key for the same lock. Barry Wels and Julian Hardt of The Open Organisation Of Lockpickers (TOOOL) developed the technique in 2008 to mill the side bit milling so the finger pins remain in one position as the key is moved slightly forward during bumping.

designed to open the target lock because it has different bitting values. As noted in Part V, keys can be modified in a subtractive or additive process. This can be accomplished by removing material from the key's blade or adding material to build up a lower bitting value.

Tolerance Exploits

Locks can be defeated by exploiting tolerance errors, primarily between the plug and shell, because they control how the pin tumblers perform their blocking function at the shear line. Tolerances involve a manufacturer's assignment of depth increments and the vertical distance between depths, which translates to the different lengths of individual pin tumblers. This assignment can affect key interchange, picking, impressioning, jiggling, and tryout keys. The number of depth increments also controls the number of key changes available in a keying system.

Code-Setting Keys

This attack type is based on the tolerances in a Medeco cylinder, as documented more fully in Chapter 24 and Parts VI and VII. In 2008, it was predicated on an exploit of the rotation angles of the pins that allowed the development of four different keys for setting the sidebar code for all non-master keyed Medeco locks. Once this was accomplished, the lock could be picked and bumped like a conventional cylinder. The four patented keys are a subset of tryout keys, allowing the sidebar to be set to make picking possible.

Jiggle Keys

Jiggle keys are a form of tryout keys combined with a kind of lockpick. They can have multiple bitting combinations equal to or slightly different from those in the target lock. Any key that can enter a keyway can be employed as a jiggle key, but for it to open the lock, its bitting pattern must be able to simulate the bitting for the correct key that opens the lock. The term *jiggle* refers to how the key is used to pick the lock. It is often moved back and forth or jiggled to trap each pin at a shear line with tension applied. Old or worn keys can make excellent jiggle keys because their bitting values may differ slightly from the original factory values. They can simulate different depth increments and move in the keyway up and down and back and forth. Figure 18-13 shows a set of jiggle keys produced by Wendt.

Figure 18-13: This set of jiggle keys can be used to open pin tumbler and wafer locks by moving them back and forth and up and down while applying torque.

In a system with poor tolerance between the plug and shell or a limited number of depth increments, jiggle keys can be a real problem and present a serious legal and security issue. In an office building, for example, one tenant's keys can open another unintended office because the difference between bitting for different keys is insufficient to prevent the jiggling of keys. The problem can be more complex if jiggle keys are used as bump keys and shock or vibration is applied. The trick is to move pins to the shear line—they may be very close to it but not exactly there. Vibration, shock, or impact can move the pins and cause the lock to open. Theoretically, any key whose bitting values are similar to those of an unintended lock can be used as a jiggle key.

Signature Picks

The signature picks shown in Figure 18-14 were developed many years ago to replicate different bitting patterns that may be common in pin tumbler or wafer tumbler locks. They can be considered jiggle keys because they're normally moved in and out and up and down within the keyway to manipulate detainers to various levels and set them at the shear line.

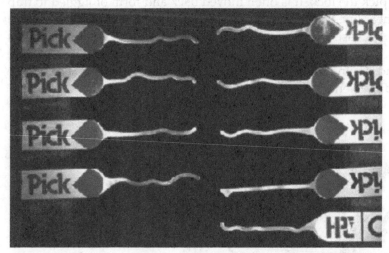

Figure 18-14: By manipulation within the keyway, many different signatures can be simulated. The set of rocker picks shown was computer-generated in Israel for HPC.

Gate-Fence Tolerances

The tolerance between the gate and fence can be exploited in key and combination locks if it isn't tight enough. This is important when sidebars are the primary security layer because if the gate is too wide, keys can operate unintended locks and reduce the number of usable key bittings. The same issue exists in combination lock wheel packs. The combination is based on the fence dropping into a gate for each wheel. If the fence is too wide, more than one number will work in a combination. It's the same theory as with tryout keys. Robot dialers and SoftDrill were based on the premise that not every combination needed to be tested to open a lock. In Group 2 locks (those not rated for high security), the tolerance may exceed ±1.5 dialed numbers. To derive the correct value, fewer numbers have to be tested in a combination lock with 100 wheel divisions. A robot dialer, which is programmed with software and motor-driven to precisely turn the dial, does exactly that: it dials every combination number for each wheel, considering gate-fence tolerance. The SoftDrill system automatically dialed each combination, sensed by feel and sound the fence-gate relationship of a combination lock, and effected an opening in as little as 15 minutes. It was withdrawn from the market because of its risk to high-security combination locks.

Width of Keyway

The design of the keyway affects the ability to pick a lock and simulate keys, especially for restricted keyways. This directly relates to the exploitation of tolerances. The wider the keyway, the easier it is to manipulate the lock with a pick and tension wrench. In the case example of Medeco locks, we produced blanks for restricted keyways, turned them into bump keys, and picked the high-security cylinders.

Tryout Keys

Tryout keys rely on and exploit the tolerances and gaps or space between the plug and shell. Keys can be specially cut with bitting that doesn't equal the normal pin depths for the bitting in the lock. Rather, the bitting is cut for altered depth increments, either slightly below or above the standard factory measurement. For example, older Kwikset pin tumbler locks had tolerances allowing depth increments of up to a one-step difference to raise the pin to the shear line. Tryout keys used this shear-line attack to produce far fewer keys to open a target lock. Thus, tryout keys could be cut with only three bitting depths in some older locks with six-depth increments. That meant a pin length of 2 could be operated with a key cut with a 1 or 3. Likewise, a 3 cut would operate a 2 or 4, and a 5 cut would operate a 4 or 6. If all the key codes were matrixed, 81 keys could theoretically open all permutations for a 5-pin lock, which normally requires 5^6 or 3,125 different keys.

The extrapolation of a master key system and its top-level master key (TMK) also relies on tryout keys but with known values for testing each bitting based on the values of a change key in the system being probed. The difference is the extrapolation process and the goal, which is used to determine the values of the top-level master key for a specific lock or system. Tryout keys, in contrast, are designed to consider all the bitting values possible in a keying system, where the specific value of a target lock is unknown.

Vibration and Rapping Attacks

The bitting combination of a lock can often be simulated by applying vibration or rapping to a key or the lock body. This is a problem if springs aren't employed to bias the detainers, as occurred in Winfield locks many years ago (as discussed in Part VI), exposing a vulnerability for millions of locks worldwide. These locks could be opened with vibration, which is another form of shear-line attack. Vibration can randomly move pins or detainers to a shear line, much the same as bumping.

Wendt makes a tool to open safes by applying extreme vibration to the door to move internal components such as solenoids. This tool is affixed to a reciprocal drill motor and can open a safe quickly.

Impressioning

Impressioning locks is another method to attack the function of a shear line, as mentioned previously. It differs from picking because it's based on the tolerance between plug and shell to produce a physical key rather than manipulating the detainers to move them to the position where the plug can be turned. There are many impressioning techniques, but they're all based on the same premise. The goal of any impressioning procedure is to produce a fully cut key with the correct bitting to open the lock without disassembling it.

If done properly, tiny marks are produced on the surface of the key blade when upward and downward pressure is applied on the key blank when the bitting value is *not* at the shear line and binding between plug and shell.

This approach is based on the idea that the gap (or tolerance between plug and shell) will create a space between the top and bottom pins when the pin tumbler being tested is exactly at the shear line. When the cut on the key raises the pin to the shear line, it can be said to be floating in that gap. Applying pressure will not cause the pin to mark the key blade because it isn't binding. Impressioning can be considered an exploit of the physical gap between plug and shell and the impossibility for a pin tumbler to be at the shear line and cause marking when upward pressure is applied.

A normal impressioning procedure uses a blank key, a special holding tool, and a special file that produces fine cutting. The blank is inserted, and torque is applied to bind each pin tumbler. Marks will appear on the key's surface until the pin is at the shear line. Pins will not mark when they are at the gap between the plug and the shell.

Several impressioning systems have been designed for lever locks; as we've mentioned, John Falle invented a system that relies on steel pins and nylon fishing line to determine the position of tumblers. LuckyLock created a far more sophisticated system based on the same principle. It's a self-impressioning system using movable inserts that automatically sense and physically indicate the gate position for each lever. It is shown in Figure 18-15.

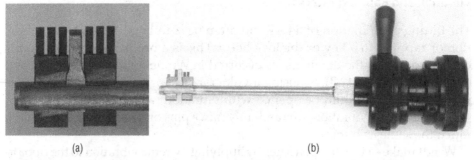

(a)   (b)

Figure 18-15a, 15b: The LuckyLock self-impressioning system for lever locks works on the same principle as the original Falle system. Lever locks are still popular in many parts of the world, and this tool can open them quickly. (a) shows the different tines in their normal state. (b) shows the tool with the adjusted tines that opens a decoded lock.

John Falle developed the auto-impression system shown in Figure 18-16 that relies on metal foil to indicate the positions of pins. It is discussed more thoroughly in Chapter 20. It's effective for pin tumbler locks and particularly for dimple locks. A Bulgarian company named Turbo Decoder (LuckyLocks) produces an excellent set of automatic and extremely versatile impressioning tools. They're all designed to detect when pins or other detainers are at the shear line.

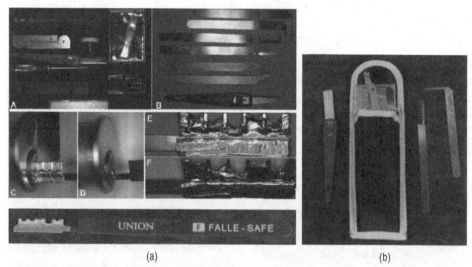

(a)   (b)

Figure 18-16a, 16b: The Falle foil impressioning system relies on a carrier inserted into the keyway (C, D), which is then lifted up and down against the tumblers with tension applied. The carrier is then withdrawn, and the pattern of the tumblers is reproduced. If done correctly, the depressions match the precise position of the pins at the shear line (E, F). Falle produces a complete kit with all required implements (A, B). The tool at the bottom of (F) is an impressioned key that opened a target lock. (b) are different tools that are used to create and trim the foil impressioned key.

A similar foil impressioning system by Tampke was disclosed in U.S. Patent 2,763,027, resembling the Falle technique (see Figure 18-17). A carrier with channels to correspond with the individual chambers is covered with foil and then inserted into the keyway. The tool is forced up and down with tension applied to freeze the tumblers and cause depressions in the foil. When the pins are at the shear line, they no longer depress the foil on the carrier.

The Martin impressioning system (U.S. 4,817,406) shown in Figure 18-18 utilized a composite brass and lead key to record impressions from pin tumblers. It was highly effective but not a commercial success.

Banks also have clever self-impressioning systems for pin tumblers and safe-deposit lever locks, shown in Figure 18-19. Lock Defeat Technology developed such a system. In a simple procedure, a blank piece of brass is placed over the carrier and inserted into the lock. The special key is turned against the levers, causing the blank to bend in proportion to the height of the bellies. The brass blank is removed and can be decoded.

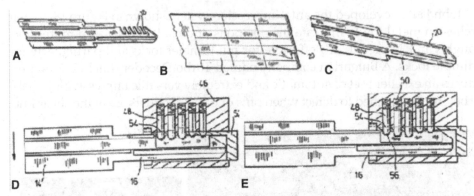

Figure 18-17: The Tampke system resembles the John Falle tool, using foil to impression a pin tumbler lock. The system utilizes a carrier (A) covered with foil (B) so that the top edge (C) is flat and has the same dimensions as the bitting of a blank key. When the key is manipulated within the keyway, the tumblers produce greater depressions as the movement continues (D) until all tumblers are at the shear line (E).

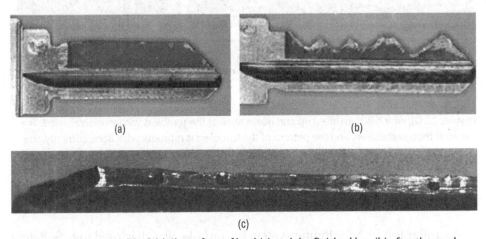

Figures 18-18a–18c: A blank blade surface of lead (a) and the finished key (b) after the marks were filed after multiple insertions. Each of the five tumblers produces an easily readable mark (c).

LuckyLocks also developed the series of three extremely sophisticated tools shown in Figure 18-20. These systems have been designed for lever locks, pin tumbler cylinders, and certain automobile locks. The system for pin tumblers is an impressioning, picking, and decoder tool designed to self-impression a cylinder.

Variable Key-Generation System

Systems to replicate keys have been designed by John Falle, Madelin, and others to generate bitted keys of thin metal that can be cut to any bitting depth. They're

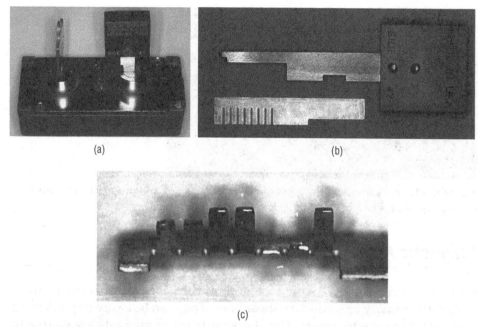

(a)   (b)

(c)

Figures 18-19a–19c: The Lock Defeat Technology system can impression safe-deposit locks in seconds. The result is a brass strip with different bitting values. This clever system is designed for specific lever tumbler safe-deposit boxes. (a) shows the complete lock with the guard and customer keys inserted. In (b) the parts of the impressioning system with the brass blank are bent when pressure is applied against each lever tumbler. In (c) the finished key replica has been produced.

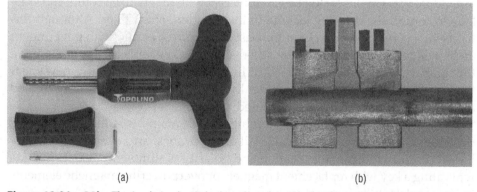

(a)   (b)

Figure 18-20a, 20b: The LuckyLocks pick, decoder, and auto-impressioning tools effectively open pin tumbler locks. (a) shows the pin tumbler decoder, and (b) the lever lock impressioning and decoding tool.

all intended to simplify generating cut keys without concern about keyway warding. Refer to Part V for more detailed information about these systems and 3D-generated keys and blanks. See Figure 18-21 for an example of impressioning marks on the blade of a key, viewed through a light box.

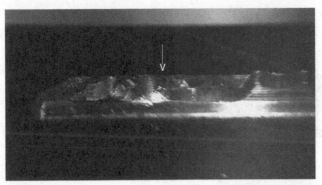

Figure 18-21: This is an example of impressioning marks visible through a special light box for viewing key blades. The arrow is pointing to an impressioning mark.

Magnetic Attacks

Magnetic elements have become integral to many locks to enhance security and create primary or secondary shear lines. They can be easily implemented and are often easy to defeat. The characteristics of magnets are simple to understand, decode, and replicate. The characteristics of different polarities of the lines of magnetic flux can be utilized to create several forms of movable elements implemented to create shear lines in card locks, pin tumblers, and many other designs.

One of the most famous is the EVVA Magnetic Code System (MCS). Four rare earth magnets are embedded in a double-sided key to control and move eight individual gates in this lock. The gates interact with magnetized rotors and side-bars to control the primary locking of the plug and shear lines. Although this has been a very popular lock for the past 30 years, especially with government and intelligence services, it can be decoded and its key replicated to circumvent the sidebar design and, thus, the shear line. Even more problematic, new shear lines can be created in seconds in older lock versions, so all the security created by magnetic rotors can be circumvented.

The fundamental security vulnerability with magnets is that they can be decoded. Gauss meters, magfilm, Hall effect probes, and even magnetically biased pins can indicate the location and polarity of tumblers. Defeats include replicating a key with replacement magnets or overpowering magnetic elements in keys to defeat the internal systems in the lock.

Many years ago, a magnetic card system based on barium ferrite vinyl was developed for hotel locks, parking garages, and government facilities, including the U.S. Mint in San Francisco. As described in Part VI, this system involved a design based on the action of multiple magnetic pins that repelled a movable platform that held magnetized pins, which controlled unlocking and was equivalent to the shear line. The position and polarity of the pins could be easily decoded and replicated with tiny magnets mounted on a piece of stiff paper.

In profile cylinders in Europe, ferrous components controlled a form of shear line. The Ring of Fire was a series of magnets placed in an aluminum housing designed to defeat these locks. When spun around the outside of a profile cylinder, a few revolutions caused the lock to open, depending on whether the rotation was clockwise or counterclockwise. Strong magnetic fields have also successfully defeated electric strikes on doors and the most popular mechanical push-button lock in the United States. The manufacturer didn't consider the effects of a magnetic field against the critical ferrous component that controlled locking and was equivalent to a shear line.

Magfilm is a material used to decode magnets in locks and keys. It can be employed to locate magnetic pins and determine their polarity with a Gauss meter. It can be an effective tool to circumvent shear lines created by magnets and the interaction of magnetic elements. Shear lines can also be decoded by determining the position of individual pins or ball bearings in certain lock designs. That was how the Trioving hotel lock was defeated: by determining the location of the positions of multiple ball bearings that, as a composite, created a shear line. I was granted a patent for this form of attack (U.S. 5,355,701). It was accomplished using a wire and a piece of carbon paper. Magnetized wire can also be employed to move ferrous components within a lock.

Processor Reset Attacks

Although these attacks are identified as forced attacks, they can also be thought of as nondestructive and covert. Regardless of the classification, they should be considered potential threats by design teams. Techniques to circumvent locking mechanisms include destabilizing control chips, interrupting power to reset vital functions, and intentionally reducing power to integrated circuits to force a reset. Access to reset switches within locks and safes should be analyzed because in many instances, it is possible to insert a shim to depress buttons physically or cause a circuit run to be shorted on a printed circuit board. More information can be found in Part VI, in a case example that involved the Kaba 5800 push-button electronic lock.

Decoding Information from Within the Lock

Information about the shear line and bitting values can be derived externally or using special tools and instruments that can probe the plug. Pick-decoding tools by Lishi, Turbo Decoder, Madelin, and other companies can perform dual functions to determine the bitting combination and maintain that information mechanically to open the lock like the original key.

Borescopes made by Olympus and other vendors feature fiber optics linked to video cameras with probes as small as 0.6 mm in diameter. Most borescopes contain a light source for illuminating the target. Companies have developed tiny, self-contained video cameras that can be inserted into plugs to read tumblers and derive measurements. One such company, Lock Tech Supply, specifically developed a camera system to decode the popular Kwikset reprogrammable locks. Other systems have been designed to interface with many locks to accomplish the same result. Some offer wireless links for remote viewing, which is especially valuable in covert operations with off-site teams.

Viewing from outside the lock is possible with ophthalmoscopes, an optometrist's precision tool. They're perfect for reading wafer locks because they can have multiple focus depths. They're also excellent for viewing the first and second pin tumblers with short lengths, which can provide their bitting code below the shear line.

Other more sophisticated decoding techniques exist for determining bitting values and correlating them to shear lines. Electronic decoders produced by Madelin and C.O.F.E.D. use ultrasonic sound to map the positions and values of detainers in pin tumbler and lever locks. These techniques are discussed in Chapter 23.

Audio Frequencies and Sound

The lengths of pin tumblers can be measured based on their resonant frequency when excited properly. This is why Medeco inserts steel pins into its tumblers for high-security installations. Sound can also indicate false gates and when pins are at the shear line. Listening to binding pins is a favorite technique for decoding locks using contact microphones and amplifiers.

Piezo Measurement

Part V examines techniques for decoding precise bitting values in pin tumbler locks with piezo decoders that use ultrasound to excite the pins. With the proper software and hardware, this is an extremely effective technique. This technology has been incorporated into handheld decoding systems, with the output correlated to extensive databases for many lock manufacturers.

Feeling, Friction, and Decoding

Mechanical decoding is based on feedback from internal components. When different moving parts interact, they offer information about their functions, measurements, position, binding, and the shear line if there is a direct relationship between them and moving elements. Sidebars and side pins can mask some of this information, which is why they're employed. But fence-gate information can also be derived by feeling with probes in the form of picks and keys. Determining a true or false gate in a sidebar is critical for decoding certain locks. Combination locks for safes and vaults can be decoded with auto-dialers and the SoftDrill, using mechanical and audio feedback in conjunction with software programs to map and determine drop-in points for the sidebar and wheel gates. This information yields the combination that will open the lock.

Belly Reading and Markings

John Falle developed a system to decode the bellies in a lever lock using plasticine and scratch marks caused by the interaction of a key and each lever tumbler. This technique can be utilized to decode other locks. One of the classic cases that relied on markings produced from internal components used a thin wire to determine the positions and values of ball bearings within a popular card lock.

Against Any Openings into the Lock Body with Shims and Wires

Any opening can provide a method to exploit potential vulnerabilities in internal components. Some of these are discussed in Chapter 20, but many attacks can be accomplished covertly with little or no trace. It is often difficult for lock designers to understand what can be accomplished using a shim with a diameter as little as ten-thousandths of an inch and any openings into a lock body.

Openings, channels, holes, and tolerance differences between external components provide entry points to reach and manipulate critical components, actuating levers, gates, and mechanical or electronic release systems. Even seemingly immune data ports may have enough clearance for a shim. Designers often wrongly believe that minute openings are blocked from direct access to critical components and that a shim couldn't possibly go around internal obstacles, curves, or other blocks. In many cases, I have employed Nitinol memory wire to overcome such issues.

Shims can be fashioned to manipulate actuating mechanisms, bolts, latches, and other mechanisms in simple attacks. In one case, we circumvented a high-security lever lock for a vault by introducing a shim. This permitted the entire internal locking design to move slightly, allowing the lock to be opened. It can't be repeated enough: any opening may allow circumventing or bypassing critical components and result in unlocking the target mechanism.

The next chapter looks at electromechanical and electronic locks and some defeats involving the interface between software and hardware. As more of these locks are developed, there will be further opportunities for attacks to defeat their security.

Attacks Against Electronic Locks

The integration of electronics into traditional mechanical locks was inevitable. The commercial, private sector, and government facilities are migrating to systems that are either hybrids of mechanical elements with electronic credentials or fully electronic cylinders. Every major lock manufacturer offers a full range of products that incorporate mechanical keys and encrypted elements. Many provide electronic cylinders that rely solely on a credential embedded in a simulated key or use some form of wireless or contactless technology to replace traditional keys. The locks can be networked, with or without wired connections. They can validate credentials through a local server or the cloud. The systems are growing in popularity and utilization due to the security they can offer and the enhanced options they provide.

These systems can be vulnerable to different forms of attack against their hardware and software. The physical interface between digital and analog is always a weak point and often the target. The rule that "Electrons don't open doors, mechanics do" applies to these systems, so the hardware–software junction is always the most vulnerable. Every lock must control moving elements to create a locked or unlocked condition. When the correct credential or key is inserted into the lock, it must activate a movable part that may cause a pin, latch, or bolt to be released. Electronics often communicate with a motor, worm gear, or solenoid where this movement is generated. It's always a question of how to access that element directly and thus bypass the lock's security.

There are many forms of attack and levels of sophistication. Design teams, especially for companies that don't have a long history and experience with this type of hardware, must understand the various vulnerabilities. Because electronic-based mechanisms function somewhat differently than traditional mechanical locks, it's important to focus on potential areas of inquiry and assessment. Common vulnerabilities and bypass techniques are identified in this chapter for cylinders that mimic traditional systems, which are referred to as *electromechanical*. These are based on my experience in hundreds of cases for my clients in which their locks and those of competitors were analyzed and defeated. They included many variations of designs that relied on the use of radio frequency identification (RFID) and encrypted elements within keys that communicated with a processor inside the lock.

The designs of all electromechanical locks have certain basic hardware configurations and functions in common, which creates a vulnerability to covert and forced attacks. By design, these locks contain a mechanical locking system with a bitted key and an electronic credential. Both systems must be concurrently validated. The mechanical locking portion can easily be configured to integrate into legacy systems for pin tumblers, wafers, sliders, or discs. The detainers prevent the plug from rotating without the correct credential and provide a second security layer, so the mechanical cylinder's benefits are combined with electronic credentials. Many systems can be configured to be backward compatible with presently installed locks so they can be mixed to meet optimum access control requirements.

The locks are configured with an electronic credential-verification system. Communication between the key and processor may require an embedded circuit that runs along the key's surface to communicate with the validation system within the lock's body. Inductive coupling, a system that relies on contactless communications using energy transmitted via magnetic fields, may also be employed for data exchange. In principle, it is the same fundamental method of energy transfer as found in power transformers, but for the transfer of information. In practice, there is no physical electrical connection between the key and the lock – just a form of induced energy.

Unless energy-harvesting systems are implemented, a battery in the key head or lock powers the system. Newer locks have up to a 10-year battery life, so introducing energy-harvesting technology may lose popularity unless environmental concerns about batteries and their replacement and disposal are paramount to users.

When a key is inserted, some form of validation matches the identification (ID) to the one programmed into the lock's memory. After this occurs, the internal electronics typically activate a small motor, which turns a blocking rotor, worm gear, solenoid, or some form of magnetic system to allow the plug to turn. Many systems capture and store an audit trail of key insertions so access logs are created. Current lock designs typically require power to store such information.

Many locks can be attacked mechanically to circumvent the hardware responsible for securing the plug against rotation, just as in traditional cylinders. Attacks can include bumping, rapping, using a shim to access a critical component, and compromising the reset system. Some locks can also be attacked electronically by spoofing the credentials and by a focused application of force. Reset timing windows can be exploited and allow attacks against relock elements. Magnetic fields can be applied to move critical components, and direct access to blocking elements can be achieved to neutralize the electronic security layer.

Information in this chapter relates specifically to defeating the components in electromechanical and electronic locks. It doesn't explore hacking techniques, which will become more prevalent as these systems are increasingly embedded in facilities. Many vulnerabilities in electronic locks have been demonstrated and publicized at DefCon, in the media, at lock-picking sites, and elsewhere. Those attacks aren't within the scope of this chapter and will be reserved for a later work.

Electronic-Based Locks: Common Design Vulnerabilities and Attacks

Electronic locks are subject to many unique forms of attack based on their specific hardware designs. The following vulnerabilities should be thoroughly explored because they lead to a rapid and, most often, nondestructive defeat of the mechanical components and electronic credentials. For design engineers, the problem with these methods is that they aren't obvious or readily apparent, so they're most likely never considered. They don't appear in the literature and are unknown by most manufacturers. Not addressing these issues in initial lock designs or upgrades can create a security vulnerability for covert and surreptitious attacks. A checklist of possible issues appears at the end of this chapter. The scenarios described were all identified in investigations conducted by myself and my colleague for different manufacturers.

Bumping and Rapping to Move Rotors

Many conventional and electromechanical locks can be bumped or rapped open, as described in Part V. This attack still presents a significant problem, even though many designs have been updated in electronic-based locking systems to mitigate the threat. Earlier versions of almost every lock were easily opened by applying energy to the mechanical key in the correct sequence. Major manufacturers developed shock fuses to detect and lock critical components when these attacks were attempted. Before these lock types had matured in design, it was relatively simple to open them through vibration, rapping, and bumping the lock's key or its face. Most manufacturers claim their locks can't be bumped or are highly resistant to such attacks. But even the latest iterations of these locks can be subject to these attacks, so it's incumbent on design and testing teams to determine whether any component can be affected by shock, vibration, or rapping. In my experience, many of these locks can be defeated after the battery in the key is removed.

Attacks Against Electronic Elements Blocking Movement

Electronic-based locking systems must contain some form of blocking devices and actuators that release those devices. They prevent mechanical components, which can be accessed by a user, from being moved. Unless an actuator receives the requisite signal from the electronic control unit to release the blocking mechanism, it can only be moved to a locked or unlocked position by circuitry controlled and authenticated by a valid credential. This credential can be in the form of a key, a card, or a token, or by some type of wireless system. This process allows users to turn (or slide) a mechanism to extend or retract a bolt, latch, or other system. Depending on the design of the actuator and release mechanism, these systems can be vulnerable to different attacks.

In electromechanical locks with traditional bitted keys combined with an electronic element, the blocking elements can be of various designs. They're usually a motor or some form of magnetic field, including a solenoid. They may release a cam associated with the plug or retract or move a pin. In one magnetic-based approach by Yebo Tech, the cam at the plug's end is freely spinning until it engages a clutch after a valid key has been presented (European patent [EP] 1 960 622 B1).

The utilization of a small motor is the most common design. It can take the form of a worm gear or a tiny unit that rotates some kind of blocking element to prevent movement of the plug until an authentication signal is received. Attacks against motors can take many forms. They may involve gaining direct physical access to the blocking element that the motor controls. The application of rotational energy against a mechanism linked to a worm gear, such as the actuating knob outside a door lock, transmits the motion to move a latch or bolt. Motors can be moved by induced vibration, rapping, or magnetic fields.

Care should be taken in the design and placement of motors to protect against mechanical and electrical attacks. The design of printed circuit boards must ensure that there isn't a way to run a shim through any feedthrough holes to manipulate and move rotors directly. Attention must be paid to the motor's direct power input. The defeat of a popular electromechanical lock was inconceivable to the engineers responsible for its design. The attack required a special key with an embedded shim and could be executed in seconds.

If blocking elements are free-floating, they can often be vibrated or rapped to an unlocked position without triggering an audit trail or reset system, leaving no trace of the attack. Protective fuses or relocking systems can be implemented to guard against such an attack. Still, there's always a tradeoff in the sensitivity of these systems and how they respond to shock and vibration. If they're too sensitive, they can cause a lockout or malfunction. If they aren't sensitive enough, they won't be effective.

A worm gear is a motor-driven mechanism linked to a spring or threaded screw that moves as the motor is energized in a forward or reverse direction. Some form of interface to the gear part revolves as the motor turns. This element controls other parts that block or allow the actuator to function and permits locking or unlocking. The designs are simple in concept, allowing them to be easily defeated.

Worm gears are subject to an attack based on Newton's First Law of Motion if rotational energy can be applied to a mechanical element linked to the gear's movement. Typically this occurs in electronic cylinders with protruding free-spinning knobs that the user turns to lock or unlock a door when the correct credential is presented. Testing protocols against this defeat must be understood and executed properly to be valid. Such procedures aren't defined or enumerated in any lock standards. Worm gears can be defeated by rapid acceleration and deceleration in the correct sequence. Doing so advances or retracts the gear movement, resulting in a covert opening or locking without any audit trail.

Rotor Manipulation by Application of Energy

My colleague and I have evaluated many electromechanical lock designs and identified at least three vulnerabilities that can neutralize a blocking element moved by a motor. These attacks involve altering the rotor position by tapping and stepping, shim wire access, and shock and vibration to create a whiplash effect.

Rotors and movable locking elements are subject to attacks if energy is applied to the lock body using two different methods. In many designs, these elements are free-floating and not spring-biased. Their position can be altered by repeatedly tapping or vibrating the lock and applying the proper amount of force for each strike. If there's no internal design to protect against this attack, the electronics can be neutralized once the blocking element has been moved to an unlocked position. A variation of the application of controlled force is more violent and creates a form of reverse movement consistent with Newton's Third Law of Motion. Applying a focused, staccato set of strikes can cause elements to move in some locks.

The direct wire-manipulation attack requires the preparation of a special key configured to allow precise placement of a shim that can be extended and retracted once the key is inserted into the target lock. It only works if there's direct access to the rotor, usually through a feedthrough hole in the circuit board. The procedure allows the operative to insert a key with the wire retracted to the special key's surface. Once inserted, the wire is then pulled back to extend upward and at the proper angle to exactly mate with the hole in the printed circuit board immediately underneath the rotor. The wire then moves the rotor to its unlocked position. After that occurs, the electronic-controlled element is neutralized, so only the bitted mechanical key becomes active.

Piggyback Attacks

Electromechanical locks employ a traditional bitted key that controls detainers and an electronic credential, normally in conjunction with a sidebar. The security of these cylinders consists of multiple layers that must be accessed simultaneously. An electronic reset mechanism times out after a few seconds once a valid key is inserted, turned, and removed. If the reset system and sidebar are circumvented, the lock may be vulnerable to improper or unauthorized access.

In some cylinder designs, it's possible to execute what we call a "piggyback" attack. It is so named because it relies on an electronic credential's physical and electrical linking from one key to a bitted portion from a second key. The exploit requires using the proper electronic credential for the target lock with a specially modified mechanical key portion providing sidebar access. It must have a small channel to allow a shim to run along its length or to provide access to a channel precut within the lock's cylinder wall adjacent to the sidebar. Neutralizing the sidebar and the reset mechanism can defeat these cylinders.

This is a sophisticated attack based on several steps that can provide access to a target cylinder via a mechanical key without electronic credentials. The security and legal ramifications are significant, as one benefit of electronic-based systems is the options and features programmed into each lock, which rely on the electronic credentials of a key rather than its bitted portion. Many or all locks in a system may have the same bitting combination. Suppose a lock can be altered through a piggyback attack. In that case, there's no accountability for *any* mechanical key that can open that lock because the electronic credentials are no longer present and have become irrelevant.

The two critical procedures to perform for this attack are the placement of a shim and interrupting communications between the key's electronic element and the processor within the lock. A shim is inserted to neutralize the sidebar by turning the plug slightly with the correctly bitted key and then applying torque to remove the authorized key immediately and replace it with a key with no electronic component. At the same time, the electrical contact on the key that normally communicates with the processor is either disabled or shorted out, thus disabling the communications that would normally occur.

A manufacturer can claim that opening one of these cylinders is impossible without concurrently using an electronic credential and a bitted key. In my experience, that is incorrect based on certain design flaws that allow the sidebar and reset system to be disabled once the attack is executed.

Once the attack is completed, the lock functions properly with *any* mechanically bitted key. No electronic credential is required, and no audit trail is produced. The lock, in effect, reverts to a conventional cylinder. This is possible because the reset mechanism that's normally active is circumvented, signaling to the processor that the authentication process is complete and the electronic-controlled block has been reset.

The lock manufacturer changed its design to block access to the sidebar in the locks examined after this attack was discovered. The attack can be more complex if a simulated bitting of the key is implemented. This capability is discussed subsequently.

Replicating the Original Mechanical Key Bitting

It is often difficult to obtain blanks to reproduce mechanical bitting, especially if they're restricted or utilize different keyways. This is required to facilitate an attack on a system by duplicating different bitting key codes for an electromechanical lock. There are several ways to create a simulated or duplicate key that can properly mate with the mechanical portion of the lock. An original metal key can be modified for different locks with individual bitting codes, or keys can be simulated in metal or plastic.

Dimple pin tumbler locks are particularly vulnerable to this type of attack. A channel must be created longitudinally across the bitting surface to allow an insert made of plastic, nylon, or metal to replace the original bitting code. Once accomplished, the special key can be inserted into a key machine and cut to the required bitting code. The insert is then replaced and recut to alter that code for another lock. This process allows a blank to be reused to attack different locks in a system. As noted in Part V, keys can also be reproduced in various materials, including metal and plastic.

A Modified Piggyback Attack: Drilling to Create Access to the Motor

Depending on the cylinder's design and anti-drilling protection, a tiny hole can often be drilled through the plug, allowing shim insertion alongside the sidebar to neutralize it. In typical attacks of this type, the wire segment is "deposited" into the lock once the plug is turned to the correct angle. When the plug is returned to its home position, the wire remains in the channel until removed. It doesn't affect the normal operation of the key or the lock. This attack allows the use of a key that doesn't contain electronic credentials – only the valid bitting code.

This technique can be distinguished from the piggyback attack in that a fully credentialed key containing an electronic element is *not* required, but a properly bitted key must be employed. This hybrid forced entry attack isn't detectable unless the lock is disassembled. A custom tool is required for the procedure and is specially designed as part of a key that must perform two functions. The tool is a drill jig for the placement of a tiny drill bit, which is precisely placed at the exact angle required to intersect with the rotor through the plug's wall. It must also raise and neutralize a relocked pin.

The special key is positioned in the keyway to carry out this procedure. First the drill bit is placed into the jig and positioned to make an angled hole by drilling through the plug. The hole allows the rotor to be manipulated, which normally blocks the sidebar's action. The rotor is then manipulated to an unlocked position. A tension wrench is placed in the keyway to apply torque, the jig key is removed, and a noncredentialed key replaces it. The sidebar is then trapped through the shim's relock control. The torque application is required; otherwise, the reset mechanism would physically reset the rotor.

The key is correctly bitted for the mechanical portion of the lock and has a milled groove along its side edge in which to insert the shim wire to neutralize the sidebar. The reset system is then manipulated.

The piggyback and modified exploits are classic hybrid attacks requiring a careful examination of each critical detainer involved in blocking the sidebar's action and the reset mechanism's release. Although these attacks may seem complicated, they can be executed rapidly and pose a significant security vulnerability for high-value targets. The fact that no current security standards define them makes them even more troublesome, as design teams rarely contemplate these attacks.

Magnetic Fishing and Shim-Wire Movement

In some earlier cylinder designs, an attack could defeat the sidebar by fishing a wire to the critical mechanism using a magnetic field. This defeat was possible because manufacturing created an open channel and such an attack was never contemplated. The attack required a properly bitted and credentialed key to be inserted and rotated 90 degrees. Protective mechanisms were later implemented to block such access, but they were insufficient to mitigate the threat. A syringe-type delivery system was developed with a magnet to fish the shim wire to the lock's center to reach the critical component. A piggyback attack could then also be executed. The same theory was implemented with a shim wire segment deposit to neutralize the sidebar. The net result is that the lock opens without any electronic credentials.

In practice, a wire is deposited through a syringe to the back of the plug and dropped into place. The plug is rotated until the wire can be aligned with the sidebar slot in the shell and moved into that opening. The magnetic wire then fishes the piece of shim to the front of the cylinder, which neutralizes the sidebar's operation. A traditional mechanical key can now operate the lock. The result is three different key types: the properly bitted and credentialed key, a properly bitted key without a battery, and a key with the proper bitting and no electronic credentials.

Direct Electrical Access to the Motor

There are many instances of a lock with any type of motor drive that can be defeated by directly accessing the electrical connection of the power leads. I have noted this design issue in consumer digital door locks and with the most sophisticated electromechanical cylinders and small safes installed in hotel rooms. The ability to circumvent the power supply to a motor or solenoid presents a significant vulnerability that is often difficult to detect and is overlooked during the design process.

Many locks employ plastic to shield electronic components. If a power lead can be reached by drilling and feeding an insulated wire to the critical point on a printed circuit board, the lock may easily be opened. This is especially true with electromechanical cylinders, where the blocking rotor can be electrically manipulated to an open position.

A tiny 1/32" hole is created through the plastic body and keyway for this purpose and then slightly enlarged. In many cases, the wire's placement isn't critical. Therefore, care must be exercised in the layout of a printed circuit board to ensure that the runs aren't accessible from outside the lock. If a properly bitted key is utilized with this simple attack, the lock can be opened without any audit trail. Any such lock design must assess the potential of directly connecting to a run and possible drill points that provide access to power the motor or the driver chip energizing the motor circuit. The keyway is often the most vulnerable point because of the use of plastic, which can easily be pierced with a drill bit at the proper angle.

The lock's body is usually at ground potential, so only one power lead with a positive polarity is required. A carrier key is designed with a predrilled hole to guide the drill's path through the plug to the printed circuit board. The wire is routed through the same hole, and a modified key with the correct bitting is inserted. The lock can then be opened. This is a silent attack that isn't easily detected without disassembly. The lock's operation isn't affected by a mechanical bitted key or the normal credentialed key.

Auto Reset of Relock Exploit

In some electromechanical locks, an automatic reset occurs after several seconds. This function can be exploited if other systems aren't properly protected, and it should be considered in a security assessment because it controls the rotor and, indirectly, the sidebar. The operating system software will characteristically time out after a few seconds when it's assumed that the user has inserted and removed their key. The reset's purpose is to change the state of the rotor and return it to a locked position, which is critical because the lock can remain unlocked if the reset system is defeated. This is like the attack against the iLOQ cylinder, discussed in Part VI as a case study, where the reset mechanism was physically disabled and allowed any key to work.

We have analyzed designs where if a valid key remains inserted and a timeout occurs, torque can be applied to the plug and the key removed. In this sequence, the relocker is trapped and can't release the rotor because the sidebar traps the motor. A special key with a slot and a piece of wire must then be inserted and rotated to cause the wire to drop into the sidebar channel. Once completed, any properly bitted key will open the lock. Attention must be paid to how the reset system is programmed and what it controls due to the possibility of altering the action of critical components to result in covertly reconfiguring the lock's operation.

Exploiting Reset Functions in Electromechanical Locks

A special jig key must be created to exploit this type of vulnerability. This attack targets a potential design defect involving reset mechanisms that block the sidebar from working until an opening cycle is properly completed. Common in electromechanical cylinders, these systems are vulnerable if not executed properly because they control how the sidebar works. The scheme can bypass electronic credentials by using any key for a particular facility or system as a drill guide. This provides direct access to manipulate the movable blocking element rotor.

A design issue that allows the relocker to be trapped can often be exploited. In this attack, the locking cycle is interrupted *electrically* with a small shim wire. The battery can also be removed to accomplish the same step to fool the processor into believing that the cycle has been completed.

In practice, a properly bitted and credentialed key is inserted into the cylinder and turned, and the communications contacts are interrupted. Torque is then applied to the plug as the key is removed to maintain the status of the sidebar and relocking system. Another key is then immediately inserted and turned, providing direct access to the functionality of the cylinder. This second key has the correct bitting but no electronic credentials.

The rotor is left in the open position. The only action that causes locking is removing the original key. When this operation is completed, any mechanical key or simulation can turn the plug and allow access to other components. The goal of this exploit is to open locks in a system without the required electronic credential. Only a properly bitted key is necessary.

Drilling for Rotor Access

The rotor that performs the blocking function can be directly accessed by drilling a small hole and manipulating it with a fine wire shim. A special jig key is created from a mechanical key that guides a tiny drill at the proper angle to reach the rotor. In many electromechanical locks, plastic is used throughout to shield critical components. It makes them easy targets because it's simple to penetrate the locks with a few turns of a drill bit by hand. Once a hole is created, a shim wire can be inserted to move the rotor to an unlocked position, and the lock can be opened with any properly bitted key.

Drilling to Force the Sidebar to Retract

In many electromechanical locks, the sidebar must be retracted by the proper key bitting and released by the action of the blocking rotor once it receives a signal from the processor that the key's been validated. It's possible to drill a small hole to reach the rotor directly, but in such an attack, the mechanism that creates the sidebar block must be released before the lock can be opened. The goal of this attack is to be able to insert any properly bitted key without any electronic credentials and open the lock. Although the sidebar properly aligns with the detainers' gates when a valid mechanical key is inserted, it can't retract into the plug until the block from the rotor is fully released. The sidebar can be forced into position by dropping a small wire into the channel that provides physical blocking. Once that occurs, a properly bitted and authenticated key is again inserted into the plug and turned so the wire moves to the correct position.

After that action is completed, any mechanical key with the correct bitting will open the lock. This is a one-time detectable attack that leaves forensic traces. The process requires a special key to guide the drill bit into the plug. The lock can then be set for unauthorized entry later and function properly with its regular key. To open the lock with a mechanically bitted key, torque must be applied to force the sidebar to retract. The wire insert's function is to allow force to be applied to the sidebar.

The lesson for design engineers is to analyze the protective mechanism of the rotor and how it can be forced to move. This isn't assessed as a highly reliable attack, but it deserves notice because it can compromise a cylinder. Insiders or others can set a lock for an unauthorized opening at any time. All of the attacks described in this chapter are design flaws that could lead to security breaches and are important to consider. They may seem esoteric and remote, but they constitute real threats to the design of many electromechanical cylinders.

Potential Design Vulnerabilities to Review

The following hardware and software designs and configurations should be analyzed to ensure that they protect against the exploits identified in this chapter. This list involves access to critical components and certain software parameters that can create vulnerabilities:

- How can credentials be bypassed?
- Can the functionality of credentials be split between software and hardware?

- Can keys be simulated to replicate valid credentials?
- Can shims or magnets directly access and manipulate the blocking rotor?
- If there are free-floating parts, are they subject to shock, vibration, bumping, or rapping to move their position?
- Can audit trails be defeated by removing the battery from the key or the lock?
- Can a credential be spoofed as part of a technique to open a lock?
- Can any form of the piggyback attack work with the current lock design?
- Does the current design rely on a relocking mechanism for a reset?
- Can a relocker be mechanically trapped in a position to prevent the sidebar from functioning?
- Can an electrical reset be forced to occur?
- Can torque be applied to trap a component in the reset mechanism?
- Can any exposed channels or slots in the lock body be exploited?
- Is it possible to insert a shim wire into any channel affecting sidebar operation?
- Is it possible to neutralize individual security layers to affect a lock opening?
- Can the lock be opened with one valid credential and a simulation of the other?
- Can one security layer be leveraged against another?
- Is it possible to bypass mechanical bitting components within a lock?
- Is there a method to control a relock system to defeat it?
- Can a rotor be moved to an open position other than with a key?
- Are detainers subject to rapping, bumping, or tapping to cause them to reach the shear line?
- How can you neutralize the sidebar's operation by inserting a wire?
- How do you simulate the bitting portion of a key and use that technique to produce multiple keys?
- Can you open a lock and defeat any audit trail of entry?
- Can the lock be opened by a correctly bitted key, coupled with shock or vibration, to bypass electronic credentials?
- Can a lock be preset to be opened by any properly bitted mechanical key?
- How can the sidebar be neutralized?
- How can the lock be set to bypass its sidebar?
- Can a lock be opened without any valid electronic credentials?

- Can you defeat a reset system using an electrical short circuit of contacts?
- How can a hybrid attack be executed with torque to the plug to neutralize the sidebar?
- Can you identify points to drill to enable access to critical components?
- Is there a direct power connection to a motor?
- What is the effectiveness of anti-rap or anti-vibration protection?
- Can a wire segment be used to apply leverage to a sidebar?
- How do you force a reset by destabilizing controlling circuits by injecting conductive liquids?
- Is it possible to bypass worm gears and solenoids by applying Newton's Laws of Motion?
- Are components secure against drilling through plastic or very thin metal barriers?
- How do you use a correctly bitted key and simulated electronic credentials to open a lock?
- How can a simulated mechanical key and correct electronic credentials be used to open a lock?
- Can two keys share electronic credentials?

The following chapters describe advanced attacks against high-security locks. Much of this material was derived from spending time with experts in different parts of the world who are known for their covert-entry tool designs. Many videos of demonstrations of these tools are contained in *LSS+*, the multimedia edition of *Locks, Safes, and Security*.

Advanced Attacks Against High-Security Locks

The compromise of high-security locks has always been a problem for law enforcement, government, intelligence agencies, and even locksmiths. Such locks can be difficult to open covertly because they're designed to resist attacks, especially by sophisticated actors. Lock manufacturers constantly refine their designs to keep up with the latest techniques against their products. Understandably, tool developers who produce instruments to defeat specific locks try to keep that information secret from the manufacturer.

The producers of sophisticated and expensive government-only tools don't want the exploits they devise and discover to become known to anyone other than their clients. This is for two reasons. First, the manufacturer will likely fix the problem if possible once it's aware, so these tools may not work properly. Second, others will copy the tool designs, reducing revenues. Patents aren't generally filed for these tools, so there's no way to protect intellectual property (IP) and prohibit copying and knockoffs. For designers, the investment in tool production and research is often very high.

I have had the privilege of knowing or working with a few covert-entry tool designers throughout my career. These designers have dedicated their lives and business models to analyzing locks and figuring out often ingenious ways to defeat them. They've pioneered unique tools and provided them to virtually every government agency that isn't prohibited from buying them due to export controls. They're recognized worldwide for their expertise and support of government missions against terrorists, spies, and criminal gangs. They include

John Falle and Addi and Sascha Wendt (Germany), Frederic Madelin (France), Clay and Harry Miller of Lockmasters (United States), Martin Newton of Safe Ventures (UK), and Aldo Silvera (France).

This chapter summarizes some of the most unique, clever, and effective methods to compromise lever and pin tumbler locks. It offers a roadmap to lock manufacturers about the tools and techniques they may not know so that countermeasures can be implemented. The methods are also instructive as an insight into developing secure locks and envisioning exploits often unimagined in the lock manufacturing industry.

Very few patents exist for the tools developed for this niche business because public disclosure isn't in anyone's interest. Lockmakers must recognize some of these unique methods because they relate directly to their devices' security. Manufacturers need to know about exploits against their highest-security mechanisms so they aren't misrepresenting them to their customers as being secure. It's also important for those who recommend, purchase, install, and rely on specialized locking systems to understand what's available to those intent on defeating them and the security risks involved.

Considerations in Developing Attack Strategies, Techniques, and Tools

Conceiving and developing attacks against specific locking mechanisms is often complicated because it simply hasn't been done before. High-security locks can appear invulnerable, so the task may initially seem daunting or even impossible. Creativity and knowledge of similar designs are critical to success in analyzing a lock. But that's only the beginning of the process because once possible bypasses are considered, they must be tested. This testing requires creating and prototyping tools, usually in high-tolerance processes that employ advanced manufacturing techniques such as electrical discharge machining (EDM).

EDM can produce intricate and precise shapes, often required for custom picking and decoding tools. For designers, an advanced understanding of materials and the capability of EDM and other manufacturing processes is essential to determine what tools need to be created and their technical parameters and functionality.

Once a prototype is created, it must be tested and refined before the final product is released to clients. This creation process often requires multiple iterations. Some locks have significant barriers for tool designers due to their precise construction and unique mechanisms that frustrate manipulation.

Tool designers initially examine a lock from many perspectives. Their experience with other locks that exhibit similar designs and characteristics is always a primary consideration. Exploits identified in Chapters 17 and 18 should be factored into any possible solution because they always form the basis of how to compromise every locking mechanism. Regardless of a lock design's complexity, all locks are based on the same principles insofar as primary components and what they must accomplish.

In addition to the issues described in Chapters 17 and 18 on destructive and nondestructive entry, the following basic exploit techniques and questions should always be considered before developing prototype tools:

- Are there any special tactical considerations for clients using tools developed to open locks?

- Are the proposed techniques to open a lock considered feasible or possible?

- What are all the possible methods to compromise all known attack vectors against a specific lock?

- What are feasible techniques for bypassing the security of a target lock, and how should you focus on viable possibilities?

- What's the most important goal for a specific client involving a target lock: opening time, forensic traces, or key production?

- What are the advantages and disadvantages of each proposed system?

- How much skill will be required to use a proposed system effectively?

- What are the system limitations for the proposed design?

- How fast can a lock be opened with the proposed system design?

- How should active locking components be analyzed in a locked and unlocked state, and how will they be controlled?

- What forensic traces might be created with any tool design? How is this issue critical for certain intelligence operations?

- Can you identify and determine the locking elements and what they accomplish?

- Will the proposed attack vectors give a false indication of readings or data that can invalidate the result?

- Can previously developed decoders be adapted to work with a target lock?

- Can a proposed tool design be stuck in the lock during an entry attempt?

- Can an estimated opening time be validly computed?

- Can audio and resonant frequencies be employed to measure components?

- Can advanced viewing devices, including borescopes and endoscopes with tiny fiber optic probes, gather critical information to produce a key or open the lock directly?

- Is there a way to create or add shear lines with comb picks and other methods?

- Can you employ the advanced use of shims and tools designed around shims, such as the core shim decoder, to open the lock?

- Is it possible to simulate credentials through variable key-generation systems and foil impressioning?

- Can decoding systems be developed based on feeling and detecting contact points and shear lines?

- Has the use of marking systems to indicate the contact between internal locking elements and keys been considered?

- How will detainers react to torque, pressure, movement, feel, and position at the shear line?

- Can you probe the position and measurement of pin tumblers in both the bottom and top chambers?

- Is there a way to measure the dimensions from the base of a pin tumbler to the shear line?

- Can marks be created and read from the interaction of moving components to yield usable information?

- Can individual depth increments be reliably decoded?

- Can electronic decoding systems measure or determine critical component placement or operation or decode and measure internal components?

- Can physical contact points be identified to aid in measuring and manipulating components?

- Are critical components tensionable?

- Can electrical probes be employed to detect and measure movable detainers?

- Can impressioning be accomplished with blank keys?

- Are multiple shear lines involved in the lock?

- What are the tolerances of the keyway and pin chambers that would allow shims to be introduced for the measurements of detainers or movement of components?

- Are there sufficient tolerances to insert shims between pin tumblers and chamber walls to permit measurements to be made?

- Is it possible to map contact points from within the lock with a special system such as lasers and a marking material like plasticine?

- Is it possible to determine the position of false and true gates and notches on security pins or by the symmetry of gates?

- What is viewable from outside of the keyway?

- What kind of shear line is used, and is it independent or isolated from the primary active locking components?

- What stops the plug from rotating?

- What mechanism unlocks the lock?

- How many detainers are in the target lock, and what is their design?

- Are protective shields blocking access to picks or other tools, such as the barrel and curtain designs in lever locks?

- Are any false notches, pins, or levers designed to give false indications during picking?

- Is it possible to develop a system to lift each pin during the picking or impressioning process to provide better and more controlled feedback on its location related to the shear line?

- Can a specially designed system be modified to work with different lock manufacturers and lock configurations?

- Does the target lock contain more than one system, such as the pump lock in Europe that requires multiple key actions before it can operate the mechanism?

- If lock picking is interrupted due to the nature of a covert operation and because of a specific lock design, can the operative return to the lock without losing the decoded information? In other words, is there any reset mechanism to prevent an attack requiring multiple visits?

- Does the target lock have any mechanical restrictions requiring a full revolution of the plug before a pick can be removed before decoding? Is there any relocking system to frustrate picking? Is there a limitation of turning the plug that can be circumvented so that decoding can occur and the picking tool can't be trapped?

- Does the lock have to be picked before it can be decoded?

- Are there any key-retaining mechanisms that can prevent picking or make it difficult?

- How many locks are on the target door? Do they require multiple pick and decoding tools to be used simultaneously?

- How many detainers are in the target lock, and can they be jiggled open?

- How many levers are in the design?

- Has the lock manufacturer implemented any changes to prevent using a pick or decoder tool? Can changes be circumvented if they've been incorporated based on a new tool release?

- Does the keyway contain complicated warding that could prevent using variable key-generation systems?

- Is there a geographic limitation for using a specific decoder on a target lock because only certain manufacturers are available in that region?

- Has accurate information been gathered to determine which tool will work on a lock?

- Can tension be applied to the lock to pick or manipulate the mechanism successfully? Are there any barriers to picking, such as the barrel and curtain, that require special two-in-one wheel picks?

- Does the target lock have any lockouts or a detector system that prevents using specific tools or foil impressioning?

Unique Design Approaches to Opening Lever and Pin Tumbler Locks

Designers of specialized nondestructive entry tools focus on the two primary lock types utilized in most parts of the world: the lever tumbler and the pin tumbler. Some hybrid versions are recognized for their high-security designs, including the disc tumbler; versions of laser track such as the EVVA 3KS and 4KS; and dimple locks by Keso, Mul-T-Lock, Assa Abloy, dormakaba, and other manufacturers.

Regardless of the lock brand, the primary attention for developing opening systems is always on decoding, picking, or impressioning mechanisms relating to the shear line. Using shims, applying pressure to detainers, generating keys, and having a marking system are fundamental to the designs discussed in the following pages. Specialized hardware for generating keys is analyzed, including variable systems, programmable bitting insert systems, exchange of bitting elements to build sections of a composite key, and foil impressioning systems. Electronic decoding systems are discussed in Chapter 23.

Pin and Cam Systems

The Pin and Cam system was developed by John Falle in 1991 for lever tumbler locks and was a revolutionary idea that essentially mechanized the impressioning process (see Figure 20-1). It improved the classic impressioning technique, which relies on using a blank key that is inserted into the lock and marked by each lever as it binds with torque application. The theory is that marking will occur whenever the lever is *not* aligned with the fence. In normal impressioning, the user must file a blank key where the marks appear and then repeat the process until there are no marks and bitting is created that matches the levers' position. The genius of the Pin and Cam system was that it offered the same functionality but in a more controlled and precise way.

The original concept for the Pin and Cam tool was based on a technique that Falle conceived and demonstrated for me in his garage in Jersey, the

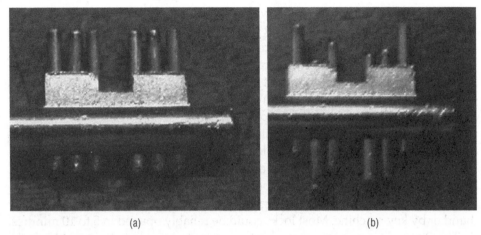

(a)   (b)

Figures 20-1a, 1b: This is the genesis of the Pin and Cam system for a lever lock. The key post is drilled for each lever position, and steel pins are inserted (a). They're moved during the impressioning process to replicate the bitting (b).

Channel Islands. He took the post of a lever lock key, drilled holes along its surface corresponding with the location of the levers in a test lock, and inserted nylon fishing line into each hole with a steel pin that replicated the key's bitting. With torque applied and the key rocking, the lock was opened in seconds.

TIP Watch the video I shot in the Czech Republic of some Russian locksmiths demonstrating this process with a lever tumbler lock: `https://youtu.be/-n0YdI g7Vuw`.

Developing the Pin and Cam system was a natural outgrowth of the original idea. The final tool was different in several important ways. Rather than pins of fixed length, a set of different pin lengths is provided with a tool for each lock or lock class based on the bitting values. As the lock is impressioned, different pin lengths are inserted until the correct one to match the bitting is determined. A hardened steel cam is positioned within the tip and directly below the pin. It is free to slide forward and backward. When the cam is rotated, the pin positioned directly above it is raised exactly .5 mm.

In practice, a user inserts the longest pins into each hole in the tip, replicating a blank key. With the tip fully inserted into the lock, torque is applied by twisting the tool. Each pin position can be tested by pressing a button on the tool that slightly elevates each pin through a camming system. If the feeling from the button is stiff, the pin length is incorrect. If there is play, the pin is in the correct position at the shear line. The pin segments are changed for each position until each yields a certain amount of play when tested. The tool design and concept are very versatile and can open many different locks based on changing the tip design and pin sets.

The Pin and Cam tool creates a variable key-generation system that can be adapted to most lever locks. It isn't affected by false notches, which cause difficulty in picking. One of the interesting advantages of using this tool is the ability to take readings over time rather than all at once. Thus, a covert team can make several passes at a target lock to read one or more tumblers, which only requires a few seconds. Once a lock is decoded, a key can be produced by reading the values of the different pin inserts.

The idea for the Pin and Cam system changed how lever locks were compromised and resulted in advanced pin-lock decoders for pin tumbler cylinders. Falle released many versions of the tool for most high-security lever locks in Europe. It was recognized for its ease and speed of operation and the ability to generate a working key directly by decoding the pin values and then creating a key by hand or by key machine. Most locks could be reliably opened in 5 to 10 minutes.

The Pin and Cam system has also been adapted to open disc tumbler locks such as Abus and Abloy, which have always proven difficult to compromise. The tool can be used as a pick to open the lock before the bitting values are decoded. This system works on any tensionable lever lock without regard to the number of levers.

It's important for engineering teams to understand the concept and technique and translate its operation to current or proposed locking mechanisms. An ability to change bitting values and apply controlled torque and pin elevation should be considered if the process could apply to defeating current designs.

The Universal Belly Reader

Another tool for decoding lever locks is the Universal Belly Reader, which is effective for any mechanism in which the levers fall to different levels. The operating theory of these systems is the use of a shim probe to determine positions. The tool is only a decoder and will not open the lock. The advantage of the system is that it can be used for numerous locks and those with or without a barrel and curtain protector. The downside is that the operator must return with a key after taking readings. These readings may not be accurate because they can apply to different lever sizes. In this event, several keys must be constructed to ensure that the correct bitting values are read. Opening speeds vary, depending on the time it takes to construct a key. Torque isn't required, so the decoding time is less than 2 minutes.

Pin-Lock Pin and Cam Systems

This system uses replicated segments of an actual key rather than insertable pins as required for the original Pin and Cam system (see Figure 20-2). The unit is self-contained and allows the operative to select the correct bitting pieces by moving a lever associated with each tumbler's position. The user inserts the decoder into the keyway and selects the lever to change bitting values. The process is repeated with multiple insertions until the correct code is determined. No calibration is required, and no forensic trace is left after decoding. The system uses the same principle as the original Pin and Cam by sensing the contact at the shear line.

(a)   (b)   (c)

Figures 20-2a–2c: This system contains all the different bitting values for a specific lock. Two versions are shown. Two versions are shown. In (a) the tool contains bitting segments for each tumbler position, which can be selected with a corresponding lever for each tumbler. In (c) individual components are inserted for bitting values.

Systems Based on the Use of Shims

Several unique systems are based on shims and the measurement of internal components and detainers in locks. The pin-lock decoder, core-shim decoder, and Medeco decoder are three examples that should be a warning to those responsible for designing locks that shims have been used to defeat even the highest-security mechanisms. Extremely thin shims can be routed around pin number chambers and can be very useful for accessing areas within a lock that are almost unimaginable.

The Basic Pin-Lock Decoder

The Falle basic pin-lock decoder is recognized worldwide as a unique way to open virtually all pin tumbler locks, irrespective of the number of pins in the plug (see Figure 20-3). The system also works with dimple locks and functions by measuring the length of the lower pins. A later generation of the Pin and Cam system combines the functionality of the pin-lock decoder and Pin and Cam. Information from the decoder can be used to construct a working key. The system is far more precise and much easier to use than picking or impressioning systems. No forensic trace is left within the lock.

In use, the needle tip is positioned upside down into the forward recess on the key blank. The decoder is then inserted into the lock so the pins and drivers are situated above the needle. The needle is rotated 180 degrees into its upright position, directly underneath and to one side of the pin to be measured. With the needle in this location, the inner gauge is pushed forward, forcing the fine shim wire up the side of the pin until it engages at the base of the driver at the shear line.

Figure 20-3: The pin-lock decoder, developed by John Falle, is a precision tool for measuring the length of bottom pin tumblers within their chambers.

Core-Shim Decoder

Also created by Falle, the core-shim decoder was initially designed to function with dimple pin tumbler locks but was modified to operate with conventional cylinders. This extremely innovative system relies on a simple technique known to most locksmiths: a shim is inserted into the rear of the plug between the plug and shell and then slowly forced across each breakpoint as a blank key is withdrawn. This procedure forms the premise for the core-shim decoder.

The tool was designed to circumvent the shear line in a pin tumbler lock. Core shimming works across all pins in a different sequence rather than serially, as with a blank key.

A tool introduces a shim through the bottom of the keyway to travel between the plug and shell. It is thin enough to revolve around the plug's outer circumference. Using a geared mechanism, it is forced to move from the base of the keyway 180 degrees to where the pin stack intersects the plug and shell.

The decoder consists of a hypodermic tube with two slots on either side of its tip. The distance to insert the tube can be calculated by reading the markings on the gauge body based on the specific lock, which allows precise determination of which tumbler is being probed. A slot is located on the side of the tube, where the blank key is inserted into the lock. Contained within the tube is a miniature gear that can be rotated by turning a knob at the rear of the tool. A micro-perforated shim, measuring exactly 10 mm long and 4.5 mm wide and resembling a 35 mm filmstrip, is fed into the slots. It can be extended and retracted using the gear.

In use, the shim and the tube are inserted into the keyway at a position as far to the right as possible against the inside of the plug. The shim is then extended around the outer ridge of the plug until it contacts the sides of the pins. If the diameter of the plug is known, the point at which the shim reaches the sides of the pins is always constant. A series of step keys are then inserted into the lock. When the correct bitting depth raises the target tumbler, the shim can be extended further between the pin and the driver, thus verifying the correct depth. Once the first pin has been decoded, the shim can be extended to the second pin, and the procedure is repeated for all pins and the plug can be turned.

The Medeco BIAXIAL Shim Decoder

Falle invented a decoding system for Medeco BIAXIAL locks in the 1990s; it was the first effective tool to compromise this high-security lock using a shim for measurements (see Figure 20-4). A syringe delivered a wire to each bottom pin. It then decoded the length by probing each pin chamber from the tip of the bottom pin to the shear line. The tool decoded the pins' lengths, yielding the bitting data to produce a key. It could determine the rotation angle of the pin, which yielded the sidebar code and whether the chisel point tips of the tumblers were positioned fore or aft.

The rotation angles, which my colleague and I named the *sidebar code*, originally could be determined by probing the channel that ran the length of each pin. Medeco recognized this vulnerability and changed the design of the bottom

Figure 20-4: The Medeco shim decoder tool.

pins to close the slot so it couldn't be decoded. This is a good lesson for lock designers because no one ever considered this potential, as it wasn't obvious. Once Medeco implemented its special security pins, identified as ARX (Attack Resistance X-tended), the system wouldn't work.

The tool's design wasn't effective on the Medeco cam lock, as described in Chapter 14. This is important to consider in analyzing the design of any high-security lock and whether the capability could exist to produce a working key.

The drawback to this system was the requirement that special key tips be used: one for the slot probe and one for the decoder. They're created from BIAXIAL key blanks and must be precise to work properly. The important issue for lock manufacturers is key control on restricted banks and the policies to prevent the use of keys for such decoding systems. Other systems have been designed around key blank tips and segments.

Material Impressioning System

Dimple pin tumbler locks can be easily impressioned using foil systems, some of which have been previously discussed. See Figure 20-5. Although there are locks that can't be impressioned with these systems, most can be rapidly opened. Foil is an excellent impressioning medium, far more responsive than hard metal keys. Other materials also work for this technique, but I have found that foil is the best. These systems require little skill or time to implement.

Figure 20-5: A dimple key can be impressioned with wax or plastic tape; the principle is the same as with metal foil.

The Bates impressioning system utilizes plastic tape, which is pressed over a dimple key containing a complete matrix of tumbler positions for a specific lock. When the key is pressed against the pins, the tape depresses in direct relation to its position on the shear line. The matrix may also be filled similarly with wax and impressioned.

A variation of this system utilizes the end of a plastic pen to impression small-format axial pin tumbler locks, such as those used on computer locks and alarm systems. The inner diameter of the keyway is almost exactly the outside diameter of some pens. The end of the pen barrel is inserted and pressed against the tumblers. Torque is applied, followed by forward pressure, causing plastic deformation to occur equal to the length of each pin below the shear line.

The process is repeated, as in the conventional impressioning technique, until each pin rests at the shear line. The plastic compresses equivalent to each pin's length. Many of these locks can be opened in a few seconds with essentially no skill level using a ballpoint pen.

Foil Impressioning System

This self-impressioning system utilizes foil as the medium to derive bitting values (see Figure 20-6). Once a key has been created with a foil overlay, it may be inserted into the lock a few times before the process forces the metal foil to deform equal to the pressure of tumblers at the shear line. These systems are unique to a specific lock and aren't universal. They may not yield accurate results for all locking systems.

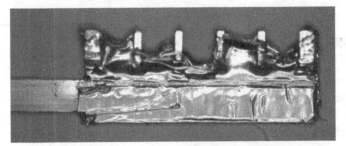

Figure 20-6: A key carrier with a foil overlay that has been impressioned for a pin tumbler lock.

Impressioning Lightbox

Impressioning marks can be difficult to read, especially in covert operations, so an *impressioning lightbox* was developed to make viewing marks easier to see and more efficient. A key blank is inserted into an opening on the box's side where it can be closely examined under three different light sources. The illumination is only visible to the user, allowing a lock to be impressioned in total darkness for certain operations. See Figure 20-7.

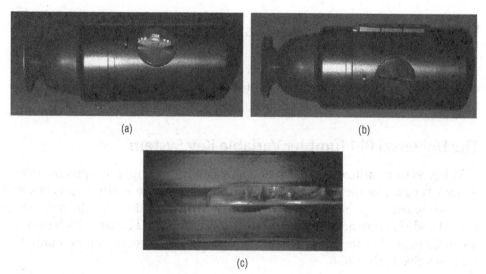

(a)   (b)

(c)

Figures 20-7a–7c: Several lightboxes have been designed for covert use. They provide viewing that is far better than during the normal process. (a) shows a device with a key inserted for viewing, (b) shows the control buttons for the LEDs, and (c) shows an impressioning mark that is visible on an inserted key.

Plasticine Reading Systems

This system can be employed to decode many lever tumbler locks. It's based on an impression of the lever bellies with a specially prepared key. The markings created by the levers can be interpreted to derive the bitting code. A variable key system can then be used to generate a key. (These systems were described in Chapter 15.) When a plasticine-coated key is inserted into a lever lock with nonlinear bellies, the material directly correlates, as a reverse image, to the dimension between the belly and the gate. From this information, a key can be decoded and produced because the amount of lift required for each lever is displayed. Plasticine allows decoding in both rotation directions.

Plasticine is an excellent medium for recording marks to indicate the detainer movement in a lock. Two methods exist to impression and decode a lever lock. A coated key may receive an impression of the levers at the initial point of contact (i.e., at rest) or as they're lifted to their maximum height. Two different readings may be taken depending on the lock, the type of levers, and whether the process occurred in the locked or unlocked position. Because the portion of the key that controls the bolt throw has already been removed, only the bitting that contacts the levers is present.

Each mechanism must be studied to use plasticine effectively, and a determination must be made about which technique provides the most information. Some lever packs always contain one particular lever that may have a special characteristic.

Variable Key-Generation Systems

Several systems have been developed to generate keys with movable segments or precut strips that can be fashioned to replicate a key. Special decoders like the Pin and Cam can also generate keys after decoding the lock.

The Universal Pin Tumbler Variable Key System

This key system utilizes precut metal sheets with multiple designs for over 50 lock types. The metal is very thin, allowing a key to easily bypass most keyway wards. A scissor cuts the keys to desired bitting depths once the correct code is known. Each key is only 0.2 mm thick and is flat, which means it can be jiggled in the keyway so that even incorrect codes can be made to function. See Figure 20-8.

Figure 20-8: A key produced with a variable system.

Reusable Variable Key Systems

This key system requires precut key segments for a specific keyway to be assembled as a complete key once the code has been derived. The system is reusable. A kit has individual segments for each bitting level and rotation (see Figure 20-9). The lock is decoded, and the proper segments are added to the key. They're held in place magnetically.

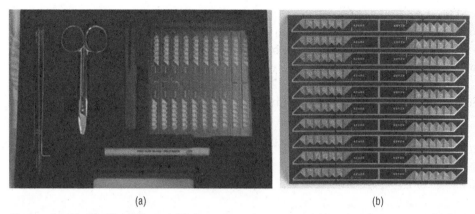

(a)   (b)

Figures 20-9a, 9b: The Falle variable key-generation system. (a) keys can be cut to any bitting value. (b) shows a blank strip of key blanks that can be easily cut with a scissor.

The composite resembles a key vertically sliced into segments, one for each chamber. A selection of all possible depths is provided in the kit, and a key is "built" by abutting the proper segments (see Figure 20-10). This system has the advantage of providing a precisely fitting key that does not have to be manipulated to operate the lock. A Japanese patent was issued in 1975 (Kokai No. 52-51298) for a magnetic segmented key system to open Medeco locks.

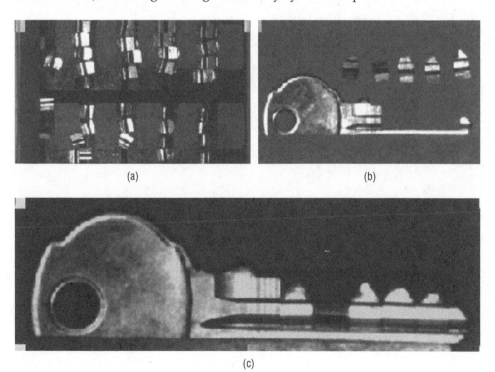

Figure 20-10a-10c: The Medeco lock's Falle magnetic key generation system. The kit contains a carrier and different inserts. (a) are individual key bitting segments that are magnetic, (b) is a carrier key, and (c) is a constructed key with different magnetic inserts.

The next chapter focuses on attacks on keys and special keying systems, including master keys. There have been many advances in compromising these systems, including using 3D-printing technology and electronic decoders. Locks are opened primarily by their keys. If the correct key code can be derived, a system can be defeated. Chapter 21 examines different approaches employed in attacks against keys and systems.

Attacks on Key Control and
Special Keying Systems

Compromising credentials and key systems is often the first line of attack against locks and security systems, as locks are always opened by some form of credential, whether mechanical, electromechanical, or electronic. Because it's vital to understand the different methods that can be employed to defeat a lock and keys, Part V introduces the various forms of keying systems and advanced methods to attack key control. A detailed discussion is presented on specialized software for 3D printers that can allow almost any mechanical key to be replicated, simulated, or duplicated. Unfortunately, many engineers are not thoroughly conversant with the current capabilities of 3D technology and how it can be applied to defeating most of the conventional and high-security locks that are relied on to protect people, assets, and facilities.

Yet the capabilities of 3D printing, as described in the following chapters, are only part of the security risk inherent in almost every mechanical and electromechanical lock. The introduction of handheld electronic scanners has allowed for the rapid and accurate decoding of locks and the data to produce keys from the bitting codes of a target lock, so I describe one of these scanners in detail. A complete understanding of the combination of 3D and scanning technology by every lock manufacturer that engages in some form of key control is vital to lock security.

The final chapter summarizes a case study of the defeat of one of the highest-security locks in the United States. It provides an insight into the evolution of a methodology that the manufacturer never conceived of, which resulted in the ability to defeat their locks worldwide. This summary offers valuable lessons for those tasked with creating mechanical systems that resist the ability to pick and bump their locks.

CHAPTER 21

Attacking Keys and Keying Systems

Keys are the primary credentials for all locks. The type of mechanism, whether mechanical, electronic, or electromechanical, dictates the forms of required credentials. The ability to compromise whatever opens the lock will defeat all the embedded security designed into any system. That is why manufacturers go to great lengths to protect keys, keying systems, and internal mechanisms from attacks that can neutralize any security enhancements related to keys and render the system vulnerable.

The capability to attack these systems depends on whether the lock is classified as conventional or high-security, as defined by applicable standards. Do internal mechanical designs make the simulation, replication, or duplication of a credential more difficult? For example, Medeco employs rotating pin tumblers and a second set of pins controlled by side bit milling in the key, making the keys more difficult to copy and the lock more complicated to pick, decode, bump, or impression.

Other manufacturers embed some form of a movable, interactive, or magnetic element and control multiple shear lines in their keys. Many years ago, EVVA developed its Magnetic Code System (MCS) with four embedded rare earth magnets in the key that mate with eight rotors in the lock. In another design, the lock had a magnetic wafer impressed into the key's surface, which mated with a corresponding magnetic pin inside the lock. All these features are meant to stop criminals, thieves, spies, or malicious actors from defeating a system through their credentials. But regardless of the design, unfortunately most can be easily circumvented.

This chapter is about vulnerabilities of keys and keying systems, including the design of keys and keyways, interactive elements, and their corresponding internal systems. It encompasses the interface with whatever security is designed into or embedded in the key, making it more difficult to either spoof the locking mechanism or manipulate it open through recognized covert techniques. Hybrid attack methods must be imagined and considered because using multiple attack vectors is to be expected, especially in more complex systems. This is especially important with the advent of advanced 3D printing capabilities to generate keys.

In an electromechanical system, where the credential consists of a mechanical and electronic element, each element must be neutralized separately. This may require that the functions of the key's mechanical portion (i.e., the bitting in whatever form) be split and separated from the part of the key containing the electronic credential.

Using this formula, my colleague and I have compromised many high-security designs. When an engineering team states that such an attack is impossible, they often do so because of a lack of understanding and failure of imagination. Both characteristics in engineers can be fatal to a lock design and the company that produces it.

Design engineers must consider and understand many recognized methods to defeat whatever they think is secure in their locks, keys, and key systems. The relevant considerations for these systems are explored in this chapter.

Summary of Attack Strategies Against Keys, Plugs, and Detainers

When analyzing the security of keys, bittings, and detainers, certain primary areas of inquiry can lead to discovering system design vulnerabilities. These areas are summarized next and discussed in detail in this chapter:

Credential simulation, replication, and duplication: It's essential to examine the ease of creating credentials by modifying similar blanks, creating keys from different materials, and 3D printing. How keys can be easily copied or duplicated is often the question.

Amplification of rights of credentials: Can keys be easily modified to alter their bitting values or keyway warding? Organizations that don't implement a physical key control policy are at risk if keys that are lost, stolen, deleted, or not accounted for can often be altered to open locks for which they aren't authorized.

Standardized keys and codes: Many industries offer keyed-alike locks for ease of maintenance or to facilitate access. This is common in utilities, transport, energy, and many critical infrastructures. A search should always be conducted to see if these keys are available online, especially for luggage, physical restraint kits, building access systems, disaster temporary housing, remote utility sites, and other applications.

Magnetic elements embedded in keys: Manufacturers embed magnets within their keys for added security, for secondary security layers, and to create virtual keyways. Depending on the sophistication of the magnetic designs, they can often be easily defeated.

Attacks against secondary mechanical locking systems as part of keys: Almost all high-security locks have secondary security layers involving complex key designs. To defeat these layers, a careful analysis must be conducted to envision the different attacks, especially hybrids.

Attacks against movable interactive elements: A huge variety of movable elements have been embedded into keys to increase the difficulty of copying or the simulation of original credentials. However, once an attacker understands how the elements function and integrate with internal mechanisms, it's often possible to simulate their actions. Many such designs have been defeated. This is especially problematic regarding patent-protected counterfeit blanks distributed and sold to local locksmiths. Such copies can defeat the security of the locks they're designed to protect against attack. In a major counterfeit investigation that I led in Taiwan that resulted in identifying a factory producing hundreds of thousands of knockoff blanks with movable elements, we discovered that the engineers had figured out how to make them work by circumventing the original patented design.

Attacks against primary or critical locking elements that interact with a key: Many primary locking elements can be compromised, especially with hybrid attacks. Sidebars, sliders, side bit milling, and special tumbler designs can be vulnerable. A careful analysis should be conducted to determine whether embedded design issues make these elements vulnerable.

Attacks against keyways and wards: Keyways and their wards can often be easily defeated with simulated blanks or blanks that that aren't designed for the target lock but can be milled to fit. Blanks can also be 3D printed or produced in plastic or other materials. In the case example of the Medeco code-setting keys, keys were produced from thin brass stock. Paracentric keyways can prove more difficult but can be circumvented similarly. Milling machines and the EasyEntrie machine make replicating blank keys trivial.

Intelligence from Locks and Keyways

Analyzing keys or a keying system is the easiest way to compromise critical locks controlling access to secure areas. Significant intelligence can be obtained about a lock or system from one or more keys and by examining lock cylinders, either externally or with an optical viewing aid such as a borescope, ophthalmoscope, or fiberoptic video camera. Usually, only depth and spacing data is involved once the manufacturer and keyway have been identified. Deriving critical information about high-security locks and keying systems can be significantly more complicated due to the addition of multiple security layers and more complex key designs.

Obtaining certain information can be critical to successfully compromising a lock and key system. An inquiry must begin with identifying the type of lock, keyway, and technical specifications. If intelligence can be gathered to yield key codes for the target locks, a key can be produced. Data about the type of master key system, the number of keying levels, and how the division between change keys and master keys is organized can aid in decoding master key bitting codes to compromise some or all locks in a system.

Research about how key blanks can be obtained or generated and how properly cut keys can be produced is crucial. Many conventional locks have nonrestricted keyways that are easily obtained from locksmiths, hardware stores, or Internet vendors. Many keyways are similar, and a key can often be modified to work in a lock with a slightly different keyway or ward pattern. It's also possible to evaluate the keyway's design, which can lead to the production of a key blank that bypasses all the wards. Complex ward patterns, especially in paracentric keyways, can be defeated using very thin pieces of brass or other material that slide between the wards in the keyway.

Much of the information needed to compromise a system can be derived by examining one or more keys in a system. If the target is a key that opens a master keyed lock, the cylinder and evaluated key should be common to the same master key system.

Critical information and system intelligence can be derived about many important parameters from an analysis of locks and keys. Such an analysis can be simple and may only require the physical examination of one or more keys in a system, taking a short amount of time to accomplish. Gathering information can take many forms, from visual inspection to taking a high-resolution photograph with a smartphone. It can be a physical impression of a key as well. A specially designed key micrometer, or other tools to read and display depth information, can directly decode a key in seconds. These and other techniques may all be necessary to defeat a system's security.

Developing system information and intelligence can help answer preliminary questions that engineers may raise in evaluating a design by a covert-entry operative. Initial questions may include the likelihood of picking, impressioning, or decoding a lock, such as the following:

- Can the lock be bumped open?
- Can the top-level master key be easily extrapolated?

- Is there a way to compromise key control procedures?

- Can the rights associated with bitting values be amplified?

- Will a hybrid attack be necessary, or even possible, if there are multiple security layers?

- Is there a simple method to mechanically bypass the lock or the system without replicating the key?

- Does the system have a sidebar or side bit milling codes common to all keys?

- Can any internal components within the lock be viewed externally that will provide relevant information?

The following data can be derived from the inspection of one or more keys and an external analysis of one or more locks in a system.

Lock Manufacturer

Often, the lock manufacturer's name and a key blank number are stamped on the key head. This information can simplify the acquisition of key blanks. Manufacturer numbers may also be cross-referenced if the examined keys aren't original blanks, which is often the case. The key head's design can be important in identifying the original manufacturer. Many comprehensive reference manuals provide a master listing of thousands of keys, keyways, and manufacturers.

Signature of the Keyway

The signature of a keyway, which is an image of the profile, can often be easily identified through key code programs and key blank reference books. If the keyway is proprietary or restricted, it may not be referenced. If the keyway can be identified, it can yield information about the manufacturer and possibly the number of pin tumblers or other detainers. Often, the blank number is stamped on the key head.

Special Industry Keys and Identification Data

Many keying systems have identification numbers that allow keys to be acquired from online vendors, locksmiths, and manufacturers. These include power and utility cabinets, Transportation Security Administration (TSA) luggage locks, emergency housing in trailers by the Federal Emergency Management Agency (FEMA), control panels, access-control systems, building intercom systems, and many low-security applications. These numbers identify keys and specific bitting values that allow the compromise of certain systems.

Key Codes and Other Data Stamped on Keys

Direct or indirect key codes may be stamped on the faces of keys and padlocks. These codes can provide information that leads to producing a valid key. Indirect codes, especially for padlocks, can be found in multiple reference books to provide the direct code for the bitting. Other information may also appear on the surface or key head, including a customer number that can be used to obtain keys copied by unauthorized individuals. Information may also indicate the level of the master key system to which the key belongs.

The Key's Physical Design

A key's physical characteristics can offer a clue about the type of master key system, if one has been implemented. The two primary keying types are those that use some form of *progression* or rotating constant of bitting positions and those that are *positional*. An analysis of multiple keys in a positional system can yield critical master key information because the master key combines the bitting positions for individual keys. There are no master pins in the positional keying system. I investigated a major hotel's master key system that used a barium ferrite vinyl magnetic key card and a positional master key system. The grand master key was decoded by analyzing the lock data from 25 rooms. The case is discussed in Part VI.

The Key's Bitting Data

Critical information can be derived from examining the key's bitting values and correlating them to internal components within the matching cylinder. This information includes the following:

- Position of each active locking component on the bitting surface
- Number of active locking components
- Depth of each bitting position
- Spacing between chambers
- Design or shape of each active locking component
- Presence of security enhancements such as mushroom tumblers, false gates, serrations, movable elements, interactive components, sidebars, or side bit milling

Movable Elements

A physical key can also offer information about the design of movable elements and how they work inside the lock. Many types of interactive elements exist. Some are fixed, whereas others move vertically within the key's surface and can extend above the key when inserted into the plug. They can be designed to slide or depress within the key.

The physical placement of movable elements can be determined from the key. A manufacturer can alter their position to create added virtual keyways or heightened security. Mul-T-Lock began this practice many years ago by changing the placement of interactive elements to different bitting positions. The company also changed physical characteristics to deter the use of counterfeit copies. For design engineers, the important issue is how the elements function and how easy the scheme is to defeat. This translates directly to the ability to replicate keys and how a system can be defeated.

Magnetic elements are becoming popular in key design due to their unique characteristics. Although they may appeal to design engineers because of these special capabilities, they can provide attackers with information about their placement and polarity. This information can subject them to compromise and lead to counterfeit key production. Some elements mate with their counterpart in the lock to be attracted or repelled, depending on the orientation of the magnetic fields. The polarity of these elements is easily determined with electronic probes, such as a Gauss meter or even a magnetized needle suspended above the key's element.

My colleague and I evaluated one very clever implementation whereby a fixed magnetic wafer was placed in a certain position on the key's surface. A corresponding element was then mated with it inside the lock. The design was for the two elements to attract each other and then move and retract the internal component to allow the plug to turn. However, there was a fatal problem with this concept. A strong magnetic field could be placed around the key head, causing the same result as the placement of the correct magnetized wafer in the key. Placing a magnet near the key head negated any security advantage such a design offered.

The Number of Pin Tumblers, Discs, or Wafers

A physical examination of a key provides information about the number of detainers that may be present in the lock. This information indicates the overall difficulty of picking, bumping, or impressioning but does not provide relevant data about the actual bitting code.

Correlation Between Physical Key Design and Master Key Systems

If the keying system is based on a positional master key system, the number of detainer positions may not reveal specific bitting information. This is particularly true with dimple locks, such as those offered by Keso and dormakaba.

The number of dimples can denote a change key or a master key, depending on the total number of pin positions on the key's surface. Dimples can also be placed on other key surfaces, including the edges opposite the primary bitting. These are often used to create virtual keyways and are a form of positional system in that some dimples may not be active.

Conventional master key systems are based on the placement of master pins to create different shear lines for each keying level. Their coding involves defining a *key bitting array (KBA)*, which denotes the actual bitting and division between change and master key codes. How the KBA is defined is important for reverse engineering a system based on analyzing several keys in the same system. It's possible to derive the keying sequence, which yields critical information about the definition of the master key. The master key can often be derived, depending on the progression in the KBA.

Depth and Spacing

Depth and spacing information can be determined with a key micrometer or gauge from different manufacturers. These tools are readily available and can display critical depth increment information and other parameters in the case of high-security locks. Key machines automatically measure a key with lasers, providing immediate information about depth and spacing.

The center-to-center spacing between bitting cuts can be measured. This depth and spacing information indicates the total number of divisions for each bitting position (i.e., depth increments) and the vertical spacing between each depth increment for a specific system. Whether the system is set for odd or even keying progression in the assignment of individual key coding can indicate how a master key system is defined. Identifying depth increments can reveal the required number of system test keys needed to probe each chamber for the top-level master key. Keys can be visually decoded to extrapolate the number of depth increments and the bitting code for a target key. This can be done with the physical key in hand or from a photograph. Direct codes can be derived from indirect codes stamped on a lock or key using reference sources.

This data indicates how a master key system may be configured and the tolerances that can be exploited for tryout keys. The information can guide key cutting during the impressioning process. Depth and spacing information, combined with the number of active pin tumblers or other detainers, can also provide the total number of theoretical differences or key combinations available for the specific lock. Information about plug-shell tolerances can provide an approximation of the number of real key changes and the ability to approximate bitting values in tryout keys.

Information about depth and spacing and the manufacturer and specific lock data can indicate restrictions for maximum adjacent cut specifications (MACS), which can affect the total number of useable combinations and indicate pick resistance.

Decoding Depth and Spacing Information

Once accurate depth and spacing information has been acquired, the actual bitting code for the key can be determined. Other secondary locking system parameters may also be found if the key is for a high-security lock. During an investigation, this data can determine the location and facility where the system for the target key is utilized. Depending on the security level, a manufacturer may be able to search its database to identify and match a specific location to a key. If a manufacturer assigns secondary locking system codes such as side bit milling to individual locksmiths, a key can be traced to that locksmith, depending on the geographic assignments.

Decoding provides the means to produce a key when an original is unavailable. The process can take many forms, both mechanical and electronic. Often, picking or impressioning must be accomplished before code information can be derived. In some cases, traditional forms of bypass aren't an option, thus making decoding necessary. In certain instances, disassembly of the lock may be required. There are four primary reasons to decode a lock or its key:

1. Production or simulation of a key for immediate use

2. Derivation of code information for later production or simulation of a key

3. Derivation of information that allows the determination of code patterns for a system

4. Derivation of information that allows the production of keys other than for the target lock

Two primary sources for gathering bitting data through decoding are the *key* and the *lock*. In essence, decoding involves a process wherein the key is analyzed or the lock's internal components are examined for their number, position, and measurement. The decision about which technique to use to produce a key, either directly or from derived bitting data, depends on many factors and questions.

For Keys:

Is the target key available? Can keys be copied by physical duplication using a key machine or 3D printing? Are key blanks readily available, or will molds, milling, or other techniques be required to simulate restricted keyways? Is key code information readily available from internal lists, manufacturers, locksmiths, or other sources? Can an impression be made from the target key and then either decoded or used to create a duplicate?

For Locks:

The information derived from decoding a lock can provide data about active locking components, the type and coding of pin tumblers, the length of pin stacks and secondary security layers, and the required key design. There are different procedures to gather this information, depending on the ability to gain access to the cylinder to conduct an analysis. It's possible to scan the lock using a piezo or ultrasonic measuring system to learn detailed information from inside the lock. I define two approaches for gathering such information: external and internal analysis.

External procedures pick, decode, electronically scan, or visually examine internal components without removing the cylinder or requiring disassembly. They can involve extrapolation of the top-level master key or the use of system keys if certain prior intelligence is available. The relevant question is whether disassembly is necessary or even possible. The lock's design will dictate whether a pick-and-decode tool can provide the necessary information or whether traditional impressioning techniques are an option to produce a working key.

An *internal analysis* can be carried out in stages, again depending on the circumstances of the operation and whether it must be covert. If the cylinder can be removed, even temporarily, the simplest and least intrusive method can be a partial disassembly, which entails removing the plug endcap to allow shimming of the shear line or releasing the staked strip or set screws that seal each pin chamber. Access to each chamber allows the pin stack to be measured by removing whatever mechanism is employed to seal the chambers.

Depending on the lock's design, a shim can be inserted from the back of the plug and advanced, catching each pin at its breakpoint. If a blank key is advanced from the plug, separating the pins will allow the plug's removal using a following tool. A *following tool*, or *follower*, is a piece of metal or wood that is the exact same diameter as the plug and is inserted into the lock to physically replace the plug as it's removed from the lock. The tool's purpose is to keep all the top pins in the shell so they don't fall out when the plug is removed. Once the plug is removed, a key can be fitted to the pins, and any master pins can be calculated for the bitting of master keys.

The other option is to shim the lock in combination with depth keys that have been precut for each depth increment. This is a rapid way to decode the lock and can quickly yield the bitting combination without running the risk of total disassembly.

Depending on whether mechanical or electronic procedures are utilized, the following information can be available:

- For each component, the position or distance from or to the shear line
- Number of active locking components, which can be especially important in a positional keying system
- Position, angle, magnetic polarity, or other feature of each component that provides security for the locking mechanism
- Length, exact dimensions, and material composition of each active component
- Shape or angle of each component
- Individual tumbler marking, identifying depths

Manufacturer-Imposed Rules About Bitting and Key Codes

It's important to understand certain manufacturer restrictions describing how they establish valid bitting codes. Certain systems can be defeated because of internal mechanical limitations related to the interaction between key bitting and internal detainers. Medeco is a prime example. The BIAXIAL has certain prohibited bitting combinations between the fore and aft values because some are interchangeable. This means a key with one cut can open a different combination. Although this is a rare event, it can be a problem in certain systems if the definition of the keying program is done incorrectly.

Information Appearing on the Lock Face

Information may be imprinted on the lock face that can yield important clues about the keying system. This may include a manufacturer name (or no name), keyway, security designation and rating, profile type or identification, the type of keying system, trademark indication, and lock vintage and version. Interchangeable-core, reprogrammable, and standard configurations can also be easily determined.

A name printed on the lock can indicate the quality, tolerance, and security rating, whether it's a conventional or high-security lock, the keyway, and the availability of bypass tools. If there is no manufacturer name, it can be inferred that it's a knockoff of a primary brand and possibly of substandard quality and security. A knockoff can provide a clue about whether the lock can be easily picked or bumped open. The keyway may be easy to extrapolate, especially for the most popular brands such as Kwikset, Weiser, and Schlage.

There may be a stamped indication of the vintage and security level on the lock. Medeco, for example, provides different logos and trademarks to indicate BIAXIAL, m3, and M4 cylinders. This information provides specific indications about the internal security layers, how the keys are configured, bypass capability, possible restriction levels in obtaining blanks and cut keys, and system information. Whether the lock is rated for high security by Underwriter's Laboratory (UL) or the American National Standards Institute (ANSI)/Builders Hardware Manufacturing Association (BHMA) also appears on its face.

If the system is determined to utilize interchangeable-core technology, the size can indicate whether it's a small- or large-format system. This offers insight into how to defeat or decode the lock's control key portion, including how many pin tumblers are active in the control key.

A special security feature and trademark may be present that clearly defines the system's security rating. With side bit milling, Schlage imprints "Primus" on the plug to denote its high security.

Master Keys and Keying Progression

Analyzing several system keys and their depth and spacing information can provide clues about odd or even programming for pin tumblers and the keying progression and division between change and master keys. This information can potentially allow the extrapolation of master keys. If enough sample keys are available, they can offer clues about the type of master key system, the KBA, and possible partial change key or master key coding.

Secondary Locking Systems

Examining keys can easily determine secondary security layers and locking systems, including virtual keyways, side bit milling, undercuts to control added locking pins such as with Schlage Everest, slider controls and position for the Medeco m3 and M4, interactive elements and placement, ball bearings, spring-biased elements, and magnetic pins, discs, or wafers.

Sectional Keyways and Counterfeit Blanks

In larger systems, sectional keyways may be employed to add security and segregate different access areas. Key markings may indicate a blank's or keyway's identification that can be traced back to a manufacturer to identify the system. Additionally, sectional keyways may be altered to allow unauthorized or unintended keys to access areas with different keyways. In one major investigation, we identified locksmiths selling counterfeit blanks with multiple keyways that could access different systems without the proper authorization.

Maison Keying Systems

Maison systems can be found in apartment complexes where all residents require access to perimeter doors with individual apartment keys. The locks in this system type are often set with fewer tumblers, with their bitting depths common to all locks in the system. The cylinders can be easily defeated if the common parameter can be defined. Unless they're high-security, the locks can be easily picked or bumped.

Photographing or Scanning Keys for Later Reproduction

The capability to easily replicate keys to defeat a system must be a continual concern. High-resolution photography, scanning, and 3D printing, which makes it simple to create keys in plastic or other materials, can seriously threaten key control. The implementation of additional layers of security for keys must always be considered when designing a system.

Restricted Keyways

A *restricted keyway* means there are security controls on the availability of blanks or cut keys, usually by the manufacturer or government agency. Keyways for the postal service, military, and Department of Defense (DoD) are prime examples. Possessing or duplicating these blanks is often illegal, thereby limiting unauthorized access. The control keys for removable-core systems may also be restricted due to the facility's security risk if keys can be easily acquired.

Attacks Against Keying Systems

Covert attacks against keying systems can take many forms and often require the development of intelligence about a specific set of locks and how they're configured. Attacks that target vulnerabilities in various systems differ from deriving information *from* and *about* keys. The primary objective of any attack is usually the production of a working key or the ability to covertly open one or more locks by picking, bumping, or decoding using special tools such as those produced by Lishi, John Falle, Madelin, Wendt, or other vendors.

Virtually all conventional locks, some high-security cylinders, and their associated systems can be compromised by attacks based on the design and mechanical functions of the open keys. This methodology is distinct and set apart from the procedures that have been outlined involving analyzing a locking cylinder.

An initial assessment is often conducted to determine the best attack option. Developing intelligence about locks and keys involves many factors that relate to security levels and enhancements, tolerances between plug and shell, the number of active detainers, the keyway's design, whether the lock is master keyed, and the type of master key system (i.e., progression or positional).

The most common methods of attack against keys and their associated systems include but aren't limited to the following techniques.

Rights Amplification of Keys and Locks

Depending on the target key's design, amplifying rights can allow the key's security components to be altered. The goal is to allow the modified key to gain unauthorized access to cylinders. In some instances, locks can be externally modified so they can be opened in an unauthorized or unintended manner. iLOQ was a prime example of two scenarios: the lock was externally modified to be set to open by any key, or a key was modified to cause the mechanical reset mechanism to be circumvented and fail, allowing any key to open the lock.

Rights amplification of a key can take several forms, including adding or subtracting bitting material from the key's surface (the most common approach), changing the bitting on old discarded keys in a system, modifying keyway warding, altering virtual keyway systems, and modifying side bit milling or other secondary locking systems. It can denote the substitution of bitting material to allow the reuse of a blank key to open different locks. This can often be easily accomplished by altering a key's primary characteristic to fit a different lock. Removing bitting is simple and often accomplished with a file. A surface can be built with solder or other substances bonded to a key's surface.

Rights amplification of a lock can mean a mechanical modification that allows it to operate unanticipatedly, as with iLOQ. Another example was the older Kwikset and Weiser reprogrammable locks that could be circumvented by inserting a partially cut blank key to bring all the sliders to the shear line, allowing the plug to be torqued open. This case is discussed in Part V as a case example.

Recutting a Key to Change the Bitting

A failure to track and account for keys that have been issued, lost, stolen, deleted from a system, or taken out of service; that belong to terminated employees; or that are extra released duplicates can be deadly to a system's security. Unless the keys are for high-security cylinders and have sufficient protection to guard against rights amplification, most can be successfully modified to work in an unauthorized manner. Design teams should focus on keys as a crucial part of any lock design and imagine how keys can be changed to work in a lock. Any key in a system that can be modified is a threat, even restricted keyways that management may believe are immune to duplication or other forms of attack.

Modification of Keyway Warding

Changing the keyway's warding can often be easily accomplished with a file or milling machine. This can take the form of creating new warding tracks, widening or deepening matching patterns, or other modifications to allow a key or blank to enter a keyway it was not designed to enter. Ward patterns can also be modified using a milling machine such as the Keyway King or EasyEntrie with special software that works with Adobe Photoshop.

Altering Virtual Keyway Systems

Many manufacturers include virtual keyway systems to increase the number of available keyways, especially for large systems. These systems can take the form of added bitting surfaces; adding sliders or other devices (e.g., in the Medeco m3) to distinguish one type of key from another; using check pins to block the entry of a key unless an undercut or other mechanism is present (e.g., Schlage Everest); embedding magnetic pins or wafers (e.g., EVVA); and using interactive movable pins, bearings, or other devices. These virtual systems can often be easily modified and circumvented because they're designed not for security but to create additional keyways.

Modifying the Secondary Locking System

It's possible to alter the geometry of secondary locking systems, such as side bit milling, to create a bump key or circumvent anti-duplication or security measures. The tolerances of secondary bitting can be changed to allow keys to function where they shouldn't work. The older Medeco m3 slider system could be modified, or the slider could be circumvented by inserting a paper clip or wire.

Inserting an Overlay into a Blank or Cut Key

In one case I investigated, the bitting material on a high-security restricted dimple key was removed, and a nylon insert was set. It could be easily cut to any required bitting and was easy to remove and replace with a blank nylon strip to work in a different lock.

Converting a Change Key to a Blank Key

A change key with any bitting value can be scanned and used to create a blank key with an EasyEntrie milling machine. The EasyEntrie, developed more than 20 years ago in Germany, can mechanically scan a pin tumbler key and re-create it as a blank that can then be cut to any bitting value.

Creating a New Shear Line

A new shear line can be created by using a comb pick, injecting ball bearings, or drilling the plug in two different ways. John Falle developed a professional set of comb picks to raise all bottom pins above the shear line if balanced top pins haven't been properly installed. The pick raises all pins simultaneously, creating a new shear line that allows the plug to rotate.

A new shear line can be created in dimple locks by injecting ball bearings into each chamber, creating another shear line like a comb pick. In one investigation, my colleagues and I had to develop a special delivery tool, like a hypodermic needle, to deliver the bearings. It's a very effective way to neutralize many dimple locks.

Drilling the plug is the most common method to create a new shear line. This can take two forms: one well known and the other quite rare. First, a drill bit is placed at the breakpoint outside the plug. Usually, a 1/8"-diameter bit is run across the plug from the first to the last chamber. If done properly, this creates a new shear line, and the plug can be turned.

In the second method, the procedure is more complicated and obscure. A small diameter bit is placed outside the plug's normal shear line position. A fully inserted blank key will raise all the tumblers to their highest point. The blank is removed, and the bottom pins will drop to the bottom of the keyway, eliminating any block to plug rotation. This method was attempted in a triple homicide case in which I worked in Canada, where entry was attempted. It's discussed in Part VI.

Replicating or Copying a Target Key

Keys can be copied or replicated with materials other than an original or actual blank. I've employed plastic sheets, adhesive labels, plastic, copper wire, and plastic credit cards cut with an X-ACTO knife. A variable key generation system, produced by John Falle, can also replicate the bitting values with thin metal and bypass most keyway wards. Blanks can be modified to fit different keyways. Keys can also be produced with 3D-printing technology, including for hybrid attacks.

Design engineers must consider how they're protecting their keys against copying, simulation, or replication. Imagination is critical because almost any thin material can be shaped to accomplish the same function as bitting and can be inserted into a keyway to mate with pin tumblers or other active components. The finished product's appearance is irrelevant, but how it interacts inside a lock is critical. Even high-security keys with advanced copy protection can be replicated, especially with 3D-printed blanks or carriers.

Generating System Keys

A lock can be attacked by system keys specially coded to replicate all the bitting combinations in a master key system. They're employed by manufacturers and locksmiths to rapidly test all the different incidental shear lines and bitting combinations once locks are pinned. System keys can eliminate the need to test each cylinder with its various keys to ensure pinning accuracy. Another use is to exploit the virtual shear lines in a master key system to create precut keys that open locks rapidly.

Brian Chan, a locksmith at the University of California at Berkeley, conceived using system keys. The underlying theory of system keys requires that all locks be pinned using the Total Position Progression (TPP) or Rotating Constant (RC) algorithm. The keys work because many chambers are grouped and have the same bitting values. The importance of this technique can be useful in attacking a master key system when it's desirable to open locks and decode the master key. See the following discussion about the extrapolation of the top-level master key.

Extrapolation of the Top-Level Master Key

This concept derives the bitting value of the top-level master key (TMK) by sampling each chamber with a series of cut keys to determine which bitting depth *other than the change key* will open the lock. In a master key system using TPP, the top-level master keys bitting values are usually different than the change key's.

Secondary Locking System Decoding

Secondary locking systems, such as side bit milling, sliders, wafers, and other mechanisms, can often be modified or decoded to deduce the top-level master keys values in a system. The geometry can be changed to allow the production of a bump key, which is required because the milling will not mate with that of the key when forward movement is required during the bumping process.

Chapters 4 and 20 discuss hybrid attacks in detail and involve using two or more different methods to neutralize security layers in a locking system. A hybrid attack contemplates splitting each layer and considering it individually. When all layers are compromised, the lock can be opened. An example is the very early versions of the Ikon CLIQ electromechanical lock. It had a mechanical bitting component and an electronic credential component. Both had to be active at the same time. This lock was compromised by simulating the bitting on the key and circumventing how the electronics worked. My team produced a hybrid key that opened the lock in seconds.

A hybrid attack can also use both covert and forced techniques in combination. How we were able to compromise high-security deadbolts was a classic hybrid attack and is described in Chapter 17 and Part VI. It required shearing the retaining screws of the plug's endcap and then manipulating the tailpiece through the end of the keyway.

Creating Bump Keys

Bump keys can be easily created by cutting down the bitting on a discarded, deleted, stolen, or lost key, regardless of its bitting combination. Bump keys always have all their bitting set at the deepest value so energy is properly transmitted to the base of each pin tumbler. Any key with the same keyway and number of pin positions can be used to create a bump key.

Decoding Control Keys

If the control key can be decoded or extrapolated in an interchangeable-core system, access to every lock is guaranteed and a top-level master key is unnecessary. Depending on the coding scheme for a specific manufacturer, the control key for some interchangeable-core systems can be easy to determine. It's important to remember that the ability to decode the control key allows access to any lock and can create a lockout condition by exchanging cores.

Mechanical Bypass

Many locks can be compromised by techniques that involve the mechanical bypass of critical components. These are often simple methods that are either overlooked by engineers or not imagined by design teams. The circumvention of security can neutralize sophisticated and multiple layers designed into locks and their keys. Attacks can employ conductive materials and liquids, methods to short-circuit electronic systems, shim wires, vibration, torque, shock, force, sound, air pressure, temperature extremes, or alteration of the geometry of primary components.

A recurrent problem in lock design is the failure to identify one or more components that can hurt overall security if modified, manipulated, or altered. Parts that appear inconsequential or unrelated to security can cause serious problems, especially if an attacker uses the failure of one part to gain access to others that may end up being critical. It's incumbent on design engineers to look at every component, regardless of how insignificant its function, and consider all "what if" scenarios in the event of failure.

The problem with most lock designs is that there can be infinite possible weaknesses or failures to consider when identifying potential security design flaws. The following list provides insights and suggestions about the scope of issues and possible attacks:

- Isolating and neutralizing each security layer separately, thus allowing functionality to be split into separate components that can be individually bypassed

- In a system that uses side bit milling or a unique sidebar code, obtaining a blank or cut key with the same code to compromise a different system

- Replicating or modifying the side bit milling code in plastic or metal

- Inserting a thin plastic or metal key with the correct bitting to match the depth of pin tumblers to replicate a key, and applying torque, if required, to turn the plug

- Neutralizing a secondary locking system with shims or plastic to bypass any mechanical elements

- Inserting a partial blank key to align all sliders, and applying torque in the older Kwikset reprogrammable cylinders

- In a wafer-type lock, inserting a partial blank key cut to specific depths to align all detainers to the shear line, and applying torque to turn the plug (this procedure is similar to raising all pin tumblers to a shear line in a lock with sidebars as a second security layer; torque can be introduced to bypass the sidebar design)

■ Inserting a piece of brass stock .025″ thick and cut to the correct bitting to bypass all keyway wards

■ Producing a bump key with all deepest cuts for a pin tumbler lock on the correct blank or on a discarded or out-of-service key

■ Cutting a metal shim .025″ thick to create a bump key to bypass most keyway wards

■ Impressing a pin tumbler lock with the correct blank to create a properly bitted key

■ In a tubular lock, inserting a plastic tube with the correct diameter and applying forward energy and torque

■ Examining the design of electromechanical locks to determine whether the mechanical bitting can be separated from the electronic credential, and then determining whether a path has been created to access the rotor or other blocking mechanism that keeps the lock from opening unless the correct credential has been submitted

■ Determining whether the electric contacts that control locking mechanisms can be directly accessed externally or on a circuit board

■ Locating a critical control circuit accessible from the outside of a lock or container

■ Determining whether a system reset or reprogram switch can be accessed externally

■ Determining whether critical circuitry can be accessed by releasing a keypad, lock, or other access point covers and whether it's possible to complete a circuit through the keypad or opening or with a shim to activate critical circuitry

■ Determining whether a system reset button can be controlled externally using a shim, wire, or other material

■ Determining whether critical access can be obtained to spring-loaded release pins external to a lock or keyway

Compromise of Key Control Procedures

Manufacturers, especially of high-security locks, must implement key control procedures and systems to protect the access, distribution, and cutting of restricted keys. Key control has two elements: control of key blanks and related issues and organizational controls to ensure that the administration of locks and keys is protected and secure. The following questions must be considered when evaluating key control systems and measures:

- Can key control cards or documents be counterfeited or electronically circumvented to allow a locksmith or lock manufacturer to cut restricted keys? Can proprietary or restricted key blanks that are the basis of the control of keys be reproduced, simulated, or replicated?

- Can key control procedures be circumvented to allow access to blank or cut keys from the factory, distributor, or locksmith?

- Is the control of deleted, out-of-service, lost, or stolen keys in place to prevent keys from being cut as bump keys?

- Can keys be scanned and 3D printed?

- Can hybrid 3D-printed keys be produced with inserts for movable elements?

Tryout Keys

If locks—especially conventional low-tolerance cylinders—are used, tryout keys can be a serious threat. Risk managers and manufacturers should consider the following issues to assess the risk from the use of tryout keys to circumvent the security of the locks installed in a system:

- Can internal tolerances be exploited within a lock or between plug and shell to allow tryout keys to be employed to lessen the number of test keys that must be generated to defeat a system?

- Are sets of tryout keys for vulnerable locks offered for sale on the Internet or by locksmith supply facilities?

- Can keys for secondary security layers be produced to exploit tolerances and reduce the number of test keys required to open a lock?

See the discussion of Medeco code-setting keys and how they were used as tryout keys.

Exploiting Key-Interchange Issues and Tolerances

Some locks, especially dimple pin tumbler cylinders, have key-interchange and tolerance issues, especially if there are insufficient differs in a large system. *Key interchange* refers to the number of depth increments a manufacturer assigns to a lock design and the tolerance between plug and shell. If the tolerances aren't tight enough, bitting values altered from the factory-established measurement can open the lock.

- Will the differences between depth increments in a keying system allow keys with different bitting values to be manipulated?

■ Will the differences between depth increments in a keying system allow keys to be jiggled to enable access to one or more locks with different combinations?

Defeating Virtual Keyways

Manufacturers implement virtual keyways to enhance or multiply the number of available keyways. This can be important in a large and complex keying system where thousands of cylinders must be managed with different sub-master keys and other ways to increase the number of locks that must be controlled. Virtual keyways aren't real in the sense that they prevent entry of an unauthorized key into the plug, or by a cut key with specific warnings. *Virtual* means a keyway created using other means, such as dimples or movable elements designed into the key itself.

■ Can virtual keyway schemes, whose function is key control, be easily defeated mechanically or magnetically?

■ Can ferrous components be magnetically manipulated?

Defeating Ferrous Elements with Magnetic Fields

Regarding defeating ferrous elements using magnetic fields, you must ask yourself the following questions:

■ Can critical components be moved or affected by strong magnetic fields?

■ Can magnetic-based locks be easily decoded to determine field polarity and the location of critical locking elements?

Incidental Master Keys, Online Key Information, and Electronic Credential Cloning

The following information must be known when dealing with incidental master keys, online key information, and cloning electronic credentials:

■ Can a keying system be decoded to determine the combinations for incidental master keys?

■ Is the complexity level of a master key system conducive to producing keys for virtual shear lines?

■ Can photographs of critical keys be found online that allow decoding or duplication?

■ Can radio frequency identification (RFID) or near-field communication (NFC) credentials be easily decoded and cloned with readily available and inexpensive tools?

Compromising the Master Key Other than by Extrapolation

Obtaining the bitting code for the master key with techniques other than extrapolation is possible under certain circumstances and may prove easier to accomplish. Design teams and security managers should review the following attack methods to minimize the ability to circumvent a system by gaining access to a top-level master key.

Physically Copying, Photographing, or Decoding a Master Key

If physical access to a key is possible, even briefly, a photograph can be taken that can then be translated into a key. It can be decoded visually, especially if there are limited depth increments. There are simple tools to measure each depth, and keys can be 3D-printed from a scanned photo.

Accessing One or More Cylinders to Decode the Pin Segments

Cylinders (with or without a change key) can be removed and disassembled to decode the actual pin lengths for each chamber. There is a danger in this procedure if pins are dropped or lost or their sequence is altered by error. If there are multiple pin segments in each chamber, this can complicate the determination of change keys and master keys. Done properly, key codes can be easily derived by disassembly. This method was used to produce keys to the Brinks facility in Boston before the robbery in 1953.

Using a Falle Pin-Lock Decoder to Measure Pin Segments Using Shim Wires

The John Falle pin-lock decoder can measure pin segments using shim wires that run alongside each chamber. This older tool has been replaced by more modern techniques, including the inexpensive Lishi pick and decoder.

Falle Pin and Cam Decoder

This decoder tool probes each tumbler for its position at the shear line. It also allows the operative to quickly decode a master keyed cylinder to extrapolate the top-level master key and generate a key. The operative senses the position of each pin when at the shear line, and the tool then displays the bitting values. The tool is very expensive and available only to government agencies.

Shimming the Cylinder with Depth Keys

This method requires access to the cylinder shear line to insert a shim wire from the plug's rear to determine the code for each pin segment. The shim slides between the pins and is moved to the shear line. A prepared blank key with the correct bitting raises each pin until the shim moves forward.

Visual Inspection of Bitting Values

A key can be visually decoded to determine each bitting value. This technique depends on the operative's expertise and the depth increments' complexity. If there are limited depths, then it can be simple to determine the bitting values. For example, keys with six depth increments, such as Medeco and Kwikset, can be rapidly and accurately decoded. Dimple locks and advanced bitting designs make this process much more difficult because of complex drill patterns and multiple drill points and depths. Keys for Keso and dormakaba dimple locks can be extremely difficult to visually decode because of their complex bitting arrays.

Viewing Tumblers, Discs, Wafers, or Active Detainers with Optical Devices

These locks lend themselves to visual decoding because of their design. It's often a simple matter to look into the keyway with optical viewing devices and determine the bitting codes of each detainer because in wafer tumbler locks, the way the wafers sit in their idle state can reflect the actual code of the lock.

Optical viewing devices, including borescopes and ophthalmoscopes, can directly view pins, discs, and wafers. Tiny video-chip cameras have also been developed for this purpose.

Radiographic Techniques

Portable X-rays, piezo measurements, and ultrasound are available to measure active detainers. These systems require expertise, are expensive, and are usually limited to government agencies. An X-ray can show gate positions, especially in safe locks, which may correlate to the combination. The Russian government developed techniques for reading safes more than 75 years ago.

Analyzing Change Keys to Reverse-Engineer the System

Depending on how a system has been configured, it's possible to reverse-engineer the architecture of the KBA to derive the values of change keys and even top-level masters. Master key systems, unless extremely simple and with very few change keys, must *divide* the key bitting between levels and the number of key codes that can be assigned to change keys and master key levels. It's sometimes possible to analyze change-key coding to determine how the system is designed and to predict the coding for master keying levels.

Top-Level Master Key Extrapolation

Top-level master key extrapolation is one of the greatest threats to the security of a pin tumbler lock. The vulnerability, known as *split-pin master keying*, is inherent in all master key systems that employ a bottom pin, master pin, and top pin in one or more chambers to create virtual shear lines. Extrapolation works best when there are only two bottom pins in each chamber. The process requires access to one lock with one change key and several blank keys that can be cut for each pin's depth increment until the correct values are identified. No disassembly is required to probe a lock, and as few as three keys are required to decode a five-pin system.

The extrapolation process is simple. A lock can be considered an oracle that either accepts or rejects keys. It doesn't matter whether the pin tumblers or the change key are at the shear line for the master. In its simplest form, the process is designed to identify each virtual shear line's height for the master pin.

For a six-tumbler lock with 10 possible depth increments, sampling each chamber can require up to 54 keys if the progression is a single step. Most systems are defined by a two-step approach, which means the depth increments are varied by two divisions rather than one. In that case, as many as 24 key samples would be required to determine the master key. Far fewer test keys are needed because multiple cuts can be made on one test key for each chamber. Thus, as few as five or six keys may be required to probe the master key's value.

Other than facilities found in government service, many facilities are master keyed. Compromising a master key system through extrapolation presents a minimal discovery risk for an attacker and offers absolute access once the top-level master key is decoded. There is no forensic trace, the attack isn't high-tech, and there's no time limit to execute the attack. In a five-pin tumbler system, as few as three test keys are required to derive the master key.

Master key systems have inherent security issues and limitations. If the top-level master key is compromised, there is significant liability exposure as well as the cost to rekey the system. *Double pinning* to create virtual shear lines almost always results in reduced pick resistance. There is unwanted key interchange, incidental master keys are created, and a potential for cross-keying. Rights amplification of change keys can turn them into master keys.

A master key system's security can be measured by the difficulty in acquiring or replicating blank keys and associated key control. Enhancements of key blank design include side bit millings, sidebar codes (e.g., Medeco), undercuts, unique ward patterns, and paracentric keyways. As our team has repeatedly demonstrated, secondary-locking systems may not provide the expected level of security they represent. The security of cylinders and physical access must be monitored, controlled, and restricted. Unauthorized access to code data for a system must be prevented to ensure that only those who need to know can obtain the information for change keys and master keys.

Extrapolation, Defined

Extrapolation is the process of deriving the top-level master key by probing the pin stack of each chamber, using a change key as a constant. Vulnerable systems must be pinned by TPP, partial position progression (PPP), or RC systems, because the ability to decode the top-level master key is based on the double pinning of one or more chambers. The security threat exists because any change key can be employed to determine the value for the top-level master key, assuming the change key is part of the same master key system.

The Security Threat

The security threat results from several related factors. No special tools or expertise are required. Keys can be cut by hand or with a handheld cutter or portable key machine. The operation is covert, and no forensic trace is left. The operation can be accomplished in one session or over an indeterminate period. All that is needed is one change key as the constant to probe each chamber.

Practical Considerations, Variables, and Tactics

Several practical considerations and variables exist when evaluating the potential to compromise a system or its vulnerability. The availability of key blanks is essential, and how they can be cut for taking samples is important. For many popular conventional locks, blanks are easily obtained. Others may be controlled or not available through normal channels. Blanks can be simulated or modified. If keys are restricted, overlay material can be inserted for certain blank types, allowing one blank to be reused with different bitting values. Likewise, consideration must be given to using sectional keyways and how they can be circumvented.

The lock to be decoded must be confirmed to be pinned with one of the accepted three methods of master keying (TPP, PPP, or RC). The lock can't use a *master ring*, an old system with two distinct physical shear lines. It must be confirmed that chambers employ double pinning and that the test cylinder is on a master key system, not a non-master keyed lock. A determination must be made that single- or two-step pinning progressions have been utilized and that standard depth-increment values have been implemented. If a deviation from standard depths has been employed, this must be known before sampling each chamber.

Suppose a system from Medeco, Assa, Schlage, or another manufacturer utilizes multiple sidebar or side bit milling codes. In that case, blanks must be available for the specific system being probed. If two side bit milling or sidebar codes are mixed, the keys will not work. Likewise, if different pinning systems are employed, the results will be invalid for deriving the top-level master key. The process becomes much more complicated and unreliable if there are more than two lower pins in each chamber. If the target lock isn't on the master key system, the results will not be valid.

Issues that may be encountered in planning to extrapolate a system are as follows:

- *Is extrapolation the best method to obtain top-level master key bitting data?* There are other procedures for deriving the bitting codes for master keys, such as decoders and lock disassembly.

- *Does a master key system exist?* Before attempting to extrapolate the top-level master key, it must be determined that only one system, with one top-level master key, exists, especially in large facilities or multiple locations.

- *Is a change key to be used for sampling the target lock?* Care must be taken that the key used to test a specific cylinder is a change key associated with the same master key system. This is because the change key is the constant used to probe the value of the top-level master key pin. If the change key isn't associated with a system being probed, it's of no value in the process.

- *Have the proper blanks been obtained?* Ensure that the proper key blanks are sufficient to execute an operation. If not, there is no way to probe the lock and cut test keys.

- *Should the secondary locking mechanism be the same for the target?* If there are secondary locking systems, such as sidebars and side bit milling, ensure that the change key and blank keys are compatible. To probe a system where sidebars or side bit milling is in use, the keys used for probing must match the secondary security layer bitting, or the keys will not work.

- *Should you consider and determine what time frame the decoded top-level master key requires?* A preliminary decision must be made about whether the extrapolation will occur in one pass or over time and whether there are constraints on the operation. This factor depends on access to the target lock, the secrecy level of the operation, and the risk of being caught.

- *Are the number of pins in the sample key and target lock the same?* Ensure that the length of the blank key is correct for the target cylinder. If there are different numbers of pins in certain locks, the key blanks must be available to accommodate the proper number of pins. A five-pin blank will not work in a six-pin lock.

■ *Do you have access to a cylinder associated with the top-level master key?* Confirm that access to the target lock is available at the required time of the operation. This is essential if a successful operation is to occur. The procedure requires access to probe a target lock.

■ *If sectional keyways are employed, is the proper blank available?* Verify whether sectional keyways are involved and key blanks are available to test the target lock. Sectional keyways are subsets of main keyways. If a keyway is a sectional keyway, the proper blank for that keyway must be available, or key blanks that contain the individual sections must be used.

■ *Is access to more than one cylinder required?* You must determine whether top-level master keys for multiple sites or areas are required. In large facilities, there may be different locks that must be accessed and that may have their own top-level master key.

■ *Can you assess the visibility of the sample and target locks?* Analyze the area where the target lock is located and its associated work area, considering the potential to discover the attack during the process. This issue must be resolved before an operation is undertaken to reduce the exposure of operatives.

■ *What is the specific location of the target and sample locks?* Ensure that the location of the target lock is established so the operative is in the correct area. This is important to be certain the correct lock is decoded.

Information and Intelligence Before an Extrapolation Attempt

Obtaining certain information and intelligence may be helpful before attempting to extrapolate the top-level master key. Although the process is straightforward, difficulties can arise unless certain this is available to facilitate probing different bitting values and cutting keys. Here are a few examples of what you can expect:

■ *Relationship between the target locks to be opened and the lock to be tested with the change key*: Be certain that the target lock to be probed and the rest of the system are on the same master key. This is especially true in facilities where certain cylinders aren't set up on the master key for security reasons so that mal actors can't access and decode easily.

■ *Change-key code*: Determining the change-key code is your first step in the extrapolation procedure.

■ *Conventional or positional master key system*: Information must be gathered to determine whether the pinning system is based on standard algorithms or a positional keying system. A positional system can't be decoded similarly and may require multiple changes in key samples to derive the master key.

- *Multiple sidebar codes (Medeco or Assa)*: Does the system employ multiple secondary locking systems, such as sidebars or side bit milling with different coding for specific areas in a facility or different buildings? Medeco, for example, can deploy up to 729 different sidebar codes for maximum flexibility in a large system.

- *Utilization of a standard method of progression*: Extrapolation tests will only work with pin tumbler systems programmed with TPP, PPP, and RC systems. Otherwise, the scheme will not work.

- *Standard depth increments have been utilized*: It's important to determine that the factory's original depth increments have been employed in the pinning scheme. Otherwise, there is no reference for how much material to remove from a test key when probing each chamber.

- *Manufacturer data*: Sufficient manufacturing data must been ascertained to determine the name of the lock's producer, blank key and keyway identification, availability of blanks, number and measurement of depth increments, whether the lock has one or two-step programming and has odd or even parity, and whether secondary-locking systems are employed.

- *Maison-keying system implemented*: It must be verified that the target cylinder isn't Maison keyed, because if it is, it may not contain the number of pins employed for the other cylinders in the system.

- *Local or factory keyed*: Was the master key system designed and implemented by the manufacturer directly or by a local locksmith? If it was set up by the manufacturer directly, are there any special keying restrictions or requirements or invalid combinations of bitting?

- *Number of keying levels*: How many keying levels are present in the target system? This is important because the derivation of the top-level master key can be confused with incidental master keys and virtual shear lines, especially if there are more than two bottom pins in any chamber.

- *Construction-keyed cylinders*: Be certain that the target cylinder isn't construction-keyed to a special bitting and not on the master key system.

- *Information from systems with implemented visual key control*: Some systems have stamped numbers on keys or locks to indicate their ID in a system. This information can be of value when attempting to reverse-engineer how a system is configured.

- *Identification of sectional keyways*: If sectional keyways are utilized, identify all the potential subsections and keyways that control each section and which would be utilized for the top-level master key.

- *Number of active chambers within each cylinder*: Determine the number of active chambers within the target cylinder. Sometimes a six-pin plug may be set up with only five active chambers.

Decoding Options and Logistics

There are many ways to decode the top-level master key through the extrapolation technique. However, which procedure to follow depends on many factors that involve the target system, the venue, logistics, and security concerns. The choice of how to proceed is also dictated by the attacker's identity and the danger or likelihood of being discovered during the process.

Decoding the top-level master key with a Change Key in One Session

The normal procedure is to decode the top-level master key in one session while at the test cylinder. However, it can also be done at different times, depending on the nature of the operation. Functionally, there's no difference in the result. Extrapolation isn't like lock picking because analyzing all chambers simultaneously isn't required.

Decoding the top-level master key with a Change Key in Multiple Sessions

In a covert operation, this procedure can be carried out in one or more separate passes. Regardless of the time frame, there is no difference in the result, making the procedure even more dangerous in terms of security vulnerability. An attacker can execute multiple steps, each taking a few seconds. This is especially true if precut system keys are employed, which means sample probes can be carried on in a few seconds and the result recorded.

Decoding the top-level master key with All Possible Permutations Precut in One or More Sessions

Up to 32 (for a five-pin lock) or 64 keys (for a six-pin lock) are generated in this process, but the actual value of the top-level master key is not known until the correct combination is tested and opens the lock.

The next chapter introduces advanced methods of attack on key control. These can involve the use of 3D printers and sophisticated software. An analysis of one of the best examples of software developed for law enforcement and intelligence agencies is presented to demonstrate the capabilities for producing keys for hundreds of different cylinders and lock manufacturers and thousands of different keyways. For design engineers, this chapter should provide serious concerns and demonstrate the need for more imaginative key control measures that are designed into their keys.

Advanced Attacks on Key Control: 3D Printers and Special Software

Advanced capabilities and technologies that target keys, key control systems, and locks have developed and matured over the past 10 years. This has occurred partly due to the availability of a wide array of 3D printers, sophisticated sensing hardware, processing speeds, and applications designed to analyze the critical parameters of security components in mechanical locks. The ability to rapidly decode a lock's secrets and translate that information to usable credentials has provided necessary tools for law-enforcement and intelligence agencies in their fight against terrorism, organized crime, espionage, and criminal gangs. These capabilities have increased the risks for locking manufacturers in their high-security designs because many of these designs are vulnerable.

The design of some mechanical locks has advanced in terms of the security of their keys, so law-enforcement agencies may experience added difficulty in operations that require them to be able to open the locks. Lock manufacturers must understand that some enhanced designs may not be sufficient to deal with threats from the latest printer and decoding technology.

These enhancements are meant to make it more difficult to obtain or produce key copies or employ manipulation procedures with traditional covert or sur-reptitious entry methods such as picking, impressioning, and decoding. Private companies and government agencies have spent millions of research dollars developing more sophisticated approaches to exploiting design vulnerabilities in attacks on key control. Such problems for law enforcement can be complicated, especially in sensitive operations where portability of equipment, speed, detection, silence, result reliability, and lack of forensic evidence of compromise are important.

For lock manufacturers, the result is the availability of hardware and software solutions that may render many of their best security designs ineffective against these attack forms. Although export controls may be considered effective, the technology isn't guaranteed to be unavailable to jurisdictions, foreign agents, and criminals who can't acquire these capabilities legally.

Some of the underlying technology is described in patents found in the United States and the United Kingdom, and commercial hardware components are readily available. Expertise in writing software for these tools is available and only requires time, funding, and a basic understanding of how the systems work. Lock manufacturers that design hardware and supply it to major customers, including diplomatic, critical infrastructure, and government facilities, must understand how their mechanisms can frustrate or deter successful attacks by malicious (mal) actors. They must educate their customers about potential risks so these consumers can upgrade to more secure locking systems.

The flip side of this equation is equally important and problematic. Governments must understand the vulnerabilities of the locks they encounter in covert operations and how to circumvent them when necessary. This is a real conundrum because the same locks they employ to protect their facilities may be too difficult for them to attack as adversaries.

Specialized tools can be identified in three categories: software to generate keys, 3D-printing hardware, and electronic scanners for pin and lever tumbler locks. These technologies, individually or in combination, allow for the covert compromise of mechanical credentials for most conventional and high-security locks.

Only a few companies offer such systems, usually to government agencies. The primary vendors are Wendt (Germany), Madelin, ATS Security, C.O.F.E.D. (France), and Lockmasters (United States). The hardware is expensive and requires special training to become proficient in its usage. The United States and many other governments require all manufacturers, importers, exporters, and brokers of items, technical data, or services designed for the defense to meet certain rules known as the International Traffic in Arms Regulations (ITAR). Export is restricted under ITAR regulations in the United States and Europe and certain other countries.

Covert-entry systems may qualify for treatment under these regulations and exclude countries that don't comply or that have been banned from sales or imports of such tools. Unfortunately, this doesn't mean banned countries haven't developed or stolen this intellectual property (IP) and aren't producing their own tool versions. So, it's even more important that lock manufacturers consider this eventuality when designing high-security locks to resist such attacks.

They must factor into their designs the advanced capabilities of 3D printing and electronic scanning of locks that employ piezo decoders and ultrasound to sense and map internal components.

The process of *3D printing* is a specific manufacturing technology in which a machine creates three-dimensional objects in an *additive manufacturing* process, meaning building up layers of material. In contrast with more traditional forms of manufacturing that typically rely on *subtractive* technology, these processes are typically found in machining, molding, or casting. *Subtractive manufacturing* involves the removal of material.

Technology can significantly threaten key control, even for high-security locks and the facilities they protect. The equipment and required expertise are within reach of everyone, including mal actors, criminals, thieves, and spies. The available hardware has rapidly advanced, and prices have continued to decline. Although more sophisticated software is available only to law enforcement and government agencies, most is commercially available, and the basic 3D capabilities aren't restricted. They are limited only by cost and programming time if the software must be developed rather than purchased.

The 3D-printing process is now an integral part of many global manufacturing facilities for prototyping and producing parts on demand. In the context of key control, it can neutralize even the most sophisticated and ostensibly secure designs. Therefore, it's incumbent on design engineers and those tasked with threat assessment to understand the current capabilities of 3D printing in conjunction with specialized software and electronic scanners. They must recognize the ability to compromise their locks by circumventing almost every aspect of key control and restrict access to blank and cut keys and the ability to replicate, simulate, and duplicate mechanical credentials.

The maturation and advancement of this technology have provided new weapons to law enforcement and intelligence agencies. Several leading companies in the United States and Europe have pioneered and developed sophisticated software and hardware systems to decode a target lock and its keyway. These systems can map internal detainers, output bitting values, and generate a key in various materials. They can display this information, allowing a covert operative to cut a key with a machine, by hand, or by using an interface between the decoding and printer hardware.

Early on, there were many misconceptions in the lock industry about what could and could not be created with a 3D printer and its associated software. As described in this book, the awakening began at DefCon when two MIT engineering students simulated Schlage Primus keys that opened high-security locks on campus. In retrospect, they made an unsophisticated, simplistic, and yet effective attack—one that set off alarm bells for my clients.

As the technology advanced, it became clear to the major lock manufacturers that regardless of the mechanical security enhancements they designed, implemented, and patented, it wouldn't matter in a contest with sophisticated printer hardware and software. Notwithstanding the statements by manufacturers as they touted, advertised, and represented their security against 3D printing, they realized that the security could be circumvented, bypassed, and reproduced in 3D-printed keys with the appropriate expertise and hardware. In my experience and via testing by our security labs team, I can attest that almost every high-security rated lock today can be defeated—not all of them, but most. It simply is a question of time and the ability to employ available software coupled with requisite hardware.

Any manufacturer suffering under the illusion that its key and lock designs can't be defeated with direct or hybrid attacks is doing their clients a disservice and misleading them. If a manufacturer publicly represents that its key control systems are immune from attack by 3D techniques, it may create unacceptable security risks and potential for legal liability.

The good news is that many lock manufacturers have implemented systems to frustrate efforts to bypass their mechanical security enhancements. As described in Chapter 14, such measures can take many forms. Any such innovations and improvements still rely on the same premise: that one or more parts must move, expand, contract, be magnetically attracted or repelled, be (or not be) present in a specific key location, or interact with internal components to allow or block plug rotation.

The 3T2R rule, described in Chapter 4, is the security index that can gauge the threat from 3D printing for a specific design. It's all about time, tools, training, and the required expertise to produce a credential that opens a target lock or provides access to a system. Every design team must understand that almost every concept is open to some form of attack. Imagination is critical because 3D technology can directly produce a key or an intermediate step that, combined with movable elements, can generate a piece of plastic or metal that will open the lock.

3D Printing vs. EasyEntrie Milling Machines

As noted previously in this book, the EasyEntrie is a special milling machine specifically designed to produce blank keys for various profiles. Its primary function is to scan a sample key (bitted or blank) and re-create the warding on a new specially designed blank so a traditional key machine can cut it. Multiple versions of blanks that are supplied with the EasyEntrie are selected by their thickness, length, and width. Although the machine re-creates a scanned blank, it isn't an exact replica, meaning there's no patent infringement for specialized or protected keys.

The EasyEntrie technology is dated but still has its use for locksmiths and law-enforcement operations. Its capabilities are far different from that of a 3D printer because the 3D output can create a fully bitted key. If there are secondary security enhancements, EasyEntrie can't replicate them. Still, a 3D printer can create a hybrid key, allowing secondary security mechanisms to be inserted separately.

3D Printer Technology

Although this isn't intended as a treatise on 3D-printer principles and technology, it is helpful to understand the basics and the differences between the three primary systems. This can allow for an informed decision about which system offers the best options for working with and printing keys. Different output materials depend on which type of printer is selected. Printed keys are primarily made of plastics, nylon, metal, and special wax for casting. The three primary printing systems are fused-deposition modeling (FDM), stereolithography (SLA), and selective laser sintering (SLS). Each has its characteristics, limitations, resolution, and costs. I have found that the SLA hardware is the most applicable and cost-effective for most jobs that involve the generation of keys, key carriers, or lock parts.

Fused Deposition Modeling Technology

Fused deposition modeling is the most popular and least expensive printing technology, although it wasn't the first technique to be invented. It was patented three years after SLA was developed and one year after SLS. FDM's inventor was Scott Crump, who went on to found one of the most recognized and successful companies in the industry, Stratasys.

FDM became popular in the non-commercial community and was known as fused-filament fabrication (FFF). The FFF patent expired in 2009, and its developers went on to found MakerBot Industries. This was one of the first commercializations of open-source FDM 3D printers. The primary characteristic of FDM is the extrusion and selective depositing of thermoplastics into layers, which are continually added to create a 3D object.

An FDM printer has two primary components: an extrusion and deposition head and a mechanical platform to move the mechanism to precisely place the filament material. Spools of filament feed the printer. The critical function is to control the rate of feed (flow rate) or how the material is deposited to create the object. The filament is delivered through a nozzle in a spray-liquid form. Technology allows the correct amount of material to build layers at the right temperature and physical state. These systems build two-dimensional layers that fuse to create a 3D part.

My first experience after the DefCon presentation was with a MakerBot printer. Although it's suitable for simple projects and relatively rapid output, it isn't conducive to reproducing objects requiring high tolerances, such as a key. The

MIT students accomplished their task of replicating the Schlage Primus keys because they approximated the side bit milling not exactly, but close enough to work (see Figure 22-1). The output didn't look like a Primus key, but that didn't matter.

Figure 22-1: This is the 3D-printed Schlage Primus key created by MIT students to open locks on campus.

The genie was out of the bottle. It ignited research by engineers, law enforcement, intelligence agencies, lock manufacturers, hackers, and ultimately criminals to exploit the technology to compromise key control previously thought to have been secure against copying. It was soon recognized that FDM was unsuitable for serious jobs because of its inability to work with the tolerance required of most keys.

Stereolithography Technology

Stereolithography employs a different method than FDM to print layer by layer. It is a photochemical process that uses light to bond chemical monomers to form polymers, creating the infrastructure of a solid. Such characteristics allow the printing of small features with tight tolerances (see Figure 22-2). The system uses an ultraviolet (UV) laser aimed at the surface of a liquid resin that sets with heat. The finished object is washed in solvents to remove extra material, and any support structures are manually broken away. A UV curing cycle solidifies the outer surface parts. Care should be taken not to expose the finished parts to UV and humidity, to prevent them from degrading. One of the leaders in the industry is Formlabs in the United States, which supplies high-quality SLA printers. Its printers can produce high-tolerance keys and key carriers.

Figure 22-2: This is a complex Fichet key. It was replicated with a 3D SLA printer and special software.

The process of 3D printing is especially adaptable to printing dimple keys and carriers that can contain movable elements. The key shown in Figure 22-3 demonstrates this capability. It allows the placement of a movable element and the bitting for a specific lock. Laser tracks and grooves can also be easily printed, as shown in Figure 22-4b for the EVVA 3KS and 4KS.

Figure 22-3: A key for a Mul-T-Lock Interactive+. Note the hole for the insertion of the movable element.

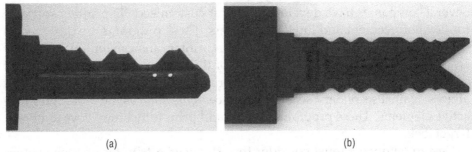

| (a) | (b) |

Figure 22-4a, 4b: (a) A FAB key with holes for side pins. (b) The EVVA 4KS is the latest iteration of the popular 3KS with various slider tracks.

SLA differs from FDM because it relies on a thermoset liquid, not a thermoplastic. The system works using a layer of liquid activated by UV light to produce each succeeding layer. The material properties are different, including tensile strength, which can be important for specific applications involving keys. Many materials are available for printing, including polycarbonate-like acrylonitrile butadiene styrene (ABS) and polypropylene-like materials. Metal plating is also possible on finished parts.

SLA is ideal for printing keys because of its ability to attain high resolution, accuracy, and sharp detail (see Figure 22-3). Finer output is possible because the printing temperature is lower than in thermoplastic-based systems that melt the raw material. SLA uses light instead of heat, so the process occurs near room temperature, eliminating the potential for thermal expansion and contraction. The laser spot size is 85 microns, compared to 250- to 800-micron nozzles for FDM machines.

The printing system is very versatile because of the different resin formulations. The materials have a wide range of optical, mechanical, and thermal properties. Compared with traditional technologies, SLA 3D is between standard and fine machining.

Selective Laser Sintering Technology

Selective laser sintering uses a laser to sinter and fuse powder material to create solid output. No support structures are required, and the system offers the advantage of a low cost per component. The output resembles injection-molded parts. This technology is best for mechanical prototyping.

Wax Casting

Special wax is output by 3D printers to create casting molds to produce metal parts. It's an ideal format for creating keys.

Specialized 3D Software for Keys

Several companies have developed or offer customized 3D-printing software for law enforcement and intelligence users. These programs are designed to communicate with or input data to 3D SLA printers and can replicate virtually any mechanical key design. They allow for the scanning or manual creation of custom profiles. AT Security and other programs create "carriers" for hybrid attacks against secondary security enhancements such as movable and interactive elements. These programs encode and print fully bitted keys to open a target lock.

Design engineers must consider the advanced attributes of such custom software when implementing mechanical enhancements to make their keys and locks more secure. The capabilities of many of these programs anticipate almost every function that might be needed to execute a covert-entry operation involving the duplication or creation of keys. These capabilities must be factored into high-security lock designs to ensure that key control enhancements provide at least some protection against compromise and defeat.

AT Security and other programs offer the following advanced functions:

- *Ability to scan keys or images*: Many programs can input scanned images of target keys to decode, replicate, and create a custom profile or match the profile to existing information in the database.

- *Complexity of mechanical keys*: Mechanical keys, regardless of their design, are pieces of metal with different shapes, angles, dimples, grooves, tracks, protrusions, bitting, surface contours or irregularities, and movable elements. With the proper software, most can be copied or replicated, even with sophisticated secondary security mechanisms.

- *Secondary security mechanisms*: Manufacturers constantly introduce new key and lock designs and modifications to keep their patents alive and extend their IP protection. Changes in current designs to create newer products reduce security against copying. Many enhancements don't matter in 3D printing because they are often vulnerable regardless of how secure they appear.

- *Characteristics of movable elements*: The characteristics and designs of movable and interactive elements in keys are as diverse as the lock industry. Every conceivable combination can be found in various locks because they can be a prime consideration in obtaining patent protection. Movable or interactive elements include wafers, ball bearings, springs, pins, magnets, sliders, expanding pins, key tip special shapes, and many other variations. The process of 3D printing allows a wider latitude in placing actual or simulated elements and their functions. In one popular lock, a ball bearing is used as the security element and moves laterally across the key's surface. Its end position is important rather than the fact that it moves. That functionality is easily accomplished with a 3D-printed key carrier.

- *Virtual keyways*: Most can be defeated, depending on the scheme. Their mechanical attributes rather than appearance are relevant, especially where part of the protection is based on a positional keying system. Many of these designs can be circumvented by printing critical key portions.

- *Hybrid attacks and 3D-printing-generated key blanks*: Hybrid attacks are employed against multiple security layers in keys and locks. They require creating a special carrier key that usually comprises the primary bitting and warding but doesn't include any specialized holes, inserts, or movable elements. These are added to the carrier so it functions like a factory original. Special elements can be obtained from other key samples, manufactured, or printed. They are often pressed into the plastic carrier to replicate the functions of the original key.

- *Keys with interactive elements*: Keys containing interactive elements can appear secure against a traditional mechanical attack because of the difficulty in replicating their multiple designs or actions. Employing a 3D-printed carrier can simplify the compromise of these enhancements in a two-step process because it allows each layer to be individually attacked.

- *Cuts with a different geometry*: Keys that are 3D printed can have cuts of different angles, shapes, and sizes, which can be much more difficult to produce with traditional manufacturing processes and may become important when inserting uniquely shaped elements into a carrier. Printing complex shapes and configurations such as undercuts and laser tracks is relatively simple to do with 3D printing.

An Overview of Typical Program Capabilities

One industry expert, Alexandre Triffault of AT Security in France, has spent the past 10 years creating specialized programs and extensive databases. These contain profiles, keyways, depth and spacing information, and critical data about internal detainers in locks that law enforcement agencies may encounter. Some of the capabilities of his programs are described in this section.

The ATS3DKEY program is Windows-based software specifically designed for law-enforcement operations. It allows for the instant generation of almost every profile type, including patented ones that may even contain movable or magnetic elements. The program's output can be in high-resolution metal or plastic for direct field use. The program includes a database of more than 9,000 key profiles and can re-create more than 99 percent of all keys—even those that are extremely complex.

I have evaluated and utilized the AT Security software to generate keys to open several high-security locks. It closely reflects the capabilities of other competing programs I have reviewed for use by government agencies. The software is loaded on my laptop and interfaces directly with a Formlabs Form 3 SLA printer for optimum results. Bitted keys generated as tests have included the EVVA 4KS, FAB 1000, Mul-T-Lock Interactive+, and Fichet F3D. These represent a good selection of different shapes and complex designs.

Special 3D software typically provides many functions required for law-enforcement operations. The AT suite includes three separate modules. The *3DKEY* module can create a printed key based on an existing profile in the database or created by the user. Inputting the depth, spacing, bitting information, and any moving elements allows a key to be generated.

The Lock Profile Identification or *LOPID* module can identify a profile from an image of the target lock. It cross-references to the Silca master database for a specific lock if it exists.

The *DxDraw* module is like the LOPID module but without a database. This module allows the user to draw the profile freehand but doesn't provide a search for similarly identified locks. This software is designed to create the profile from a picture and then export it to ATS3DKEY. A separate copy of *InstaCode* is also supplied with the software. This detailed database contains depth and spacing information for every lock manufacturer in North America and is a primary reference for locksmiths (see Figure 22-5).

Some options are designed into the software, allowing a key to be created and printed based on various lock facts and its access, depending on whether information about a target is already stored in the database or a new profile must be created.

The program anticipates the following scenarios that can precede an operation and require a key to be produced that can open a lock (see Figure 22-6):

- *It is possible to photograph the target key or keyway.* If a photograph of the key or keyway can be captured, that information can be input into the system. In some cases, a picture of the key can be obtained, which is sufficient to create a profile. Suppose the target profile is already in the LOPID database. In that case, finding and generating a key is simple after transferring that information to the ATS3DKEY module together with bitting parameters.

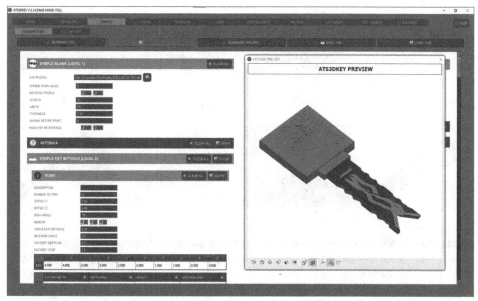

Figure 22-5: A profile is imported, and the parameters are entered into the database.

■ *A target key can be obtained.* This allows the key to be photographed or decoded, and the information is entered into the system.

■ *A target key is unavailable.* The different software modules must be utilized to identify the lock to produce a working key.

■ *The target lock can be impressioned, decoded, or electronically scanned.* It is possible to pick, decode, or impression the lock with special tools to derive needed information for the program.

■ *The lock manufacturer is known, and the keyway has been identified.* In this instance, it's a simple matter of searching the database or inputting the depth, spacing, and bitting information to find what you need. The software can identify a keyway from an image taken from the target lock.

■ *The lock manufacturer is identified, but the keyway is unknown.* A photograph can be taken of the lock and input into the program to either identify it or create a new profile from which a print can be generated. A profile can be generated without knowing a specific keyway. In such an event, a very thin, flat piece of plastic or metal is created with the bitting. This technique can bypass all wards within a keyway.

■ *Neither an identification of the manufacturer nor the keyway can be established.* A photograph of the keyway can be utilized to create a new profile. If information about the target lock isn't contained in the Lock ID software or the profile is patented, a drawing can be created and exported to the ATS3DKEY software to generate the key.

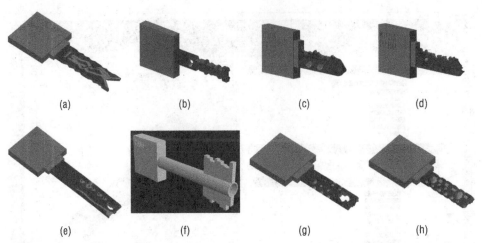

Figures 22-6a–6h: These images represent ATS3DKEY previews of created keys. Each profile is complex, and some have movable elements or laser tracks. They include CISA, Mul-T-Lock, EVVA, Wilka, Kaba, and DOM keys.

Other important capabilities of this software include the following:

■ It's easy to modify profiles stored in the database. Based on a picture of the target lock, the software can draw the keyway contour exactly using drag-and-drop anchors. An offset can also be set to fit the plug's key precisely. Once a profile has been created, many parameters can be input, including the number of pins, distance from the shoulder, inter-pin distance, and all possible depth increments. A root length and specific angles can also be set.

■ There are no maximum adjacent cut specification (MACS) restrictions. The program allows the generation of any bitting values. If MACS rules are violated, it's simple to modify the root angles for proper mechanical operation within the lock.

■ Spaces or holes can be created in a printed key to allow movable or interactive elements to be inserted.

■ Measurements for depth, spacing, and bitting information can be added once the keyway is identified or drawn.

■ Photographed, scanned, or modified images can be saved to the database. Bitting values can be added or changed to generate different keys on demand.

■ A custom profile can be created for almost any keyway, as shown in Figure 22-7.

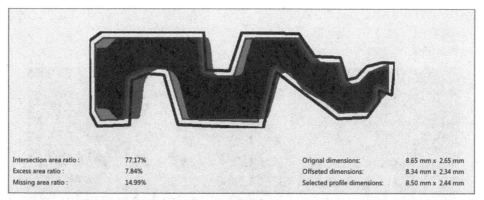

Intersection area ratio :	77.17%	Orignal dimensions:	8.65 mm x 2.65 mm
Excess area ratio :	7.84%	Offseted dimensions:	8.34 mm x 2.34 mm
Missing area ratio :	14.99%	Selected profile dimensions:	8.50 mm x 2.44 mm

Figure 22-7: A key profile is mapped and modified from a photo of the lock.

- An existing key in the database can be modified. Figure 22-8 shows a keyway scan and how it can be modified.

- The program can create multiple bitting surfaces in different formats such as laser track or side bit milling.

- The user can verify the program's output to visualize the finished key before printing it.

The available key profiles and models usually include these:

- Conventional and high-security pin tumbler keys

- Regular keys with side bit milling

- Dimple keys with up to 6 rows and 22 pins per row

- Laser keys (e.g., vehicles, EVVA, Mul-T-Lock MT5+, Yuema, Mauer, and others)

- Lever lock single-bitted keys

- Lever lock double-bitted keys

- Tubular keys

- Specific or custom profiles including disc tumbler, tilting-wafer, and high-security lever lock keys for safes

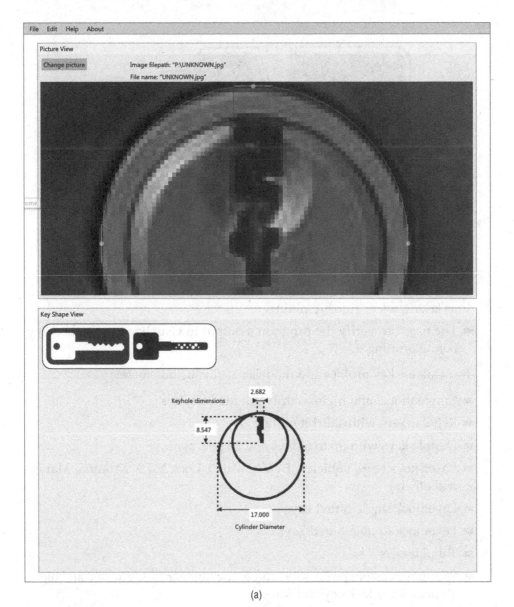

(a)

Figure 22-8a, 8b: Two keyway scans generated from LOPID profiles. They are from macro photos of a target lock. It's possible to add measurements from point to point to map the keyway. Once that is accomplished, bitting values can be added and the key can be printed.

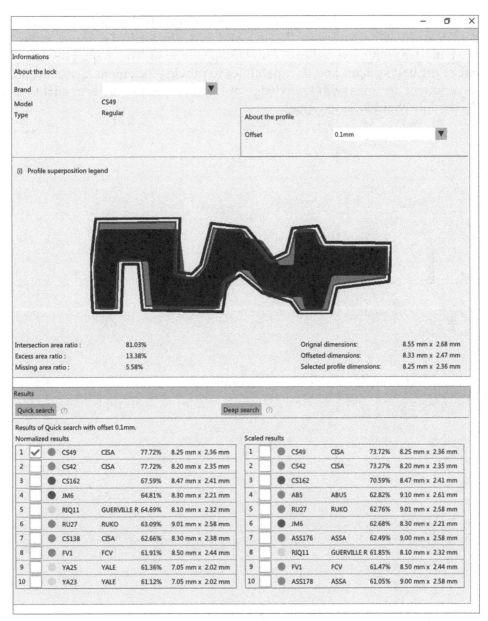

(b)

Figure 22-8a, 8b (Continued)

The next chapter details how locks can be electronically decoded with a hand-held device that measures each detainer and provides detailed output matched in a database within the device or on a laptop computer. The chapter discusses one of the best systems and its capabilities to provide lock manufacturers and government agencies with knowledge of the sophisticated tools available to derive data about locks externally.

CHAPTER 23

Digital Fingerprints of Locks: Electronic Decoding Systems

Locks are designed to frustrate the ability to easily determine the bitting data of their credentials. That information is supposed to be protected by the features embedded in keys and internal mechanisms. Any lock's security is partly based on the difficulty of opening it without the correct key and by an unauthorized person. Still, there are many instances when it's important to learn the bitting code for a key. They can involve lost keys, lockouts, mechanical problems, emergencies, and access by fire, medical, law enforcement, or government personnel. In most instances, there's no need for advanced tools or techniques to produce a key.

Sometimes the need to obtain the codes for keys is for unlawful purposes, such as the famous Brinks robbery in Boston in the 1950s. In that case, the thieves picked perimeter door locks and had them disassembled and decoded by a local locksmith. Keys were then produced to access the armored-car facility, where the thieves stole millions of dollars.

There are many methods for opening locks. They involve picking, impressioning, decoding, bumping, or using more advanced tools and procedures. The result is often the simulation of the key's function or generation. These traditional methods and tools require less sophistication and are usually reliable. They normally succeed, but there can be serious impediments based on the many variables in the lock and external conditions.

High-security locks can be especially problematic due to their multiple layers of protection, specifically designed to resist attacks against their key control and physical manipulation. Law-enforcement and intelligence operations encounter many different types of locks. They need tools that can account for multiple manufacturers and designs encountered in the field, over which they have no control. Their operations usually require careful consideration and minimalizing the risk of detection, time delay, and the potential to leave a forensic trace. These and other issues favor using more sophisticated methods of attack. Certain tools described in this chapter can quickly optimize the chances of success against almost any lock. Depending on the selection of advanced systems, the quality and accuracy of data derived from the lock can be assured.

Electronic scanners are the next generation of tools for mapping, decoding, and measuring the internal components of thousands of profiles of pin tumbler and lever tumbler locks. Government agencies need to understand what is available as the latest and most reliable technology for covert-entry teams and how handheld scanners can assist in their efforts.

These advanced tools, techniques, and systems have specific capabilities and drawbacks. A thorough analysis can be especially important in selecting vendors and their ability to offer their clients the latest technology, stored databases, technical support, and training. This is especially true because criminal gangs, spies, and terrorists often select high-security locks that they believe can't be easily opened by police. So, the proper selection of advanced covert-entry tools may be critical. It's equally important that manufacturers of high-security locks understand the potential limitations of their designs against attacks from these tools and systems. That knowledge allows them to implement countermeasures to prevent or hinder successful decoding and measurement of critical components that may lead to the production of a key.

This chapter describes the latest generation of electronic-scanning technology offered to the government sector by two French companies. Similarities and differences in hardware, software, and operational capabilities can be critically important. Both systems are based on the same physics and electrical principles, but their functionality, operational use, and output data quality are different and very significant.

Scanner Tools, Technology, and Physics

These systems are based on piezo crystals that directly measure pin tumblers and other solid surfaces in locks. *Piezo* is from the Greek *piezein*, meaning "to press." Piezo crystals can be found in many devices and products, including quartz watches, computers, microphones, and almost every industry involving some form of measurement.

NOTE The *piezoelectric effect* was discovered in 1880 by Pierre and Paul-Jacques Curie, two French physicists working with quartz, tourmaline, and Rochelle salt crystals.

It was discovered that certain crystals have a unique property that was called *pressing electricity*. The concept is simple: a crystal converts mechanical energy into electricity or does the inverse, using electricity to create mechanical movement. If an electric current is applied to the crystal's surface, it's energized, which causes a minute change or alteration of its shape while the current is present. In other words, the crystal causes microvibrations and expands.

This principle explains how quartz or synthesized crystals can precisely measure solid surfaces like pin tumblers. If a crystal is configured as a small sensor and mechanically linked to the base of a tumbler and activated, it "pings" the solid object. With the appropriate hardware and software, minute changes in characteristics can be deciphered and translated into the object's dimensions.

It can be compared to sonar and ultrasound: pulses energize the crystal at a high frequency, and the return signature is read. To determine the length of an individual pin, the tumbler is stimulated with an impulse of mechanical energy. The vibrational response of the tumbler is then detected over time. Each depth increment or length exhibits a different response. The manufacturers of these scanners have tested them against all the locks in their databases for reference information, so there's a standard for comparison. That data can be interpreted to correlate with a known target to determine the depth increment of each pin.

Although this process sounds relatively simple, it's actually complex. It requires sophisticated software to process the return energy signals from the crystal in conjunction with advanced hardware to energize the crystal accurately at high voltage and various frequencies. Both scanners employ a 1 mm × 1 mm sensor designed into a special tip. In normal operation, it's guided by a key profile that can mate with the lock's keyway and act as a carrier. Protecting the probe tip from mechanical damage is paramount because it's fragile and expensive. Using these scanners without guides isn't recommended.

To optimize the accuracy of readings, the scanner is usually positioned with a properly indexed reference key segment in the lock for mechanical stability. This allows for precise alignment with each pin tumbler as the probe is moved laterally through the plug. It also allows for controlled and measured movement of the probe tip so each reading of its position and contact with the base of each pin is accurate. A liquid medium must also be introduced between the probe tip and the tumbler to facilitate energy transmission. Depending on the scanner's design, this can be accomplished manually or automatically.

One challenge of a successful scan is for the operative to have the proper keyway segment before analyzing the target lock. The selected hardware must be supplied with preconfigured keyway guides encompassing most lock profiles a customer may encounter in any selected operation venue. This depends on the resources and technical capabilities of the company that developed, sells, and supports the selected system. This technology is evolving and dynamic due to the proliferation of mechanisms from different countries and the requirement to maintain an up-to-date reference database of key profiles. These scanner tools are expensive, so the financial stability of the selected vendor should be established before making a purchase.

Primary Patents

The scanning technology was originally patented by Nedwell in 2018 but was in development for many years before the patent's filing in 2013 (U.S. 9,366,056 B2 and UK EP 2 834,438 B1). The design's concept is to allow an operative to approach a lock, insert the tip of the scanner into the keyway, and very rapidly scan, measure, compute, and store each pin tumbler's length. The internal measurements are visually displayed from this saved information, and a code can then be produced to cut a working key. It's desirable for a covert operation to spend as little time as possible at the target to obtain the necessary data. Disassembling the lock is usually not an option, nor are more traditional entry techniques, so the need for this type of technology is obvious and essential.

As described in the patent and its claims, the scanner must have certain components and perform critical functions and processes to derive a useful measurement from one or more tumblers accurately. Let's break them down.

A Common Transducer

A *transducer* is a device that converts energy from one form to another. A common or combination driving and detecting transducer can transmit and receive signals to and from the surfaces of the probed tumblers. The piezo or similar crystal is the transducer. It's formed into a 1 mm^2 assembly mounted on a shaft or blade for insertion into the lock.

The crystal transducer moves in response to an electrical-driving signal, and the resulting movement is transferred to the tumbler's base. Then the detecting step of the transducer generates an electrical signal in response to the movement of the crystal's surface, which is caused by the tumbler's response to the driving signal.

The process can be likened to an audio speaker and a microphone, both transducers. In this example, electrical energy in sound waves energizes a coil that physically moves the speaker's cone, which is equivalent to the crystal's surface. The crystal then becomes a microphone that *listens* to the sound vibrations of the pin tumbler response. The micro-movement of the pin—the "sound"—is converted into electrical energy processed by the decoder software to ultimately display a precise measurement of the pin's movement.

Transducer Assembly

A *transducer assembly* includes a gauge to display the depth to which the shaft or blade is inserted into the keyway. It may contain a register to show the longitudinal position within the lock to allow the transducer to align with the tumblers.

Reference Software

The *reference software* compares known tumbler measurements to the pins being probed and then identifies which cut of the plurality of possible cuts the tumbler possesses. The manufacturer stores at least one reference domain response time history from the detected response for each possible cut. The software compares the detected time history with the reference histories. Each comparing step uses an algorithm that produces a value that depends on the match quality between the detected time history and the respective reference time history. The tumbler value is determined from one or more reference time histories that produce the best quality-of-match value.

Scanner Designs: Current State-of-the-Art

Two primary approaches to scanner designs for decoding locks are offered by Madelin (www.madelin-sa.com) and C.O.F.E.D. (cofed-sas.com). Figure 23-1 shows one of the probes produced by C.O.F.E.D. These companies provide support services to government agencies and have been engaged in the research and development (R&D) of scanner hardware and software for many years. It's believed that Madelin conceived of the initial approach to decoding locks and expended significant funding to develop the technology, now in its second generation. C.O.F.E.D. uses a similar approach to serve law enforcement, special forces, and government users. One of the primary distributors of this technology is Wendt (www.zieh-fix.com) in Germany. Wendt is intimately familiar with both systems and has represented both manufacturers.

Figure 23-1: The small SWD 1 mm probe with the tip partially extended.

M-SCAN Ultrasonic Lock Decoder and Sound Wave Decoder (SWD Version 4): An Overview

The decoders from both companies appear outwardly to perform the same functions: they utilize a handheld electronic device to scan a target lock electronically, with a small probe to map and measure internal components. They're self-contained and can provide the necessary information to generate a key. Scanning can be performed in a couple of minutes without any trace.

Although the underlying scanning technology is similar, there are significant differences in the hardware configurations, databases, system performance, and ease of use. Major updates appear to have been made to the system software for the M-SCAN, but not to the same extent as the SWD, partly due to C.O.F.E.D.'s reliance on Android for the electronics interface unit.

Both systems employ piezo 1 mm^2 sensors and recommend using individual key profiles for increased tip stability within a keyway. The hardware configuration is different because the electronics that drive the transducer are combined in one package with the M-SCAN and are separate and distinct from the SWD. The method to gather information and measurements is similar, but the output of display capabilities and details differs. The M-SCAN may be more user-friendly and intuitive to use in the field, although detailed training is required for both tools.

> **NOTE**   Certain information isn't described in this chapter by request of the vendor due to the security concerns of its clients. More data and videos demonstrating the functionality of each decoder can be found online at www.wiley.com/go/ tobiasonlocks. Some of these videos are restricted to government-only access.

Operational Features

The decoders we're reviewing contain several operational features that are important in their use. These features are discussed next.

Handheld Probe

The two companies take very different approaches to the configuration containing the sensor inserted into the lock. The C.O.F.E.D. titanium probe comprises the piezo tip, extension, extension adjustment and registration, USB connector, and ability to retract the tip to protect it from damage. The decoder Version 4 weighs 58 grams, and its dimensions are approximately 15 × 10 × 126 mm. The usable probe length inside the lock is 55 mm. It's extremely light and easy to manipulate during the scanning process. The other version is the slightly larger OPS, which measures 18 × 30 × 148 mm and weighs 180 grams. It combines electronic functionality on one circuit board but uses the same technology as the two-piece unit.

The M-SCAN is completely self-contained in a small, easily concealable package that measures 52.5 × 77 × 217 mm. The unit has all the driver electronics and a small display for directly viewing the results of probing a lock. It can be linked to a computer to upload and download information for better results and visual detail. The module has an optical scanner to identify and register the probe's position while it moves within the target lock. There's a tip-interlock feature for the different keyway guides.

Hardware Configuration

The configuration that C.O.F.E.D. has chosen is a two-piece system. The ultrasonic encoder–decoder hardware is in a separate pocket-sized package manufactured by LeCoeur, a French company specializing in ultrasonic measurement electronics. This module connects to the probe with a cable and transmits its output to a smartphone by Bluetooth or USB.

Piezo Crystal Technical Specifications

Both decoders employ a one-channel detector that powers and measures the 1 × 1 mm sensor embedded in the delivery structure. The frequency of the transducers runs at approximately 13 MHz.

Waveform Displays

The manufacturers have taken a different approach to their hardware designs. The C.O.F.E.D. unit employs an Android smartphone or tablet as its primary display, as shown in Figure 23-2. The M-SCAN has a built-in monitor as part of the handheld probe, designed to provide limited information during scanning; decoding is performed later using the large screen on a laptop when running the M-SCAN software. The M-SCAN software also displays a huge scan image and can be used as the primary screen. The larger display and internal database help identify pin materials and shapes. These issues can directly influence the quality and validity of a scan, so as much information as possible must be included in the cylinder database.

A complex key like the Keso 2000S is a good example. There are many different pin shapes and materials in these locks. One pin may be construed as a different value, which provides an error in the output. If the automatic decoding feature is turned on, many "no-name" foreign locks can be easily decoded by cutting several versions with different depth increments.

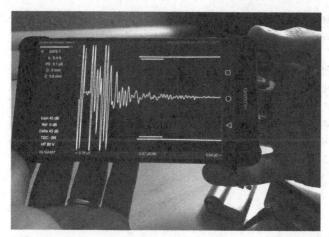

Figure 23-2: The software display for the LeCoeur electronics module is at the heart of the Sound Wave Decoder.

Commands and Menu Items

Each device has touchscreen capabilities to select different menu options. The M-SCAN display may be more practical in the field than a separate system requiring a smartphone. The M-SCAN initial menu items provide rapid access to the most important features of the system, which are discussed next.

Connectivity and Information Transfer

Each device can have a wireless or wired connection between the probe and a computer or a remote feed for storage, data transfer, and profile information input.

Database Entry

All the devices provide for entering and storing images of keys and locks and establishing reference databases. The units can provide real-time analysis of a scan or can process the data later. The M-SCAN software has a large database of reference scans, including most pin variations inside these different lock models. The manufacturer has specifically requested that detailed information about what is in its database not be disclosed.

Software and Operating Systems

The C.O.F.E.D. units rely on an Android-based system that interfaces with a LeCoeur electronics module. This software is available from the Google App Store for free download. The M-SCAN is a proprietary internal system.

Information About a Key

Both companies have compiled extensive databases of lock manufacturers and key profiles. These can be utilized to identify a specific manufacturer after the target lock is scanned. The availability of a complete, detailed database is vital for a valid scan. Many lock companies like to deploy steel and brass pins in their highest-security cylinders. This material difference often means a discrepancy of two to three depth increments displayed. The database must provide information for all pin shapes and materials encountered within a target lock. Clients have reported issues with certain decoders due to a lack of complete database information, which can lead to invalid scans in the field.

Scanning Capabilities

Each device can scan the pins individually as the probe is moved across a pin stack. This is referred to as an *A scan*. A graphical output shows and captures the waveform signature for later analysis. The entire interior of the keyway can be probed to provide an image of all pins. This is referred to as the *B scan*.

Key Tips and Profiles

Each manufacturer recommends using prefabricated key profiles as a guide for the probe tip. As of this writing, many tips available from Madelin for the M-SCAN support a significant number of lock manufacturers. Each tip has a unique RFID address for identity. Information isn't available from C.O.F.E.D. about the number of tips or key profiles it can support.

Internal Storage and Memory

The system should have enough memory (at least 16 gigabytes) to store mission and system data, the operating system, and a reference database of profiles.

The Process of Scanning a Lock

The Madelin and C.O.F.E.D. systems are similar in how they scan the interior of a mechanical lock. Figure 23-3 shows a lock being scanned. First an operative inserts the probe, which is usually affixed to a reference keyway segment for stability. It's moved through the keyway to scan each pin stack. That information can be displayed in real time or stored for later evaluation. The M-SCAN's software may be more sophisticated in its capabilities to measure and evaluate the pin or lever tumblers, but this is a subjective observation because it depends on the preference of the person using the probe as well as the target lock.

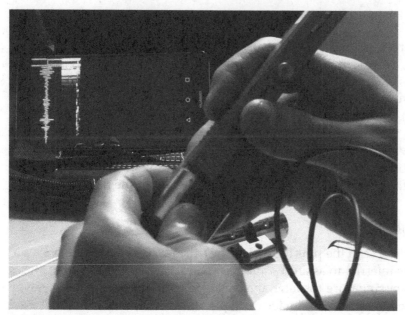

Figure 23-3: A demonstration of the handheld probe for the C.O.F.E.D. system: probing a cylinder, and display on an Android phone.

Before a valid scan can be performed, a liquid such as glycerin must be applied to the piezo crystal or the base of each pin tumbler because there can't be an air gap between the probe and the solid object. This ensures the reliable transmission of energy.

Scanning a lock requires less than 1 minute if done properly. After the probe is removed, the resulting information can be displayed directly on the unit, a computer (M-SCAN), or an Android smartphone or tablet. The software can identify individual pin tumblers and provide different graphical displays to accurately determine their measurement and composition. As described in Chapter 22, the information can be used with a key machine or 3D-printing software to generate a key to open the lock.

Scanner Capabilities: A Summary of Required Features

There are many important features that an electronic scanner must offer and functions they must perform to be considered useful as a reliable covert-entry tool. Many are available as standard with the M-SCAN and SWD, but not all, so any agency considering adopting this technology should determine the required and available options. The features listed here are considered essential:

- Identifying the lock manufacturer from the decoded length of pin tumblers.
- The ability to scan and decode a lock in 5 minutes.
- Wireless feeding of the output from a small display to a larger monitor.

- Cylinder decoding a cylinder with or without a reference database.

- Automatic lock decoding if there's a comparison with a known manufacturer in the database.

- Accurately measuring the distance between the key stop and first pin, and inter-pin distances. There should be sensors to determine the probe-insertion distance with a suggested minimum accuracy of 500 points/mm.

- Offering precise information about the position and insertion point of the probe for each pin tumbler, which can be done with an integral system to read the probe's movement.

- Storing photographs of locks, pins, keys, drawings, pin materials, sizes, and other relevant mission data and information in a database immediately accessible to the scanner for use in the field.

- Wirelessly sharing information between users.

- Software available in multiple languages, including English, French, Spanish, Italian, and German.

- Performing a 2D B scan of the entire length of the keyway and all pin stacks.

- Information about the material and form of the pin tumblers.

- Using the stored database of pins to match what is shown in the scan for rapid identification.

- Creating a new data entry for a target lock not found in the stored database.

- Ability of the client to manufacture key tips without relying on or being supplied by the manufacturer. (The use of key tips and segments is important because using a probe without a guide is inherently less accurate and can also lead to the breakage of the probe.)

- Detailed training seminars for clients.

- A database containing most lock manufacturers in a specific jurisdiction a client may encounter.

- An automatic or manual method to apply glycerin, gel, or other liquid for coating pin tumblers or the probe tip to eliminate any air gap.

- Accurately scanning pin tumbler, dimple pin tumbler, pump, tubular, and lever tumbler locks and other special configurations.

- Ability to do a live feed to other distant team members during the decoding process.

Visualization of Scans

Significant differences exist between the visualization of scans by the M-SCAN and SWD. Although measurements are available on both platforms, their details are presented in different formats. Whether one is more usable than the other must be determined by an operative deciphering the information in the graphical representations. The A and B scans contain more information on the M-SCAN device than the SWD. The author photographed the device output from the C.O.F.E.D. device in Figures 23-4–23-6. Detailed information about the M-SCAN has been omitted because of security concerns to protect sensitive operations.

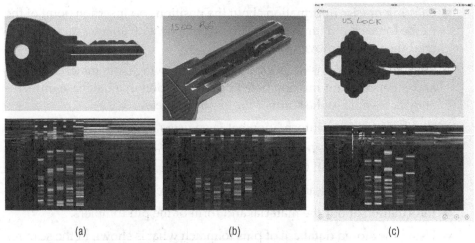

(a)   (b)   (c)

Figures 23-4a–4c: These are scans of different keys using the C.O.F.E.D. decoder.

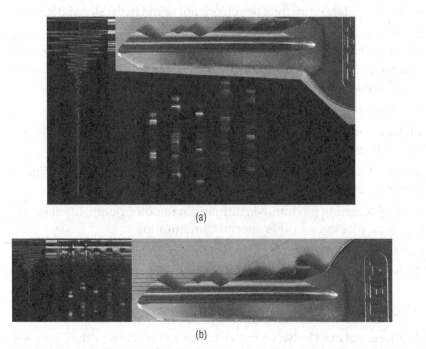

Figure 23-5a, 5b: This scan of an ABUS pin tumbler lock shows the detail and corresponding key with its different bitting. (a) is a composite image of the key and scope output of the scanner. (b) is the detail of each pin tumbler bitting value, correlated with the actual cuts of the working key.

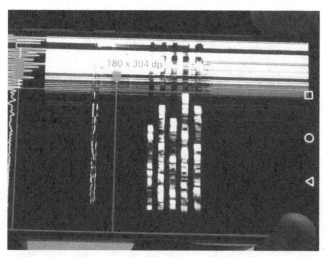

Figure 23-6: This scan from the SWD device is shown on a smartphone.

Chapter 24 provides an overview of deciphering the various security layers of one of the most sophisticated and popular high-security locks in the United States. The case is an example of embedded security deficiencies that were not discovered for more than 25 years and led to the ability to pick and bump open these cylinders in less time than that required by the standards for these locks.

Code-Setting Keys: A Case Study of an Attack on High-Security Key Control

This case study describes a project to attack key control and the related protective mechanisms of the most popular and respected high-security mechanical lock in the United States: Medeco. This case is important because it started with one simple question:

Could a high-security lock be bumped open?

This question took more than a year to answer and led to the discovery of serious embedded design issues and the creation of four keys that allowed Medeco locks to be bumped and picked worldwide. The Medeco design is analyzed in detail in Chapter 14.

My colleague, Tobias Bluzmanis, is a locksmith in the Miami area. He worked for one of the largest Medeco lock shops and is an expert in all aspects of Medeco designs. He can also pick open high-security cylinders and invented a Medeco decoder. We decided to collaborate on a project to defeat Medeco security by bumping. We had no idea if we could accomplish that goal or where it would lead. But our research became an industry model and case study for developing a systematic attack methodology for a lock that had never exhibited any vulnerabilities that would allow it to be easily compromised.

For 18 months, we worked our way through a multistep process of developing hypotheses, analysis, and testing that resulted in our writing *Open in Thirty Seconds*, receiving four U.S. patents, and demonstrating that the security of the

Medeco locking system could be compromised in many significant ways. The book and the Medeco case study offer insight into how to conduct a vulnerability assessment (VA) of a lock that seemed perfect and impervious to security vulnerabilities.

> **TIP**   For a detailed treatment, I recommend reading *Open in Thirty Seconds: Cracking One of the Most Secure Locks in America* by Marc Weber Tobias and Tobias Bluzmanis (Pine Hill Press). Parts of the material for this chapter are taken from this book. It is also available online as a PDF at `https://lss-dame.com`.

Background Facts and the Initial Problem

In 2006, the threat of lock bumping became public in the United States. Consumers, law enforcement, risk managers, security experts, and locksmiths from the private and public sectors began questioning the locks they depended on to protect people, facilities, and assets. It was more than unsettling to think there was a technique that a kid could learn (and rapidly execute) to open a high percentage of conventional pin tumbler locks. Not surprisingly, this concern soon focused on the possible vulnerability of high-security locks. This was partly due to certain manufacturers announcing the heightened security of their cylinders against bumping. Companies had stated that their locks were bump-proof or "virtually resistant" to bumping attacks. However, they didn't fully understand the threat or techniques that could bypass their mechanical designs.

Our initial question was whether we could open Medeco locks with a bump key. They were the logical target because of the company's industry leadership and the news releases about their locks' security against bumping. We developed hypotheses both for and against the premise that we could defeat the actions of Medeco sidebar and rotating tumblers. With our detailed knowledge of the locks' design, we knew there were technical obstacles that would and should prevent bumping techniques from being practical or dependable or from working at all.

As it turned out, all our assumptions were wrong. That should be a lesson for every VA team of the hazards of predicting ideas and beliefs based on history and the preconceived notions of design engineers, management, and the lock industry. Nothing we did was obvious; in fact, quite the opposite was true. Like any vulnerability research and testing, it required imagination, positive thinking, and experimentation.

We sought a method that would allow an operative to approach a target lock with no prior information (other than possibly identifying the keyway) and have a high probability of success in opening it with a bump key. If such a method was possible, we decided it would be easy to learn and execute. Any technique in the field should be easy to accomplish and not require sophisticated or expensive tools. The method shouldn't create too many variables that could make the results less certain or more time-consuming. Our methodology shouldn't require extensive training, nor should it be difficult to acquire the materials to produce keys with the correct bitting.

An Overview of the Medeco Design

There were three generations of Medeco locks, from the original in 1968 until 2008, when we completed our research and released the results. In 2022, Medeco introduced a new generation, the M4. It is much improved over the versions we compromised but isn't immune to certain forms of attack that are irrelevant for discussion in this chapter.

Medeco is famous for designing and developing a high-security pin tumbler lock with rotating tumblers. Figure 24-1 shows the Medeco plug with sidebars. They interface with a sidebar that provides two different layers of security. In 2003, the m3 was Medeco's next generation of locks. It contained a sliding element that blocked the sidebar's movement until a protruding step on the side of the key properly aligned it. That modification didn't affect the lock's basic design or its security.

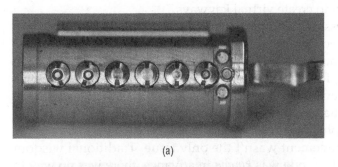

(a)

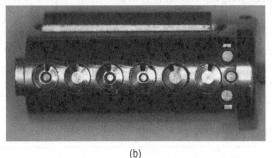

(b)

Figures 24-1a, 1b: Two Medeco plugs with all the pins properly aligned at the shear line. (a) shows the rotations set for the sidebar legs to enter the gates. (b) shows the pins out of alignment, which prevents the sidebar from retracting.

The key bitting has special cuts that rotate each pin in one of three angles separated by 20 degrees. Each bottom pin tumbler has corresponding chisel points that rotate the pins when they contact the key's bitting to the proper angle. This feature makes the design very resistant to picking, impressioning, and bumping.

Experts prefer these locks for high-security environments, including the Pentagon, the White House, the royal palace in London, embassies, and other venues worldwide. Locksmiths, law enforcement, and intelligence agencies had a real problem opening these locks due to the difficulty of bypassing their design.

The objective of creating a bump key is to open a lock, but it's really the compromise of key control. The permutations for Medeco locks and possible key combinations are daunting. There are six depth increments and three angles of rotation for each pin. For a six-pin tumbler lock, there are 46,656 theoretical differs if you consider the possible number of keys.

But that isn't the end of the problem. It is also necessary to calculate the rotation angles in the equation. There are 729 (3^6) possible angle combinations in a six-pin lock. We named these *sidebar codes,* and they represented all the permutations of selecting a matrix of rotations for the pins. Adding the number of pin tumbler permutations and the number of sidebar angles totaled more than 34 million theoretical key changes for each keyway. In 2003, the possible number of permutations increased dramatically when Medeco added different slider steps to the design to create virtual keyways.

The prospect of successfully bumping the lock seemed improbable because the normal procedure required applying energy to the head of a bump key. The key was simultaneously moved forward to contact all the bottom pins. The theory was that *any* forward movement of the key would cause the pins to rotate. That would prevent the sidebar legs from properly aligning with the channels in each pin. If that occurred, the sidebar could *not* retract into the plug and would prevent the plug from turning.

The key's forward movement wasn't the only issue. Traditional wisdom was that unless the sidebar code was *known* in advance, there was no way to create a bump key that could work. This was the problem not only with the Medeco design but also with every high-security lock that contains any form of movable, interactive element or side bit milling. These systems all rely on secondary locking elements that must remain in the correct position during the key-validation process: bumping interrupts that alignment.

Could We Bump Open a Medeco Lock?

There were reasons to believe we could *not* open these locks with bump keys, and there were also reasons to believe we could succeed. We reduced them to two primary issues: having the correct key blank *and* having the correct sidebar code. Conventional locks pose less of a problem with blanks, and they don't have secondary security levels like angled bitting or side bit milling. Because of the design of the Medeco cylinder and key control procedures, those two requirements were complicated, especially for restricted keyways. We had little doubt that the Medeco pin tumblers could be bumped traditionally. The problem was always the sidebar.

We also needed to research mechanical issues, including timing, torque, the sequence of applying energy simultaneously with a turning motion of the key, and the amount of torque and energy to apply. We were also concerned about the tolerance between the plug, shell, and sidebar, which took mechanical priority when turning the plug. As we later found, this was critical because it was easier to bump open a Medeco lock by turning the plug counterclockwise rather than to the right. So, our simple question of whether these locks could be bumped became complicated and, as it turned out, was only the first step in our research because it opened the door to other vulnerabilities.

We began by considering the premise that it was possible to apply bumping to the locks and the other premise that the first was invalid due to overriding mechanical restrictions.

The Premise That Medeco Locks Could Not Be Bumped Open

Primary mechanical designs had to be circumvented for a bump key to work:

- The timing of the application of energy and attempt to turn the plug.
- The interaction of the sidebar legs with the channel in each of the pins.
- The relationship between the physical sidebar and the corresponding slot in the shell of the lock.
- Slight forward movement of the bump key during the process would cause the pins to rotate slightly, causing a failure to align with the legs of the sidebar properly.
- Possible creation of a bump key with the correct blank to match the keyway.
- If we didn't have the right sidebar code, there would be no way to retract the sidebar because the bump key required the correct angle rotations.

The sidebar made all these locks impervious to such attacks. Unless the sidebar code was known in advance, there was no way to create a bump key that could work. Even if the correct sidebar code was known, the preparation of a key was problematic, as locksmiths and others have discovered.

The Premise That Medeco Locks Could Be Bumped Open

As part of our initial hypothesis, we considered why a lock *could* be bumped open. Our answers were not as persuasive:

- If we had access to one change key in a system, we could modify it as a bump key, assuming it had the same sidebar code. We could also decode the angles and re-create them on our bump key. If we didn't have such access, we didn't know how to circumvent the rotation angles of the pins as well.

- We could fashion a narrow, flat piece of metal as a key with the correct bitting and rotation angles. This might be possible because of a wider keyway.

Through trial and error, we determined we could bump open Medeco locks with the correctly bitted key and sidebar code. As a result, we developed a way to bump most high-security locks. It involved changing the amount of torque, which way to turn the plug, and how to slightly withdraw the key before striking it. We thought we could reliably open the locks once we determined all the variables.

We realized that just being able to bump open a lock with the right blank and correct sidebar code didn't accomplish much other than proving our original hypothesis. Unless the attacker was an insider, had access to a key, and modified it by cutting down to all number "6" depth cuts, they couldn't reliably open a lock. It was a nice trick but wasn't practical in the world of covert entry or for locksmiths or law-enforcement operations to open a lock they couldn't pick. It didn't threaten Medeco customers much because creating a bump key for a specific keyway and set of pin rotations would be difficult.

The real question was whether we could develop a system that allowed the creation of one or more keys to bump *and* allow picking, because picking was incredibly difficult. If we could accomplish a method for field personnel to open these high-security cylinders reliably and quickly, we knew it would have significant value for government agencies. It would present serious design issues for Medeco and cause the company to upgrade its locks to be safe from advanced attacks. However, it took Medeco 15 years to redesign its locks to completely prevent our primary method of attack.

As any VA team should do, we evaluated what we had accomplished, expanded the scope of our inquiry, and considered what we thought were the next critical steps to accomplish. We developed a task list with our updated goals:

- Analyze the interaction and tolerances between the sidebar legs and bottom pin tumbler gates to develop a method to simulate multiple sidebar codes.

- Analyze Medeco codes to determine the numbering scheme and potential vulnerabilities in their progression and assignment of bitting values.

- Develop the concept of code-setting keys based on tolerances within the lock.

- Reduce the number of keys from 729 to a smaller number that would open non-master keyed systems.

- Produce four keys to open all non-master keyed locks for bumping.

- Develop the concept of utilizing code-setting keys to pick Medeco locks.

- Develop a method to pick the locks in any system by using a change key to set the sidebar code.

After reviewing our progress, we had to solve two fundamental problems. The first was to develop one or more keys that would bypass *all* keyways so we wouldn't have to depend on the requirement to obtain the proper blank for a target lock. Solving that problem was easy, as shown in Figure 24-2. We cut our keys on .025" to .030" brass stock. We could still create angled cuts with this metal thickness and reliably rotate the pins.

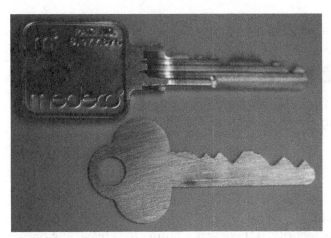

Figure 24-2: A Medeco key and a simulated blank replicating the bitting and rotation of pins.

The next problem was more difficult. We had to reduce the number of sidebar permutations so a reasonable number of keys could open the lock.

We analyzed the code book that every Medeco locksmith consulted to determine valid bitting codes for keys in any system. We found that the mathematicians who devised the coding scheme had separated the codes into master keyed and non-master keyed cylinders. We then reverse-engineered the book to sort the sequences numerically.

Before assessing any issues, we needed to determine whether there was a way to exploit the tolerances that Medeco had defined for its rotation angles. The company had always utilized 20-degree separation, which meant there were three angles: left, center, and right. That created 729 (3^6) permutations in a six-pin lock. Our question was, would changing the 20-degree angle to 10 degrees affect the operation of the key? If so, we could reduce the number of sidebar codes, but in our view, there were still too many to be practical.

After experimentation, we determined that the pins would reliably rotate with a 10-degree bitting angle. We could reduce the total number of permutations of sidebar codes to fit on *four keys*. To do so, we had to *double-cut* the keys for each tumbler position.

After analyzing the code book, we determined the codes for our set of four keys. We also realized that the interface design between the sidebar legs and the pin channels allowed us to "set" the tumbler rotation with one or more of our keys. Figure 24-3 shows the pin configuration and rotation angles. The process held the position of the pins in place, which allowed us to pick the locks like a conventional cylinder. Our ability to compromise the cylinders with special code-setting keys is related to the tolerance between the sidebar legs, vertical gating of the bottom pin tumblers, and angled bitting of the key. We cut the code-setting keys on our .030″ brass stock and demonstrated bumping and picking.

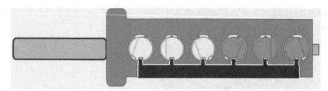

Figure 24-3: This diagram represents a six-pin plug with all bottom pins rotated to the correct position so the sidebar legs enter the true gates of each pin. Note that each pin can rotate in one of three angles.

Lessons Learned

The design of a Medeco lock required that we overcome many independent actions to compromise its security. If there was a failure to achieve any one or more of these, the lock would not open. Our challenge was determining how to override these requirements nondestructively and covertly.

Our approach, as it progressed, utilized each piece of information depending on the attack method. In our first scenario, we concentrated on developing a bump key to open a cylinder rather than picking, impressioning, or decoding. All our methods of covert attack evolved and relied on our use of keys. We want to think that our approach to "cracking" Medeco security was logical and that our progression of techniques from simple bumping to complex picking was predictable once we made certain basic assumptions and findings. It was a creative process that didn't follow preordained or defined rules or concepts. In retrospect, the various bypass levels we accomplished were simple, obvious, and inherent to the Medeco sidebar design.

The next chapter provides many case examples of insecurity engineering that are instructive for design engineers. Some vulnerabilities involved simple exploits; others were more complex and far less obvious.

Specific Case Examples

Part VI offers many examples of simple to complex design errors in locks and security systems that I have encountered with clients and other lock manufacturers. These examples demonstrate and are illustrative of different design problems and defects that often violate the basic principles enumerated in Part VII. Categorized and keyed to specific design rules, the cited examples offer the reader different perspectives on evaluating their current products and designs to aid in the identification of potential security flaws and vulnerabilities.

Case Examples from Part VII Rules

Insecurity engineering is a concept and protocol that in its purest form is meant to connote and ensure that certain long-standing and adopted standards in the lock industry are considered, anticipated, and met during the design, testing, vulnerability assessment, and manufacture of a new or modified lock. The "theory" is that these basic engineering concepts and rules are understood and adhered to, to protect the finished product against certain recognized covert and forced entry attacks and safeguard mechanical or electronic credentials against counterfeiting, spoofing, simulation, or copying.

In my experience, theory is too often not reality. Those responsible for engineering often forget the basics of lock design and may not be aware of past mistakes. This is especially true with experienced engineers retiring or being let go due to budget cuts and cost savings; there is little or no "institutional memory" of past security issues and design flaws. Therefore, manufacturers are bound to repeat the same mistakes.

I have been involved in projects where some of our clients have spent years and millions of dollars researching, developing, and manufacturing what they thought were secure locks and safe designs. To their surprise, these were often defeated in seconds, sometimes by simple attacks as described previously in this book.

Most electrical, mechanical, and electronic engineers lack the skills to meticulously execute and test their designs against real-world security threats from criminals, insiders, hackers, spies, and even young kids. They're great at making things work properly, but they're *not* great at reverse-engineering their designs to detect or understand security vulnerabilities and what can go wrong.

This problem is compounded by the ease with which thousands of resourceful and knowledgeable individuals worldwide collaborate on the Internet to figure out how to attack and defeat any security system. They post videos on YouTube and other sites showing how to compromise even the highest-security locks and safes. Social media can become a real problem for any company that manufactures security hardware, especially if excessive security claims have been published. Engineering and marketing divisions should be incredibly careful when making claims about a new product because representations about security invite attacks.

In my career, I've had the luxury of working on many criminal investigations involving technology. I got to know and interviewed some very smart and clever offenders, from thieves to killers, who researched a target lock, safety, or security system before their successful attacks. One such event (described later in this chapter) involved the theft of more than $100 million in diamonds from a secure facility in Belgium. It's imperative that those responsible for lock design are cognizant of attack vectors. Even more importantly, they must be able to think like a bad guy.

Over the years, my work with my partner analyzing the design of locks and security systems for mechanical and electronic vulnerabilities has provided valuable insight and perspective and forced a unique way of thinking about reality versus design theory. Our clients, some of the world's largest lockmakers, were often wrong in their beliefs about the security of their designs even against the most elementary challenges.

Often, they relied on computer-aided design (CAD) programs to create, analyze, and debug the interactions of components. Unfortunately, these programs can only go so far. They're incredible at allowing engineers to visualize 3D models, animate their designs, and translate them to metal and plastic. But what CAD can't reliably do is assess the ability of each component to be attacked.

In 2006, I released two detailed whitepapers analyzing the vulnerability of pin tumbler lock designs to a technique invented and patented in England in 1925. The papers looked at the technical, legal, and security ramifications of lock bumping. They were cited in several U.S. patents and technical books due to their discussion of instantly recognizable security dangers posed by a simple key that just about anyone could make and that could open most locks in the United States and many parts of the world.

As described in Part IV, *lock bumping* is a process used by hackers, criminals, locksmiths, law enforcement, intelligence, and sports lockpicking groups to open many locks quickly and often very easily, with little skill and sometimes no trace. Why is this important? Because this type of attack was not known to most design engineers at the time, *but it should have been*. It had been a popular burglary technique in Denmark for many years. In fact, I learned it from Hans Mejlshede, the leading forensic locksmith in Copenhagen in the 1990s.

Lock bumping mutated as attackers became more proficient at it. It now takes many forms and is recognized as a legitimate threat to a specific class of mechanical and electromechanical locks. Most manufacturers originally scoffed at the idea that their locks could be so easily compromised. Now most understand how the introduction of *directed energy* or *force* can defeat or neutralize critical internal components in many different mechanisms, both mechanical and electronic. Unless designers are conversant with relevant laws of physics, they'll never be able to produce a secure mechanical design.

In 2007, I asked the 11-year-old daughter of computer experts to open several popular pin tumbler locks in front of a large audience at DefCon, the largest hacking conference, which is held yearly in Las Vegas. In seconds, young Jenna Lynn bumped open two of the most popular locks in America. As a result, she became a YouTube star. The following year, she succeeded in cracking one of the most secure pin tumbler and sidebar locks produced in the United States, which is employed in government security applications worldwide.

I cite this example because of the important lesson for lock manufacturers and design engineers: bumping is much broader in scope than simply attacking a lock with a simple key and a device like the handle of a screwdriver. The fundamental problem with lock bumping is that manufacturers were either unaware of the issue or ignored it and thought it didn't apply to them. It wasn't just this one type of attack that was critically important, but also other straightforward design mistakes that led to product recalls, large legal damages, and other ramifications. Many of these problems could have been avoided had the basic rules of insecurity engineering been considered, understood, and followed, coupled with examples of past failures in lock designs that these companies and their engineers should have studied and conceptualized.

Many case examples in this chapter highlight the failure to contemplate, understand, or imagine possible attack vectors. Most often, this occurs through a lack of understanding by engineers of the many different attack capabilities that their designs help to create. In the following pages, I present a collection of problems with mechanical designs that translated into product failure, legal liability, loss of credibility, and, most importantly, a lack of the protection for which the end user purchased the product. Cases cited in this chapter have a key number for easy reference to rules found in Chapter 27.

The Introduction of Focused Energy Against Internal Locking Components

Originally invented by Linus Yale in 1860, today's pin tumbler locks comprise about 95 percent of the locks found in America and worldwide. Pin tumbler designs appear in thousands of configurations because they're inexpensive to produce and adaptable to any size requirement.

The problem is that they're all vulnerable to lock bumping, which relies on introducing directed energy against all the pin tumblers simultaneously while applying a slight torque or turning motion to the plug or central core. If executed properly using a few strikes with a mallet or bump hammer, the lock will open. The reader must understand that this technique translates to many different modes of attack against distinct locks, both mechanical and electronic.

Jenna Lynn, the 11-year-old daughter of computer experts whom I mentioned previously, unknowingly set in motion a series of events that changed how many lock manufacturers thought about the security of their mechanical cylinders. Her actions caused significant modifications to the design of many locks and a serious self-examination by leading lock manufacturers worldwide.

Furthermore, our demonstrations in which Jenna Lynn was involved were reported by global media, although an exposé of the security problem with lock bumping had already been presented on national television in Germany and the Netherlands in 2005. The video of her opening the lock in a few seconds is at https://youtu.be/D1LH7lrftKA.

Initially, industry experts thought that lock bumping was impossible as a viable attack mode. Then they believed bumping only applied to conventional pin tumbler cylinders. That changed, however, when my co-author and I defeated America's highest-security mechanical lock. We did so through several covert methods of entry described in this chapter and in Part IV, as well as in our book *Open in Thirty Seconds: Cracking One of the Most Secure Locks in America*. These attacks are all based on Sir Isaac Newton's Third Law of Motion: For every action, there is an equal and opposite reaction. The introduction of directed energy at internal components within a lock has been shown to have serious and immediate consequences. Such action can defeat all the internal security designed into the mechanism by a manufacturer.

Introducing focused energy into a locking mechanism is relevant in the following examples and cases. Design engineers and vulnerability assessment (VA) teams must understand the consequences of not designing for and testing against these forms of attack.

As a result of the DefCon demonstration and the attendant intense publicity, Medeco announced that its locks were not subject to bumping and were essentially "bump proof," believing this statement was a marketing bonanza. Eighteen months later, the industry realized that the statement was inaccurate and that conventional pin tumbler mechanisms could be compromised, as well as high-security locks. The important lesson here is that every lock should be thoroughly tested against different attacks involving the introduction of energy directed against internal locking components.

A Paper Clip Defeats a Clever Security Enhancement

Lock manufacturers are continually seeking to update their designs, often so they can file for new patents to demonstrate to customers their latest security enhancements and increase the marketability of their locks. Sometimes these enhancements aren't thoroughly vetted in terms of potential security vulnerabilities. That was the case with an extremely popular high-security lock that added a third security layer to its design. In this design, a slider was made a part of the sidebar. This metal block moved horizontally to interface with the bottom of the sidebar. Not only did the sidebar have to mate with each of the pin tumblers precisely, but it also was prevented from entering their gates until a protrusion on the key's side moved the slider into the correct horizontal position. This modification of the original lock design also created a subset of keyways, increasing the complexity of keying systems.

There were 26 key designs or step combinations to move the slider to the correct position. These were created by protrusions on the side of the key and would mate with the corresponding step measurement on the slider. When the key was inserted, the protrusions moved the step on the side of the slider into the correct position to allow the sidebar to retract and the lock to open.

I was invited to the factory to review this new design before its release. The problem was immediately apparent: the slider could be easily defeated, regardless of the step combination. The engineers failed to realize that regardless of the combination of the measurements of the key step protrusion and corresponding slider position, the slider *always* moved to the *same position* under the sidebar. If the slider was physically moved to that precise mating position, the sidebar could function properly. The designers failed to realize that the required movement of the slider was about 0.040″, which is precisely the diameter of a standard paper clip. So, all that was necessary to defeat this system was to insert a paper clip into the keyway and wedge it between the plug's body and the edge of the slider. The manufacturer has redesigned this system for its latest generation of locks.

Defeat of Electronic Credentials

We had a very sophisticated electronic cylinder to analyze for security vulnerabilities. I knew the project's lead engineer, who had a reputation for excellence and had been with the company for more than 20 years. His team's lock was groundbreaking, leading the industry in designing advanced electromechanical locks.

This mechanism featured a mechanical-locking portion controlled by a key and an electronic element within the key head that communicated with a processor inside the lock. The key contained a high-tolerance set of bittings that controlled wafers within the lock housing. The key also had an encrypted element that authenticated to the lock via a contact alongside the key. A liquid crystal display was also built into the key head, indicating the lock's battery status and whether pairing and authentication with the lock were successful.

In many systems, all the keys for every lock in an installation were keyed alike; only the digital credentials were different based on security and access levels. That meant if we could obtain one key from any lock in the system, we solved half of the puzzle if the bitting could be copied or replicated. To us, that was one of the system's vulnerabilities. A single lost key or a key deleted from the system could be utilized to attack the entire facility if the software, or what the software controlled, could also be compromised.

From the mechanical perspective, our initial analysis was that the lock would be exceedingly difficult to pick, impression, or subject to other forms of traditional attacks. Pin tumblers weren't employed, so that eliminated bumping as a possible attack vector. The key bitting was curved, which made it more difficult to replicate. The lock couldn't be opened unless the electronic authentication scheme could be defeated simultaneously.

We've developed many attacks against electromechanical locks, mostly based on accessing and defeating the interface between the lock's hardware and software. Our expertise is in mechanical bypass, not software. In this example, we had to isolate the element that allowed the locking mechanism to be activated. At the same time, the key operated the mechanical portion of the lock, which wasn't enough to open this device. We also had to activate the electronics and simulate the software control of a blocking element. The internal program controlled a small motor that moved a 90-degree rotor to unblock the system and allow the plug to turn.

My rule that states "The key never unlocks the lock" was demonstrated in this example. The mechanical-locking element and wafers were only one part of the puzzle. If the key could be replicated and, at the same time, the rotor driven by the tiny motor could also be controlled, we surmised that the security of the lock could be defeated. We knew we couldn't hack into the software to cause the rotor to turn, so the question was how to turn the rotor 90 degrees by bypassing the software.

First we succeeded in duplicating the bitting on the key. (Today, this might be easier with 3D-printing technology.) We took a key for this lock and modified it to be inserted into the keyway to move the wafers to their correct position. However, the problem remained as to how to move the blocking rotor.

On closer examination, we determined that a feed-through hole had been placed on the PC board directly below the rotor block. This was a real failure of imagination on the part of the designers because it gave us a channel for direct access to the lock's critical security layer. Our answer was to insert a correctly bitted key and place a very thin wire through the feed-through hole on the lateral surface of the key blade. Then we bent the wire in such a way that when extended, it interfaced directly with the rotor. That way, we could move the rotor out of the way and unlock the mechanism without a trace or audit trail. The wire was formed to interface directly with the rotor once extended. That way, we could move the rotor out of the way and unlock the mechanism without a trace or audit trail. The electronics were irrelevant at this point, and the lock was opened.

Defeat of an Electronic Access Control Lock Remote Using a Pin

We also dissected an electronic keypad lock designed for access control for commercial, government, and military installations. In addition, it had a common access control (CAC) card reader to authenticate federal government employees. This lock was the advanced version of the Simplex 1000 mechanical push-button lock, which has been the primary access control lock in millions of facilities for more than 50 years. It's described later in this chapter due to its simple defeat with a magnet.

This lock is made of metal and has a keypad, a CAC reader, and two status LEDs on the front panel. It also features a trigger for an electric door strike, allowing a dispatcher, guard, or attendant to control access remotely. This access is accomplished by running a pair of wires from the lock to the remote-control points. The ground is communicated to the lock, which then causes the electric strike to activate. On examination, we found nine significant design issues that provided some serious security vulnerabilities. The first we concentrated on was the easiest: the remote-open circuit.

The design engineers never considered the placement of the printed circuit runs on the board mounted immediately behind the lock's front face. Soldered to it were the two status LEDs above the keypad. The remote-control option runs were immediately next to one of the LEDs. Again, there was no consideration of what would cause the lock or door to open. It wasn't the entry of the correct combination on the keypad or the reading of the CAC. In this case, it was the communication of a ground signal to the electric strike. This problem was replicated in another case example in this chapter that deals with master intercom systems for apartment buildings.

This lock's design required mounting the status LEDs within a protective grommet made of silicone or similar material. The security flaw was the failure to imagine that if the circuit board, which ran directly behind the LED, were accessed, it would defeat the entire remote unlock system.

How did we accomplish this? We correlated the placement of the run and its direct proximity to the grommet that held the LED in place. We inserted a metal straight pin through the soft grommet and shorted out the contact, and the door opened. It was a critical failure of imagination that could have dire consequences, especially for high-security facilities.

Other design deficiencies of this same lock are described later in this chapter.

Defeat of the Most Popular Vehicle Anti-Theft Device with a Shim Wire

Known as "The Club," this anti-theft device was simple in design and marketed as being able to prevent a vehicle from being stolen by blocking the rotation of the steering wheel once the long lockable bar was attached. The company employed law enforcement representatives to tout its product, including the superior strength of the South African steel from which it was constructed. The two-piece device was a telescoping assembly interlocked with a ratchet mechanism. The two rods could be joined together and compressed to fit the steering wheel, where they were secured into place by the locking dog entering angled grooves, much like the operation of a handcuff assembly. Once in place, a key was required to release the ratchet by rotating about 90 degrees.

A colleague and FBI agent called me one day to ask if I had seen it. I had not, because we didn't have an auto theft problem where I lived. He told me it was simple to pick and that I should look at it because it had a wafer lock that was easily defeated. I purchased one because I was curious about its design. It was immediately clear that that wasn't the problem and that the manufacturer had completely missed the security vulnerability.

I contacted the company's owner in Pennsylvania and told him his product wasn't secure and could be defeated by just about anyone with a five-cent piece of wire! He said numerous police departments had thoroughly vetted his products and that his company would file a lawsuit if I made any public statements. This was a typical engineering failure by a company with no security engineering experience.

I was flown to Sharon, Pennsylvania, to demonstrate how The Club could be easily opened and removed from a steering wheel. I was provided with several different Clubs, along with a very skeptical group of engineers and executives watching to see if I could open their products.

I pointed out the problem: the ratchet mechanism was improperly designed, with an excessive gap between the locking dog and the teeth of the ratchet. This space allowed for the insertion of a .015″ shim between the two rods where the ratchet contacted and locked into the teeth. Once accomplished, the two rods could be instantly removed from the steering wheel. The designers failed to understand or perceive that the shim could be inserted between the two moving sections if forced forward a few millimeters so the locking dog rose above the ratchet teeth. At this precise point, the shim slid between the two locking elements, thereby neutralizing their effect. It was a failure of imagination on the part of the designers to understand this simple problem. And their claims that "law enforcement had thoroughly tested" their product were meaningless because, in my experience, most law enforcement agencies have no expertise in physical security other than certain crime lab personnel who routinely investigate burglaries.

The net result of our meeting: The Club was redesigned based on the patent (5,277,042) I obtained to change the tolerances of the ratchet mechanism.

The Hundred-Million-Dollar Diamond Heist

Antwerp, Belgium, is the uncut-diamond capital of Europe; about 85% of the world's diamonds flow through this city. It's an armed fortress, with 24-hour SWAT teams guarding a six-square-block area housing the buildings where diamonds are received, stored, cut, processed, and distributed. No unescorted vehicle traffic is allowed, and pneumatic barriers are built into all streets that lead to the critical central buildings.

The Diamond Center was one of the many buildings home to diamond cutters and merchants. It was 15 stories high, 13 of which were above ground. A total of 225 merchants ran their businesses there. A vault in the basement was accessible to all the tenants by stairs or elevators. In 30 years, there had never been a security problem. Each of the 225 customers had a safe deposit box in the vault. The Diamond Center had its own internal security guards and team to ensure everything was protected for its tenants.

Access to the building was by street or the underground parking garage outside the Diamond Center's protected perimeter. Passing through a security checkpoint was required to get into the building, and an electronic access control system controlled garage access.

In February 2003, the largest theft in the history of Antwerp occurred over Valentine's Day weekend. The burglary, which involved the participation of seven career criminals and was two years in the planning, was perfectly executed. The stolen diamonds and other jewels were never recovered. It's a crime that was possible because each of the multiple security layers in the building was neutralized by simple means, which security experts could have anticipated with some imagination by "connecting the dots." The thought processes, logic, and methodology in assessing the target that made this crime possible are instructive for VA teams tasked with analyzing locks because the neutralization of individual security layers is precisely what must occur with more complex locks or security systems.

I visited the vault with the chief of detectives to assess the burglary from the perspective of the crime, the criminals, and the criminal and forensic investigation and physical evidence. I spent several hours in the building, vault, and garage figuring out how the crime occurred and how it could be accomplished again.

The vault was a heavy, high-security-rated strong room with a massive door that had a four-combination anti-manipulation high-security dual-control lever lock. That means a key *and* a combination were required to open the vault. The key for the vault lock was stored in a key cabinet in a locked room with a high-security dimple lock next to the vaulted entry. The vault contained hundreds of safe deposit boxes with three separate combination locks.

The vault had alarms for shock, vibration, and door entry, and there were video surveillance and light sensors inside the vault. It was believed to be impregnable. The alarm system also utilized infrared and microwave motion sensing within the vault and audio sensors outside of the vault. On the actual vault door were high-security balanced magnetic sensor trips.

During the heist, four criminals worked for six hours in the vault. They even brought their wine, sausage, and cheese because they didn't want to get hungry while they broke open 109 safe deposit boxes. Once all the boxes were opened, they gathered up the remnants of their burglary, tools, food, and other potential evidence, put it all in trash bags, and proceeded to leave. But before they left the building, they stopped at the first-floor guard desk and removed all the videotapes and logs, which meant there would be no trace of the crime. The criminals then went to the ringleader's apartment, split up the jewels, and drove home to Italy. About 30 miles outside Antwerp, they stopped at a remote shelter belt on a farm and buried the trash bags.

Monday morning, the farmer who owned the land realized that someone had buried garbage on his property. He dug it up and found receipts from the Diamond Center around the same time the news broadcasts started announcing the theft. The following week, one of the thieves was caught returning home to Antwerp, where the police had executed a search warrant and found diamonds and other jewels.

One hundred million dollars in jewels were stolen because the "security experts" who designed the facility and its protective systems failed to imagine how the impregnable fortress could be compromised with planning and a simple attack. The thieves had analyzed the facility for over two years. They even conducted covert video surveillance walkthroughs with a disguised camera hidden in a gym bag, all to study how the building was laid out and any methods of compromise.

This real-world major crime has important lessons for lock and safe designers. Part of the problem was the arrogance of the building staff in thinking that the appearance of security was enough. Evidently, no one ever thought to plot a theft and work their way through each security layer relied on to protect the millions of dollars in assets.

The seven thieves realized that the security layers that protected the Diamond Center involved six critical elements, all of which worked in tandem but could be individually defeated in sequence on careful review. We employ that same methodology to defeat high-security locks. Multiple security layers are designed to prevent easy compromise, but their weakness is often the ability to neutralize each one with no time constraints.

The security layers that were defeated in Antwerp were obvious. And once the thieves were inside the building, with time to test each system, it was easy to attack successfully. They were:

- Obtaining building access
- Bypassing all the locks

- Bypassing the vault's alarm systems
- Accessing the vault
- Achieving entry into the safe deposit boxes
- Exiting the secure area of the building without attention

How did they do it? They already had building and parking garage access by being a tenant!

The locks that protected the room next to the vault where the second key for the safe was stored were easily picked with a modified Allen wrench specially ground as a rake pick. Even the detectives on the Diamond Squad, who had no special training in opening locks, were able to jiggle the pin tumbler mechanism open in seconds.

The alarm system consisted of multiple components. There was a vibration detector outside the vault's door, a four-wheel high-security combination lock, and a set of balanced magnetic trips to sense when the vault door was opened. The way this was installed, as is customary, was to attach the sensor to the vault frame and the magnetic portion to the door so that when the two parted, the magnetic field would trip. During the day, the thieves cleverly removed both parts of the balanced magnetic switch (BMS) and remounted them on one piece of aluminum stuck to the outside of the safe with tape to appear normal. The thieves obtained the combination earlier via a camera mounted in the ceiling directly above the combination lock. During the burglary they moved the entire sensor assembly out of the way so the alarm system never knew the door was open.

The vault's light sensor camera had been defeated days before with a simple piece of black electrical tape placed over the lens. The combination infrared/microwave motion sensor was defeated by spraying it with silicone, so it didn't detect any signal. This old detector didn't have an anti-masking capability, which should have detected this problem.

Access to the safe deposit boxes just took time and wasn't difficult. Each lock was removed with a simple dent puller, a common locksmith tool used when a bank customer loses their keys.

Before leaving the facility, they removed their audit trail and took the evidence to be destroyed later.

The exit with the loot was through the garage, which was outside of the protected perimeter of the Diamond Center, so there was no alarm system to deal with.

Although all the thieves were all caught and prosecuted, none of the loot was ever recovered.

Vulnerable Design of an Electromechanical Door Lock, and the Murder of Three People

I received a call from the Calgary Canada Police Forensic Laboratory and the chief of the Homicide Bureau. He asked if my partner and I would be willing to assist in a triple-murder investigation where entry was made by compromising the door lock. This immensely popular push-button design also had a bypass cylinder, allowing a homeowner to use a key if the battery was dead or the electronics failed.

The murders of two elderly grandparents and a five-year-old little boy had occurred in a private residence. It turned out to be a vengeful crime; the killer thought he had been cheated out of credit for a patent design. He methodically planned the entry and murders and then took the bodies with him.

It took the laboratory experts five days to process the crime scene. After several days, one of the technicians called the lab and asked if it was normal for very small holes to be present in the door lock. They didn't know, which is one of the problems with many police departments; they aren't lock experts in covert and forced entry or in analyzing how a crime involving locks or safes may have occurred. At that time, there was no expert forensic locksmith or member of IAIL, the International Association of Investigative Locksmiths, in Canada.

At our request, the crime lab sent us photographs of the lock that showed the two small holes drilled in the front. One was 1/16" above the plug's center line in the bypass lock; the other was about 1/4" at the shear line. We ordered a sample of this lock to examine before traveling to Canada. I wanted to develop possible entry methods before going to the lab and examining the lock from the crime scene. We determined there were eight separate ways to open it. Two involved picking and bumping the cylinder. Others involved drilling the lock at the shear line, impressioning, picking, analyzing the keypad with ultraviolet (UV) to determine the keys that were pressed, and drilling a small hole on the lock's side to activate and simulate the action of the electronics portion of the lock.

Our best clue to the entry mode was the two holes in the plug. We speculated that the killer had attempted to make a small opening *above* the shear line to insert a shim after using a blank key to lift all the pins, trapping them, and then letting them drop, which would allow the plug to rotate. We also speculated that, for some reason, this procedure didn't work, so the killer then drilled the lock in the normal way to create a shear line and turn the plug.

We traveled to Canada and spent two days with the forensic examiners and the detectives who worked the case. We dissected the lock for six hours and utilized a comparison microscope to examine each pin tumbler within the bypass cylinder. Indeed, the killer had drilled above the shear line to trap all the pins. It didn't work, however, because he drilled at an angle and tried to pick the two end pins to raise them. He then took a 1/4" drill and bypassed the lock normally to create a shear line with the drill bit.

It would have been just as easy to open the lock by drilling a tiny hole to activate the electronics. The lock's design didn't protect against this circumstance. In addition, the bypass cylinder wasn't protected against drilling because it wasn't rated as high-security. Nor were there any significant anti-drilling guards to protect the electronic mechanism that activates when the proper keycode is entered.

Although this lock has been extremely popular with consumers and is well designed, there are security engineering enhancements that could have been implemented to make forced entry more difficult.

Absence of Evidence of Entry Doesn't Mean a Lock Wasn't Opened

Burglaries accomplished with bump keys can present a significant problem for law enforcement investigators and insurance companies in the United States and Europe. A failure to provide evidence of entry is grounds to deny claims. With bumping attacks there is typically no evidence of forced entry to document a loss. Many carriers refused to pay claims that likely were caused using a bump key, where little or no forensic trace is left on or in the lock. Additionally, crime labs have little expertise with certain kinds of toolmarks. There may be no evidence that any focused energy was applied in very sophisticated attacks where specialized tools are employed. Companies that produce mechanical locks with hardened materials, such as nickel silver, should be on alert for such attacks if queries are received from their customers. A proficient attacker can operate without fear of detection, at least from the evidentiary standpoint.

Unknown Tools Specified in Standards Can Produce Invalid Results

Standards for locks and safes have testing protocols that rely on certain specified tools for covert and forced entry. The individuals performing the analysis, especially for high-security mechanisms, may be unaware of certain restricted tools that are only available to government agencies or known to the hacker community. In such cases, the testing doesn't accurately identify vulnerabilities that can result in opening locks well under the time requirements in different Underwriters Laboratories (UL), Building Hardware Manufacturing Association (BHMA), and America National Standard Institute (ANSI) ratings.

I've been personally involved in VAs where the manufacturers had some of the best U.S. and European laboratories run tests on locks to determine whether new attack vectors could open them. With lock bumping, the labs failed to understand different techniques that could be employed and thus came to wrong conclusions about the locks' security, to the manufacturers' detriment. Several simple and sophisticated tools are available for rapidly compromising security layers. Companies should conduct independent investigations and determine whether specific opening tools are offered to open their cylinders. Expert tool designers in Europe, including John Falle (England), Wendt (Germany), and Madelin (France), are perhaps the best in the world. Any high-security lock makers should retain consultants who have contact with the restricted tool-makers and the hacker community.

Any Opening in a Lock Body or Accessible Component Can Provide a Manipulation Path

I've found on countless occasions that it's difficult for design engineers and test teams to envision using what appears to be an inaccessible hole to access and manipulate a lock's internal components and cause it to open. Yet it's a frequent problem that can have serious consequences. My colleagues and I have opened hundreds of locks by inserting and probing with tiny shims, sometimes measuring .0010″ in diameter. Part IV of this book describes them as some of our favorite tools. Complete sets of shims are excellent covert-entry tools and have surprised even the best lock designers in the world. Engineers should be alert and attempt to exploit *any* available or visible opening in any lock.

Attacks Against Integrated Circuits, Causing Them to Become Unstable

Years ago, I interviewed a Bulgarian safe technician who reported that he could open many electronic combination locks by injecting human urine or other liquid directly into the lock's body. He demonstrated this for us, and we confirmed the vulnerability. I then traveled to Israel, where I met with the safe engineer who discovered the problem but did not understand *why* it worked. The "why" was relevant to my clients who manufactured the high-security safe locks that had been compromised. When our team analyzed the chips within the lock, we found that one of them was the motor driver circuit controlled by the microprocessor, which validated the correct entry of the combination number. The designers of this lock (which had been in use worldwide for many years) failed to investigate the technical data on the integrated circuits thoroughly. If they had, they would have discovered that any change in impedance on some of the inputs could cause the chip to become unstable, thereby resetting it. When this occurred, the "reset" to a normal state also caused the system to extend and retract the bolt mechanism. The solution was to add a protective potting compound like epoxy to isolate all the surface-mount contacts around the chip on the printed circuit board. The takeaway: analyze every component on any printed circuit board, be certain to understand the technical specifications for each component, and run tests for forced changes in impedance, electrostatic discharge, radio frequency (RF) and electromagnetic pulse (EMP), and high voltage, such as from a stun gun.

Simple Attacks Against Sophisticated, High-Security, or Complex Locks May Be All That's Required

I was asked to evaluate several electronic and mechanical integrated door locks for security vulnerabilities. Some had fingerprint readers, and others had keypads. The one common element: they all had bypass cylinders to provide a key override. The team that designed two of these locks forgot one of the most basic rules: *any* opening can provide a way to reach critical internal components.

One of the locks was designed for high-security government facilities; the other was primarily for the home and business sectors. The problem is that manufacturers can make locks appear well made and secure, but a shiny finish and sleek designs don't equal security. The government lock had a lever handle with a high-security interchangeable core cylinder. Although it was extremely difficult to bump, pick, or otherwise compromise, it had an open-ended keyway at the rear of the plug that allowed a paper clip to enter and easily manipulate the controlling component in seconds. The fingerprint lock had a similar lever handle with a low-security dimple pin tumbler lock, a knock-off of a Mul-T-Lock design. It, too, could be bypassed with a large paper clip faster than the fingerprint reader would recognize the valid user.

I see this problem repeatedly: a lack of understanding of access points and often a culture that doesn't fully comprehend even the simplest threats to hardware design.

The Most Popular Bike Lock in the World Opened by a Ballpoint Pen

It was perhaps the world's most recognized and secure "made in America" bicycle lock. Its name, Kryptonite, was synonymous with the Superman comic and television series and connoted strength and security. It was designed to ensure that expensive bikes couldn't be stolen once attached to a fixed object like a bike rack. It's also a classic example of a "failure to connect the dots" by design engineers and accountants who ultimately control parts costs for a project.

One Sunday afternoon, I was bored, so I decided to post a security alert about the design of a tubular pin tumbler lock common to bicycle locks, alarm panels, elevator controls, motorcycles, and laptop cable locks. Identified as an axial pin tumbler lock, it's recognizable because it has a round keyway. The pins are placed in a circle rather than in a straight line, as with traditional pin tumbler cylinders.

The lock designed into the Kryptonite had an industry standard keyway diameter of 0.375"—one of the "dots" that were not connected. A combination of size, cost, and convenience determined the selection of this lock by the manufacturer. Tubular locks were favorites because they're easy for consumers to unlock, and they're very inexpensive solutions for securing hardware.

The engineers who selected this lock weren't familiar with the technique of impressioning, which is a traditional way to produce a key for a pin tumbler lock without taking it apart. It involves inserting a blank to contact the pins and then applying pressure to create marks where the pins are binding against the shear line. Technically, when a lock is impressioned, there are micro-depressions on the blade's surface. The engineers failed to comprehend the use of a lock with the same diameter as that of several popular soft plastic ballpoint pens.

A plastic pen barrel was inserted and pressed against all the pins at once and moved in a circular motion. The tumblers depressed and deformed the plastic equal to the depth of each pin. After a few seconds, a key was produced that turned the plug and opened the lock.

This oversight failure and lack of understanding of how to impression a lock translated to a recall of about 350,000 bike locks at an estimated cost of $10 million. The company failed to correlate the keyway diameter and the ability to easily impression soft material.

Axial Locks: Targets for Easy Opening by Bumping and Impressioning

The Kryptonite wasn't the only lock that was affected. The design problem that I outlined in my security alert reverberated through many other companies because the media coverage was intense. This is a prime example of the power of the Internet, even in its infancy. Postings live forever. They're proliferated on hundreds of search engines worldwide, so if an internationally known company is attacked, it can be devastating in terms of sales, reputation, and economic damage.

Impressioning wasn't the only way to circumvent the security of these locks. Bumping became a favorite because it was fast and easy. Locks on expensive motorcycles, elevators, alarm systems, and many other applications were simple to open in seconds. I was sent to a factory in Taiwan that produced locks for the cable lock giant and attempted to solve the problem. I worked with the company's engineers to mitigate and prevent the effect of bumping. They produced about 30 different iterations with what I thought would have different bump resistance. Nothing worked, however, and I kept opening the locks.

I analyzed the root problem: all the pins were accessible to a bump key, which meant the current configuration could *never* solve the problem. The solution was to place one of the pins below the shear line. A key was produced with a protrusion of a few millimeters that entered the pin chamber. The problem was solved, and a patent was granted for the design (7,441,431).

Experts Think High-Security Locks Can't Be Bumped Open

Most leading lock manufacturers denied that their high-security cylinders could be rapidly opened by bumping. They were wrong. Some had testing labs verify their claims, which turned into a marketing bonanza, given the media coverage of young kids and locksmiths opening doors in a few seconds. There were no standards to cover this attack, so there were no criteria by which to judge the security of any cylinder.

Medeco issued press releases claiming its locks were bump-proof, as did other companies. My colleagues and I figured out how to move each security layer so that bumping would work. Some locks had side bit milling, a second set of bitting to control a separate sidebar. Although these locks were initially thought to be impervious to the attack, it turned out that they could be opened with a slight amount of milling. The companies continued to argue that it couldn't be done until they were shown incontrovertible proof that bump keys could be produced and were highly effective. The lesson was hard learned for manufacturers and the standards organizations: never say never. A simple bump key was shown to defeat many of the best locks in the United States and Europe.

Multiple Security Layers Don't Make a Lock Secure

High-security mechanical and electronic cylinders frequently start with simple and direct designs. In initial testing, the original versions are often easily defeated, so increased layers are added to protect the critical locking components. My colleagues and I were involved in the design of many electromechanical cylinders. When we were shown the designs, usually on AutoCAD, we noted that if one critical component was bypassed, the lock could be opened. The senior design teams' answers were "It could not happen" or "It is impossible."

Multiple security layers present more opportunities to defeat a design because there are more points of potential failure. Complex locks are subject to many different attacks, including bypassing the interface between hardware and software components.

A Key Isn't Ever What Unlocks a Lock

My first critical design rule is always to consider that the key never unlocks the lock! Although this may seem counterintuitive, it's the first concept that design engineers must remember. You must always consider what action you take to unlock the lock. The key actuates the mechanism that unlocks the lock but usually doesn't do it directly. If this tenet is kept in mind, then different attacks can be imagined. It's the point of least resistance. The simplest examples are the locks on office filing cabinets and combination padlocks that are so popular. A simple wire can be inserted in each case to manipulate a critical component.

ILCO produced a five-button mechanical lock that has been employed in millions of facilities since it was invented in 1965. It was the standard in this type of lock for banks, government agencies, airports, businesses, pharmacies, hospitals, and every imaginable application. The design relied on an internal metal bar allowing the mechanism to release and move a lever handle to retract a bolt. The problem with this configuration: the release bar was ferrous. Although this wasn't an issue in 1965, by 1980, when rare earth magnets debuted, it became an incredibly significant security vulnerability. An inexpensive magnet purchased on the Internet could move the locking bar in a couple of seconds. This design caused several class-action lawsuits to be filed. As a result, the lock was updated, and the lessons were clear. If a lock is being sold today, it doesn't matter when it was developed, patented, or initially offered. Today's standards judge locks.

I've used magnets to open many locks, safes, and electric strikes. They're available in many sizes, shapes, and strengths. Magnets are one of our best bypass tools, and the capability of attacking ferrous components should never be ignored or not tested.

Attacks on Power Sources Can Affect Electronic Circuits and Cause Locks to Open

Electronics must have the power to function properly. Consider what happens if the power is interrupted, shorted, reduced, or cut. This can cause circuits to destabilize and attempt to reset or erase audit trails. I worked on one investigation in a bar with video lottery machines, all online to the state capitol gaming division. Our team conducted remote surveillance with cameras on a microwave link so we could watch the theft in real time from down the block. The manager was a thief who'd stolen more than $100,000 when we caught him. He thought he was very clever in disconnecting the power to the machines near certain internal cameras. He would then open the cash vault, take the money, lock the machines, and restore the power. He thought the power failure would wipe out the audit trail. His primary mistake was not killing all the power in the bar, rather than only to the machines he wanted to steal money from. The logs at the state told the story.

We have succeeded in defeating locks by pulsing power or interrupting the supply to electronic circuits within a lock. This can be highly effective, especially if driver chips can be made unstable. The rule for designing these circuits is to set reset modes to the last state rather than an unlocked condition.

Arrogance and a Lack of Imagination Never Works

As I've mentioned, I've been involved in many cases where management and the design team told us they had vetted a new lock design and knew it was perfect. In my experience, this is a prescription for failure. In one case involving an electronic cylinder with an RFID keycard as the credential, the company was certain its research and development had been completed and there were no vulnerabilities to exploit. When our team analyzed the lock and that of similar manufacturers, we found that Newton's First Law of Motion could open the mechanism in about 30 seconds without any audit trail or trace. The lock could then be relocked after entry with no forensic evidence.

The manufacturers of similar locks were all required to modify their designs to prevent the attack, some taking several years to remedy the issue. There was a total failure to understand how the locking mechanism worked and how it could be activated. The locks all used a motor-driven worm gear that moves in and out to control a release mechanism. We manipulated the outer free-spinning knob to cause it to advance or retract the gear to an open position by rapidly spinning and stopping the knob. The design engineers missed the application of force to the knob in a particular way. They tried to use a drill motor or similar device to rotate the knob at high speed. In that manner, it would never open. However, they didn't try accelerating and then decelerating the knob rapidly multiple times. If they had studied the worm gear movement, they would have observed that it moved slightly as the knob was rotated and stopped. It took about 30 "spins" to open or relock the lock.

Small or Uncomplicated Design Changes Can Create New Security Challenges

Every time a lock's design is modified significantly, it can trigger security vulnerabilities. A perfect example was a large computer cable lock manufacturer that experienced a fundamental problem with its locks being impressioned and bumped open. The company modified the design of the lock and changed the diameter of the keyway–plug relationship. It felt that if the diameter was less than that of the original lock, it would solve the problem. In doing so, the manufacturer changed how the cable was secured internally to the lock body—a minor change, but a fatal error.

A "C" clip held together the lock assembly at the tip of the mechanism, where the key rotated the interface and locking element that entered the computer. The company failed to analyze and discover that the clip could be easily removed with a jeweler's screwdriver while the lock was still connected to the laptop. This allowed the cable assembly to be completely removed from the lock's body and a laptop to be easily stolen. A small and simple modification required the release of a new lock and the expense of all the locks manufactured with the defect.

A 25-Year-Old Embedded Design Defect

In 2007, lock bumping was the primary subject of discussion among locksmiths and lock manufacturers. Claims were made that certain locks were bump-proof and thus far more secure than conventional cylinders. My partner and I engaged in a project to examine Medeco locks, which were and still are the predominant product chosen by businesses and governments to secure facilities. We determined that the company's locks could be bumped open, but only if the collection of rotation angles for a given system was known. We viewed the fact that they could be bumped as a nice theoretical exercise but one meaningless in the real world of covert entry.

An ingenious design invented in 1968, Medeco locks' security is based on the premise that pin tumblers are both elevated and rotated to their correct position, in contrast with traditional locks where pins are only raised to the correct shear line position. Six depth increments are possible for each pin in a six-pin Medeco lock, allowing for a theoretical 46,646 key combinations. Add to that the three rotation angles for each pin, for a total of 729 different sidebar combinations, and the lock now has a possible 34,012,224 key combinations.

We discovered a design defect that allowed us to put torque on the plug while withdrawing the correct key for a given lock. This action trapped the pins in a way that could lock the sidebar legs into the channels in the pin tumblers so the lock was easily picked. Medeco locks were known as exceedingly difficult to pick. This allowed us to open them, but we weren't satisfied. We sought to develop a set of keys to open all Medeco locks by bumping or picking.

All keys for Medeco cylinders worldwide must be cut to meet specifications in the company's codebook because conflicts must be accounted for due to the locks' chisel-pointed pins. We analyzed the codes and determined that we could matrix different sidebar codes into far fewer than 729 combinations. We found that the rotational tolerances of 20 degrees could be reduced to 10 degrees, and double cutting the key bitting allowed us to produce four keys that would likely allow the opening of all the non-master keyed cylinders worldwide.

Medeco has since released its M4 design, with added key codes to make this process more difficult, but some critical issues remain. We published a book in 2008 titled *Open in Thirty Seconds* that described the methodology we developed to neutralize each security layer in this lock. See the more detailed account of this exploit in Chapters 24 and 26.

Man-in-the-Middle Attacks Can Allow Your Expensive Car to Be Stolen

A series of car thefts in the United States and Europe revealed the introduction of sophisticated devices to initiate a man-in-the-middle attack on key fobs that controlled keyless access to some of the most expensive cars. The word *fob* likely came from the German word *fuppe*, which means "pocket." Key fobs are electronic keys for cars carried in one's pocket. These bypass devices are being sold to governments and car thieves. One of the prime distributors for these systems is Wendt in Bergheim, Germany, the leading company with a wide range of government covert-entry tools. The release of these systems has prompted certain lock manufacturers to invest in intellectual property (IP) that can protect against this attack. A chipset can determine the location and range within a few inches between the key fob and the vehicle, which can block the man-in-the-middle attack.

Keyless entry is based on a low-frequency radio beacon in a vehicle and an ultra-high frequency (UHF) return path for an authentication code from the key. When the owner touches the door handle, it triggers a 20 KHz radio signal transmission with an extremely limited range of a couple of feet. Car designers thought this low range was sufficient to authenticate the owner of the car and their key fob with the vehicle rather than cars nearby. They were wrong, however, and never considered the potential for a man-in-the-middle attack where the communications to and from the key fob could be intercepted and repeated. It was a security flaw that was first denied, resulting in warnings to consumers and changes in how these systems operate.

The devices sold by Wendt and others can be placed near the holder of the key fob and another radio transmitter-receiver near the target vehicle. The signals are relayed back and forth, so when the thief touches the door handle to trigger the radio beacon in the car, it's received hundreds of feet away by the key fob, just as if it were next to the car. Once that signal is received, the key transmits an encrypted signal in the UHF band relayed back to the car. The thieves don't need the key to steal the car or drive it away.

All the car manufacturers that have implemented keyless entry failed to understand or imagine a man-in-the-middle attack and design safeguards to prevent the occurrence. It is, again, a failure of security engineering with serious consequences.

Hidden or Unknown Security or Design Information About a Device Doesn't Make It Secure

I have been involved in hundreds of cases where manufacturers believed that the nondisclosure or attempted obfuscation of their security "secrets" would prevent the defeat of their devices. Such a premise is rarely, if ever, true in the long term. The argument is always made that consumers shouldn't be told about security flaws because it places them at risk. I've never agreed and believe this policy can have serious liability implications.

I've analyzed one of the premiere protective systems for retail security sales. A U.S. manufacturer developed very clever electronic and mechanical locking systems to protect against the theft of items in stores, especially electronics and jewelry. Locks for glass display cases, counters, and hanging merchandise are all secured by these devices, which are controlled by infrared encoders built in the form of keys. This key is placed against the locking device and communicates with the processor to release the locking mechanism.

The lowest level of the antitheft device employs a Nitinol wire designed to change shape when activated by an electric current. The electronic key induces a voltage in the wire and causes it to move, thereby releasing the locking mechanism slightly. The designers of this unit, which is secured to a hanging peg to prevent merchandise from being removed, failed to understand that a tiny shim wire could be inserted into the gap in the plastic housing and used to lift the Nitinol wire to change its position physically. In a couple of seconds, this security device could be removed, thus allowing thieves to steal the merchandise it's designed to protect.

A more serious design flaw is in the electronic lock offered by the same company. In this example, an infrared encrypted code is exchanged between the key encoder and lock. The system isn't online, so the codes programmed into each locking device worldwide are fixed. I wanted to understand what would happen if the locks malfunctioned or the keys were lost or stolen, so I called engineering support for the company and spoke with a technical support supervisor. Through innocent questioning, I learned there was a global master key that could be used to unlock or reprogram any lock (or group of locks) in the world. That critical information would allow us to potentially reverse engineer one or more locks and develop a key that would open all of them anywhere. It created a significant liability problem for the company because once that information was in the possession of thieves, every store would be at risk. This is a perfect example of the social engineering of employees who possess critical information about products that, if disclosed and exploited, can lead to serious liability.

This is just one example of how information can provide insight into a product's undisclosed security issues. Management should be aware of the potential liability for releasing critical information or disclosing inaccurate statements or representations regarding product security.

The Most Likely Attack Against an Electronic Lock May Not Be the Most Serious

We were tasked to look for vulnerabilities in two new electronic lock designs that the manufacturers thought could not be opened other than with the correct credentials built into the key or by utilizing Bluetooth credentials from a smartphone. After analyzing each lock, it was determined that both designs could be manipulated by inserting tiny shims about 0.005" in diameter. In one case, the wire was routed through a small opening that provided a manufacturing clearance into a critical component. In the other lock, it was determined that the small motor that controlled unlocking could be similarly manipulated by forcing a wire into its release gear, because it was designed to turn in one direction, facilitating the attack.

In extensive conversations, it was decided that the attack risk in both lock designs took more skill than a traditional attacker would possess, and thus so did the threat. However, it could be executed in under 1 minute and should be the priority. The manufacturer with the motor issue contacted the motor provider and got it to rewind the coils. Hence, the rotation was opposite of normal, partly solving the security problem.

Although we discovered other potential vulnerabilities in both lock designs, the attacks with shims that proved most deadly became a lower priority than those that were more obvious but took more time and were more likely to occur.

VA teams should concentrate on and prioritize the attacks that are most likely and easiest to accomplish and minimize the impact of more exotic attacks, even though they may yield faster results but require much more skill.

In both cases, I asked the critical question: are you willing to not fix the issues involving the use of wire shims, gambling that criminals will not discover the exploits? Ultimately, the companies fixed the issues, reducing the likelihood that all but very experienced attackers could compromise these new locks.

The following chapter categorizes the cases discussed in this chapter by attack methods. I felt it was important to analyze what went wrong in the designs of the locks that were the subject of attack with regard to why they were vulnerable, not just that their designs failed and were vulnerable.

Case Examples by Category

This chapter presents detailed case examples illustrating common security engineering failures in designing and testing locks and security hardware. Of the many cases my colleagues and I have worked on during my career, I've selected those representing various issues that should or could have been imagined, foreseen, or discovered. I've classified them into 13 categories reflecting the most common and critical elements that must be understood and considered in any serious vulnerability assessment (VA) conducted before, during, and after a product is developed, modified, or upgraded. These classifications closely follow the organization of the chapters in Part IV.

It's important to understand the required methodology and thought processes for everyone involved in a project to analyze different known or potential design deficiencies, failures, or attack vectors. These various issues can lead to significant security breaches and the failure of a product to accomplish its intended purpose or to meet its direct or implied security representations.

Note that you will find some duplication of case examples and descriptions between Chapters 25 and 26 because they're categorized differently in each chapter based on the type of attack. Many of these cases are documented with detailed videos in the accompanying multimedia edition at www.lss-dame.com.

Failure to Connect the Dots and Lack of Knowledge About Locks

Many of the cases I have analyzed that involve deficient or defective designs result from a failure of design engineers to "connect the dots" about what can go wrong. Often, the issues are simple and aren't recognized for their potential impact on security and how they can create vulnerabilities that can allow locking systems to be defeated and compromised. Much of the problem stems from a lack of understanding of bypass techniques and mechanical configurations that can be easily compromised.

A fatal flaw in building entry control systems can allow unauthorized access in 30 seconds.

Most apartment and condo complexes have an integrated access control system that allows visitors to call a tenant from the front door and be "buzzed in" when recognized. One industry leader provides a typical design of such a system: a metal enclosure with a keypad, liquid crystal display, speaker, and microphone. All the electronics necessary to integrate with a "back-end" system are present, including the radio frequency identification (RFID) readers at every door so residents can activate the electric strike on a nearby door to the building or garage entrance. Internal relays within the panel control the strike and other accessories. Many systems also incorporate a lever lock for the U.S. Postal Service to allow a second means of building access for mail delivery. The lock is embedded into the panel and constantly activates a microswitch against the extended (i.e., locked) bolt. When the postal key is inserted, it retracts the bolt. It triggers the *normally open* microswitch connected to one of the internal relays that communicates with the electric strike on the door.

The entire security of the electronics in this enclosure is based on the manufacturer's selection of an inexpensive four-wafer lock that can be shimmed or picked open in seconds. That means a five-dollar lock is the only barrier between a criminal and all the building residents. Why is this possible? The circuit design provides for a normally open switch to sense the status of the postal bypass lock. The two contacts can be shorted out easily once the panel is open. The electric strike relay is triggered when that occurs, and the adjoining door can be unlocked.

When I discussed this design with the engineering team that created the product, they admitted they didn't know locks, nor did they know how easy it was to compromise the one they'd chosen for thousands of installations. To make matters worse, I could order keys for their locks from Amazon, which also opened other similar systems.

This industry leader never considered the capability to circumvent the entire system with a paper clip or piece of wire by shorting out the two adjacent contacts on the microswitch once the cabinet was opened. Their failures put every building resident at risk because they didn't connect the dots between the ease of bypassing the lock and the ability to control the electric strike on the access doors. This liability could have been significant had there been a loss. Once informed, the company notified its customers and upgraded all enclosure locks to higher-security Medeco cam locks, which are far more difficult to pick and decode.

Good ideas don't necessarily mean good security.

One of the most innovative examples of a good idea for a lock design is the 3D-printed "stealth key" patented by Urban Alps in Switzerland. The inventor, Dr. Alejandro Ojeda, has extensive 3D-printing and manufacturing expertise. He conceived a key with hidden bitting that could be printed in titanium for strength and durability. The idea was that the bitting code couldn't be copied through a normal analysis process by viewing and extrapolating the various depth increments. The key was designed to hide the bitting completely and has been patented in many countries.

The internal locking components consisted of a series of rotating discs that were moved by a laser-track–type bitting with the capability of three different depth increments. The printed and embedded bitting in the key caused the discs to rotate and move their corresponding gates to the correct positions for a sidebar to enter, thereby allowing the plug to rotate when all were properly aligned.

This idea was groundbreaking and quite clever for the lock industry. The ability to print an unlimited number of keys on demand seemed like a logical solution, especially for locksmiths who were required to keep an inventory of blank and special key machines. Unfortunately, the execution of the idea and turning it into a secure lock was more difficult to achieve. The key's design dictated the lock body's mechanical configuration, which drastically limited the capabilities for different security layers and the number of theoretical differences or key combinations. Several compromises were required to make the key work. This ultimately resulted in the manufacturer's inability to meet recognized market demands for differs, key duplication, keyways, effective master keying, and the ability to resist picking and decoding techniques.

The manufacturer had little expertise in lock design and was hampered in its ability to enhance the security of its original lock model. It had to select a currently available shell to make the plug design control the discs. The company's inventiveness limited how far it could advance its technology. The fact that the keys could be 3D printed meant little to the industry insofar as marketability and meeting any large quantity demands. This lock had a niche market, but it could meet security demands in certain environments where the ability to hide bitting information entirely was important, such as in a prison.

The lesson to be learned from this very costly startup lock company is as follows: a patent ensures neither security nor marketability. It only prevents others from duplicating the idea for 20 years. The requirements for a successful locking product are complex and involve engineering, security, local customer support, multiple security layers, key control, endurance, compliance with standards, and many other criteria. All these issues must be considered whenever a new design is presented or embarked on.

Electronic cylinders rely on a tiny motor for locking; many systems can be compromised.

Virtually all electronic and electromechanical cylinders rely on tiny internal motors to control moving elements that block or unblock associated barriers to the movement of the plug. Unlike solenoids (which can often be easily defeated by shock, vibration, or magnetic fields), motors or worm gears are the favored technology. Regardless of how the lock is powered (i.e., internal battery or a battery within the key), something must move to initiate a locked or unlocked state, and some form of motor usually drives that movement. Even the two most recognized and sophisticated energy-harvesting locks produced by Abloy and iLOQ in Finland rely on motors. The important issue is the ability to directly access the motor and thus bypass all the credentials contained within the key.

I've personally seen many successful direct access attacks, including the use of a shim or wire to manipulate the rotor or blocking element activated by the motor. In many designs, it's possible to connect a power supply directly to the motor input. Often, only one lead is required to drive the motor in these designs because the lock body is at ground or has a negative potential. Physical access can be achieved by drilling tiny holes through the often-plastic lock bodies. We don't like using this material because it can be penetrated easily with tiny drills or a high-temperature wire or probe.

Design teams must always consider the primary axiom that "the key never unlocks the lock" when considering direct access to motors and the elements they control. There is often a method to input power directly to the motor or to access whatever the motor controls mechanically. Don't ever discount the ability to route shims around or through what appear to be insurmountable obstacles within a lock to reach a critical element. Memory wires that can retain shape are especially well suited for this purpose.

Failure of Imagination and Engineering Incompetence

In the following cases, solenoids are discussed because of their prevalence in lock and safe designs. Many engineers fail to understand their vulnerabilities to simple attacks. Therefore, extreme caution should be exercised whenever a design calls for their use.

Defective safe designs based on solenoids can result in deaths.

In 2010, the Vancouver, Washington police department required all off-duty deputies to store their weapons in a provided gun safe, in response to a fatal accident a few years before when a three-year-old boy had accessed his father's gun.

I was retained as an expert witness to analyze the gun safe to determine any design defects that could cause it to open, tragically allowing the service weapon to be retrieved and the child killed. We installed a high-speed video camera inside the safe to record how the locking system worked. In the video, we found that the solenoid could be jiggled and bounced to cause the bolt to move and the safe opened. It was a classic case of design engineers employing a very popular and inexpensive locking mechanism to substitute for a reliable security solution. As a result of this investigation, we analyzed several of the other safes produced by this company and found that all could be opened with vibration, shock, or shim wires. The net result: the manufacturer settled a federal class-action lawsuit.

Nitinol-shaped memory wire is a great idea for a locking device, but it isn't secure.

Nitinol wire is a nickel-titanium alloy with elasticity that has shape-memory characteristics. The wire can be deformed at one temperature and will then return to its original formed shape after being heated above its transformation temperature. Its shape can also be altered with an electric current because of the wire's resistance.

A group of software engineers thought they knew about lock design and decided that Nitinol wire, shaped as a blocking device, would make a unique locking mechanism that was easy to control and manipulate. They designed a profile cylinder for the European market and asked that we test their design. Surely it was secure, they thought, because there was no easy way to access or manipulate the wire with any conventional technique.

They didn't fully understand the physics of Nitinol, however, and how it could be activated in a way other than with an electric current that generated the appropriate temperature to reshape and move the wire-blocking element they designed. What they failed to imagine was that the wire could be activated by high temperature. We attacked the lock using a hair dryer, blowing hot air into the cylinder for 2 minutes and opening the lock. The lock designers failed to consider what would happen in a fire recognize the potential threat to life and safety if the locked body heated up and was frozen in the locked position. The lesson to be learned: always consider what unlocks the mechanism other than the obvious, and extrapolate potential scenarios to exploit such possibilities. In this case, the designers ignored the wire's physical characteristics and all the means to create similar conditions.

Solenoids used as locks don't make safes secure.

Solenoids are a substitute for higher-security traditional combination locks. These devices are designed to block the movement of internal bolt works in less-expensive safes and storage containers. They comprise a coil and a spring-loaded magnetized pin that floats in the windings' center. When energized, the pin retracts. The solenoids are placed to block the movement of locking bolts. They're typically activated by an electronic keypad that sends voltage to the coil when the correct combination is entered. This allows the pin to be retracted and the bolts to move.

One of the most popular fire safes was designed with a solenoid mounted in the door's upper-left corner. The manufacturer, which had been in business for more than 80 years, failed to consider a primary attack method of using a strong magnetic field to retract the movable pin inside the solenoid coil. It could be opened in 2 seconds with a rare earth magnet. The way the manufacturer placed the solenoid allowed for the perfect mating between the magnet and the pin. The design engineers either did not fully grasp the simplicity of how solenoids worked or failed to understand that a strong field would easily move the pin and open the door.

Solenoid-type magnetic release mechanisms in storage containers aren't secure.

A company that produced many products such as tote bags, plastic boxes, tables, umbrellas, and beach tables thought it could capitalize on the anti-theft business by producing a storage container for package deliveries called CleverMade. The manufacturer produced and sold a steel container with a keypad combination lock and a bypass keylock to allow homeowners to leave a locked box on their porch or near their front door so UPS, FedEx, or the postal service could securely leave packages without fear of them being stolen. The company had zero expertise with locks or locking mechanisms. It designed the system to release a form of solenoid that would allow the top of the container to be opened. When the design was analyzed, I found that the lock was conducive to external shock applied to the side of the container. One strike with a rubber mallet or a swift kick causes it to release and open. The wafer lock could be easily shimmed open in seconds by reverse picking.

When the manufacturer was advised of the problem, the company denied it, notwithstanding that each container sold for about $150. This is a prime example of the failure of a manufacturer to understand how magnetic-based locking systems work and how they can be very easily compromised.

Failure to Consider or Deal with Hardware Constraints or Material Limitations

Consideration should be given to the materials employed for locks, safes, and storage containers. Although they may appear secure, it depends on the characteristics of the materials relied on for their strength, hardness, and ability to be bent, flexed, or penetrated by drills or the application of different forces.

The internal construction of locks can also be deceptive and hide vulnerabilities that may not be apparent.

A gun storage case that appeared to be secure was not, with tragic results.

The single mother of a 10-year-old boy was dating a police officer near Las Vegas, Nevada. As a gift and for protection, he gave her a .357 magnum revolver and a gun case to securely store it. This seemed like a very responsible thing to do, especially because guns are *attractive nuisances* for children, which means children are drawn to guns—with often-deadly results. The gun case was made of Lexan, known for its toughness and endurance. The case allowed the weapon and ammunition to be stored in a padded foam rubber interior and was secured by two padlocks. The locks were connected to the case through a hole on either side of the enclosure, which locked the two halves of the case together. It was advertised as TSA-approved for transporting weapons and appeared to meet the requirements to securely store a weapon, especially one as powerful as the .357 magnum revolver.

I was retained to analyze the gun case and learn how a weapon could be removed without unlocking the two padlocks or doing any damage. On viewing it, I noticed there was no evident damage to the plastic or deformity in the Lexan material. I found it obvious that the manufacturer had no expertise in locking systems or containers because it was simple to grab the carrying handle, separate the two halves of the top and bottom of the container, apply pressure, and create a gap to expose the contents. This action allowed about 1.5" clearance to reach in and retrieve the weapon easily. Tragically, that's exactly what occurred, and the single mother's 10-year-old son shot himself in the head.

Lock and container designs have real-world consequences. In this case, the manufacturer denied liability, claiming no one reasonably believed such a case was secure. The company settled a lawsuit partly because of its advertising photographs showing a weapon and clips of ammunition in the case. If the designers of this enclosure had done any vulnerability assessment (VA), they would have realized that Lexan could be flexed to deform the opening without any damage. The material had acted as a spring to reveal the opening.

Failure to Understand or Correlate Attack Methods

Insecurity engineering is all about a failure to contemplate or perceive potential methods of attack against locks, safes, and security systems. In the following example, an award-winning lock manufacturer did not correlate the design of its electromechanical locking system with the capability of multiple defeats that involved fundamental mechanical designs within the lock. The exploits that my colleague and I developed created significant security issues for every installation of these locks until the manufacturer updated the designs to minimize the threat.

An award-winning electromechanical lock could be easily defeated.

iLOQ, a Finnish lock manufacturer, designed perhaps the first energy-harvesting electromechanical lock requiring no batteries in the key or lock body. This system worked like a wind-up watch and utilized a dual-mode motor that provided current to power an internal processor. Inserting the key caused the motor to act first as a generator. After the encrypted code in the key was validated by the processor, the "generator" turned into a motor to lift a pin, allowing the plug's rotation to unlock the connected latch.

The design was patented, won many awards for innovation and excellence, and was well accepted in the Finnish security market. It received a high-security certification from that country's standards group. All the locks had the same mechanical key, but each key had unique electronic credentials. This was a critical failure due to the way the hardware was designed. It should have been foreseen during the initial planning and VA testing.

iLOQ was founded by several software engineers who weren't lock experts when the original designs were created and marketed. They were very creative and prescient in understanding the need to eliminate batteries, from both maintenance and environmental standpoints, but they failed to conceive of potential attacks.

Two critical flaws existed in the interface between the keys and the reset mechanisms. The entire system was based on the premise that once the key was fully inserted and authenticated, the system was reset when the key was fully withdrawn. A hook in the tip of the key performed this function by pulling a lever to return the locking system to idle status. If there was no reset, the single-pin tumbler that controlled physical locking and plug rotation could be easily lifted with a screwdriver by inserting it into the keyway.

There were two ways to alter the reset system in a way the designers didn't intend: the first method was to grind about 1/32" off the tip of a valid key, and the second was to insert a battery-operated Dremel tool cutter and slightly reduce the contact material of the tip of the key. If either attack was completed, the lock could be left in an open state until it was reset using another valid key.

Ignoring the electronic authentication, the entire mechanical security of this lock was one pin tumbler lifted by the tip of the key. That system could be easily circumvented by modifying the interface mechanism at the front of the keyway or by modifying an actual key. iLOQ made significant modifications and upgrades to deal with this issue. Some very critical software problems were also discovered and are discussed in another part of this chapter under attacks on credentials.

Failure to Consider the Application of Force

Lock bumping is the most popular and best-understood attack that relies on applying focused energy in a pin tumbler lock. However, it's only one of many techniques successfully applied to internal components in many different locking systems to cause reactions that release bolts, latches, spring-loaded parts, blocking rotors, and virtually anything else that moves. Never underestimate the ability to move or alter components through different energy applications against keys, lock bodies, keyway endcaps, retaining screws, gate designs, and systems on combination lock wheels. Likewise, applying force can cause the movement of discs and the advancement of motor drives and worm gears. It can result in using and defeating shock fuses specifically designed to thwart energy attacks, much like relockers acting as secondary and independent locking systems to block bolt movement on safe and vault doors.

Torque is another way to apply energy to deform and defeat locking systems, especially those that rely on sidebars. The important rule to follow is that if it moves, stores kinetic energy, or is spring-loaded, it has the potential to be successfully attacked.

High-security and standards-rated padlocks appear secure but often aren't.

Many padlocks can be easily opened by subjecting them to shock and vibration. In one case, I was asked to analyze a high-security-rated padlock produced in China. It was an electronic credentials-based lock that appeared to be secure. However, when we tested it, we could rap it open with a plastic mallet with a few strikes. The problem was a floating and rotating internal locking part. The manufacturer never considered that the critical element could be rotated to the unlocked position by rapping at the correct position on the face of the lock. The rule: locks without any spring-biased components can often be compromised. We found similar issues with locks produced in Europe by major vendors. They were unaware of the problem until we discovered it by analyzing many competing products for a major public utility concerned with compliance issues in the locks the utility was proposing to purchase. We opened the locks in 10 seconds. The security risks caused a major liability issue and mandated a recall.

A patented programmable mechanical cylinder for hotels and universities could be opened in seconds due to a fatal design flaw: no springs.

Hotels had a major security and liability problem before magnetic card locks were common and replaced traditional key locks. If a guest didn't return the room key, the key or lock had to be exchanged to ensure that the rooms couldn't be improperly accessed later. In the hospitality environment, liability became, and continues to be, a serious concern and problem. The issue plagued hotel administrators until magnetic stripes and smartcard locks were introduced.

One of the leaders in the hospitality industry was a company called Winfield. It patented (U.S. 4966021) one of the first programmable locks in the late 1970s. It was a cylinder with two separate keyways: one for guests and one for security and maintenance. The two plugs worked in tandem to allow keys for guests to be instantly changed. This was accomplished by inserting the security key in the left keyway and the guest key on the right side of the cylinder. To change the guest key, it was turned slightly and withdrawn, and a new key with a different combination was inserted, turned back to the home position, and removed.

The design of the keys was based on a series of sliders in the plug that were raised to a shear line. These sliders or wafers were free-floating to one of two positions for each bitting combination. It was a binary lock, so there were only two possible positions for each slider.

Because the sliders weren't spring-biased, they could be vibrated to one position at either the top or bottom of the plug. This meant the lock could be easily opened or decoded. This design was fatally flawed because the manufacturer couldn't fix the problem of injecting vibration into the plug to move the sliders. This was accomplished with a handheld vibrating tool connected to a key blade inserted into the keyway. We used an inexpensive scribing tool from a hardware store whose primary purpose was to engrave or mark items through a vibrating stylus. If the stylus was removed and a key blade was inserted, it made a very effective tool to introduce force, via vibration, into the lock.

This also created a critical problem that allowed the lock to be decoded externally by inserting a borescope through the keyway to read the position of each slider when set at the shear line. Once that information was observed, it was simple to cut a key for each bitting position to correspond to a 0 or 1 cut (i.e., no cut or full cut) for the center of the key blade. This design flaw allowed the master programming key for an entire facility to be easily and rapidly decoded without any trace. My "Winfield rule" for lock designers is as follows: a mechanism without springs invites attacks because tumblers, sliders, and other critical components (as with different padlocks discussed previously) can be moved into position through the introduction of vibration.

The design's defect also allowed bitting combinations to be changed by unauthorized persons to prevent the proper key from working. This could cause a lockout from critical areas and facilities. These problems resurfaced 30 years later when one of the largest lock companies in the United States introduced an updated version of the Winfield to the U.S. and Canadian consumer markets and encountered extremely bad press and the compromise of many locks by locksmiths and criminals.

A programmable lock can be opened by applying torque to the plug.

In 2011, I filed a complaint with the Builders Hardware Manufacturers Association (BHMA) to challenge the security rating of the Kwikset design specifically because of its ability to be easily compromised with a screwdriver inserted into the keyway. If sufficient torque was applied, the sliders could be compressed and the plug easily turned. My partner and I consulted with Kwikset to change the design and revert to the original 1935 General Motors sidebar lock. This change vastly increased the torque resistance of the programmable wafer-lock SmartKey.

In 2017, Spectrum Brands, the parent company of Kwikset, was sued by the estate of a female victim who was raped and killed by a security guard in a condo complex in Orlando, Florida. He had watched our presentation at DefCon on his smartphone as we demonstrated the compromise of the Kwikset. He then allegedly replicated the attack in a condo complex he was guarding.

During the lock-bumping frenzy in 2006 and 2007 in the United States, Kwikset introduced its programmable wafer lock called SmartKey. Because of our work releasing information about bumping, I was flown to the Kwikset corporate offices for a briefing about the new lock, which the company understood was bump-proof. The design engineers were unaware of the concept of bumping, and they had created a bump-proof lock by accident. During their PowerPoint presentation, I explained to their engineering staff that their design replicated the first generation of a lock produced by Rielda in Italy that was then upgraded by Winfield for the hospitality market.

Like its predecessors, the Kwikset lock relied on two sliders with teeth that meshed or moved apart to change the bitting pattern for any given key. All that was required was to insert the proper key, press a deprogramming link that separated the two bitting components, and then insert a key with a new combination and release the programming link, causing the two halves of the sliders to come together with the new bitting values.

The problem with the design was the ability to physically warp the sliders by applying torque to the plug with a screwdriver inserted into the keyway. In normal operation, the sliders rested above or below the shear line as a key was withdrawn. That relationship could be altered by inserting a piece of a blank key cut to a depth between a three and a four cut, with a possible total of six depth increments on a Kwikset key. The lock could be easily torqued open if all the sliders could be brought to their mid-position.

For years this caused Kwikset a significant engineering and liability issue, which was resolved when my colleagues and I suggested that the company modify its sidebar and gate design to mirror the original Briggs & Stratton sidebar lock for automobiles invented in 1935. That solved the problem but was a lesson for all lock companies to pay attention to applying focused energy against internal locking components and to be knowledgeable about the history of different lock designs.

A high-security deadbolt mortise cylinder was opened in seconds with a two-dollar screwdriver.

The Medeco Maxum deadbolt is one of the industry's best and highest-security cylinders. It's utilized in hundreds of thousands of locations due to its design, toughness, and resistance to force attacks. Its appearance exuded security, and nobody doubted its ability to withstand an external attack. The problem was that none of its designers, installers, locksmiths, or other experts seem to have considered what kept the lock secure and what its critical weakness was.

The reality was that the entire security of this deadbolt was based on two tiny screws, each with a diameter of about 0.083". Nobody imagined that if these two screws that retained the endcap for the keyway were somehow removed, there was the potential to manipulate the tailpiece. It was seated in a slot at the end of the plug and was the critical element to transmit turning motion to actuate the bolt for locking and unlocking.

Again, it was a cascading failure to connect the dots, with significant consequences. The designers failed to comprehend that the end of the keyway was open, which allowed a tool to be inserted to grip and turn the tailpiece if it was somehow disconnected from the plug. We first fashioned a tiny, inexpensive screwdriver as a two-pronged fork designed to grab the tailpiece and turn it once pushed outside the channel in the plug. We needed to find a way to isolate the operation of the screw-on endcap that retained the tailpiece from the back of the plug. We realized that the only things keeping the endcap bound to the plug were those two tiny screws. The question was how to unscrew them from outside the lock. The answer to this problem was simple: insert a thin piece of spring steel into the end of the keyway and abut against the endcap, and then strike the metal three times with a hammer. Doing so applied excessive force against the endcap and sheared the two screws. It was simple to push the tailpiece backward about a millimeter and then turn it to release the bolt.

Medeco urgently fixed the problem after *Wired* magazine and other news media widely reported the attack. This caused the manufacturer to implement a fix that didn't work; they had to repeat the process by implementing another fix.

The interim fix resulted in our ability to *reverse-pick* the lock and remove the plug, which wasn't contemplated when the modification was made. Ultimately, Medeco remedied the problem, and the Maxum remains one of the best deadbolts in the industry. The lesson to be learned is this: always consider what components keep the entire assembly together and what moving element, if compromised, becomes critical. In this case, the metal tailpiece connected to the plug's end was the link to transmit energy between the turning of the key and the movement of the bolt. Nobody ever considered what would happen if the two pieces became disconnected.

Failure to Consider Decoding Methods and Attacks

Decoding methods to determine critical bitting, shear line, and sidebar information are a primary means of compromising the security of a lock. Decoding techniques can be based on mechanical feedback of internal components, visual observation of the detainers' movement, or the use of electronic instruments to read and measure different internal detainer values. The failure of lock designers to understand different decoding techniques and available hardware can be fatal. The examples that follow show how imagination can be applied to the decoding of different mechanisms, with serious security consequences.

Carbon paper and a piece of wire decodes and defeats a programmable hotel lock to produce a key.

The VingCard was one of the first programmable card locks for hotels worldwide and can still be found on thousands of doors. Its design was unique because it allowed hotel management to change a lock's coding instantly if guests didn't return their key on checkout. The system was based on a pin tumbler mechanism set in a 7 × 5 matrix of ball bearings. Each plastic keycard had a separate hole pattern of varying positions and several holes that mated with the individual steel balls inside the lock. The card combination determined which steel balls were allowed to protrude through holes in the card and which were blocked by blanks or no holes present. The guest inserted the card horizontally into the lock to open the door. Doing so forced a movable platen to move forward if the correct combination was encoded on the card. The platen's movement was the equivalent of clearing a shear line in a conventional pin tumbler lock design.

Although the system was extremely clever, it also had an embedded design flaw that the creators never conceived. The system could be easily and rapidly decoded to render an exact image of an individual room key, and then one could be created based on that image, presenting a significant security issue for the hotel and any guest.

In 1992, I was tasked with determining how to defeat the system. When I realized the entire lock's security was based on the pressure exerted on each bearing, the solution was relatively simple. The result was a mechanical and electronic method to decode the lock and issuance of a patent for the process (U.S. 5355701A).

To determine the coding of a specific keycard, I needed to learn the position of each steel ball that protruded above the shear line and the ones that were blocked. Mechanically, that was accomplished by inserting a metal sandwich comprising two thin pieces of brass, a layer of carbon paper, and a .002″ diameter U-shaped metal wire. One of the brass pieces was withdrawn, and the wire scraped across the carbon paper for each row of balls. This action marked the carbon paper as the wire was forced against each ball bearing.

After the "sandwich" was removed, the carbon paper showed the position of the steel balls that protruded through the keycard's holes. A complete matrix of a plastic card with all 35 holes was utilized as a master key. It was covered with thin cellophane tape, and wherever holes were indicated on the carbon paper by pressure marks, the tip of a ballpoint pen was used to punch a hole through the tape to replicate the action of the actual plastic room key.

An electronic decoder was also devised to defeat the system by inserting a printed circuit board into the lock, which had 35 electric-printed grids that were positioned to rest under each bearing position. The circuit detected the steel balls electrically on the circuit runs and caused them to create a short if they were under pressure. An LED display was connected to the circuit board with a 7 × 5 matrix to replicate what the keycard looked like. A key could then be produced from the master matrix card as described previously.

The lesson for design engineers in this type of attack is clear: a determination must be made of the methods to figure out the "security secret"—the code for the lock—to defeat it. Always remember that every lock with internal mechanical movement communicates its code by exploiting tolerances and interacting with critical components. As a result of the risks that resulted from the exposure of this security flaw, major hotel chains replaced these locks with more secure ones.

Magnetic locks at the U.S. Mint and hotels were decoded with video-recording tape that defeated multiple security layers.

Corkey, a Hong Kong company, invented and produced an extremely innovative magnetic card lock used in hotel rooms worldwide, parking garages, and at the U.S. Mint in San Francisco. It was based on barium ferrite vinyl (BFV) cards. This material could be magnetized in multiple spots or domains across the surface of a card with a special encoding gun. These magnetized domains attracted or repelled correspondingly placed magnetic pins within the lock's body. The security of this lock was based on two things: whether each domain was north or south polarity and the location and number of each pin.

In operation, the keycard was magnetized in different areas to correspond with the coding of magnetic pins in the matching lock. Remember that magnetic poles repel, so the trick was to encode the domains to repel certain pins that were pushed above the shear line. The lock could be opened if all the repelled pins and attracted pins matched. I was asked to analyze this locking system and determine whether security vulnerabilities would allow its compromise. They would, but it required some research and consultation with experts in reading magnetic fields and available instrumentation. It was critical to determine whether the system could be defeated, because these locks were master keyed using a positional system in many hotels. That meant the master keycard was a *composite* of all the individual keys. To decode the master key for a given property, samples had to be taken of the many different locks in the facility.

Defeating this locking system required several steps: determining how many magnetized pins were in the lock, determining each of their polarities, determining their physical positions within the lock, taking enough samples of various locks to make a composite master keycard, and creating an actual card that would operate any or all the locks.

This was accomplished by mounting a piece of low-coercivity 2"-wide videotape on a stiff paper card that matched the size of the keycard. Then an anti-magnetic shield surrounded the videotape like a metal sandwich. This was done so that the blank videotape card could be inserted into the lock and could read each of the randomly positioned pins. If a card were inserted and removed without the magnetic shield, all that appeared were magnetic tracks that yielded no relevant information. We needed to determine the position and polarity of each pin. I employed a thin stainless-steel shield that was withdrawn once the sandwich was inserted. This allowed each pin to magnetize the videotape. The shield was then reapplied and the card removed.

Next, a piece of visa mag or plastic magnetic viewing film was overlaid on the videotape sample. Each domain was displayed as well as its location. A Gauss meter probed each of the domains for polarity. After all the cards were processed, a composite could be created using exceedingly small magnets spray-glued onto a stiff piece of file-folder paper.

This was a complex procedure to defeat the security of the lock, but it was important because of the risks involved in the protected facilities. The relevant issue for the VA teams involved in the original lock's design was to understand what constituted the "secrets" that kept this lock from being opened and how that information could be discovered by analyzing each security component.

Electronic hotel safes at major resorts were decoded to produce master keycards for thousands of rooms, with no concern about security by the manufacturer.

An Israeli manufacturer developed and patented one of the first in-room hotel safes that utilized a credit card to set the lock and open code. This scheme is also used aboard some cruise ships. A customer's credit card is swiped through the embedded reader on the front of the safe, which reads and stores the credit card number. In case a customer loses their card or the magnetic stripe is damaged, the manufacturer issues each venue a master programming card that security personnel can use to open the safe.

I was contracted to circumvent the security of this container, which was installed at several hotels in the United States, including major installations in Las Vegas and Florida. I first traveled to Israel to meet with the electronics designer. When I asked him about the electronic security within the safe and how the memory chip that stored the code for the master programming and access card was protected, the developer said he didn't understand because the printed circuit board was locked in the safe. I asked him whether the data for the access card was encrypted. It was not. The two critical security design criteria that were of immediate concern were the security of the program chip inside the safe and the security of the data on the programming/access card.

Next, I checked into a Las Vegas hotel with 2,000 safes installed. I removed the four non-security screws from the internal back cover protecting all the electronic circuitry inside the safe door. I then removed the electrically erasable programmable read-only memory (EEPROM) chip. This type of non-volatile memory doesn't lose its contents due to a power failure or if it's removed from its socket. It wasn't soldered onto the board, either, which was another security engineering failure. I then placed the chip in a reader and obtained a readout of its data.

Before traveling to Las Vegas, I ordered one of the safes, which was supplied with a master programming card. When I ordered the safe, I asked customer service what would happen if the master card was lost. I was told they would send us a new card and a replacement EEPROM to be installed on the printed circuit board inside the safe.

I contacted the U.S. safe manufacturer representative a couple of weeks later, told them we had lost the master card, and asked if they could send us another one and a new chip. I received these materials within two days. I then had a comparison chip and card that I could read against the original chip and card. I found the 24-byte master code that could open this or any other safe. To verify, I encoded a new blank card with this code.

To validate our analysis, I traveled to Disney World in Florida to a hotel that used these safes. I repeated the same procedure: removing the chip, reading it, and then encoding a credit card with the 24-byte code. I found I could open the room safe and any others in the hotel.

This is an excellent example of using a multi-stage approach to defeat the security of a locking system because the manufacturer failed to understand the different security layers that could easily be compromised. This wasn't a difficult or sophisticated attack. It simply required a methodology to determine each security engineering failure and how to neutralize it. If criminals had acquired the master cards, every room in each affected hotel would have been at risk, and the liability would have been significant for both the hotel and the safe manufacturer. It's also a good reminder that the patent office, in determining that the design was unique, non-obvious, and had utility, did not rule on security, which, as noted in this text, isn't its job or responsibility.

Complex Attacks and Security Failures in Designs

Embedded vulnerabilities in both conventional and high-security locks may require the development of complex attacks to circumvent multiple security layers. Two multilevel attacks are illustrative of the issue. The first was the subject of Chapter 24, which discussed our analysis of Medeco high-security locks, briefly summarized below. The other case, also in this chapter, was a complicated attack to decode and replicate magnetic keycards produced by Corkey in Hong Kong.

One of the world's most secure locks was picked and bumped with special code-setting keys.

The following case example is one of the most complex cases of my career to date. The target required a very imaginative analysis of the multiple problems that had to be identified and overcome to be successful. My partner and I created a new method of attack and, in the process, educated many design engineers on potential vulnerabilities in their designs. The result, after 18 months, was the publication of a detailed account of the methodology titled *Open in Thirty Seconds: Cracking One of the Most Secure Locks in America*. It also resulted in the issuance of four U.S. patents for code-setting keys that potentially enabled virtually all the non-master keyed Medeco locks in the world to be picked or bumped open. Patents were also issued for special high-security pick-resistant pin tumblers (7,775,074, 7,963,135 B1, 8,302,439, and 9,719,275).

Most American locksmiths said it was impossible to open Medeco high-security cylinders. The lock had been secure for 40 years and was the bane of law enforcement and intelligence agencies for covert entry teams. Even John Falle, one of the world's leading government tool designers, had only developed a decoder to measure the length of each pin (as described in Part IV) but had not identified a way to pick the lock rapidly.

Because of the 2007 media coverage and close attention by manufacturers, lock-bumping issues became especially important due to their security threat. Many high-security lock makers claimed their cylinders were bump-proof and difficult to pick. These claims were backed up by their UL and BHMA standards certifications for high security, which attested to their resistance to covert and forced entry.

Why was this lock so difficult to compromise, and why did governments worldwide select the design to protect palaces, embassies, banks, and commercial facilities? The lock, as of 2003 with the introduction of the m3, had three distinct security layers: five- or six-pin tumblers, a sidebar that could retract only if all the pins were correctly rotated by each key's bitting values, and a slider that physically blocked the sidebar legs from contacting the pins unless the key's step protrusion was also correct. In short, Medeco cylinders are extremely secure. Government versions can have special anti-pick micro-milled pins, steel inserts, and other security enhancements as well. All these issues were factored into our assessment of whether the locks could be rapidly compromised.

Our goal was to develop a technique that would allow us to approach and rapidly pick or bump open a target lock. In the world of covert entry, the time specified by the high-security standards promulgated by UL and BHMA is under 10 minutes—the minimum delay to open a lock.

Our initial test was whether we could modify a known key for a specific lock to turn it into a bump key. After much testing, we produced a working bump key. However, that discovery didn't buy us much because we still had to have the correct sidebar code (i.e., collection of angle rotations) to produce that key accurately. We wanted the ability to insert some form of special key into a lock with an unknown combination and have a high probability that we could open it.

Our research analyzed the rotation angles, internal lock tolerances, and designation of key cuts or bitting. We determined that we could exploit the angles, which were normally 20 degrees, reducing them to 10 degrees. We then realized we could "double cut" each bitting position on a key to produce a complex bitting pattern. Finally, we analyzed the code book that Medeco had developed and required each Medeco locksmith to follow anywhere in the world. We found that we could reduce the number of keys that could open a lock to four. With four code-setting keys, we could reliably pick and bump open a vast majority of the world's Medeco cylinders that weren't part of a master key system.

This case is a lesson for every engineer who believes they know everything about their design and each security vulnerability that may exist. Medeco is one of the highest targets in the world due to its reputation and deployment of its locks in the most secure places. We found and exploited an embedded design defect that had existed for over 25 years. VA teams should have discovered it and resolved the issue. The lesson is that engineers and Red Teams (those who are responsible for attempting to compromise the designs of the engineers responsible for the original concept) will never discover all the potential vulnerabilities in any given product. It requires diligence, imagination, and an understanding of different attack methods.

Another case that required the development of a complex attack was the compromise of the security of the magnetic card lock made by Corkey. There were several problems to overcome to defeat this lock. As noted earlier in this chapter, the "security secrets" were based on the physical location and polarity of multiple magnetic pins in the lock. There was a possibility of up to 44 magnetized pin tumblers held in a physical matrix that was different for each lock. Usually there were about 11 pins in each lock, but they were in different positions. When the keycard—a piece of magnetized material called barium ferrite vinyl (BFV)—was encoded with several magnetic domains that corresponded with the pins in the lock, it repelled and attracted the pins based on its individual code.

To defeat this security, it was necessary to determine the location and polarity of the pins and then replicate them on another card. I solved this problem by using a piece of 30-year-old 2"-wide videotape. I used this to sample each test lock in a hotel complex. It was then required to analyze the magnetic domains created on the tape and determine their polarity. The result was the production of a master key for the entire hotel that was constructed from tiny magnets glued to a stiff piece of paper the size of the original keycard the company used.

These examples illustrate complex attacks requiring several steps to complete and, most importantly, imagination to figure out the process.

Attacks on Lock Bodies and Integrity

Many attacks can be successful against lock bodies and the integrity of their physical components. It's critically important to understand that almost *any* opening may allow the use of shims to reach and access critical locking components.

These attacks can be both covert and forced. I have worked on many cases where it appeared impossible to activate internal mechanisms, yet this was done with shims and Nitinol-shaped wire.

An opening anywhere in a lock can provide unanticipated access to its critical components.

This example deals with a popular single-deadbolt RFID-controlled mechanism installed in many apartment complexes, military installations, and commercial facilities. The design uses a simulated plastic key containing RFID electronics to communicate with the internal processor for validation. As with any conventional design, the key is inserted into the lock. The lock provides full programming and audit capability via a USB port at the bottom of the enclosure. It's barely noticeable and doesn't draw any attention.

The lock's manufacturer paid no attention to the capability to fish a very thin shim wire around the internal mechanism to reach the critical spring-loaded plunger located at the system's heart. We inserted a wire between the USB receptacle and the metal lock case. It provided us with just enough clearance for a long shim, and we easily reached and lifted the plunger at the heart of the locking system. Within seconds, the lock was compromised, and a screwdriver was inserted where the plastic key would normally be used to exert a turning motion to retract the bolt.

The importance of this example is the very small and insignificant opening in the lock body. It provided enough clearance to access the critical component and open the lock.

A high-security electronic combination lock could be defeated by creating a secondary-interface gear to actuate the bolt control mechanism.

The Mas Hamilton X-07 was one of the most revolutionary locks of the last century. It was a combination lock, an evolving series produced by dormakaba that is used in safes, banks, ATMs, and federal facilities to protect top-secret materials. It was designed by two industry leaders and was tested by multiple government agencies before being vetted for the highest security classification. Its unique design utilized a specially engineered Intel low-current processor, yet it contained no batteries or power supply. Its electronics were based on using a magneto-type generator to produce electricity to power the liquid crystal display, bolt mechanism, and processor when the combination dial was turned. It also meant the lock could be inactive for many years and brought to life with just a few dial turns.

I received a call from a respected safe technician in upstate New York one evening, stating that one of his colleagues had found a way to defeat the lock. Although skeptical, I've learned to never say never to a defeat, no matter how unlikely. After all, many federal testing agencies had spent over a year trying to defeat this lock with everything from X-rays to high voltage, EMP, vibration, and so on. They were unsuccessful, so the lock was cleared to protect the highest-value assets.

I had a sample of the X-07 that I had received from the company's president a few months before the call. I carefully analyzed the components for the first time because I'd never imagined any design flaw that could result in a vulnerability. I was wrong. It turned out that the safe technician telling people he had found a way into the lock was repeating information from a colleague at one of our National Laboratories. He had discovered that injecting grease could cause the drive mechanism to be altered, which could lead to the ability to retract the locking bolt. The problem with this approach, I would discover, was that it wasn't reliable.

I analyzed the mechanical linking between the dial and the small motor drive that forced two independent gears to mesh when a valid code was entered. This created a direct link between the dial and the bolt, allowing it to be retracted. I realized the problem and determined that grease wasn't the answer but rather silicone. I drilled a small hole in the lock's case and squirted in some of the quick-setting liquid that dentists use. If this is done at the precise spot between the two gears, the silicone can create a third interface gear within 2 minutes. In one step, the lock could be opened and locked repeatedly due to the newly created link to the lock's critical component. Once it was done, all the electronic security was bypassed and largely irrelevant.

I contacted Mas Hamilton (the original creator of the lock) and told the company of my findings. It admitted that it was aware of the issue and had made corrections to remedy it. The company sent me a second-generation lock, which I believe still didn't fix the problem.

I then contacted the General Services Administration, which is responsible for government lock certification, and discussed the issue with them. Because the lock was and is utilized in the commercial and government sectors, I asked if it was permissible for the problem to be published. Normally, they're only concerned about forced entry, which this attack certainly is. They said the material could not be made public in this case, even though non-governmental facilities could be at risk. That was 20 years ago, and the problems have since been rectified.

This is an excellent example of a failure to review every internal component in a locking system, especially one rated at the highest level of security. We refer to this as *component failure analysis*, meaning designers and vulnerability teams must look at every internal component and whether it could be attacked. After the problem was discovered, it should have been obvious, but the method of attack was not. The rule is that regardless of how minor or insignificant the component appears in the overall security design, it can often be very significant in developing a new attack vector.

A high-security cylinder was attacked using a plastic key and vise grips.

This example involves one of the most recognizable mortise cylinders for commercial metal doors in the United States. The lock fits into a special bolt and lockset case mounted inside the door in a pocket or hidden area. The mortise cylinder screws into the internal assembly and is retained by a set screw tightened from the door's side edge. This cylinder has a .065" protrusion on the plug's face.

My colleague and I were tasked with circumventing the security of this lock and its sidebar design.

The sidebar offers a second security layer against covert entry and was believed to add a physical barrier to defeating the lock.

In this case, we analyzed the design and wanted to determine if the lock could be defeated with spoofed credentials—a key made of thin plastic. We went to an office supply store and found a .030" thick plastic report folder we thought we could use to fashion a key. The lock's primary security was the five- or six-pin tumblers that kept the plug from rotating unless the key had the correct bitting combination. The question was whether the sidebar offered any significant physical barrier to rotation. As it turned out, it did not.

We cut the plastic key with an X-Acto knife to reproduce the bitting but not the angled cuts of the key. The question was whether we were also required to reproduce and match the rotation angles for each pin tumbler as would occur with a metal key. We believed that if the pin tumblers were raised to a shear line, we could alter the sidebar's geometry so it would become irrelevant in preventing the plug from turning.

The plug's protrusion was the critical element that allowed us to compromise this lock. Using vise grips, we grabbed the plug's outer ridge at the bottom of the keyway and applied a lot of torque or compression motion. This changed the relationship of the sidebar to the pins and keyway. With the plastic key inserted, we could turn the plug with a screwdriver because there was no longer a barrier (i.e., the sidebar) to protect it.

The designers of this lock and other similar electromechanical versions had always believed that the pins and sidebar were coequal in preventing the plug from rotating. The issue would have been discovered and properly dealt with if this had been properly tested in a vulnerability assessment. In a later example, we compromised an electronic design using the same basic attack form.

Attacks on Credentials

Innovative attacks on credentials, both mechanical and electronic, must be considered in analyzing key control and how to protect the generation of unauthorized copies. The flip side of this issue is the compromise of locks in covert operations that require access to blanks for restricted keyways. One of the problems with the duplication of keys for such keyways is obtaining blanks, unless they're generated with 3D printing.

An electromechanical lock's security was defeated using plastic keys and torque.

One iteration of an electromechanical lock is the combination of an encrypted credential within the key and a bitting pattern that controls pin tumblers or discs and moves them to a shear line. The mechanical portion and the electronic authentication must work in parallel before the lock can be opened. In one lock, the pin tumblers were conventional, with no sidebar protection. The security in the cylinder was the key's electronic chip and the lock body's internal processor. The lock could never be opened unless the key was authenticated, even if the mechanical bitting portion was correct and all the pins were raised to the shear line.

The lock I analyzed was extremely popular and appeared secure. It was a mortise cylinder that was primarily installed in commercial installations. How was the lock circumvented? With a plastic key cut to the proper combination and torque applied to the face of the plug. Several manufacturers believed the pins protected the plug sufficiently from turning. All that was necessary was to satisfy the mechanical security requirements of this group of locks and then eliminate the electronic blocking element that was controlled by the encrypted chip in the key.

The security assessment for this design should have included an application of my first rule—"The key never unlocks the lock"—and a determination of what it would take to open the cylinder. The only real security was the pin tumblers, not the blocking element controlled by the processor. If the key's physical properties could be circumvented, the lock could be opened. It was a simple matter to bypass all the encryption and electronic elements. Steps should have been taken to strengthen the parts that controlled the rotation of the plug.

Attacks on Electronic Elements

Locks that rely on internal electronic elements for their security can have vulnerabilities that may not be obvious but can lead to the defeat of the entire mechanism, often simply and rapidly. This was definitely the case in any electronic lock that contained ferrous materials that controlled any moving elements.

Toilet paper rolls, glue, and magnets have defeated many electronic cylinders.

The idea began and was conceived at the Wendt company in Bergheim, Germany, just a few miles from Cologne. Addi Wendt had founded the company many years before and was known for creating, designing, locksmithing, and government covert and forced-entry techniques and tools. He and his team intended to develop a way to use magnetics to open some electronic cylinders around 2006. They realized that certain locks could be subject to magnetic fields that were controlled and applied a certain way. The company experimented with many locks and settled on a small manufacturer, Uhlmann and Zacher, that produced a series of electronic profile cylinders for the European market. Addi Wendt realized that a properly placed and configured rotating magnetic field could cause internal elements to move, potentially causing an unlocking or locking condition.

The original prototype consisted of a stripped-down roll of toilet paper and four magnets glued to the inner core that were equally placed around its circumference. The initial sample was rotated around the outside of the lock several times, which caused it to open. The lock could be relocked without a trace if the direction was reversed. This technique was ultimately known worldwide as the *devil's ring* and was manufactured within an aluminum shell by Wendt. It opened many locks, much to the chagrin of various manufacturers. I interviewed the president of Uhlmann and Zacher, who agreed that his company had a significant problem and notified all their customers that the locks were being recalled and retrofitted.

Lock manufacturers couldn't believe magnetic fields could attack internal components in this orientation and method. It was a difficult lesson because the engineers had never considered the possibility of such an attack. The important issue is the application of magnetism and the power of magnetic fields to act on any ferrous component. I've found that magnets, especially rare earth neodymium, are powerful tools that should always be tested against any lock design in vulnerability assessments.

Direct electrical access to motors in electronic locks can harm their security.

Most electronic and electromechanical locks have internal plastic layers and are relatively easy to compromise by drilling with tiny bits. This is a problem when there's potential access to the tiny motors that move blocking elements to stop the plug's rotation.

Access to the motors can be relatively simple using shim wires, small-diameter drills, or other means to penetrate the plastic. Engineers should be cautious about using plastic or other soft materials because bypassing the barriers to motors, chips, leads, or other components may be easy. The paths to any actuating mechanism should be checked to ensure that all routes are blocked.

Attacks on Internal Locking Components

During the design process of locks and secure containers, the focus is often on the one critical component that controls locking. This can result in failing to recognize other routes to access critical components that can lead to a complete compromise of security. This was the case in a popular in-room hotel safe installed worldwide. The design team never considered the potential to directly access the motor control that allowed the bolt to withdraw, thereby unlocking the safe.

A paper clip and a sharp reamer tool easily compromised an electronically controlled safe.

The vulnerability in one of the most popular in-room hotel safes was obvious and should have been discovered during its design. It was not and allowed the safe to be opened in less than 1 minute.

I received a call from a safe technician, asking whether I was familiar with a problem with hotel safes in Hawaii and a locksmith who was being threatened with a multimillion-dollar lawsuit if he disclosed what he had discovered about one very popular in-room safe. So, I traveled to Winnipeg, Canada, to a hotel with 246 rooms that used these safes. I checked into a room with one of the older El Safe keypad-controlled electronic safes. When I opened the door of the safe, the problem was immediately apparent.

The keypad, batteries, and communications electronics were mounted outside the safe door. A ribbon cable from the assembly to the internal motor drive was connected to the bolts that locked the door. The problem was the slot in the door: It provided access to the motor drive's gear mechanism from outside the safe. If the keypad panel was removed by unscrewing its retaining screws, a long paper clip could be fed through the slot and through a very small hole in the plastic internal back cover, made with a sharp reamer tool. Once this was accomplished, fishing the wire straight down to the large gear attached to the motor drive was simple. Pushing on the gear could move the bolt to an unlocked condition, resulting in no audit trail created.

The manufacturer should have discovered or contemplated this vulnerability, and as a result, a shield was installed to protect against this attack. The rule that any opening in a container can provide a vulnerability should have been adhered to.

Attacks on Openings with Shims and Wires

Many companies produce security-related products without understanding the fundamentals of locks and their design requirements. The result is often serious vulnerabilities that could have been avoided and that present unnecessary risks to consumers. One of the most interesting cases involved an electronic padlock designed for storage containers protecting delivered parcels. It demonstrated the lack of knowledge on the part of the design team that created the product.

A clever electronic padlock allowed direct access to critical lock components.

The padlock was designed by a company intending to offer a product to deter package theft from residences and apartment complexes. This was a different approach than that taken by CleverMade with its locked storage container, discussed earlier in this chapter. This padlock was all electronic, with a motor drive controlled by a microprocessor, a Wi-Fi link, and an internal scanner that could be pointed at the barcode label on shipping invoices by the delivery agent. If the code matched what the shipper and carrier entered into the system, the lock opened and the contents could be placed in the secure container, which was then locked again. The recipient repeated the process to open the lock and retrieve the shipment.

We found two fatal design flaws that should have been immediate red flags. The leads that activated the small internal motor were accessible by drilling one small hole in the case. This hole provided direct access to feed power to the motor and release the two ball bearings holding the shackle. The second fundamental problem was a small hole at the top of the padlock under and to the center of the shackle. The entire assembly could be accessed and circumvented if a drill or center punch were inserted and forced downward.

This was a classic case of the manufacturer not understanding lock design and defeat techniques. The vulnerabilities should have been identified earlier and corrected.

Shear Line Attacks

Attacks against the shear line can be the most effective and problematic because virtually every lock must have some form of breakpoint between fixed and moving components that control locking and unlocking. Traditional attacks usually involve picking by manipulation of pin tumblers or other detainers. The following example describes a unique method that my colleague and I developed to compromise a high-security lock that resulted from a modification by the manufacturer to correct another security vulnerability described earlier in this chapter that involved the Medeco Maxum deadbolt.

A unique and unheard-of method of picking a high-security deadbolt lock defeated its security.

After we defeated the Medeco Maxum deadbolt with a two-dollar screwdriver and sheared the tailpiece retaining screws, the manufacturer urgently implemented an interim modification to the plug and how it was secured to the shell, believing this would prevent our attack. It's a classic example of too rapidly implementing a modification without considering the problem and its potential ramifications. Admittedly, it would have taken some thought on the company's part to realize the vulnerability. The problem was that traditional logic overshadowed the designers' ability to think outside the box about the possibility that the lock could be somehow physically compromised by picking the plug in a very unconventional manner: pulling it out of the cylinder.

Most design engineers know the theory of lock picking, at least on a basic level. They understand that picking is based on tolerances and the ability to trap bottom and top pins at the shear line, thereby exploiting the gap of a few thousandths of an inch precisely at the shear line. When all the pins are "set," the plug will turn because there's nothing blocking rotation. Lock picking has always been taught as an exercise in applying torque to the plug in a clockwise or counterclockwise direction using a tension wrench. There's no way to pick the lock and turn the plug other than clockwise or counterclockwise rotation in virtually every instance because the plug is retained and linked to the lock body (i.e., shell) by either screws or a clip. This prevents the plug from being pulled forward and out of the lock when the correct key is inserted and turned. But for the retaining screws at the back of the plug, any reverse pressure would release all the pins as the plug is pulled forward. It never occurred to the engineers that such a condition could be created if the endcap screws were removed and the lock was picked and pulled forward. Their modification created precisely that condition.

We inserted a spring steel shim, applied force to the back of the plug to shear the two screws, then used a paper clip wedged to the front side of the front of the keyway to pull the plug forward. Picking wasn't difficult, but it used an illogical technique. Rather than rotating the plug, it was pulled forward to apply binding pressure at the shear line. The result was the same: trapping the pins at the shear line. When they were all set, the plug was pulled out of the cylinder, allowing a screwdriver to be inserted to actuate the bolt mechanism.

This was a classic failure to connect the dots and to consider all the potential results in the modification that effectively prevented our manipulation of the tailpiece but created yet another more fundamental problem. The lesson for design engineers is this: Very carefully consider what can result from what appears to be a solution to a mechanical security problem. Any modification to a design often creates additional vulnerabilities that must be conceived of and considered as well.

The final chapter presents a listing of my rules, axioms, and guidelines that should be considered in evaluating any design proposal, either new or modified. I have developed these rules during my career based on the cases my colleagues and I have investigated. In one form or another, they're all applicable when evaluating lock designs and what can become a security vulnerability.

Design Rules, Axioms, and Principles

Drawing on my investigation and review of hundreds of lock designs, deficiencies, and defects has provided me with a database and the knowledge to identify common mistakes. Often, those omissions or errors result in serious security flaws and liability. These results can be caused by engineers, vulnerability assessment teams, and project managers, as well as installers and system designers. This experience has resulted in my development of design rules, axioms, and guidelines. They are based on my experiences analyzing locks and how they can be defeated or forced to malfunction or fail.

I recommend reading and considering each rule and how it might apply to current or proposed designs. They are all based on often hard-learned and costly experiences that lock manufacturers have encountered. I hope they prove helpful as you navigate the complexities of secure lock designs and often-unimagined problems that may be exploited in any design.

Design Rules, Axioms, and Guidelines

Those responsible for the conception, design, and execution of projects that involve security-related devices, especially those related to locks, safes, and allied systems, must always be mindful of certain "rules of the road." The assessment of potential security vulnerabilities, risks, and liability in the products they're responsible for creating, modifying, or updating should be guided and tempered by problems, pitfalls, traps, errors, and insights experienced by their colleagues throughout the industry.

Companies and design engineers often pay the price for mistakes that could have been mitigated or avoided if they had kept in mind certain basic maxims. The failure to consider the experiences of engineers, inventors, vulnerability assessment (VA) teams, and other critical design team members can be very costly in terms of delays, unexpected outcomes, security failures, product reliability, recalls, public relations disasters, and the loss of certifications and/or profits. Often, such problems can be traced to a failure to remember certain basic design tenets.

My collection of such rules, axioms, and guidelines stems from being involved in hundreds of cases of design and analysis, in addition to reverse-engineering, compromising, defeating, litigating, and attacking locks and safes produced by some of the largest worldwide manufacturers. In this chapter, I have tried to encapsulate important philosophies, thought processes, hazards, and common mistakes, especially those made by mechanical engineers who are often far better at making things work than conceiving ways to break them.

These same rules have been highlighted in different chapters throughout this book where applicable. They aren't presented here in any relevant order and will hopefully provoke thoughtful discussion. Certain design nightmares can occur when those responsible for producing a satisfactory, safe, and secure result don't consider such rules. Case examples referenced in these rules are discussed in more detail in Part VI and are denoted in this chapter with a key symbol in the margin and a reference number.

1. *The easiest way to open a lock is with a key.* There may be many other ways to open the same lock; it only requires your imagination.

2. *Never say that a design can't be compromised.* What can't be opened today will surely be opened tomorrow. There are no absolutes regarding the security of a lock, safe, or device.

3. *Research and development (R&D) costs money, and many companies take short-cuts.* The failure to invest in significant product R&D can, and often does, have serious or fatal consequences.

4. *Just because a "high security" label is given to an intended product doesn't make it so.* Beware of such designations given without the verification of supporting research and vulnerability testing to verify that the product is more resistant to compromise.

5. *What is initially considered a very clever lock design may not be used by consumers, may be used improperly, may result in unreliable operation, or may be exploited to compromise the security of the design itself.* A perfect example is programmability in locks that allows for instant key change by the consumer. This option is rarely used.

6. *Never dismiss or underestimate the fact that adversaries can be inventive and clever.* Those who design locks, safes, and other security devices frequently miss potential vulnerabilities and attack vectors. Unfortunately, such myopic vision is often due to ego and lack of imagination on the part of the design team and a failure to understand how a device may be subject to an "outside the box" compromise. Don't ever think that adversaries are too stupid to figure out an attack or problem, regardless of how sophisticated or tested the design appears.

7. *The allocation of security resources is often based on or indexed to the value of the perceived target asset.* Another approach may be to consider the potential costs of the risks involved.

8. *Be clever, but don't get clever in designs.* Engineers tend to overdesign products and incorporate technical options and enhancements that may be desirable but are often expensive or overkill, require excessive power (e.g., increased battery size and device dimensions), and don't add anything to the functionality. Just because it can be done doesn't mean it should be.

The premise of "keeping it simple" is always good advice, especially because the more options or enhancements built into a design, the more potential exists for security compromise. I've seen this problem in countless proposals for new lock designs. A reality check is always required.

9. *Designers and teams should always encourage change, flexibility, and critical thinking about what makes a lock secure, especially in upgrades to current products.* Always ask yourself the following: do the proposed design changes enhance security, or do they appear to do so but accomplish nothing? Are they solely to extend patents?

10. *Encryption is irrelevant in digital lock designs because electrons don't open doors, mechanics do.* There is an obsession with encryption in electromechanical and electronic lock designs. In my experience, all the encryption and microprocessor integration are irrelevant to traditional attack vectors. All locks function because something must move to release critical elements; that's usually what is most vulnerable. The intersection between software and hardware allows us to attack and compromise a lock. It's as if design teams are mesmerized by the sophistication of encryption algorithms, wireless options, and clever enhancements. Still, they miss what opens the lock: the part that must move. Attack that part, and the lock will be opened.

11. *Every key has a signature. Always consider how difficult it is to clone, spoof, or replicate the key.* The easiest way to open a lock is with the correct key, but this doesn't mean it's the key provided by the lock manufacturer or a legitimate copy. Always consider the ease or difficulty of simulating or replicating a mechanical key.

12. *The description or use of the phrase "high-tech" in conjunction with a security product doesn't mean it's secure.* When discussing locks and safes, a reference to being *high-tech* is meaningless. When the term is bandied about in the industry or by other knowledgeable engineers or "experts," that may only mean they can't figure out how to compromise such technology.

13. *Manufacturers often believe that "not invented here" is a good policy.* I've dealt with many companies worldwide that believed they were the only experts in their industry and that if ideas and inventions didn't come from internal sources, they were invalid or wouldn't work. This mindset isn't true and can have serious security and cost consequences.

In 2007, we methodically analyzed the best high-security lock in the United States and determined how to defeat all of its patented security features. The company couldn't comprehend how that was possible because it thought it knew everything about its products and 40-year tested designs. But it didn't: the manufacturer had no idea there was an embedded design defect that allowed its exploit. The result was the publishing of a detailed book on the company's lock designs and the issuing of four U.S. patents, two of which detailed the four keys that would allow all of the company's non-master keyed locks in the world to be picked or bumped open, often in seconds.

14. *Many customers don't care about security, only the appearance of security, and often they don't know the difference.* Many locks appear secure but aren't. Customers, except those requiring high-security locks that must meet certain standards, care about price and local service. Manufacturers must always do a reality check on the products they're developing to determine what their intended users require.

 15. *Simple attacks can defeat many security devices.* Even highly sophisticated designs may be compromised by remarkably simple means. For example, in 2006, U.S. lock manufacturers weren't briefed about or aware of the ability to "bump open" their pin tumbler locks with special keys, a plastic mallet, or even a screwdriver handle. Yet an 11-year-old girl demonstrated how to open different locks in seconds at DefCon. Lock bumping, one of the simplest and most effective attacks, raised serious security issues, even though the technique had been patented in 1925.

16. *Security is a continuum, not a binary equation.* "Security" is a relative term, as pointed out throughout the book. A lock, safe, or device is rarely "secure" or "not secure." Rather, it's a continuum: on the one hand, very secure, and on the other, not secure at all. There are often multiple ways to defeat a security system, so it's an intellectual analysis of what constitutes security in any given environment and use case.

17. *Security is usually complicated.* Achieving the desired product's security can be exceedingly difficult and complex, which should cause uncertainty and angst on the part of a design team. There's never a guarantee that all security vulnerabilities have been considered or discovered. Unfortunately, there is no rigorous and "right way" to do security. Often, the worst problem and common element is arrogance—the belief that every issue has been discovered—and everyone is confident that security has been attained.

18. *Security needs to be both effective and convenient.* Most employees, users, and anyone impacted by security measures don't like or follow them because they're often burdensome, limiting, and aggravating. If security measures aren't designed for ease of compliance and use, they will be circumvented or ineffective. This should always be kept in mind when designing products, especially locks.

A perfect example of Rule 18 is the very sophisticated lock manufacturer in Finland that figured out how to produce an electronic door lock and padlock that required no batteries; it derived its power from a near-field communication (NFC) connection from a smartphone. Although it was a great idea and very environmentally friendly, it required a delay of up to 1 second for the lock to open. For the consumer used to the instant gratification of inserting a metal key into a lock and instantly opening it, a delay of a second is aggravating and, after a while, intolerable.

19. *Security theater is a sham or ceremonial security only.* This concept was created by Dr. Roger Johnston, PhD, in a video produced at Argonne National Labs. It describes a "magic security device" that solves all security problems in a 10,000-square-foot space. It denotes over-confidence by those unfamiliar with security complexities and enamored with recent technology or gizmos. They're often imbued with over-confidence and driven by arrogance and ego as a substitute for knowledge.

20. *Encryption doesn't necessarily make a product secure.* Many companies don't understand the difference between the encryption of data embedded in a product and simply moving data blocks around in a sequence. This should be an important lesson for design engineers and legal counsel for every manufacturer.

A major security company that developed sophisticated bypass products for government agencies reverse-engineered a series of legacy hotel locks produced by two global hospitality lock manufacturers. The security company learned to use a standard magnetic stripe room card and a programming smart card inserted into the lock. Within 1 minute, they could decode the system master key to access every room. I investigated several lock manufacturers to determine this security threat to their thousands of properties and guest rooms. Although the manufacturers believed their systems utilized encryption to protect the card information for each room, it wasn't encryption but simply rearranging information blocks within each lock. The legal result: we couldn't pursue a criminal case under the Digital Millennium Copyright Act (DMCA) because it required electronic protection of the information not present in the lock.

21. *You don't need to understand encryption in an electronic lock to defeat it.* Encryption is only the scrambling of 1s and 0s: it has little to do with what unlocks the lock, which is the intersection of hardware and software. Something must move or be moved to cause a physical unlocking, and that's what is relevant. As noted in another rule, *electrons don't open doors, mechanics do.*

22. *Don't make security the enemy of productivity.* If security, whether in hardware, software, or procedure, interferes with the ability to work efficiently, it will not be effective or utilized by those affected.

23. *We don't like using plastic in the design or construction of locks.* All electronic locks utilize plastic parts in their internal design or construction. As noted in Part IV, any external or internal plastic provides potentially serious security vulnerability, allowing many and often almost undetectable forms of attack.

24. *Look for simple solutions to solve complex security problems.* The ability to compromise or defeat the security of a lock, safe, alarm system, or other product appears overly complicated. But the solution is often elementary. Always look for the simple and obvious first.

> A high-security U.S. lock manufacturer received a patent for a clever new design that added a third security layer to its keys. This sliding element blocked the movement of a sidebar (i.e., the primary locking system within the cylinder) until a protruding step on the side of the key physically moved the slider to one of 26 positions. In the original design, all variations of the sliders were required to be moved by the key approximately 0.40″. The lock's security against picking and other covert entry attack forms seemed secure until it was discovered that a standard paper clip could be wedged between the slider and the lock's body to defeat the system. This was a simple answer to a clever design that originally required a complicated solution to overcome.

25. *Clever designs don't mean secure designs.* See Rule 24 above and its excellent real-life example.

26. *You can't get around the laws of physics.* The exploitation and reliance on the laws of physics and the application of force, heat, temperature, and other related parameters are often employed to open or defeat locks and safes covertly and without any trace. Design engineers often forget the discoveries and inventions of Sir Isaac Newton (i.e., laws of motion), Tesla (i.e., alternating current and rotating magnetic field), Roentgen (i.e., the X-ray), J.J. Thomson (i.e., electrons), Gilbert (i.e., magnetism), Dr. Buehler (i.e., Nitinol shaped wire), and many others.

27. *All exploits can be said to replicate the function that the key performs to open a lock.* Whether picking, impressioning, manipulation, bumping, key jiggling, or other forms of covert entry, virtually all techniques replicate what the key does: it actuates the mechanism that allows the lock to be opened. The most important question any lock designer can consider is, "What opens the lock?"

28. *All secrets in a lock are self-contained.* A lock is a puzzle with internal secrets. Knowing, learning, or decoding those secrets will open the lock. If an attacker "listens to the lock," all its internal secrets can be learned.

> Famous American locksmith Alfred C. Hobbs demonstrated Rule 28's maxim in London in 1851 during the Great Exhibition, when he succeeded in opening the famous Bramah lock that had not been defeated in 40 years. He accomplished this feat in about three weeks by listening to the lock and probing its internal components. He won a significant prize for doing so and caused a great deal of consternation in the lock industry at that time.

29. *All security is about liability.* The defective or deficient design of a lock, safe, or security product can have serious implications, especially involving legal liability other than for governments or their agencies. Design engineers must always consider the liabilities if a device causes injury, loss, or other damage. If that happens, someone will likely pay for the errors.

30. *Electrons don't open doors, mechanisms do.* Locks relying solely on hardware and software must still cause something to move to extend or retract a bolt or a similar locking mechanism. The popularity of electronic locks has drawn many lock manufacturers to develop and market a myriad of products. In my experience, many can be defeated because they ignored or didn't understand the potential attacks against the interface between software, microprocessors, and hardware that accomplishes locking. It's a fatal error that is often repeated.

31. *"If everybody is thinking alike, then nobody is thinking."* This statement by General George S. Patton is one of the primary rules in any project that involves collaboration in the design of hardware or its defeat. Individual thought processes and creativity that can contribute to a successful conclusion are essential. Without individual thought, there's no chance for unique ideas.

32. *Locks are designed to be attacked, tampered with, and tested.* By their nature, all locks should be designed to be targeted for attack. Insecure designs invite compromise. Many years ago, the chief counsel for a global lock manufacturer stated that the security of locks and corresponding liability only applied when its products were utilized in a normal and standard manner. She stated that no liability should attach if a lock was manipulated or attacked. No lock manufacturer should adhere to this policy because it isn't the law. The concept that "all locks can be opened, so nobody should be liable" is legally faulty logic.

33. *Always believe you can defeat a lock.* Believing that a lock can be defeated is half the battle in finding one or more ways to compromise it. One of the problems I've found, especially in VA teams, is the belief that a lock is secure because no one has been able to defeat it in the past and no issues have been reported. This belief, attitude, and arrogance can be disastrous and lead to significant liability, damages, recalls, and loss of certifications. Don't ever believe that a lock can't be defeated. If not today, then surely tomorrow!

34. *All exploits replicate a key's function within a lock.* Whatever mechanism the key actuates can usually be replicated by bypass tools or a simulated key. Any lock designer should always consider this primary rule.

35. *Don't rely on standards to guarantee the security of a rated lock or safe.* Standards are often outdated, don't reflect current attack methods, and don't allow for any inventiveness or initiative in assessing a device's security or the way to defeat it. After serving on the Underwriters Laboratory (UL) Standards Technical Panel on locks and safes for more than 15 years, I can attest to the deficiencies in standards specifically for covert entry testing of rated devices. These standards are rigid guidelines for testing and often don't cover most methods to circumvent the rated security of a lock or safe. In one case, a leading manufacturer relied on tests conducted by U.S. and European standards labs, which tested the susceptibility of its high-security cylinders to lock bumping. The labs reported that the company's locks were impervious to these forms of attack. As the record shows, they weren't, which resulted in a great deal of negative publicity and end-user concerns about the security of their products.

36. *Defeating the credentials of an e-cylinder may appear difficult or impossible, but the process may be simple.* Electronic and electromechanical locks may appear immune to attack because of their sophisticated encryption algorithms and integration of processors within the keys and locks to prevent bypass. Some of these locks can be easy to bypass, and their appearance of security is often an illusion. Their design teams should always consider what keeps the lock in a secure mode. Remember that electronic credentials, encryption, and their interaction with other components may be irrelevant when considering what opens the lock.

37. *Every lock can be compromised: always remember the 3T2R rule.* The 3T2R rule, my succinct summary of what the standards teach, states that all lock defeat is a matter of time, tools, and training. The exploitation is further measured by the attack's reliability and its repeatability. Design engineers and VA teams should always look at a security device in terms of 3T2R.

38. *In assessing security vulnerability in a device, everything should be examined.* Every security device's hardware and software aspects should be suspected and analyzed. This includes assessing and considering all movable parts, springs, motors, solenoids, ferrous materials, magnetic components, inertia attacks, coils, mechanical bypass circuits, mechanical overrides, microswitches, drain holes, entry points, and data ports.

39. *When designing a new lock or modifying a current design, identify all the perceived problems and probable solutions.* This is the optimal way to begin a project. Then continue to expand and evolve the project's parameters and goals.

40. *Just because it's patented doesn't mean it's secure.* Patent examiners don't evaluate or test for the security of a proposed patented device or concept.

No reliance should be placed on the fact that a patent is pending or has been granted; in the context of security, it means nothing.

41. *Always look for ways to exploit a design or a combination of designs to defeat a product.* Finding one minor design flaw can often lead to discovering much more significant vulnerabilities.

42. *Look for the path of least resistance to open or circumvent a lock or its critical mechanisms.* Always focus on what action or mechanism opens the lock; it's often not the key.

43. *Rarely do you know where a vulnerability analysis will end up in assessing what is perceived as an impenetrable lock.* The mindset of "it can't be done," "nobody has been able to defeat this lock," or "our engineering team is unable to discover any methods of defeat" is the mode of thinking that will doom a vulnerability review to failure.

44. *Never say never: what can't be opened today will be opened tomorrow.* Every lock, whether mechanical or electronic, can be compromised and opened. It's always a question of the 3T2R rule: the required time, tools, and training to do so. Many high-security lock manufacturers believe their locks are virtually impenetrable, at least to covert attacks. They're rarely aware of sophisticated tools and techniques available to government agencies, hackers, and criminals. Such tools can also be purchased in certain countries outside the United States with no export controls, even though they're restricted for sale in the States.

45. *Patent protection for a key's mechanical elements or design doesn't ensure security or duplication protection.* The mechanical elements of many keys are patented to make them more difficult to replicate and to impose civil liability on anyone who traffics in the manufacture, distribution, or cutting of such keys for the patent's duration. Although such features may enhance key control, virtually all mechanical keys can be copied, simulated, replicated, and duplicated by various methods discussed in Parts IV and V. Two distinct types of patents come into play: utility and design, which are discussed in Part II. These can make it more difficult to circumvent key control. All mechanical keys are simply pieces of metal, and anything a manufacturer does to add to its security can be defeated, especially with 3D-printing technology.

46. *The warning "Don't Duplicate" on a key means nothing.* There is little legal significance in prohibiting the duplication of a key, even if patent-protected. Some manufacturers have also stamped patent numbers on their keys to warn against copying or improperly altering the factory-original blank keys. Locksmiths who supply cut keys for restricted keyways and high-security locks will usually honor the warning to comply with contractual obligations with the manufacturer.

47. *Electronic cylinders' programming access and audit capabilities can provide security vulnerabilities.* An electronic lock offering many options is often more vulnerable to attacks. A description of an attack of a very sophisticated push-button and common access card (CAC) lock is presented in Part VI. This lock was designed for commercial, military, and government services. We discovered nine ways to defeat the lock's mechanics and electronic circuits with simple attacks that could be executed in seconds.

48. *Management may often object to, quash, or ridicule creative thinking about vulnerability assessment, as it's the fastest way to stifle innovative thinking about the problem.* Management typically has little understanding of or tolerance for what is involved in the creative process of discovering and analyzing vulnerabilities in security devices. They often think they can force creativity and compress the required time to develop answers. They can't, and such an approach can lead to significant design and liability issues.

49. *Attackers usually develop intelligence about their target before they attack.* They obtain their information from the lock, sales engineers, and other insiders through social engineering or public documents found on the Internet. In contrast, the typical VA team usually tries to discover everything independently and rarely asks for technical data from the product developers.

50. *Engineers, police, and locksmiths aren't experts in finding vulnerabilities in locks and safes.* They can provide valuable input but aren't usually experts in discovering security flaws.

> The case of the Club vehicle anti-theft device provides an excellent example of Rule 50. Many years ago, I analyzed the incredibly popular steering wheel-locking device and found it could be compromised with a five-cent piece of wire in a few seconds. The company that produced the patented devices relied on locksmiths and police departments to test its products and attest to their elevated level of security. Although the company generated hundreds of millions of dollars in sales, some of its products were insecure. Winner International should have employed experts to design and evaluate its products, not *apparent* experts.

51. *Security is a concept that must be considered in the context of its application and environment.* It isn't a binary definition: either secure or not secure. The concept is far more complicated and should be considered as it usually involves multiple parameters, considerations, and value judgments.

52. *A failure of imagination in developing attack vectors can be fatal.* Discovering security and design flaws requires imagination. It's often the essential ingredient to foster creativity and a successful result.

53. *A "high-security" product label can often be very misleading, especially for an uneducated consumer.* The term denotes complex issues and requirements, including compliance with testing standards promulgated by the American

National Standards Institute (ANSI), Underwriter Laboratories (UL), Builders Hardware Manufacturers Association (BHMA), and other standards organizations. Lock manufacturers may use the term as a marketing statement, which often is not factually based.

54. *Security vulnerabilities may not be evident, but that doesn't mean they don't exist.* The failure to learn of an incident involving the compromise of a device isn't dispositive of anything. The lack of a reported incident or a surreptitious attack shouldn't be relied on as evidence that there's no significant issue.

55. *Don't ignore a vulnerability that has little apparent significance.* An issue that appears minor in its relation to security can often lead to more significant problems that can be exploited and compromise a device's overall security.

56. *Security standards have limited value in assessing security vulnerabilities.* Standards are promulgated to define covert and forced entry, endurance, environmental, and other forms of testing. They aren't about testing for attack vectors, both simple and sophisticated, especially those that test exploits of which examiners aren't aware. One of the major problems with standards is that you can't test against an attack you haven't conceived of.

57. *Adversaries can be incredibly resourceful.* Design teams should never underestimate the capabilities of potential attackers, especially for high-value targets. They're often much more creative and technically capable than those who designed and built locks, safes, and support systems. Unfortunately, it's often all about ego on the part of engineers. The diamond heist in Antwerp described in Chapter 25 was a perfect example.

58. *Don't ignore possible equivalent "back-door" attacks and tampering with locks and their internal components to compromise security.* Locks and safes can be subject to simple and clever attacks involving the manipulation of internal components, which are rarely contemplated by design engineers, with serious consequences. One such attack I was involved with involved an award-winning electromechanical lock from Finland (discussed in Chapter 19). I demonstrated that our attack method could open all of the company's locks.

59. *All locks are mechanical, whether they contain electronic elements or not.* Attackers can focus on various aspects of a lock's design to exploit or create vulnerabilities. Whether purely mechanical, a hybrid of mechanical and electronic components, or solely electronic, every lock can be attacked by means of what moves internally to cause an opening.

60. *All security, like politics, is local.* The security of locks must always be considered in the context of local threats, conditions, environment, and service.

61. *The allocation of security resources shouldn't be based solely on the value of the asset rather than the risk.* The asset's value is only one consideration, but the risk to that asset should take priority.

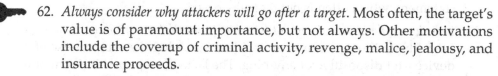 62. *Always consider why attackers will go after a target.* Most often, the target's value is of paramount importance, but not always. Other motivations include the coverup of criminal activity, revenge, malice, jealousy, and insurance proceeds.

> One interesting Canadian case involved the compromise of a popular electromechanical push-button lock that protected a private residence, as discussed in Chapter 25. The perpetrator entered the building and killed two adults and one child by drilling the mechanism obscurely to gain entry. The case illustrates the exploit of design issues that allowed the lock to be opened.

63. *An absence of evidence of the lock's compromise can't be relied on as an absence of evidence that it was compromised.* Lock bumping and certain covert entry tools have caused insurance companies to reconsider their position on the validity of loss claims. Typically, they require evidence of entry to pay claims. The rules have changed, especially in residential burglaries, because the tools that allow locks to be easily and quickly opened through lock bumping have become popular. Similarly, cars can be stolen by simple mechanical bypass techniques or by defeating keyless entry systems without forensic evidence of entry.

64. *A design team that can't conceive of or envisage a potential security vulnerability will not be able to avoid one.* The ability to imagine and then exploit unknown vulnerabilities is the key to a successful vulnerability assessment.

65. *Security analysts rarely know all the tools to compromise a lock or safe design.* This is especially true for standards organizations and lock manufacturers that can't adequately test for covert entry requirements. Government tool suppliers such as Wendt (Germany), Madelin (France), John Falle (UK), and Lockmasters (U.S.) design, develop, and manufacture very specialized tools solely for use by government agencies. These tools can often defeat even the highest-security locks.

66. *Any opening in a lock can create a vulnerability.* Most design engineers can't imagine the compromise of even the most sophisticated mechanisms by exploiting an opening of a few thousandths of an inch in a lock's body or component.

67. *Arrogance by design engineers and management about their capabilities, knowledge, and product security is a recipe for disaster.* There are thousands of examples of design security failures in locks and safes because the manufacturers thought they knew everything about their hardware, their

software, and capabilities to exploit them. They often couldn't conceive of viable ways to defeat their security. In one case, developers compromised high-security safe locks in a completely unimaginable manner by introducing urine into the lock. This lock utilized electronic circuitry, including a chip to control the internal motor drive. The manufacturer never potted the critical chips, which made them vulnerable. As described in Part IV, there is a commercial tool to accomplish this kind of attack.

68. *Attacks are often directed at interfaces between critical locking components.* Designers should never compartmentalize design team expertise or the possibility of an attack. They should be allowed and encouraged to examine the entire system.

69. *Attacks may be low- or high-tech.* Don't ignore or dismiss one possibility for another.

70. *Assume that adversaries understand your security and vulnerabilities better than you do.* As noted throughout the book, attackers may gather significant and critical information about vulnerabilities that can be exploited in hardware and software designs. Two of the highest-profile cases involved the Kaba Simplex 1000 push-button lock and the Medeco BIAXIAL defeat. The Kaba lock was defeated with a rare earth magnet, and the Medeco locks were compromised due to an embedded design vulnerability that allowed the status and function of the sidebar to be defeated.

71. *Auditors and accountants can compromise security by cutting costs when they don't understand the ramifications.* Don't cut costs when designing secure engineering in locks. Design engineers and budget analysts can fail to "connect the dots" when creating their designs by cutting costs. Doing so can result in numerous costly vulnerabilities and vastly compromise the security of whatever the lock is tasked with protecting. One prime example of this was the design of the Kryptonite lock, discussed in Chapter 25.

72. *Be afraid of the Internet and what it can cause regarding an attack on a security product.* Social media platforms and video delivery services such as YouTube and Vimeo have radically changed the security world in regard to the availability of information about every conceivable subject, including bypassing locks, safes, alarm systems, and Internet of Things (IoT) devices. The Internet allows for the collaboration of unlimited resources worldwide for free. Every lock manufacturer should be especially careful with every aspect of product design, marketing, and publicly available specifications.

73. *Be careful when designing security hardware so as not to drive the method of attack.* Designers must always consider whether their designs will promote, encourage, or facilitate specific forms of attack.

74. *Just because it can't be conceived of doesn't mean it doesn't exist.* When lock bumping was first introduced into the American market, industry leaders and trade groups for locksmith organizations made public statements that locks couldn't be opened with simple keys and techniques, that the issue had been exaggerated, and that nobody should talk about the issue. One leading lock executive stated that if he couldn't view the technique personally, it didn't exist. Every major lock manufacturer attempted to address the real threats from bumping and parallel attacks, even for high-security locks.

75. *Beware of tech people on VA teams who are engineers.* In my experience, design engineers often can't conceive of attack vectors or design deficiencies that can lead to the compromise or defeat of a lock or safe.

76. *Burglars rarely pick locks.* There are many ways to defeat a lock; picking is only one. Obtaining copies of keys, using bump keys, and other exploits, including hacking attacks, are far more common, especially for high-value targets. "Smash and grab" or brute-force attacks are the most common entry methods.

77. *VA teams should select people who can make reliable observations.* Team members should be chosen according to those knowledgeable about how locks work and those who don't have any preconceived opinions about the security or insecurity of the project they're working on.

78. *Complex security layers can almost always be defeated.* The more complicated the lock design is, the more likely that one or more security layers will be defeated. Often, adding more layers may create more vulnerability. I've been involved in many initially simple and very clever lock designs. Exploits were found, so more layers of security were implemented to fix the original design concept. Such an exercise can be expensive because of time delays, material changes, personnel costs, and redesign requirements.

79. *Consider the cost to a manufacturer of not fixing a known vulnerability versus the risk to a customer facility.* This is always the tradeoff of priorities and what constitute the most probable threats for any security device. Many manufacturers have been aware of what they perceived to be minimal threats, only to face serious legal liability when they failed to understand the extent of the ramifications of such "minimal" threats.

80. *Consider what unlocks the lock and how it or its credentials can be spoofed.* The first rule in designing any security device is "the key never unlocks the lock." It doesn't matter whether it's a physical key for a mechanical lock, an encrypted key for an electronic lock, or a software-controlled element such as radio frequency identification (RFID) that allows the lock to be opened.

81. *Covering up or ignoring known security vulnerabilities can be lethal in terms of legal and moral responsibility and liability.* Policies must be established to respond properly to known security flaws in a product. A protocol should be in place to guide action when a problem is discovered or brought to the attention of the manufacturer. Such an action plan is detailed in Part II.

82. *An irrational or crazy idea raised during the assessment of a vulnerability can be expanded until it isn't outside the realm of probability.* Design team members should be encouraged to think of all scenarios for attacks, no matter how crazy they may sound. It's often such creativity that leads to understanding and discovering security vulnerabilities.

83. *Creative ideas come from individuals, not groups.* Although creativity is a unique attribute, ideas can be spawned from group collaboration.

84. *Always investigate unexplainable occurrences that lead to a security breach. There's always an identifiable cause.* Don't discount obscure causation in the creation of a security vulnerability. A prime example is the cutting of power to systems that don't provide power backup to protect audit trails.

85. *Defense is always more difficult than offense in vulnerability assessments.* The VA process is analogous to a jury trial; failure to find one or more design flaws can cause serious security and legal consequences. In a jury trial, all it takes is one juror to vote against the others to stop the process.

86. *Design against attack vectors, not how secure a lock appears.* The security or insecurity of a specific lock or design is only part of the evaluation process. The focus should first be on the potential threat and then the hardware solution.

87. *Design errors always favor bad guys, especially in recent technology.* If there's a security flaw, it will usually be discovered by mal actors and then exploited.

88. *Designs should encourage change, flexibility, and critical thinking about what makes a lock secure.* Design teams should consider whether any proposed changes or upgrades enhance security or only appear to do so. Unfortunately, many upgrades and changes are only implemented to extend patents for marketing purposes, with little understanding or appreciation of how they can affect security.

89. *Developing and testing exploit scenarios and strategies will result in failures.* This is the normal course of testing and is to be expected. Understanding what works and what doesn't is important.

90. *The discovery of security vulnerabilities is inevitable and indicates positive results.* A failure to discover any design issues should be cause for concern because usually they exist, whether discovered or not.

91. *Discovering attack vectors shouldn't limit a search for others.* Don't be distracted or satisfied that one or more vulnerabilities have been discovered. There are often more of them waiting to be exploited.

92. *Don't believe in current assumptions or thinking about a security device or technology.* Design teams and companies must be open to possibilities, imagination, and creativity. It's always an attitude *about* the problem, not the problem itself.

93. *Don't blame or kill the "security messenger" because of a possible or actual breach.* Reporting security flaws should be encouraged, regardless of the ramifications.

94. *Don't implement a permanent modification or fix to remedy a temporary solution.* Any design modification must be carefully analyzed before implementing it into a security device. Changes always lead to additional vulnerabilities.

95. *Don't restrict vulnerability analysis by time or budget.* Creativity and discovery of security flaws can take time and can't be rushed, regardless of the pressure that is brought to bear by management.

96. *Don't be overly impressed or swayed by new patented designs in security hardware.* Just because they're thought to be clever or advanced doesn't mean they are so. Their technology may not be thoroughly understood.

97. *Don't be distracted or fooled by a lot of hype about security technology.* It may mean that engineers or others don't understand it fully.

98. *Don't believe statements from management about a potential security problem.* It's highly unlikely that they know about or have enough background to grasp the significant issues.

99. *Don't assume that all is secure with a product because no one has presented evidence to the contrary.* A negative doesn't prove a negative. A lack of information can't form the basis for not finding any security flaw or vulnerability.

100. *Just because "everyone" uses a security technology or component means nothing.* It's inadvisable to jump on the "everyone uses it" bandwagon, because everyone may be wrong.

101. *Don't make security decisions or conclusions based on too small a sample.* Ensure that you have enough expertise and have included a group of experts when forming a valid conclusion.

102. *Focus on the larger picture, not product design and analysis details.* Don't miss the forest for the trees.

103. *Don't rely on facilities management personnel for security.* They rarely understand complex security issues, problems, or vulnerabilities.

104. *Don't ignore the potential to defeat or disable software-based systems with denial of service (DoS) attacks.* Consider the possibility of radio frequency (RF)-based attacks from electromagnetic fields (EMF), electromagnetic pulse (EMP), and jamming.

105. *Design engineers should always be thinking of "what ifs."* Even if some of the ideas are crazy or are thought to have no merit, they should always be discussed and considered.

106. *Even high-tech devices can often be defeated with simple attacks.* A full understanding of how a device works may not be required to defeat it. Never underestimate the effect of a simple attack on sophisticated technology.

107. *Everything we know or understand about a technology or device may be wrong.* We don't know what we don't know what we don't know.

108. *The existence of vulnerabilities is often denied.* This mindset comes from a lack of understanding, arrogance, or an attempt to avoid liability. Whatever the cause, it's a dangerous policy.

109. *Failure to identify vulnerabilities can stem from the person responsible for such an assessment.* Such a finding may be because the one making the assessment can't foresee the problem.

110. *Forensic evidence of an attack may not be present or may be missed.* Most crime labs are especially ill-suited to forensic investigation of locks and safes. They don't have the cases to work on or the expertise. This was especially evident in a triple homicide case I was involved in, where it took the lab technicians five days at the crime scene to realize two small holes had been drilled in the lock on the entry door.

111. *Always consider all products' security and liability implications, even if they don't appear to have any.* Remember, all security is about liability. This mantra must always be kept in mind by every member of a design or product team.

112. *Lawyers, design engineers, public relations, and management are rarely prepared to speak with the media about any issue involving the security of products.* A protocol should be developed with specific action plans before there's a fundamental problem with a lock, safe, or security product design. A detailed threat-level assessment and response are presented in Part II.

113. *"Groupthink" isn't recommended for promoting creativity in solving design and security issues.* In my experience, a group of like-minded engineers may be entirely counterproductive and inhibit creativity in envisioning and solving a problem.

114. *"High-tech" in a product description doesn't mean high security.* Complexity means vulnerability in product design. Design engineers may be unaware of certain types of attacks.

115. *Not talking about a security issue or vulnerability may cause it to be considered irrelevant.* If a potential or perceived threat is never discussed or reviewed, intentionally or not, it may never be considered important. Lock bumping is a perfect example. Many manufacturers ignored the problem and mounted a campaign to downplay its significance and threat.

116. *If everything is confidential, then nothing is.* There are no longer any secrets. Defining information as confidential means there's a high likelihood that such confidentiality will be breached and disclosed.

117. *Erroneous assumptions may be made by security personnel and design engineers if they can't figure out a way to compromise a lock or system.* If critical employees can't defeat a system, it may be assumed that nobody else can. Such a mistake shouldn't be made because design engineers, especially, may not possess the requisite skills.

118. *Expecting a vulnerability can often mean you will not be prepared for it.* It's possible to mentally ignore findings in a product analysis or to dismiss them as already known, which means they may not be addressed.

119. *Anyone who thinks a lock or security system is "foolproof" may prove that fools exist.*

120. *There should be two primary considerations in assessing security vulnerability: when an attacker is most likely to strike and how soon it's detected.* These issues go to the seriousness of the threat, especially detection. Attacks on locks are most concerning with covert attacks if there's no forensic evidence of entry.

121. *In designing a security device, addressing or eliminating every security vulnerability may not be necessary.* There must be a balancing of interests in assessing threats. Although caution is required, a threat assessment must include a realistic approach to analyze and prioritize the reality of the probability of threats.

122. *IT staff and locksmiths in an organization aren't experts in finding vulnerabilities in locks and safes.* Experts in covert and forced entry should be employed to analyze devices and systems unless such expertise exists in a company.

123. *Just because a lock design has been available for a long time doesn't mean it's secure.* There may be embedded security issues that no one has found. One of the highest-security locks in the United States was found to have serious design flaws that allowed it to be picked and bumped open within seconds.

124. *Just because there was never a security problem doesn't mean one doesn't exist.* Just because no one has reported or found a vulnerability doesn't prove there isn't one. Negatives don't prove negatives.

125. *Confidence about security is not enough.* I've worked with many design engineers who had high confidence that their designs had no vulnerabilities, when in fact they did. Confidence is no substitute for proper testing for security flaws.

126. *Being intelligent doesn't mean one can think like a bad guy.* Many highly intelligent engineers with whom I've worked didn't have the mindset to think like a criminal and figure out vulnerabilities in products.

127. *The inability to envision an attack vector doesn't prove there isn't one.* A lack of imagination about potential vulnerabilities has little bearing on whether they exist. It requires a special kind of thinking to consider security issues, and most engineers don't possess this skill.

128. *Lawyers with an understanding of lock design and imagination should be involved in assessing security and its risks.* This is important because lawyers can have a unique perspective on product design and liability.

129. *Repeatedly look for vulnerabilities in a device. With continued analysis, you are likely to find some that were missed.* A vulnerability assessment (VA) is often an incredibly detailed process that requires time to think about attack modes. It involves creativity in thinking and is a maturation process that can't be forced. If you search hard enough, you will find design issues that can be exploited.

 130. *Never rule out a "man in the middle attack."* They can be amazingly effective in compromising electromechanical and electronic locks.

131. *Don't believe many of the security claims of biometric access control systems.* Most of these systems offer little security and can be spoofed.

132. *The fact that security appears to be working and sufficient can often be misleading.* It may mean that nobody is preparing for an attack.

133. *Most organizations will not be prepared for the ramifications of new security technology. Their first impulse may be to ban its implementation.* This can be a very short-sighted policy that may allow competitors to develop advanced products. On the other hand, recent technological advances may be subject to serious security vulnerabilities that take time to discover and rectify.

134. *The proper mindset is required to discover vulnerabilities. Without it, they may never be found.* If you believe you will not discover a design vulnerability, you likely will not find one. You must always believe there is a security flaw to be found.

135. *The application of common sense is the first rule in assessing vulnerabilities.*

136. *Only good guys follow standards.* Criminals or attackers don't carry a copy of the applicable lock standards in their pockets when planning or executing an attack. Reliance on the standards to protect a device will rarely be effective.

137. *Openness and transparency in security design is the best and most effective policy.* Manufacturers should be transparent in disclosing security defects to their customers and advising them how they're resolved. I believe there are no more secrets. Nondisclosure of serious security problems can create liability.

138. *In assessing security, people often see what they expect to see, not what they actually see.* Engineers often miss critical failures or deficiencies because they've been so deeply involved in a specific product that they're blinded to obvious issues.

139. *A high price doesn't make a product secure, nor is it a guarantee of security.* The fact that expensive security hardware is expensive doesn't provide a true index of its security. I have evaluated a lot of expensive locks and safes that can be easily compromised.

140. *Remain flexible during vulnerability testing. Return to the same problem with new attacks, techniques, or thoughts.* Developing new attack vectors can be particularly challenging. Often it requires looking at a problem from many different perspectives before a breakthrough solution can be achieved.

141. *Vulnerability is a risk, and risk is vulnerability. It's a value judgment considering context and cause.* Risk minimization must occur in all designs.

142. *Sales engineers and tech support for lock companies are unprepared to answer security vulnerability questions.* Statements they make regarding security should never be assumed to be accurate.

143. *Security arrogance and ignorance go hand in hand.* One of the recurring problems I have encountered when dealing with lock manufacturers is arrogance about how they totally understand their product far better than an outsider. Such arrogance actually can denote ignorance and can lead to serious ramifications for the company and its customers.

144. *Security by obscurity can work in certain lock designs, but as a rule, it isn't a good policy or effective, except in government security devices.* Long-term secrets don't exist; information can always be obtained deliberately or inadvertently. I've found that sales engineers are usually the ones who disclose critical and confidential security design details.

145. *Security complacency works best for attackers.* If a manufacturer believes their product is perfect and no further research or review is necessary, it's not only a prescription for liability and other adverse actions, but it always works to the advantage of attackers. This is especially true if a security vulnerability has existed for some time and is either unknown or has been ignored by the manufacturer.

146. *Security engineering mode is far different from pure engineering.* There is a significant difference between mechanical engineers designing a lock and

security engineers designing one that can't be compromised. Mechanical engineers typically learn how to make things work properly. Security engineers have the skills to understand design vulnerabilities.

147. *Security is about time delay, deterrence, and discouragement of adversaries.* It's rarely, if ever, perfect, especially with determined attackers.

148. *Security is an optimization problem.* There are many complex tradeoffs and value judgments, human factors, and management issues.

149. *Security measures are going to fail, and security is rarely predictable.* Any security measure, whether in hardware, software, or procedures, will predictably fail at some time. That can be due to a design error, customer misuse, or other factors. The important issue is to attempt to forecast and anticipate such failures before they occur so they can be effectively dealt with.

150. *Security standards aren't the gold standard for security.* They're often too general, overly simplified, and flawed by special interests. Compliance isn't legal proof of security, especially when a standard doesn't cover all vulnerabilities.

151. *Security starts when the project starts, not at the end.* Security engineering of a project or device must begin with the conception of the design and continue through all phases. If not, it will end up being without security.

152. *Security vulnerability can't be reduced to mathematical formulas and numbers.* The concept of security in a device, product, or system is a complex mix of ideas, hardware, and consideration of multiple known and potential attack vectors. There is no valid means to reduce such variables to a mathematical equation.

153. *In any new or modified design, seek input, welcome questions about why or why not, and be open to criticism.* Be careful of over-confidence in design team members or by others.

154. *Don't discard the possibility of signal or signature spoofing to defeat a biometric device.* A classic example was using jelly beans or gummies to defeat a fingerprint reader. Biometric authentication by fingerprint, voice, or facial recognition can be spoofed, so such potential should never be discounted. Although technology is becoming increasingly secure against attacks, they are always possible. It's critical to have up-to-date information about the defeat of biometric systems because they're becoming so prevalent for identification and authentication.

155. *Beware of simple design errors.* They can cause larger errors that experts will miss and will often lead to their exploitation and the bypassing of devices.

156. *Take care not to rely on the premise that "Somebody must have considered it because it's so important or obvious."* This mode of thinking can be fatal to the security of a product. Never count on it.

157. *Security standards may not be good enough to ensure actual security.* Standards may reflect the minimum requirements. Unfortunately, testing criteria often restrict protocols and provide no incentive for innovation and finding problems. Just because a testing lab says a lock is secure doesn't mean it is. This was especially true when locks were tested against bumping techniques.

158. *Every lock manufacturer should implement a crisis protocol to respond to reports of security vulnerabilities in its products.* Once notified of a problem, there should be a plan to carefully respond to what may be a crisis. It defines who will address what and who will talk to the media. It provides a grading scale as to the severity of the alleged problem and what to do about it. This is thoroughly discussed in Chapter 9.

159. *Don't discount an attack involving tampering with a security device or component to circumvent a system.* Classic examples include replacing a target lock, ATM skimmers, and access control system keypads. The defeat of a system can involve altering security hardware that may be difficult to discover. In two cases discussed in this text involving Kwikset locks and iLOQ, the locks were modified or altered, which allowed their compromise. Once the issues were discovered, the manufacturers made changes in their designs to mitigate the threat.

160. *Never think that the compromise or alteration of a noncritical component can't cause or lead to a security vulnerability.* Analyzing every component is essential in a locking system and can reveal a potential cascading failure effect.

161. *The appearance of security doesn't equal security.* Many locks, safes, and security systems appear secure to the uninformed. Unfortunately, many aren't.

162. *The belief that all security devices can be defeated means that none will be fixed.* Circular thinking is wrong and can lead to significant legal liability and security breaches.

163. *Companies should be careful not to subscribe to the Galileo Rule (by Dr. Roger Johnston): "The more significant is the value of the asset or facility being protected, the less willing management will be to learn of vulnerabilities."* Like Galileo and his telescope, in 1633 church officials refused to investigate his telescope for fear of what they might see. I've found that many corporations and facilities, including banking, hospitality, and medical, may decide they don't want notice of a security problem, nor do they want to take any action for fear of liability and adverse publicity.

164. *Being unable to handle the truth about vulnerabilities means you will not have good security.* If those responsible for implementing security policies and

ensuring that design changes are made don't acknowledge a factual basis that is brought to their attention about design issues, there will never be good security. Ignoring a problem doesn't make it go away; it only exacerbates it.

165. *Don't base the vulnerability testing results of locks on arbitrary or limited criteria and then translate those results as applicable to all locks.* Locks may be tested with jigs or other setups that may or may not replicate real-world conditions. Management may also base their opinions on false claims or beliefs that the test didn't apply to other locks because of such perceived limitations. The perfect example relates to lock bumping. Often, cylinders were held in hand and easily bumped open. Many manufacturers, especially high-security lock makers, believed and represented that these tests were not valid because the cylinders were not mounted indoors. Often, this was an invalid assumption and is as ludicrous as saying the attack was demonstrated on Thursday, but today is Tuesday, so such a test isn't viable today.

166. *Fix demonstrated security vulnerabilities rather than blame someone for the problem.* In my experience with major lock manufacturers, the policy should always be to assess the risks associated with a security vulnerability, establish evaluation criteria, and fix the problem. Blaming someone for the issue will solve nothing. It will always be less expensive to deal with an issue early rather than later when discovered by customers or the news media, or when there is litigation.

167. *Don't make a security analysis overly complicated, detailed, or structured.* The result can be less attention to detail and less creativity, which can thwart imagination.

168. *For attackers, the value of the target is often the prime motivation for an attack.* A high-value target dictates information gathering, preparation, intelligence, and knowledge. Always consider probable targets and why they would be attractive.

169. *There are no more secrets; it's called the Internet.* Everything is on the Internet, on YouTube, and in the public domain. This is especially true for different attacks against locks and safes.

170. *Threats are more likely to come from insiders or the exploitation of information from knowledgeable employees.* This may include technical data gained from the social engineering of employees or public sources.

171. *Threats aren't vulnerabilities, but a vulnerability may constitute a threat.* The terms aren't interchangeable. A vulnerability can constitute a security threat that is exploited, but a security threat may have no relation to a vulnerability.

172. *Using "good locks" doesn't mean they're secure or can't be compromised.* The definition of a "good lock" can be very misleading and only relates to quality, not security.

173. *Vulnerabilities are found through creative thinking, first by individuals and then in collaboration.* It often takes a lot of thought to perceive a security flaw in a design. This process is usually done first on the individual level, and then team members can consult for their feedback.

174. *Vulnerabilities should define methods of attack.* Discovering vulnerabilities may identify different attack vectors and lead to multiple security design failures.

175. *A common management position when vulnerabilities are discovered is, "We will worry about it down the road."* This posture never works and can be extremely costly, especially if legal liability is found. Once a company is on notice of a vulnerability that results in some form of economic or personal injury, serious damages can arise when this management action is exposed on discovery.

176. *"Not making any sense" about vulnerabilities doesn't mean you're wrong in your belief.* Others, especially in management, may not understand or have the imagination or technical background to make a valid assessment that a statement is "wrong" or doesn't make any sense about vulnerabilities.

177. *Believing that vulnerabilities can be found will often result in finding them.* The opposite is also true: if you don't believe they exist or can be identified, they won't be discovered.

178. *Never believe that all the vulnerabilities have been discovered in a specific lock, device, or system.* You can't prove that you have found all the vulnerabilities in a product.

179. *Those who are sure they can't be fooled are often the easiest to fool.* Arrogance and ignorance go hand in hand. A good example is the seasoned expert in the lock industry I dealt with to obtain cylinder samples for testing against bumping attacks. He told the news media that if he did not see a vulnerability, it did not exist.

180. *Bad guys don't follow the rules or use attack modes defined in a security standard.* They may use flaws that are defined in standards to defeat a device.

181. *Bad guys, not good guys, should define potential security vulnerabilities and risk analysis.* In my experience working with some very clever and knowledgeable criminals and hackers, lock manufacturers would be wise to employ those who can be properly vetted to conduct certain vulnerability analyses. This is no different than software companies offering rewards to hackers to find zero-day exploits or those that are unknown.

182. *Security vulnerabilities are often found after being missed by other examiners.* Don't believe that vulnerabilities don't exist in locks or security products just because others haven't been able to identify them.

183. *Beware of people without the requisite knowledge who are making judgments about security and vulnerabilities.* The Dunning-Kruger Effect states that people lacking knowledge or expertise about a subject don't know they lack it. Mark Twain said it best: "It isn't what you don't know that gets you into trouble. It's what you know for sure that just isn't so."

 184. *Prioritize valid and realistic potential attack scenarios, not the rare ones.* Be certain that a lack of knowledge or imagination doesn't bias the definition of realistic scenarios.

185. *Very few engineers have the proper design mindset for security and security devices.* Engineers have a methodical approach to solving problems. They're often not creative thinkers and may lack the proper mindset to think creatively about security vulnerabilities or even recognize when they exist.

186. *Minor changes in a patented design can introduce major security vulnerabilities.* I've seen many cases where a small change in a product's design has created significant and serious security vulnerabilities. In my world, there is no such thing as a simple or minor design change in a lock or safe design. Always consider what can go wrong.

187. *In the security world, things are rarely what they appear to be.* Apparent security is often mistaken for actual security.

188. *The General Moshe Dayan Rule states, "The same road that leads from Damascus to Tel Aviv also leads from Tel Aviv to Damascus."* Dayan was a famous Israeli General who drove the Syrians back during the 1973 war. His words apply to lock designs, where the technology or components can be utilized to attack and compromise the lock.

Epilogue

Throughout this book I have reiterated, "Whatever is secure today will not be tomorrow." The capabilities of attackers are continually evolving with the availability of more innovative methods and enhanced and cheaper technology that can be applied to a specific lock. It's also because many people are interested in collaborating to defeat a lock or mechanism without restrictions or borders. Locks are universal, as is the interest in compromising or "breaking" them. The Internet and availability of information have made it possible to focus a great deal of expertise on a problem, and locks are a favorite target.

Security is always a dynamic concept and a metric in lock design because it can easily change. It depends on many factors involving hardware, software, operating environments, standards ratings, and consumer use cases. Perhaps most important, it relies on the competence of the design engineers who created the initial product and any upgrades and the vulnerability assessment (VA) team that vetted them.

I have stressed the need for imagination on the part of everyone involved in developing locks. They must conceive and forecast how any part can be vulnerable. In my experience, this has always been the principal requirement and ingredient for success in making a product secure. The absence of imagination can lead to a vulnerability and resulting security breach. Implementing insecurity engineering principles and procedures must be a discipline for all manufacturers that create or modify products to keep people, assets, data, and facilities safe.

Mechanical locks will be here for the foreseeable future, as the need for them isn't going away. Engineers must always remember that mechanical operation is based on physics and the movement of internal components. Without intelligence from embedded software, they are dumb devices, regardless of how clever, sophisticated, or complicated they or their credentials appear. To paraphrase one of the most recognized American lock experts, Alfred C. Hobbs, almost two centuries ago, "Any part that moves against any other component in a lock can yield information about how to defeat that lock."

Likewise, mechanical keys are credentials that act on and control internal mechanisms. They are simply pieces of metal with no intelligence, so they can most often be defeated, regardless of how much security is designed into them and the locks they open. Advances in 3D printing have made this possible. Those capabilities will only accelerate and become easier and less expensive to implement as time goes on.

The migration toward electronic locking systems and integrated approaches to security that combine many different technologies will require even more education, understanding, vigilance, and sensitivity about what can go wrong and how to ensure that it does not. I hope the information in this book has given you a better appreciation of the multifaceted complexity of the lock industry and helped prepare you to deal with what will surely happen in the future: more attacks against what were perceived to be secure designs.

Innovation has been the hallmark of the development of locks and their defeat for the past 4,000 years. The problem as I see it today is the desire to integrate newer technologies that have not been thoroughly vetted. This is a prescription for failure that can be exceedingly costly and put users at risk.

I hope the information, case examples, and guidelines in this book help those with the difficult task of creating security products. If so, this book will have been worth the effort to write. We often don't know what we don't know. That's always the problem with lock designs and methods to defeat them.

I welcome feedback from readers at mwtobias@securitylaboratories.org or my secure email at mwtobias@protonmail.com.

Patents Issued

The following is a list of patents that I hold:

5,355,701 VingCard hotel lock decoder

5,277,042 Club vehicle anti-theft device

7,441,431 PC Guardian laptop lock

7,775,074 Medeco ARX programmable security pin

7,963,135 B1 Medeco ARX Pin-2

8,302,439 Medeco process patent for code-setting keys

8,997,538 Magnetically repelling lock

9,719,275 Medeco code-setting keys

9,767,315 Biometric patent to erase information

10,120,991 Biometric patent to delete information, advanced

10,337,207 High-security electro-mechanical lock

10,443,267 B2 Lock integrity sensor

10,565,839 Medallion portable device protection

10,832,111 Medallion added technology

11,319,727 B1 E-lock for laptop

11,319,745 B1 Protection of space and medication

11,321,980 B1 Alarm–Safe combination

11,357,212 B1 Pet notifications at the door

11,447,984 Securing device enhancements

11,458,781 Tire pressure monitoring system for tracking vehicles

11,587,380 System for transmitting an authorization code

11,828,264 Encrypted system for transmitting authorization code

11,828,065 Keyway monitoring system assembly

11,828,086 Deadbolt monitoring system enhanced

11,629,525 B1 System for multifactor authentication with porosity sensing

11,640,757 Use of infrared for energy saving system

11,739,560 B1 Deadbolt status monitor

11,774,267 Deadbolt status monitor enhanced

11,828,086 Deadbolt status monitor

11,828,264 System for transmitting authorization code

11,828,065 Keyway monitoring system

Trademark Listing

The following are registered trademarks. The terms are referred to in the text.

TRADEMARK	HOLDER
3KS, 4KS	EVVA Group (Austria)
ACE, ACE 11	Chicago Lock Corporation (USA)
Akura 44	EVVA Group (Austria)
AirKey	EVVA Group (Austria)
Aperio	ASSA ABLOY (Italy)
AVIONAL	Silca, dormakaba (Italy)
BHMA	Builders Hardware Manufacturers Association
BIAXIAL	Medeco, ASSA ABLOY (North America)
Bluetooth	Bluetooth SIG (USA)
CleverMade	CleverMade (USA)
CLIQ and eCLIQ	ASSA ABLOY (Switzerland)
CodeMax	HPC, Inc., division of Hudson Lock (USA)
CUMULUS	Abloy, ASSA ABLOY (Switzerland)

Continues

(*continued*)

TRADEMARK	HOLDER
Data-on-Card	SALTO Systems (Spain)
Delrin	DuPont (USA)
Diamant	DOM Security Group (France)
DIAMATIP	Magnum (USA)
Disc Lock	Abloy, ASSA ABLOY (Finland)
DPI	EVVA Group (Austria)
Everest	Schlage and Allegion (USA)
Extrude	Kerr Endodontics (USA)
Futura Pro	dormakaba (Switzerland)
GEMINY	Drumm GmbH (Germany)
Granit	ABUS (Germany)
iLOQ	iLOQ Oy (Finland)
InstaKey	InstaKey Security Systems (USA)
InSync	dormakaba (Switzerland)
Interactive, Interactive+	Mul-T-Lock Israel, ASSA ABLOY (Switzerland)
Keso	Sargent, ASSA ABLOY (Switzerland)
KeyMe	KeyMe LLC (USA)
Kryptonite	Schlage and Allegion (USA)
LeFebure	Lock Defeat Technology LLC (USA)
LOCKMASTERS	Lockmasters, Inc. (USA)
m3	Medeco, ASSA ABLOY (Switzerland)
M4	Medeco, ASSA ABLOY (Switzerland)
MARLOK	Marlock Corporation, dormakaba (Switzerland)
Maxum	Medeco, ASSA ABLOY (Switzerland)
Mogul	Folger Adam, Southern Folger (USA)
M-SCAN	Madelin (France)
MT5, MT5+	Mul-T-Lock, ASSA ABLOY (Switzerland)
OMNILOCK	OSI Systems, Inc. (USA)
Peaks	dormakaba (Switzerland)
Prime-Cut	Broco Rankin (USA)

TRADEMARK	HOLDER
Primus	Schlage and Allegion (USA)
PROTEC	ASSA ABLOY (Finland)
Quattrocode	Silca, dormakaba (Switzerland)
READ-EZE	Lockmasters, Inc. (USA)
Saflok	Winfield, dormakaba (USA)
SecureKey	Schlage and Allegion (USA)
Simplex 1000, 5800	dormakaba (Switzerland)
SmartKey	Spectrum Brands, ASSA ABLOY (USA)
Spark	ASSA ABLOY (Switzerland)
Spra-Ment	3M Scotch Brand (USA)
SWD and Sound Wave Decoder	C.O.F.E.D. (France)
The Club	Winner International (USA)
Triax	dormakaba (Switzerland)
TuBAR	Chicago Lock Corporation (USA)
Turbo Decoder	Lucky Locks (Bulgaria)
Ving, VingCard, TrioVing	ASSA ABLOY (Norway)
X-07	Mas-Hamilton, dormakaba (USA)
XT	Medeco, ASSA ABLOY (Switzerland)

Index

A

Abloy disc lock
  disc tumbler, 252, 288, 319
  figure 13-3, 289
  figure 13-17, 301
  Han Fey, 288
  patent disc tumbler, 319
Abloy Pulse
  energy harvesting lock, 310
abstract
  of patent, 176
access control systems
  attacks against, 552
  keys, 305
  wireless door locks, 312
acoustic pick
  figure 15-23, 369
Acura 44 system
  EVVA, 299
advanced attacks
  against locks, 459
advancements in RFID
  lock design, 255
adversaries knowledge and resources
  design rules, 600
advertising
  misleading, 211
AFTE
  forensic analysis of locks, 36

alarms
  attacks against, 314
ALOA
  development of, 235
  organizations, 258
alternative designs
  failure to consider in locks, 101
  legal liability, 124
American Inventors Protection Act
  patent, 169
American National Standards Institute
  definition, 258
analysis of keys
  master key systems, 229
ANSI
  definitions, 258
  standards, 138
anti-bumping pins
  lock, 301
anti-drill barriers
  locks, 34, 300, 398
anti-theft device
  vehicles, 13
Antwerp diamond heist
  locks, 370, 555
apparent security
  design rules, 623
appearance of security
  design rules, 620

application of force
  failure to consider, 578
application of torque
  to a lock, 580
arrogance in designs
  design rules, 610
ARX Medeco pins
  figure 13-13, 298
  figure 13-18, 302
  Medeco, 302, 468
ASIS
  development of, 235
ASSA Abloy CLIQ
  figure 13-23, 307
  lock design, 306
ASSA Abloy eclair
  lock design, 306
ASSA Abloy Spark
  energy harvesting, 310
  figure 13-27, 310
ASSA sidebar design
  figure 14-6, 324
ASSA twin
  lock design, 321
ASSA V10 lock
  figure 14-5, 325
  lock design, 321
  side pin design, 323
assembly retaining
  locks, 384
assumptions about security
  design rules, 614
ASTM
  standards, 138
AT Security software
  3D printing, 514
attack methods
  failure to correlate, 577
  lever locks, 355
  prioritization design rules,
    623
attack motivation
  design rules, 621
attack resistance times
  UL 437, 141
attack types
  locks, 385
attack vector discovery

design rules, 613
  imagining, 617
attacks against locks
  against cars man-in-middle, 566
  against high-tech design rules, 611
  against keying systems, 489
  against tolerances, 387
  electronic cylinder, 146
  electronic locks, 445
  design rules, 605
  forced entry, 36
  history, 341
  hybrid, 80
  inside, 62
  intelligence about locks, 608
  key control advanced, 508
  security ratings, 83
  shear line, 44
  simple, 560
  time computation, 68, 69
audit trails
  BHMA 156.30, 155
  characteristics of, 46
  compromise of, 46
  covert entry, 76
  defeat of, 77
  defeating of, 392
  locks, 46, 76
  vulnerabilities, 608
avoiding legal issues
  legal liability, 89
axial pin tumbler locks
  attacks against, 562
  bumping attacks, 562
  decoder, 431
  definitions, 258
  figure 12-1, 258
  figure 13-11, 297
  utility patent 7441431, 296
axioms and guidelines
  lock design, 599

B

back doors
  design rules, 609
bad guys and security vulnerabilities
  design rules, 622
balanced driver attacks

covert entry, 428
    definition, 259
ballpoint pen attacks
    axial pin tumbler locks, 562
    impressioning, 14
banks
    figure 11-15, 250
barrel and curtain design
    lever locks, 365
Barron Robert
    lever lock, 354
    lever tumbler lock, 244
battering ram
    forced entry, 411
belly decoding and reading
    figure 15-21, 362
    lever lock decoding, 362
    lever locks, 356
bending
    forced entry, 404
Best lock company
    definition, 268
BHMA 156.30 High security standards
    bumping resistance, 160
    data from the lock, 157
    decoding, 156
    deficiencies, 148
    definitions, 261
    electronic attacks, 159
    electronic audit trails, 155
    forced entry, 153
    internal tolerances, 158
    key control, 155
    lock standards, 133, 139
    mechanical bypass, 154
    pick resistance, 158
    standards, 133, 138, 142
    testing deficiencies, 153
BHMA 156.5
    deficiencies, 148
    lock standards, 139
    standards, 146
BIAXIAL (Medeco)
    Decoder, 469
    Medeco design, 259, 328
    Medeco pin diagram, 329
bike locks
    attacks against, 561

biometric access
    gun safes, 392
biometric devices defeat
    design rules, 619
biometric security claims
    design rules, 617
bitting of keys
    attacks against, 388
    change keys, 490
    definition, 260
    depths figure 12-3, 260
    inserts on keys, 221
    key design of, 482
    keys, 43
    locks, 301
    rules, 485
    sequence decoding of, 229
    systems for keys, 301
blackmail
    against lock manufacturer, 203
blacksmiths
    development of, 233
blade of key
    definitions, 260
blank key
    definition, 261
blocking elements
    locks, 384
blows against locks
    forced entry, 411
Bo Widen patents
    lock designs, 325
    locks, 321
bolts and mechanisms
    attacks against 389
    definition, 261
    locks, 384
    pressure against to open, 366
    warded locks, 347
bottom pin
    definition, 261, 276
Brahma lock
    attacks against, 342
    figure 11-11, 246
    figure 15-22
    Great Exhibition, 246
    lock design, 368
    security of, 245

breaker tools
 forced entry, 403
Briggs & Stratton locks
 sidebar lock, 255
 wafers, 284
Brinks robbery
 Boston, 370
broaching of plug
 locks, 240
brute force attacks
 locks, 37
Builders Hardware Manufacturers
  Association (BHMA)
 lock standards, 133
bump key
 creation of, 225, 493
 definition, 261
 diagram, 8
 diagram of bumping, 8
 figure 1-1, 8
 figure 11-19, 252
 figure 13-7, 293
 locks, 42, 293
 theory of operation, 8
 UL 437, 150, 152
Bumping
 Attack theory figure 1-12, 19
 axial pin tumbler locks, 562
 covert entry, 41, 438
 definition, 261
 electronic locks, 447
 forced entry attacks, 411
 high-security locks, 562
 locks, 34, 41, 428
 Medeco, 83, 538
 rapping of locks, 392
 resistance BHMA 156.30, 160
 security rating, 83
 testing, 57
 time required, 71
burglars don't pick locks
 design rules, 612
burglary resistant mechanisms
 Underwriters Laboratories, 138
bypass of locks
 bumping, 16
 combination, 23
 definition, 270

electronic cylinders, 20
electronic locks by drilling, 452
expertise, 37
fundamentals, 35
gun locks, 15
iLOQ locks, 14
impressioning, 17
Kryptonite bike locks, 14, 83
Kwikset lock, 83
lever tumbler locks, 352
with liquids, 14
Luckylock, 436
Medeco m3, 23
nitinol wire designs, 575
paperclips, 12
padlocks, 579
plugs, 14
push button locks, 13
shimming, 16
using shims, 443
wafer locks, 12

C
cam
 definition, 261
case examples
 absence of evidence of
  compromise, 610
 by category, 571
 the Club vehicle protection,
  608
 great Exhibition, 605
 iLOQ, 602
 Medeco m3 lock, 604
 push button lock attack, 610
caveat emptor
 legal liability, 108
chamber of lock
 definition, 261
change key
 definition, 261
 locks, 42
 modifying, 491
 reverse engineering of, 499
chemical attacks
 forced entry, 414
Chicago Tubar lock
 Brahma, 246

Chinese lever locks
  opening, 363
chisel and wedging attacks
  forced entry, 412
chisel-point pin tumblers
  definition, 262
Chubb detector lock
  Detector lock, 246
  figure 15-20, 361
Chubb locks
  figure 11-12, 247
Civil law
  liability, 106
claims
  patents, 175
classification system
  patents, 183
clever designs
  design rules, 600, 604
CLIQ
  lock design, 306
cloning
  electronic credentials, 497
the Club
  case example, 608
Club (anti-theft device)
  attacks against, 553
  bypass, 13
  vehicle anti-theft device, 13
CMOE (Covert Methods of Entry)
  locks, 418
Code of Justinian
  liability, 107
codes
  definition, 262
  keys, 482
code setting keys
  covert entry, 432
  definition, 262
  figure 3-1, 57
  Medeco, 127, 537, 587
C.O.F.E.D.
  decoding of keys, 223
  lock scanner, 527
  scanner figure 23-1, 527
Columbia Railroad versus Hawthorne
  legal liability, 120
comb picking patent

2064818, 429
comb picks
  figure 18-8, 428
combination locks
  bypass, 23
  opening, 363
  standards, 138
common sense usage
  design rules, 617
  in security vulnerabilities, 617
complex attacks
  security failure in design, 586
complex security layers defeat
  design rules, 612
complex security problems
  design rules, 604
complexity
  insecurity engineering, 25
  locks, 25
complicated security analysis
  design rules, 621
component analysis
  design rules, 620
compressed air
  forced entry attacks, 411
compromise of locks
  of locks, 36
  design rules, 600, 606
conceiving of attacks inability
  design rules, 612
conductive liquids
  standards, 146
confidence about security
  design rules, 617
confidential information
  design rules, 616
consequences in lock design
  unintended, 391
constructive knowledge of risk
  lock manufacturers, 128
consulting agreements
  NDA, 201
control key
  decoding, 493
  definition, 262
conventional mechanical locks
  classification, 31
  figure 13-4, 290

history, 283
security enhancements, 300
selection of, 315
vulnerabilities, 291
core
definition, 262
Core Shim Decoder
John Falle, 468
Corkey magnetic lock
attacks against locks, 584
cost cutting
design rules, 611
counterfeit keys and blanks
cutting keys on, 214
key control, 43
identification of, 216
locks, 488
protection against, 7
covert attacks
against microprocessors, 441
audio frequencies, 442
expertise, 32
feeling, 442
locks, 387
covert entry
amplification of rights, 431
audio frequencies and sound, 442
balance driver attacks, 428
covert methods of entry, 417
experts, 459
expertise required, 38
forensic traces, 32
gate fence tolerances, 434
hybrid attacks, 390
impressioning, 436
jiggle keys, 433
locks, 76
magnetics, 440
methods of, 38, 421
picking, 425
rapping attacks, 435
signature picks, 434
standards, 141
techniques of, 36
tolerance exploits, 432
tool makers, 459
traditional, 38
crazy ideas

design rules, 613
creative ideas source
design rules, 613
creative thinking and management
design rules, 608
vulnerability assessment, 622
credential spoofing
design rules, 612
credentials
attacks against, 478, 591
electronic, 12
criminal law
legal actions, 106
liability, 106
crisis protocols
design rules, 620
cross-combination
definition, 262
cross-keying
definition, 263
key design, 43
cross-picking tool
figure 15-28, 375
current assumptions about security
design rules, 614
cut angle
definition, 263
cut keys
overlay, 491
cut root
definition, 263
cutting by forced entry
attacks against locks, 396
cycle tests
standards, 147
cylinder
definition, 263
cylinder pulling
with screws, 403

D
damages
patents, 186
types of in lock defects, 197
dangerous conditions
product liability, 94
data from the lock
BHMA 156.30, 157

deadbolt
  definition, 264
  Medeco, 431
deadbolt attacks
  Medeco, 581
  Cylinder figure 12-5, 264
decoding
  belly reading, 362, 443
  BHMA 156.30, 155
  by borescopes, 442
  control keys, 493
  core shim, 468
  covert entry, 40
  definition, 264
  Falle, 41
  keys, 220, 222
  Lishi tool, 41
  locks, 41
  master keys, 44
  methods of, 41, 524
  methods of attacks, 582
  piezo attacks, 442
  pin lock, 467
  radiographic techniques, 499
  secondary security layers, 493
  standards, 145
decoding attacks
  against mechanical locks, 388
  information from locks, 441
  methods failure to consider, 582
  options master key systems, 505
  shims, 467
  standards, 152
  standards BHMA 156.30, 156
  systems locks, 524
  techniques expertise required, 41
DefCon
  definition, 264
defeat
  key control, 213
Defeat Technology Company
  impressioning system, 438
defective designs
  copying of, 393
  locks, 195
defective products
  definition of, 92, 112, 113
  design flaws, 113

disclosure policy, 12
  failure to disclose, 97
  insufficient warnings, 113
  internal procedures, 193
  knowingly selling, 126
  legal liability, 96, 118, 128
  malfunction doctrine, 124
  manufacturing flaws, 113
  notification action items, 187, 195, 200
  notification rules, 188
  procedure to follow, 188, 198
  protection, 9
  threat level criteria, 198
defenses
  legal liability, 127
  misconduct o the use, 127
  patent infringement, 185
definitions
  balanced drivers, 259
  BHMA, 261
  bitting, 260
  blade of key, 260
  blank key, 261
  bolt, 261
  bottom pin, 261, 276
  bump key and bumping, 261
  bypass, 270
  cam, 261
  chamber of lock, 261
  change key, 261
  code setting key, 262
  control key, 262
  core, 262
  cross-keying, 263
  cross-combination, 262
  cut angle, 263
  cylinder, 263
  deadbolt, 264
  decoding of lock, 264
  DefCon, 264
  depth and spacing, 265
  depth increment, 264
  depth keys, 265
  detainers, 270
  differs, 265
  dimple key, 265
  direct code, 265
  double-bitted key, 266

double-detainer theory, 266
driver pin, 266
end-cap, 266
ESD, 266
EVVA MCS, 267
feel picking, 267
fence, 267
graduated driver, 267
grand master key, 267
high-security lock, 267
impression system, 267
indirect code, 267
industry, 257
insecurity engineering, 3
interchangeable core, 268
jamb, 268
key code, 262
key gauge, 268
key interchange, 262, 268
key milling, 268
key picking, 268
key symbols, 268
keyhole, 268
keying levels, 269
keyway, 269
lock picking, 273
loiding, 269
MACS, 269
master key, 270
master pin, 270
Medeco chisel point, 262
Medeco high-security cylinder, 270
Medeco m3, 269
mortise cylinder, 270
movable detainer, 270
multi-section key blank, 272
mushroom tumbler, 272
paracentric keyway, 272
pin stack, 273
pin tumbler lock, 273
plug, 273
rapping of lock, 273
removable core cylinder, 273
restricted keyway, 273
rim cylinder, 273
security pin tumbler, 272
security pins, 273
shear line, 273

shell of lock, 273
sidebar, 274
sidebar lock, 274
strike, 274
tailpiece, 266, 274
theoretical key changes, 274
TMK, 276
tolerance, 276
top pin, 276
triple-bitted key, 276
tryout key, 276
tubular pin tumbler lock, 276
Underwriters Laboratories, 277
virtual shear line, 277
wafer lock, 277
delayed action time locks
  standards, 138
dent puller
  locks, 404
dependent infringement
  patent, 184
depth and spacing data
  decoding from keys, 484
  definitions, 265
  information about keys, 484
depth coding
  keys, 43
depth increment
  definition, 264
  key system, 43
depth keys
  decoding locks, 499
  definition, 265
  shimming of cylinders, 499
design
  patents, 170
design changes
  in locks, 565
design defects
  duty to warn, 197
  failure to remedy, 197
  legal liability, 90, 91, 115, 195
  notification procedure, 193
  post-sale duty, 197
  recall, 197
  threat levels, 198
design errors recent technology
  design rules, 613

design expertise
  high-security locks, 32
design exploits
  design rules, 607
design failures
  against complex attacks, 586
  locks, 18
design flaws
  defective products, 113
design guidelines
  locks, 599
design improvements
  lock manufacturers, 6
design issues
  Medeco, 565
design mistakes
  by manufacturers, 37
designs previously considered
  design rules, 619
design rules
  absence of evidence of
      compromise, 610
  adversaries and intelligence, 609
  apparent security, 623
  appearance of security, 601, 620
  arbitrary criteria, 621
  arrogance in engineering, 610
  assumptions about security, 614
  attack motivation, 621
  attack vector discovery, 613
  attack vectors designs against, 613
  attacker developed intelligence, 608
  attacks against high-tech, 611
  attacks on interface, 611
  attacks on locks, 605
  audit trails, 608
  back doors, 609
  bad guys and vulnerabilities, 622
  biometric devices defeat, 619
  biometric security claims, 617
  burglars pick locks, 612
  clever designs, 600
  cleverness and security, 604
  cleverness in designs, 600
  cleverness in thinking, 601
  common sense usage, 617
  compromise of locks, 600
  confidential information, 616

crazy ideas validity, 613
creative ideas source, 613
creative thinking, 622
credentials defeat, 606
crisis protocols, 620
current assumptions about
    security, 614
cutting costs, 611
cutting research costs, 600
defeating complex security layers, 612
design errors, 613
designs and security, 613
do not duplicate, 607
down the road, 622
Dunning-Kruger effect, 623
e-cylinders, 606
electrons in locks, 605
encryption, 601, 603
engineers and mindset, 623
erroneous security assumptions, 616
everyone thinking alike, 605
expecting to find vulnerabilities, 616
expertise required about
    vulnerabilities, 608
experts finding vulnerabilities, 616
exploits and keys, 605
exploits testing, 613
facility management, 614
finding all vulnerabilities, 622
fixing vulnerabilities and costs, 612
fool about vulnerabilities, 622
foolproof security, 616
forensic evidence failure, 615
Galileo rule, 620
good locks and security, 622
groupthink, 615
high-security doesn't mean secure, 600
high-security label, 608
high-tech, 601
high-tech and security, 615
Hobbs, 604
ignoring vulnerabilities, 609
iLOQ, 602
imagination failure, 608
imagining attack vectors, 617
impenetrable lock, 607
important, 23
inability to conceive attacks, 612

Internet information, 611
keys, 599
laws of physics, 604
lawyers in vulnerability
    assessment, 617
lock designs and finding
    vulnerabilities, 616
locks are mechanical, 609
Man-in-middle attack, 617
management quashes innovation, 608
management statements about
    security, 614
meaning of patents, 606
Medeco design, 604
media comments about security, 615
minor changes, 623
misjudging adversaries, 600
Moshe Dayan rule, 623
never say never, 607
new design technology, 614
new locks, 606
no more secrets, 621
non-critical components, 620
not invented here, 601
not making any sense, 622
observation ability, 612
opening locks with keys, 600
openings and vulnerabilities, 610
overly complicated analysis, 621
patents and security, 607
path of least resistance, 607
poor attitude about compromising, 600
positive attitude about attacks, 605
previously considered issues, 619
price of products, 618
prioritize effective attacks, 623
proper mindset in security, 617
ramifications of new security
    technology, 617
reliance on standards, 606
replication of keys, 604
sales engineers and security, 618
secrets and locks, 604
security and arrogance, 618
security and confidence, 617
security and delay, 619
security and efficiency, 603
security and liability, 605

security and liability
    considerations, 615
security and mathematics, 619
security and openness, 618
security and projects, 619
security and risk, 618
security as a concept, 608
security as a continuum, 602
security assessment considerations, 616
security by obscurity, 618
security complacency, 618
security confidence, 617
security decisions, 614
security defeats, 615
security device defeat, 620
security device development, 616
security effectiveness, 602
security engineering and regular
    engineering, 618
security focus, 614
security hardware methods of
    attack, 611
security idea input, 619
security is an optimization process, 619
security is complicated, 602
security is local, 609
security is working, 617
security issues ignored, 616
security messenger, 614
security resources allocation, 600
security rules and failures, 619
security standards and actual
    security, 620
security standards value, 609, 619
security technology hype, 614
security theater, 603
security vulnerabilities denial, 615
security vulnerabilities existence, 616
security vulnerabilities failure to
    identify, 615
security vulnerability blindness, 618
security vulnerability evidence, 609
signature of keys, 601
simple attacks against complex
    mechanisms, 615
simple attacks to defeat locks, 602
simple design errors, 619
source of threats, 621

spoofing credentials ability, 612
standards and good guys, 617
standards reliance on, 606
tampering with security device, 620
target valuation, 610
temporary modifications, 614
thinking like bad guys, 617
threats and vulnerabilities, 621
3T2R rule, 606
truth and security, 620
unexplained occurrences, 613
use of plastics, 603
vulnerabilities define methods of
    attack, 622
vulnerabilities missed, 623
vulnerabilities searching, 617
vulnerability analysis restrictions, 614
vulnerability assessment team
    members, 612
vulnerability assessments and
    flexibility, 618
vulnerability cover-up, 613
what ifs consideration, 615
wrong assumptions about security, 615
design teams and vulnerability
  case examples, 610
design vulnerabilities
  electronic locks, 455
designers thinking alike
  design rules, 605
designs and security
  design rules, 613
destructive attacks
  against locks, 395
destructive entry tools
  locks, 414
destructive testing
  standards, 144
detainers
  definition, 270
  hybrid attacks against, 391
detector lock
  Chubb, 246
devil's ring
  bypass of locks, 23
  figure 1-10, 17
  magnetics, 23
diamond heist

Antwerp, 370, 555
differs
  definition, 265
  inadequate number, 224
  key control, 43
  standards, 143
  theoretical, 275
digital cylinders
  key-based, 305
digital door locks
  designs, 391
digital fingerprints
  locks, 523
dimple keys
  definition, 265
  simulation of, 221
dimple lock attacks
  John Falle, 295
dimple lock printed key
  figure 22-3, 513
dimple locks
  axial, 30
  figure 13-9, 295
  foil attacks, 295
  forced attacks, 406
  lock designs, 294
  Mul-T-Lock, 295
direct codes
  definition, 265
  keys, 43
direct infringement
  patents, 184
disassembly
  of locks, 43
disassembly of locks
  decoding, 498
disc tumbler locks
  lock design, 252, 288
disclosure policy
  defects, 12
DMCA
  lock design, 203
do not duplicate
  locks, 607
door locks
  standards, 141
door opening tools
  forced entry, 409

double-bitted key
  definition, 266
double-bitted wafer lock
  figure 12-15, 277
double-detainer locking
  lever locks, 243
  theory, 266, 289
Double-sided wafer lock
  figure 11-21, 254
down the road
  design rules, 622
drill resistance
  standards, 144
drilling
  electronic locks, 452
  interchangeable core locks, 401
  pin tumbler locks, 398
  rotor access, 454
drilling attacks
  figure 17-1, 397
  figure 17-3, 399
  forced attacks, 398
  locks, 396
  sidebars, 455
driver pin
  definition, 266
driving
  forced entry, 404
duckbill
  forced entry tool, 410
due care
  lock design, 128
  in manufacturing, 102
  manufacturing, 128
Dunning-Kruger effect
  design rules, 623
duplication of keys
  key control, 217, 218
  patent infringement, 215
duty to recall
  products liability, 96
duty to warn
  design defect, 197
  legal liability, 115

E

Easy Entire key machine
  key control attacks, 510
e-cylinders
  defeat of credentials, 606

EEPROM attacks
  hotel safes, 585
Egyptian pin tumbler lock
  Development, 237
  diagram figure 11-4, 239
  figure 11-2, 238
  figure 11-3, 238
  figure 15-1, 345
  origins, 237, 344
  security vulnerability, 345
electromagnetic pulse (EMP)
  BHMA 156.30, 159
electromechanical locks
  attacks against, 557
  audit trail defeats, 392
  bypass of, 453
  designs, 29
  reset functions, 453
electronic access control
  attacks against, 552
electronic attacks
  against lock, 314
  BHMA 156.30, 159
  most unlikely, 568
electronic audits
  vulnerabilities, 608
electronic consumer locks
  figure 13-29, 312
electronic credentials
  attacks, 547
  cloning, 497
  locks, 12
electronic cylinders
  bypass, 20
  compromise of, 574
electronic elements
  attacks against, 592
  locks, 448
electronic hotel safes
  attacks against, 585
electronic laptop locks
  defeat of, 393
electronic locks
  attacks, 145, 452
  attacks against, 445
  audit trails, 46, 77
  auto reset, 453
  bumping attacks, 447
  bypass of, 452
  data port access, 393

design vulnerabilities, 447, 455
designs, 29
ion, 14
Kevo, 311
lock designs, 310
manipulation of rotor, 449
mechanical key bypass, 451
motor attacks, 453
piggyback attacks, 450
RFID, 21
rotor access, 454
rotor manipulation, 449
shim attacks, 452
sidebar attacks, 455
standards for, 138
vulnerabilities, 447
electronic locks exploits
   auto reset, 453
electronic padlocks
   attacks against, 595
electronic pick guns
   covert entry, 427
electronic rotor access in locks
   by drilling, 455
electronic scanners
   locks, 524
electrons in locks
   design rules, 605
electrons opening doors
   design rules, 605
electrostatic discharge
   definition, 266
elements of proof
   legal liability, 128
EMP attacks
   BHMA 156.30, 159
employment agreements
   patents, 174
encryption
   case study, 603
   design rules, 603
   lock design, 601
   what it means, 603
   understanding of in lock defeat, 603
end-cap
   definition, 266
energy harvesting
   Abloy Pulse, 310
   eclair, 306

iLOQ, 308
   locks, 29, 307
engineers
   expertise in locks, 26
engineers and mindset
   design rules, 623
entry holes
   locks, 22
entry tools
   warded locks, 349
Epilogue
   Tobias on Locks, 625
erroneous security assumptions
   design rules, 616
ESD
   definition, 266
ESD testing
   standards, 146
estoppel
   patents, 185
European patent convention
   patents, 167
everyone uses security
   design rules, 614
evidence
   absence of, 559
   absence of compromise, 610
   of bypass, 36
   of entry, 46
   forensic evidence, 46
EVVA
   magnetic code system, 299
EVVA Acura 44
   figure 13-16, 300
EVVA dpi lock
   figure 15-5, 349
EVVA locks
   Acura 44, 300
EVVA magnetic code system (MCS)
   definition, 267
   figure 13-15, 299
   lock design, 334
   magnetic attacks, 440
EVVA 3KS
   figure 13-2, 288
   printed key figure 22-4, 513
   sliders, 286
EVVA 4KS key
   printed, 513

examples
  insecurity engineering, 14
expanding bits
  lever keys, 364
expertise
  covert attacks, 32
  forced attacks, 32
  insecurity engineering, 25
  lock engineers, 27
  lock manufacturers, 7
expertise required
  covert entry, 38
  UL 437, 151
experts
  lock manufacturers, 128
experts finding vulnerabilities
  design rules, 616
exploit
  repeatability of, 83
exploits and keys
  design rules, 605
exploits of locks
  design rules, 607
exploits testing
  design rules, 613
explosive attacks
  locks, 368
  small keyholes, 365
  small keyholes preventing, 365
external locking elements
  attacks against, 389
extortion attempts
  civil remedies, 204
  criminal investigation, 203
  design defects, 202
  federal statutes, 203
  insider threats, 206
extrapolation
  master key systems, 44
  TMK, 267, 493, 501
  top-level master key, 225
extrapolation of TMK
  intelligence required, 501
  master key systems, 500
  practical considerations, 501

F
facilities management and security
  design rules, 614
failure of imagination

design rules, 608
failure to connect dots
  insecurity engineering, 572
failure to warn
  legal liability, 94
Falle impressioning system
  covert entry, 437
  figure 15-17, 359
Falle (John)
  Pin and Cam systems, 464
  pin lock decoders, 41
Falle pick set
  covert entry, 424
false advertising
  liability, 211
false gates
  lock design, 301
false keys
  lever locks, 357
  traps, 355
false representations
  legal liability, 129
  product liability, 93
federal statutes
  extortion, 202
feel picking
  definition, 267
Fenby permutating key machine
  key cutting, 364
fence
  definition, 267
ferrous components
  attacks against., 36
  locks, 35
Fichet locks
  3D printed key, 512
field of invention
  patents, 176
figure 1-1
  bump key, 24
figure 1-2
  side bit milling, 9
figure 1-3
  worm gear, 10
figure 2-1
  simulated keys and key control, 32
figure 2-2
  master key system, 42
figure 2-3
  plug and sidebar, 45

figure 3-1
  Medeco code setting keys, 45, 61
figure 11-1
  Greek lock, 236
figure 11-2
  Egyptian lock, 238
figure 11-3
  Egyptian pin tumbler lock, 238
figure 11-4
  Egyptian lock diagram, 239
figure 11-5
  warded lock design, 239
figure 11-6
  warded lock design, 240
figure 11-7
  warded lock and key, 241
figure 11-8
  warded lock mechanism, 241
figure 11-9
  warded locking mechanism, 241
figure 11-10
  lever tumbler lock, 243
figure 11-11
  Brahma lock, 246
figure 11-12
  Chubb locks, 247
figure 11-13
  Parsons lever lock, 248
figure 11-14
  lever locks, 249
figure 11-15
  time locks banks, 250
figure 11-16
  Yale pin tumble, 251
figure 11-17
  pin tumbler locks, 251
figure 11-18
  pin tumbler lock with sidebar, 251
figure 11-19
  bump key, 252
figure 11-20
  wafer lock, 254
figure 11-21
  double sided wafer lock, 254
figure 12-1
  tubular lock, 258
figure 12-2
  Medeco BIAXIAL lock, 259
figure 12-3
  bitting depth and measurement, 260

figure 12-4
  pin tumbler lock components, 263
figure 12-5
  deadbolt cylinder, 264
figure 12-6
  keyway, 269
figure 12-7
  MACS, 270
figure 12-8
  Medeco sidebar lock, 270
figure 12-9
  pin tumbler cylinder, 270
figure 12-10
  mushroom pin tumbler, 272
figure 12-11
  paracentric keyway, 272
figure 12-12
  shear line, 273
figure 12-13
  sidebar diagram, 275
figure 12-14
  top pins, 276
figure 12-15
  double bitted wafer lock, 277
figure 13-1
  Kwikset SmartKey, 287
figure 13-2
  EVVA 3KS, 288
figure 13-3
  Abloy disc lock, 289
figure 13-4
  conventional pin tumbler lock, 290
figure 13-5
  creating a shear line, 290
figure 13-6
  paracentric keyway, 291
figure 13-7
  bump keys, 293
figure 13-8
  Sargent Keso, 295
figure 13-9
  dimple locks, 295
figure 13-10
  Mul-T-Lock pins, 296
figure 13-11
  axial pin tumbler locks, 297
figure 13-12
  laser track keys Mul-T-Lock, 298
figure 13-13
  Medeco ARX security pins, 298

figure 13-14
  Medeco cam lock, 299
figure 13-15
  EVVA magnetic code system, 299
figure 13-16
  floating magnetic wafer, 300
figure 13-17
  Abloy disc lock false gates and
      security pins, 301
figure 13-18
  security pin tumblers, 302
figure 13-19
  key designs, 17, 303
figure 13-20
  interactive pins movable element, 304
figure 13-21
  Schlage Everest, 304
figure 13-22
  Mul-T-Lock mt5+, 305
figure 13-23
  Assa Abloy CLIQ, 307
figure 13-24
  Ikon eCLIQ, 308
figure 13-25
  iLOQ, 309
figure 13-26
  iLOQ, 309
figure 13-27
  Assa Abloy Spark, 310
figure 13-28
  RFID in locks, 311
figure 13-29
  electronic consumer locks, 312
figure 13-30
  Schlage electromechanical locks, 313
figure 13-31
  Kwikset Kevo, 314
figure 14-1
  ABLOY disc lock, 319
figure 14-2
  side bit milling, 322
figure 14-3
  unique sidebar design, 322
figure 14-4
  finger pin design, 323
figure 14-5
  ASSA V10 lock, 325
figure 14-6

ASSA sidebar design, 324
figure 14-7
  Schlage Primus design, 325
figure 14-8
  Schlage Primus, 326
figure 14-9
  Schlage Primus, 326
figure 14-10
  Medeco sidebar design, 327
figure 14-11
  Medeco BIAXIAL diagram, 329
figure 14-12
  Medeco rotation angles, 329
figure 14-13
  Medeco BIAXIAL lock, 330
figure 14-14
  Medeco pin position, 330
figure 14-15
  Medeco m3 lock, 331
figure 14-16
  Medeco cutaway m3 lock, 331
figure 14-17
  Medeco m3 slider, 332
figure 14-18
  m3 lock cutaway, 332
figure 14-19
  Medeco M4 lock design, 332
figure 14-20
  Medeco M4 key design, 333
figure 14-21
  Medeco M4 sidebar, 334
figure 14-22
  EVVA MCS design, 334
figure 14-23
  magnetic code system
      design, 336
figure 14-24
  MCS rotor design, 337
figure 14-25
  magnetic code system profile, 338
figure 14-26
  magnetic overlay film, 338
figure 15-1
  Egyptian lock, 345
figure 15-2
  Roman warded keys, 346
figure 15-3
  warded lock, 347

figure 15-4
  warded key and lock, 348
figure 15-5
  EVVA dpi lock, 349
figure 15-6
  warded keys, 350
figure 15-7
  skeleton keys, 350
figure 15-8
  keys for warded locks, 351
figure 15-9
  warded lock impressioned,
    351
figure 15-10
  warded bypass tools, 352
figure 15-11
  warded locks picking tools, 352
figure 15-12
  lever tumbler lock diagram, 353
figure 15-13
  Canadian postal locks, 354
figure 15-14
  silicone impressioning, 356
figure 15-15
  plasticine impressioning, 356
figure 15-16
  impressioning of bitting, 358
figure 15-17
  Falle impressioning system, 359
figure 15-18
  2-in-1 lever tool, 360
figure 15-19
  KGB impressioning system, 361
  programmable lever lock picking
    tool, 361
figure 15-20
  Chubb detector lock, 361
figure 15-21
  belly reading decoders, 361
figure 15-22
  Brahma lock, 368
figure 15-23
  acoustic pick, 369
figure 15-24
  KGB picking tools, 372
figure 15-25
  KGB picking tool pin tumbler
    locks, 372

figure 15-26
  KGB magnetic lock decoder, 373
figure 15-27
  Aldo Silvera tools, 374
  specialized picking tools, 374
figure 15-28
  cross-picking tool, 375
figure 15-29
  Sputnik picking tool, 375
figure 15-30
  Lishi picking tool, 376
figure 17-1
  drilling attacks, 397
figure 17-2
  forced attacks, 398
figure 17-3
  drilling of locks, 398
figure 17-4
  drilling of locks, 399
figure 17-5
  shear line drilling, 400
figure 17-6
  shear line drilling, 400
figure 17-7
  shear line creation, 401
figure 17-8
  interchangeable core locks, 401
figure 17-9
  profile lock breaker, 402
figure 17-10
  forced entry, 403
figure 17-11
  dent puller, 403
figure 17-12
  lock mounting, 404
figure 17-13
  torque pipe tool, 404
figure 17-14
  torque tool, 405
figure 17-15
  torque tools, 406
figure 17-16
  breaking tools, 406
figure 17-17
  breaker tools, 407
figure 17-18
  Sigma security tools, 407
figure 17-19

Sigma Hooligan tool, 407
figure 17-20
Sigma breaking tools, 408
figure 17-21
forced entry tools, 408
figure 17-22
jamb spreading tools, 409
figure 17-23
jamb spreaders, 409
figure 17-24
K-tool, 410
figure 17-25
forced entry wedge tool, 410
wedge tool, 410
figure 17-26
Broco thermic lance, 413
figure 18-1
picking tools, 424
figure 18-2
picking tools, 425
figure 18-3
picking tools, 425
figure 18-4
turning wrench, 426
figure 18-5
rocker picks, 426
figure 18-6
pick guns, 426
figure 18-7
electronic pick guns, 427
rake picking, 427
figure 18-8
comb picks, 428
figure 18-9
comb picking, 429
figure 18-10
Sputnik pick, 430
figure 18-11
Peterson decoder, 430
figure 18-12
side bit milling modification, 432
figure 18-13
jiggle keys, 433
figure 18-14
signature picks, 434
figure 18-15
impressioning attacks, 436
figure 18-16
Falle foil impressioning system, 437

figure 18-17
foil impressioning system, 438
figure 18-18
lead impressioning system, 438
figure 18-19
Defeat Technology system, 439
impressioning system, 439
figure 18-20
Luckylock system, 439
figure 18-21
impressioning marks, 440
figure 20-1
lever lock opening, 465
figure 20-2
pin lock decoder, 467
figure 20-3
Medeco decoder, 468
figure 20-4
Pin Lock Decoder, 469
figure 20-5
mpressioning systems, 470
figure 20-6
foil impressioning system, 471
figure 20-7
light box, 471
figure 20-8
variable key systems, 472
figure 20-9
variable key generation system,
473
figure 20-10
Medeco reusable key, 473
figure 22-1
Schlage Primus key, 512
3D printed key, 512
figure 22-2
Fichet printed key, 512
figure 22-3
3D printed key, 513
figure 22-4
3D printed keys, 513
figure 22-5
Imported key profile, 513
figure 22-6
3D printed keys, 518
figure 22-7
key profile, 519
figure 22-8
keyway scan, 520

figure 23-1
  SWD scanner, 527
figure 23-2
  Sound Wave Decoder, 530
figure 23-3
  lock scanning, 532
  scanning of lock, 532
figure 23-4
  scanner displays, 534
figure 23-5
  3D printer output, 517
  lock scanner output, 534
figure 23-6
  Sound Wave Decoder, 535
figure 24-1
  Medeco plug, 539
figure 24-2
  Medeco simulated keys, 543
figure 24-3
  Medeco sidebar legs, 544
finding vulnerability beliefs
  design rules, 622
finger pin design
  Schlage Primus, 325
  side bit milling, 322
first to file rule
  patents, 173
fixing vulnerabilities
  design rules, 612, 621
foil impressioning keys and locks
  locks, 41, 470
  patent 2763027, 437
fooled about vulnerabilities
  design rules, 622
foolproof systems
  design rules, 616
force
  applied against locks, 396
  force application failure to
      consider, 578
forced attacks
  covert hybrid, 391
  expertise, 32
  locks, 385, 396, 398
  special tools, 369
forced entry
  application of force, 407
  application of torque, 405
  attacks, 36
  bending, 404

breaker tools, 406
  compression attacks, 411
  dent puller, 404
  duckbill tool, 410
  fracturing, 404
  impact, 411
  K-tool, 410
  locks, 75
  Medeco deadbolt, 431
  peeling, 406
  shear line creation, 399
  standards, 141
  techniques of, 36
  temperature attacks, 412
forced entry attacks
  battering ram, 411
  chisel and wedging,
      412
  punching, 412
  slam hammer, 412
  thermic lance, 413
  with chemicals, 414
forced entry methods
  locks, 405, 414
forced entry resistance
  UL 437, 151
forced entry standards
  BHMA 156.30, 153
forced entry tools
  door opening, 409
  figure 17-20, 408
  figure 17-21, 408
  locks, 403
forensic analysis and evidence
  locks, 36, 559
  design rules, 615
  traces covert entry, 32
foreseeability
  product liability, 95
Formlabs
  SLA printers, 512
fracturing of materials
  locks, 404
fraud and misrepresentation
  legal liability, 129
  product liability, 93
fused deposition modeling
  3D printing, 511
future attacks
  locks, 373

G

Galileo rule
  design rules, 620
gate designs
  locks, 34
gate fence tolerance
  covert entry, 434
gates
  lever tumblers, 244
  locks, 383
General Moshe Dayan
  design rules, 623
good ideas
  failure of security, 573
good locks and security
  design rules, 622
Gossman
  Henry, 235
graduated driver
  definition, 267
grand master key
  definition, 267
Great Exhibition
  Brahma lock, 246
  Hobbs, 366
great train robbery
  locks, 370
Greek lock
  figure 11-1, 236
groupthink
  design rules, 615
guard rings
  prying, 406
guidelines
  lock design, 599
guilds
  development of, 234
gun lock stamped keys
  figure 1-9, 16
gun safes
  biometric access, 392
gun trigger locks
  bypass, 15

H

Han Fey
  Abloy expert, 288
hardware constraints

failure to deal with, 576
Hawthorne case
  legal liability, 120
  Supreme Court on liability, 119
Hemingson versus Bloomfield Motors
  liability case, 111
hidden information
  about locks, 567
high-security
  definition, 267
  design rules, 600
  high-security label design rules, 608
  locks, 32
  mechanical locks, 304
  standards, 131, 142
high-security locks
  attributes of, 304
  comparison of, 318
  criteria, 304
  design expertise, 32
  high-security standards
    recommendations, 160
  meaning in rules, 601
  mechanical designs locks, 302
  selection of, 315
  side bit milling, 20
  simple attacks against, 560
high-tech and high-security
  design rules, 615
history
  lock development, 27, 233, 343
Hobbs
  American locksmith, 604
  Great Exhibition, 366
Hobbs protector lock
  locks, 248
Hooligan breaking tool
  figure 17-19, 407
horizontal privity
  legal liability, 122
hotel locks
  case study of defeat, 63
  encryption defeat, 603
  insecure designs, 579
hotel safes
  attacks against, 585
  decoding of chips, 585
  paperclip attacks, 594

hybrid attacks
  against detainers, 391
  against security layers, 390
  covert entry, 41
  covert forced, 391
  forced, 386
  locks, 30, 41, 294
  methods of, 80
  modes of, 80
  standards, 79
  3T2R rule, 78
hybrid electronic
  lock design, 311
hydraulic jacks and spreaders
  breaking tools, 409
  forced entry, 411

I

identification
  counterfeit key blanks, 216
ignoring vulnerabilities
  design rules, 609, 622
Ikon eCLIQ
  figure 13-24, 308
iLOQ
  bypass of, 14
  cylinders bypass of 83
  defeats, 578
  design rules, 602
  energy harvesting, 308
  figure 1-7, 14
  figure 13-25, 309
  figure 13-26, 309
imagination and failures
  locks and attacks, 564
  failure of, 574
impenetrable lock
  design rules, 607
implied warranty claims
  liability, 110
impressioning
  ballpoint pen, 14
  bypass of locks, 17
  covert entry, 39, 436
  definition, 267
  figure 20-5, 470
  figure 20-7, 471
  foil system, 41

light box, 470,
locks, 14
of keys, 222
keys figure 15-14, 356
marking figure 18-21, 440
marks, 440
plasticine systems, 471
technique for dimple locks,
  295
tools, 41
UL 437, 150
warded locks, 350
impressioning system
  figure 18-17, 438
  KGB, 361
  lever locks, 359
  locks, 469
  Luckylock, 439
  Tool figure 15-16, 358
  variable, 438
improper use
  locks, 102
improving designs
  lock manufactures, 6
incidental master keys
  key systems, 43
  locks, 497
index of security
  locks, 68
indirect code
  definition, 267
  keys, 43
indirect infringement
  patents, 184
industrial property
  Paris convention, 167
industry standards
  definitions, 257
  failure to adhere to, 100
  legal liability, 128
information
  hidden about locks, 567
  from keys and locks, 479
infringement of IP and patents
  lock manufacturers, 6, 7
  patents, 183
injunctions
  patents, 186

innovation
  not invented here problem, 601
input devices
  lock standards, 147
  locks, 146
insecurity engineering
  case examples, 571
  categories of cases, 571
  definition, 3
  examples, 14
  expertise, 25
  failure of imagination, 574
  liability, 4
insider threats
  against lock companies, 205
  locks, 62
Instakey
  programmable lock, 248
insufficient warnings
  defective products, 113
integrated circuits
  attacks against, 560
integrity of locks
  attacks against, 388, 588
intellectual property
  lock manufacturers, 6
  protection of, 163
intelligence
  within locks, 32
intelligence about targets
  design rules, 608
interactive pin design
  figure 13-20, 304
  Mul-T-Lock, 304
  interactive pins
interchangeable core locks
  control key, 262
  control key decoding, 493
  definition, 268
interface attacks
  design rules, 611
internal components
  attacks against, 593
internal tolerances
  exploit of, 158
Internet information
  design rules, 611
interstate communications

threats, 203
inventions
  definition under patent law, 170
  naming of inventor, 174
  nondisclosure of, 180
Iowa American company
  forced entry tools, 407
  K-tool, 410
IP protection
  by lock manufacturers, 6

J
jamb
  definition, 268
jamb spreaders
  forced entry, 409
  figure 17-23, 409
jiggle keys
  covert entry, 433
  figure 18-13, 433
jimmying
  forced entry, 405
John Falle
  decoding system, 41
  dimple lock attack, 295
  Pin and Cam decoder, 498

K
Kaba 5800 lock
  figure 1-6, 13
Kaba InSync lock
  figure 1-4, 11
Kaba simplex 1000 lock
  figure 1-11, 18
  legal liability, 128
key
  3D printed, 512
key-based
  digital cylinders, 305
key bitting
  rules of manufacturer, 499
  visual inspection of, 499
key blade
  definition, 260
key blanks
  definition, 272
  expired patents, 216
  impressioning marks, 440

lead impressioning system, 438
overlay, 491
picking by, 431
key changes
standards, 144
key codes
rules about, 487
standardized, 478
key control
advanced attacks on, 507
attacks on, 43
authorization cards, 213
BHMA 156.30, 155
compromise of, 217, 495
concept, 43
copying with wax, 357
decoder, 268
liability for statements, 211
locks, 32
locksmiths defeat, 212
manufacturers, 212
organizational, 229
security policies, 229
standards, 143, 149
3D printer technology, 43, 511
3D printing, 509
UL 437, 149, 153
key designs
EVVA 3KS, 288
figure 13-19, 303
Mul-T-Lock, 305
security issues, 209
key duplicating
key duplicating machine, 235
key duplicating shops, 213
restricted, 215
3D printers, 219
violation of law by locksmiths, 216
warranty violations, 215
key gauge
definition, 268
key generation systems
figure 20-10, 473
key interchange
definition, 262, 268
exploit, 496
key locks
standards, 138

key machines
computer right, 218
Fenby permutating, 364
Henry Gossman, 235
permutating, 357
sophisticated, 218
3D printers, 219
key milling
definition, 268
key picking
definition, 268
key profile
mapping of, 520
key simulation
key control, 217
key systems
incidental master keys, 43
reusable, 472
variable generation, 472
keyhole
definition, 268
keying levels
definition, 269
keying symbols
definition, 268
keying systems
attacks, 477, 489
change keys, 42
legal issues, 209
locks, 42
maison, 488
reverse engineering, 499
keyless entry
car attacks, 566
keys
access control, 305
actual combinations, 43
attack strategies, 477, 478
attacks against, 388
bitting, 482
bitting designs, 43, 301
bitting sequence, 229
bitting system, 301
bump key creation, 493
changing bitting, 490
copying, 492
copying methods of, 498
counterfeit, 43

counterfeit blanks, 488
counterfeit protection against, 7
cut angle, 263
decoding of, 220, 222
depth and spacing, 265
depth and spacing information, 484
depth coding, 43
depth keys, 265
design rules, 599
differs, 224
direct codes, 43
double-bitted, 266
double-cutting, 266
duplication of, 44, 218
electronic locks bypass, 451
figure 13-19, 303
iLOQ, 14
impressioning of, 222
indirect code, 267
information about online, 497
information from, 44, 479, 482
key codes, 482
key control, 43
legal restrictions, 215
locks, 42
Madelin, 223
magnetic pins, 300
master key systems, 483
milling, 268
modification of, 491
movable elements, 304, 482
movable elements attacks, 479
overlay insertion, 491
patent infringement, 215
physical design of, 482
physical examination of, 483
positional master key system, 229
protection of, 477
replication of, 44, 222, 492, 601
reusable systems, 472
rights amplification, 43, 223, 489
scanning of, 488
signatures of, 601
simulation of, 32, 43, 44, 220
software and hardware-based, 305
special industry, 481
spoofing, 601
stamped, 16

system keys, 492
theoretical combinations, 43
tryout, 435
variable key generation systems,
    221
visual decoding of, 220
visual inspection of, 499
keys and credentials
    attacks against, 591
    locks, 381
keys and locks
    rules, 23
keys 3D printed
    figure 22-6, 518
keyway access
    latch or bolt, 392
    locks, 300
keyway designs
    keying systems, 44
keyway restrictions
    circumvention, 216
keyway warding
    attacks against, 479
    modification of, 490
keyways
    attacks against, 479
    attacks through, 300
    compromise of, 435
    definition, 269
    figure 12-6, 269
    figure 13-6, 291
    locks, 381
    open ended, 15
    paracentric, 272, 291
    restricted, 49, 215
    scan 3D printer software, 521
    sectional, 488
    secure in locks, 34
    signature, 481
    virtual, 22, 225
    virtual defeat of, 497
    wards, 240
    width for covert entry, 435
KGB
    lock design, 255
KGB picking tools
    figure 15-24, 372
    warded locks, 352

knock-off keys
  cutting keys, 214
knowledge of locks
  failure of, 572
knowledge required
  vulnerability assessment, 623
Kryptonite bike lock
  attacks against, 561
  bypass, 14
  opening, 83
K-tool
  forced entry, 410
Kwikset Kevo
  electronic locks, 311
  figure 13-31, 314
  lock design, 311
Kwikset lawsuit
  patent infringement, 163
Kwikset locks
  design failure, 580
  opening, 83
Kwikset SmartKey
  Lock, 300
  figure 13-1, 287
  wafer lock, 286

L
laches
  patents, 185
laptop locks
  defeats magnetics, 393
laser track
  lock design, 296
laser track keys
  figure 13-12, 298
latch or bolt
  keyway access, 392
Laws of Motion and physics
  Newton, 24, 394
  Rules, 23
lawyers
  role in vulnerability assessment, 617
lead impressioning system
  Martin, 438
legal defense
  state-of-the-art, 129
legal issues
  keying systems, 209

master key systems, 226
Twelve Tables, 107
warning exemptions, 116
legal liability
  alternative design, 124
  caveat emptor, 108
  civil law, 106
  constructive knowledge of risk, 128
  consumer safety disregard, 101
  criminal law, 106
  defective product, 113, 118, 128
  defenses against, 127
  design defects, 115
  due care in design, 128
  duty to warn, 115
  elements of proof, 128
  expert lock manufacturers, 128
  failure to disclose defects, 97
  failure to fix products, 98
  false representations, 93
  fraud and misrepresentation, 92, 129
  industry standards, 100, 128
  Kaba simplex lock, 128
  knowingly selling defective
    product, 126
  locks, 103
  MacPherson versus Buick Motor Car
    Company, 120
  malfunction doctrine, 124
  manufacturing defects, 114
  marketing defects, 115
  Medeco case study, 127
  merchantability, 118
  misconduct in products, 99
  misrepresentation about products, 99
  misuse of product, 128
  negligence and privity of contract, 118,
    120, 121
  negligence proof, 128
  non-manufacturers, 129
  origins of, 106
  post-sale warning, 95
  privity of contract, 109
  post-sale issues, 115
  product design, 125
  products liability, 90
  reasonable foreseeability, 128
  risk-utility analysis, 124

security, 89
sophisticated user doctrine, 117
specific actions, 102
state-of-the-art, 128
strict liability, 121, 122
use of product, 95
warning of design defects, 115
warranties, 118
levels of threat
design defects, 198
lever tumbler locks
advancements of, 243
barrel and curtain design, 365
Barron Robert, 244, 354
belly decoding, 356
belly reading decoding, 362
bypass, 352
Canadian postal, 354
Decoder, 466
decoding by sound, 369
development, 242
early methods of picking, 359
figure 11-10, 243
figure 11-14, 249
figure 15-12, 353
figure 15-13, 354
figure 20-1, 465
gates, 244
impressioning techniques, 358
keys expanding bits, 364
KGB impressioning, 360
locks, 30
mapping of the tumblers, 359
methods of attack, 355
methods of opening, 366
Newell, 247
opening, 363, 464
over-lifting tumblers, 360
Parsons balanced lever, 247
picking programmable tool, 360
picking tool figure 15-18, 360
pressure against bolt, 366
security pins, 364
traps for false keys, 355
Tucker and Reeves, 249
Universal Belly Reader, 466
leverage
forced entry, 405

liability
attack times, 74
defective products, 112
design defects in locks, 195
false advertising, 211
keying system design, 209
legal, 4
lock standards, 151
standard of care, 107
3T2R rule, 68
liability avoidance
privity of contract, 111
liability case
Hemingson versus Bloomfield
Motors, 111
liability law
locks, 105
liquids
bypass of locks, 14
Lishi picking tool
figure 15-30, 376
picking, 41
lock assembly
attacks against, 389
lock attacks
last 100 years, 371
laws of physics, 24
time measurement, 70
lock bodies
attacks against, 588
lock bumping
advertising, 211
bump keys, 225
covet entry, 41
definition, 261
examples of bumping of locks, 15
figure 1-1, 8
Medeco, 538
methods of, 58
protocols, 57
standards, 141
time delay, 71
lock cylinders
shimming of, 499
lock decoders
Sound Wave Decoder, 528
lock defeats
Antwerp diamond heist, 555

positive attitude, 605
lock defects
  reasonable foreseeability, 128
lock designs
  alternatives, 101
  ASSA twin, 321
  damages for defects, 197
  design rules and vulnerabilities, 616
  eCLIQ, 306
  good ideas, 573
  KGB, 256
  laser track, 296
  legal liability, 103
  lessons, 29
  MACS, 224
  magnetic fields, 299
  Medeco, 298
  Medeco M4, 294
  Middle Ages, 294
  nitinol wire, 393
  rotating pin tumbler, 296
  rules, 64
  side bit milling, 320
  3T2R Rule, 67
  use of plastics, 394
  VA team selection, 54
  vulnerabilities, 52
  vulnerability assessment teams, 50
lock developments
  history, 28
lock engineers
  expertise required, 27
lock experts
  covert entry, 459
lock manufacturers
  arrogance, 102
  as experts, 128
  design mistakes, 35
  disclosure of defects, 13
  expertise, 6
  extortion attempts, 202
  insider threats, 206
  intellectual property, 6
  responsibilities, 4
  threats of exposure, 203
lock materials
  characteristics, 33
lock modification

design rules, 606
lock openings
  shims, 594
lock parts
  visual decoding, 499
lock picking
  burglars, 612
  covert entry, 425
  England, 366
  figure 18-2, 425
  kits, 424
  reverse, 255
lock plug
  figure 2-3, 44
lock scan displays
  figure 23-4, 534
lock scanners
  C.O.F.E.D., 527
  capabilities, 532
  Madelin, 527
  output display, 535
  process, 531
  visualization, 534
lock security
  sidebars, 228
  threats, 53
lock standards
  BHMA 156.30, 133
  bump key, 152
  decoding attacks, 152
  key control, 149
  liability, 151
  mechanical bypass, 154
  rapping test, 146
  rules relating to, 133
lock types
  basic designs, 29
locking components
  movable, 383
locking elements
  attacks against, 479
  external attacks, 389
locking systems
  figure 13-28, 311
  first of, 235
  mechanical bypass, 36
  secondary, 488
  sidebars, 319

locks
advanced attacks against, 459
AFTE, 36
anti-bumping, 34
anti-bumping pins, 301
anti-drill barriers, 34
anti-drill pin, 300, 397
application of force, 578
arithmetic attacks, 363
Assa Abloy CLIQ, 306
attack methods, 577
attack strategies, 478
attack types, 385
attacks against, 341, 460, 479
attacks against keys, 388
attacks strategies, 460
attacks with explosives, 368
audit trails, 46, 76
axial pin tumbler, 30, 258, 296
bitting design, 301
bolts, 384
Brahma, 342
broaching, 240
bump keys, 42, 293
bumping, 41
bypass buttons, 392
bypass by magnetic fields, 23
bypass fundamentals, 35
change keys, 42
choosing methods of attack, 420
clever designs, 600
comparison of high security, 318
complexity, 26
compromise of, 36
consumer use of, 102
conventional classification, 31
conventional locks selection, 315
conventional vulnerabilities, 291
copying defective designs, 393
covert attacks, 387
covert entry, 76
covert hybrid attacks, 391
covert methods of entry, 417
critical thinking about, 601
deadbolt attacks, 581
decoding, 41
decoding attacks against, 388
decoding by disassembling, 498

decoding information from, 441
decoding methods, 524, 582
defeat of credentials, 606
defective designs, 195
definitions, 257
design changes, 565
design defects, 197, 198
design failures, 18
design rules, 599
designs and testing, 379
destructive attacks, 395
differs, 224
digital door lock designs, 391
digital fingerprints, 523
dimple, 30, 294
disassembly of, 43
disc tumbler lock, 252
DMCA, 203
do not duplicate, 607
double-detainer theory, 289
drilling, 398
drilling attacks, 396, 397
drilling of, 401
Egyptian pin tumbler, 237
electronic, 310
electronic attacks, 314, 447, 568
electronic authentication, 315
electronic decoding systems, 524
electronic elements attacks, 448, 592
electronic scanners, 524
electronic vulnerabilities, 447
energy harvesting, 307
engineers, 27
enhancements, 34
entry holes, 22
evidence of bypass, 36
evidence of entry, 46
exploits of, 461
extortion attempts, 202
false gates, 301
ferrous elements in, 497
ferrous materials, 35
foil impressioning, 470
force applied against, 396
forced attacks, 385
forced entry, 75
forced entry tools, 403
forensic analysis, 36

forensic evidence, 46
forensic examination, 45
future attacks, 373
gate design, 34
gates, 383
hardware constraints, 576
hidden information about, 567
high-security, 32
high-security attributes, 304
high-security locks selection, 315
high-security mechanical, 302, 304
historical development, 343
history of, 233, 279
Hobbs protector lock, 248
hybrid, 30
hybrid attack techniques, 41, 80
hybrid electronic, 311
hybrid forced attacks, 386
hybrid mechanical designs, 294
impenetrable appearance, 607
impressioning, 14
impressioning systems, 469
impressioning tools, 470
information about, 487
input devices, 146
insider threats, 62
integrated circuits attacks, 560
intelligence from, 32, 479
internal attacks against, 593
internal tolerance exploits, 158
key control, 32
key control attacks, 509
key duplicating machine, 235
keying systems, 42
keys and credentials, 381
keys with software, 305
keyway access, 300
keyways open ended, 14
lack of imagination, 564
lack of knowledge, 572
laws of physics, 36
lever tumbler, 30
lever tumbler development, 242
magnetic components, 35
magnetic field attacks, 389
magnetic pins, 300
magnetics, 35
major crimes, 370

malfunctions and liability, 101
master keying levels, 42
material limitations, 576
mechanical and arithmetic attacks, 363
mechanical bypass, 36, 494
mechanical electronic interface, 384
Medeco BIAXIAL, 293
Medeco locks, 23
methods of entry, 421
microprocessor attacks, 441
minor changes, 125
motion transfer components, 384
movable components, 383
movable elements, 34
NDA agreements, 201
never say never, 607
notification of defect, 189
open keyways, 14
openings, 389, 443, 560, 589
organizations, 258
paracentric keyways, 291
physical integrity, 388
piezoelectric effect, 525
pin tumbler, 30, 288, 289
plug retaining components, 384
plugs and keyways, 381
primary components, 379
primary vulnerabilities, 419
product liability, 104
programmable, 43
re-keyable, 43
reverse picking of, 595
RFID, 21
rotating disc, 30, 288
scanner capabilities, 532
scanner designs, 527
scanner tools, 524, 525
secondary security layers, 384
secrets within, 604
security classifications, 31
security definition, 53
security features, 34
security layers, 390
security modifications, 614
security pins, 34, 301
security standards, 609
selection of, 315
selection criteria, 315

shear line, 290, 381
shear line attacks, 387, 595
shell or housing, 380
side bit milling, 19, 31, 34
sidebar, 30
sidebar designs, 34, 320
sidebar use, 319
sidebars, 294, 383
simple attacks against, 602
simulated keys, 32
spring-loaded mechanisms, 18
standards, 131, 138
standards and criteria, 34
standards organizations, 132, 137, 283
strengths tests, 147
surreptitious entry, 76
technology development, 233
testing using torque, 33
theory of operation, 29
threat level criteria, 198
3T2R rule, 41
tolerance attacks, 387, 496
tolerance testing, 146
torque to open, 33
trade groups, 235
tryout keys, 496
UL standards, 137
ultrasonic scanners, 525
Underwriters Laboratories, 137
unintended consequences, 391
upgrades to products, 601
use of plastics, 603
using plastic keys, 591
vulnerabilities of, 36
vulnerability analysis, 379
vulnerability assessment, 49
vulnerability assessment program, 53
vulnerability assessment reports, 63
wafer, 30
wafer tumbler, 253, 284
warded, 30
warded insecurity, 346
warded methods of entry, 347
why designs, 605
wireless authentication, 312
worm gears, 36
Yale pin tumbler, 250
locks are mechanical
  design rules, 609

locks security
  criteria for judging, 319
locks standards
  BHMA, 133
  UL, 133
locksmiths
  as experts in vulnerabilities, 608
  city ordinance violations, 216
  contract violation, 215
  dealer contracts violation of, 215
  liability for damages, 210
  patent infringement, 215
  security issues, 210
  tools availability, 83
loiding
  definition, 269
London
  Great Exhibition of 1851, 366
Luckylock
  attacks, 436

M
MacPherson versus Buick
    Motor Company
  legal liability, 120
MACS
  definition, 269
  figure 12-7, 270
  lock design, 224
  standards, 144
Madelin
  decoding of keys, 223
Madelin lock scanner
  locks, 527
magnetic attack Kaba
  figure 1-11, 18
magnetic attacks
  covert entry, 440
  visa mag, 440
magnetic code system
  definition, 267
  design figure 14-22, 336
  EVVA, 299, 334
  figure 14-22, 334
  key profile figure 14-25, 338
  rotor design, 337
magnetic components
  locks, 35
magnetic decoding

covert attacks, 440
magnetic decoding attacks
  against locks, 584
magnetic decoding film
  visa mag, 338
magnetic elements
  attacks on, 479
magnetic fields
  using to attack, 389
  application of, 497
  attacks against locks, 299
  bypass of locks, 17
magnetic fishing wire
  electronic locks, 452
magnetic lock decoder
  figure 15-26, 373
magnetic lock design
  Mul-T-Lock, 335
magnetic locks
  attacks of, 79, 584
magnetic release
  solenoid bypass, 576
magnetic ring
  figure 1-10, 17
magnetic wafer
  figure 13-16, 300
magnetics
  devil's ring, 23
  theory, 35
magnets
  bypass of locks, 23
maison keying systems
  locks, 488
malfunction doctrine
  legal liability, 124
man-in-the-middle of attack
  design rules, 617
  cars, 566
management statements about security
  design rules, 614
manipulation
  standards, 144
manufacturers
  design mistakes, 35
  due care, 102
  liability for damages, 210
manufacturing defects
  legal liability, 114

manufacturing flaws
  defective products, 113
mapping the tumblers
  lever locks, 359
marketing
  misconduct in, 99
marketing defects
  legal liability, 115
Martin impressioning system
  patent 4817406, 438
  locks, 358
Mas-Hamilton X07
  attacks against, 589
master key systems
  analysis of keys, 229
  design and information from, 483
  diagram of, 42
  extrapolation, 44
  figure 2-2, 42
  incidental keys, 43
  information from keys, 483
  legal issues, 226
  level of, 269
  procedures to decode, 505
  progression, 488
  security threats, 501
  vulnerabilities, 44, 227
master keys
  compromise of, 498
  decoding of, 43
  definition, 270
  incidental, 43
master pin
  definition, 270
materials and locks
  characteristics, 33
materials limitations
  locks, 576
maximum adjacent cut specification
  definition, 269
  lock design, 224
Maxum deadbolt
  Medeco, 15
MCS
  EVVA design, 334
  EVVA locks, 299
MCS design
  figure 14-22, 334

MCS lock
  magnetic attack, 440
MCS rotor design
  figure 14-24, 337
mechanical bypass
  definition, 270
  locks, 36, 494
  standards, 154
mechanical bypass of locks
  cylinders, 36
mechanical electronic interface
  locks, 384
mechanical locking elements
  covert attacks, 390
mechanical locks
  conventional, 283
  designs, 29
Medeco
  ARX pins, 302, 468
  case study, 537
  code setting keys, 432, 537, 586
  double cutting keys, 266
  lock design, 298
  sidebar codes, 540
  sidebar design, 165
  simulated keys, 541
  Tobias Bluzmanis, 537
Medeco ARX pins
  figure 13-18, 302
Medeco BIAXIAL
  decoder, 469
  definition, 259
  figure 12-2, 259
  figure 14-11, 329
  figure 14-13, 330
  lock design, 328
  locks, 293
Medeco cam lock
  figure 13-14, 299
Medeco case study
  lock design, 601
  possible liability, 127
Medeco code setting keys
  design, 127
  figure 3_1, 61
Medeco coding
  pin tumblers, 329
Medeco cutaway of m3
  figure 14-16, 331

Medeco decoder
  figure 20-3, 468
Medeco design
  Original, 327
  overview, 539
Medeco design issue
  locks, 565
Medeco high-security cylinder
  definition, 270
Medeco locks
  bumping, 83, 538
  differs, 540
  formation, 320
  3T2R rule, 83
Medeco m3
  bypass, 23
  case study, 604
  cutaway figure 14-18, 332
  definition, 269
  figure 14-15, 331
  locks, 23
  plug drilling attacks, 397
  sliver figure 14-17, 332
  U.S. Patent, 331
Medeco M4
  lock design, 228, 294
  side bit milling, 332
  figure 14-19, 332
  figure 14-20, 333
  side bit milling, 332
Medeco Maxum deadbolt
  attacks of, 581
  figure 1-8, 15
Medeco pin positions
  figure 14-14, 330
Medeco pin rotation
  diagram of, 329
Medeco pin tumbler design
  locks, 326
Medeco plug
  figure 24-1, 539
Medeco rotation angles
  figure 14-12, 329
Medeco sidebar design
  figure 14-10, 327
  photographs, 539
  tumbler interaction, 326
Medeco sidebar legs
  figure 24-3, 544

Medeco sidebar lock
    figure 12-8, 271
media comments about security
    design rules, 615
members
    vulnerability assessment teams,
        56
methods of attack
    choosing against locks, 420
    design rules, 611
methods of entry
    locks, 421
methods of forced entry
    locks, 414
metrics in security
    3T2R rule, 68
Middle Ages
    lock design, 242
milling
    of keys, 268
milling machines
    key duplication, 219
minor changes
    design rules, 623
    of locks, 125
    security vulnerabilities, 623
misconduct
    defense, 127
misleading statements
    lock bumping, 212
misrepresentation about products
    legal liability, 99
misuse of product
    legal liability, 128
MIT students 3D keys
    3D printed key, 512
modern locks
    history of, 279
modification of designs
    locks, 606
modification of products
    patents, 166
modifying
    keyway wards, 490
mortise cylinder
    definition, 270
motor attacks electronic locks
    compromise in electronic locks, 574
    electronic locks, 453

movable detainer
    definition, 270
movable elements
    locks, 34
    in keys, 304
    keys, 479
    of keys, 482
    magnetics in key, 300
M-SCAN
    lock scanner, 528
multi-section blank
    definition, 272
Mul-T Lock mt5+
    figure 13-22, 305
Mul-T-Lock
    dimple design, 295
    interactive pins, 304
    magnetic lock design, 335
    telescoping tumbler, 296
Mul-T-Lock pins
    figure 13-10, 296
Mul-T-Lock printed key
    figure 22-3, 513
mushroom tumbler
    definition, 272
    figure 12-10, 272

N
NDA agreements
    locks, 201
Nedwell patent
    lock scanner, 526
    locks, 526
negligence
    in design, 100
    legal liability, 118, 121
    in manufacturing, 100
    in product design, 100
    proof of, 128
negligence and privity of contract
    legal liability, 120
never say never
    lock defeats, 607
new designs
    design rules, 614
new locks
    design rules, 606
Newell parautopic lock
    lever lock, 247

Newton
  figure 1-12, 19
  laws of motion, 24, 394
  Third law of motion 3T2R, 41
NFC
  lock design, 255
nitinol wire
  defeats of, 393
  defective designs, 575
no more secrets
  design rules, 621
non-critical components
  importance of, 620
nondisclosure agreements
  consulting, 201
non-manufacturers
  legal liability, 129
non-obviousness
  patents, 177
nonprovisional patents
  application, 172
not invented here
  design rules, 601
not making sense
  design rules, 622
notification
  of defects., 200
  of lock defects, 187
notification of defects
  assessment of issue, 194
  internal procedures, 193
  priority, 195
  protocols, 188, 198
  to consumers, 189
novelty
  patent requirements, 177

O

observation ability in team members
  design rules, 612
occurrences unexplained
  design rules, 613
open keyways
  locks, 14
openings and locks
  attacks, 589
  attacks against, 389
  covert entry, 443

in locks, 22, 560
  shim wire attacks, 594
openings and vulnerabilities
  design rules, 610
organizational key control
  key control, 229

P

padlocks
  attacks against electronics, 595
  bypass of, 579
  development, 242
paperclip attacks
  bypass of locks, 12
  figure 1-5, 12
  hotel safes, 594
paracentric keyway
  definition, 272
  figure 12-11, 272
  locks, 291
parautopic lock
  lever lock, 247
Parsons lever lock
  figure 11-13, 248
  lever locks, 247
partnership agreements
  patents, 175
patent application
  primary parts of, 175
Patent Cooperation Treaty
  patents, 168
patent criteria
  United States, 165
patent EP 2834438
  scanner, 526
patent infringement
  criteria, 183
  defenses of, 184
  duplication of keys, 215
  lock manufacturers, 6
  locksmith, 215
  remedies for, 186
patent law
  England, 167
  history of, 166
  overview of, 169
  United States Overview, 169
  Venetian patent statute, 167

patent office
  web address, 182
patent origins
  U.S. Constitution, 167
patent protection
  by lock manufacturers, 6
  lock manufacturers, 6
patent requirement
  utility, 177
patent rights
  not covered, 178
  patents, 171
patent treaties
  international, 167
patents
  abstract of, 176
  acts to invalidate, 180
  advantages of filing, 181
  American Inventors Protection Act, 169
  background, 176
  claim, 175
  classification system, 183
  criteria for issuance, 176
  damages, 186
  design patents, 170
  direct infringement, 184
  employment agreements, 174
  European patent convention 1977, 167
  field of invention, 176
  filing in United States, 172, 173, 181
  first to file rule.12.8, 173
  former employee, 175
  history of, 166
  indirect infringement, 184
  injunctions, 186
  intellectual property, 163
  invalidation of, 180
  invalidation of application, 179
  laches, 185
  legal requirements for filing, 173
  life and validity, 178
  misuse of, 185
  modifications of products, 166
  naming inventor, 174
  non-obviousness, 177
  nonprovisional applications, 172
  novelty, 177
  obtaining in United States, 172

Paris convention, 167
partnership agreements, 175
PCT, 168
piezo decoder patent, 180
plant, 171
preferred embodiment, 176
primary parts of application, 175
prior art, 180
provisional applications, 172
relation to security, 165
remedies for infringement, 186
rights, 171, 178
search tools, 182
shop rights, 175, 185
specification, 175
statutory criteria for issuance, 176
Title 35, 165
Trip S Agreement, 168
types of, 170
utility, 170, 176
patents don't mean security
  design rules, 607
patents expired
  key blanks, 216
patents meaning of
  design rules, 606
path of least resistance
  design rules, 607
permutating key machines
  lever locks, 357
Peterson axial lock decoder
  covert entry, 431
Philo Felter
  wafer lock design, 284
physics laws
  defeat of, 604
  and locks, 36
pick guns
  covert entry, 426
pick resistance
  156.30, 158
  standards, 144, 145
  UL 437, 150
picking of locks
  complex forms of, 150
  covert entry, 38
  definition, 273
  England, 366

lever locks, 359
Lishi tool, 41
reverse, 431, 595
simultaneous, 431
tolerances, 41
picking tools
KGB, 372
warded locks, 351
piezo decoder patent
investigation, 180
piezo measurement
decoding, 442
piezoelectric effect
locks, 525
piggyback attacks
electronic locks, 450
Pin and Cam decoder
Definition, 464
John Fall, 498
Pin Lock Decoder system
John Falle, 466, 467, 498
locks, 467
pin tumbler lock
components figure 12-4, 263
definition, 273
development of, 237
driver pin, 266
figure 11-17, 251
figure 11-18, 251
figure 12-9, 271
Linus Yale, 243
lock design, 296
locks, 30
opening techniques, 464
pin stack definition, 273
principles of operation, 289
origins of, 344
rapping, 273
reverse picking, 431
security attacks, 344
shearing of, 406
Yale, 367
pinning restrictions
MACS, 224
plant patents
patents, 171
plastic
and lock designs, 394

plastic keys
attacks against locks, 591
plasticine
impressioning keys, 356
plasticine impressioning
locks, 471
plasticine impressioning system
figure 15-15, 356
Martin Newton, 356
plug and sidebar
figure 2-3, 45
plug of lock
definition, 273
figure 2-3, 44
locks, 381
locks bypass, 14
pneumatic pressure
forced entry, 411
police
as experts in locks, 608
positional master key system
analysis of, 229
post-sale issues
legal, 115
post-sale warnings
product liability, 95
pounding
of locks, 404
price of security products
design rules, 618
primary components
locks, 379
Primus lock design
sidebar, 325
Schlage, 324
prior art
patents, 180
prioritize realistic attacks
design rules, 623
privity in contracts
horizontal, 122
legal liability, 109, 122
vertical, 123
processor reset
covert attacks, 441
product defects
definition of legal liability, 92
product design

legal liability, 125
legal liability origin, 106
negligence, 100
reasonable care, 102
risk-utility testing, 100
product liability
consumer safety disregard, 101
defects, 96
design defects, 90, 91
development of, 104
duty to recall, 96
failure to remedy problems, 98
failure to warn, 94
foreseeability of defect, 95
improper use of product, 102
legal actions to trigger, 102
malfunctions, 101
marketing failures, 99
post-sale warning, 95
seller's liability, 107
understanding by lock
manufacturers, 9
upgrades, 119
product upgrades
liability, 119
product warnings
failure of, 100
profile cylinder breaker tools
locks, 403
programmable
lock, 43
programmable keys
warded locks, 352
programmable lever lock kit
impressioning, 359
programmable locks
Kwikset, 248
programs
3D printing, 514
progression
master key systems, 488
protection of patents and intellectual
property
by lock manufacturers, 6
provisional applications
patent, 172
prying
locks, 404

pulling attacks
forced entry, 401
punching attacks
forced entry, 412
push button locks
attacks against, 557, 610
bypass, 13

R
radio frequency attacks
BHMA 156.30, 159
radiographic techniques
decoding, 499
rake picking
pick guns, 427
figure 18-7, 427
R&D costs
design rules, 600
rapping attacks
BHMA 156.30, 160
definition, 273
electronic locks, 447
standards, 146
ratchet mechanisms
defeat of, 394
recalls
design defects, 197
reliability
3T2R rule, 83
remedies
extortion attempts, 204
removable core cylinder
definition, 273
repair doctrine
legal liability, 119
repeatability of exploit
3T2R rule, 83
replication of keys
design rules, 604
key control, 217
key duplication, 222
reports
vulnerability assessment,
62
reset attacks
electronic locks, 453
reset buttons
bypass of, 392

reset function exploit
electromechanical locks, 453
resource allocation
design rules, 610
responsibilities
by lock manufacturers, 4
restricted key blanks
circumvention of, 216
cutting of, 214
restricted keyways
definition, 273
DoD, 215
locks, 489
overlay bitting insert, 221
retailers
legal liability, 129
reusable key generation
figure 20-9, 473
reverse picking
figure 1-5, 12
pin tumbler, 431
wafer locks, 255
reverse picking attacks
against locks, 595
RF attacks
BHMA 156.30, 159
RFID
locks, 21
rights amplification
covert entry, 431
keys, 43, 223, 478, 489
rim cylinder
definition, 273
ripping
forced entry, 406
risk-utility analysis
legal liability, 124
risks
constructive knowledge of, 128
risk-utility test
product design, 100
rocker picks
covert entry, 426
Roman keys
figure 15-2, 346
Roman law
liability, 107
origins of liability, 107

Roman locks
early design, 239
warded, 239
root of key
definition, 263
Ross Anderson book
Security Engineering, 5, 36
rotating disc
locks, 30
rotating pin tumblers
lock design, 296
rotating tumbler design
Medeco, 326
rotor access
electronic locks, 454
rules
keys and locks, 23
laws of physics, 23
lock design, 599
locks, 41
suggested for a lock design, 64

S
safe
standards, 131
safe designs
with solenoids, 575
sales engineers and security knowledge
design rules, 618
Sargent Keso
figure 13-8, 295
SAVTA
development of, 235
sawing attacks
locks, 396
scanner
M-SCAN, 528
Sound Wave Decoder graphics,
532
scanner designs
locks, 527
scanner display
locks, 534
Sound Wave Decoder, 529, 534
scanners
lock process, 531
locks, 524
patents, 526

Schlage
  Smartkey lawsuit, 163
Schlage electromechanical lock
  figure 13-30, 313
Schlage Everest
  figure 13-21, 304
Schlage Primus
  figure 14-7, 325
  figure 14-8, 326
  figure 14-9, 326
  lock design, 324
  3D printed, 512
scoring of security
  3T2R rule, 83
screws
  forced entry, 403
search tools
  patents, 182
secondary locking systems
  modifying, 491
  security, 488
secrets
  about security, 621
secrets and locks
  design rules, 604
sectional keyways
  keys, 488
secure keyways
  locks, 34
security
  confidence about, 617
  criteria for judging, 319
  definition of, 53
  in products, 53
  liability, 89
  mistaken beliefs, 617
  not an equation, 619
security against attacks
  time delay, 71
security and confidence
  design rules, 617
security and designs
  design rules, 619
security and liability
  design rules, 605, 615
security and patents
  patents do not mean security, 607
security and price
  security effectiveness, 618

security and productivity
  design rules, 603
security and truth
  design rules, 620
security arrogance
  design rules, 618
security as a continuum
  design rules, 602
security as concept
  design rules, 608
security as effective
  design rules, 602
security assessment
  3T2R rule, 83
security assessment blinders
  design rules, 618
security assessment considerations
  design rules, 616
security assumptions
  design rules, 614
security by obscurity
  design rules, 618
security claims
  biometric, 617
security classifications
  locks, 31
security complacency
  design rules, 618
security decisions
  design rules, 614
security defeats
  design rules, 615
security design input
  design rules, 619
security design openness
  design rules, 618
security device development
  design rules, 616
security device tampering
  design rules, 620
security devices defeat
  design rules, 620
security engineering
  distinguished from engineering, 618
  Ross Anderson, 5, 36
security engineering differences
  design rules, 618
security enhancement
  in locks, 34, 300

security features
    locks, 34
security focus
    design rules, 614
security is about time delay
    design rules, 619
security is complicated
    security rules, 602
security is optimization process
    sign rules, 619
security is working
    design rules, 617
security issues
    ignored, 616
    keying systems, 209
    notification of, 189
security layers
    attacks against, 479
    decoding of, 493
    neutralization of, 390
    secondary for locks, 384
security measures and failures
    design rules, 619
security messenger
    design rules, 614
security metrics
    3T2R rule, 68
security mindset
    design rules, 617
security pin tumblers
    figure 13-18, 302
security pins
    definition, 272, 273
    locks, 34, 301
security problems existence
    design rules, 616
security rating
    3T2R rule, 68
    locks, 83
security resource allocation
    design rules, 600, 610
security standards and actual security
    design rules, 620
    meaning design rules, 619
    value of, 609
security technology
    ramifications of new, 617
security technology hype

design rules, 614
security testing criteria
    design rules, 621
security that everyone uses
    design rules, 614
security theater
    design rules, 603
security transparency
    design rules, 618
security vulnerabilities
    common sense, 617
    conventional lock, 291
    ignoring, 609
    inability to imagine, 617
    notification of, 188
    repeatedly searching for, 617
    what ifs, 615
security vulnerabilities and mathematics
    design rules, 619
security vulnerabilities missed
    design rules, 623
security vulnerability denial
    design rules, 615
security vulnerability evidence
    design rules, 609
seller's liability
    product liability, 107
serrated pins
    lever locks, 364
SFIC
    definition, 268
shear line
    attacks against, 44
    creation of, 290, 399
    definition, 273
    figure 12-12, 273
    locks, 381
shear line attacks
    description of, 44
    locks, 387, 595
shear line creation
    figure 13-5, 290
    pin tumbler locks, 400, 491
shear line drilling
    cylinders, 400
    locks, 400
shear line forced attacks
    locks, 411

shearing attacks
  locks, 396
shell of lock
  definition, 273
shell or housing
  locks components, 380
shim attacks
  electronic locks, 452
shim wire attacks
  against openings, 594
shim wires
  decoding of locks, 498
shimming of locks
  examples, 15
shims
  bypass techniques, 13
  covert entry width, 443
  decoding systems, 467
shock
  forced entry, 411
shop rights
  patent, 175, 185
side bit milling
  figure 1-2, 9
  figure 14-2, 321
  finger pin design, 322, 323
  in locks, 228
  lock designs, 320
  locks, 19, 31, 34
  modification of, 431
  patents, 321
side pin design
  ASSA V10, 323
  interaction with sidebar, 325
sidebar
  bumping of, 587
  attacks electronic locks, 455
  codes definition, 540
  comparison of use, 320
  defeat with plastic keys, 591
  definition, 274
  design of Medeco, 165
  diagram figure 12-13, 275
  figure 11-18, 251
  locks, 30, 294, 320, 383
  Medeco, 539
  Protection of, 228
  Wafers, 286

sidebar designs
  figure 14-3, 322
  locks, 34
  similar, 321
sidebar interaction
  with side pins, 325
sidebar lock
  Briggs & Stratton, 255, 284
  definition, 274
  figure 12-8, 271
  original patent, 255
  picking of, 587
Sigma breaking tools
  locks, 407
signature picks
  figure 18-14, 434
silicone
  use in attacks, 589
  impressioning keys, 356
Silvera (Aldo)
  picking tools, 374
simple attacks against complex security
  design rules, 615
simple design errors
  design rules, 619
simple solutions
  complex problems, 604
simulated keys
  figure 2-1, 32
  locks, 32
  Medeco, 541
  simulated Medeco keys figure 24-2,
    543
simulation
  of keys, 43, 220
skeleton keys
  figure 15-7, 350
  warded locks, 242, 349
slam hammer
  forced entry attacks, 412
SLS technology
  3D printing, 514
small openings
  locks, 22
SmartKey locks
  Attacks against, 580
  Kwikset, 248, 300
  Schlage lawsuit, 163

solenoids
  bypass of, 576
  in safe designs, 575
Sophisticated User doctrine
  legal liability, 117
sound
  used for decoding, 369
Sound Wave Decoder
  display, 532
  figure 23-2, 530
  locks, 528
  output figure 23-6, 535
source of threats
  design rules, 621
specification
  patents, 175
spreading
  forced entry, 406
spring-loaded mechanisms
  locks, 18
springs
  failure to use, 394
  failure to use in locks, 579
Sputnik pick tool
  covert entry, 430
  figure 15-29, 375
  figure 18-10, 430
standard 156.30
  testing deficiencies, 153
standard of care
  liability, 107
standards
  ASTM, 138
  BHMA 156.30, 142, 304
  BHMA 156.5, 146
  conductive liquids, 146
  covert entry, 141
  cycle tests, 147
  decoding of locks, 145
  destructive testing, 144
  differs, 143
  drill resistance, 144
  electrified input devices, 147
  electrostatic discharge testing, 146
  forced entry, 141
  high-security, 142
  high-security locks, 131
  high-security locks criteria, 304

  hybrid attack, 79
  key changes, 144
  key control, 143
  lock bumping, 141
  locks, 138
  locks and safe, 138
  manipulation, 144
  pick resistance, 145
  rapping, 146
  reliance on, 606
  rules relating to, 133
  strength tests, 147
  surreptitious entry, 144
  testing deficiencies, 78
  testing deficiencies in BHMA, 153
  tolerance tests, 146
  tools utilized, 559
  3T2R rule, 78
  visual key control, 143
standards and criteria
  lock, 34
standards and good guys
  design rules, 617
standards and testing
  false results, 100
standards deficiencies
  UL 437, 148
standards for locks
  locks, 131
standards organization
  locks, 132, 137, 283
state-of-the-art technology
  legal defense, 129
  lock manufacturers, 6
Statute of Monopolies
  English, 167
stereolithography technology
  3D printing, 512
STP 0140
  Underwriters Laboratories, 137
STP 0437
  Underwriters Laboratories, 137
strength tests
  locks, 147
strict liability
  legal liability, 121, 122
strike
  definition, 274

surreptitious entry
  locks, 76
  standards, 144
SWD decoder
  C.O.F.E.D., 530
system keys
  locks, 492

T
tailpiece
  definition, 266, 274
target selection by attackers
  design rules, 610
team members
  vulnerability assessment, 59
techniques of decoding
  locks, 41
telescoping tumblers
  figure 13-10, 296
  Mul-T-Lock, 296
temperature extremes
  forced entry attacks, 412
temporary security solutions
  design rules, 614
tension wrench
  lock picking, 426
terminology
  lock, 257
test results
  falsification of, 100
testing exploits
  locks, 613
testing of locks
  vulnerability assessment process, 60
  destructive, 144
  tolerance, 146
testing protocols
  UL 437, 148
theoretical combinations
  of keys, 43
theoretical key changes
  definition, 274
theory of operation
  locks, 29
thermic lance attacks
  forced entry, 413
thinking like bad guys
  design rules, 617

threat assessment
  locks, 53
threat levels
  design defects, 198
threats
  against lock companies, 203, 205
  interstate communications of, 203
  sources of, 621
threats and vulnerabilities
  design rules, 621
3D printers and programs
  capabilities, 514
  FDM technology, 511
  Formlabs, 512
  key control, 507, 511
  key machines, 219
  key profile figure 22-5, 517
  keys figure 22-2, 512
  mapping of keys, 520
  output, 517
  SLA technology, 512
  selective laser sintering, 514
  UL 437, 153
  vulnerabilities, 43
  wax casting, 514
3D printing software
  AT Security, 514
  specialized, 514
3T2R rule
  audit trail defeat, 77
  design rules, 606
  hybrid attack, 78
  lock design, 67
  manufacturer's use of, 83
  Medeco locks, 83
  numerical scoring, 83
  reliability of exploit, 83
  repeatability of exploit, 83
  security assessment, 83
  security rating, 68
  tool assessments, 81
  tools, 72
  training, 83
time computation
  attacks against locks, 69
time delay
  against attacks, 68
  lock attack, 71

time measurement
  attacks against locks, 70
time to attack
  locks, 74
Title 35
  U.S. patent code, 169
TMK
  definition, 276
  extrapolation of, 225, 228, 267,
    493
TMK decoding
  procedures, 505
TMK extrapolation
  intelligence before, 501
  master key systems, 500
tolerances
  attacks against, 387
  definition, 276
  exploiting of, 432, 496
  lock picking, 41
  standards and tests, 146
tool assessment
  3T2R rule, 81
tools
  attack methods, 83
  available to locksmiths, 159
  for testing, 159
  impressioning, 41
  locksmith, 83
  special, 36
  traditional, 36
  3T2R rule, 72
  use in standards, 159
tools and vulnerabilities
  design rules, 610
tools in standards
  unknown, 559
top level master key systems
  decoding options, 505
  definition, 276
  extrapolation of, 225, 493
top pin
  definition, 266, 276
  figure 12-14, 276
torque
  application of, 33
  application to plug, 580
  forced entry, 405
  forced entry technique, 33

torque testing
  locks, 33
torque tools
  forced entry, 406
trade groups
  locks, 235
train robbery
  great train, 370
training
  3T2R rule, 83
treaties
  patents, 167
Triffault Alexandre
  3D printing programs, 514
Trip S Agreement
  patents, 168
triple-bitted lock
  patent 2030837, 276
triple-bitted key
  definition, 276
truth and security
  design rules, 620
tryout keys
  attacks by, 363
  covert entry, 435
  definition, 276
  key systems, 44
  locks, 496
tubular pin tumbler lock
  definition 276
  figure 12-1, 258
Tucker and Reeves
  lever lock, 249
tumbler over-lift
lever locks, 360

U
U.S. patent 1514318
  ABLOY, 319
U.S. patent 1965336
  sidebar lock, 255
U.S. patent 2030837
  triple-bitted key, 276
U.S. patent 2064818
  comb picking, 429
U.S. patent 2763027
  foil impressioning, 437
U.S. patent 3080744
  original Medeco patent, 326

U.S. patent 3499303
  Medeco, 327
U.S. patent 3722340
  Medeco, 327
U.S. patent 4377082
  sidebar design, 320
  sidebar designs, 320
U.S. patent 4393673
  side bit milling, 321
U.S. patent 4434631
  sidebar design, 320
U.S. patent 4635455
  Medeco BIAXIAL, 327
U.S. patent 4638651
  sidebar design, 320
  sidebars, 320
U.S. patent 4715717
  Schlage Primus, 325
U.S. patent 4723427
  Medeco, 327
U.S. patent 4756177
  Schlage Primus patent, 325
  side bit milling, 321
U.S. patent 4815307
  Schlage Primus, 325
  side bit milling, 321
U.S. patent 4817406
  foil impressioning, 438
  William Martin impressioning, 358
U.S. patent 4966012
  lock designs, 579
U.S. patent 5067335
  side bit milling, 321
U.S. patent 5277042
  the Club, 553
U.S. patent 5640865
  side bit milling, 321
U.S. patent 5715717
  side bit milling, 321
U.S. patent 5809816
  Schlage Primus patent, 325
  side bit milling, 321
U.S. patent 5845525
  side bit milling, 321
U.S. patent 6134929
  side bit milling, 321
U.S. patent 6477875
  Medeco, 327
  Medeco locks, 327

  Medeco m3 lock, 330
U.S. patent 6945082
  Medeco, 327
U.S patent 7213429
  re-keyable lock, 163
U.S. patent 7434431
  keying systems, 163
U.S. patent 7441431
  tubular lock design, 296
U.S. patent 7775074
  ARX pins, 301
U.S. patent 7963135
  security pin, 301
U.S. patent 8074479
  EVVA MCS attack, 335
U.S. patent 8997538
  magnetic lock design, 335
U.S. patent
  10563426, 79
U.S. patent 11629525
  authentication of lock, 315
  definition, 277
  locks standards, 133
UL 437
  attack resistance, 141
  bumping, 150
  complex picking, 150
  deficiencies, 148
  definitions and tests, 140
  expertise in testing, 151
  forced entry resistance, 151
  impressioning, 150
  key control, 149, 153
  liability, 151
  lock standards, 139
  pick resistance, 150
  standard Underwriters
      Laboratories, 138
  3D printed key, 153
  vulnerabilities, 148
UL 768
  Underwriters Laboratories,
      138
UL 887
  Underwriters Laboratories, 138
UL 1034
  Underwriters Laboratories, 138
UL 2058
  Underwriters Laboratories, 138

UL and BHMA
standards, 139
UL standards
locks and safes, 138
ultrasonic scanners
locks, 525
undercuts and keys
Schlage Everest, 304
Underwriters Laboratories
definition, 277
standards, 133
STP 0140, 138
STP 0437, 138
Underwriters Laboratories 437
standards
different tests, 140
Universal Belly Reader
lever locks, 466
universal pin tumbler system
John Falle, 472
upgrades
design rules, 601
lock design, 601
USB port
and locks, 393
use of products
product liability, 95
USPS
restricted keyways, 215
USPTO
web address, 182
utility
patent requirement, 177
patents, 170, 176

V
V10 ASSA
lock design, 321
VA team members
criteria, 56
variable key generation systems
figure 20-8, 472
impressioning, 438
John Falle, 472
keys, 221
locks, 472
vehicle anti-theft system
attacks against, 553
anti-theft device, 13

Venetian patent statute
origins of patents, 167
vertical
privity and liability, 123
vibration attacks
covert entry, 435
locks, 394
virtual keyway systems
altering, 490
defeat of, 225, 496
locks, 22
virtual shear line
definition, 277
visa mag
magnetic code system decoding, 338
magnetic field attacks, 440
visa mag images
figure 1-10, 17
figure 14-26, 338
visual decoding
of keys, 220
of lock parts, 499
visual key control
standards, 143
vulnerabilities
Bypass, 419
electronic locks, 455
identification of, 51
3D printing, 43
master key, 228
of lock, 36, 379
methods of attack, 622
notification of, 188
search for, 617
understanding of lock
manufacturers, 6
vulnerabilities and risks
analysis restrictions design rules, 614
analysis tools design rules, 610
conceived of by design teams design
rules, 610
design rules, 618
expecting to find design rules, 616
failure to identify design rules, 615
lock designs, 52
vulnerability assessment
design rules, 606, 617, 618
lock design, 49
program, 53

process lock design, 60
reports, 63
team selection of, 50, 55, 59, 612
vulnerability cover-up design
    rules, 613

W

wafer locks
  attacks on, 285
  bypass, 12
  characteristics of, 285
  definition, 277
  EVVA 3KS, 286
  figure 11-20, 254
  hybrid designs, 286
  Kwikset SmartKey, 286
  locks, 30, 253
  Philo Felter, 284
  reverse picking, 255
  tumbler, 284
  Winfield, 285
warded
  keyways, 240
  locks, 30
warded bypass tools
  figure 15-10, 352
warded key impressioned
  figure 15-9, 351
warded keys
  15-6, 350
warded keys and locks
  figure 15-4, 348
warded locks
  design figure 11-5, 239
  early designs, 239
  figure 11-6, 240
  figure 11-7, 241
  figure 11-8, 241
  figure 11-9, 241
  figure 15-3, 347
  figure 15-8, 351
  impressioning techniques, 350
  insecurity, 346
  limitations of, 243
  methods of entry, 347

multiple bolts, 347
picking tools, 351
programmable keys, 352
Roman, 239
skeleton key, 242, 349
warning of defects
  exempt from liability, 116
  legal liability, 115, 118
warranty of merchantability
  legal liability, 118
warranty violation
  keys, 215
wedge tool
  forced entry figure 17-25, 410
wedging
  forced entry, 4-5
what ifs
  design rules, 615
white hat hackers
  3T2R rule, 83
Widen (Bo)
  lock patents, 321, 325
Winfield locks
  attacks, 285
Winterbottom versus Wright
  legal liability, 110
wireless authentication
  door lock, 312
  lock design, 312
wireless door locks
  lock design, 312
worm gears
  attacks against, 36
  figure 1-3, 10
  locks, 36
wrenching
  forced entry, 405
wrong assumptions about security
  design rules, 615

Y

Yale lock design
  figure 11-16, 251
  locks, 250
  pin tumbler, 243, 367